WISCONSIN

A History

THE STATE HISTORICAL SOCIETY OF WISCONSIN

WISCONSIN

A History

ROBERT C. NESBIT

THE UNIVERSITY OF WISCONSIN PRESS

Published 1973

The University of Wisconsin Press
114 North Murray Street
Madison, Wisconsin 53715

The University of Wisconsin Press, Ltd.
1 Gower Street
London WC1E 6HA, England

Printings 1973, 1977, 1979

Printed in the United States of America

Designed by Sylvia Solochek Walters
Pictorial essay designed and selected by George Talbot

ISBN 0-299-06370-4; LC 72-7990

To James W. Nesbit

(1853–1912)

Principal of the Free High Schools of
Durand, Wisconsin (1885–1898)
and
Mondovi, Wisconsin (1898–1905)

Superintendent of Schools
Ellensburg, Washington (1905–1912)

CONTENTS

MAPS

A section of illustrations constituting a pictorial essay on the history of Wisconsin will be found at the end of the volume.

PREFACE

State history is a difficult medium. Many historians would say that the form imposes artificial limits which vitiate its usefulness. The author is all too aware that others of his readers will have an antiquarian interest. They want to find the unique, the particular, and the familiar. My apologies to these readers. The particular was chosen primarily as illustration rather than for itself, and the familiar for its meaning.

State boundaries—even the arbitrary line between Wisconsin and Illinois—do make a difference. The societies enclosed within them do see themselves as units with separate histories. Regionalists are always bumping into this stubborn fact, as well as the difficulties of limiting and defining what one means by the Midwest.

Wisconsin history offers an unusually good vantage point for a long view of much of our national history. The Fox-Wisconsin waterway between the St. Lawrence and Mississippi drainage basins made the Wisconsin country a focus of French and British imperial policy from the late seventeenth century. The Wisconsin country was the meeting place of the eastern woodlands Indians and those from the plains. It was an important crossroads for the fur trade and therefore important in diplomacy and Indian policy well into the nineteenth century.

Wisconsin Territory's Organic Act of 1836 represented a landmark in the interpretation of the Northwest Ordinance of 1787. The settlement of the territory offers examples of a variety of frontiers: fur-trading, mining, agricultural, lumbering, and urban. The mingling of native-born and European-born Americans began early in Wisconsin and continued on a scale which provides rich material for the study of immigration history. The state has a higher proportion of her people engaged both in agriculture and industry than the national average, reflecting that both made difficult transitions from a careless exploitation of finite resources to intensive use of capital and labor. As for politics, a state that offered two such contrasting generic terms to national politics as La Follettism and McCarthyism must command attention. Finally, the most generally satisfying explanation of the American pioneer experience and one which continues as a commonplace in the national rhetoric found expression in Frederick Jackson Turner's "The Significance of the Frontier in American History," published in 1893. Turner's generalizations started with his home town, Portage, Wisconsin.

There is one aspect of Wisconsin history that I have not attempted to deal with here. The book lacks a chapter on "Literature and the Fine Arts," "The Advancing Arts," "The Theater and the Book World," "The Pattern of Culture," or similar efforts by the local historian to pick his way through the gardens of the other muses. The results would not be worth the trip. The reader who has a special interest in regional art, literature, architecture, or music doubtless knows as much or more about it than the author, as well as where to look for more informed guidance. Lists of artists, authors, their works, cultural organizations, architectural examples, performances, and institutions are a mind-numbing exercise for both author and reader. The same applies to the famous and the notorious who may have a Wisconsin connection.

I wish to thank the Research Committee of the University of Wisconsin's Graduate School for providing leave for a semester to work on this book. Alice E. Smith, a mine of information on Wisconsin history, cheerfully shared her knowledge and ideas. William F. Thompson and Paul W. Glad read substantial parts of the manuscript and offered helpful suggestions. Vernon Carstensen and the late William B. Hesseltine deserve thanks for encouraging me to work in local history and to write this book.

My wife, Marie, took notes, typed, worried over my syntax, kept a record of editorial changes, did indexing, but maintains a steadfast loyalty to the Pacific Northwest as the truly habitable region of the United States.

A NOTE ON
THE BIBLIOGRAPHIES

Wisconsin history is a much-plowed field with an embarrassment of riches for the scholar, making it clear that some ground rules had to be established to keep the chapter bibliographies within reasonable limits. The first assumption, then, is that there are available bibliographic guides that will carry the student or general reader beyond the capacities of the average city library. Leroy Schlinkert's *Subject Bibliography of Wisconsin History* (Madison, 1947) is a standard. Larry Gara's *A Short History of Wisconsin* (Madison, 1962) is a later guide with suggested readings at the end of each chapter. *The Wisconsin Magazine of History* has cumulative indexes published in separate volumes. Since 1935 the useful *Wisconsin Blue Book,* published biennially, has had compilations of special articles that have appeared in earlier issues. The twenty-volume series of the State Historical Society of Wisconsin *Collections* (Madison, 1855–1911) is indexed in volume 21. William F. Raney's *Wisconsin, A Story of Progress* (New York, 1940; Appleton, 1963), the standard scholarly history in wide use, has selected bibliographies by chapters. Library card-catalogues are, of course, the most current guides.

The bibliographies in this book concentrate upon recently published materials which are presumed to be widely available. Some older works that have been quoted or summarized and unpublished masters' theses and doctoral dissertations of particular usefulness are noted. Entries from serial sets are a suggestion of the series for the interested reader. A few publications of a general nature which were not cited in the chapter bibliographies are listed in the general bibliography. The Wisconsin History Foundation is sponsoring a six-volume work, *The History of Wisconsin.* Volume I, *From Exploration to Statehood,* by Alice E. Smith (Madison, 1973), and Volume II, *The Civil War Era, 1848–1873,* by Richard N. Current (Madison, 1976), are available.

WISCONSIN

A History

THE LAND,
ITS PEOPLE, AND
EUROPEAN EMPIRES

part one

A fair landscape, rich in natural food resources but harsh in climate, Wisconsin offered the Woodlands Indian an environment suited to his style of life which, though precarious, was in harmony with Nature's gifts and demands. With the penetration of European economic and social institutions all balances were set askew, between tribe and tribe, among the numerous sub-cultures, and most important, between a way of life in harmony with the environment and one based upon the exploitation of a single resource, the fur trade. To acquire the simple utensils, the weapons, the comforts, and the debaucheries of European culture, which the Indian suddenly found essential, he abandoned much of his own civilization. His fate is one of the embarrassments of American history.

The struggle of the Europeans for imperial hegemony over the Midwest was part of a prolonged series of international wars broken by periods of uneasy truce and maneuver in the interior. The prizes here were the water route which provided the main lines of communication, control of the fur trade, and influence over the natives, but in the eyes of the European combatants, these were dwarfed by other prizes in other lands. The wars were won or lost on distant fields in Europe or even Asia and on the high seas of the world. Britain finally triumphed, inheriting the prize of French Canada and the fur trade of the interior for the most part unchanged. The use of the land and its people continued much the same. A new breed of invaders, the Americans, would change all of this.

THE LAND
AND PRIMITIVE MAN

1

Wisconsin has the advantage of natural boundaries which give a sense of geographic unity often absent in many of the United States. Two of her man-made boundaries are limited to sparsely populated stretches across the northern highlands separating the two Great Lakes on the Michigan border and a shorter reach from the upper St. Croix to the mouth of the St. Louis River which separates Superior, Wisconsin, from Duluth, Minnesota. The longer longitudinal boundary on the south, stretching directly across from Lake Michigan to the Mississippi River, ignores topographical features.

In area, Wisconsin covers 56,154 square miles, or just over 36,000,000 acres. It is almost exactly the size of the neighboring states of Illinois and Iowa, but with more variety of landscape and much more lake surface. Wisconsin stretches 300 miles north and south, and its greatest width is 280 miles.

Wisconsin's topography has more variety than that of the other Lakes states because of the vagaries of the continental ice cap, which was the most recent, in the scale of geological time, of the major agents in its formation. Geographers identify five geographic provinces in the state, readily seen on any relief map. Coming down from the north they are (1) a narrow shelf of lowlands on the shore of Lake Superior cut by streams from the highlands into relatively deep, narrow valleys; (2) the gently rolling northern highlands formed from a glacier-shorn old mountain range into a high plain dotted with many small lakes, marshes, and stream beds; (3) the central plains making a crescent below the highlands and characterized by buttes and mesas; (4) the western uplands, in roughly the southwest quarter of the state, largely unaffected by the later glacial action and of a pleasingly rugged aspect, and (5) the eastern ridges and lowlands, containing the most conspicuous examples of glacial action, and comprising about a quarter of the state in a north and south band some 80 miles deep running back from the shores of Lake Michigan. This last province contains Lake Winnebago, the Kettle Moraine, Horicon Marsh, and the coastal and interior lowlands.

The soil created by the glacial movements varies in character. The largest area of prime glacial soil lies in the southeast quarter of the state; others are found around Lake Winnebago, in the Fox Valley, and along the shore of Lake Michigan nearby. The soil of the driftless area, sometimes called loess, is also prime in the relatively few places where it lies level. These areas are limited generally to the coulee bottoms and small flood plains of streams. The soil of the central plain, usually of a glacial character, is apt to be sandy and less desirable for agricultural purposes. Only lately has it been exploited, by means of expensive pressure irrigation.

Wisconsin is subject to what is known as a continental forest climate. Lying between 42 degrees 30 minutes and 47 degrees north latitude, it is nearly 1,000 miles from the Gulf of Mexico and from the Atlantic Ocean and 2,000 miles from the Pacific. Lakes Superior and Michigan have some moderating effect upon the severe winters and hot summers. There is a considerable variation in the climate from south to north. The southern counties lie within the influence of "corn-belt" summers, with normally hot, humid air from the Gulf controlling the weather. Winter is the dominant season in the north, where the summers are relatively short and cool and hence the growing season short. On the average, southern Wisconsin has a snow cover 85 days of the year, while along the Lake Superior shore this stretches to 140 days a year. The mean annual temperature of Wisconsin at 43 degrees Fahrenheit sounds innocuous enough, but the extreme range is from about 110 degrees above to 50 degrees below zero. The state has a summer temperature similar to that of France, Germany, and southeastern England, and a winter temperature comparable to that of northern Sweden and Central Russia.

Wisconsin's summer weather is unusually humid for a continental climate. The range of annual precipitation across the state is fairly narrow: from 28 to 44 inches, with 36 inches the average. Compare this with an

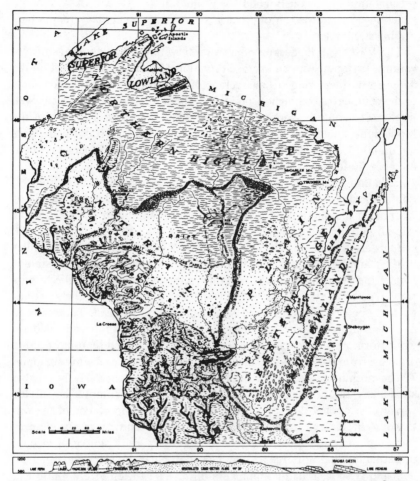

Map 1.   Physiographic Diagram of Wisconsin. By Loyal Durand, Jr., 1931. © The
Geographical Press, Hammond, Inc., Maplewood, New Jersey   *UWCL*

annual 34 inches in Seattle and 13.9 inches in Salt Lake City. Milwaukee's 29.5 inches of precipitation a year is much more evenly distributed
than Seattle's; probably one-fifth or more comes as snow, and the heaviest rainfall, from May through August, usually takes the form of short,
heavy downpours.

Wisconsin's snow is held by the cold winters for the growing season and
forms a blanket for vegetation, while the heavier rainfall holds off until
late spring, after the snow water has run off, thus minimizing flooding
and maintaining stream flow throughout the year. This distribution of

precipitation is obviously good for promoting the growth of vegetation, which in turn retards run-off, and it is favorable for agriculture and harnessing stream flow.

The Wisconsin landscape offers variety within a narrow range of elevations. It slopes from an average elevation of 1,600 to 1,800 feet on the flattened northern ridge to an average of 700 to 800 feet in the lowlands of the southeast. The highest points are about 1,950 feet above sea level, the lowest, along the shore of Lake Michigan, 580 feet. The level of the Mississippi is about 670 feet at Prescott, where the St. Croix River enters it, and 600 feet at the Illinois border. The level of Lake Superior is about 600 feet, 20 feet above Lake Michigan.

Elevation is not as important a factor in determining temperatures, rainfall, and weather patterns as it would be in more elevated terrain or where real mountain ranges exist. And since Wisconsin has a favorable rainfall pattern and relatively gently sloping land, its lakes and drainage systems are important. The state has some 9,000 lakes and 33,000 miles of river and stream frontage. The largest river system within the state is that of the Wisconsin, one of several rivers which drain into the Mississippi. The river system associated with Lake Winnebago is the most important one draining into Lake Michigan from Wisconsin. The drainage pattern south of Lake Winnebago is dominated by the eastern ridges, which form a narrow watershed for Lake Michigan and send most of the drainage from the central basin down the Rock River to the Mississippi.

The prominence of lakes, drainage systems, and a relatively reliable streamflow meant that the rivers would be an important element for whatever economy developed here. We know the importance of the waterways for the fur trade. Rivers turned the machinery of the pioneer economy and carried its products. Today, they are a source of electric power and a vital resource for the important paper industry and others.

While Wisconsin had a mining era in the lead region of the southwest, mining has not been an important industry for a good many years. Wisconsin apparently has no coal or petroleum resources to develop. She is known to have both iron and copper ores in the northern highlands, but they lie deep and are expensive to work. There was some iron mining near the Michigan peninsula which enjoyed a boom in the 1880s, but the deep shaft mines there had difficulty competing with open pit mines elsewhere. There are deposits of low-grade iron that are of interest if cheaper methods of extraction can be developed and applied.

Wisconsin, as the American pioneer found it in 1830, was heavily forested over the northern two-thirds of its land surface. Evergreens, particularly white pine, dominated the forests farthest north. Moving south,

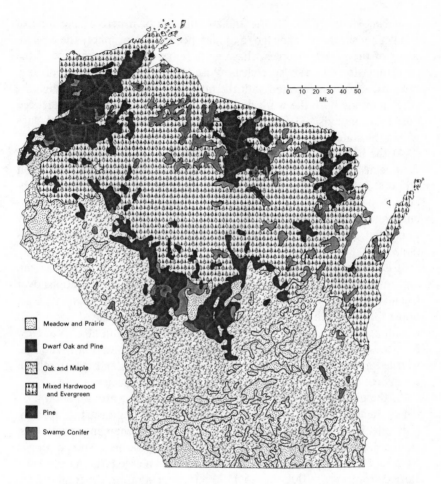

Meadow and Prairie

Dwarf Oak and Pine

Oak and Maple

Mixed Hardwood
and Evergreen

Pine

Swamp Conifer

Map 2.   Native Vegetation   *UWCL*

one would have found the evergreens well mixed with hardwoods and
then the hardwoods alone in a belt about fifty miles wide. In some areas,
such as pioneer Ozaukee County, there was a heavy, hardwood forest
cover, while across the southern third prairie grassland was dominant,
interspersed with groves of oaks and other hardwoods. According to
John Muir, the hardwoods in the south spread after the American settlers began to arrive; the Indians had held down new hardwood growth
by burning over the prairie grass to drive game.

The Wisconsin of 1830, with its forest cover, was the same environment in which the Indians had made their homes before the arrival of

Jean Nicolet in 1634. Of the Indian tribes known here at the time of Nicolet's visit, the Winnebago, a Siouan people, are probably the descendants of prehistoric peoples whose mute remains are the province of the archeologists and other specialists. Wisconsin is rich in these prehistoric remains, usually associated with the familiar effigy mounds, although the effigy mounds were the work of only one of the cultures which practiced burial in mounds. There are over 15,000 known archeological sites within the state.

At the beginning of the seventeenth century, before the penetration of Europeans had disrupted Indian life, it is estimated that there were about 100,000 Indians in the vicinity of the upper Great Lakes. This was probably 10 percent of all the people living in North America above the present United States boundary with Mexico. Some areas were very sparsely populated, of course, while others supported a relatively dense population.

It is generally accepted that the American Indian is of Asiatic origin, and entered the continent from Siberia in a succession of migrations over a land bridge to Alaska. Physical evidence of man's occupation of the upper Great Lakes area dates from about 10,000 B.C., based upon finds of chipped stone spear points similar to those first found at Clovis, New Mexico. The points belonged to men, designated by us Paleo-Indians, who led a rigorous existence preying upon mastodons and mammoths in an environment dominated by the great continental glaciers.

As the glaciers retreated northward for the last time around 7000 B.C., the character of the land and ecology changed. The land warped upward, relieved of the tremendous weight of the glaciers, changing lake levels, contours, and drainage patterns. As the climate warmed, spruce forests were replaced by pines. A new human culture emerged, thought to have existed from about 7000 B.C. to 4500 B.C., judging from the fragmentary remains found in sites of human occupation. This culture has been named the Aqua-Plano, and the stone tools of its hunting and fishing people can be distinguished from those of the earlier mastodon hunters.

From about 5000 to 500 B.C. the upper Great Lakes region was occupied by two identifiable cultural groups that may have been related, the Boreal Archaic and the Old Copper. Both peoples worked in stone and wood, but had no pottery. The Old Copper Indians were the first fabricators of metal, possibly anywhere, some of their work done six to seven thousand years ago. They worked raw copper in much the same way as they shaped stone, and learned to harden it by annealing—alternate heating and cooling. They did not smelt or cast the metal.

The Old Copper Indians moved northward. As late as one hundred years ago, copper objects fashioned in their way were found among Indi-

Map 3.   Land Classes   *UWCL*

ans and Eskimos in the Northwest Territories of Canada. The Boreal
Archaic culture underwent changes in the area south of Lake Superior,
and developed into what is generally known as the Early Woodland culture, thought to be part of a culture found in the northern forest zones of
Europe and Asia as well. Its most important changes were in the introduction of elaborated burial customs and pottery. Evidence is more complete than for previous cultures because of the new burial customs.

The Hopewell culture began to replace the short-lived Early Woodland culture about 100 B.C. A river people centered in the Illinois River
valley, the Indians of this culture followed the valleys northward as far as

they found the climate adaptable to their rather delicate flint corn. They were related to similar cultures originating in present Mexico: sedentary, with capabilities in farming, construction, tool-making, and pottery well beyond those of the preceding cultures on the upper Great Lakes. They built burial mounds as well as impressive earthen structures for defense and ceremonial purposes. Based more on agriculture than hunting, the Hopewell culture was more stable than its predecessors; nonetheless, these people were gone before the Europeans arrived. The American Indian at all times lived in a precarious balance with his environment, subject to the disasters of weather, disease, and attack from his neighbors.

The people of the last prehistoric period, roughly from 700 to 1600 A.D., shared a common culture and combined hunting and fishing with a primitive agriculture. The most distinctive sub-group in this Later Woodland period, as it is known, was that of the Effigy Mound People. A contemporary cultural group, the Peninsular Woodland tribes, lived around the shores of Lake Michigan. It is presumed that they were the ancestors of some of the Wisconsin tribes of historic times: the Menominee, Potawatomi, Ottawa, Chippewa, and possibly the Sauk and Fox, all belonging to the Algonkian language group. The Lake Winnebago culture is another recognized within the Later Woodland period. These people were probably the ancestors of the historic Winnebago tribe, but this is not firmly established. They came to this area around 100 A.D. by way of the Mississippi Valley and were possibly the builders of Aztalan, which archeologists now date between 1100 and 1300 A.D. There is no oral tradition among the Winnebago linking them with this earlier culture, but the Winnebago are a Siouan people and the Lake Winnebago culture was related to the Chiwere Sioux.

The estimate made by George Irving Quimby of 100,000 Indians in the upper Great Lakes area in 1600 A.D. places possibly one-fifth of them, about 20,000, within the boundaries of present Wisconsin. He does not count the Santee-Dakota, a Siouan people who sometimes ranged into western Wisconsin.

All of the upper Great Lakes tribes of this period figured in later Wisconsin history, as did tribes even farther to the east, after the dislocations brought about by the wars incidental to the fur trade. But in 1600, before these hegiras, the tribes on the upper Lakes were the Huron and Ottawa east of Lake Huron; the Chippewa ranging north of Lake Huron and all around Lake Superior; the Menominee, Winnebago, Sauk, Fox, and Miami in present Wisconsin; and the Potawatomi in western Lower Michigan, with the Ottawa on their east and the Miami on the south around the lower end of Lake Michigan. These Indians of historic time

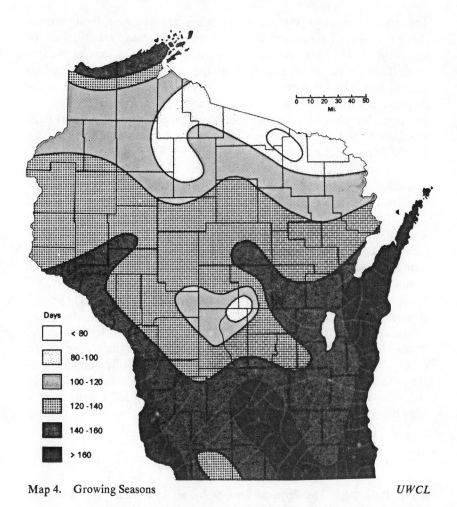

Map 4. Growing Seasons   *UWCL*

come within the purview of the cultural anthropologist and historian, since Europeans had contacts with them and wrote about them. The observations of the fur traders, priests, and soldiers were not scientific, but they form the raw material for study of these people, along with the artifacts of their cultures and the oral traditions of their descendants. But the record is far from complete, and the impact of European culture on their own was disastrous.

Anthropologists group Indian tribes by language families. The largest of these is the Algonkian, which dominated the eastern woodland from the Atlantic coast to the Mississippi, and north from Virginia and

Tennessee to Hudson Bay. All of the tribes named above, living around the upper Great Lakes, were of the Algonkian language family, with the exception of the Huron and the Winnebago. The Huron were of the Iroquois family, but were not part of the strongly organized Iroquois League which had penetrated the Algonkian range along the line of the Appalachian Mountains and occupied the strategic Mohawk valley and Finger Lakes country of present northern New York. The Winnebago were related to the Sioux tribes who dominated the plains from the Mississippi to the Rockies.

The Hurons were an agricultural people who farmed intensively the traditional corn, squash, and beans and were to become the farmers of the Great Lakes fur trade. The Chippewa, who ranged mainly north of lakes Huron and Superior, were primarily a hunting people whose land was not adapted to agriculture. The Chippewa had refined the Indian canoe and moved by water. Unlike the other tribes discussed here, they were not a sedentary people but a nomadic people who usually travelled in small family groups. The other peoples were essentially sedentary, devoted to agriculture and hunting in season on the prairie, in communal groups.

The culture of the Chippewa proved to be best adapted to the requirements of the fur trade. Before many generations, all of the Indians of the upper Lakes would be mistakenly identified as historically nomadic people primarily engaged in hunting. The fur trade was a hard taskmaster and from its pressures emerged a common, bastardized culture resembling the most rootless of these, the Chippewa.

Selected Bibliography

Black, Robert F. "The Physical Geography of Wisconsin." *The Wisconsin Blue Book,* 1964, pp. 171–77. A short, useful sketch.

Brown, Ralph H. *Historical Geography of the United States.* New York, 1948. Brief and of limited use.

Douglas, John M. *The Indians in Wisconsin's History.* Milwaukee Public Museum Popular Science Handbook Series, no. 6. Milwaukee, 1954. Their history, but mainly their adaptation to their environment in elementary terms.

Garland, John H., ed. *The North American Midwest: A Regional Geography.* New York, 1955. The emphasis is on economic development since 1800.

Hickerson, Harold. *The Chippewa and Their Neighbors: A Study in Ethnohistory.* New York, 1970. More ethnology and method than history.

Kinietz, W. Vernon. *The Indians of the Western Great Lakes, 1615–1760.*

Map 5.   The State in 1973

UWCL

Ann Arbor: Ann Arbor Paperbacks, 1965. Covers the hegira of the Huron to the western shore of Lake Michigan and contains material on individual tribes.

Leonard, William Ellery. "Ghosts in Wisconsin." In Walter Havighurst, ed., *Land of the Long Horizons*. New York, 1960. A poet evoking the landscape.

Leopold, Aldo. *A Sand County Almanac*. New York: Oxford Paperbacks, 1968. Describes the Wisconsin wilderness as it was.

Martin, Lawrence. *The Physical Geography of Wisconsin*. Wisconsin Geological and Natural History Survey, bulletin 36, Educational Series no. 4. 1st ed., 1916; 2d ed., 1932. 3d ed. Madison: University of Wisconsin Press, 1965. The standard work.

Maxwell, Moreau S. "A Change in the Interpretation of Wisconsin's Prehistory." *Wisconsin Magazine of History* 33:427–43. Useful for an appreciation of the problems of field archeologists working in Wisconsin.

Nesbitt, Paul H. "Rock River's Indians." *Wisconsin Magazine of History* 28: 416–21. Indian life in an area conducive to agriculture.

Quimby, George Irving. *Indian Life in the Upper Great Lakes, 11,000 B.C. to A.D. 1800*. Chicago, 1960. An informative book for the layman, by an expert.

Radin, Paul. *Indians of the United States*. 2d ed. New York, 1944. Radin did an earlier volume on the Winnebago; this is for the layman.

Ritzenthaler, Robert D. *Prehistoric Indians of Wisconsin*. Milwaukee Public Museum Popular Science Handbook Series, no. 4. Milwaukee, 1953. What is known and unknown about Wisconsin prehistory and why.

Ritzenthaler, Robert D. and Pat. *The Woodland Indians of the Western Great Lakes*. American Museum Science Books. Garden City, N.Y., 1970. A topical summary with a useful bibliography of available studies.

Underhill, Ruth M. *Red Man's America: A History of Indians in the United States*. Chicago, 1953. A synthesis of scholarship for the layman.

Wissler, Clark. *Indians of the United States*. New York, 1951. A readable account by a distinguished anthropologist.

FRANCE AND
THE EMPIRE OF
THE ST. LAWRENCE

2

France controlled the destinies of what is now Wisconsin for nearly a century before losing all of New France to the British in 1763. Yet the influence of that control left little to mark its passage beyond some names on the land. The tiny population of Frenchmen was simply inundated by a flood of Americans who spoke a different language, brought a quite different culture, had radically different ideas about the uses to which the land was to be put, and felt no uncertainty about their mission to impose their language and culture, their social, political, and economic order upon it. But this does not explain why, 130 years after Jean Nicolet stepped ashore at Green Bay, the French had only one permanent settlement in all of Wisconsin. Even Green Bay, although established as a fort in 1717, was only an outpost of Mackinac where residents from points west had to repair to find a priest in residence or to execute a legal instrument.

The failure on the part of the French to exploit Wisconsin as anything more than a source of furs and a portage to the Mississippi did not result from any want of appreciation of the possibilities of the country. Pierre Radisson, who wintered in the Wisconsin country in 1660, wrote that "the country was so pleasant, so beautifull and fruitfull that it grieved me to see yt ye world could not discover such inticing country to live in." The grandiose dreams of the enthusiast Robert Cavelier, Sieur de La

Salle, to found an empire between the Lakes and Louisiana displayed an appreciation of the country's possibilities for broad settlement. Nicolas Perrot prospected the lead mines on the upper Mississippi before 1700 and showed the Indians improved methods of mining. French traders and explorers reported evidences of other minerals. An agricultural and commercial people, the French were as alive as anyone to the rich possibilities of the vast empire they explored and claimed, but their ambitions and energies were thwarted by the meagerness of their numbers and means in the face of the distances and difficulties encountered.

It was the Portuguese and Spanish who pioneered the expansion of the known world to the Far East, and westward to a New World which lay athwart the route they sought to China and the Indies. Pope Alexander VI divided this unknown world between the two in 1494, and both grew rich. The new sources of wealth and the rise in European prices that resulted were serious embarrassments for monarchs whose revenues came from customary levies upon land. The two nations which were to lead in later struggles for empire were hard pressed. France, primarily a land power, was late in entering the competition for empire by exploration. England was considered a poor relation among European nations, remote and weak, but the long War of the Roses ended in 1485, and under the Tudor monarchs her maritime strength developed and became a tradition.

The Reformation made it easier for the French as well as the English to ignore the Pope's division of the unexplored areas of the world, but Spanish power kept them out of the Caribbean and South America except as freebooters. They then turned their attention to the coasts of North America and a search for the Northwest Passage to the Far East, a search which would fascinate men even in the twentieth century.

Jacques Cartier, in 1534, was to solve one of the great puzzles of this search for France. Aided by a grant from Francis I, he sailed westward, hoping to break Spain's monopoly on what seemed an incredibly rich harvest by entering the interior of America from the north. The coast of Newfoundland, occupied in season by Breton fishermen for drying fish and trading with the Indians, he pronounced to be a land bequeathed by God to Cain. Pressing on into the Gulf of St. Lawrence, he confirmed the existence of the great river. Cartier made two more voyages for Francis, sailing as far as an Iroquois-Huron settlement at present Montreal and bringing home iron pyrites which he thought to be gold. It was a fair land that he saw, but not an Indian civilization providing ready booty. Nor had he proved the existence of a Northwest Passage, although he did learn of water routes leading to other lands and peoples beyond. This was not enough to sustain the interest of a revenue-hungry monarch.

Official French interest in Cartier's discoveries languished after the reigns of Francis I and his successor Henry II. A weakened monarchy and religious wars followed, until the first of the Bourbons, Henry IV, took the throne in 1589. But other enterprising Frenchmen were drawn to the St. Lawrence by a brisk trade which had developed between the Indians and the Bretons, Portuguese, and English fishing on the Grand Banks. The fishermen went ashore to dry their fish and found the natives eager for any bit of metal gear that they might part with. Furs were soon established as the medium of exchange for these treasures—especially beaver skins, which were ideal for the best-quality felts used by European hatmakers.

With the accession of Henry IV, Samuel Champlain, who had visited Spanish America and was a recognized geographer and colonial expert, was chosen to lead in exploiting France's long-neglected rights to Cartier's discoveries. According to the prevalent mercantilist theory, colonies provided necessary raw materials without an outflow of gold from the empire, and a captive market as well. Empires were deemed essential to national health; colonies were no longer simply fortuitous sources of precious metals.

Henry granted a monopoly to a company of courtiers who were to have control of the growing fur trade in the St. Lawrence. In exchange for this privilege, the company was to undertake to found a colony there —not an easy task, surely, given the French aristocracy's disposition to look upon the environs of Paris as the limits of its world. Champlain, acting for the grantees, made a number of voyages to the St. Lawrence and in 1609, after disappointments and false starts, established what was to become Quebec. For twenty-five years, until his death in 1635, he guided the infant colony, despite the assassination of his patron, Henry IV, changes in the original grant, and intrigues at court by rivals. He proved to be one of the great colonial administrators of history.

It was the luck of the French to appropriate for themselves the valley of the great St. Lawrence River. While the British colonies clung to the Atlantic coast, developing relatively tidy colonies devoted to commercial agriculture, shipbuilding, commerce, and sometimes illegal manufacturing, the Frenchmen rapidly adapted themselves to the woodsman's and boatman's skills of their Indian allies and pressed inland over the long waterways of the St. Lawrence, Great Lakes, and Mississippi River system until they had linked up an empire from the Gulf of St. Lawrence to the Gulf of Mexico. But Frenchmen at home felt no great incentive to leave their broad, fertile land to make new farms in a wilderness. Those who came to farm were recruited, subsidized, or sent, while others came as adventurers to improve their fortunes or as missionaries zealous to harvest souls. New France was no refuge for the discontented and politically unreliable, but was a crown colony under the control of a highly centralized bureaucracy. The colony's destinies were subject to the whims of an absolute monarch whose views were swayed by courtiers and the hierarchy of the church. Once in the New World a Frenchman settled either in Quebec, which was a provincial copy of Paris with its court and a countryside burdened by a system of feudal grants, or he went on to Montreal, which was the center for the fur trade with its complicated relationships of partners, *engagés,* and credits reaching out to individual Indian hunters even beyond the Mississippi.

The fur trade, a monopoly licensed by the crown, was the life blood of the empire. It paid the costs of the civil administration and the military, built the posts in the wilderness, and transported the priests on their missions. The needs of the trade determined policy toward the Indians when the king was not persuaded otherwise by the church. Furs were the only dependable form of wealth that could be transported over the great distances involved by the means available, the canoe and batteau. The trade was prodigal in the exploitation of its basic resources, the animals that grew the pelts and the Indians who hunted and trapped them. The beaver furnished the basic pelt of the trade and was soon hunted to extinction in successively more remote areas. The trade moved on west or north, the Indian serving it, losing his civilization in the process and failing to gain a new one useful to him or to the Europeans, after the trade had stripped the land of its fur resources. He became a displaced person in his own land.

If Champlain had a failing, it was his passion for exploration, to which he was sometimes inclined to subordinate his colonizing activities and even the fur trade. A man of resolution and resourcefulness, he made a number of explorations himself, questioning the Indians closely and adding to his geographical knowledge. In his later years he entrusted explorations to younger men, among them Jean Nicolet and Etienne Brule. Samuel Champlain's writings, drawings, and maps are a priceless record of these years.

While Champlain cherished the hope that his explorations might lead to the discovery of a passage to the Pacific or to riches other than furs, they in fact affected the fur trade and the relations of the French with their Indian clients in very practical ways. The French have generally been credited with a superior ability to get along with the Indians and retain their friendship. It is assumed that this was because they exhibited less racial prejudice and readily intermarried with the Indians, adopted their mode of life, and paid them the compliment of learning their language. Furthermore, the Frenchman usually was not a farmer and therefore had no reason to dispossess the Indian, enslave him, or change his way of living. While some of this may be true, the record of French relations with the Indians does not bear out the implied comparison with the English and Americans. Seeds of trouble between the French and Indians were present from the first, and Champlain's explorations and decisions brought them to fruition.

The Indians with whom the French had their first contacts and trade were Algonkian tribes. While some Algonkian tribes recognized a degree of kinship, others met as total strangers and in their encounters with each other were every bit as savage as western Europeans. The blood feud was common, and status was gained in warfare. Only occasionally did a leader like Pontiac or Tecumseh emerge among the Indians, one who could persuade warring tribes to bury the hatchet and make common cause against the whites.

The Indians were a primitive people but not simple: they recognized the advantages which European utensils, tools, and weapons gave them over neighboring peoples who did not have them. Nor were they a rootless, nomadic people. On the contrary, they had a strong sense of communal ownership of a customary range, and of its boundaries. This, combined with a quick perception of relative values once the trade was established, brought predictable results. The Indians were going to use their rights to customary range, or the advantages in war, to levy toll on the trade or to act as middlemen for trade with the tribes more remote from the Europeans. The depletion of animals in their own ranges was an added incentive for such control.

Another fact of the fur trade that Champlain soon learned was that monopoly was not easy to enforce. Without monopoly, a sort of Gresham's Law operated which drove goods beneficial to the Indians out of the marketplace and replaced them with brandy or rum. The American Indians had not discovered the arts of brewing, fermenting, and distilling and were unprepared to handle liquor. They did have a place in their culture for a state of exhilaration or trance induced by various means. Alcohol provided a shortcut to this illusory state of well-being or revelation which they adopted with disastrous enthusiasm.

European social and epidemic diseases were catastrophic enough to the Indians to obliterate entire communities. European tools, weapons, utensils, and textiles made the natives dependent on the fur trade. Skills and crafts of their former way of life fell into disuse. A man owning a gun lost the art of using bow or lance and went hungry if the tenuous supply lines of the trade failed to bring him powder and shot. The requirements of the trade turned the warrior into an exterminator of the game which had provided his livelihood, or into an irregular soldier in the wars of European empires. Liquor gave the Indian a temporary refuge from his degradation, while it confirmed for the European his belief in his own superiority.

Champlain deplored the effects of unregulated trade in spirits upon the Indians. The church, experiencing a renewal, was also interested in the status of the trade and its abuses. The Canadian woods were to see many zealous priests, some of whom perceived the Indians' basic humanity while prayerfully courting martyrdom among them. But neither crown officials nor churchmen could entirely control the trade or the contacts of French and Indians.

The Ottawa and Huron who traded to the western Lakes maintained a tenuous contact with the French. It was through them that the French learned of the Winnebago, who as a Siouan people had a culture and language strange to their Indian informants. The Winnebago called themselves the People of the Stinking Water, rendered as *Puant* in French. Champlain seized upon this title as evidence that the Winnebago lived, or had lived, on salt water and could lead the French to the elusive Northwest Passage. To investigate this possibility, mediate the differences between the Huron and Winnebago, and incidentally contact these new customers directly, Champlain sent Jean Nicolet, who had established his usefulness as a woodsman, interpreter, and diplomat, to accompany the Huron to the West.

Other Algonkian tribes living around the upper Lakes—the Chippewa, Ottawa, Potawotami, Miami, and Illinois—had also been displaced by the westward shift of the Hurons and their efforts to control the trade. Nicolet was to contact all of these people, make peace among them as well as among the Fox and Kickapoo ranging beyond Green Bay, and bring them into alliance with the French. After various stops with tribes encountered along the way, Nicolet stepped ashore, so it is commonly agreed, at Green Bay, arrayed in an elaborate Chinese costume and firing his pistols for dramatic effect. He accomplished his mission and returned to Quebec in the following year, 1635, the year of Champlain's death.

Nicolet's visit was an isolated one. Cardinal Richelieu, who had now come to power in France, was interested in building a colony of settlers, an aspect of the work of the Company of New France which had not flourished. But the Iroquois, becoming progressively bolder, attacked the

French at Three Rivers in 1637. It seemed that only within the walls of Quebec were the French safe. The fur trade languished. The Jesuits pushed beyond the barrier of the Iroquois to work among the Huron, but occasionally they fell into the hands of the enemy, who were specialists in the Indian practices of torture. Quebec grew slowly, cut off from the West and barely clinging to the outposts at Montreal and Three Rivers.

For twenty years, from 1640 to 1660, the Iroquois controlled the situation. They made war under the very walls of Quebec, and threatened to take it as well as the other French strong points, except that they cared little for the hardships of a long siege. War, for the Indians, was the most exciting of pastimes, but piling their bodies in windrows to take a fortified post was no patriotic necessity.

The lack of unity among the other tribes had permitted the Iroquois Nation, a strong union of related tribes, to establish itself in the Mohawk Valley and to expand from there. Confident in their ability and organization, the Iroquois ranged far to bring war to their neighbors. They controlled the upper reaches of the St. Lawrence, the route to lakes Ontario and Erie.

Although the French held Montreal, the Iroquois had them cut off from the interior by way of the St. Lawrence. The alternative route was by way of the Ottawa River in a northwesterly direction. Ascending the Ottawa, the canoes were portaged to waters that led through Lake Nipissing to Georgian Bay, a part of Lake Huron. The way lay westward from there on the upper Great Lakes.

The aggressive Iroquois were bent upon the destruction of the Huron, their competitors as middlemen for control of the trade westward. Unable to stand and fight this superior foe, the Huron, an agricultural people already being converted into traders and fur hunters, were driven from their customary range, and their wanderings are illustrative of the impact of the fur trade upon the native population. Settled in one of the great concentrations of Indian population between Lake Ontario and Georgian Bay, they numbered an estimated 30,000 to 40,000 people. The Iroquois razed their fields and villages, massacred many, took slaves, and put the remnants to flight.

The Huron, Neutrals, and Ottawa made up the exodus who fled by way of Mackinac Island to Green Bay and set up a village, probably on Washington Island, then known as Huron Island. Their numbers were sadly depleted. Arrogant and overconfident, the Iroquois sent a large war party to seek them out, but failing to find sufficient food along the way arrived in a weakened condition. The Iroquois begged food from their intended victims, who had sufficient enterprise to slaughter the intruders. A truce was made with the French in the following year, 1654, but it was only a breathing spell. The Iroquois were not tamed, but they had lost some of their power to overawe the French and their Indian allies.

The Huron who had fled to the western shore of Lake Michigan moved inland to the environs of Lake Pepin on the upper Mississippi, where they set themselves up as middlemen for the Santee Sioux. They were soon at odds with the Sioux, who drove them northward. The Huron then settled for a time at Chequamegon Bay, where the Ottawa had moved. It was there that the missionaries, who had worked among the Huron before the Iroquois despoiled their lands, found them, through the agency of some Ottawa traders who brought Father René Ménard there in 1660. Ménard, lost in the wilderness of northern Wisconsin, was replaced by the more forceful Father Claude Allouez, who found a collection of displaced tribesmen, numbering only 800 warriors, when he arrived at Chequamegon Bay in 1665. His writings are among the best sources on the Algonkian tribes and Hurons whom he found there.

After the Iroquois menace abated, the Huron and Ottawa turned eastward again, settling on Mackinac and Manitoulin islands around 1670. Thirty years later they removed to Detroit at the invitation of the French. In Michigan and Ohio, in later years, the Huron remnants were generally known as the Wyandot, and were among those defeated by Anthony Wayne at Fallen Timbers in 1795. They were removed to Kansas in 1842, and subsequently to Indian territory in what is today Oklahoma.

Twenty years after Jean Nicolet's visit to the West, the St. Lawrence Valley, under the harassment of the Iroquois, had no more than 1,000 Frenchmen, French-and-Indians, and Indian wards. The people had had no contact with the western tribes for nearly four years. The defeat of the Iroquois expedition to the West in 1653, however, gave the Ottawa an opportunity to reopen trade and act as middlemen for the Algonkian tribes that had fled to Wisconsin, and they were persuaded to take two French traders with them on their return. To this circumstance we owe the journals of Pierre-Esprit Radisson recording the several trips which he and his brother-in-law, Médard Chouart de Groseilliers, made to the area that is now Wisconsin.

Radisson and Groseilliers are well known to history. After Groseilliers' first voyage to the wilderness, he and Radisson returned on three other occasions to trade around and beyond Lake Superior. The French authorities refused to license them as legal traders, calling them *coureurs-de-bois,* a term meaning illegal traders under proscription. While on one such expedition north of Lake Superior, the pair came in contact with the Cree Indians, who informed them of the rich fur country tributary to Hudson Bay. They immediately saw the advantage of tapping this trade directly by sea, for the entrance to Hudson Bay was now known. Heavily fined by the French authorities for their illegal trading, Radisson and Groseilliers carried their plans to England, where Prince Rupert, a cousin of Charles I, took up their schemes. The result was the issuance of a charter in 1670 to the Hudson's Bay Company, a venture which led to years of rivalry with the French and trading companies operating out of Montreal. Radisson's journal is a great document of early Wisconsin history. "We weare Cesars being nobody to contradict us," he wrote of their wintering near Chequamegon Bay in 1660, but it was a rugged and dangerous life in which "our gutts became very straight by our long fasting."

As the Iroquois threat receded, French fortunes improved in New France and brought a period of increased western activity under the leadership of Jean Talon and the Comte de Frontenac. This coincided with the reign of Louis XIV (1643–1715), who brought France to the peak of her power during his long rule and then dissipated it in endless wars on the Continent. Talon's objective was to open the interior to French trade and settlement. In 1667 Nicolas Perrot, seeking to break the monopoly of the Ottawa on the far-western trade, journeyed to Wisconsin, contacting the Algonkian tribes that had moved there and tying them in alliance with the French. In subsequent years he built posts on the Mississippi at Mount Trempealeau and Lake Pepin, opening trade with the Sioux beyond the river, and was among those Europeans who reported on the wanderings of the Hurons.

Daniel Greysolon Du Luth, a man of great courage and commanding presence, operated similarly in what is now Minnesota, bringing peace among the tribes. Obsessed with the idea of reaching the Pacific, Du Luth was frustrated by such happenstances as the rescue of Father Hennepin, a Jesuit missionary, from Sioux raiders. Hennepin had been with a party sent out by La Salle to explore the upper Mississippi in 1679, and was not averse to taking much credit for explorations made by Du Luth and others.

La Salle's schemes had included building an empire in the interior based upon a huge grant centered in what is now Illinois, and Talon hoped that the Mississippi might be the river that the Spanish reported running into the Gulf of California. He determined to explore this possibility and in 1673 sent Louis Joliet, with Father Marquette, across the Fox-Wisconsin route, thence down the Mississippi as far as the mouth of the Arkansas River. When they saw that the Indians there had European goods, they were assured that the river emptied into the Gulf of Mexico. Now the French had a waterway from Quebec to the Gulf and could contest possession of the latter with Spain.

Adrien Joliet, Louis's brother, had explored a new route back from Lake Huron by way of Lake Erie, and to his surprise met La Salle's party coming in by way of Lake Ontario, the first Frenchmen to use the route by way of lakes Erie and Ontario. La Salle was beginning the incredible labors of exploration, building, and scheming which ended a dozen years later in his murder, at the hands of his own men, while attempting to found a colony at the mouth of the Mississippi.

Governor Frontenac had succeeded Intendant Talon* as the guiding spirit of New France in 1672, and it was he who directed the work of exploration in this period, but despite the vigor of his administration, the long death agony of the French colony was beginning. In 1688, the Glorious Revolution in England toppled James II, who had been beholden to the French King. England now stood against the ambitions of Louis XIV, playing the role of banker to the enemies of France and using her sea power to harass French communications.

The zeal of the missionary priesthood was not rewarded by many evidences of conversion among the Indians in New France, and churchmen believed that their work was hindered by the presence of the fur traders. Many traders were rough and irreverent men who debauched the Indians with liquor, prostituted their women, and fomented quarrels with their competitors. The churchmen had the king's ear at a time when he was particularly susceptible to their arguments: the market for furs was depressed, while the trade was producing an oversupply. In 1696, Louis ordered the western posts closed, withdrew the garrisons, and threatened severe punishment for any trader who should violate his edict closing the interior to trade. The missionaries were to have sole access to the Indians, and the fur monopoly would be preserved by having the Indians come into the St. Lawrence valley annually to do their trading.

The new policy, however, did not work. The years of diplomacy by men like Nicolas Perrot, who had brought the Wisconsin Indians firmly into the French orbit and held them as allies in King William's War (1689–1701), were in danger of being thrown away. The western Indians did not come to Montreal to do their trading, but depended upon English goods reaching them through the Iroquois and the French coureurs-de-bois who evaded the law.

Another policy was called for to redeem the frontier for France and hold the western tribes. It was decided to build a limited number of

---

* The office of intendant represented the monarch directly, whereas the governorship was ordinarily a ceremonial office reserved for the great nobles. This distinction was blurred in New France, where the governorship was not established as an hereditary office. The form was retained, and created some confusion.

strong points and to concentrate the friendly tribes around them, where the Indians could be turned into Frenchmen, tilling the soil within the sound of church bells under the protection of French cannon. The strong points selected were at Detroit and Lake Peoria with posts at Chicago and other intermediate points along the route to New Orleans.

It was during the implementation of this concentration policy that the French became involved in their bootless wars with the Fox, the most intractable of the Wisconsin Indians. The range of the Fox was on the upper Fox River, strategically astride the waterway leading to the Mississippi and the Sioux Indians. They had taken advantage of this to exact toll from the trade, enforcing their rule by occasionally killing a Frenchman or an ally.

Although a large body of Fox Indians joined the other tribes in settling near Detroit at French invitation, they were not trusted but were suspected of sympathy with the Iroquois. When ordered to return to Wisconsin they refused to do so. With the connivance of the French, the Indian allies fell upon the band of Fox and annihilated them. The Fox were a fearsome people, and those remaining in Wisconsin sought revenge and regularly ambushed parties of Frenchmen and their Indian allies throughout the upper Lakes. In 1716 a large force of French and Indians was dispatched from Montreal. The Fox stood their ground at their fortified village near Little Lake Butte des Morts through a three-day siege, finally asking for terms but remaining hostile.

Indians were not interested in becoming farmers, nor were the French traders willing to go out of business, and the French policy of concentration was a failure. To the credit of the French, they did not persist in the policy, but returned to the former system of licensed traders and the maintenance of many posts. Mackinac was reopened, and replaced Detroit as the center of trade for the upper Lakes. A fort was built at Green Bay, in 1717, to command the Fox-Wisconsin route to the Mississippi. Other posts were maintained at Chequamegon Bay and among the Sioux on the upper Mississippi.

Meanwhile the Fox were biding their time. The leader of the irreconcilables among them, Kiala, anticipated the later efforts of Pontiac and Tecumseh to effect a coalition of tribes to drive out the whites. He failed, and in 1728 the French, infuriated by his dealings with the hated Iroquois, mounted a second expedition against them. It was far from a military success, but the French succeeded in detaching Kiala's allies one by one and turning them against the Fox in a war of extermination. The neighboring Sauk Indians took in the pitiful remnants of the once powerful Fox, thus incurring the wrath of the French. A second battle was fought at Big Lake Butte des Morts in which the French suffered heavy losses. They demanded action by their Indian allies against the Fox and Sauk.

Eventually the French lost much by their implacable hostility toward the Fox, and the other tribes came to realize that the French had played upon their weaknesses in enlisting their aid. They saw that the French might wreak a similar vengeance on them; as Nicolas Perrot reminded his countrymen, almost every tribe at some time had killed or threatened Frenchmen. But his call for moderation fell on deaf ears. French authority in the West sank to a low ebb and depended more and more upon the influence of individual traders. The prolonged wars with the Fox forced the French into the Ohio country and sharper conflict with the British.

It was a relative handful of hardy, heedless, and venturesome men who carried on the trade and its expansion, organized into a tight society with a carefully regulated hierarchy. The upper crust retired to France, Quebec, or Montreal, while junior members became permanent residents farther afield—the de Langlades and Grignons of Green Bay, for example. But all of New France, by 1750, mustered a population of only 60,000 to 70,000 that could be counted as French, while the English colonists numbered more than 1,250,000. Quebec was only one-third the size of Boston, which was smaller than Philadelphia or New York.

Control of the high seas enabled the English to cut off the French flow of goods on which the fur trade depended. In wartime, the French in New France had little in the way of manufactures to make up the loss. The Indians then turned to the Iroquois or British traders and found goods of English manufacture both cheaper and of better quality. Their loyalties were continually being tested by gifts and blandishments. They were not dependable as allies in the European style of warfare which characterized much of the fighting on the seaboard. They disliked open engagements, malingered at times, and were not easily restrained from their own manner of fighting, which violated the ideas of civilized warfare held by the French officers.

Except for the last of the four wars fought between 1689 and 1763, the American theater of operations was decidedly peripheral in the eyes of the French monarch. Preoccupied with monumental struggles on the Continent, he rightly assumed that colonial possessions were pawns in the game that would be won or lost on European battlefields or in ensuing peace negotiations. It was frustrating for colonial officers and completely mystifying to their Indian allies to find defeat so often snatched from the jaws of victory.

France produced such brilliant and dedicated officers as Pierre Le Moyne d'Iberville and the Marquis de Montcalm to lead her forces in

America, but the struggle was an unequal one. Despite the brilliant capacities of many civil and military officers of New France, the weaknesses which were to overwhelm the French monarchy in 1789 were all too evident in the administration of the colony. New France was the personal fief of the crown, run by a centralized bureaucracy staffed by feudal privilege and court intrigue. At one point the minister of marine, who had the administration of the colonies in his charge, was a boy of fourteen who had inherited the post on his father's death. The administration of the colony was always loaded with noble placemen. When Montcalm wished to withdraw forces from outlying posts which served no purpose and simply increased French danger, the governor's secretary thwarted the move. He was the accomplice of contractors supplying the posts with goods costing 150,000 livres, for which they collected 1,000,000 livres from the king.

In 1754, while war was in progress, the last intendant of New France wrote to a friend in command of a fort in Acadia: "Profit, my dear Vergor, by your place; trim, lop off; all power is in your hands; do it quickly so that you may be able to come and join me in France and buy an estate near mine." A fitting epitaph for the passing of New France in America.

Selected Bibliography

Adams, Arthur T., ed. *The Explorations of Pierre Esprit Raddison*. Minneapolis, 1961. Tries to reconcile the chronology in Radisson's *Journal*.

Bakeless, John. *The Eyes of Discovery: The Pageant of North America as Seen by the First Explorers*. Philadelphia, 1950. Literary in treatment but well grounded.

Bishop, Morris G. *Champlain: The Life of Fortitude*. New York, 1948. For the popular audience, but based upon the sources and available scholarship.

Brebner, J. Bartlet. *Canada: A Modern History*. Ann Arbor, 1960. One hundred pages on the French and British periods to 1783.

————. *The Explorers of North America, 1492–1806*. New York, Anchor Paperbacks, 1955. Originally published in 1933, the book in this handy edition lacks the maps of the original.

Caruso, John Anthony. *The Mississippi Valley Frontier: The Age of French Exploration and Settlement*. Indianapolis, 1966. Mixes the popular and the scholarly.

Clark, James I. *Father Claude Allouez, Missionary*. Madison, 1957.

————. *Wisconsin: Land of French, Indians, and the Beaver*. Madison 1955. Historical Society Pamphlet for public school use.

Crouse, Nellis M. *La Verendrye: Fur Trader and Explorer*. Ithaca, N.Y.,

1956. Not much on Wisconsin, but a good account of an extraordinary explorer.

Delanglez, Jean. *Life and Voyages of Louis Jolliet, 1645–1700*. Chicago, 1948. Glowing, somewhat uncritical, but a good adventure story.

Hamilton, Raphael N. *Marquette's Explorations: The Narratives Reexamined*. Madison, 1970. Sifts contrary and obscure evidence.

Innis, Harold A. *The Fur Trade in Canada: An Introduction to Canadian Economic History*. New Haven, 1930. Good on the beaver and the impact of the trade on the Indians.

Kellogg, Louise Phelps. *The French Regime in Wisconsin and the Northwest*. Madison, 1925. The principal source for this chapter.

Kennedy, John H. *Jesuit and Savage in New France*. New Haven, 1950. Useful coverage of a subject about which much has been written.

Kenton, Edna, ed. *Black Gown and Redskins: Adventures and Travels of the Early Jesuit Missionaries in North America*. New York, 1956. A useful selection from the *Jesuit Relations*.

Lanctot, Gustave. *A History of Canada*. Vol. 1, *From Its Origins to the Royal Regime, 1663*. Vol. 2, *From the Royal Regime to the Treaty of Utrecht, 1663–1713*. Vol. 3, *From the Treaty of Utrecht to the Treaty of Paris*, 1713–1763. Cambridge, Mass., 1963–65. Very readable.

Morse, Eric W. *Canoe Routes of the Voyageurs*. Pamphlet reprint from the *Canadian Geographical Journal*, May, July, Aug., 1961.

Nute, Grace Lee. *Caesars of the Wilderness*. New York, 1943. Standard biography of Radisson and Groseilliers.

"Radisson and Groseilliers in Wisconsin." *State Historical Society of Wisconsin [SHSW] Collections*. Vol. 11, pp. 64–96. Madison, 1888. Source of the material on the pair wintering in northern Wisconsin.

Rich, Edwin E. *The History of the Hudson's Bay Company, 1670–1870*. 2 vols. London, 1958–59. The company was involved in Lake Superior trade.

Vogel, Virgil J. "Wisconsin's Name: A Linguistic Puzzle." *Wisconsin Magazine of History* 48:181–86. It is an unsolved puzzle.

Wilson, Clifford P. "Where Did Nicolet Go?" *Minnesota History* 27:216–20. (Sept. 1946). Interesting argument that Nicolet landed, not at Green Bay, but on the Lake Superior shore.

Wrong, George M. *The Rise and Fall of New France*. 2 vols. New York, 1928. An older work, but useful.

THE BRITISH YEARS
1750–1775

3

It might appear that the North American continent afforded ample room for the French and English to develop their colonies without continual clash, but their imperial ambitions bore no relation to the actual space needed for their colonial settlers. The fur trade and control of the Indian tribes were inevitable points of friction. They readily found others. The claims of both parties to the continent were unbounded. As an example, Virginia's grant ran from sea to sea, with the northern border running off in a northwesterly line which cut through the Sault Ste. Marie. The Sault, of course, was unknown in 1609 when the grant was made. Virginia was still firm in her pretensions in 1783 when the lands were ceded to the American Confederation. Governor Frontenac dreamed of an empire stretching to Mexico and claimed New York for good measure, on the basis of Verrazano's voyage in 1524. Any claim might be made good in a trial at arms and therefore was not abandoned, save temporarily under duress.

The charter to the Hudson's Bay Company, issued in 1670, moved the French to a series of formal ceremonies in the interior, beginning at Sault Ste. Marie in 1671, taking possession in the name of Louis XIV "of all other countries, rivers, lakes and their tributaries contiguous and adjacent thereto, those discovered and to be discovered, bounded on one side by the Northern and Western seas, and on the other side by the South

Sea, this land in all its length and breadth." Given the comprehensive character of this catalogue, it seemed a supererogation for Perrot and Du Luth to duplicate this formula, as they did, further west.

France had the English colonies flanked by the line of communications and posts she was completing through the Lakes, down the Mississippi, and eastward into the Ohio country, meeting the British expanding westward. But when formal hostilities began, the main points of contact were the French strong points in Acadia (now Nova Scotia and New Brunswick), which offered havens for privateers attacking New England shipping; the Lake Champlain corridor pointing to Albany and Montreal; and the lands of the Iroquois, which lay across the shadowy border. The Iroquois, abetted by the English, were engaged in a fierce competition with the French for control of the fur trade around the Great Lakes and westward.

Privateering, raids, embassies, and Indian wars were constant, but official hostilities between France and England began in 1689 when William of Orange replaced James II on the English throne. The four wars which occupied over half of the next seventy-five years to 1763 were similar in pattern except for the last, which ended in an overwhelming British victory. In the American theater, the usual strategy of the British was to mount an overland attack against Montreal and a seaborne expedition against Quebec.

Most of the French on the frontier were engaged in the fur trade and accordingly were less vulnerable than communities of farm families. Just as the Iroquois were allies of the British, the French claimed the allegiance of the western tribes and called them into service in the St. Lawrence valley to counter Iroquois raids and assist in expeditions against the scattered British settlements, with demoralizing effect.

The British, despite their overwhelming numerical superiority, had difficulty concentrating their colonial militia. The southern and middle colonies were remote from the conflicts and resisted imperial levies for money and men. The New England colonies were in the habit of mounting their own campaigns, usually against the Acadian strong points which threatened their shipping. Like New York and Pennsylvania, they could claim the priorities of their own frontier settlements for protection in resisting British drafts on their forces.

King William's War (1689–97) ended in a draw and a peace based upon the status quo ante bellum in America; Queen Anne's War (1702–13) was won by the Duke of Marlborough on the Continent. The British fleet sent against Quebec was run aground by an incompetent admiral, but the French were forced to give up Hudson Bay, which they had

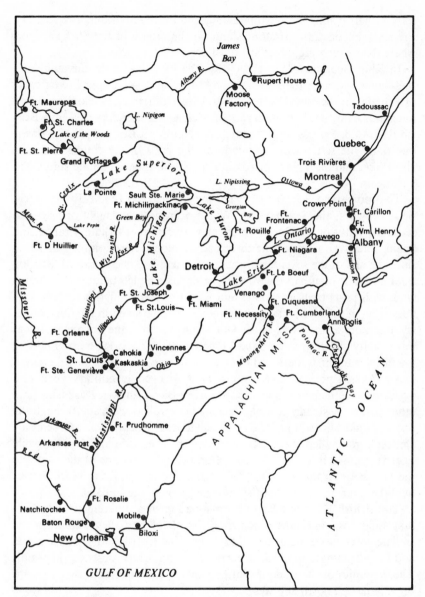

Map 6. The French Period. Jean Nicolet reached Green Bay in 1634, just one hundred years after Jacques Cartier's discovery of the St. Lawrence. After the French-Iroquois wars, exploration was resumed by Marquette and Joliet, who reached the upper Mississippi by the Fox and Wisconsin rivers. The French fur trade expanded along the new route, missionaries and the military followed, and posts and routes in the interior developed. Adapted from a map in Edward Whiting Fox, *Atlas of American History* (Oxford: The Clarendon Press, 1964)   *UWCL*

seized, their claims to Newfoundland, and more important, Acadia. The French retained Cape Breton Island, in the mouth of the St. Lawrence, where they built a great fort at Louisburg.

In King George's War (1744–48), the French had the advantage on the Continent, with the leadership of Maurice de Saxe and Frederick II of Prussia. In the New World, the growing strength of the American colonies was evident when the forces of Massachusetts, supported by a British fleet, took France's new fortress at Louisburg. But, as with the previous wars, the settlement was made on the basis of the course of events elsewhere, and the Treaty of Aix la Chapelle was based on the status quo ante again.

The fourth and decisive struggle, the French and Indian War (1755–63), known as the Seven Years' War in Europe, was fought primarily to settle the status of the North American possessions of Britain, France, and Spain. The rivalry among the three had developed new points of irritation since the end of the seventeenth century. There had been a race to develop a colony at the mouth of the Mississippi since La Salle's failure. The French won, with posts built at Mobile and Biloxi in 1699. English traders were appearing in the interior: a few on the Great Lakes and in the Ohio country, but more aggressively in the Old Southwest from the Carolinas. It was this activity which prompted the French to rescind the 1696 order closing the interior to fur traders and to build posts and missions along the Great Lakes–Mississippi route. Missions, later to become military posts and agricultural settlements, appeared at Green Bay, Cahokia, Kaskaskia, and other points. A strong post at Mackinac controlled the trade through the Sault to Lake Superior and the approach to Lake Michigan and Green Bay. Detroit commanded the waterway between lakes Erie and Huron, while Fort St. Louis (Illinois), like Green Bay, lay athwart one of the routes to the Mississippi from the Lakes. New Orleans was founded in 1718. France held the interior, despite British intrigues among the Indians.

The British Hudson's Bay Company adopted a different strategy. Establishing posts around the southern rim of the bay, they waited for the Indians to come to them, which they did. The British had superior goods and the advantages of cheaper carriage by ship to the posts on tidewater. The dynamics of the trade meant that the best hunting and trapping continually moved north and west.

The Fox Wars (1701–16, 1727–38) damaged French prestige in the upper Great Lakes and made the portages to the Mississippi by way of Green Bay and Chicago hazardous for them. Seeking alternatives, the French developed the route by way of the Maumee and Wabash rivers from the western end of Lake Erie to the Ohio. To protect this waterway, which was much shorter than the former routes to Louisiana by way of Lake Michigan, they strengthened posts, built new ones along the way, and also revived their interest in the St. Lawrence, Lake Ontario, Lake Erie route. At this point, the new posts at Fort Miami and Vincennes were less disturbing to the English than Fort Niagara, which gave the French a foothold in Iroquois territory. With their Indian allies, the French had more than held their own in the American phase of King George's War, concluded in 1748, despite the fact that English colonists held an advantage of twenty to one in men of militia age. Encouraged by this success, the French determined to secure new lines against British advance into the Ohio valley.

The British and their American colonists were equally fixed in their purpose to establish ownership over the same lands. In 1749, the Ohio Company, made up of influential men in England and Virginia, secured from the crown a grant of 200,000 acres on the upper Ohio River. The Washingtons were interested, along with Governor Fairfax of Virginia. Land speculation was a favorite form of investment among the colonists, who saw their population almost double each twenty-five years after 1700, with consequent pressure on the available land. The Ohio country was no longer *terra incognita* to them but was recognized as potentially rich agricultural land awaiting exploitation.

It was largely through their Iroquois allies, supplied by traders at Albany, that the British tampered with the Great Lakes trade. British policy was forwarded by the presence among the Iroquois of William Johnson, a young Irishman who settled among them to manage the affairs of a relative with lands in the Mohawk valley. Johnson married an Iroquois princess, and was later knighted for his work as Indian agent for Britain. In the Ohio valley itself, Pennsylvania traders ranged freely, and some attained considerable influence among the Indians there. The best known of these were George Croghan and Christopher Gist, who were later hired by the Ohio Company. Croghan, by the 1740s, was operating trading ventures as far west as the Illinois country and causing the French much concern over their own connections between Canada and Louisiana. A French captain who led a force from Fort Niagara down the Ohio in 1749 to reassert French authority reported "that the tribes of those localities are very badly disposed toward the French and entirely devoted to the English. I do not know by what means they can be brought back. . . . if we send to them for trade, our traders can never give our merchandise at English prices on account of the costs that they are obliged to incur." He went further, stating that French profits from the area were made by trading pelts with the English, who favored beaver, which the French had, while other furs purchased by the English from the Ohio Indians had a better market in France. Showing the flag, blazing trees, and burying lead plates were not sufficient to insure French dominion on the Ohio.

The French were losing their grip on the Ohio country, while the Fox Wars, general neglect, and corruption in the exploitation of trading privileges had seriously undermined their influence in the upper Great Lakes. Despite these handicaps, the Indians around Green Bay remained loyal to them and served in the eastern theater against the English. A prominent name among the western Indians at the time of the French and Indian War was that of Charles de Langlade, half French and half Ottawa, who settled in Green Bay in 1764 and is associated with its history through his own name and that of the Grignons. De Langlade was an officer in the French army operating out of Mackinac, where he had been raised.

The Pennsylvania trader, George Croghan, had boldly fortified a post at Pickawillany, a village of the Miami Indians on the upper reaches of the river of that name in present western Ohio. The post was close to the French route to the lower Ohio at Vincennes, which used the Maumee and Wabash rivers to cross the western end of Lake Erie. In 1749, Pierre Celeron had attempted to win these Indians back to their French allegiance, but without success. Three years later Charles de Langlade, leading a force of 240 of his Ottawa kinsmen and a few French, fell upon the village while most of the men were off on their summer hunt, killed an English trader, and captured five others. They ate the trader's heart and also ate the village chief, known as La Demoiselle to the French and as Old Briton to the English. The majority of the Miami changed their affiliation, although as Celeron remarked, "it is so rare . . . that a war with savages can bring about a very stable peace. . . ."

Peace was not to be. The French, determined to secure the Ohio country, were dispatching troops there to build and strengthen forts along the routes and especially at points to intercept the British traders: Presque Isle, Le Boeuf, Venango, and finally Dusquesne on the site of present Pittsburgh. To the British colonists who had claims to the same area, this was an act of war. The next act was the mission of George Washington to Fort Le Boeuf, in 1754, on behalf of the Virginia government. Washington, after an engagement in which ten Frenchmen were killed, was forced to retire under a truce. The war, which was to end disastrously for New France, had formally begun.

The story of the French and Indian War is a familiar one. Western tribesmen, including Menominee, Winnebago, Potawatomi, and others from the western shores of Lake Michigan, participated under the leadership of Charles de Langlade. Lieutenant de Langlade's Indian irregulars are generally credited with turning General Edward Braddock's encounter with the French forces, near Fort Dusquesne, into a rout in which Braddock was killed and 1,400 of his 1,900-man force were killed or wounded. They also took part in battles in the eastern theater, including two actions before Quebec. In January 1757 Langlade's command had a skirmish with the famous Rogers' Rangers. The action ended with the withdrawal of the English force with Rogers wounded. Paul Marin and his son Joseph, who shared with the governor of New France a monopoly of the fur trade through Green Bay, also had prominent roles in the war. The elder Marin had placated the western Indians after the second war with the Fox Indians, and although their exploitation of the trade was unconscionable, the Marins had great influence with the Wisconsin Indians.

The French-allied western Indians, as in previous wars with the British, were successful in most of their early encounters, but they were an embarrassment to Montcalm, who could not accept their savage customs in warfare. Their last great success was the capture of the British Fort William Henry on Lake Champlain, in the summer of 1757, where both Langlade and the younger Marin distinguished themselves. The Indian victors could not be restrained, and massacred many victims, both civilian and military. Sent home in disgrace, they carried with them the smallpox which had broken out among the English. The disease ran unchecked through the western tribesmen, greatly reducing their effectiveness as a fighting force.

The battle of Fort William Henry marked a turning point in the war. British forces struck back the next year, taking Fort Dusquesne and renaming it Fort Pitt. This success brought the Indians in the Ohio country, who had been undermined in their allegiance to the French by George Croghan, back into alliance with the British. Disaffection spread to the Potawatomi, who ranged along the shores of Lake Michigan up to Green Bay. The neighboring Menominee caught the spirit and struck at the Green Bay post, killing twenty-two Frenchmen, but they were defeated and gave up hostages. Montcalm recognized this unrest as more than a result of British insinuation, recording in his journal a passage about French administration at Green Bay: "Never have theft and license gone so far."

Europeans and Americans, looking at relations with the Indians, have seen in the Indians a fickle and treacherous people whose allegiance was never secure, but it must be understood that the Indians recognized themselves as pawns in a larger game. Dependent on the trade for their very weapons and other necessities, their apprehensions were often justified when warfare cut off their supplies. Their fickleness might better be recognized as an artful cynicism in which they required no schooling by the whites. The extravagance of Indian oratory, used to express undying fidelity, was readily matched by French, British, and American.

The war, like those preceding it, was not decided by the clash of arms on the frontier or even in the New World, the principal prize. This time, however, the British were successful in their seaborne campaign against Quebec, which fell to General Wolfe's army in September 1759. A year later, Montreal fell and Canada was out of the war. British forces already had taken the Ohio country and lower Great Lakes. The Indians, anxious to ride with the winner, drove their erstwhile French allies further west until all that remained were the posts at Mackinac, Green Bay, Detroit, and the Illinois villages.

Britain cut France off from her possessions and trading stations in Africa, India, the Far East, and America. Worried by British victories in Canada and the West Indies, and hopeful of regaining Gibraltar, which Britain had won in the Treaty of Utrecht in 1713, Spain took the field as France's ally late in the war. The British promptly seized Cuba and the Philippines while their ally on the Continent, Frederick the Great of Prussia, was bringing France and her allies to their knees.

The British victory was almost embarrassing in its completeness, and the settlement reflected England's determination to assure the security of the American colonies. France was ousted from Canada and the Northwest; her holdings were limited to two tiny fishing islands off Newfoundland. Her islands in the West Indies, Guadaloupe and Martinique, were returned. Spain was forced to give up Florida for the return of her Caribbean islands and the Philippines. From France, Spain received her claims to New Orleans and Louisiana west of the Mississippi, while England took everything claimed by France and Spain east of that river except New Orleans.

Britain's new problem was how to organize her conquests. There were several interests to consult. The colonial and English land speculators wanted the interior opened for exploitation, while the back country agricultural pioneers expected to move in on their own terms. The fur traders of Albany and the Scots who took over the Montreal trade wanted the interior reserved for the trade and its Indian clientele. The King's ministers recognized the Indians as an interest which had to be insulated from the liquor traffic and the pressure of unauthorized settlement, or the costs of future Indian wars would eat up the profits of empire. An interest which was overlooked was that of the French Canadians, whose customs, laws, and Catholic religion fit poorly into a British administrative framework. There were the American colonists, who naturally expected to enjoy the fruits of the victory, while the British administrators were planning to make them fit into a more strictly regulated mercantilist system and support the costs of their own protection. All of these were defensible interests, but not all compatible.

Faced with the need for decision, the Board of Trade, which administered the colonies, developed various proposals, but was hampered by changing ministries in an unstable political situation at home, a lack of first-hand knowledge of the situation in America, and a flood of interested advice. These deliberations were influenced decisively by news from the interior.

It will be recalled that Canada and the western posts had been surrendered by the French after the fall of Montreal in 1760, although the final settlement waited upon the Treaty of Paris signed in February 1763. The British had moved into the western posts after the Canadian surrender. Lieutenant Gorrell reached Green Bay, the most westerly, in October 1761. The western tribes, many of which had clung to the French alliance to the end, were restive. The catalyst for this unrest was provided by an Ottawa chieftain named Pontiac, who built an unstable confederacy among the northwestern tribes. The Indians recognized that the elimination of the French boded ill for them; after all, just as the Europeans had played upon their tribal animosities and feuds, so the Indians had used the rivalries of the British and French. The French had exploited them, but beyond formal pronouncements of ownership and protection, the French had taken actual possession of little land. The Indian position was that the land had never been surrendered; the French had simply been welcome guests among them. The British came as fur traders and a military presence also, but the American colonists followed. Pontiac played upon the Indian desire to retain the French presence and upon their resentment of British arrogance expressed by such commanders as Lord Jeffrey Amherst, who had ill-concealed contempt for the Indians and the customary methods of dealing with them. The role of the French traders in encouraging Indian apprehensions is obscure.

Taking advantage of the obtuseness of the new British commander at the key post of Mackinac, who refused to credit warnings of Indian unrest by men like Charles de Langlade (left behind to surrender the western posts while the French military decamped for New Orleans), the Chippewa seized the fort by a ruse and put the British garrison to the knife in May 1763. The Indians, playing lacrosse outside the stockade, pursued the ball inside and then set upon the British.

Pontiac's plot misfired. He led a force against Detroit, but failed in his deception, and the Indians would not sustain the required siege. Fort Pitt too, beat off attack, but with the exception of Fort Niagara, the other isolated posts fell. Green Bay was abandoned to bring Lt. Gorrell's small force to help the captives from Mackinac. The neighboring Ottawa were ill disposed toward the Chippewa, who had taken Mackinac without consulting them. The Sioux, seeing an opportunity to deal directly with British traders, were ready to help the British against the Ottawa and Chippewa, who had exploited the Sioux in the trade. The Menominee, neighbors of the Green Bay post, also helped the British. George Croghan, acting for Sir William Johnson, got to Pontiac's allies and further undermined Pontiac's position.

Pontiac's uprising collapsed with surprising suddenness, but not without leaving an indelible impression upon the British military. They saw the need for garrison forces of regulars on the frontier, since the colonies were slow, as usual, to respond to calls for colonial militia. The military also saw the need for imperial regulation of the contacts between Indians and colonists, and the value of assurances to the Indians relative to their lands. Their approach favored the fur trade, except for the provision for control of traders, and this common feature of French administration was pressed by men like William Johnson.

As a result of these events and of consideration of the practical problems of administration for the interior, the Proclamation Line of 1763 was hurriedly adopted, a hastily drawn line along the Appalachian Highlands through the headwaters of streams running into the Atlantic. Settlement beyond the line was forbidden, and trade with the Indians was to be regulated by licenses from the colonial governors or the military commanders of the interior. A plan for superintendents of Indian affairs to regulate the licensees was subsequently added. The direction of the developing policy was toward removing the colonies from Indian affairs and the administration of trade, as well as prohibiting individuals, companies, or colonial governments from dealing with the Indians for land rights. This was all consistent with commitments made to the Indians during the late war with the French.

It can be seen that this organization of affairs would be met with resistance by the colonists who wanted to deal in western lands, settle in the trans-Appalachian area, or engage in trade. But this was not all of the imperial package. The administration of the fur trade and the maintenance of some 10,000 regular troops in the interior would cost money, and the logical source of that money was the American colonies. The colonists had borne a comparatively light burden in the French and Indian War and had accumulated an insignificant debt compared to that of the mother country, which had only about five times the population of her American colonies. The decision to have the colonies pay for their own defense led to the Stamp Act, the tightening of the administration of the Navigation Acts, the infamous Writs of Assistance, and finally coercive measures to bring the colonists to heel.

The Americans, freed of the menace of the French at their backs, responded to the tightening of the imperial reins with increasing resistance and then open revolt. There is more to that story, of course, than the problems imposed by the interior, but these figured prominently, as they would for the succeeding governments of the Continental Congress and the new American union of 1789. Historians still disagree about the reasonableness of the reconstructed British imperial system of 1763–75, the political maturity of the colonists, and the role of the West in all of this. It is now considered that the Proclamation Line of 1763 was a minor aggravation for the colonists. Many, including George Washington, saw it as a temporary measure invoked to quiet Indian apprehensions. Certainly many Americans ignored it with impunity. No sure source of revenue was found to implement the fur trade restrictions, and as unrest developed in the colonies, the British gave less attention to the regulation of the interior.

After the British ministry had despaired of controlling the interior either through the American colonies or through an imperial system lacking financial and colonial support, they imposed the other important imperial measure affecting the West, the Quebec Act. Prior to the Quebec Act, they had put the Canadians under British law, hoping to divert American settlers into Canada as well as into Florida, away from the interior. But British legal disabilities imposed upon Catholics worked to the disadvantage of the Canadians, and the ministry finally perceived the justice of granting legal and religious privileges to the French-Canadians. At this point, in 1774, they also saw advantages in transferring the administration of the interior to Quebec. Most of the white population there was Canadian, and the administration of Indian affairs from Quebec seemed advisable, in view of the growing unrest among the American colonists. The Americans looked upon this change as another evidence of British intent to keep them from laying claim to lands in the interior which they felt belonged to their colonies. The British government countered that this was a necessary measure to placate the Canadian population and assert continued control over the Indians of the interior. It was not, they claimed, meant as a final disposition of the lands.

While the Old Northwest thus had an important bearing on the coming struggle between Britain and her American colonists, what was the status of the land at the far end of the Lakes which was to be the future Wisconsin? The British were to maintain effective control there until after the War of 1812, despite nominal ownership by the United States.

Like the French, however, the British maintained only an occasional military presence, and exploited the fur trade for which Green Bay and the Fox-Wisconsin route to the Mississippi were highly strategic.

Immediately after the surrender of Canada, the Scots had begun their long association with the Canadian fur trade. It was a business that required an extended line of credit, for it might easily be three years from the time trade goods were ordered at Montreal until the furs received in exchange were auctioned in Europe. The disruption of the trade, blockade of the sea-lanes from France, and ruin of many French trading companies in the war had created havoc with the Montreal traders. Scotland, one of the first European countries to create a free banking system and maintain an educational system open to the children of the poor, was in a position to export capital and educated young men prepared to take advantage of this opportunity. They moved in on the demoralized fur trade in Canada to compete with the French Canadians in Montreal. London replaced Paris as the auction center for the European fur market.

The Scotsmen adopted the French system of organization. The man with a license to trade in a certain area and a line of credit with or a partnership in a Montreal trading company was called a *bourgeois*. In addition to hiring voyageurs to make up a brigade for the transportation of his goods, the bourgeois required the services of men called *engagés*. These men took the goods from the western posts or supply points out into the field and dealt directly with the Indian hunters. Some of the engagés might resort to hunting and trapping themselves, but this was more true of the American fur men; the Montreal trade was directed to the Indian hunter. It was the job of the engagé to keep the mettlesome savage interested in his role as producer with whatever means seemed most effective: credit, cajolery, threats, gifts, or liquor.

Between the bourgeois and his army of voyageurs and engagés in the field was another class of officers comparable to the noncommissioned officers of the military. These were the clerks who maintained the records in the posts and subposts and might lead a party of engagés into the field. They were usually young men, with the proper education and family connections, serving an apprenticeship in the trade with the expectation of becoming bourgeois, traders, or partners. Other classifications survived the shift in ownership, for instance the *hivernants,* engagés who wintered in the fur country, as contrasted with the *mangeurs de lard,* who came out only for the season. The trade commonly left behind communities of superannuated voyageurs and engagés, often married to Indian women, who might do a little farming to supply the post and who looked to their bourgeois as protector. Green Bay was such a community when the American settlers arrived to transform the land and its institutions.

In the early years of British occupation the fur trade became atomized and highly competitive. In some ways this worked to the advantage of the Indian hunter, but the trade tended to meet the competitive tricks of the lowest order, which meant more dependence on bad liquor and shoddy goods. The normal relationships between the Indian and trader were undermined. The most beneficial form of the trade was that carried on through area monopolies, the object of governmental licensing and regulation, but the British government was even less successful than the French in this. The Scot traders, true to Adam Smith's admonitions about allowing businessmen to come together for social occasions, organized the North West Fur Company as a monopoly, tentatively in 1778 and formally in 1784. It came to include most of the trade out of Montreal, and controlled the Great Lakes trade quite effectively until John Jacob Astor extended his operations there in about 1817. Beyond the Lakes, the company competed with the Hudson's Bay Company across the continent in Canada and with the French, Spanish, and Americans on the upper Mississippi.

Figures on the value of the fur trade for any given area or the trade as a whole can only be approximations. One authority estimates that furs valued at £125,000 came through Montreal annually in the 1780s. The North West Company in its heyday had about 4,000 employees in the field. Profits were high if all went well, but the trade was a costly operation with a multitude of hazards involving the transportation of goods, credit risks, hostilities between rival traders, the uncertain temper of the Indians, poor fur seasons, the volatile European market, which was subject to style changes, and the usual factors of supply and demand. It took a cost-conscious entrepreneur like John Jacob Astor to make it profitable over the long pull, and he had the wit to invest his gains in Manhattan real estate.

One of many interesting records of the trade in Wisconsin is the journal which Peter Pond dictated in his old age. Pond, a Connecticut Yankee who started trading out of Albany and then shifted to Montreal for his goods, was one of the original founders of the North West Company. In 1773–75 Pond traded in the vicinity of Prairie du Chien, the scene of an annual rendezvous. The French and Spanish, working up the Missouri River from St. Louis, cut off much of the trade with the Sioux who came to the rendezvous at Prairie du Chien; their transportation up the Mississippi, by barge manned by oarsmen, had advantages over the long and difficult route from Montreal. The west bank of the Mississippi was part of Spanish Louisiana. The Fox-Wisconsin route retained its importance for British and Canadian traders out of Mackinac competing with traders from the lower Mississippi. During the American Revolution, the bulk of the Montreal trade came through Prairie du Chien and Green Bay.

The principal center of the western trade was at Mackinac on the lower peninsula of Michigan, commanding the straits into Lake Michigan. Here the supply brigades from Montreal unloaded where warehouses were maintained, and here partners in the field and those from Montreal met and the brigades for points beyond Mackinac were made up. In Peter Pond's words, "Hear was a Grate Concors of People from all Quorters Sum Prepareing to take thair furs to Cannadey—Others to Albaney & New York—Others for thare intended Wintering Grounds—Others trade in with the Indans that Come from Different Parts with thare furs, Skins, Suger, Grease, taller &c—while Others were amuseing themselves in Good Company—While the More vulgar Ware fiteing Each other . . ." In 1780, the new British commander moved the fort and trading operations to Mackinac Island where it is today a tourist attraction and museum of the trade.

The British did not maintain an official presence in Wisconsin during the years of their formal ownership. Lt. Gorrell's little detachment left precipitously with news of Pontiac's uprising in 1763; Mackinac was the nearest military post. Green Bay, or La Baye as the French knew it, or Fort Edward Augustus, as the British expansively named Lt. Gorrell's brief command, stood empty. An English merchant had purchased the French trading privilege there and made good his claim by having it included in the 1763 treaty. His efforts to levy tribute on the trade through Green Bay were ignored. The British officials simply refused to reestablish the post or give the claimant any aid. The de Langlade family continued in the role of bourgeois there for the small French settlement.

One of the various efforts to control the trade officially involved Major Robert Rogers of Rogers' Rangers fame. He went to England, where he was taken up by society and wangled an appointment as commandant of Mackinac, much to the disgust of Sir William Johnson, who was trying to have his own schemes for regulation of the fur trade adopted. Rogers, with large ideas but no scruples, left Mackinac in chains, was acquitted, but found himself in debtors prison in London. One of his schemes had been an expedition to discover the Northwest Passage, involving another well known character, Jonathan Carver. Like Peter Pond, Carver was a Connecticut man who saw service with the British against the French. Apparently he was sent west from Mackinac by Rogers with the idea that they would later join forces and push westward to the Pacific.

Carver spent 1766–68 travelling through present Wisconsin and into

Minnesota, but Rogers failed to make their rendezvous and Carver returned, making his way to England to press claims for a pension for his explorations. His account of the adventure, *Travels Through the Interior Parts of North America in the Years 1766, 1767, and 1768,* published in London in 1778 two years before his death, ran through many editions, was widely translated, and remained popular for many years. The story was liberally cribbed from available French accounts and a vivid imagination. Peter Pond visited the cabin in which Carver had wintered on the Minnesota River, although Carver had claimed it was far to the west among the Sioux. Pond commented that "His Hole Toure I with One Canoe Well maned Could make in Six Weeks." Nonetheless, many people drew their impressions of the Wisconsin frontier from Carver, who wrote of tame rattlesnakes and of the Carcajou which hunted the caribou by springing upon it and bringing it to the ground "by his long tail, with which he encircles the body of his adversary." The people whom Carver described were equally exotic.

While Sir William Johnson despaired of regularizing the trade beyond Green Bay, a whole generation of Scotsmen and Americans were learning the trade from the Canadians and would bring their own organization to it, built upon the social and economic structure developed by the French. The American Revolution made surprisingly little difference to this trade, although it was clearly one of the prizes in the contest and Wisconsin Indians were pawns in the game. The area which was to become Wisconsin formally changed hands again, but real changes were delayed over thirty years.

Selected Bibliography

Alvord, Clarence Walworth. *The Mississippi Valley in British Politics.* 2 vols. New York, 1959. The vital interest of the British was not Boston and New York but the West.

Connell, Brian. *The Savage Years.* New York, 1959. Brief, readable account of the French and Indian War.

Jacobs, Wilbur R. *Diplomacy and Indian Gifts: Anglo-French Rivalry Along the Ohio and Northwest Frontiers, 1748–1763.* Stanford, 1950. Demonstrates the importance of the Indians in the struggle, but one needs stamina to find it out.

Kellogg, Louise P. *The British Regime in Wisconsin.* Madison, 1935. Not as satisfactory as her *French Regime,* but the standard work.

Krenkel, John H. "British Conquest of the Old Northwest." *Wisconsin Magazine of History* 35:49–61 (Autumn 1951). A concise treatment of the French-British rivalry in Wisconsin.

Morton, W. L. "The Northwest Company, Pedlars Extraordinary." *Minnesota History* 40:157–65 (Winter 1966).

Parkman, Francis. *The Parkman Reader: From the Works of Francis Parkman.* Selected and edited with an introduction by Samuel E. Morison. Boston, 1955. Condensing the work of forty years and sixteen volumes on the French and British struggles in America.

Peckham, H. H. *The Colonial Wars, 1689–1762.* Chicago History of American Civilization Series. Chicago, 1963. Condensed, clear version of the French and British wars in America.

———. *Pontiac and the Indian Uprisings.* Princeton, 1947. The materials are scarce, but he brings Parkman up to date.

Phillips, Paul Chrisler. *The Fur Trade.* 2 vols. Norman, Okla., 1961. A life's work in the sources, but he ignored others working them.

Quimby, George Irving. *Indian Culture and European Trade Goods.* Madison, 1966. The early impact of the fur trade.

Saum, Lewis O. *The Fur Trader and the Indian.* Seattle, 1965. An interesting treatment of the clash of cultures.

Sosin, Jack M. *Whitehall and the Wilderness: The Middle West in British Colonial Policy, 1760–1775.* Lincoln, Nebr., 1961. Starts with Alvord's argument that British policy in the period was determined by the American interior.

———. *The Revolutionary Frontier, 1763–1783.* New York, 1967. Has a recent account of Clark's expedition.

FROM AMERICAN OWNERSHIP TO CONTROL, 1775–1816

part two

The British, for reasons of diplomacy, accepted a settlement at the end of the American Revolution that was particularly generous to the United States in its definition of the borders of the new country. On its western perimeter, the Mississippi River was established as the boundary, although American settlement and practical control did not extend much beyond Pittsburgh in the country north of the Ohio River. Not until Anthony Wayne's victory at Fallen Timbers in 1794 did Americans claim effective control over most of the present state of Ohio, leaving the remainder of the Old Northwest in the hands of the Indians. It would be more than twenty years after Wayne's triumph before the Americans could establish a convincing presence in the area now included in Wisconsin.

This combination of legal ownership without the power to make it effective, in a region economically tied to Montreal and strategically vital for access to the rich fur country beyond Prairie du Chien, invited efforts on the part of the British traders and military in Canada to alter the terms of the 1783 settlement. British diplomacy paid only occasional attention to these local interests which nonetheless were in a position to create mischief. The years from 1783 to 1816, for the geographic area now defined as Wisconsin, were marked by frustrated efforts on the part of the United States to make its legal ownership felt. The British-Canadian fur interests had the easier task of holding on to what they had.

It took a second war to decide the issues raised, a war accurately described as the second war for American independence. Fortunately for American success, it was not decided by the trials at arms that took place on Wisconsin soil.

THE NORTHWEST AND THE AMERICAN REVOLUTION

4

The Northwest did not play a major role in the American Revolution nor in the catalogue of growing grievances which brought it on. The present area of Wisconsin was far from the main theaters of the conflict, little known to the American colonists, and beyond the range of their aspirations except as it impinged upon the security of the Ohio country, which they did want. It was, of course, within the bounds of the east bank of the Mississippi, which became the western boundary of 1783. Nevertheless, the course of the Revolutionary War and the fortunate diplomatic circumstances which ended it were crucial to the future of the Wisconsin country.

The American colonies were maturing politically and economically, and with the removal of the French as a threat to their existence, found the assertion of a tightened imperial policy, in place of former "salutary neglect," abrasive and too limiting. The new imperial legislation and administration may have been enlightened and reasonable in the light of contemporary political and economic theory, and the American response therefore immature and parochial, but a growing American sentiment accepted the final solution of separation and revolution.

While the administration of the western lands and regulation of relations with the Indians figured prominently in the revision and administrative overhaul of the British imperial system, the weight of colonial complaint was concerned with the impact of the system upon the Atlantic seaboard population. Except for those engaged in western land speculation or trading beyond the mountains, the voice of the West was not a loud one in the colonial assemblies, although there was a growing western population even before the war. As for the speculators, the Proclamation Line of 1763 already had proved to be quite flexible by 1768 and speculative interest reached even within the circle of the king's ministers, making them indulgent toward land schemes stretching far into the Ohio country.

The American fur traders were in a somewhat different circumstance. An active trade continued from the middle colonies, particularly Pennsylvania, into the upper tributaries of the Ohio. Men like Daniel Boone, who explored this area and beyond into present Kentucky before the Revolution, brought back principally deer hides for the trade. More desirable pelts came from around the Great Lakes and the Illinois country. Most of them probably originated even farther west where the French and Spanish operated out of St. Louis on the Missouri River, and farther north where the Mackinac traders were competing with the Hudson's Bay Company. George Croghan realized the potential of the Illinois country in a trip he made there in 1765 as a deputy to Sir William Johnson, and he induced a wealthy Philadelphia trading firm to undertake an ambitious trading venture in Illinois. But the French, who still occupied the old posts at Vincennes, Kaskaskia, and Cahokia, as British subjects now, kept their ties with their compatriots at St. Louis, as did the neighboring Indians. Croghan's venture failed and turned the Philadelphia trading company into one of many supplicants for a western land grant.

Farther north, the New York fur traders working out of Albany traded on the Great Lakes as far as Mackinac and beyond. Johnson's plan to regulate the trade closely was no longer taken seriously by 1767, and open competition was the order of the day. Peter Pond noted, in 1775, that furs gathered at Mackinac were packed for transport to Montreal and Albany. While Pond had started his trading out of Albany, he shifted to Montreal, as did a number of other Americans, partly because the Quebec Act of 1774 put the fur country within that province for administrative purposes and partly because Montreal was a better base for operations on the upper Lakes. The colonies were moving toward an open rupture with England by then, but the Candians gave little indication that they would join in. The British were more suspicious of the American fur-trade colony in Montreal than they were of Canadian loyalty.

Although the role of the West in the developing revolution was minor, it could not be ignored in the conduct of the war. Previous wars between the French and British had involved the western tribesmen, and there was every reason to assume that they would be engaged now. Control over the Indians depended in turn upon control over access to their territory and over trade with them, a reality that had to be faced even though little could be done about it. With armies of British regulars installed on the Atlantic seaboard, the colonists had few resources to divert to the western frontier, whatever their aspirations there.

The Americans realized that their vital interest in the West would be served if they could keep the Indians neutral, but this turned out to be a larger order than mere intentions could fulfill. Congress could never find the money or the goods to supply the trade requirements of the Indians, much less provide the necessary gifts to buy their neutrality. The alternatives were to overawe them with an ever ready military force or to cut the British off from the interior by taking Montreal and holding it. Unable to maintain an army in the interior, the Americans adopted the latter course early in the war, with two armies directed at Montreal and Quebec. The British commander, Guy Carleton, had insufficient forces to meet both attacks, and Montreal fell to the Americans. But Carleton withstood the attacks of the combined American forces at Quebec, where winter, the indifference of the French-Canadians to the American cause, the arrival of a British force by sea, and smallpox forced American withdrawal from Canada in the spring of 1776. The Americans had delayed British offensive operations from the St. Lawrence valley, but left their foes in possession of the routes to the Great Lakes and the Ohio country.

As the war progressed the British officers, charged with the defense of the interior, overcame their reluctance to use the Indian allies they had inherited from the French. Always short of regular military forces, they found the French-Canadian officer class and men of property firmly attached to the British cause. For this they could thank Governor Carleton's rule and the Quebec Act. Illustrative of this was the career of Green Bay's Charles de Langlade. Just as he had led his Ottawa and Chippewa followers east to meet the British invaders in earlier years, he now responded to Carleton's call for aid in the defense of the St. Lawrence valley against the Americans. De Langlade arrived too late to be of service, but returned the next year to aid Burgoyne in his invasion of New York. Although Burgoyne readily threatened savage war, however, he abhorred the notions of warfare held by de Langlade's Indian auxiliaries, and they left his command before Saratoga. De Langlade's efforts, in the later years of the war, were needed in the Wisconsin and Illinois country to counter the activities of George Rogers Clark.

Loosing the western Indians on the exposed American frontier was not of great advantage to the British. The American frontiersmen were inclined to be even more local in their interests than their fellow colonists, and had failed to respond to pleas that they enlist in regular forces to undertake organized campaigns. This reluctance was partly justified by the lack of support received from the East and by the exposed position in which they had placed themselves and their families. But when the British turned the fury of the western Indians on them, some American frontiersmen finally saw the wisdom of mounting organized campaigns to keep the Indians occupied defending their own homes.

The western Indians were the key to the security of the American frontier, and in general they preferred the British cause to the American for a variety of reasons. British officers and Indian agents had endeavored to protect the Indian lands and regulate the trade in the interest of the Indian. Aside from the military and other officials, Indian contact with the British had been with fur traders, and these contacts were in the tradition of the years of French control. The local French trader or bourgeois remained, and there was no pressure from the fur trade, under its new owners, to usurp the Indian's land or his accepted role in the trade.

The Americans were something else again. The western Indian's first contact with an American was likely to have been with an explorer-hunter on the order of Daniel Boone. Boone was a self-sufficient hunter who enjoyed solitude, complete freedom, and matching his wits against the wilderness. Typically, Boone penetrated the Kentucky country in search of deer hides, which he took with his own rifle, and as a land-looker for the speculator who financed his wanderings. There was no place for the Indian in this scheme of things.

We tend to think of the Indian as a free agent, perfectly adapted to his habitat, able to challenge any interloper who had to meet the environment on equal terms, and being less tied to a place and material possessions, able to evade danger more readily. Put European weapons in the Indian's hands and who could challenge him? But the truth was quite otherwise. Daniel Boone and his fellows carried a little kit of hand vises, files, and plates which enabled them to keep their deadly long rifles in repair far from civilization. The Indian, with his cheap trade rifle, was dependent on the skill of the gunsmith at the trading post. The first request that the Indians made of Lt. Gorrell when he arrived at Green Bay was that he "send for a gunsmith to mend their guns, as they were poor and out of order; the French, they said, had always done this for them."

Nor was the Indian a freer spirit in the wild than the American hunter. The American mastered the Indian's skills and those of his own technology as well. The American left his family behind in a settlement while he indulged in exploration and the life of a free hunter. If this was not his bent, he stayed home, where there was doubtless duller work to be done. The Indian left for the hunt because it was his livelihood, leaving his family as a hostage to fortune in another part of the forest. He did not fear for them less because he was a savage. Every stranger whom the Indian met was a potential enemy, white or Indian, whereas the American hunter had his relations with other whites regularized for him by a distant government. The Indian was well aware of the hazards of trespass upon the hunting grounds of a neighboring tribe, but the displacements caused by the fur trade and consequent migration had upset traditional boundaries. The American assumed that he could look any land over with the expectation of eventual possession, although it didn't pay to get caught in some places.

The Indians neighboring the American frontier were restive but awed. The frontiersmen believed that the best defense against them was a swift offense, and their enmity was not discriminating. An inexcusable but not untypical action was the Gnaddenhutten Massacre, where ninety friendly Delaware of the Moravian faith were cut down by a group of land-hungry Pennsylvania frontiersmen after the Indians had been their generous hosts for three days. On the southern frontier the Creek, Cherokee, and Choctaw initiated raids which brought a crushing response from the Carolinas and Virginia. The Iroquois, in contact with Canada and under the influence of the British, were a serious threat to the Americans at all times, and the New York frontier was swept by many terrible raids until the Iroquois power was broken, in 1779, by a contingent of Washington's continental forces. The Indians from the Ohio country and westward were another irritation. They operated from bases seemingly beyond the American reach and were supplied and encouraged from British posts on the old French routes to the Mississippi.

Frontiersmen who were persuaded that they must strike into the Ohio country in force to bring an end to this privileged sanctuary found their leader in George Rogers Clark, a Virginian who had moved to the Kentucky country just before the war. In the absence of tangible aid from the Continental Congress, Clark persuaded Governor Patrick Henry of Virginia to give him a commission and support in raising a small force to invade the Ohio country. The Virginians were interested, because their original charter included the country to be invaded as well as the Kentucky frontier. A successful expedition could confirm Virginia's claims against other contenders.

Colonel Clark, who was twenty-five when he led his "army" into the Ohio country in the summer of 1778, was a tall man with great physical stamina. Confident and decisive, he led a campaign which has remained a model of audacity and endurance. Clark was informed of the disposition of British forces in the interior and had taken soundings on the probable sympathies of the French *habitants* there and of the Spanish at St. Louis. As it turned out, he had little to risk with the French and Spanish, as word of the formal French-American alliance reached him before he started from his advanced base.

Clark took his forces down the Ohio by boat and marched them overland to Kaskaskia, which he persuaded to surrender without a fight. Cahokia and Vincennes fell with equal ease to his emissaries. Like Vincennes, Kaskaskia and Cahokia were former French posts with a remaining population of habitant farmers and fur traders.

It was the Indians whom Clark wanted to reach, and the influence of the Spanish and French, who had been trading up the Mississippi at Prairie du Chien, was helpful to him. He called a formal council of the Indians at Cahokia and was astonished by the turnout. It is estimated that nearly 4,000 warriors appeared, most of them from the upper Mississippi and Wisconsin. Clark hit just the right note of toughness, indifference, and conciliation. The Indians, who naturally were pleased by a politician and orator who said he was neither, were also struck by the news that the French had joined the Americans, and readily agreed to Clark's offer of peace. He had not, after all, demanded that they go to war against the British, but only that they choose peace or war with the Americans.

Indian neutrality was certainly a valuable asset from Clark's point of view, for his next objective was to advance upon the sources of British power in the West, especially Detroit. If nothing else, his success at Cahokia would cause the British apprehension and divert their attention to the western Indians and the mischief which the French and Spanish could do there. Wisconsin Indians, including the Potawatomi, Sauk, Fox, southern Winnebago, and those around present Milwaukee, as well as some Osage and Miami, had accepted Clark's terms. A similar group around Vincennes, on the Wabash, defected to Clark's agents.

As expected, Clark's successes created a number of diversions among the British. The commander at Mackinac sent de Langlade and others out to bring the defectors back into the fold, but their proximity to St. Louis and the Mississippi posts in Clark's hands made them independent. An Indian caught between two fires could be expected to respond with prudence, or without regard to his sacred obligations, according to the observer's point of view. The British found them fickle.

Colonel Hamilton at Detroit gathered his forces and retook Vincennes. Clark's Kentuckians stationed there decamped for home, and the French offered no resistance. Two Americans constituted the garrison when Hamilton arrived. No man for half measures, Clark set out from Kaskaskia overland, in early February, to take Hamilton by surprise.

The Illinois and Wabash rivers were in flood, and the little troop of 172 men waded much of the way in icy rain, covering the last miles through deep water with a skim of ice. They had run out of food, but Clark brought them through, and with the cooperation of the habitants they silently entered the town and surrounded the unsuspecting British. There was a sharp fire fight which ended with the British surrender. Colonel Hamilton was sent to Virginia, where he spent some time in irons. This was the high point of Clark's career. He spent the rest of the war putting out brushfires and never got to Detroit.

The news of Clark's victory at Vincennes deepened the gloom of Colonel De Peyster at Mackinac and his fear of the Americans along the south shores of the Lakes. The rebels were buying horses near Chicago, and the licensed trader there was transformed into a captain of Virginia militia. De Langlade and his nephew Gautier, wrote the colonel, "are rather a burden upon me. To send them upon an expedition without troops is doing nothing [and] they cannot live at this extravagant place upon their allowance having a constant run of Indians who snatch the bread out of their mouths." There was little pleasure in being a "white father" during a run of bad luck. The only bright spot was provided by the Sioux, who were far from the American's wiles and yearned to kill some Fox, Sauk, or Chippewa for the British if the occasion would allow it.

The war in the West looked more encouraging for the British the next year, 1780, although an expedition over the Fox-Wisconsin route from Mackinac to Cahokia was bluffed out by Clark and sharply repulsed by the Spanish at St. Louis. The British presence did serve to return most of the Wisconsin Indians to their fold. Another force out of Detroit undid Clark's work elsewhere by advancing down the Miami and terrorizing the Kentucky frontier. The Indians returned to their British alliance there, and Clark abandoned the Mississippi posts in order to rally the Kentuckians. He succeeded locally, but still failed to gain support for an advance on Detroit. The French in Illinois were disenchanted with the American alliance when the western Indians returned to the warpath on the British side. Virginia was losing some of her interest in the West, because the cession of all western claims was a central issue in the Confederation. As it turned out, the Americans won the West at the peace table.

It was the good fortune of the Americans, in the peace negotiations ending the war, to be represented by men of the stature of John Adams, Benjamin Franklin, and John Jay. It was in the interest of French and British diplomacy to allow these men to treat separately with a conciliatory Britain. The negotiations and interests involved were complicated and full of nuance, but their main outlines are these: (1) After it became apparent that Britain must lose the American colonies, France wanted out, but was pledged to continue the war until Spain regained Gibralter. Allowing the Americans to treat independently made continuance of the war impractical. (2) Treating independently with the British, the Americans got territorial concessions at the expense of Spain's claims. (3) The bankruptcy of the policies of George III brought to power in Britain men whose policy was one of conciliation and generosity toward the Americans. The turning point was the surrender of Lord Cornwallis in October 1781.

The French minister, Vergennes, knew that the settlement was going to cost France's ally Spain something, for Spain had notions of recovering much of interior America west of the Appalachians. Britain was more than generous. She returned the Floridas to Spain without definition of the boundaries. With the Americans, she narrowly defined the Florida boundary on the north to the benefit of the United States. And to Vergennes' astonishment, the British conceded the western boundary of the United States at the Mississippi River and gave up all of the land between the Ohio River and the Great Lakes. As Vergennes remarked, "the English buy peace rather than make it."

Our interest is in the northwest boundary and Britain's apparent abandonment of her Indian allies south and west of the Great Lakes. At one point in negotiations, Franklin had the British unofficially committed to the concession of Canada as a really generous gesture. On the American side, Congress was prepared to accept something very like the old Proclamation Line moved westward only a nominal distance. When they got to serious negotiation between these extremes, the Americans offered a choice between a line on the 45th parallel from the Connecticut River to the Mississippi or what is essentially the present boundary through the Great Lakes. If you look at the line of the 45th parallel, you will see that it cuts through Wisconsin just below Marinette, above Wausau, and strikes the Mississippi at Hudson. Had the line continued west it would divide the northern suburbs of Minneapolis. The present boundary through the Lakes had a greater appeal for the British, since the other would have cut off present Toronto and Canada's shoreline on lakes Ontario, Erie, and much of Huron.

The puzzle is the concession of the Ohio country and the abandonment of the Indians there, apparently a reflection of the fortunes of English politics at the time. Britain had not arrived at a settled policy for the interior before the American Revolution, partly because the fur interests and land speculation interests seem to have offset one another. The

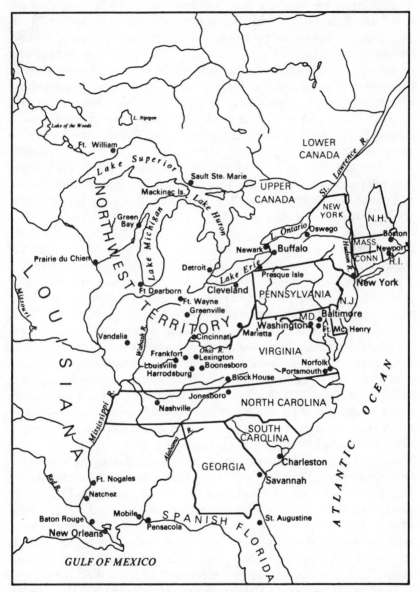

Map 7.   The Early American Period. Adapted from a map in Edward Whiting Fox,
Atlas of American History (Oxford: The Clarendon Press, 1964)   *UWCL*

fur trade, which had gravitated into Scottish hands, was represented in Parliament by the members from Scotland. Scotland was a model of the rotten borough, and the king had its representation in his pocket. When the peace was written, by men who opposed the king's party, the Scottish members had little influence. Also, a prejudice was current that the cost to the empire of maintaining the fur trade was all out of proportion to the returns. Those interested in the trade were aghast at the final terms abandoning to the Americans vital posts including Oswego, Niagara, Detroit, and Mackinac. British officials and army men in Canada were equally indignant. The treaty did provide that Britain and the United States should share navigation rights on the Mississippi from its mouth to its source, but this was no great limitation. American power and population were several hundred miles away, and since Spain controlled the river's outlet, the Americans doubtless hoped that British interest would be involved in keeping it open.

The terms of the peace were one thing but their implementation another. English commercial interests showed no disposition to make important concessions to the new nation, particularly since each American state retained the right to regulate its own commerce. The new Pitt ministry was sympathetic to the voices of British businessmen, and the foundations of the War of 1812 were laid. In the Northwest, this meant a refusal to evacuate the important posts which fell within American territory, a continued domination of the fur trade, continuance of relations with and support of Indian allies, and the hope of erecting an Indian buffer state in the Ohio country at the expense of the United States. This policy probably owed as much to British concern for her Indian allies as to her concern for the fur trade; Britain had as much to fear from a repetition of Pontiac's conspiracy as did the Americans.

British-American relations continued to worsen even as a stronger central government was emerging in the United States. There had been no exchange of accredited ministers and no commercial agreements, which meant that American commerce in England was regulated by the whims of municipal corporations. England was again at war with France, a revolutionary France this time, and using her seapower with heavy pressure on neutral shipping. This culminated, in the spring of 1794, with the seizure of 300 American vessels trading in the French West Indies.

Relations of the United States with British power in Canada were also reaching a head in 1794. The premise of the American frontiersmen that the way to handle a discontented Indian was to shoot first might have worked to the Americans' satisfaction had the British officials not harbored the hope that the numerical superiority of the Indians could be organized to stay the American advance into the Ohio country. The British planned to win the concession of an Indian buffer state there—a demand they had failed to press in 1783—and were quite open in the arrogant assumption that they could force this solution, even sending an informal diplomat to argue the case with Secretary of State Jefferson. The Americans contributed to this British arrogance by mounting two federal campaigns against the Indians in 1790 and 1791, those of Generals Harmar and St. Clair, which ended in disaster for the Americans. Then, in 1794, the news of the seizures of American shipping in the Caribbean coincided with a report of a fiery speech by the governor-general of Canada to a delegation representing Indians from American territory whom General Anthony Wayne was making a third federal attempt to pacify. War threatened. Such a war would have been a serious inconvenience to Britain, but possibly fatal to Washington's administration.

Conditions had changed in the intervening ten years since the Treaty of Paris, signed in 1783. President Washington had experimented with the executive powers of the new federal government in foreign affairs, found them considerable, and used them vigorously. Britain was embroiled in a war with a new French government which was exporting revolutionary ideas and backing them with a revolutionary army. The United States was still bound to France by treaty obligations to help protect her West Indies possessions. Both Britain and Washington's administration viewed this obligation with a wary eye. Britain had worried briefly that the United States and Spain would come to some mutual agreement and strike at her positions on the Great Lakes during the brief Nootka Controversy between Britain and Spain in 1790. This action had not occurred to the Washington administration, which on its part feared the British might ask for the right to take an army across American territory to strike the Spanish in Louisiana. The various fears abroad illustrate American apprehensions but also her opportunities. She was a militarily weak but isolated country with a considerable merchant marine readily convertible into a harassing force. Nor had the British forgotten that their former colonies consumed some 17 percent of their exports.

For Pitt, the war with France was the central concern. His indifference to American protests was replaced by a desire for accommodation. The result was Jay's Treaty of 1794, named for John Jay, who negotiated the instrument for the United States. The treaty contained few satisfactions for American commercial interests but assured peace and regularized relations with the British Empire. This was the *sine qua non* of Treasurer Alexander Hamilton's financial policy; the United States, however, conceded much to get it. In the Northwest, Britain agreed to evacuate the posts on American territory by 1796 in return for American recognition

of Loyalist claims. Arbitration was accepted in principle for settlement of
the northern boundary dispute, but Britain refused to treat on her relations with the western Indians. Instead, both parties were free to trade
with the Indians on either side of the boundary, which of course favored
the British, who controlled the trade on the Lakes and beyond. In addition, Britain won the right of access, across United States territory, to the
Mississippi. This gave her legal use of the Fox-Wisconsin route.

Jay's Treaty was immensely unpopular, but passed the Senate with the
bare two-thirds majority required. The Indian situation was somewhat
relieved, and open war with Britain over her Indian policy was averted
by Wayne's victory at Fallen Timbers, under the very guns of the British
at Fort Miami. The British commander prudently refused aid to the Indians. In the Treaty of Greenville, Wayne won the cession of most of Ohio
from the Indians. Britain had held that the earlier Treaty of Fort Stanwix
guaranteed the land to the Indians, hence Wayne's definition of the status
of the Indians and the land in his treaty. The British refusal to aid the
Indians directly, on Wayne's obvious dare, had severed their alliance,
and now the British were to give up their posts south of the boundary.
But the idea of the Indian buffer state was not dead, nor were the Americans in possession by occupation of their lands west of the Wabash
River. The Wisconsin River country awaited the tread of its first United
States officials. It was not yet within the ken of American homeseekers.

Selected Bibliography

Abernethy, Thomas Perkins. *Western Lands and the American Revolution.*
2d ed. New York, 1959. Essential volume on land speculation and its role.
Alden, John R. *The American Revolution, 1775–1783.* The New American
Nation Series. New York, 1954. Has a good account of the war in the
West.
Bemis, Samuel Flagg. *A Diplomatic History of the United States.* 5th ed.
New York, 1965. Standard work on the diplomacy of the American Revo-
lution and the early national period.
Campbell, Marjorie Wilkins. *The Northwest Company.* New York, 1957. A
popular account.
Darling, Arthur P. *Our Rising Empire, 1763–1803.* New Haven, 1940. A
diplomatic history.
Gipson, Lawrence H. *The British Empire Before the American Revolution.* 3
vols. New York, 1958–60. A complete revision of the original 14 volumes
published by Caxton, of Caldwell, Idaho, 1936–68.
————. *The Coming of the Revolution, 1763–1775.* The New American

Nation Series. New York, 1954. Following his argument of British reasonableness.

Morgan, Edmund S. *The Birth of the Republic, 1763–1789*. Chicago History of American Civilization Series. Chicago, 1956. Better balance than Gipson.

Philbrick, Francis S. *The Rise of the West, 1754–1830*. The New American Nation Series. New York, 1965. Takes up the argument about British intentions and actions in the West.

Pond, Peter. "Journal of Peter Pond." *SHSW Collections*, vol. 18, pp. 314–54. Madison, 1908. A rough character in a rough trade.

Sosin, Jack M. "The Use of the Indians in the War of the American Revolution: A Reassessment of Responsibility." *Canadian Historical Review* 46: 101–21 (June 1965). British restraint vs. savage fury.

AMERICAN IN FACT

5

Americans took over the British posts on United States territory, according to provisions of Jay's Treaty, in 1796. This brought the American military presence as far west as Mackinac, but the British simply moved across the line and established new posts: Malden across the St. Clair River from Detroit, and St. Joseph Island some forty miles east of Mackinac Island. The Canadian traders continued the use of their facilities on Mackinac.

The surrender of the posts to the Americans made little difference to the Montreal traders for a number of years. They had the techniques of the business mastered to the point where they competed with the Spanish out in the Missouri country successfully, and indeed, supplied many of the St. Louis traders illegally across the Mississippi from Prairie du Chien, Cahokia, and similar points. The Spanish ruefully admitted that they hired Canadians to carry on their own fur trading because the Canadians knew the business so well and could gain the confidence of the Indians. Even the superior transportation route by way of the Mississippi did not permit the Spanish to supply the upper Mississippi and Missouri trade more cheaply than could the Canadians.

The Americans had been kept out of the trade before 1783 by British vigilance at Oswego, where goods from New York, by way of Albany and the Mohawk valley, would enter the Lakes. During the Revolution and for some time after, the Canadian traders were not allowed to have private vessels on the Lakes and had to depend upon vessels in the king's service. This served to implement regulations requiring the trade to center in Montreal. Furs had to be shipped to London, under the regulations, regardless of their final destination. John Jacob Astor, who started his career dealing in local New York furs, visited Montreal regularly, as his business broadened, and bought in that market. It was about 1810 before Astor entered the Great Lakes trade directly with his own men.

With the Canadians maintaining their monopoly on the Lakes by imperial regulation and their own superior organization, American fur men had only their own frontier to draw upon. The incessant Indian wars and the pressures of American settlement made this poor pickings; the fur trade was a phase in western expansion that could not survive extensive agriculture, mining, or cattle raising. By 1794 when the British agreed to abandon the northwest posts, Detroit, which depended on the Ohio and Illinois country, had declined sadly as a source of furs. Mackinac, controlling the trade from Lake Michigan and beyond, even into the Missouri basin and upper Mississippi, was in its heyday, while the Lake Superior trade stretched to the Pacific, after Alexander Mackenzie's expedition there in 1793 for the North West Company. The trade through Montreal was worth £250,000 in 1794, about a third of it through Mackinac and two-fifths through the Grand Portage on Lake Superior.

The fur trade was a truly big business in its time. As the wilderness receded westward, the logistics involved became more complicated, some risks greater, the credit requirements heavier and longer-term, and the necessary managerial talent of a higher order. The marked tendency toward monopoly in the business, a growing impatience with government regulation, and the power to counter it are therefore not surprising. Government could not escape an interest in the fur trade, because of its intimate involvement in Indian affairs, nor could it escape a dependence upon men in the trade for information and advice. It was a unique business with a fascinating history.

Americans would have liked to inherit the rich fur trade of the upper Great Lakes along with the posts of Mackinac and Detroit, which had once controlled a good share of it, but the Canadian hold on the trade was not broken. It is true that an American was to inherit much of it, but by the time John Jacob Astor gained control of most of the Mackinac trade, after the War of 1812, the great years had passed. Astor is supposed to have remarked, on hearing the news of Jay's Treaty, "Now I will make my fortune in the fur trade," but he continued to buy through the Montreal traders for another fifteen years, and the bulk of his fortune was gained elsewhere. A few Americans tried to break into the trade around Lake Michigan, but without success. The British traders had better goods, could sell them cheaper, and had the confidence of the Indians. Their competition was among themselves. The brief rivalry between the new X Y Company and the older North West Company for the business in Wisconsin from 1798 to 1804 was an example of this. The Louisiana purchase was to put the Americans back in the fur business.

For the American government, effective control over the tribes west of Lake Michigan would depend upon an American presence there. The provisions of Jay's Treaty gave the Montreal traders a legal right to be in what is now Wisconsin and to trade with the Indians. American traders were not in a position to challenge them. The intervening country south of the Lakes, from about the Wabash River, was Indian country and recognized as such by the Treaty of Greenville. The trade there was quite demoralized and tended to go down the Mississippi, through the hands of the French habitants and their countrymen. It was a tough nut for the Americans to crack.

The United States did not garrison a post in present Wisconsin until after 1815, possibly because the British had maintained no such post after the recall of Lt. Gorrell from Green Bay in 1763. Green Bay was still a modest outpost of the fur trade in 1796, and old Charles de Langlade was the patriarch of the French-Canadian community there. An enterprising British trader described their ramshackle agricultural arrangements and his disgust that there were never any foodstuffs for sale there, although everyone in the trade went by Green Bay's doorstep and would have been glad to buy. Jacob Franks, a Jewish fur trader representing a Montreal house, established himself there in 1792, as did a French-Canadian, Jacques Vieau, representing the North West Company. Green Bay was a less bustling place than Prairie du Chien, where the British traders repaired to trade across the river in Spanish territory and with the Sioux from up river.

Casting about for some way to establish evidence of its ownership, the United States government included the west shore of Lake Michigan in Wayne County, created as a subdivision of the Northwest Territory in 1796. Detroit was the county seat. Inasmuch as the inhabitants of Green Bay and the mixed village of Indians and traders in Milwaukee were unaware of this new jurisdiction, the move did not have the desired effect. Ohio was made a state in 1803, and the remaining Northwest was organized as Indiana Territory in 1800, with the enterprising William Henry Harrison as governor. Harrison created a new county in what is now Wisconsin, naming it St. Clair, and commissioned a number of fur traders in the area as justices of the peace and militia officers. Such honors could do these men no harm in the eyes of their Indian customers, but

Harrison's appointments were not a convincing show of American power.

An unexpected diplomatic coup suddenly shifted the balance, when President Jefferson's agents, seeking an accommodation on the prickly question of use of the lower Mississippi, were confronted with the dazzling opportunity of purchasing the whole of the Louisiana Territory from Napoleon. The boundaries of the 1803 purchase were somewhat indefinite, but the territory included the Missouri River basin, where much of the fur trade passing through Prairie du Chien to Mackinac originated. It also flanked the Indian boundaries, roughly on the western border of Ohio, and made St. Louis an anchor of American power beyond the lands of the tribes confronting American settlement north of the Ohio.

The Montreal traders realized that the game had been changed. The competing X Y and North West companies, which at times had been competing hotly in Wisconsin and along the upper Mississippi, composed their differences and organized the Michilimackinac Company to control the trade of the upper Great Lakes and upper Mississippi. North West Company operations were now confined to the country beyond Grand Portage at the western end of Lake Superior. The object of the Michilimackinac Company was to strip the Wisconsin area of furs, thus keeping the American traders out. They were careful not to challenge American legal authority directly, paying duties on goods taken into American territory at Mackinac, where a customs office was established. A new threat, however, loomed when General Wilkinson, at St. Louis, declared the Louisiana territory across the Mississippi out of bounds to the Canadians. They argued the application of Article 3 of Jay's Treaty, but Wilkinson replied, correctly, that Louisiana was not included in the terms of that treaty. Spanish efforts to keep the Canadians out had been totally ineffective, but the Americans might prove more determined and resourceful.

General James Wilkinson has been described as "an individual about whom trouble always gathered. Vain, bombastic, and incompetent, he was a master of petty treason with a gift for scandal." It was this paragon who commanded at St. Louis. For twenty years he had intrigued intermittently with the Spanish and was probably involved in the Burr Conspiracy in 1805. This was the year that on his own initiative he authorized the expedition to the upper Mississippi led by Zebulon Pike. Apparently Wilkinson was interested in a possible venture in the fur trade for his personal profit.

Lt. Pike, whose career was advanced by Wilkinson, is better known for his later expedition in 1806–07 up the Arkansas River into the area of present Colorado, where his name is memorialized by Pike's Peak.

Pike shared Wilkinson's later disgrace, possibly unjustly, but in 1805 he was a competent choice for a difficult job. The resources at Pike's command were modest, as was the federal military establishment. Commanding a seventy-three-foot keelboat manned by twenty-one enlisted men, Pike was the only officer, a circumstance which he, as a man of considerable ambition and vanity, preferred. Equipment for the expedition, plus trade goods, cost the government about $2,000, certainly a modest outfit. Pike had no interpreter along, no doctor, and the instruments were inferior, even by existing standards. His instructions were to ascend the Mississippi to its source, making suitable maps and notes, select sites for military posts, establish peace among the Indians, procure specimens of flora and fauna, investigate the Indian trade, and show the flag.

Pike left St. Louis in August 1805, visiting the principal Indian villages and trading posts along his route. He reached what he thought were the headwaters of the Mississippi on February 1—he was only a few miles off—after a journey that taxed his perseverance and command abilities. He wintered on Swan River in northern Minnesota, leaving on April 8 as the ice was breaking up. The expedition was back in St. Louis three weeks later after traveling over 5,000 miles during the nine months. Pike had shown the flag, rebuked numerous Indian chiefs for their adherence to the British, and reminded traders of their obligations to be licensed properly by American authorities—that is, to pay customs duties, avoid the use of liquor in the trade, stop distributing and displaying the British flag, and stay on the east side of the Mississippi. In one of the earliest formal real estate transactions in Minnesota, Pike purchased the site of the future Fort Snelling from the Sioux. He also thought he had made peace between the warring Sioux and Chippewa.

The attitude of the British traders varied. Many of them found Pike quite presumptuous for the commander of a force of twenty-one men several hundred miles from his base. But they did feel the breath of American power at their backs and a surprising number, even of those on the St. Croix River and above, had paid the small fee for an American trading license, sending to Detroit for it. Robert Dickson, Governor Harrison's appointee and an important trader out of Prairie du Chien, extended numerous courtesies to Pike and gave him much valuable geographical information. Pike recorded his impressions of all these men whom he met.

The Indians along the way were probably a better gauge of the trader's sentiments toward Americans and the real degree of their cooperation. Pike had no success in his efforts to gain Indian allegiance to the United States, although he asked them to give up their British medals and flags in return for the promise of suitable American medals and the presentation of flags. He could not find a single Indian to accompany him to St. Louis. As he approached Prairie du Chien he recorded in his journal with what dread the Indians viewed the Americans as "a very vindictive, ferocious, and warlike people. . . . but when they find our conduct toward them is guided by magnanimity and justice . . . it will have the effect to make them reverence at the same time they fear us." The traders and Indians were not wrong in their apprehensions. When Americans came in other than official guise, their lives were going to be transformed more profoundly than they had been by the previous transfer from French to British jurisdiction.

Pike's brief invasion was merely a forecast of American efforts to establish possession of the land west of Lake Michigan. The key to this was control of the Indian trade and relations with the tribes. The Americans had inherited the same problems left unsolved by the British: how to restrain the frontiersmen from war-provoking pressures on Indian lands and how to regulate the trade in the interest of national policy. It may seem, in retrospect, that the federal government had no policy beyond forcing the cession of Indian lands, but it had developed an official attitude that was benign in intent and devoted to the interests of the native. The gap between official expressions and enforcement only proved that the law, as a practical matter, is represented by what citizens will support in any given situation. The frontier would not support a policy based upon humanitarian considerations, nor a concept that Indians had rights which Americans were bound to respect.

Congress and the president had puzzled over the question of controlling the fur trade, which was, after all, more amenable to solution than the problem of halting or diverting the inexorable stream of American settlers into the West. President Washington and others held the interesting view that the trade was so intimately a part of the federal government's Indian policy that the government should undertake the role of trader. Only in this manner, it was argued, could the Indian be protected from liquor and commercial chicanery on the one hand and be encouraged in the arts of agriculture, civilization, and true religion on the other. When war resulted from unsatisfactory trade relations, the burden fell upon the federal government. Control of trade relations would give the government control over the vital issue of peace or war.

Congress was persuaded to finance a system of federally owned and operated trading posts, which remained in existence from 1796 to 1822. Historians have enjoyed the incongruity of George Washington sponsoring an experiment in "state socialism," but in fact, the federal fur factories, as they were called, were a mercantilist solution for the control of a situation vital to the government. Unfortunately, the solution was characteristically a compromise. The state factories existed alongside a system of licensing and regulation of private traders, administered by a superintendent of Indian affairs and his agents, which was very like Sir William Johnson's plan of a generation before. The regulation was nominal or nonexistent, and the private traders eventually overwhelmed this experiment in economic paternalism.

It was natural that the federal factories would be placed where Indian relations were a special problem, and so, until President Jefferson took a renewed interest in the device, they operated only in the South among the Creek, Cherokee, and Chocktaw. Jefferson turned his attention to the Northwest and the new Louisiana Purchase, and government factories were set up at Fort Wayne and Detroit in 1802, at Chicago in 1805, and on Mackinac Island and at Fort Madison (Iowa) in 1808. By 1809 there were twelve in operation, but none in present Wisconsin until after the War of 1812.

It is a question how effective the factories were. They did show a small profit until the disruption of the war. They were not expected to be profit-making ventures, however, but existed on a revolving fund established by Congress, and the administrative hazards included keeping the system solvent. Furthermore, congressional generosity in paying part of the salaries had its drawbacks: as an example, the agent at the new factory on Mackinac Island was the son of the speaker of the House, a Massachusetts representative. Political appointees generally came from the more populous states and more often than not had no experience in the Indian trade.

The government factory system was administered by a superintendent of the Indian trade, who was an official in the War Department. A summary of instructions to a new factory at Chicago gives an idea of the bureaucratic and policy limitations imposed: (1) "The principal object of the Government [is] to secure the Friendship of the Indians . . . in a way the most beneficial to them and the most effectual and economical to the United States." (2) The normal mark-up on goods was 66⅔ to 100 percent on invoice, and the prices for pelts such as to give satisfaction to the Indian but not diminish the revolving fund. (3) No credit except to "Principal Chiefs of good character." (4) No Liquor. (5) Watch out for tricks by private traders, and (6) Keep a good set of books. The instructions did not mention that there was no provision for gifts or other marks of favor. The Indian trade was largely built upon a personal relationship between the trader and the Indian hunter. Gifts, rum, seasonal credit, and taking the trade to the Indian were important elements of this relationship. An inexperienced place-holder, sitting at a government post waiting for customers without a keg or even an inconsequential gift to bestow, was working under serious handicaps. But Indians were inveterate shoppers and ungrudging of their own time and travel, therefore the government posts got some business.

Jefferson, who was a practicing idealist about affairs which he ordered at a distance, assumed that the companion system of licensing and regulating private traders insured a high-mindedness which would be devoted to the government's interests in the trade. He encouraged traders to follow the federal factories and uphold American interest on this new frontier. John Jacob Astor answered the call, pressing his operations into the Great Lakes from the New York backcountry. The competition of the federal system of fur factories, license requirements backed by American posts at Detroit, Mackinac, and Chicago, and official encouragement of private American traders made the Montreal traders increasingly nervous. In 1809, Jefferson's Embargo Act was replaced by the Non-Intercourse Act closing American ports to British and French ships. The customs officers on the Lakes interpreted this as a ban on Canadian goods entering American territory. Where the traders at Green Bay, Chicago, and Prairie du Chien had been inconvenienced before by American tariffs collected at Mackinac, they were now forced to depend upon smuggling or to adopt American connections for the receipt of trade goods. The Montreal traders adopted John Jacob Astor as their front; he shortly swallowed them. But many of the traders were embittered and stayed in business precariously by smuggling, awaiting an opportunity for revenge. Among these was Robert Dickson, whose disenchantment with the Americans was to be expensive for them.

The American embrace drew even closer with the appointment of a new Indian agent at Prairie du Chien, the only one on Wisconsin soil before the War of 1812. A British trader, John Campbell, had received such an appointment as early as 1802, but this was an American gesture of sovereignty with no great effect. Campbell was killed in a duel with another British trader near Mackinac in 1808, with Robert Dickson acting as second for Campbell's opponent (compounding Dickson's difficulties with the Americans). The new agent for Prairie du Chien was Nicholas Boilvin, who despite his name and Canadian birth had moved in 1774 to what is now Missouri, and faithfully served the Spanish and then American governments in various capacities. Boilvin was more active than Campbell had been in the American interest, but unfortunately his reports and recommendations to the War Department were written in French and sometimes accumulated for months before anyone got around to translating them. The transmittal of his pay, gifts for the Indians, and other reimbursements were equally dilatory, limiting his effectiveness.

When war with Britain was finally declared, western agitation over British tampering with the Indians in the Northwest had been aroused to fever pitch by the success of a Shawnee chief, Tecumseh, who was building a confederation of tribes, from Wisconsin to Alabama, to drive the Americans from their lands. It was no conspiracy, as it has often been described, for Tecumseh was quite open about his plans and purpose in confrontations with his principal antagonist, Governor William Henry Harrison of Indiana. Harrison was aggressive in his drive for Indian land cessions and undeterred by any feelings of sympathy or common humanity. He took every advantage of traditional divisions among the Indians, pressuring them ruthlessly to cede their lands or fight.

Tecumseh was encouraged in his plans by the British officers at Malden and by the fur traders scattered through the Northwest. Tecumseh had a brother, known as the Prophet, who spread a new religion among the Indians, calling on them to abjure the white man's ways. He had spent a dissolute youth, but had been converted by Shaker missionaries, from whom he derived some of his religious ideas. A disgusted trader among the Ottawa reported that "they do not wear Hats, Drink or Conjur . . . Whisky & rum is a Drug [on the market], the Indians do not purchase one Gall^n per month." Tecumseh, whose mother was a Creek, ranged widely and recruited warlike members of the Prophet's cult to spread the word. The Winnebago were early converts, and the crusade won recruits among the Sauk, Potawatami, Chippewa, and the mixed village at Milwaukee.

Boilvin, the Indian agent in Prairie du Chien, reported early in 1811 that the situation there was growing dangerous. The Canadian traders were "constantly making large presents to the Indians, which the latter consider as a sign of approaching war." Boilvin suggested that a strong garrison be sent and a federal fur factory established to control the situation. He said that many of the Sauk, Fox, and Iowa Sioux were engaged in lead mining and should be encouraged in this pursuit. The Canadians would leave of their own accord, he argued, as the fur trade declined.

The Indians in Indiana became more bold, and warlike incidents occurred. The Prophet gathered a large town of his followers on the upper Wabash at Tippecanoe, which became the center of the cult. They worried Harrison, not only by their new spirit of amity among diverse tribes hostile to the Americans but also by the fact that they had turned to agriculture on a large scale and had given up rum. Harrison held some parleys with Tecumseh, who, without guile, told him he was going south to bring his mother's people and neighboring tribes into his confederacy. Harrison took the opportunity to advance on the Prophet's town at Tippecanoe with a military force, in November 1811. A fight was provoked, ending in a standoff but winning a presidential election handily in 1840. Although the Indians were not decisively beaten, Tecumseh's prestige suffered by their failure to defeat Harrison, and the confederation declined. The Winnebago had had a prominent role in the battle.

The American frontiersmen were aroused by what they considered the perfidy of the British, who had all too openly encouraged Tecumseh. Whatever the causes of the War of 1812, the American frontiersmen and the British in Canada were both spoiling for a fight. The latter still hoped to see an Indian buffer state in present Indiana and Illinois. The Americans wanted to crush Indian resistance and get rid of the troublesome British influence in the Northwest, and they were not averse to seizing Canada as a prize. It was the only British territory within reach.

Napoleon's diplomacy and American willfulness maneuvered us into our declaration of war. The warlike West was nevertheless not prepared for the fight that came, and the war there turned into a military debacle. The British happily recalled a defect in the design of the fort at Mackinac which they had built. A mixed force of fur traders and Indians, largely recruited in Wisconsin by Robert Dickson, appeared on an undefended height above the fort and demanded its surrender. The American commander, who hadn't heard that there was a war going on, had no choice but to comply.

The commander at Detroit, General William Hull, who had failed to warn Mackinac, now ordered the forces at Chicago (Fort Dearborn) to abandon that post, although they had provisions and ammunition to withstand a siege. The order was carried out, but not with dispatch. This gave hostiles from Milwaukee and other points an opportunity to gather and massacre the garrison and many of the civilians, including a dozen children, as they retreated along the lakefront. (Others were saved by friendly Potawatomi.) Hull by this time was beleaguered at Detroit by Tecumseh, the western Indians who had helped take Mackinac, and a small British and Canadian militia force under General Isaac Brock. Brock warned Hull that he could not answer for the manners of his Indian allies, and the incompetent Hull, who didn't want to be a general anyway, surrendered Detroit to the grateful General Brock.

In Wisconsin, the energetic Robert Dickson took command of the situation, boldly recruiting Indian allies for the British with borrowed trade goods and promises which he hoped the government would uphold. As his efforts met with success, his initiative was rewarded and his commitments were honored. A collection of his letters from this period give insights into the state of the economy and the attitudes of the Indians. Dickson spent much of his effort simply trying to feed his charges while faced with the task of accumulating food surpluses for a marching army. A typical letter to trader John Lawe complained, "I am now entirely destitute of provisions. Since Mr. Powell left me upwards of forty Sauks came here, having eat nothing for two days, & had not Askin taken up his Cache & given them full avoins [wild rice which the French called *folle aviones*, "wild oats"] they must have perished, they are gone off well pleased and proud."

Dickson's correspondence also illustrates the hazards of categorizing Indians and assigning historic roles to them by tribes. Their normal political group, in many instances, was a village or even a single family unit. They had the wit to know that they were the men in the middle in a war. They cheerfully sold out to the highest bidder, or to both sides if they could find the paymasters. A "good" Indian was hard to find even at a price—they were continually faltering and consulting their own interests. "The Poutewatamies have always been villains to both parties and will continue so untill the end of the Chapter," groused Dickson. Again: "I will give nothing more to the Indians of Millwackie they are a sett of Imposters." Or: "The Renards [Fox] . . . with the Sauks are playing a double game."

At about the same time, Governor Ninian Edwards of Illinois was writing to an agent: "[My] object is the preservation of peace between us, and the Potawatomies. As . . . there can be no neutrality with savages, in the vicinity of conflicting powers, and as we have found them faithless in all their promises . . . you will therefore use your utmost exertions, to engage them in a war. You will insist upon their striking a blow upon some of our enemies as a proof of the sincerity of any professions or promises they may make." The Potawatomi maintained no diplomatic archives for our enlightenment.

After such an inauspicious beginning for the Americans, the course of the war in the West was reversed. General Harrison was reclaiming American honor, rather ineptly to be sure, and managed a victory at the battle of the Thames River in Canada on October 5, 1813. Tecumseh, a British general now, courted and met death there. But, unexpectedly, the decisive battle in the West was the naval engagement on Lake Erie, won by Commodore Perry on September 10, 1813. British sea power on the Atlantic made it prudent for the Americans to send their large naval guns to the fleet built on Lake Erie. The British flag was being swept from the Lakes, and the situation of the British west of Lake Michigan was serious.

A logical American step was to mount an attack from St. Louis across the Fox-Wisconsin waterway. The first order of business was to secure Prairie du Chien. It was this threat which found Robert Dickson touring the Wisconsin woods with his gloomy thoughts about the inconstancy of Indians and the uncertain prospects of his next meal. With the reversal of British fortunes around Lake Erie, his Indian allies had lost their earlier enthusiasm.

In the spring of 1814 General William Clark, commanding at St. Louis, got together a force of 140 militia and 61 regulars to ascend the Mississippi in five keelboats and build a "fort" at Prairie du Chien. This was bringing war into the enemy country. There had been a battle with Fox Indians on the way, and the Winnebago earlier had attacked Fort Madison in Iowa, which was later abandoned by the Americans, but the landing at Prairie du Chien was not contested. General Clark left Lieutenant Perkins to complete Fort Shelby there, leaving two of the keelboats mounting small cannon to aid in its defense. Perkins had 60 men in the fort. Part of the militia left on one boat, as their enlistments were running out; the others were quartered on the remaining "gunboat."

The British answered the threat with a force of 75 volunteers and 136 Indians gathered at Mackinac. Since Dickson was having a controversy with the commander, the force was led by a Colonel McKay, who collected an army of 650 on the way, largely Indians who were a trial to him. It developed that the most valuable man in his army was a sergeant of artillery with a three-inch cannon. McKay put the fort under siege while his cannoneer put the American gunboat to rout, then turned his attention to the fort. The Indian allies laid the village to waste and did much firing from a safe distance. The fort, without water, surrendered as the cannoneer was searching for used cannon balls to supplement the six he had remaining. Now both sides could worry about McKay's Indian allies. "I beg you will excuse my not having it in my power to give you a full account of the things taken in the fort, for a man having to do with Indians in my present situation is more tormented than if in the infernal regions," McKay wrote to his commanding officer.

Some of McKay's Indians redeemed themselves in British eyes. An expedition from St. Louis under Major Zachary Taylor, come to reclaim Fort Shelby, was turned back by a force of Sauk Indians at Rock Island led by a Scots trader with two cannons from the fort. The American Fort Shelby had become the British Fort McKay and remained so for the duration of the war.

As in the Revolution, American and British commissioners were meeting as the war progressed, to discuss terms of peace. The Americans in the West feared a settlement on the basis of the lines of battle, but the

British realized that their victories at Mackinac and on the lower Wisconsin would be of little use to them if they did not control the upper Lakes, and this control Perry had won. After nearly a quarter of a century of war with Napoleon, the British public refused to support any further efforts to win territory on the Canadian frontier. The war was a draw. The Treaty of Ghent in 1814 reflected this, with a return to the boundaries as they existed in 1812. President Madison insisted upon British abandonment of Article 3 of Jay's Treaty—the right of access to the Mississippi across American territory. The Indians of Wisconsin had lost another White Father.

Selected Bibliography

Beirne, Francis F. *The War of 1812*. New York, 1949. A journalist's useful account taken from secondary works, primarily Henry Adams

Bemis, Samuel Flagg. *Jay's Treaty: A Study in Commerce and Diplomacy*. Rev. ed. New Haven, 1962. The standard study, dealing with the Lakes forts and access.

Burt, A. L. *The United States, Great Britain, and British North America, 1783–1815*. New Haven, 1940. A careful account of the diplomacy.

Clark, James I. *The British Leave Wisconsin: The War of 1812*. Madison, 1955. A concise treatment for school use.

Gilpin, Alec R. *The War of 1812 in the Old Northwest*. East Lansing, Mich., 1958. His interest is the military phase of the war.

Hollon, W. Eugene. *The Lost Pathfinder, Zebulon Montgomery Pike*. Norman, Okla., 1949. The best account of Pike's explorations of the upper Mississippi.

———. "Zebulon Montgomery Pike's Mississippi Voyage, 1805–1806." *Wisconsin Magazine of History* 32:445–55 (June 1949).

Horsman, Reginald. "The British Indian Department and Resistance to General Anthony Wayne, 1793–1795." *Mississippi Valley Historical Review* 49:269–90 (Sept., 1962). Wayne called the British bluff.

———. "British Indian Policy in the Northwest, 1807–1812." *Mississippi Valley Historical Review* 45:51–66 (June 1958). The British did not incite the Indians, but did take advantage of their discontent to save Canada.

———. *Expansion and American Indian Policy, 1783–1812*. East Lansing, Mich., 1967. A thoughtful extended essay making much clear.

———. "Wisconsin and the War of 1812." *Wisconsin Magazine of History* 46:3–15 (Autumn 1962). Sorts out a complicated story nicely, putting it in context.

Peake, Ora Brooks. *A History of the United States Indian Factory System, 1795–1822*. Denver, 1954. Confused, but it leads the reader to the documents.

Prucha, Francis Paul. *American Indian Policy in the Formative Years: The Indian Trade and Intercourse Acts.* Cambridge, Mass., 1962. Good coverage on the fur factory system.

Scanlon, P. L. "Nicholas Boilvin, Indian Agent." *Wisconsin Magazine of History* 27:145–69 (Dec. 1943). One of Harrison's "officials."

SHSW Collections. Vols. 19 and 20. Madison, 1910, 1911. Documents on the post-1800 fur trade in Wisconsin and on the factory system.

THE
MILITARY FRONTIER

6

Wisconsin in 1815 was what we today, with a more extensive vocabulary for describing our stages of belligerence, would term a power vacuum. The Indians east of the Mississippi never again confronted the American military in force, nor could they regain their shattered faith in their British allies.

The Duke of Wellington warned that the British public would not support the military effort necessary to compel American agreement to British terms for the Northwest. The fact that Britain's best diplomats were required at Vienna for the liquidation of the Napoleonic years also helped the American cause. This, in effect, pitted Britain's second team against Henry Clay, John Quincy Adams, Albert Gallatin, Thomas Bayard, and Jonathan Russell. Clay and Gallatin were well acquainted with western interests, and President Madison was firmly opposed to any concessions there. Wisconsin, although indisputably in British hands throughout the war, was surrendered to the Americans at Ghent in the treaty ending the War of 1812.

The problem of the Americans was to fill the power vacuum that existed west of Lake Michigan, maintain peace with the Indians, deal equitably with the whites who chose to remain, and yet firmly detach both the Indians and the fur trade from their British connections. This was accomplished with astonishing ease and only occasional incidents, some of which have been dignified as wars but in retrospect can be seen as minor inconveniences to American power and population. The effect upon the Indian population was much more profound, of course.

To appreciate the surprising ease of transition to American de facto control requires some knowledge of the conditions in the Wisconsin country in 1815. The Indian tribes there were almost universally hostile to the American interest and continued so. Most of them had actively aided the British, but none had been directly defeated by American arms. Quite the contrary, they had helped drive an American force from Prairie du Chien and turn back two relief forces. Wisconsin Indians had been parties to British victories at Mackinac and Detroit. They had prudently decamped from General Proctor's army before the Battle of the Thames and had not shared in that British defeat. They had, therefore, every reason to be intractable.

The fur traders had reason to be apprehensive and resentful. They had won all of the local engagements but lost the war. Some were also concerned about their legal status. Those who had continued residence on American soil after Jay's Treaty went into effect in 1796 were legally American citizens after a year, unless they had declared themselves otherwise. This provision had been largely ignored by the traders and the British government. Many had readily volunteered or been impressed into British service during the war. Some, both Canadian and British in origin, had taken prominent roles in the fighting.

It might appear that the hazard of establishing citizenship was a small one on a frontier where so few Americans lived, records were scanty, and a man's legal residence difficult to establish in such an itinerant calling. But the fur trader left quite a paper trail behind him. He very probably had bought a license to trade from an American official at Mackinac or Detroit and paid duty on trade goods. Montreal and St. Louis traders had regularly repaired to Prairie du Chien to meet the annual concourse of Indians there. The St. Louis traders had accepted American citizenship, and some were happy to identify Canadian competitors who had turned their coats. In a society which numbered so few white men, geography did not confer anonymity, and everyone knew everyone's business or had a version of it.

Aside from concern about his legal status, the fur trader had his living to worry about. The Treaty of Ghent did not renew the right of the British subject to follow the Indian trade across the international border, or guarantee access to the Mississippi. Except for the voyageur or engagé, who could ply his trade wherever it took him in the interior, the fur trade was not a footloose business. The trader, if he had any standing, was caught in a skein of credit arrangements and personal ties which made it difficult for him to pull up stakes. He naturally considered his Indian clientele and their range as his business property, in a sense, and was accustomed to warn against American trade goods, traders, and motives. It was the trader of substance who had to worry about his legal status under a de facto American regime. He also had some capacity for mischief if he chose to use his influence with the Indians against American interest.

Americans were slow to work themselves into the economic life of the area, which remained the preserve of the French Canadians and the Scots who had come by way of Montreal. James Lockwood, an American from upstate New York, had settled in Prairie du Chien in 1816 and recalled that his was the only wholly American family in the community as late as 1827. There were half a dozen Americans: an Indian agent, three or four men lately discharged from the army, and a trader with a French wife. The army post, which would develop into Fort Crawford, had been temporarily abandoned. Green Bay was not being Americanized any more rapidly.

Given the situation—Indians who were hostile, defiant, and undefeated in war, American failure in attempts to win the area by conquest, an alien white population in control of the economy and hostile to American interests, and American settlement a generation and some hundreds of miles away—why was the transition to American control and final settlement accomplished with such relative ease? The answer seems to lie in the eroded energies of Wisconsin's tribesmen, the effectiveness of the United States Army, the adaptability of the fur trade to another change of allegiance by conquest, and John Jacob Astor.

The Wisconsin Indians, while undefeated by the Americans in battle, were not an impressive force, if we except the Sioux, who ranged mostly west of the Mississippi. We have noted how the fur trade displaced the various tribes and sent them westward, where their struggles to establish new ranges exacerbated old rivalries and created new ones. Warfare with neighbors was the Indian way of life, and the migrations of the fur era had given the Wisconsin Indians ample opportunity. Incidents with whites frequently grew out of these intertribal clashes.

As one reads of the encounters between Americans and the Indians on this frontier, it appears that most incidents grew out of individual acts. The American trader James Lockwood tells of a nervous journey on the Wisconsin River when a Winnebago was patently "laying for him." He had refused credit to the man for an unsatisfactory performance the previous year as a fur hunter. The man was emboldened by the fact that the garrison at Prairie du Chien had been called up the river to Fort Snelling by a presumed emergency. The precipitancy with which the troops left encouraged the Winnebago, who were particularly resentful over the arrival of Americans at the lead diggings on their land, and the so-called Winnebago War of 1827 followed.

The *causus belli* was the Red Bird incident. Red Bird, who always wore a red coat and referred to himself as English, went to Lockwood's store with two other braves while Lockwood was away. The Indians were acting in a threatening manner toward Mrs. Lockwood, but were persuaded to leave by Duncan Graham, who happened to be in the store with Mrs. Lockwood's brother. Graham had been a captain in the British Indian department and commandant at Prairie du Chien during the late war. He had been trading in the country for some forty years and was well known to the Indians as an Englishman. Red Bird, who had taken it into his head that honor required the blood of some Americans and had reinforced this conviction with a keg of spirits bought on credit from another trader, proceeded to the home of Registre Gagnier, a friend well known to him. The Indians accepted Gagnier's hospitality, then suddenly rose up and slew him and his hired man. Gagnier's wife escaped with some difficulty, but her daughter was scalped, although she miraculously survived. Red Bird's conduct was doubly astonishing, for he made clear distinctions even between Americans and Englishmen, and Gagnier was French-Canadian and black.

The Winnebago averted war, after American troops were in the field, by persuading Red Bird to surrender himself. This he did with such grace and dignity as to win himself a place in local history. His squalid deed is forgotten in the poignancy of his surrender and death while awaiting trial in the guardhouse. Colonel McKenney, who headed the Indian Bureau (and earlier, the federal fur-factory system), was with the troops called out for the "Winnebago War." In extenuation of Red Bird, he wrote that "the murders committed at Prairie du Chien were not wanton, but in retaliation for wrongs committed upon his people by the whites. The parties murdered at the Prairie, were doubtless innocent of the wrongs and outrages of which the Indians complained, but the law of Indian retaliation does not require that he alone who commits a wrong, shall suffer for it. One scalp is held to be due for another, no matter from whose head it is taken, provided it be torn from the crown of the family, or people who may have made a resort to this law necessary."

Indian traders recognized the Indian as a touchy customer, but one thing they were generally agreed upon: he must be handled with firmness and no hint of fear. Occasionally they overplayed this. In one such miscalculated encounter, a trader became enraged by a minor Sauk chief who refused to honor a previous debt after he was denied further credit.

The trader vowed to take a valuable horse from the Indian in payment. Meeting the chief mounted on the animal, he pulled him down, gave him a drubbing, and took the horse. The Indian returned, put a bullet through the trader's head, and took back his horse. If the story has a point, it would seem to be that the trader had reason to assume that the Indian would not retaliate, a conclusion he had generalized from contact with these people. His premises may have been perfectly sound as a general proposition but were obviously faulty in the particular instance.

The melancholy results of the years of contact with the whites were observed by many contemporaries. The Indians were aware of how their star had fallen. A pioneer missionary, who fell in with a band of Winnebago fleeing from the lead diggings in 1828, recorded their old chief's lament:

> But, My friend, the Winnebagoes are not now wise. Once they had many thousand fine warriors. But every year we grow smaller. Too much our young men go into the white man's house, and strive to live like him. They drink strong drink, and soon die. Traders buy our skins, and give us strong drink, calico and beads, which are not good for Indians. The skins of our game we want for clothes, and we could raise corn for ourselves were we left alone; but soon, my friend, we shall be no more. A few short years and our nation will be unknown.

Americans who recorded their impressions of Wisconsin Indians were apt to see them as cowardly beggars with only occasional flashes of pride. But when one belatedly asserted his manhood, according to accounts, it was well to be out of range. As one who had little to lose, the Indian could be careless of consequences. Acts of desperation were usually individual or involved only a small number, while the white's assessed responsibility collectively—just as Red Bird did when he murdered his friend Gagnier as a representative American. The Wisconsin Indians seemed incapable of collective action. Even Black Hawk carried only a fraction of his own tribesmen with him. As an old Winnebago chieftain remarked, the white man was a catastrophe for his people, but the Sacs and Foxes were their "sworn and eternal enemies."

Counting Indians was an exercise in futility indulged in by agents of the French, British, and American governments with widely divergent results. They ordinarily got their information from traders and chiefs who were guessing or exaggerating. One enterprising American agent suggested that a cooperative chief make a nose count and bring him a red bean for each man, a yellow for each woman, and a white for each child. The chief was presumably still sorting beans when the agent's report was sent off. James Duane Doty's estimate, in 1827, of 24,000 Indians within the present limits of Wisconsin is probably as reliable as any; not a formidable number, as scattered and divided as they were. The pressure of white penetration was felt only by a fraction of these at any one time, and the usual response was to give way after an interval of tension and alarms over isolated incidents.

The United States Army was not an impressive force in 1815. It seldom numbered more than 6,000 men before 1830. The Sioux tribes along the upper Mississippi, trading regularly at Prairie du Chien, could alone raise four times that number of warriors, and the tribes living within the confines of present Wisconsin, exclusive of the Sioux, constituted a warrior force probably as large as the entire regular army. But sheer numbers were quite meaningless, for the army represented a disciplined force under a unified command, competent for the task proposed. This task was to control the routes used by the fur traders to reach the Indians ranging on American territory. To this end, garrisons were posted and forts built at Chicago, Green Bay, and Prairie du Chien immediately after the War of 1812, and at Fort Snelling by 1819. The initial complements at Green Bay and Prairie du Chien each numbered about four companies of infantry. A full-strength company counted fewer than eighty enlisted men, and probably few companies approached full strength. The army was becoming a frontier garrison force, a policy reinforced by John C. Calhoun, secretary of war under President Monroe from 1817 to 1825. The increasing American population in the Ohio Valley and the breaking of Indian power there made this policy feasible.

The military played a pioneering role on the frontier well illustrated by the posts in Wisconsin. Inspectors complained regularly that drill in the manual of arms was neglected while garrisons engaged in the necessary pursuits of farming, road-building, lumbering, and the like. As at Prairie du Chien, the usual procedure was to land a body of troops at a site with instructions to build and man a fort, calling any number of trades into play. It was well that the small regular-army officer corps had the advantage of the best civil-engineering education offered in the country at the time.

Prairie du Chien, by 1820, was a village of fifty or sixty houses and a permanent population of two hundred or more. Most of the men were engaged in the fur trade, and as James Lockwood remarked, Indian traders possessed little instinct for other enterprises which would foster the growth of the country. A garrison had a considerable impact upon such a community. There was more farming at Prairie du Chien than at Green Bay, but the surplus wheat had no other market than the Indian trade based upon barter. Money, or at least government requisitions, entered the economy when the army discovered that local flour was superior to that brought by keelboat from Pittsburgh. Officers brought their families, and enlisted men had occasional paydays which put the economy partly on a money basis. The need to ship basic supplies from supply points as far away as St. Louis and Pittsburgh was a source of contracts for boat operators. In 1823, an enterprising contractor tried out a small Ohio steamboat, despite the prevailing notion that they could not negotiate the rapids at Rock Island. His success in bringing supplies in this manner to forts Crawford and Snelling brought other and larger steamboats to this part of the river. Such activity and the protection of the garrison brought other Americans, although in these early years most of them were traders rather than farmers, Lockwood for example.

The regular army in this period was a rough outfit, and the gulf between officer and enlisted man was a wide one. Military life for the enlisted man was Spartan, discipline harsh. A man who soldiered under Zachary Taylor at Prairie du Chien described how Taylor grasped a German recruit by the ears and shook him while the man was in ranks. The action was not unusual, but the outraged private knocked Taylor down; he had not understood the command which Taylor expected him to execute. The point of the story was that Taylor generously saved the man from a flogging, the usual consequences of striking back at an officer. Some officers, however, harbored the notion that they had been set down in conquered territory and acted accordingly.

Americans did not ordinarily join up unless they had good reason to seek the anonymity of the ranks and travel in distant parts. The army was more apt to attract recent immigrants looking for bed and board and $5 a month. In one typical period, out of 5,000 recruits more than 3,500 were immigrants, and more than 2,100 of these were Irish. In the year 1830 there were 1,250 desertions, which accounts for the high recruiting rate for such a small force. It was an officer's war and an enlisted man's fight. To compound the difference, in 1832 the army imposed temperance on enlisted men. Officers were presumed to be able to handle their liquor.

Troops were fine to have around when trouble threatened, but their constant presence on the frontier, where the civilian government was only a sketchy presence, encouraged military officiousness. One witness records that as late as 1827, when Judge Doty of the district court was passing Fort Howard at Green Bay he was ordered ashore by a sentry, who threatened to fire if not obeyed. It is true that the judge was riding in the usual conveyance available, an Indian canoe, but he was not a man to submit to such assaults upon his dignity. The luckless commandant of Fort Winnebago, Major David Twiggs, soon found himself named as defendant in a lawsuit before Judge Doty in a case involving trespass by a trader on Indian land. Major Twiggs had evicted him. Doty seemed sympathetic to the plaintiff.

While the military was sometimes officious, there was another side to the story. The want of civil courts and local government could be an embarrassment to conscientious army officers who found themselves the sole source of local authority. Father Paul Prucha, an authority on the army's frontier role and American Indian policy, has a delightful illustration of the dilemma. Colonel Stephen Kearney was in command of a new post near the mouth of the Des Moines River in 1834. He addressed a series of questions to his superiors in Washington that went beyond relations with the Indians. Was the land adjacant to the post Indian land, public land, or could it be privately owned? Assuming it was either Indian or federal land, could he forbid settlement? He had evicted some neighboring grog shops, but it bothered him that there was no civil government in existence to share his jurisdiction over civilians. Finally, he asked, "What is required of this command while stationed here?" The answer he received was a rebuke from the adjutant general. "So much of [your letter] as refers to *settlers,* to the introduction of *ardent spirits,* in the part of the country in which Fort Des Moines is situated, to *public lands,* and to *Indian Affairs,* could not be satisfactorily *answered* by the Genl-in-Chief—/nor is it competent for him . . . to give you the light you aske for . . . touching these subjects. . . ." Finally, "it is required of your command, as of all other garrisons, to be well instructed in all its duties, and to be always ready to perform them, as the exigencies of the public service may require—."

The military filled a necessary but sometimes uncomfortable role on the Wisconsin frontier in a time of transition. Its principal duties were to enforce the federal government's Indian policy and to regulate the fur trade. This may have seemed perfectly straightforward, especially since the other federal agents involved were employees of the Indian Bureau within the War Department or were territorial governors, who in this period doubled as superintendents of Indian affairs. Many were men of military background, such as Lewis Cass and William Clark, who negotiated the Indian Treaty of Prairie du Chien in 1825. But the very presence of the military attracted American civilians and broadened the base of the American traders' operations into lumbering, transportation, supply contracts, and whatever other economic opportunities beckoned. The responsibilities of the military were ill defined in dealing with the new element in the community and would be until civilians became numerous enough to erect a local government, however sketchy. This phase depended upon the appearance of a new settler class, farmers and lead miners, who would create more problems in Indian relations.

Like the fur trade, the military frontier was a passing phase. The officers and their families helped set the social tone of the communities where they found themselves, but they were essentially transients (Zachary Taylor and his son-in-law Jefferson Davis are the best known) and usually did not share in the economic and social goals of their neighbors. Enlisted men and militia, called in for emergencies, were more apt to join the community on completion of their service.

The army was more secure in its relations with the Indians and the fur trade. The federal Constitution has little to say about relations with the Indians, because with the cession of western land claims to the central government, it was tacitly acknowledged that the regulation of Indian affairs and treating for Indian lands lay with the federal government. The 1795 Treaty of Greenville had defined Indian sovereignty; their ownership of the land was recognized but limited by the higher sovereignty of the United States, which alone could treat for changes in Indian boundaries or alienation of land. Despite this limited theory of sovereignty, the federal government invoked the treaty power in dealing with the Indians as if they had full and unlimited sovereignty. This method of dealing with a people who as a practical matter were becoming more and more dependent proved increasingly unsatisfactory, but was continued to 1871. The American pioneer usually discerned no property, civil, or human right belonging to an Indian which he was bound to observe if he could avoid reprisal. The army and the Indian agent had the unpopular duty of keeping this contempt within bounds, and as we have seen, were often harassed by local courts, officers, and juries in the process.

In theory, then, the United States recognized Indian property rights and its own right to treat for Indian land, buy it, or win it by conquest as from a sovereign power. Trade was so intimate a part of these sovereign relations that the right and duty of the federal government to control or regulate it was assumed. There was an obligation on the part of the government to protect the Indian and mete out justice evenhandedly for offenses committed involving Indians and whites. Accounting itself a Christian nation, the obligation to Christianize, "civilize," and educate the Indian was another assumption of American policy. It has still to be settled exactly what he is being educated to be, although it is easy to smile at some of the notions of the past.

The elements of this policy of most concern to the military and Indian agents on the Wisconsin frontier were the regulation of trade and white contacts with the Indians, maintenance of peace in Indian country, and protection of the inviolability of the Indian lands while other agents, under the treaty power, sought if possible a peaceful cession of the lands ahead of pressure for settlement. A new element had been added to the theory of cession after the acquisition of Louisiana. This made possible the isolation of the Indians east of the Mississippi by removal to suitable lands west of the river, beyond what were assumed to be the limits of white expansion in the foreseeable future. There is no evidence of an intent to remove these people to inferior, useless lands, but rather beyond the pressure of white settlement where they could be guaranteed perpetual rights to the lands reserved for them. The Indian Removal Policy, as it was called, was articulated as early as Jefferson's presidency, but it was not until Jackson's administration that it became official policy. It was not strictly a western or frontier policy. There was a growing humanitarian movement directed toward justice for the Indian which agreed with removal as a solution that would save them from further degradation and despair.

Indian removal had at first implied only a *cordon sanitaire* between the whites and Indians, with the eastern Indians moving to land ceded by western Indians. The Indian population was decreasing, while instruction in agriculture and other civilized arts was expected to reduce the need for vast tracts of hunting land. It was under this arrangement that the Oneida Indians from New York, the group under the influence of the Reverend Eleazer Williams, were given a small reservation by the Menominee in 1823. The Stockbridge Indians were similarly accommodated by the Menominee and in turn ceded land to the Brotherton Indians. Except for the Brotherton, these tribes are still represented in the vicinity of Green Bay.

This phase of Indian removal had an interesting chapter. The Reverend Jedediah Morse of New Haven, Connecticut, was commissioned in 1820 by Secretary Calhoun to make a study of the status of the Indians under American jurisdiction, and to make recommendations. Morse was a well-known American scholar of the day, author of the widely used *Universal Geography*. He set out to visit Wisconsin in May 1820, accompanied by his son, coming ninety-six miles by way of the uncompleted Erie Canal and from Buffalo on the pioneer steamer *Walk-in-the-Water*. Morse conceived of Wisconsin as an excellent site for an Indian state, where he proposed that the eastern Indians be gathered and protected, but not completely isolated. He would send among them what he called "education families," by which he meant missionary groups of farmers, blacksmiths, and teachers, to instruct by example. The idea, he thought, was a particularly happy one for Wisconsin, inasmuch as he found no

American population at Green Bay, but only a few mixed French and Indian families. He cannot have been much of an economic geographer, having ridden partway on the Erie Canal and drawn no conclusion from the experience about Wisconsin's destiny.

More practical men were soon to begin dealing with Wisconsin's Indians. A great concourse of the Wisconsin Indians was called at Prairie du Chien in 1825, presided over by General William Clark and Lewis Cass, governor of Michigan Territory. The purpose of the negotiations was ostensibly to set the boundaries of the various tribal lands precisely, with the idea that intertribal wars were based on territorial claims. Cass and Clark were too experienced to accept this simplistic view of Indian warfare, but they shared the Anglo-American reverence for an unclouded land title. What better way to establish eventual American land titles than to have the various tribes agree to precise metes and bounds before entering into treaties of cession with individual tribes? This purpose was admirably served at the proceedings, and the Red Bird incident in 1827 led to a cession, in 1829, of the lead region south of the Wisconsin River. Other cessions followed in regular order, usually ahead of American settlement.

The other responsibility of the military during its years of ascendancy in the area was the regulation of the fur trade. This came within the purview of officers of the War Department especially assigned as Indian agents. Their first concern, like the military's, was to cut the ties that bound the fur traders to Canada, and the Indians to the British Indian agents and military officers who still had influence with the Wisconsin tribes. The British continued to dispense gifts annually, near Mackinac, where many Indians repaired for renewal of old loyalties. These pilgrimages could not be controlled.

John Jacob Astor Americanized the Wisconsin fur trade, but did not endear himself to the Indian Bureau in the process. Before the War of 1812, the Canadian traders found themselves embarrassed in their trade across the border by the Non-Intercourse Act, closing American ports to British goods. Attempting to solve this dilemma, the Canadians took Astor into partnership and sold him the Michilimackinac Company, their instrument for trading into Green Bay and Prairie du Chien. Astor had larger ambitions: a monopoly of the fur trade in the entire United States and on the Pacific Coast through the American Fur Company, a corporation chartered by the State of New York, for which he subscribed all of the stock himself.

After the war, Astor administered the *coup de grâce* to his onetime Canadian partners. In 1816 Congress, with Astor's urging, passed a law forbidding aliens to engage in the fur trade. This gave him full control of the major company trading in Wisconsin and the opportunity to develop his operations in the more valuable fur territory to the west, without Canadian competition. The traders in the Wisconsin country, who had openly supported the British cause almost to a man, had the choice of asking for American citizenship, with a degrading oath disavowing their recent allegiance, or going to work for Astor under the "supervision" of an American clerk who could be licensed. Astor's habitant agents were really on commission. The company provided the goods on credit and the agent turned in his furs at company prices. The Canadians had been vigorously reaping the harvest before the war and the annual catch was declining. Only Astor made a profit while his "agents" accumulated debts to him.

American control of the Wisconsin frontier was secure by the mid-twenties. The frontier of American agricultural settlement still lay to the east, but the lure of another sort of frontier, a mining frontier, had already fastened upon a few hundred hardy souls who were digging in the hillsides along the Fever River in back of present Galena.

Selected Bibliography

Barsness, Richard W. "John C. Calhoun and the Military Establishment, 1817–1825." *Wisconsin Magazine of History* 50:43–53 (Autumn 1966). A military policy for the frontier.

Blegen, Theodore C., and Sarah A. Davidson, eds. *Iron Face: The Adventures of Jack Frazer, Frontier Warrior, Scout and Hunter.* Chicago, 1950. Frazer, born in 1806, half Sioux, left a record of tribal life in western Wisconsin.

Carter, Clarence E., ed. *The Territorial Papers of the United States.* Vol. 10, *The Territory of Michigan, 1805–1820.* Vol. 11, *The Territory of Michigan, 1820–1829.* Vol. 12, *The Territory of Michigan, 1829–1837.* Washington, D.C., 1942–45.

Cooper, Jerry M. "The Wisconsin Militia, 1833–1900." Master's thesis, University of Wisconsin, 1968. The militia had to be led, and Dodge led it.

Foreman, Grant. *The Last Trek of the Indians.* Chicago, 1946. Covers removals from the Old Northwest, too.

Goetzmann, William H. *Army Exploration in the American West, 1803–1863.* New Haven, 1959. Mostly about the army engineers in the trans-Mississippi West, but also discusses the Great Lakes and the Canadian boundary.

Hagan, William T. *American Indians.* The Chicago History of American Civilization Series. Chicago, 1961. Covers the whole sweep of Indian relations and the fate of the Indians.

Hamilton, Holman. *Zachary Taylor, Soldier of the Republic.* 2 vols. Indianapolis, 1941, 1951. Good chapters on his service in Wisconsin.

Harmon, George D. *Sixty Years of Indian Affairs, Political, Economic, and Diplomatic, 1789–1850.* Chapel Hill, N.C., 1941. Title is sufficient description.

Haskins, R. W. "Legends of the Winnebagoes." *SHSW Collections*, vol. 1, pp. 86–93. Madison, 1903, reprint of 1855 original. The old chief's lament on what the whites had done to the Indians.

Lavender, David. *The Fist in the Wilderness.* New York, 1964. Scholar who writes well for a popular audience. This volume is on Ramsey Crooks, who imposed order on the fur trade after 1815.

Lockwood, James H. "Early Times and Events in Wisconsin." *SHSW Collections*, vol. 2, pp. 98–196. Madison, 1903, reprint of 1856 original. Contains Lockwood's account of the Red Bird incident.

McKenney, Colonel Thomas L. "The Winnebago War." *SHSW Collections*, vol. 5, pp. 178–204. Madison, 1907, reprint of 1868 original. Sympathetic head of the Indian Bureau.

"Papers on the North American Fur Trade." *Minnesota History* 40:149–220 (Winter 1966). The entire issue is given to papers read at a conference on the subject at the University of Minnesota.

Prucha, Francis Paul. *American Indian Policy in the Formative Years: The Indian Trade and Intercourse Acts, 1790–1834.* Cambridge, Mass., 1962. Draws upon federal records; a standard work.

———. *Broadax and Bayonet: The Role of the United States Army in the Development of the Northwest, 1815–1860.* Madison, 1953. A gold mine of a book.

Prucha, Francis Paul, and Donald F. Carmony, eds. "A Memorandum of Lewis Cass: Concerning a System for the Regulation of Indian Affairs." *Wisconsin Magazine of History* 52:35–50 (Autumn 1968). Just that.

Snelling, William J. "Early Days at Prairie du Chien and Winnebago Outbreak of 1827." *SHSW Collections*, vol. 5, pp. 123–53. Madison, 1907, reprint of the 1868 original. Another account of the Red Bird Incident.

Terrell, John Upton. *Furs by Astor.* New York, 1963. Easier to follow than the standard biography by Kenneth W. Porter.

SETTLEMENT, EXPLOITATION, AND ORGANIZATION, 1816–1848

part three

In the score of years between the end of the War of 1812 and the creation of Wisconsin Territory in 1836, some 10,000 Americans made their way to the new land between Lake Michigan and the Upper Mississippi. Their advance was tentative in all but the lead-mining region, however, until after the Indian cessions, prompted by the Black Hawk War of 1832, assured that land titles would soon be available. The census of 1830 found only 3,245 whites within the present area of Wisconsin.

The American of an entrepreneurial temper was a conspicuous element in the early frontier advance in Wisconsin. The Erie Canal and steam vessels on the Great Lakes gave the Yankee a new and varied view of his opportunities. The lead miner, who was most likely to come by way of the Mississippi, drew commerce behind him as mining frontiers are wont to do.

The pioneer farmer came and quickly built a commercial agriculture based upon the transportation facilities of the Lakes. For the best farm-ing sites close by Lake Michigan, he had to elbow his way through a crowd of urban pioneers feverishly speculating in city lots. Quarter-acre lots in Milwaukee were trading as high as $600 already in 1835, when the future city was as yet only a promising site.

All of this activity was based upon the American's assumption that a system of land titles, an orderly government, and charters for commercial and industrial enterprises would be immediately forthcoming. This ex-pectation created a frontier of a different order from that presided over by the French-Canadian *bourgeois* and his Scottish successor.

THE
FIRST TEN THOUSAND

7

Who were these Americans who sought a new frontier? Most of them remain simply names in the first territorial census, and it is difficult to treat them other than as numbers or as representative groups. Some of them were men who rose to positions of leadership, or were particularly enterprising and imaginative. It is interesting to notice these men briefly for a comparison with the popular image of the American frontiersman and for a perception of the vision that drew them. As for being representative of the "first 10,000," they doubtless did more to shape the Wisconsin frontier than did the average men and women whose stories have been lost.

When Wisconsin was created a territory in 1836, one of the first official acts of Governor Henry Dodge was to have a census taken by the county sheriffs. In the area comprising the present state of Wisconsin (the western boundary of the Territory was the Missouri River in 1836), there were few centers of population. Green Bay and settlements on the Lower Fox were in Brown County; Iowa County took in the portion of the lead region in Wisconsin; Crawford County's population centered in Prairie du Chien, and Milwaukee County included the settlements at Milwaukee, Racine, and Kenosha. The total count was 11,683 (Indians were not counted), but the returns included the soldiers posted at Forts Crawford, Howard, and Winnebago.

To start with, almost half, 5,234, lived in Iowa County. As one would expect of a mining community, the men outnumbered the women two to one, but the numbers of males and females under twenty-one years of age were almost equal: 1,134 and 1,092, respectively. There were 2,317 men over 21 to only 691 women. The census was certainly rough in form; however, it reflected the fact that by 1836 the lead-mining frontier in Wisconsin was maturing. We do not know how many of the females under twenty-one were wives, although the number of children indicates a large number of families. The returns are by head of household, but very few indicate bachelor households. Probably most of the single men shared diggings with or were employees or boarders of the household in which they were counted. Households of over a dozen were not unusual —one had 46 members—indicating that this was the way the count was made. Something else we know about the lead region is also confirmed: most of the names were Scots-Irish or English in origin.

Crawford County was the smallest of the four, with a population of 850, counting 260 officers and men of the fort. Excluding the garrison and the few connected families, there were 573 enumerated persons in the county. Ninety-four were women fifteen or over, and 193 men over twenty. The high proportion of single males indicates that Indian wives were not counted and probably not their children either. French names predominate, fancifully spelled, with a sprinkling of Scottish.

Brown County numbered 2,706, including the garrison at Fort Howard. One of the principal traders, Daniel Whitney, had a "family" of 49, which included his workmen in various enterprises around the territory, for he operated sawmills and the shot tower at Helena in Iowa County. The number of males reported between the ages of twenty-one and forty-five outnumbered the women in the over-twenty-one age group by more than three to one. Despite this disparity, which again reflects the exclusion of Indian wives in a largely French-Canadian community, over one-third of the population was under twenty-one. As in Crawford County, French names were in the majority, but Scottish, English, and Irish names were more numerous than at Prairie du Chien.

Milwaukee County, with a population of 2,893, had just surpassed Brown County at the time of the census. Only four years before, it had been a trading post and Indian settlement, and there was no white population as yet in present Racine and Kenosha counties. On this newest frontier, it was not surprising to find that the men twenty-one and older outnumbered the women 1,406 to 438 but it was a family frontier also, with one-third of the population under twenty-one. The farmer's frontier was just arriving, but had been preceded by an army of speculators who foresaw that Milwaukee in particular was going to be an urban center of some importance. The prevalence of Anglo-Saxon or "Yankee" names was pronounced, and the informal appellation Yankees of the Lake came into common use.

The French-Canadian society, soon to be overwhelmed in a sea of Americans with a quite different view of the prospects and possibilities of the country, was a conservative, highly stratified society tied closely to the fur trade and loath to give it up. Solomon Juneau, who considered himself a resident of Green Bay running a trading post at Milwaukee for Astor's American Fur Company, was later persuaded to make a land claim at the post. Morgan Martin recalled Juneau's astonishment that the future site of Milwaukee could possibly excite anyone's avarice. The speculators would have picked the Frenchman clean in short order, had he not had the good fortune to accept Martin as a partner in the prospective townsite. Juneau typified his people in many ways: hospitable, open, and easygoing but not adjusting readily to the changes taking place around him.

The Americans who first appeared in Wisconsin, aside from the military, were fur traders. They were a good deal like the Scotsmen who had preceded them, except that the Americans, who generally came from a less remote frontier which they had seen develop rapidly, had higher expectations and entrepreneurial notions that often outran their resources and the available markets. A good example of this group was James Lockwood, who came to Prairie du Chien in 1817 as a fur trader.

James Lockwood was born in 1793 in northern New York near Lake Champlain. His father was a farmer who, as Lockwood put it, got "Ohio fever" in 1803 but decided not to move, since although the Ohio soil promised more, the markets were uncertain. James had a meager education and after a brief try, gave up his ambition to be a lawyer. Instead, he apprenticed himself as a clerk to a regimental sutler in the War of 1812. Sutlers were civilians, usually retired officers, who had the concessions to furnish goods to an army unit or post—a sort of post exchange. In 1815 Lockwood worked for a sutler supplying a regiment posted at Buffalo, soon moving on to forts farther west on the Lakes.

Stranded for the winter in Mackinac, Lockwood hired out as a school teacher for the season. In 1816 Astor was tightening his grip on the fur trade, and the Montreal traders, who used Mackinac as a field headquarters and warehouse center, found that Congress had proscribed foreigners as fur traders to American Indians. Americans were suddenly in great demand to front for the British traders. Lockwood got a license to trade and became the "legal" trader for a British group which included Jacob Franks, a Green Bay trader. His destination was a post on the St. Peters

River (the Minnesota), which he reached by way of Green Bay and Prairie du Chien.

After two seasons on the St. Peter, Lockwood decided to make Prairie du Chien his base, and spent a season there as trader for Astor's American Fur Company before branching out on his own. In 1818 the area between Lake Michigan and the Missouri was annexed to Michigan Territory. Governor Cass had Brown and Crawford counties created to bring a modicum of local government to the communities in present Wisconsin. He sent blank commissions to Nicholas Boilvin, who had been Indian agent and justice in Prairie du Chien before the war, to find suitable Americans for the jobs, and although Lockwood declined a judgeship, he accepted appointment as justice of the peace, reluctantly. The problem was to find enough Americans upon whom to confer the political preferments. Lockwood, the sutler to the garrison and his clerks, the factor of the United States fur factory, and the official interpreter for the Indian agent about exhausted the list. A friend and counsellor of Lockwood, James Duane Doty, lived in Prairie du Chien briefly, and always one to improve his opportunities, got the settlement designated as a post office and himself as postmaster. When he left in 1824, he passed this favor on to his friend and persuaded him to take up reading law and practicing.

Lockwood traded on his own and in 1830 branched out into the sawmill business on the Chippewa River. He was probably the first to raft lumber out, made up into cribs. The enterprise, on disputed ground between the Sioux and Chippewa, was well ahead of its time. Running a waterpower mill was beyond the capabilities or interests of the voyageur help available. American labor was scarce or nonexistent, and the Indians frightened prospective employees. Lockwood anticipated by more than a generation the timber fortunes to be made from Chippewa Valley timber. Lockwood continued trading and practicing law, becoming a county judge in 1830 and a member of the first territorial legislature in 1836. That same year, he was one of the incorporators of the Wisconsin Mineral and Transportation Company, which operated the shot tower at Helena, a sawmill, and a store. Lockwood died in 1857.

James Lockwood's career illustrates his comment that a Yankee had a better eye for an opportunity than the older generation of fur traders. Daniel Whitney at Green Bay had a similar and financially more successful career. Two years younger than Lockwood, he was born in New Hampshire and came to Green Bay in 1819, where he competed successfully with the American Fur Company, was a sutler from time to time, and built some pioneer sawmills and the Helena shot tower. He was interested in the Fox-Wisconsin Canal and various land speculations.

Whitney laid out the townsite of Navarino, now part of Green Bay, and made money in speculations at Sheboygan and elsewhere.

James Duane Doty, one of the best known of the pioneer lawyer-politicians, came to Wisconsin very early, with a federal appointment in his pocket. He was a Yankee, born and raised on the Vermont border of New York State, with New England antecedents and the advantage of an academy education beyond the village school. He was well connected, and his father was prominent in local and state politics. As to Doty's character, his biographer writes that "from early manhood he seems to have been activated by a burning desire for success in life, an ambition that was never satisfied with moderate prosperity nor quenched by adversity."

The way of many an ambitious lad lay westward, and so in 1818, at the age of eighteen, Doty came west to Cleveland and then on to Detroit, a village of 770 souls and the capital of Michigan Territory, to which the area west of Lake Michigan had just been annexed. An engaging and obliging young man, he was soon making himself useful to public officials, business, and professional men.

At the ripe age of nineteen, Doty was admitted to the bar and became a partner in a prominent law firm. He cultivated important people and became favorably known to Governor Lewis Cass, who took him along as secretary on his 1820 expedition through Lake Superior to the Mississippi and back by the Fox-Wisconsin route. After his return, Doty conceived the notion of a separate judicial district for the detached portion of Michigan Territory beyond Mackinac. With the support of Governor Cass and the managers of the American Fur Company, and with other influence Doty could bring to bear through his father and friends, he prevailed in Congress against rival plans and rival appointees. At the age of twenty-three, James Doty assumed the dignity of a federal judge of a practically independent district. He will make frequent appearances in our narrative as politician and land speculator.

The greatest number of Americans counted in the 1836 territorial census lived in the Wisconsin lead region, which lay north of Galena, Illinois. The Galena mining district had been known for many years. Men are drawn to any ore field by the prospect of a fortunate strike, even of such a common metal as lead. Americans from St. Louis made cautious attempts on the Fever River district before the War of 1812, but the Sauk and Fox were working the diggings there and drove them away. The region was claimed on the basis of the 1804 cession that Governor Harrison had arranged with these tribes, but a militant group of tribesmen identified with Black Hawk refused to recognize this cession or the

Portage des Sioux cession of 1816. The Winnebago also claimed part of the diggings and had made no cession. Nonetheless, the government assumed that it had reserved a five-mile-square section at the Fever River diggings, and in 1822 issued a license to Colonel James Johnson to begin large-scale mining.

A boost in lead prices brought miners in increasing numbers after 1825, when there were 40 counted in the district. The number increased to 432 in 1826 and to 10,000 in 1828, most south of the Illinois line; threats of Indian reprisal made them cautious about isolating themselves from the main body of miners centered in Galena. The United States recognized Winnebago ownership north of the five-mile square claimed by the federal government. There were miners, however, ready to contest the claims of both the Indians and the federal government. Generally southerners, they had made their way up the Mississippi from the Missouri lead area around Potosi, and had served their apprenticeship on an Indian frontier. Their beau ideal was Henry Dodge.

Dodge was born in Vincennes, Indiana, in 1782, raised in Kentucky, and, in 1796, the family moved to the lead diggings in Missouri. Dodge grew up in the lead trade and mining. A turbulent character, he made an effort to join the Burr Conspiracy in 1806 and was alleged to have whipped a jury—consecutively, not concurrently—for threatening an indictment. He rose to the rank of brigadier general of the Missouri militia in the War of 1812. As a military commander his audacity often outran his judgment, but this was a valuable quality in directing undisciplined militia against Indians. Dodge moved to the Galena mineral district in 1827 with a family of nine children and his slaves.

The Red Bird incident, or Winnebago War of 1827, found Dodge in the thick of things. Restive about the growing number of miners on their own lead diggings, the Winnebago were overawed by the prompt concentration of militia and regular forces. As soon as the emergency passed, Dodge moved onto the Winnebago land near present Dodgeville, built a stockade, and defied the Indians or the federal government to move him. The government acknowledged that the lands belonged to the Indians, but preferred to arrange a cession by the Indians rather than attempt to move out the encroaching whites.

Spoiling for a fight, Dodge wrote to a friend, "we are not to have peace with this banditti collection of Indians until they are killed up in their dens." He was not to be denied his fight.

So much has been written about the Fox-Sauk chief, Black Hawk, that our story will be brief. Black Hawk was not a chief, but an irreconcilable war leader who gathered the like-minded around him in opposition to the leadership of Keokuk, a chief friendly to Governor William Clark. The tribe centered in the lower Rock River country's good agricultural land in Illinois. They were being squeezed from the east by settlers moving into their corn lands when they moved out to hunt, and by the lead miners on their northwest. By 1830, Black Hawk was a man in his sixties who had led his tribesmen in victories against the Americans in the War of 1812. He continued to go annually to Malden, a British post near Detroit, for presents, and to cling to unrealistic hopes of aid.

Black Hawk refused to move permanently west of the Mississippi with the main body of the tribe led by Keokuk. He hoped for an alliance with the Winnebago and other tribes as well as for British aid. In the spring of 1832 he moved his people, called "the British band," across the river to their former Illinois home. A thrill of alarm ran through the frontier and back beyond it as fear of a general Indian outbreak fed on rumors. Many frontiersmen welcomed this as an opportunity to wipe out the "savages." Besides, a small Indian war would circulate some federal money among the militia and give political aspirants an opportunity for military leadership.

Black Hawk obliged them despite a belated change of heart. The military began to surround him with such a force of regulars and militia that the old warrior decided to surrender to General Atkinson, and ask permission to recross the Mississippi. Unfortunately, the first force Black Hawk ran into was undisciplined militia. His emissaries, seeking to parley under a white flag, were unceremoniously cut down, and the militiamen rushed out to complete the work. Black Hawk, who understood warfare, ambushed them with 40 braves and sent the 300-man militia force fleeing in panic, carrying other militia with them, many of whom did not stop until they were home. The Potawatomi and the Winnebago, who had encouraged Black Hawk, were mobilized by the whites against him.

The beleaguered Indian band retreated up the Rock River, striking at outlying settlements while evading the military. The chief concealed his people for some time around Lake Koshkonong, until they were ferreted out by the milita, now numbering over 4,000 men in the field. James Henry and Henry Dodge, leading militia ranger forces, were restive under General Atkinson's control and eager for action. It was their force, operating independently, that came on Black Hawk's trail, plainly marked by discarded equipment and occasional starving stragglers who were shot and scalped by the whites—two within the present limits of Madison.

From present Lake Mendota, the retreat turned into a nightmare for the Indians, although Black Hawk proved his mastery of tactics. Some of

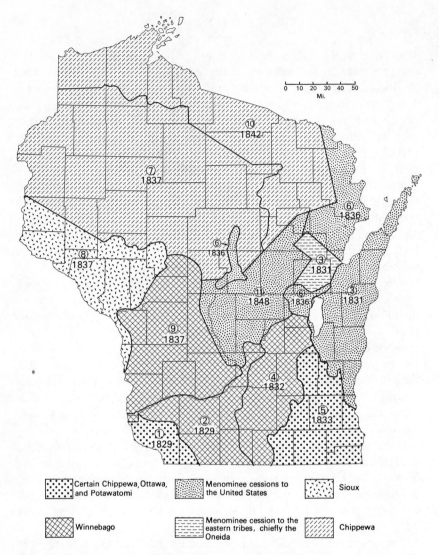

Map 8. Principal Indian Cessions. The area comprised in the state of Wisconsin was acquired from various Indian tribes by eleven treaties of cession. The first five were negotiated while Wisconsin was part of Michigan Territory, and covered all the land south and east of the Fox and Wisconsin rivers. The treaties were executed at 1) Prairie du Chien, 2) Prairie du Chien, 3) Washington, D.C., 4) Fort Armstrong, Rock Island, Illinois and 5) Chicago, Illinois. The next five were executed while Wisconsin was a territory, at 6) Cedar Point, on the Fox River below Appleton, 7) St. Peter's, at the confluence of the St. Peter's and Mississippi rivers, 8) Washington, D.C., 9) Washington, D.C., and 10) La Pointe of Lake Superior. By the time Wisconsin had become a state, Indian title was extinguished to all land except what the Menominee retained in the east-central part of the state. The cession of this soon followed, at Lake Pow-aw-hay-Kou-nay (Lake Poygan). Drawn from a map in William F. Raney, *Wisconsin: A Story of Progress*   *UWCL*

the women, old men, and children were sent down the Wisconsin River. Black Hawk hoped these would be allowed to cross over the Mississippi, but a force of regulars intercepted them, killed some, captured a few, and a good many others were drowned, while the remainder escaped to the woods. There a force of Menominee led by whites cut them down, until only a dozen remained. Black Hawk's fighting force made for the Mississippi, leaving a trail of starved and wounded, with the army in hot pursuit, Atkinson now restraining the militia by posting it in the rear. The whites, unfamiliar with the country north of the Wisconsin, allowed Black Hawk to reach the Mississippi about forty miles north of the mouth of the Wisconsin, at a small stream named the Bad Axe River. The Indians had more bad luck here. An armed transport, the *Warrior,* was coming downstream, after alerting the Sioux at Winona. Black Hawk's surrender was ignored and no quarter was given; between the *Warrior* and the army at their rear, the slaughter was almost complete. Of the 350 Indians involved, 150 were killed, as many drowned, and only 50 captured. About 300 others, mostly women and children, got across the Mississippi before the *Warrior* appeared. The alert Sioux intercepted these and massacred half of them.

Of the 1,000 Indians who set out with Black Hawk on his venture, about 150 made it back to Keokuk's people. The other 850 had ceased to care, and left to the whites the problem of dividing the honors of victory. Oddly, the two principal heroes identified with the Black Hawk War today, both sympathetically, are Black Hawk and an Illinois militiaman, Abraham Lincoln. Black Hawk, who had escaped the carnage by flight, after his many vain efforts to surrender before the final bloodletting, was turned over to the Americans by the frightened Winnebago who had helped him. He was imprisoned briefly and then taken to Washington D.C. There followed a triumphal tour of the Atlantic seaboard cities, where he was lionized and bold ladies kissed his handsome son.

Black Hawks' autobiography, written with an amenuensis, admonishes us: "Rock River was a beautiful country. I loved my towns, my cornfields, and the home of my people. I fought for it. It is now yours. Keep it as we did." On the other side, sometime captain Abraham Lincoln, a member of Congress in 1848, disparaged the heroics of his own military experience in the Black Hawk War and those of the Democratic presidential candidate, Lewis Cass. "If General Cass went in advance of me in picking whortleberries," he said, "I guess I surpassed him in charges upon the wild onions. If he saw any live, fighting Indians, it was more than I did; but I had a good many bloody struggles with the mosquitoes."

Although even in that day the indiscriminate slaughter, with whites taking scalps, evoked sympathy for Black Hawk's cause, protest had little practical effect. As long as reality was ultimately determined by those Americans in immediate contact with the Indians, official policy made little difference, and savagery was answered with savagery.

News of the war was read avidly, and the result was a flood of florid descriptions of the running battles and of the previously little-known country where they took place. The severity of the defeat put any ideas of similar ventures out of the minds of other Wisconsin Indians. By 1833 a series of treaties had opened to survey and settlement all of the land south of a line from Green Bay to Prairie du Chien. The Indians along the shore of Lake Michigan—Potawatomi, Chippewa, and Ottawa—were soon bundled off across the Mississippi.

Protestant missions to the Indians brought a few men to the Wisconsin frontier before 1836. The Episcopalians were among the first. One of the colorful characters in Wisconsin history was the Reverend Eleazer Williams, a St. Regis Indian who led the Oneida, Stockbridge, and Brotherton Indians to Wisconsin from New York and New England. Williams was a bit unstable, convincing himself and a few believers that he was the lost Dauphin, heir to the French throne. These eastern Indians made the move around 1822, and the Episcopalians maintained a mission and school for the Oneida.

The missionaries to the Indians often found other fields of endeavor more congenial. Albert Ellis, a teacher and newspaperman, came to teach at the mission school for the Oneida. After a few years he left to be a government surveyor and later, in 1833, was one of the founders of the Green Bay *Intelligencer*. Ellis moved in and out of political offices and the newspaper business until his death in 1885.

Cutting Marsh, a Vermont man educated at Dartmouth, came to Wisconsin in 1830 as a missionary to the Stockbridge Indians for the American Board of Commissioners for Foreign Missions, a joint Congregational and Presbyterian body. After 1848 he turned to the more congenial work with the Yankee population after sadly concluding that the Indians were not a fertile field for missionary efforts.

The Baptists and Methodists, successful frontier denominations, looked for white settlers in their mission work. Alfred Brunson, a Methodist minister raised in Connecticut, came to Prairie du Chien in 1835, after more than twenty years of riding circuit in Ohio and western Pennsylvania. The vicissitudes of this style of proselytizing were too great and he gave it up after 1839 for the law and a political career. He returned to his ministerial calling after it became possible to maintain a settled pastorate in southwestern Wisconsin.

As we have seen, Morgan Martin was among the first to see the possibilities of what was to become the site of Milwaukee. His judgment was soon confirmed by the arrival of men from Chicago in the fall of 1833, some of them ready to contest for the ground with Solomon Juneau. Within the year there were other newcomers driving stakes, cutting trees, and building cabins. Martin, who was a partner with Juneau in his claim, came to Green Bay in 1827 and was a resident there for almost fifty years. He served in the territorial and state legislatures, was a delegate to Congress, chaired the second constitutional convention in Madison, and was otherwise active in politics. When he arrived, Martin found himself in a community of perhaps one hundred civilians, which limited his legal practice. He became a land speculator and promoter, identified for years with the Fox-Wisconsin Canal project.

Another imaginative Yankee who was to make his mark in the promotion of Milwaukee and efforts to tie the hinterland to the growing port was Byron Kilbourn. Born in Granby, Connecticut, in 1801, he was raised in Ohio, where his family moved in 1803. Benefiting from a superior education for the day, young Kilbourn worked as a surveyor on Ohio's canal system. He arrived in the vicinity of Milwaukee in 1834 as a federal deputy surveyor, to conduct the survey along the lakefront from Fort Dearborn (Chicago) to Green Bay. M. T. Williams, surveyor general of Michigan Territory, was interested in townsite opportunities and had access to the capital that would forward his schemes. He allied himself with Kilbourn, who settled upon a claim on the west side of the Milwaukee River. Solomon Juneau had possession of the east side and the lakeshore. Kilbourn counted on Williams for funds and on his own talents to make good his claim.

The land immediately behind Lake Michigan interested agricultural settlers. Most of the Milwaukee townsite and similar choice locations were taken on the basis of "floats" or land warrants, which will be discussed later. Townsite booming preceded large scale agricultural settlement by several months, partly because of peculiarities of the land laws. All but a negligible fraction of the farm population in this area by 1840 had come in the four years since 1836. Most of them were from western New York, the New England states, and the northern edges of the Ohio Valley—transplanted Yankees. Most came on the Lakes, but many by wagon around the lower end.

Wisconsin had little subsistence agriculture in the American pioneer period. Farmers moving from upstate New York and New England were covering, in reverse, the route to their prospective markets. The oak openings and prairies, particularly in back of Racine and Southport

(Kenosha), were especially adaptable to grain growing. They were relatively easy to break to the plow, and a crop of wheat needed little attention while the homesteader proceeded to extend his cultivated acreage. The grain had a cash value if it could be carried to a market with a reasonable expenditure of money or labor. The result was a commercial agriculture based upon cash or credit rather than a self-sufficient subsistence frontier.

There were a few traditional pioneers around in 1835 to fill the classic role of Frederick Jackson Turner's "cutting edge" of the Wisconsin frontier. Henry Janes was born in backwoods Virginia in 1804. His father moved to Chillicothe, Ohio, in 1819, and Henry, at twenty-one, "left the parental roof, on an old one-eyed horse, with two shirts and four dollars in my pocket, all told." He married in Lafayette, Indiana, moved to La Porte County in the same state, and three years later, in April 1835, loaded his growing family into a wagon for Racine, Wisconsin. He had visited the area the year before and found one white family in the whole country. Janes settled six miles west of Racine when "there was not a house, nor any sign of civilization between Grove Point, twelve miles north of Chicago, and Skunk Grove, now Mount Pleasant, in Racine county." The townsite of Racine was bustling with activity.

Janes's settlement was ahead of the survey. When this was underway, he realized that he had squatted on the school section, and decided to strike inland to the Rock River Valley to little-known country. He made one false start, and because of the carelessness of his preparations for a winter exploration, had to turn back. On his third attempt, he located a claim which proved to be open for filing on the books of the land office in Green Bay.

The new claim to which Janes moved the family in the spring of 1836 became, of course, the present city of Janesville. Despite his early start, Janes soon found competing paper towns up and down the river, Wisconsin City, Rockport, Humes Ferry, and St. George Rapids among them. Janes's enterprise was too much for them. By lobbying the first territorial legislature at Belmont, he got a ferry charter, mail route, and a post office located at his claim. The county preempted the claim, but compensated Janes with adjacent land. He sold out and decamped.

Lyman Copeland Draper, first director of the State Historical Society of Wisconsin, discovered Henry Janes in Humboldt County, California, in 1855 and got an account for the society's *Collections:* "In the fall of '49 I reached the Pacific, and yet the sun sets west of me, and my wife positively refused to go to the Sandwich Islands, and the bark is starting off my rails, and that is longer than I ever allowed myself to remain on one farm; so I am at a loss how to act in the present dilemma."

There is an accompanying reminiscence from a man who as a youth helped Janes to move to his Rock River claim. In typical feckless fashion, Janes went through rather than around the marshes of Lake Koshkonong with much hauling of oxen, horses, and barrels of flour out of the mire. "He was of a roving disposition, and liked the excitement incident to a new country, and not inclined to work himself, but to plan for others. He never was wanting for a good excuse to change his location."

The populating of Wisconsin was, of course, part of a larger process. The trans-Appalachian West grew twice as rapidly as the United States as a whole in the years between 1820 and 1840. A look at the growth of neighboring populations gives us an idea of why a vanguard began to find its way into Wisconsin. In 1820, Indiana had a population of 147,178, Illinois 55,211. Twenty years later, Indiana had 6°5,866 and Illinois 476,183. There were lesser currents and eddies within the mainstream. New England was exporting an excess population from her hill farms and villages to the westward, while receiving an immigrant population from Europe which would concentrate, along with some of her surplus agricultural population, in growing industrial cities. Financial panics in 1819 and 1837 were preceded by speculative excesses in western lands and an optimistic movement of people. The reactions after these panics slowed the movement of population and helped shift the attention of prospective immigrants from one part of the country to another.

Much of the West was open and federal land was available in many places when attention began to center on Wisconsin. Why Wisconsin? Just as James Lockwood's father had had a brief spell of "Ohio fever" in 1803, attention in 1817–19 centered on Alabama and Mississippi in the Old Southwest and on Illinois and Indiana in the Old Northwest. By 1835, there was a growing Wisconsin fever developing from a variety of causes. The Black Hawk War had publicized the attractions of the newly opening agricultural land. The opening of the Erie Canal in 1825 put the prospective ports on the west shore of Lake Michigan on an all water route to the Port of New York. In 1833, 60,000 people went through Buffalo on their way west, and 80,000 the next year. Wisconsin's Lakeshore boom, as we have seen, was largely an urban phenomenon, with more interest at first in town lots than in farm land. It is difficult to overestimate the influence of the Erie Canal. It drew people into western New York, raising land values there and sending the latecomers and young people westward to cheaper land. It put the shores of the Great Lakes in communication with world markets, stimulating the development of cheaper and better shipping on the upper Lakes. Wisconsin, all at once, was the place talked about where speculative profits were to be made, fat farms awaited the plow, and a new American Eden beckoned.

Selected Bibliography

Berkhofer, Robert F., Jr. *Salvation and the Savage: An Analysis of Protestant Missions and American Indian Response, 1787–1862*. Lexington, Ky., 1965. Mutual understanding was a missing quality.

Bloom, John Porter, ed. *The Territorial Papers of the United States. The Territory of Wisconsin. Executive Journal, 1836–1848. Papers, 1836–1839*. Washington, 1969. Continuing the Carter series.

Buley, R. Carlyle. *The Old Northwest Pioneer Period, 1815–1840*. 2 vols. Bloomington, Ind., 1950. An enjoyable work, strong on social history.

Clark, James I. *Henry Dodge, Frontiersman*. Madison, 1957. There is no satisfactory biography of Dodge.

Craig, Lois Marie. "The Role of the Missionary on the Wisconsin Frontier, 1825–1840." Master's thesis, University of Wisconsin, 1949. New England saves the West.

Derleth, August. *The House on the Mound*. New York, 1958. Wisconsin novelist's treatment of the life of Hercule Dousman, fur trader to railroad builder.

Duckett, Kenneth W. *Frontiersman of Fortune: Moses M. Strong of Mineral Point*. Madison, 1955. Yankee turned southerner in the lead region.

Ellis, Albert G. "Fifty-Four Years' Recollections of Men and Events in Wisconsin." *SHSW Collections*, vol. 7, pp. 207–68. Madison, 1908, reprint of 1876 original. Ellis was brought to Wisconsin in 1822 with Eleazer Williams as an Episcopal missionary.

Hagan, William T. *The Sac and Fox Indians*. Norman, Okla., 1958. Black Hawk's people and the war.

Holbrook, Stewart, *Yankee Exodus*. New York, 1950. Popular treatment of the New England migration along the Great Lakes.

Jackson, Donald, ed. *Black Hawk: An Autobiography*. Urbana: Illinois paperbacks, 1964. Black Hawk's side of the argument.

Janes, Henry F. "Early Reminiscences of Janesville." Isaac T. Smith. "Early Settlement of Rock County." *SHSW Collections*, vol. 6, pp. 426–35, 416–25. Madison, 1908 reprint of 1872 original. Hilarious.

Josephy, Alvin M., Jr. *The Patriot Chiefs: A Chronicle of American Indian Leadership*. New York, 1961. Black Hawk, and also Pontiac and Tecumseh.

Lawson, Marion. *Solomon Juneau, Voyageur*. New York, 1960. Literary, but adequately based.

Lockwood, James H. "Early Times and Events in Wisconsin." *SHSW Collections*, vol. 2, pp. 98–196. Madison, 1903, reprint of 1856 original. Lockwood came to Wisconsin in 1816 as an agent for fur traders.

Marsh, Cutting. "Documents Relating to the Stockbridge Mission, 1825–1848." *SHSW Collections,* vol. 15, pp. 39–204. Madison, 1900. Why Marsh gave up on Indians.

Martin, Morgan L. "Narrative of Morgan L. Martin," as told to Reuben G. Thwaites. *SHSW Collections,* vol. 11, pp. 385–415. Madison, 1888. Martin was a businessman and political figure who arrived at Green Bay in 1827.

Monaghan, Jay. "Black Hawk Rides Again—A Glimpse of the Man." *Wisconsin Magazine of History* 29:43–60 (Sept. 1945). The familiar story.

Nichols, Roger L. "The Battle of Bad Axe: General Atkinson's Report." *Wisconsin Magazine of History* 50:54–58. ". . . with the greatest zeal, courage, and patriotism."

Pratt, Harry E. "Abraham Lincoln in the Black Hawk War." In Fritiof O. Ander, ed., *The John M. Hauberg Historical Essays.* Rock Island, 1954. Lincoln was a "hero" of the war, and got political mileage from it.

Rooney, Elizabeth B. "The Story of the Black Hawk War." *Wisconsin Magazine of History* 40:274–83. (Summer 1957). Clear summary.

Smith, Alice E. *James Duane Doty, Frontier Promoter.* Madison, 1954. The most important biography done on the territorial period.

———. "Daniel Whitney: Pioneer Wisconsin Businessman." *Wisconsin Magazine of History* 24:283–304. Whitney successfully competed with Astor.

"The Territorial Census for 1836." *SHSW Collections,* vol. 13, pp. 247–70. Madison, 1895. Given by counties and families.

Trowbridge, Frederick N. "Confirming Land Titles in Early Wisconsin." *Wisconsin Magazine of History* 26:314–22 (March 1943). The French land titles at Green Bay and Prairie du Chien.

THE WISCONSIN
LEAD REGION

8

We generally think of Wisconsin's lead region in terms of its picturesque past as a pioneer American mining frontier. As a mining region today it is a marginal producer, with operations small in scale and so overshadowed by the agricultural development that one must be reminded of its historic importance.

The Wisconsin-Illinois lead region has had a greater impact upon American history than appears upon its bucolic face today, however. Lead was once a more effective magnet for American penetration of Wisconsin than either furs or farming. The unconcern with which the pioneer miners treated formal boundaries and federal promises led to Indian wars and accelerated cessions of Indian lands, which then were opened to other enterprise and settlement. The population attracted to the lead region was different in origin, customs, and politics from the other mainstreams of Wisconsin settlers, and although soon outnumbered, these people made their influence felt in political, economic, and social affairs. Producing a commodity in sometimes limited national supply and with a growing market, the region was a target for transportation improvements, thereby helping to shape patterns of settlement and of road, canal, and railroad promotions. Mining frontiers are notoriously careless of costs and usually have to be sustained from outside, which gives rise to opportunities for suppliers and freight forwarders. A fortunate few in the lead-mining region became sources of capital for other enterprises. The handsome homes of Galena, Illinois, the principal center of the region, looked out upon the river steamers which in their heyday were largely financed by money made in the lead trade.

Wisconsin's mining frontier set precedents which were to be repeated often in the trans-Mississippi West. An interesting federal effort to control the development of the Galena district mines by a system of leasing and regulation, although unsuccessful, gave rise to some commonplace features adopted by common consent on other unregulated frontiers.

The idea of the federal government reserving ore-bearing lands from entry and sale, to be developed on a leasing basis, is an interesting one, because it was actually tried in the upper Mississippi lead region and there only. There was nothing unique about the reservation, but there was in the effort to develop a leasing and tax-in-kind arrangement.

It had been customary for the sovereign, in land grants, to make reservations relating to minerals, particularly the precious metals, gold and silver, on the assumption that their presence and discovery on the land was strictly fortuitous. It was in the nature of a tax on an unearned increment and was usually placed at one-fifth of value. The Land Ordinance of 1785 reserved for the disposition of Congress "one-third part of all gold, silver, lead and copper mines." It did not reserve the land or mineral rights, but only the third portion of the production of any such mines. Nevertheless the reservation was without effect and was not included in subsequent general land laws passed in 1796, 1800, and 1804, possibly because no worthwhile mineral strikes had been made on the lands immediately affected.

Jefferson's influence on the development of the Wisconsin lead region followed from his interest in the Missouri lead region acquired by the Louisiana Purchase in 1803, and the lead mines on the upper Mississippi which Frenchmen had written about. An 1807 land law applying to lands in Indiana Territory reserved lead lands from sale and provided for leasing them. It is likely that Secretary of the Treasury Gallatin had a hand in this for the purpose of insuring a source of federal revenue from producing mines. There was also concern over the fact that the United States continued as a net importer of lead for which Britain was the principal source.

Jefferson and Gallatin had hoped to apply the leasing law to the lead mines around Potosi, Missouri, but they were already being exploited, under Spanish patent, before the United States acquired sovereignty. The miners were defiant about leasing or paying a royalty on the mineral raised. They were encouraged in this attitude by their senator, Thomas

Hart Benton, who kept up a tirade against the provision until he won his point in 1827 and the Missouri lead lands were put up for sale. By that time the upper Mississippi mines were proving themselves and provided a ready field for the application of the federal leasing system. Jefferson had been correct in his earlier observation (1783) in *Notes on the State of Virginia* that the lead region north of the Rock River was richer than the developed Potosi field. Had he known more about the country he might have been aware that the more northerly lead deposits were in an area of good agricultural land, which the Missouri lead mines were not.

The Treasury Department had been given the unwelcome task of administering the leasing of Missouri lead lands and the collection of government royalties under the 1807 law. It met with little success, and the responsibility was shifted to the War Department in 1821, when John C. Calhoun was secretary. The theory was that the royalties from the mines would be collected in kind. The army's Bureau of Ordnance was the logical agency to administer the program and arrange for storing the lead collected as royalty; the lead would be stockpiled for future government use. For this purpose, an arsenal was authorized at St. Louis, the officer in charge to administer the reserved lead lands. The 1807 statute was quite vague in its language, leaving a great deal of initiative to the president and his agents in working out the scheme of administration. Lieutenant Martin Thomas, the first superintendent of the arsenal and lead district, made up a good many of the rules and set many precedents for American mining practice.

An interesting aspect of the American approach to the Galena or Fever River mining district, which includes the Wisconsin lead region, was that it was accomplished by the Army Bureau of Ordnance advertising in the St. Louis papers and elsewhere for lessees to develop the upper Mississippi lead mines. Posting a $10,000 bond, the lessee received mining privileges to a 320-acre tract on which he could use the stone and timber. He had to work his lease with a minimum of twenty men, and the government took 10 percent of the finished product as its royalty. This was no Klondike or Sutter's Mill and was unlike many other American mining rushes of the nineteenth century. It was a sober business proposition offered to men of substance who could command a $10,000 bond, hire twenty men for a year before any return could be expected, and afford the necessary outfit to open a mine, build a smelter, and house and feed the crew.

Two men answered the advertisements. Moses Meeker was a manufacturer of white lead in Cincinnati who bought his raw material, pig lead, in St. Louis. He got information on the Fever River district from an Indian trader at St. Louis who had been smelting ore and tailings from

Indian workings in the Dubuque fields. Meeker prudently visited the Fever River country in the fall of 1822 before committing himself and found that the other lessee, Colonel James Johnson of Kentucky, had an operation going near present Galena. Johnson had been mining in desultory fashion since 1819 on sufferance from the Indians, but he now had a legal lease arrangement and the cooperation of the army in enforcing his privileges. Meeker decided to try his luck the next year, hurrying to beat winter down the river in late November.

Meeker's narrative illustrates the hazards of a relatively large-scale industrial operation on an undeveloped frontier. He was also an example of the confident assault of the American entrepreneur upon the wilderness. Meeker was simply a manufacturer intrigued by the possibilities of cutting out the middlemen in acquiring his raw material. He was not a dreamer or empire builder.

Meeker set out from Cincinnati in April 1823 with a $7,000 outfit, a crew of nineteen, two with their families, assorted passengers making up a list of forty-three men, women, and children, and three dogs. The passengers apparently were going just to look; only two families remained after a couple of years. They were a mixed group: two families with children, a man and his son, two single women, one of them accompanying her two brothers, and the rest single men. Their keelboat was fifty-eight days running from Cincinnati to the Fever River, fifty-three of them, by Meeker's account, spent ascending the Mississippi from the mouth of the Ohio by poling, warping on a line secured ahead, bushwhacking by pulling on overhanging trees, and a bit by sailing.

The enterprise went slowly. They had to go across the river for timber for their buildings, and Meeker thought the sidehill furnaces used by the Indians and other miners too crude. He found a clay supply on an island and had a man make up 60,000 bricks, most of them ruined in firing. Nonetheless, Meeker built a brick furnace "on the English plan of a cupola. My fire brick were good, but I had not enough of the common brick to make it strong enough to resist the pressure of the heat. I learned that I must creep before I could walk. I had always done business before where I could obtain anything I wanted by paying for it. But here I had to make everything by my own means."

His neighbor, Colonel Johnson, decided that the hazards and inconveniences outran the opportunities and left at the end of 1823, advising Meeker to do the same, but Meeker had only had a good start, he said, "and being fully satisfied of the fertility of the soil, and its vast mineral resources, I concluded to go on with what I had hardly made a beginning." His reason is interesting, considering that he could not acquire title to the land, and farming was actively discouraged by the army officers administering the lead lands. He apparently knew his public lands history and determined to bide his time. Meanwhile during the season he had produced 170,000 pounds of lead, worth probably $7,000 in St. Louis, just the cost of his outfit without figuring housing, feeding, and paying his workmen, and the costs of building and transportation. The charm of mining was that, while the costs were fairly constant, the amount of ore raised might be increased spectacularly simply by luck.

Meeker and Johnson were not the first or only Americans to mine in the district, but they preceded the rush which had brought 10,000 people by 1828. The competitors Meeker found there in 1823 were Winnebago Indians numbering about 500, "their women quite industrious miners, but the men would not work." The Indians' tools and methods were crude, but the lead ore was found near the surface and could be followed through substantial fractures in the rock. Colonel Johnson worked a mine which he had purchased from an Indian who had found a "nugget" of lead ore requiring the efforts of the whole tribe to raise. It was the possibility of such finds that brought a rush of miners within a few years.

As more footloose men began to find their way up the river, Lieutenant Thomas modified the federal regulations to meet new conditions and keep the leasing system intact. The 320-acre lease, now requiring a $5,000 bond, remained, but permits were issued for claims measuring 200 yards square. They were prospectors' permits, really, since they could be abandoned for others, or rich strikes could be sold and new permits obtained. In an economy in which $20 worth of equipment would put a man in business as an independent miner, wages were naturally high, running from $17 to $25 a week plus board. This is difficult to compare with wages elsewhere, for local prices were also high and goods scarce. Since farming was actively discouraged by the army, almost all food, as well as manufactured or processed articles, came a long and expensive distance. It was not unusual for a merchant to have a corner on flour or some other article and charge what the traffic would bear.

As with all mining frontiers, it was the fellow who hit it rich who was remembered. An average claim would yield the worker about 150 pounds of ore a day; over the early years ore averaged about $15.65 for 1,000 pounds. Yet a miner near Hazel Green, in 1824, hit block mineral and took out 17,000 pounds in a single day. Another sold his claim to a smelter for $1,300. It was not unusual for miners to average as much as $60 a day on a rich claim, and this is what drew the others. The fellow who did not share in such good fortune could at least be where the action was and the jobs were plentiful.

Lieutenant Thomas controlled the rush through the agency of the smelters. The ore ran fairly consistent and was assigned a value based on a constant percentage of extractable metal. This ran something over 75 percent and made it possible for the royalty to be collected through the smelter. Since the lead was shipped only in the refined state, the government agents needed only to keep track of the licensed and bonded smelters, which cooperated by withholding the government's 10 percent from the total run. This system, of course, was ready-made for the smelters to agree on a price to pay the miners for their ore. Lieutenant Thomas, a benign dictator, solved the problem by decreeing that the miners should receive 350 pounds of refined ore for each 1,000 pounds of raw ore, or the cash equivalent, a solution accepted with little complaint. The smelter operators were the ones who made money in the long run. Their raw material cost was tied to the market, whereas most of the miners' costs were fixed and their production unpredictable.

Lead prices, particularly on the frontier, were quite volatile. The market rose vigorously in 1824 and continued on a high level into 1828, breaking sharply in 1829. Ore prices on the Fever River fell from an average $17 a 1,000 pounds to as low as $3, and in 1829 it took 5,000 pounds of ore to buy a barrel of flour. The break in the market likely came as a result of the increased production coming from the new Fever River field.

The sudden depression in lead-mining, which lasted until late 1831, brought the practical demise of the federal system of leasing and regulation. Lieutenant Thomas had run it with a minimum of friction, adapting his rules to changing conditions and using only a few civilian agents to audit and administer the program in the field. This harmony is surprising in view of the fact that there was no provision for appeals from the lieutenant's rulings. He was stern about the use of the limited timber, which was needed in large quantities for the smelters as fuel, and he was most reluctant to grant permission for anyone to garden or farm. He was hostile to anyone interested in land purchase or speculation in claims. The miners were expected to accept the role of tenants at will of the federal government and their function was to raise lead. By 1829 there were 4,253 miners on permit or lease and 52 smelters in the district. In the two-year period ending in June 1829 the federal arsenals collected 3,400,000 pounds of lead in royalties, almost all of it from the upper Mississippi mines.

This happy state of affairs ended with $3 ore and $15 flour. While some miners responded by digging more furiously, others saw that flour and other foodstuffs did not have to come up the river. They turned quite naturally to farming; the land was rolling, well watered, easily cleared and broken, and fertile. The interruption of low lead prices and the brief

Black Hawk War was ended by 1832, and the local market for farm produce began to grow with a new expansion of lead mining. Lieutenant Thomas had been transferred before things began going badly awry. His authority had been more assumed than real and was not to be regained by his successors, once the miners turned to farming and complaining about the 10 percent royalty. It was impossible to get the stopper back in the bottle. More and more people began to treat the land as if it were open for squatters to take possession and await survey and sale, and Congress passed the first of a series of general preemption acts in 1830 confirming them in this view. A real complication in the Galena mining district was that prime agricultural land and mineral land were one and the same.

Captain Thomas Legate, Lieutenant Thomas's successor, sought to halt the defection of miners from the lease, permit, and royalty system by reducing the royalty from 10 percent to 6 percent, but this only confirmed the opposition of the miners to a system which they now characterized as oppressive and un-American. Only about one-fifth of the lead raised in the district in 1835, after the market had recovered, was reported to the Bureau of Ordnance and the royalty paid. The smelter owners followed the miners sentiments and ignored the government's regulations.

The federal officers answered this wholesale defection by taking the large smelter operators to court. Thomas Hart Benton, defending some of these operators, took their case to the Supreme Court but lost; the court upheld the leasing system. Its demise could not be halted without resort to the police power, however, and no administration courted the obloquy which this would occasion. Although the Bureau of Ordnance was a part of the army and the lead leasing was under the direct supervision of an army officer, the bureau hired civilians as local enforcement agents. These agents reflected local sentiment and considered their appointments as licenses to turn a dollar in whatever way opportunity might suggest.

Immediately after the Black Hawk War, the interest in Wisconsin land was so great that the surveyor-general of Michigan Territory was authorized to begin surveys on the recently ceded lands. Land offices were opened in 1834 at Mineral Point and Green Bay for the auction of newly surveyed lands, but President Jackson reserved from entry and sale the lead lands lying within the Mineral Point jurisdiction. The problem now was to segregate the mineral lands from the agricultural lands, which would have been difficult even if pursued honestly. It was not.

The opening of the Mineral Point land office brought a new federal officer on the scene. John Sheldon had been a Detroit editor, Democrat, and friend of Lewis Cass. As a politician he was formidable in the isolated community of Mineral Point. As the new register of the land office, it was his responsibility to segregate the lands and mark those reserved as mineral or timber lands, and Captain Legate was to advise him on these points. Both the Captain and Register Sheldon were opposed to reservation. As was common at the time, both were engaged in land speculations involving mineral deposits, and their positions attracted associates interested in having the lands freed for sale. Legate consequently suggested few reservations, and the land office did not seek his advice. Only the protests of the dwindling number of miners operating on the old system of lease or permit kept some of the land reserved as mineral land.

Captain Legate was removed for his speculation and resigned from the army to remain at Galena and manage his holdings. It was better than chasing Seminoles in Florida, where he had been ordered. Register Sheldon was harder to reach politically, but no effort was spared on the part of both Democrats and Whigs. The Van Buren administration finally removed him after a Whig-inspired investigation reported that Sheldon "made himself master . . . of the vast mineral domain in his district, and disposed of it as if it were indeed his own, uniform only in helping himself and his friends." This partisan rebuke was not overdrawn.

Except for the few miners still working on lease or permit, agreement was general that lands should be declared non-mineral-bearing so that they could be auctioned as agricultural lands. Both settlers and speculators pressed for this solution. Land laws which ran counter to local sentiment were seldom effective, and Congress could be expected eventually to make the desired adjustment. The controversy was resolved in favor of the majority, and the remaining mineral land reserves were put on sale in 1847. Most of the lead lands had already been sold as agricultural land, through false swearing that they did not contain significant mineral deposits. Those who sold, leased, or traded in mineral claims on these lands felt no embarrassment. Indignation was reserved to eastern Whigs and later generations.

With the passing of the federal leasing system, the character of the frontier changed to a mixture of agriculture and mining, and the mining that remained became more specialized as the surface deposits were worked out. The original mining frontier had been typical in many ways, attracting an adventurous, unruly, itinerant population with a high proportion of unattached males; when people named their settlements Blackleg, Red Dog, Burlesqueburgh, Nip and Tuck, Scrabble, and Grab, they were not planning a permanent community with a church and an academy on the hill. Now the area was turning to farming, and more decorous names replaced the earlier ones. Alfred Brunson, a Methodist circuit rider from Ohio, found Galena in 1835 made up of people "mostly intelligent, enterprising & healthy but too much absorbed in the cares of the world to think of religion. They came here to make a fortune, & to leave, but have since concluded to stay here." One suspects that Moses Meeker's keelboat ark that left Cincinnati in 1823 for the Fever River, with four families aboard, was a harbinger of the frontier it became.

The mining frontier brought a rapid economic development in its train. Men with their eyes on the main chance of a rich strike were dependent upon a long and expensive line of supply that stretched back to St. Louis and beyond. This was still true in 1835 when Alfred Brunson recorded his impression that "most of the provisions consumed, are brought up the Mississippi River, from Missouri and Illinois." Moses Meeker, twelve years before, had met the first steamboat to ascend the rapids at Rock Island. It was supplying the forts at Prairie du Chien and St. Anthony Falls. Brunson found "the trade of this mineral district occupies 6 or 8 steamboats which ply constantly between St. Louis & Galena, Dubuque & Prairie du Chien."

Galena, Illinois, was the metropolis of the Fever River lead district from the beginning. It had been platted by Lieutenant Thomas in 1826 and by 1839 was reputed to have a population of 3,000. As the center of the lead trade, it developed the many subsidiary services required. Money made in the trade accumulated there. Even after the lead trade had waned, Galena for a number of years was the Queen of the Upper Mississippi, her excess capital invested in steamboats and commission houses, which had become more attractive speculations than lead claims. Galena's days of prosperity and glory were thus extended beyond the time when her relative disadvantages of location, on the narrow Fever, made it clear that Dubuque, Prairie du Chien, and La Crosse would eclipse her. These were the days when the fine mansions were built on the hills where today's tourist finds them an attractive curiosity in the somnolent village.

Mineral Point was the center of that portion of the Fever River fields lying north of the Illinois border. It was the center of a rich mineral field which had been located before 1830 when the town was designated the county seat of Iowa County, Michigan Territory. The addition of the federal land office in 1834 added to its business. By 1845, it had probably 1,500 people, and a missionary reported that "on the whole, the morals of the place would compare favorably with those of most Eastern villages." About half of the population by then were Cornish, God-fearing people of Wesleyan persuasion.

As agriculture developed around the mines, it served to provision the mining population and diminish the need for outside supplies. The transportation needs of the lead area were to haul the ore to the smelters and the finished lead to the Mississippi or to Lake Michigan ports. Illinois farm settlers, during the summer season, would appear with teams and wagons to haul ore and finished lead while the trails across country were dry enough to bear the loads. These settlers appeared and disappeared with the seasons, like the migrating suckers in the creeks. Those miners who stayed through the winter—some in the holes they had dug in the hillsides for ore—were called "badgers." Wisconsin residents today proudly call themselves badgers, but the Illinois "sucker" did not find such favor.

The early market for lead lay down the Mississippi and then up the Ohio, or else to New Orleans for transshipment to New York. The traffic was first carried on by keelboats, which could be worked upstream only with much labor. By 1823 they were already being replaced by river steamers; riverboats were entering a period of great technological evolution. Despite protective tariffs, the lead producers found themselves at the mercy of distant and unpredictable markets, capricious freight rates based upon rapid changes in competitive conditions, and water levels which could halt river traffic for months, or even for a season.

The growing Lake ports, after 1835, cast envious eyes on the rich lead haul going down the Mississippi. Many were the schemes to divert it to the Great Lakes and Erie Canal route by way of Green Bay, Milwaukee, Racine, or Chicago. Every promoter doing arithmetic for a proposed canal, waterway, road, or railroad from these ports aimed at the lead mines and calculated tonnages. Lead was heavy and not as seasonal as wheat. The Mississippi River ports, in reply, agitated for navigation improvements.

New Orleans receipts of lead hit their peak in 1846—785,000 pigs, or about 27,475 tons. By 1856, the river was getting less than half of the production of the Galena field. By 1857, Milwaukee and Chicago had rail connections to the river, the culmination of a long period of promotion and effort to divert the lead trade by other means. A note in a Milwaukee paper in 1847 called attention to the "lead schooners," large wagons drawn by twelve to sixteen oxen which came in trains from the lead mines to the Lake. The attraction of lead hauling and the development of pioneer transportation lines, first by oxen and finally by rail, tied the isolated populations of the lead region and the Lake Michigan ports together. It became much easier to fill the intervening miles with farms and towns.

The shot trade was largely the story of the Helena Shot Tower, whose remains can be seen at Tower Hill State Park, between Arena and Spring Green. Making shot of the finished lead was one step in processing to add value to the product. The process involved pouring molten lead down a long shaft. The lead fell free, formed into spheres, solidified, and dropped into a tank of water at the bottom of the shaft. It was sized by putting the shot through a series of buckskin sieves, packed, and loaded aboard scows on the neighboring slough.

The Helena Shot Tower was conceived by Daniel Whitney, a man with access to men of capital in Buffalo and elsewhere. A store, barracks, warehouse, cooperage, and blacksmith shop, in addition to the tower, were on the site. The enterprise passed through a number of hands before finally closing in 1861. Helena was quite a trade center and road junction in the years before the Milwaukee and Mississippi Railroad made a quiet backwater of the village. Teamsters hauled shot to Milwaukee, bringing settlers along the route on their return. The tower also figured in schemes to develop the Fox-Wisconsin waterway.

The lead region had a distinctive population dominated by people from the southern and southwestern states who came up the river. The region was Jacksonian Democrat in politics, and even the Yankees like Moses Strong who moved among them took on their attributes. William Hamilton, Alexander Hamilton's youngest son, a pioneer lead miner near Dodgeville, met with indifferent political success because of his Whiggish tendencies. The stamp of the lead district Democracy will be found on Wisconsin's territorial period, as Jackson, Van Buren, and Polk favored Henry Dodge and his friends. At the same time, the district was losing its early population advantage, dropping from 23 percent of the representation in the first territorial legislature to only 10 percent by 1860.

After about 1840, the character of lead mining changed quite radically. The surface ore had been taken, and that below the surface presented problems of shafting and drainage. The technological solution was brought by the Cornish miners who began flocking to the Wisconsin lead region in the early 1830s. There were eventually about 7,000, their largest settlement at Mineral Point.

The Cornish came for purely economic reasons. The principal occupation available in Cornwall was mining. Since ancient times, tin had been raised from deep mines there, and the industry was in decline, whereas the opportunities in the Wisconsin mines had become widely known abroad and attracted the Cornishmen. Contemptuous of the Americans as miners, they readily took up where the Americans had left off, accustomed as they were to hard-rock mining, water diversion, and other techniques. They were all powdermen, which the Americans generally were not. The possibility of owning a mine or working one on shares was a great temptation to men who had always worked for others in their trade. The Cornish kept the Fever River field productive until about 1860. Many of them moved on to California after 1849, while others turned to farming as the lead mining declined.

The federal lease system was abandoned after the experience in the lead region of the upper Mississippi, but the experiment had long-term implications. The framework of the typical American mining camp of the West was laid here, and Lieutenant Thomas set a precedent in the administrative code he devised as the first supervisor of the federal mines, defining a legal claim in terms of discovery, area, and required work on the ground. Wisconsin's lead-mining frontier furnished more than a quaint historic tradition in a now predominantly agricultural section.

Selected Bibliography

Carter, Margaret Smith. *New Diggings on the Fever, 1824–1869*. Benton, Wisconsin, 1959. Amateur historian using a journal of a relative who was a pioneer lead miner.

Clark, James I. *The Wisconsin Lead Region: Frontier Community*. Madison, 1955. Short Account.

Gara, Larry. "Gold Fever in Wisconsin." *Wisconsin Magazine of History* 38:106–8 (Winter 1954–55). Effects of the California gold rush on the lead region.

Keppel, Ann M. "Civil Disobedience on the Mining Frontier." *Wisconsin Magazine of History* 41:185–95 (Spring 1958). Miners and the federal leasing system.

Lake, James A. *Law and Mineral Wealth: The Legal Profile of the Wisconsin Mining Industry*. Madison, 1962. Has a chapter on federal leasing.

Meeker, Moses. "Early History of Lead Region of Wisconsin." *SHSW Collections*, vol. 6, pp. 271–96. Madison, 1906, reprint of 1872 original. The account of his pioneer mining and smelting venture.

Schafer, Joseph. *The Wisconsin Lead Region*. Wisconsin Domesday Book, vol. 3. Madison, 1932. The standard work on the lead mines.

Van Tassel, David D. "Democracy, Frontier and Mineral Point: A Study of the Influence of the Frontier on a Wisconsin Mining Town." Master's thesis, University of Wisconsin, 1951. He's not sure what he found, but the early years were turbulent.

Wright, James E. *The Galena Lead District: Federal Policy and Practice, 1824–1847*. Madison, 1966. An interesting study of federal leasing.

TERRITORIAL
WISCONSIN

9

The hand of the federal government in the affairs of Wisconsin citizens was probably more noticeable in the years before 1848 than it would be until the New Deal. This was true partly because there was no state government intervening between the citizen and his national government, but also because the pioneer, although a model of self-sufficiency by today's standards, was dependent upon the federal government for services, security, and the definition of his status. An American citizen gave up important rights and privileges when he took up residence in a territory. He lost his franchise in national elections, and many of his officials, including even municipal ones, were appointed rather than elected. Title to what the pioneer wanted most, the unoccupied land, rested with the United States government, in which he had no direct voice. That the American pioneer's hopes would not be disappointed depended upon a well-defined tradition and a body of statutes which were unique to the American experience. Wisconsin Territory marked a major milestone in the development of these.

The famous Northwest Ordinance of 1787 set the pattern for the territorial government of Wisconsin. This ordinance, one of the best known pieces of legislation enacted under the Articles of Confederation, grew out of the cession of western land claims by the original states, particularly Virginia, to the central government. A long controversy had preceded the cession of these lands. Beginning a new controversy which was to last for many years, a majority in Congress saw the western lands as a source of revenue for the future, while others worried that the lands would fall into the hands of speculators who would impede settlement and encourage the creation of great estates in the interior. The development of the land laws would depend much upon the attitude of Congress toward those pioneers who had already taken the road west and squatted on land without regard to the niceties of clear title and ownership. George Washington, an enthusiastic speculator in western lands, viewed these people as lawless banditti. His fellow Virginian Thomas Jefferson saw them as builders of new American commonwealths whose rights and futures should be protected.

At the time of Virginia's cession of her western lands, Jefferson was made the chairman of a committee of the Continental Congress to draw up a plan for the government of the unorganized territory north of the Ohio River. This plan, adopted with little change from Jefferson's draft, is sometimes called the Northwest Ordinance of 1784. It was never acted upon by Congress, but contained some important provisions incorporated in the later Northwest Ordinance of 1787.

Jefferson, who abhorred the idea of an urban America, thought that western settlement should be encouraged. His ordinance embodied what is often referred to as the compact theory, whereby unorganized territory would go through regular stages of development and would finally, by meeting certain conditions, achieve full statehood within the Union. The complement to this was the idea that the westerner retained his rights of American citizenship, except for direct representation in the national government. This right would be held in trust for him, to be restored with statehood. Jefferson's plan was thoroughly democratic, providing that the citizens of a territory should establish their own temporary government and achieve full statehood whenever the population became equal to that of the least populous of the original states. Congress added an interim step whereby the territory would adopt a constitution of its own and have a nonvoting delegate in Congress whenever its population reached 20,000.

The 1784 Ordinance never became effective for a variety of reasons. The need for a scheme of government arose again in 1787 when the Confederation was in its twilight. The important elements of the Northwest Ordinance of 1787 were drawn from Jefferson's earlier legislation, but the principal architects were James Monroe and Nathan Dane, a Massachusetts lawyer. The committee was conservative in character. In part, their conservatism grew out of the determination to hold the western territories in the Union—something Jefferson had not been sure of earlier—and partly from doubt that the West would attract a population compatible with that of the older states. They envisioned a long period of apprenticeship. The ordinance was far from being a democratic instrument. It did, however, adopt Dane's bill of rights, the abolition of slavery in the Old Northwest, and Jefferson's compact leading to statehood.

The 1787 Ordinance provided for the appointment by the Congress— by the president under the new constitution—of a territorial governor, secretary, and three judges, all required to own from 500 to 1,000 acres in the territory. The governor and the three judges sat as the legislative body, adopting laws from the older states for the territory. The governor held an absolute veto over their deliberations. There was no provision for the exercise of the franchise, for the governor held the power of appointment of all subordinate, local officials such as sheriffs, justices, and militia officers. Governor Harrison of Indiana, it will be recalled, made these appointments at Green Bay and Prairie du Chien in 1803.

The second stage of territorial development was reached when a population of 5,000 free male inhabitants of full age was attained. A voter was defined as a white male citizen over twenty-one with a fifty-acre freehold and two years residence in the district. Such property qualifications were standard in the original states, although the wide distribution of land made them less restrictive than would seem. The voters were to elect, by district, members of the lower house of a territorial legislature. The upper house, called the council, was to be chosen by the president from a slate of candidates presented by the territorial house. The governor retained his unrestricted veto, could end a legislative session by decree, and continued to hold the appointment and dismissal power over local officials. One office, that of delegate to Congress, with no vote but with the privileges of the floor, was filled by a legislative election. When a territory reached a population of 60,000, the ordinance provided that it should petition Congress for admission to statehood, which was to be accomplished by an enabling act establishing the conditions for admission.

The astonishing thing is that this essentially undemocratic system of rule not only worked with reasonable satisfaction for more than a century, but was soon acclaimed such a triumph of democracy that its makers were fit subjects for memorials. Dane County, Wisconsin, for instance, was named for Nathan Dane, chairman of the committee which drafted the ordinance. The fact that Moses Strong, a Wisconsin pioneer, could refer to the 1787 ordinance as the Northwest's Magna Charta was a tribute to the unusual compact provision which promised eventual statehood and to the genius of Americans for political accommodation. The ordinance provided the governmental framework, with modifications, for not only the five states of the Old Northwest but for all of the American West, with the exceptions of Texas and California. Wisconsin's organic act—the congressional statute, based upon the 1787 Ordinance, which served in lieu of a territorial constitution—was the model for subsequent organic acts for territories west of the Mississippi. Despite modifications in the direction of more democratic control, one student of the subject oberved that the government of Wisconsin Territory was more like that of Massachusetts in 1691 as a crown colony than of the State of Wisconsin.

Territorial status was less onerous than the 1787 ordinance and territorial organic acts would imply. Congress took little interest in its reserved right to review all territorial legislation, although it often put restrictions reflecting current concerns into the organic acts. The federal executive exhibited little interest in the administration of the territories after they had served as sources of patronage appointments. Like the early British Empire, the system flourished under a policy of salutary neglect. On the positive side, the federal government paid administrative and judicial salaries and some of the legislative costs of the territories, as well as treating them as dependencies in other ways. Although a frequent sore point with territorial citizens was the appointment of outsiders to territorial office, the equalizer was that even rank outsiders usually "landed running" for future elective political offices.

The pattern of territorial development in the Old Northwest had been for new territories to emerge, incorporating the largely unsettled portions, as the maturing sections prepared for statehood. There were various arguments for the creation of a Wisconsin Territory, and from 1823 on, James Doty, who had successfully lobbied for himself the creation of a separate judicial district in the portion of Michigan Territory west of Mackinac, was their tireless advocate. For one thing, it was normal congressional practice to create a separate land district for a new territory, although in 1823 all of present Wisconsin was unceded Indian land which could not legally be alienated to individuals. Territorial status might, presumably, hasten the process of Indian cession. But the main argument was that Detroit, the capital of Michigan Territory, was a long way off, and the bulk of Michigan's population, which controlled the territorial legislature, had little interest in affairs west of Lake Michigan. Doty found support among the growing American population in the lead area, and sympathetic ears in Congress, where the prospect of adding new territorial offices to the patronage was always attractive, but not enough interest to put the measure over before the issue of statehood for Michigan pushed Wisconsin's territorial aspirations into the background.

The desire for territorial status was far from universal. In 1830, the present area of Wisconsin had a population of about 3,000, exclusive of Indians and the military, over half in the lead district of the southwest. The light of executive and legislative concern might shine dimly from distant Detroit, but the fur traders and their habitant employees found it bright enough for their purposes. They already had been organized into geographically large counties, which brought the dubious blessings of assessors and tax collectors. The urge to multiply and distribute these refinements was not compelling, nor could the traders perceive any advantage in packing their Indian customers off across the Mississippi. A heavier population of Yankee farmers and urban lot-holders, accustomed to the amenities of civil government, was required to support territorial status. It was not long in coming.

Statehood for Michigan was delayed by the growing sectional split which tied her aspirations to a balancing slave state, in this case Arkansas. There was also a controversy growing out of congressional tampering with the borders outlined in the Ordinance of 1787. Michigan claimed, under the earlier dispensation, a strip of shore along Lake Erie including the present city of Toledo. Tampering again, Congress gave Michigan the Upper Peninsula, thus outraging James Doty and other Wisconsin partisans, who already felt aggrieved that the northern border of Illinois had been moved sixty-one miles north from the ordinance line running due westward from the southern end of Lake Michigan. Generations of pious Badgers have since congratulated themselves that the congressional interference placed turbulent Chicago in Illinois.

Michigan enjoyed a phenomenal increase of population in the decade from 1830 to 1840. A special census taken in 1834 showed a population of 85,000, more than enough to qualify for the final step under the 1787 ordinance. The citizens of Michigan, impatient to achieve full statehood, did not wait upon Congress to pass an enabling act but proceeded to call their own constitutional convention, adopt a state constitution, and demand admission to the Union in the summer of 1835. Their admission was delayed until early 1837 by the boundary dispute with Ohio and by other considerations, but favorable congressional action seemed assured. This assurance gave rise to an interesting attempt, in which Michigan's acting governor Stevens T. Mason cooperated, to transfer Michigan's territorial government intact to the area west of Lake Michigan.

The scheme worked to the extent that the last Michigan Territory congressional delegate was a political ally of Henry Dodge—George W. Jones, a resident of the lead region. Congress accepted Jones's election but did not recognize the transfer of the Michigan territorial government. It was the political neophyte George W. Jones who pressed for territorial status for Wisconsin in Congress. Jones was complacent about Michigan's boundary compensation on the northern peninsula and had no objection to the Illinois boundary which so exercised Doty. The result was that the organic act for the creation of Wisconsin Territory sailed through Congress smoothly, after Michigan statehood was settled, accompanied by the usual hyperbole about the hazards of lawlessness and Indian depredations from which this new status would somehow shield the intrepid pioneers. The new territory stretched westward to include present Iowa, Minnesota, and much of the Dakotas.

Wisconsin was the first new territory since the creation of Florida Territory in 1822. The Organic Act of Michigan Territory was a more immediate model, as it had been the subject of congressional tinkering in 1825 and 1827. Curiously, Congress had dispensed with the lower house in this revision, placing the legislative power in the council, but in 1827 made that body elective rather than appointive. The direct election of township and some county officers had been provided two years before, but the governor retained the veto and much of his appointive power.

In the hands of the Jacksonians in Congress, the Wisconsin Organic Act consolidated democratic features. There was a return to the two house legislature, with members of both elected directly by the voters. Property qualifications for voters and officeholders had disappeared, as they had generally in the older states since 1800. Like the recent revisions of Michigan's territorial government, the act made local and county officers elective, except for sheriffs, justices, and court clerks, who were appointed by the governor with the advice and consent of the council. The congressional delegate was popularly elected.

For Wisconsin Territory, the franchise was liberal and more widely used. The legislature was entirely elective. The governor was still appointed, as were the other enumerated territorial officers: the territorial secretary, attorney, marshal, and judges. The governor retained broad powers: ex officio superintendence of Indian affairs, an absolute veto over legislation by withholding approval, and some appointive power. All territorial legislation was subject to congressional review and repeal. Congress forbade taxing nonresident property owners at a different rate, reflecting a current concern. Restrictive clauses in later organic acts would increase as these concerns multipled.

A normal accompaniment to territorial status was the plea to the president to look among the worthy and able residents for appointees to territorial office. Andrew Jackson, still surrounded in 1836 by importunate claims of the faithful, knew that territorial citizens did not vote in presidential elections. He had, however, a high regard for the lead region's

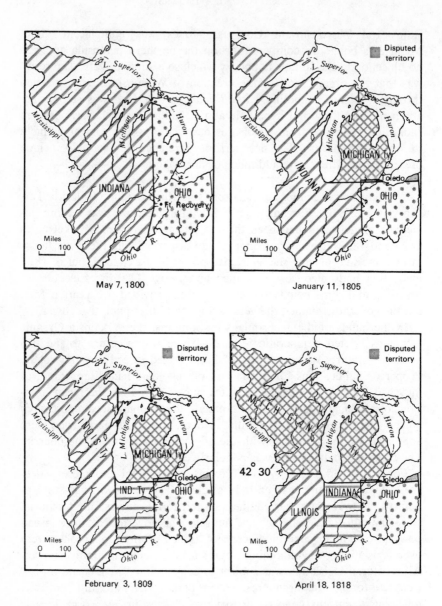

Map 9. Territorial Jurisdictions, 1800–1838. Wisconsin was included in Indiana Territory created in 1800, but in effect remained the preserve of the Montreal fur traders until after the War of 1812. Its inclusion in Illinois Territory in 1809 was an administrative convenience. American occupation and settlement followed the war and organization as a part of Michigan Territory in 1818. Wisconsin Territory, when established, included, generally, present Iowa, Minnesota, and the Dakotas,

facsimile of his own virtues, Henry Dodge, whom he had appointed earlier to a colonelcy of dragoons patrolling the Indian frontier. It was no surprise when Dodge received Jackson's nomination for governor of Wisconsin Territory. The president filled other posts with the deserving from more remote political fields.

Most of the advantages of territorial status were reserved for those with political yearnings or an entrepreneurial temper who had schemes to forward that would benefit by some legislative action. This is not to say that there were not necessary services for a territorial government to render a growing population, or that territorial status did not serve a purpose in attracting new settlers. But an examination of the index to the first legislative session reveals that fully one-fourth of the entries are concerned with the incorporation of banks, railroads, toll roads, mining companies, and other such ventures. There were no general incorporation laws, and therefore each stock company had to get a special charter through a legislative act.

Territorial politics were primarily concerned with office seeking, the dispensation of privileges, and appeals for federal largess to help develop the territory. This was a natural reflection of a sparse population, always short of capital, confronting a combination of opportunities and obstacles beyond its resources. In a nice division of labor, the lead area contin-

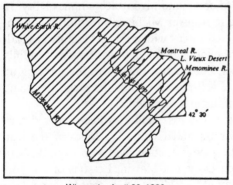

Wisconsin April 20, 1836

Wisconsin June 12, 1838

but settlement did not yet extend much beyond the Dubuque lead area and Fort Snelling. Wisconsin lost the area northwest of the present boundary in the 1846 enabling act. (On May 7, 1800, Indiana Territory was established; on January 11, 1805, Michigan Territory; on Feb. 3, 1809, Illinois Territory; on April 18, 1818, the state of Illinois; on April 20, 1836, Wisconsin Territory; and on June 12, 1838, Iowa Territory)   *UWCL* gent controlled most of the offices, while the Yankees of the Lake pursued the dispensation of special privilege.

Henry Dodge and his friends, armed by their rapport with Andrew Jackson in the White House and their early but rapidly vanishing numerical superiority in the territory, had the territorial offices in a firm grip. Their influence did not disappear all at once but was diminished by the creation of Iowa Territory in July of 1838, removing the miners around Dubuque from Wisconsin politics. Whereas the lead area had counted nearly one-half of the territorial population east of the Mississippi in the 1836 census, by the 1840 federal census it had only a large one-fourth; the impressive growth had taken place around Milwaukee and Racine. The Jacksonians lost the presidency in 1840 and with it the appointive power.

Territorial politics in Wisconsin are usually summed up in terms of a personal rivalry between James Doty and Henry Dodge, and in many respects legitimately. Distinctions of party were blurred by the fact that Wisconsin citizens had no vote in national elections, and by the overwhelming ascendancy of the Democratic party, which claimed a majority of the Yankees as well as the southerners in the lead region. With no presidential election politics to force territorial candidates and voters to take a clear party stand, they all crowded under the Jacksonian tent while the Democrats controlled the patronage.

This situation was made to order for James Doty, who as one wag aptly put it had only one party to command his loyalty—James Doty. In the interest of his earlier scheme to transfer Michigan's territorial government to Wisconsin, Doty had joined forces with a group identified as radical Democrats. This was out of character for him, for he was certainly conservative in most of his views, but his real talent was for showing up in any winning camp, with some well-placed friends there and the bland assumption that he had been with them all the while.

In 1835 Doty had run in what was essentially a three-cornered race for delegate, against Morgan Martin and George W. Jones of the lead area. Jones, the candidate of the Dodge faction, had won handily, with the Lakeshore vote split between Doty and Martin. Lessons of this sort were not lost upon Doty. He assured himself, in 1838, that his candidacy would not be contested on the Lakeshore by asking for a territorial convention to tender the nomination to him. This was managed by a small group meeting in Madison. As further insurance, a candidate from Crawford County was encouraged to run to split the vote in the southwest. Delegate Jones, who was running for reelection, was smothered by these tactics. Identification by party was not a feature of the 1838 territorial election.

In a sea of troubles growing out of his speculations in land, Doty made good use of his new position in Washington. He had acted as fiscal agent for $40,000 of federal money appropriated to build the capital at Madison. The temptation to borrow from these funds for his real estate speculations had been too strong to resist. President Jackson's Specie Circular and the panic of 1837 caught him before he could turn a profit on the land. He could not cover the debt or offer an accounting, and his opponents were in full cry. He threw himself on the mercy of John Jacob Astor, for whom he was agent at the townsite of Astor, now part of Green Bay. Doty's services in Washington and Wisconsin were too valuable for Astor to let him go under, and he was rescued at a price. Astor took most of his widespread land holdings.

Doty is a fascinating character in early Wisconsin history. His knowledge of Wisconsin was encyclopedic, gained the hard way: in the field, many times alone, on long trips by horseback or canoe, often with only a blanket for shelter even in approaching winter. He was equally at home in the milieu of Washington, a gifted raconteur and very evidently a man of considerable fascination as well as usefulness. While he inspired respect, trust, and support from many men, no one in Wisconsin politics was more vilified, disliked, and distrusted than this master of the game. Doty could turn the tables on his enemies, thwart their strongest moves, and skim over thin political ice with imperturbable assurance. He kept an easy conscience.

The successes of James Doty owed much to his opposition, the supporters of Henry Dodge. Dodge's loyalties and principles were self-evident. He was a faithful follower of Andrew Jackson and a military and political hero to his constituency. He wore pistols and Bowie knives in his belt, even on civic occasions when he was not in uniform—a commanding figure of considerable vanity. The rough exterior that endeared him to his friends and supporters gave pause to the growing Yankee population on the Lake, who saw a bit of the border ruffian in his behavior. Dodge was patently honest and straightforward, but the characteristics of a good Indian fighter did not necessarily make a successful politician. Dodge's political allies understood Doty better than did Henry Dodge. Like Doty, many of them were not above making a deal with the devil if the terms were right.

The antagonism between Dodge and Doty was personal as well as political and antedated Dodge's elevation to the governorship. In their first brush after Dodge's appointment, Doty won out. Wisconsin's organic act provided that the governor should select a temporary capital, and that then he and the legislature together should fix upon a permanent seat. This of course became a great bone of contention in the first legislative session after Governor Dodge had organized his administration, taken a census, fixed legislative districts, and called the election.

Dodge exhibited his political naiveté by yielding to the persuasions of a hopeful townsite promoter in the lead area and designating Belmont as the temporary capital. Nearly half of the territorial population in 1836 lived across the Mississippi in present Iowa, justifying this choice, Dodge felt, although it was already understood that Iowa would be created a separate territory. It was, in July 1838. Dodge's geography may have been defensible, but Belmont was not a happy choice, even though its selection gave the promoter a gratifying flurry of interest in his townsite and the opportunity to advertise an auction of lots in New York City. This was 1836, when paper fortunes were being made in western townsites, and New York was presumed to be full of greenhorns who would not read Wisconsin's Organic Act to discover that the capital location was temporary. But for the legislators, Belmont proved to be short of some elementary comforts, including for many a roof over their heads.

Governor Dodge was so affronted by the grumbling over his choice of Belmont and the unseemly scramble over the selection of the permanent capital that he vowed to approve whatever decision the legislature should make. Into this melee rode the sly and insinuating James Doty, fresh from the stimulating work of laying out a town on the isthmus between what were known as Third and Fourth Lakes and are today Lakes Monona and Mendota. The way in which he came into possession of the site belongs in another chapter, but the location is a tribute to his perspicacity and its promotion a commentary on territorial politics.

There were many candidates for the honor of becoming the permanent territorial capital. Many were communities in being, from Burlington, Iowa to Green Bay, while others were only prospective sites, such as Belmont, whose promoters were bidding for the capital with a variety of inducements. Every county had its proposals and arguments in its favor. A four-story brick hotel in the modest village of Cassville, on the Mississippi, is supposed to have been built as a lure for the uncomfortable legislators at Belmont.

The ardent logrolling that was accompanying the feverish legislative interest in the capital selection was a situation made to order for that "consummate political manipulator, master of chicane, and lobbyist of unusual charm and impressiveness," James Doty. While others were busy talking, Doty was lining up votes with the most practical of persuasions —the gift of choice lots in the future Madison. It should not be overlooked that geography favored this site, given the distribution of population and the probability of a geographical compromise. Doty was in a good position to argue for a compromise, since he controlled townsites at

Madison and at Fond du Lac. But the selection of Madison came as a surprise to many, for the site was virtually uninhabited, as was the land for many miles around.

Governor Dodge was a man of his word, although a reluctant one in this case. He would have relished a chance to renege on his earlier promise, but Doty had him outmaneuvered. Not one to depend upon the governor's rash promise to honor any choice made by the legislators, Doty had disarmed him by gifts of lots to Dodge's allies, including congressional delegate George W. Jones and the governor's son Augustus C. Dodge. Doty had not neglected those legislators from west of the Mississippi who were reasonably sure of separation from Wisconsin Territory in the near future. It is claimed that even Governor Dodge was offered lots in the future capital, which he indignantly refused. Rather than reopen the abrasive question, Dodge accepted the result, after canvassing the possibilities of overturning the decision without resort to his veto. A quarter of a century later some of the rancor had cooled, and one of Doty's devoted opponents was willing to concede the fortunate character of the decision and to remark upon Doty's "foresight and patriotism."

After this coup, Doty made his second race for the office of congressional delegate, defeating Jones for the seat. He had to stand for election again in 1839 because of the separation of Iowa Territory, and for the first time anti-Doty forces made an effort to organize as a formal party. Doty supporters, however, packed the Democratic convention they held in Madison, and endorsed his candidacy. Doty went on to win the election, even though he was under fire for his handling of federal funds as commissioner for the building of the Capitol and his role as principal stockholder in two defunct banks. His instincts for political survival, in the face of seemingly insurmountable obstacles of his own devising, were truly remarkable.

With characteristic energy, Doty almost got congressional support for a comprehensive system of canals to tie Wisconsin's rivers—and his various townsites—together, but such support was out of fashion after the 1837 panic. His main accomplishment was the passage of an act limiting Governor Dodge's veto power by providing for a legislative override with a two-thirds vote. Doty could not foresee his own political fortunes. He was to succeed Dodge.

The famous Log Cabin campaign of 1840 that elected William Henry Harrison disappointed the Democrats and brought the Whigs to the control of patronage. The adjustable Doty, despite the "Democratic" convention which had endorsed his candidacy in Madison in 1839, was the pleasant companion of prominent Whigs Henry Clay and Daniel Webster, the latter a speculator in Wisconsin lands. Doty stayed in the same boardinghouse with Clay—most congressmen did not maintain Washington homes then—often conferred with Webster, and cultivated the New Yorkers who opposed Van Buren, especially Senator Nathaniel Tallmadge, a conservative Democrat.

These associations served to bring Doty forward as a candidate for the governorship of Wisconsin. President Harrison scheduled his appointment, which President Tyler honored after Harrison's death. Confirmation in the Senate was slow, fought savagely by Doty's enemies, but national politics were confused at this point. Back in Wisconsin, neither Whigs nor the majority Democrats claimed Doty, although he had friends and some newspaper support in both parties. It was Doty's powerful support in Washington, particularly from Webster and Tallmadge, that carried the day. Democrat Henry Dodge, having lost the governorship, was rewarded by Wisconsin voters with the office of congressional delegate, thus changing places with his political adversary.

Doty's three years in the governor's chair brought out his capacity for bullheadedness, which contrasts strangely with his suavity as a lobbyist and special pleader. He sought every opportunity to thwart his enemies, who in turn were untiring in their efforts to make Doty a heavy burden for President Tyler. There is little positive that can be said of Governor Doty's administration. He was identified with no particular program or popular cause, and was not respected as Dodge was. If he was identified with any theme it was early statehood for Wisconsin. This measure he placed on the ballot four times during his tenure, and saw it defeated each time.

Doty recognized the improbability that President Tyler would renew his appointment at the end of his statutory three-year term in 1844. He therefore chose to step aside for Nathaniel Tallmadge, who still had some claims on Tyler. Tallmadge's tenure was brief; the Jacksonian Democrats returned to national power with the election of James Polk of Tennessee, in 1844, and Polk offered the Wisconsin governorship again to Henry Dodge. With a congenial governor and a Democratic legislature, Wisconsin moved now in earnest toward statehood.

There were, of course, men other than Dodge and Doty in territorial politics who are worthy of mention. Moses M. Strong of Mineral Point was a transplanted Yankee from Vermont who came to the lead region in 1836. Strong identified himself with the Dodge faction and soon became a southern Democrat of the deepest dye. Always in a hurry, like his antagonist Doty, Strong established a reputation for political untrustworthiness, but he had great nerve and energy. More admirable characters abounded. Morgan L. Martin of Green Bay, Doty's cousin, held a number of important territorial offices and was less controversial than Doty. Marshall M. Strong of Racine was a lawyer from Massachusetts and one of the many graduates of Union College in Schenectady, New York who made a mark on the Wisconsin frontier. John H. Tweedy, a Yale graduate from Connecticut, was one of the few avowed Whigs to have a broad political following. The ambitious men of talent like Doty, Moses Strong, and Bryon Kilbourn capture our interest. They were in many ways typical of a frontier community: a collection of strangers whose political values had been shaken up in transit, lacking the assurance of long acquaintance with one another and with territorial problems.

The problems of territorial government that faced them had to do with such mundane matters as perfecting the organization of county and municipal government, taxation, schools, and roads, all complicated by a sparse population and the severe deflation following the panic of 1837. The territory was also engaged in the common frontier activity of trying to create credit and capital where little existed. To this end it chartered banks, granted corporate privileges, and petitioned for federal land grants to stand in lieu of capital. The panic and depression brought most of these projects to grief and curbed congressional generosity. Much energy was devoted to recriminations and investigations, more to the point of finding political scapegoats than solutions and all exacerbated by the character of territorial politics.

The elements which stand out in Wisconsin territorial politics are rancor and spite. In a measure, surely, this grew out of the dependence built into the territorial system. Political mudslinging is even less attractive in personal letters addressed to the president and prominent political figures around him than it is in a hard fought campaign with party lines clearly drawn. The stakes were usually petty and the public interest suffered without the usual avenues of recourse. Politics may have continued rancorous and petty with statehood, but the voter counted for more and the appointive power for less, giving politics more scope for dignity and meaning.

Selected Bibliography

Benson, Lee. *The Concept of Jacksonian Democracy: New York as a Test Case.* Princeton. 1961. New York furnished the model for Wisconsin politics, and the language.

Bloom, John Porter, ed. *The Territorial Papers of the United States.* Vol. 27, *The Territory of Wisconsin, Executive Journal, 1836–1848, Papers, 1836–1839.* Washington, 1969. See also volumes of Clarence Carter, ed.,

Michigan Territory, listed in the chapter 7 bibliography. The basic records of the administration of the territory.

Clark, James I. *Henry Dodge: Frontiersman.* Madison, 1957. The first territorial governor.

Duckett, Kenneth W. *Frontiersman of Fortune: Moses M. Strong of Mineral Point.* Madison, 1955. A central figure in territorial and early state politics and in land speculation and other promotion.

Eblen, Jack. *The First and Second United States Empires.* Pittsburgh, 1968. Draws on the Wisconsin experience.

———. "Origins of the United States Colonial System: The Ordinance of 1787." *Wisconsin Magazine of History* 51:294–314 (Summer 1969). Contributions of Jefferson, Monroe, and Nathan Dane.

"Four Wisconsin Capitals." *The Wisconsin Blue Book,* 1948, pp. 125–40. Madison, 1948. Belmont and Doty's embarrassment.

Kuehnl, George J. *The Wisconsin Business Corporation.* Madison, 1959. A good chapter on the territorial period.

Pease, Theodore C. "The Ordinance of 1787." *Mississippi Valley Historical Review* 25:167–80 (Sept. 1938). Compare with Eblen.

Pomeroy, Earl S. *The Territories and the United States, 1861–1890: Studies in Colonial Administration.* Seattle: American Library Paperbacks, 1970. Wisconsin's Organic Act was the standard.

Smith, Alice E. "James Duane Doty: Mephistopheles in Wisconsin." *Wisconsin Magazine of History* 34:195–98, 238–40 (Summer 1951).

———. *James Duane Doty: Frontier Promoter.* Madison, 1954. A central character in the territorial period.

———. "Stephen H. Long and the Naming of Wisconsin." *Wisconsin Magazine of History* 26:67–71 (Sept. 1942). Anticipated Doty.

Woodford, Frank B. *Lewis Cass, the Last Jeffersonian.* New Brunswick, N.J., 1950. Cass was Doty's patron and Michigan's territorial governor for many years.

THE LAND SYSTEM
AND FRONTIER
OPPORTUNITY

10

The present-day traveller, driving through the well-ordered farmlands of southern Wisconsin, imagines with difficulty a time when no man had title to these acres which lay unsettled, unplowed, unfenced, unmeasured, and, indeed, untrod by white Americans until well into the nineteenth century. Lieutenant Jefferson Davis camped on the site of present Madison in 1829. "Nothing, as I think, was known to the garrison of Fort Winnebago about the Four Lakes before I saw them," he wrote. "Indeed, sir, it may astonish you to learn . . . that I and the file of soldiers who accompanied me were the first white men who ever passed over the country between the Portage of the Wisconsin and Fox rivers, and the then village of Chicago." Buffalo was already a city of 8,000, commanding the routes to the West on the Great Lakes from the recently opened Erie Canal, and St. Louis numbered 5,000. Chicago was an isolated trading post, located in an unprepossessing swamp, and Morgan Martin had not yet informed the incredulous Solomon Juneau that he had squatter's rights to a future city at the mouth of the Milwaukee River.

Those who make the imaginative effort to see this empire of land before it was settled may wonder how the property lines were fixed and how the long progression of titles, mortgages, conveyances, easements, and so forth, that make up such an important part of the business in county courthouses, were begun. The property lines and the initial transfers of title were the business of the United States government, which at one time held title to most of the land west of the Appalachian Mountains, including all of present Wisconsin. The lure which brought men here in the days before cities and jobs existed was land. Land was many things to these men: a farm, a speculation, a site for a town or city, a power site on a stream, a stand of timber, or any of a number of things which spelled opportunity. The Wisconsin frontier, for some, may have been a refuge from something left behind, but for most it was the chance to transform a relatively easily acquired commodity into something of value. The commodity was land and the transformation might come through luck, shrewdness, hard work, chicane, political action, the application of capital, or simply the passage of time. The varieties of opportunity and of approach to its realization brought a variety of pioneers. We miss much if we see it only in terms of agricultural pioneers spreading across beckoning acres, bringing towns, cities, transportation lines, and industries in their wake. The order was often reversed, with the farmer bringing up the rear.

The philosophy animating American public land policy was as varied as the opportunities offered by the land. As with much of American history, we have adopted convenient simplifications which come from nineteenth-century rhetoric about the public lands and from the popularization of scholarly theories. The popular ideas of one of the most persuasive of American historians, Frederick Jackson Turner, for example, about the influence of the frontier and free land upon American institutions and character have been eagerly seized upon by generations of Americans. They are part of the fabric of what Americans believe about themselves, and they are readily adaptable to the shorthand of political sloganeering, as witness John F. Kennedy's "New Frontier." Slogans and myths have a way of obscuring the processes of history, however. Most of Wisconsin was not homesteaded, and the land was free only in the sense in which Turner used the term, that it quite readily and cheaply passed from the public domain into private hands. The means by which it did so are our immediate concern.

When Virginia surrendered her claims to western lands, assuring the creation of the public domain in the hands of the central government, the Congress of the Confederation was faced with three overriding concerns: How was the public land to be governed? How was title to land to be determined and conveyed? Upon what terms should it pass into private hands? The first question was answered by the well-known Northwest Ordinance of 1787, providing for the establishment of territories and their transition to statehood. The less-familiar Land Ordinance of 1785 established the processes of survey and title conveyance by creating a means of legal land description. The conditions of sale or transfer to territories, states, and particularly private hands made a longer story and were never settled with entire satisfaction.

The system of survey before sale, defined in the 1785 ordinance, seems simpler today than it did at the time it was passed. Borrowed from New England practices, it established geographical base and meridian lines from which the land was set off into townships six miles square, divided into thirty-six sections, each one mile square. These sections, 640 acres each, divided into quarter-sections of 160 acres each, and these into quarters of 40 acres each, and so on. Any piece of land which is a measured quarter of those described can be accurately and legally identified by its position within the quarterings of the section, the section by its number within the township, and the township by its number on the meridian line either north or south of the base line, and by its range number east or west of the meridian along the base line or parallel.

An example will make this more understandable. Americans moved up into what is now Wisconsin following the lead outcroppings in the Galena lead-mining district. They were pressing for title to the land and forced the first Indian cessions there in 1829. For survey purposes the government therefore set the northern Illinois border as the base line, and the meridian, known as the Fourth Principal Meridian, was extended due north. This meridian line forms the present boundary between Grant County on the west and Iowa and Lafayette counties on the east. Measuring from this base, most of the City of Madison lies in T 7 N, R 9 E, meaning seven townships north of the Illinois line and nine ranges east of the Fourth Principal Meridian. This places the southwest corner of that township thirty-six miles north of the Illinois line and forty-eight miles east of Grant County's eastern boundary.

The advantages of the survey system are readily apparent. With a public domain which eventually encompassed about 3,000,000,000 acres, the survey permitted accurate description of any piece of land within the survey. After any area was surveyed and staked, the government could convey ownership with reasonable assurance as to the title with respect to metes and bounds.

There were some disadvantages to the system. It ignored topography, with the result that legal corners might be in rivers, lakes, swamps, or on bluffs. The survey lines ignored such natural features as streams, springs, arable bottomlands, timber, and heights. The system imposed an artificial order and method of thinking about land which were ill suited to many areas, most particularly to the arid West. Yet its advantages have far outweighed its disadvantages. A system of land claims based upon natural features and not upon a rectangular survey worked fine for the man who set out his claim or applied his warrant to a body of acreage according to the lay of the land. Southerners were accustomed to such a system. But it led to generations of litigation associated with establishing legal metes and bounds without the lines of a rectangular survey.

There were many different approaches to the disposition of the public domain. As a great national resource, should it be marketed in such a manner as to return the greatest amount possible to the Treasury directly, or was there a greater return implicit in rapid settlement and development, encouraged by low prices and easy terms? Did cheap land encourage emigration and thereby make labor dear in the older, established sections? Should speculation in land be discouraged by acreage limitations in favor of actual settlement? Should illegal squatting on public land, before survey or sale, be dealt with as a crime, or were squatters the salt of the earth—the cutting edge of the frontier—to be rewarded for their enterprise? Should the land be sold at public auction to the highest bidder, without regard to improvements made by those squatters or their claims, or should a flat price be established and priorities given to the squatters? How could the land officers distinguish between a squatter who claimed to have improved his land and a speculator? Should certain lands such as water powers, natural townsites, fords, salt springs, and mineral or timber lands be withheld from sale? If not, should enterprise be rewarded by recognizing the prior right of squatters on such sites and resources, or should the marketplace determine value by public auction?

By the time land sales began in Wisconsin in 1834, a new pattern in land policy was emerging favoring the western settler, yet leaving plenty of opportunity for speculators. The triumph of western agitation would come with the passage of the Pre-emption Act of 1841, recognition of the prior right of the squatter, or homesteader, to the land he had selected and improved before it was ready for public sale. Meanwhile the Jacksonians pressed for recognition of the rights of squatters or preemptors and won limited preemption laws in 1830, 1832, 1833, 1834, and 1838. Unlike the 1841 law, these applied only to settlement made before the passage of the respective acts. The dates are significant, since the early rush for Wisconsin land came between 1835 and 1837, requiring these squatters to wait for the 1838 act to confirm their claims. It was assumed that Congress would continue the policy, and extralegal measures were taken by the settlers to enforce the spirit of the needed legislation. A mass meeting was called at Milwaukee in March 1837, attended by over 1,000 people, to organize a claims association. After asserting their virtue and their presence "for the purpose of bettering their condition by agricultural pursuits," they perfected an organization to register their claims, defined a claim in terms of acreage and improvements, and agreed that an agent for the association should bid in all claims "and no person shall in any case be countenanced in bidding in opposition to such agent." This meant, as it implied, the use of force against an outsider should this be necessary.

There was never any doubt where virtue lay. Speculators were considered the worst of vultures, preying upon honest settlers and the government alike. There was a problem of definition, however. It was a rare settler who was satisfied with title to only as much land as he could till himself. It was a popular saying that all the land a man rightly wanted was his own claim and any land that joined it. A government surveyor told of finding a squatter, miles from the neighbors, who said he had a basis for six claims—any dependent child or relative over twenty-one could claim 80 acres—and hoped to dispose of some of it in order to pay for what he kept. Practically every man on the public domain was a speculator who hoped somehow to get control of more land than he could use, and to realize something from the expected rise in price which his own settlement and improvements adjacent would bring. Therefore when a settler spoke of speculators, he usually meant someone from outside of the community who bought land near his own. Some speculators, because they dealt in large acreages, were readily recognized. Still, the definition was equivocal. The president of the Milwaukee Claims Association was Byron Kilbourn, whose main interest was the promotion of his holdings, 440 acres divided into town lots in the present city of Milwaukee. It took a considerable stretch of the imagination to describe Kilbourn as one engaged in "bettering his condition by agricultural pursuits." He was a speculator on a large scale, but having cast his lot with Milwaukee where he lived, he was transformed into an enterprising settler.

Congress had taken the government out of the credit business in 1820. Before this the minimum price had been $2.00 an acre, with one-fourth down and four years to pay. The panic of 1819 left citizens owing the Treasury over $21,000,000 on land purchased, and demanding relief. Congress adopted a new minimum price of $1.25 an acre and required cash payment. Naturally, a good many congressmen worried that the change would favor the speculators, who could bring more cash to bear at the auction. The logical answer would have been to limit the acreage allowed to a single purchaser, but opposition to speculators was largely rhetorical. A more palatable formula was to reduce the minimum amount of land that a person could buy. This had been the standard response to the needs of the poor man. The minimum was lowered to 40 acres in 1832, at a minimum price of $50. Remember that 160 acres was assumed as a standard in the preemption acts and in the final triumph of the western settler, the Homestead Act of 1862.

Critics of public land policy argued over the prevalence of speculation without taking any practical steps to measure it. Many thought that a limitless public domain, available at $1.25 an acre, rendered land speculation an exercise in futility, but they did not take into account the relative desirability of the land as determined by location, fertility, timber, and water. A study of land-sale records by Congress showed that most sales were made at the minimum price, and this was taken as proof that speculation was not a problem. It was in fact more a reflection of poorly administered auctions, the operation of bidders' combinations, and land sales made well ahead of settlement than it was a proof that no speculation was at work. Let us see how all of this worked in terms of the early sales of land in Wisconsin.

Remember that land was not sold until it had been surveyed, and that no one who came after December 1833 had a valid claim under the preemption laws until the passage of the 1838 act. In the rapidly settled southeast corner, where this mattered most, there were probably not over 500 people in 1835, but an estimated 6,000 by March 1837. Hence the activity of claims associations there.

The pattern of early land sales in Wisconsin is interesting for what it tells us both about the administration of the national land system and about how Americans reacted to the opening of a new and desirable portion of the public domain. It is not a simple story of retreating Indians followed by settlers establishing their claims to the virgin soil. The Indians left, reluctantly, and the settlers came all right, but they found the wilderness oddly transformed. Typical was the story of a group of Norwegians who intended to immigrate as a colony at the time when Illinois, Wisconsin, and Missouri were the centers of attention for their countrymen seeking open public land. In late 1839, they sent two scouts to seek an appropriate site. The pair came to the Rock River valley, in northern Illinois, where many Norwegians were already settled, but found the land largely taken up. Rejecting Missouri in favor of Wisconsin, which was less settled and promised a more familiar climate and landscape, they pressed northward, looking for a favorable combination of timber, prairie, and water. There were many such sites along their route, but all were taken, although still uninhabited. They pushed on to Koshkonong Creek, west of Lake Koshkonong, passing only one settler in seven miles, and found a town staked out at a prospective mill site but not a soul about nor any sign of habitation.

The cause of the Norwegians' dilemma was a strong current of American speculative fever which, as it had in 1819, was reaching epidemic proportions in the years 1835–37, just when Wisconsin was drawing attention to its newly opened lands. Like the earlier epidemic, this one ended in a financial panic in 1837, brought on by the fiscal policies of the Jackson administration and the bursting of the speculative bubble. It is estimated that some 38,000,000 acres of public land were sold from 1835 to 1837, and probably 29,000,000 fell into the hands of speculators. While many were interested in choice farm lands, waterpower sites, or timber, the favorite targets of speculators were prospective townsites. The Mississippi Valley was carpeted with townsites in these years. One cynic suggested that the townsite speculators in northern Illinois should take care to leave some land for cultivation. This was the spirit which animated Wisconsin's early years of settlement.

The career of Moses Strong of Mineral Point gives us some notion of the process. A young Vermont lawyer, Strong was captivated by the idea of making a fortune in Wisconsin. The names of Milwaukee and Wisconsin were household words, and everyone knew of someone, second- or third-hand, who was bound to grow rich there. Strong came to Wisconsin in 1836, with appropriate letters of introduction, to get an appointment as a deputy land surveyor, a job assumed to be within the competence of any moderately educated man. He attracted the favorable notice of Senator Henry Hubbard of New Hampshire, who organized a syndicate with two friends to establish a $30,000 credit through a Detroit bank to add to Virginia land scrip for 8,000 acres, bought at discount. The twenty-six-year-old Strong was to use these at his discretion.

Hubbard instructed Strong to be on the lookout for good townsites, especially along the Mississippi or Wisconsin rivers, for good farm land, and for prospective county seats. "Be faithful," he admonished, "and we'll both have $100,000 within three years." Strong got diverted into a bootless scheme to force the General Land Office, under considerable pressure from Hubbard and Daniel Webster, to sell the reserved mineral lands in the lead region to another syndicate. Before this, he had, however, invested the Hubbard syndicate funds in various townsites and farm lands, the most promising seeming to find their way into his own hands as his share. There was a time when the syndicate owned forty lots in Madison, a paper townsite, St. Lawrence, across the Wisconsin from present Sauk City, and the village of Arena.

After the speculative bubble burst, Moses Strong, who remained long on schemes and always short on cash, sent his brother in the East the clear title to the Arena site and 600 acres adjoining, but his brother could not raise a dime on the property. Senator Hubbard had, largely through Strong, invested $33,000 of his own money in Wisconsin land. His dreams of $100,000 in profits had turned into a nightmare of debt. He asked President Polk to appoint him governor of Wisconsin Territory in 1844 in hopes of retrieving something, but it was another prayer unheeded. In 1847 he wrote plaintively, "How could land on which I have paid taxes for ten years be worth less than $2 per acre?" After the senators' death his son was still, in 1852, liquidating the investment at less than $2 an acre, when he could find buyers.

Not all speculations in Wisconsin in these years ended on such a gloomy note, but very few were profitable over the short term. A list made from the land sales records of 1834–39 shows twenty-one nonresident speculators and the acreage they owned. Hubbard, with 5,191 acres, had the least. Six had from 20,000 to 26,830 acres and another half dozen from 10,283 to 16,233. Many hundreds speculated through agents, relatives, or friends. The virus was widespread. Even Ralph Waldo Emerson, whose thoughts were supposed to be on less worldly matters, took a fling at speculating in Wisconsin land.

When speculative interest revived, about ten years after the 1837 panic, a new group of absentee owners was attracted and holdings were even larger. Resident speculators matched them. C. C. Washburn and Cyrus Woodman of Mineral Point accumulated 130,220 acres, much of it in timber north of the Wisconsin River; holdings in the newly opened pine lands were of a different order of size.

Apparently speculators in southern Wisconsin were generally disappointed in their expectations, unless they were fortunate enough to buy good land just in advance of settlement. American settlers were reluctant to pay more than the established government minimum of $1.25 an acre, even for superior land. They had no qualms about going beyond the rim of established settlement in search of government land. They had seen the transformation worked on interior lands by canals, roads, and railroads in New York and Ohio and expected to see the process repeated in Wisconsin. European immigrants, who made up an increasing share of the agricultural population after 1836, did not generally share this faith. If they came with money, they paid the speculator's price for land close to Lake Michigan and its markets. If they lacked the price of the more expensive lands, they took what was left of government lands near the Lake, usually land with a heavy cover of hardwood that took years of patient clearing to make farm land.

The continuing availability of federal land at the $1.25 minimum, and after 1848, large tracts of state lands selling on generous credit terms, made land speculation a hazardous field for the uninformed or unlucky. Nevertheless there were several speculators, including the uniformly gloomy Cyrus Woodman, who came out handsomely over the long pull. It was the absentee speculator who most often knew despair.

It was a truism that sales of public lands followed a boom and bust cycle. Land sales hit 20,000,000 acres in 1836 and fell to about 3,000,000 in 1838 after the panic. Credit dried up, loans were called, and paper profits vanished. The man who used his credit to make land purchases in flush times was often ruined by the turn in fortune's wheel. The resident speculator—and this included every enterprising Yankee who was holding land beyond his immediate needs—simply learned the art of subsistence and waited out the return of easier times. If he had borrowed money to buy his land he might lose the excess and more, but with land a glut on the market, his creditor often preferred future prospects of cash to foreclosure. Meanwhile, the settler knew that the opprobrious term *speculator* referred not to himself but to the absentee owner of the section down the road where the settler, with a clear conscience, pastured his livestock and cut his firewood and fence rails.

More than debt threatened the absentee speculator. The settler not only made free use of his land and timber but could burden him with unwanted taxes. Desiring the amenities of roads, county government, and schools, the settler voted these things for himself and his absentee neighbor with the knowledge that he could work out a large part of his taxes. If his farming returned a little cash, he went to the new county seat and paid the taxes on the land of his absentee neighbor. The latter likely did not know that his land had been put in a new tax district—notice was not required—and assumed that no news was good news. In three years the honest settler could thus get a tax lien against his absent neighbor's land.

While the speculator's land taken and held off the market created hardships for the scattered settlers, the results were not all malign. The absentee speculator brought cash into the country, and while he might tie it up unproductively in land, his cash went to the local land office and from there into neighboring banks, or was drawn upon to build territorial roads, pay territorial officers, and finance territorial buildings. If the speculator tried the more lucrative promotion of a townsite he probably built a mill, a store, or a tavern to prove his serious intentions. If he simply held unimproved land, his neighbors might vote taxes upon him along with themselves. If, like senators Hubbard and Daniel Webster, he had influence and his heart lay with his treasure, he was sure to take an interest in petitions for harbor improvements or requests for canal and railroad subsidies, postroads, postoffices, and surveys coming before

Congress. With the land in private ownership, an army of lawyers and county officials, dependent upon fees, moved in to minister to the litigious and maintain the records.

The absentee landowner was as often a victim as he was an unwitting oppressor. He was usually at the mercy of a local agent. Moses Strong, as an agent, simply took the best for himself, by one means or another. Cyrus Woodman's habitual melancholy frightened his eastern clients into the surrender of their holdings to their lugubrious agent, at his price. The active speculators who made money were those on the scene who could establish lines of credit or act as agents on a partnership basis. A number of the most successful were onetime government surveyors or land office officials. It was a time when few people worried about conflict of interest if it did not involve the direct theft of cash from the till. The surveyor's instructions were to be informative in his descriptions of the land as he surveyed it. Those descriptions were on the plats available to the public. But the requirements were not detailed, and more specific information was apt to go into the surveyor's personal book with which he set himself up in business as a land agent. Much surveying was done under contract, and men moved readily from this employment to private business or worked in both at once. Congress abandoned rather early the special reservation of lands, except for salt springs and the Section Sixteen in each township for school purposes.

A recent study of speculation in southern Wisconsin estimates that the examples chosen averaged only about 4 percent a year on their investments, and many lost money. Very few justified the stereotype of the hard-hearted mortgage holder. Most of them fervently wanted out of a risky investment and preferred a deferred promise of repayment to foreclosure. Speculators were gullible too. They bought land along prospective canals that never were built and adjacent to paper townsites that remained on paper. But the image of the absentee speculator endured, contributing to the westerner's traditional distrust of the easterner. The distrust was present before the era of the railroad and industrial monopolies.

Why did men invest in such speculative ventures? Because quick profits were made by the shrewd and the lucky. Because the corporation in its present form, as a limited liability investment, was not yet available for investment. Because interest rates in the West were traditionally higher, and western banknotes, which were accepted for land until Jackson's Specie Circular of 1836, traditionally sold at a substantial discount for eastern banknotes. Because Americans shared an unappeasable land hunger, and the lure of fertile acres for $1.25 was irresistible to those who saw all around them $30 land that had been wilderness within the memory of many. This also explains why congressmen could go into a passion over the evils of speculation but fought shy of firm proposals to counter them.

Why did speculative buying stray so far into the unsettled interior of Wisconsin in 1834–37? Largely because of the way in which the land was brought onto the market. Early settlement and agitation for land sales began in the lead region. The Fourth Principal Meridian was therefore established in the southwest corner of Wisconsin, and the government surveys started from there and worked eastward, south of the Fox-Wisconsin. Later, a subsidiary base line was established sixty miles north of the Illinois-Wisconsin border to survey the lands around Green Bay and Lake Winnebago. These were the lands that went on sale at the Mineral Point and Green Bay land offices in 1834 and 1835. The lands around Milwaukee, Racine, and Southport (Kenosha) were surveyed in 1835, but Presidents Jackson and Van Buren, attempting to stem the speculative tide, held them off the market until 1839. Thus the area of most rapid settlement, on Lake Michigan, was spared many of the speculative excesses that characterized the unsettled Rock River valley lands to the west.

It was fortunate for Wisconsin that the pattern of land sales went as it did. Less than 1,000,000 acres in Wisconsin were sold before the end of 1836; by comparison, the entire state contains about 36,000,000 acres. Moses Strong estimated that of the 878,014 acres sold through 1836, as many as 600,000 went to speculators. The proportions are about the same as the estimated 29,000,000 acres taken by speculators out of a total 38,000,000 sold from the entire public domain during the boom years 1835–37. Yet the full force of the speculative fever that consumed Michigan and Illinois land bypassed Wisconsin. In each of these states nearly 2,000,000 acres were sold in the year 1835 alone, sowing the seeds of future tenancy and land monopoly, particularly in the Illinois cornbelt.

The mechanics of land sale had much to do with the processes of speculation. The pressures to hurry land to survey and sale were many, and the Jackson administration was sympathetic to western impatience to get lands opened. All lands were cried at public auctions held at the land offices of the districts, in accordance with the presidential proclamation of townships to be offered. The lands were usually placed on the block in a regular order. The sale would go on for several days. What is not generally appreciated is that land which found no bidders was then open to public sale at the minimum $1.25 an acre. The early Wisconsin land sales were of land in the sparsely settled interior, because of the way the surveys had been made, and most sales at auction were to speculators who picked and chose the best lands. They bought up waterpower sites, townsites, lands along supposedly navigable waters, and timber adjacent to open prairie. The feast of land offered was so great that the auctions seldom brought lively competition, and much land went begging. The man with a long purse could buy several thousand acres of choice land, seldom going over the $1.25 minimum. James Doty found the site of Madison open for private sale after auction.

The land in the Milwaukee land district, which received the lion's share of settlement after 1835, was treated differently. Milwaukee, in particular, received a good deal of unfavorable notice for the speculation there based upon a misuse of special and general preemption laws. It figured prominently in the 1836 failure of Congress to renew the 1834 Preemption Act expiring that year. As a result of the debate over Milwaukee, Chicago, Racine, and Southport, a provision to exclude townsites from preemption entry was incorporated in the 1838 Preemption Act and in the broader act of 1841. The exclusion was not effective.

The 1834 Preemption Act was limited to those who had improved their claims by the 1833 season. About the only person in all of southeast Wisconsin with a valid claim under this act was Solomon Juneau, who had maintained a trading post at the mouth of the Milwaukee River for some years. Juneau preempted 132 acres there for $165.82 and an additional 157 acres in the name of his brother, who worked for him. By the summer of 1836 this land, which became downtown Milwaukee, was bringing as much as $4,000 an acre. The townsite was swarming with speculators.

Much of the remainder of Milwaukee's site was taken up in 1835 with special preemption claims at $1.25 an acre. James Doty helped to show the way to this coup. Congress had passed a special land act in 1820 recognizing the rights of the habitant population at Green Bay to preemption claims to land upon which they were settled. Most of these people were engaged in the fur trade rather than in farming and had little use for the 160-acre claims awarded. They received land warrants for the excess over the plots on which they were settled, as well as for dependents who were eligible. These claims were in the process of confirmation from 1823 to 1828. The French-Canadians of Green Bay, who lacked the Americans' land hunger, were easily traded out of the transferable land warrants, known as "floats." James Doty, examining the law and the records, selected sixty-two such claims, which he pressed on a contingency basis before the commissioners adjudicating them. His avarice got out of hand on some, and he was often reminded of two claims in particular: one in the name of Joseph Boisvert and the other of Joseph Greenwood, which students of French will recognize as the same name. Doty handled similar land claims for various Menominee and Winnebago chiefs, head men, and part-Indians. These floating warrants were applicable to land anywhere in the district and were widely used by Doty, Morgan Martin, Daniel Whitney, and others who were on the scene early enough. Doty used his mostly at Green Bay and at Neenah, Fond du Lac, and other interior townsites, while Martin and Byron Kilbourn were the principal beneficiaries on the Milwaukee townsite.

Fortunately for the agricultural settlers in the Milwaukee land district, the unfavorable notice given to speculative activities at the neighboring townsites gave President Jackson, a scarred veteran of similar speculations in Alabama in the boom period 1816–19, the excuse to delay opening to sale the lands attached to the Milwaukee land office. Sales opened there in 1839. With the passage of the 1838 Preemption Act, most of the farmer-squatters were secured in their holdings if they could find the cash. Thus granting mortgages on established farms favorably located became a profitable business. The common device was for the creditor to take a deed to half of the squatter's claim. The initial flurry of speculation in Milwaukee ended in disaster for many speculators in the 1837 panic, but the basis for solid growth remained in Milwaukee and in Wisconsin generally. They continued as names to conjure with, holding hope for those with courage and optimism.

Selected Bibliography

Agnew, Dwight L. "The Government Land Surveyor as a Pioneer." *Mississippi Valley Historical Review* 28:369–82 (Dec. 1941). Mostly on life in the wilderness and the technology of the survey.

Brunson, Alfred. "A Methodist Circuit Rider's Horseback Tour from Pennsylvania to Wisconsin, 1835." *SHSW Collections,* vol. 15, pp. 264–91. Madison, 1900. Description of a claim association.

Carstensen, Vernon, ed. *The Public Lands: Studies in the History of the Public Domain.* Madison, 1963. A collection of important essays and articles on the subject.

Duckett, Kenneth W. *Frontiersman of Fortune: Moses M. Strong of Mineral Point.* Madison, 1955. Senator Hubbard's land agent.

Fischer, Duane D. "The Disposal of Federal Lands in the Eau Claire District of Wisconsin, 1848–1961." Master's thesis, University of Wisconsin, 1961. The public got about what it wanted in the administration of the public lands.

Gates, Paul W. "Frontier Land Speculators in Wisconsin." *Wisconsin Magazine of History* 52:306–29 (Summer 1969). The author has never lost his sense of indignation.

————. *History of Public Land Law Development*. Washington, D.C., 1968. You are bound to find something you want to know.

————. *The Wisconsin Pine Lands of Cornell University: A Study in Land Policy and Absentee Ownership*. Ithaca, N.Y., 1943. An important book on the hazards of land and timber speculation.

Pomeroy, Earl S. "Wisconsin in 1847: Notes of John Q. Roods." *Wisconsin Magazine of History* 33:216–20 (Dec. 1949). Speculator looking at farm lands.

Robbins, Roy M. *Our Landed Heritage: The Public Domain, 1776–1936*. Lincoln, Nebr.: Bison Paperbacks, 1962. The standard work.

Rohrbough, Malcolm J. *The Land Office Business: Settlement and Administration of American Public Lands, 1789–1937*. New York, 1968. Appointments and procedures of the land office.

Smith, Alice E. "Caleb Cushing's Investments in the St. Croix Valley." *Wisconsin Magazine of History* 28:7–19 (Sept. 1944). A case history in northern Wisconsin.

————. *James Duane Doty: Frontier Promoter*. Madison, 1954. Up to his ears in land speculation.

Still, Bayrd. *Milwaukee, The History of a City*. Madison, 1948. Covers the early years of rampant speculation.

Whitaker, James W. "Wisconsin Land Speculation, 1830–1860: Case Studies of Small-Scale Speculators." Master's thesis, University of Wisconsin, 1962. The returns were modest.

Williams, Mentor L. "Philip Hone, Wisconsin Land Speculator." *Wisconsin Magazine of History* 33:479–84 (June 1950). Trials of an Eastern speculator visiting his Wisconsin holdings.

YANKEES
AND EUROPEANS
BUILD A STATE, 1830–1860

part four

Once started, the Americanization of the Wisconsin frontier was exceptionally rapid. Only 11,000 in 1836 when the territory was organized, the population rose to 31,000 in 1840, 305,000 in 1850, and 776,000 in 1860. While the older Lakes states, Ohio and Illinois, had drawn greater numbers of people, the Wisconsin growth was unchallenged in its rate, and even in absolute numbers it exceeded the 1840–60 increases in Indiana or Michigan. Aside from the well-advertised attractions of the newly opened land, the phenomenal growth owed much to the conjunction of two factors: the application of steam to inland transportation and the new scale of European immigration.

Steamboats were a familiar sight on western waters before 1840—they were running on the lower Mississippi by 1813, and the *Walk-on-the-Water* was launched on Lake Erie in 1818—but it took some years before steam vessels provided cheap, reliable transportation in significant tonnage to serve the growing commercial frontier at the western end of the Lakes. By the 1840s they provided a standard of speed and reliable scheduling not available earlier to the immigrant or land seeker. It was 1855 before the traveller would be able to reach Milwaukee from the Atlantic seaboard by rail.

The new standard of western transportation paralleled a remarkable increase in European immigration to the United States. The annual influx surpassed 100,000 for the first time in the 1840s and exceeded a quarter of a million in each of the six years 1849 through 1854. Wisconsin received a large part of this immigrant stream, which provided one-third of her 1850 population. But there was never any doubt of the economic and social dominance of the Yankees who made up a less conspicuous part of the flow of settlers moving on the Lakes.

Where did these people settle and why? The answers are interwoven with the patterns of land sales by the federal government, geography, topography, ethnic preferences, economic resources, and familiarity or lack of familiarity with the prevailing land laws. Once settlement was made, transportation became the central problem of the Wisconsin frontier. The presence of superior transportation facilities hastened settlement, but their absence retarded development as people moved inland from Lake Michigan and the Mississippi River. With the example of the highly successful Erie Canal before them, many Wisconsin pioneers saw canal-building as an answer to the problem of isolation, but it was to be the railroad that offered the better solution. Wisconsin missed the euphoric era of heavy public debt contracted for internal improvements by the older Lake states, then brought to a close by the panic of 1837. The railroad building boom of the 1850s, however, came at a high social cost.

The salient fact of Wisconsin pioneer experience was its variety. Some people pioneered in the comfort of middle class circumstances in a city or town, while others a few miles away endured hunger and uncertainty. These pioneers built a society divided along ethnic and religious lines, uneven in its rewards, and promising continuing disparity.

PATTERNS OF
SETTLEMENT

11

The United States in the 1840s and 1850s was very conscious of its new continental dimensions. Looking westward, Americans now saw beyond the Mississippi to the Pacific, and many even extended their vision to the Orient by way of a transcontinental railroad. Survey treatments of American history in these exciting decades are usually concerned with the annexation of Texas, the Mexican cession, the Oregon controversy, the California gold rush, the Mormon trek to the Great Salt Lake, the pioneers of the Oregon Trail, and the looming sectional struggle over extension of slavery into the new western territories. When we think of western pioneering in the period we are likely to picture the wagon trains gathering at Independence, Missouri.

Not many movies are made about Americans emigrating from Vermont to Milwaukee or about the 1,250,000 German immigrants who came to the United States between 1845 and 1860, moving by tens of thousands into the Mississippi Valley. Romance may be on the side of the Oregon Trail, but census figures favor the Erie Canal. The population of the United States almost doubled between 1840 and 1860, growing from 17,069,453 to 31,443,321, an 84 percent increase. The five Great Lakes states, from Ohio through Wisconsin, had a great absolute growth, from 2,924,728 to 6,926,884, a 137 percent increase. The very nominal increase of Vermont's population from 291,948 to 315,098 in the years from 1840 to 1860, while Wisconsin was growing from 30,945 to 775,881, gives us a notion of the mobility of population. As for the migration to California and Oregon, these two states plus Washington Territory numbered only 444,053 people in 1860, a little over half as many as Wisconsin.

Wisconsin's great competitors for American and European immigrants moving westward were her sister Lake states and Missouri, Iowa, and Texas. In numbers added, Wisconsin was behind Ohio, Illinois, and Missouri, but these all started from a larger 1840 base, and had a higher proportion of internal growth. The character of Wisconsin's population was established in these early years of growth: a high proportion of foreign born and of Americans of New England background.

A vital factor in Wisconsin immigration in this period was the Erie Canal. Completed in 1825, this great public work of the State of New York dominated passenger and freight traffic with the Lake states well into the 1850s. Ten separate railroad lines paralleled the canal to Lake Erie, but it was 1853 before they were linked together to form the New York Central. Railroads of the period were generally conceived as local enterprises to connect ambitious towns with their immediate hinterlands. There was no uniformity of gauge, and railroads did not usually exchange equipment, run upon one another's tracks, or use common terminal facilities. This made long-distance train travel more of an adventure than coming through by the slower water route. One finds advice to immigrants weighing the pros and cons of water or rail travel by the mid-fifties, when rail travel was feasible beyond Buffalo.

The Erie Canal and through the Lakes by sail or steam was the common route for those who peopled the cities and farmlands of Wisconsin and beyond. Milwaukee became the main port of entry. Visitors came to look and to wonder at this hustle of activity on a new frontier which could be viewed by a passenger on a steamer. Margaret Fuller visited Milwaukee in 1843, coming by a packet making scheduled sailings. These boats were new enough that arrivals and departures drew a good deal of interest from the townspeople. Milwaukee's explosive growth was something no visitor could miss. A village of 1712 persons in 1840, it counted 20,061 in 1850 and 45,246 in 1860. All was bustle, but of the new recruits arriving daily some were more easily noticed than others. Miss Fuller marked them at once: "The torrent of emigration swells very strongly towards this place. During the fine weather, the poor refugees arrive daily in their national dresses all travel-soiled and worn. . . . Here, on the pier, I see disembarking the Germans, the Norwegians, the Swedes, the Swiss. . . ."

The most conspicuous immigrants were these Continental Europeans, different in dress, language, and demeanor. The Yankee, on the other hand, was less visible. He was apt to come out alone to select his land before moving his family, and when he did return with his family, travelled light. He came as a homesteader to an area which to him was simply an extension of "back home." Other enterprising Americans would fill his requirements for tools and equipment across a store counter. By contrast, John Muir remembered that his father, like many other foreign home-seekers, brought luggage, including a beam scale and counterweights, wedges, carpenter's tools, and other heavy items readily available in Milwaukee. "At Buffalo, as if on the very edge of the wilderness, he gladly added to his burden a big cast-iron stove with pots and pans, provision enough for a long siege, and a scythe and cumbersome cradle for cutting wheat, all of which he succeeded in landing in the primeval Wisconsin woods." The credulity of the elder Muir, loading himself with more equipment at Buffalo, was matched by other immigrants, according to contemporary accounts. The German peasant in particular was apt to bring a tremendous kit, with the twin certainties that he was going into a wilderness and that Americans could never manufacture articles to suit his standards.

Despite the heterogeneity of her pioneer population, however, Wisconsin was a Yankee state. Milwaukee too, notwithstanding its beer gardens, shops with German signs, and authentic German culture, and the fact that by 1850 40 percent of its people were German-born, had its financial and political affairs firmly in the hands of the residents of Yankee Hill.

Wisconsin's population of 305,000 in 1850, about ten times that of 1840, divides rather neatly into three nearly equal groups: 103,000 from New England and Middle Atlantic states—the Yankees; 106,000 foreign-born, including 38,000 Germans, 9,000 Scandinavians, 21,000 Irish, and 28,000 English, Scots, and Welsh; and the remaining 90,000 made up of 63,000 Wisconsin born, 21,400 from the other Lakes states, and 5,500 southerners settled mostly in the lead region. In subsequent censuses the increase of the Wisconsin-born would obscure these origins.

There were a variety of reasons why Wisconsin became New England's frontier in this period. With a rapidly growing native population and a considerable influx of foreigners, New England had little desirable land for agricultural expansion. The small amount of prime land, in fact, was converting to intensive farming, while the rocky hillside farms began producing a surplus of young people who moved either to the growing industrial towns or westward. Vermont, which had sent 10,160 of her people to Wisconsin by 1850, was an example of New England's dilemma. She had a contracting agriculture and did not benefit much from the expanding markets of the coastal towns. Vermonters had already set up a significant migration pattern into Canada, but by 1820 the Erie Canal was diverting them into western New York and the Ohio shore along Lake Erie.

A familiar American phenomenon was taking place. As the wilderness was converted into farm land and brought into contact with growing markets by improved transportation, the price of the land went up, even as its production of pioneer grain crops fell. A period of serious readjustment ensued, while many of the younger, less advantageously located farmers pursued the cheaper, more productive lands to the west. Thus in 1850 almost one-fourth of Wisconsin's population—68,600—had come from New York, and a great many of these were transplanted New Englanders or their children. A large share of those from the other states of the Old Northwest had followed the same pattern and shared the same origins.

The Yankees arriving in Wisconsin had things well in hand. They knew the mechanics of public-lands surveys and sales, and often had a line of credit from back home to help them get started. They were the ones who took possession of townsites, waterpowers, and the best farm lands. They became the entrepreneurs, the speculators, the lawyers, the editors, the preachers, the merchants, and the politicians of the new communities. They even moved boldly into the lead region, the province of the southern Jacksonians. By the 1840s, the largest land speculators there were C. C. Washburn and Cyrus Woodman, both born in Maine, while Moses Strong of Vermont was a leading figure in politics.

The Yankees assumed their position of dominance without self-consciousness; they felt no sense of alienation on this frontier. They were of a generation which had seen other frontiers, in interior New York, Ohio, and Indiana, joined by road and canal improvements to the markets of the world. They had, perhaps, too much confidence in their ability to work the same transformation in the Wisconsin wilderness.

The Yankee settler was an activist. He expected his new wilderness home to be connected shortly with the world's markets, but he recognized that he would have to help it along with community and political action. He was ready to mortgage his own and the public domain for this purpose. The Yankee was impatient for success. He was less worried about what posterity would inherit than about his own rewards; posterity could look out for itself, very likely under easier circumstances. If success was elusive, he was not rooted in the soil he was working but readily sold out and sought luck's favor elsewhere. The most successful of pioneers, the transplanted Yankee knew how to handle the ax and other tools of land clearing. He shared in a tradition of progressive agriculture but readily adapted himself to the extensive farming methods of frontier wheat culture. It did not bother him to farm untidily among stumps. A practicing optimist, he always had his eye on what would be rather than what was. He easily imposed his institutions, ideas, and mores upon his new surroundings, for he assumed that he had never really left home. His European immigrant neighbors were all too conscious that they had.

The British immigrant, particularly the Englishman and Scot, was most readily assimilated to the dominant Yankee culture in pioneer Wisconsin. He was apt to have been in the States a number of years, and like the New Englander, transplanted readily. The British were less inclined to settle in ethnic enclaves and were more likely than other European immigrants to appear in the professions or as businessmen. But having generalized thus, one must note that the largest single British group was that of the Cornish miners in the lead region, an ethnic island, but readily assimilated to the surrounding population and to farming or small-town occupations. Probably 7,000 of the 27,000 British in Wisconsin in 1850 were these people from Cornwall.

The Scots were much like the Vermonters. Their land offered limited opportunity for an expanding population which was enterprising, aggressive, and relatively well educated. They shared a Calvinist emphasis upon education and work. Wisconsin, which was known to the Scots through the fur trade, attracted favorable notice.

The English were swept by many of the same enthusiasms which burned brightly in America. The British Temperance Emigration Society, organized by a group of factory hands in 1842 at Liverpool, bought land at Mazomanie and by 1849 had sponsored the emigration of 600 people. A similar organization, the Potters Joint Stock Emigration Society and Savings Fund, was founded in Staffordshire. The society held lottery drawings and sent the winners to prepared homesteads near Montello in Marquette County, with the hope that this would help to relieve chronic unemployment in the British potteries.

Many of the English were more concerned with their future prospects in England than with the opportunities of the American frontier:

. . . so long as they feel themselves wasting away from excessive toil and poisonous workshops; so long as they see infancy in rags, youth in decrepitude, manhood in graves, with the ever present prospect haunting the imagination like some frightful dream of blighted hopes, broken hearts and parish shells, they will fly—fly to the beautiful prairies of the fair west and the freedom of nature, to the most liberal institutions of present man, to the untaxed plains, rivers and lakes of a free country; they will abandon the loom for the spade; the factory for the farm; they will leave, with bounding hearts, this great 'unwieldy workshop of the world';—this slaughter house of human lives; with its steam, smoke, cinders and wheels; to pursue an unfettered life of happiness and content amid the varied scenes of nature and the handiworks of God.

It was characteristic that no one worried much about the colonists' lack of knowledge about farming. The land near Montello was poorly chosen and the potters lost the first blush of enthusiasm for their American venture as reports filtered back from the lottery winners. An undetermined number made the crossing, and eventually many became substantial Wisconsin farmers.

More typical English immigrants usually came as unobtrusive families and settled among the dominant Yankees. If, as some claimed, the English assimilated slowly, it was more an assertion of their heritage than because of any serious bars to their inclusion in the business and social life of Yankee society.

The Irish were the most easily identified of the English-speaking immigrants: they were poor, and especially they were Catholic. Yet many who came to Wisconsin had stopped along the way and were not strangers to American ways. Unlike the German and Norwegian, the Irish peasant did not yearn to get on the land and make a piece of American soil his own. Although many of the Irish did turn to farming, they shared the Yankee readiness to move on if the price were right or a move seemed to offer something better. They did not as consciously settle in separate ethnic communities as did the Germans and Norwegians, but in an urban setting they were often ghettoized by their poverty. The Irish were 14 percent of the population of Milwaukee in 1850, but less than 7 percent a decade later, when the city had more than doubled in size. The proportion of German-born held at more than one-third of the city's total. In any town that had been a center of construction work such as a plank road, canal, or railroad, the Irish were to be found, and many sought an urban setting where the church could reach them.

The Germans had a long tradition of emigration. Known as Auswanderers, German-speaking peoples migrated eastward down the Danube, into Catherine's Russia, and east of the Elbe and Oder rivers, as well as to North and South America. German intellectuals wrote much about the Auswanderer, and occasionally the German states worried over the problem, embarrassed by the complaints of Holland, Britain, and the United States about the unregulated nature of German immigration and the contemptible ineffectiveness of German governments. It is from this concern that the notion of founding a German state in America gained currency, but it was typical of German schemes of the time to end in impractical talk. We must remember that until the Bismarck era, Germany did not exist as a country or command national loyalty.

From 1830 to 1854 German immigration to America swelled to a flood. In 1830 there were just under 3,000 immigrants, and in 1854 more than 215,000, surpassing Irish immigration for the first time. Like the Irish, the Germans were widely dispersed in America and flowed readily into both city and countryside. Mississippi Valley cities acquired large German sections, and certain agricultural districts took on a markedly German character. Ohio, Indiana, Iowa, Missouri, and Texas attracted many, but Wisconsin, by the late 1840s, was a particular goal of this migration. The German-born population of Wisconsin rose from 38,000 in 1850 to 124,000 in 1860, amounting to 10 percent of the German migration to the United States in that decade. The flow continued until, by 1885, about one-third of Wisconsin's population was of German background.

The most careful student of German emigration finds it difficult to assign reasons for this outpouring of people. Americans liked to hear, and the immigrants liked to remember, that they came seeking religious or political freedom. The first Germans to come to Wisconsin as a group, a congregation of German Old Lutherans from Freistadt, arrived in 1839 and settled at Milwaukee and Mequon. There were about 500 of them, and their main purpose was to escape a controversy within the church in which they found themselves a minority. There were a number of German colonists, Lutheran, Catholic, and Hussite, who came to Wisconsin as groups, but the great majority emigrated by families for more prosaic reasons, reasons obscured by such popular phrases as *Kein König da,* "No king there." A generous interpretation of the phrase was that the German immigrant yearned for political freedom and self-expression. A less romantic reading was that German taxes and bureaucracy were burdensome. Only a small fraction of German immigration can be identified with the abortive Revolution of 1848, although Carl Schurz and his fellow emigrés made themselves legion through their literary efforts.

There was, of course, a push and pull effect at work in promoting immigration: there had to be reasons to leave and reasons to come. The economic reasons for leaving are the easiest to identify. As in England earlier, the old agrarian order was collapsing while a new industrial order was struggling to be born. Estimates are that the population, which had been stable for a century or so, doubled in northern Europe between 1700 and 1800 and was on a rising curve. It was noticed by contemporary bureaucrats and later students that the Germans who left in the years 1830 to 1846 were not the landless peasants and growing urban proletariat, but the taxpaying artisans from the towns and the small land-holders from the countryside. Rising food prices troubled the townsmen, and the trend toward consolidation of land in agriculture gave the ineffi-cient smallholder a chance to sell out.

Germany had what Friederich List called a "dwarf economy," one which could not support its growing population. The many internal bor-ders made commerce difficult, while the Zollverein, a customs union, opened the markets of an older, handicraft Germany to the products of the industrializing cities. The artisans and small landholders were ap-palled, in a class-ridden society, by the future they saw ahead for their children as a landless, urban proletariat. In this they had much in com-mon with their English contemporaries, except that the development of industry in the German states was well behind the English model, and a larger proportion of the urban proletariat were not working class but simply idle, impoverished, and unneeded. All that seemed to grow in the economy were the tax rate and the bureaucracy.

The first wave of German immigrants, lasting until about 1845, was made up of small farmers, shopkeepers, and artisans from the towns and countryside of Catholic Germany in the south. They felt themselves be-coming surplus, but had a landholding or shop to sell and made their escape. They wished to flee from an economy in which land and capital were dear while labor was growing cheaper.

The second wave, roughly from 1847 to 1855, rose to over six times the 1845 rate of 34,000, then subsided until the heavy immigration of the eighties. Landless peasants from Protestant east Germany, which had earlier gained from internal migrations, now joined in the emigration. In these agricultural provinces, the landlords tried to restrict the growing agricultural labor force by forbidding marriage, which they could do, since they controlled the households of their dependents. With an illegiti-macy rate of one in five and a growing surplus population, the landlords and their governments were ready to give covert or open support to the emigration of landless dependents. The growth of scheduled steamship runs on the North Atlantic, and of railroads both in Europe and Amer-ica, brought steerage rates down, although as late as 1856 over 96 per-cent of immigrants to American still came by sailing ships, mostly of American registry. German cities and employers subsidized the emigra-tion of their paupers and created scandals by sending what would today be classed as unemployables into the poorhouses of New York. German pride was hurt by the comments from abroad. Wisconsin received few of the paupers because of the expense of coming on to Milwaukee.

What, especially, attracted the Germans to Wisconsin? Wisconsin land was being placed on the market, making it a natural center of attention both here and abroad. The Germans had a great interest in America and in accounts of American travel; more than fifty books were published on the subject in Germany between 1815 and 1850, some written specifically for the emigrant and always in demand. Christian Ficker's *Friendly Adviser for All Who Would Emigrate to America and Particularly to Wisconsin* is an example, published in Leipzig in 1853 and written by an itinerant music teacher who lived at Mequon for a time. The so-called American letters from friends, relatives, and acquaintances who had already made the move were also widely circulated and influenced many.

A typical "American letter" was written in 1847 by Phillip Best, one of the founders of what became the Pabst Brewing Company, to his wife's family in Hessen-Darmstadt. He was urging them to make an early decision to come to Milwaukee, and his comments tell something of America's meaning for him after five years: "One beholds here how the farmer lives without worries, one seldom finds a farmer who doesn't have a newspaper in his house every week. . . . In Germany no one knows how to appreciate the liberty to which every human being is entitled . . . everyone [here] may express his opinion in accordance with his knowledge and judgment . . . here the officials and priests are dependent upon the people, and in Germany the people are dependent upon the officials and priests. The preacher's business is a poor trade here." Best went on to talk of Wisconsin's special attractions. The family business was growing, Wisconsin's agriculture was flourishing, and Milwaukee's vigor was enhancing the value of their property. Tax conscious as they were, it had not escaped the notice of the Bests that Wisconsin had missed the ruinous programs of internal improvements that had saddled some of the other Lake states with debt and high taxes after the 1837 panic.

The growing Lake cities, like Milwaukee, and the available water carriage route to the Atlantic seaboard were reassuring to the market-conscious Germans. The climate, soil, and topography of Wisconsin were congenial to both Germans and Scandinavians. Many shunned more southerly locations because of assumptions about the relations of climate to health. (Both European and American immigrants tended to move along lines of latitude.) As for available land, there was still government land to be had close to Lake Michigan in forested sections. After statehood, Wisconsin came into possession of a large acreage which it sold on liberal credit terms in an effort to realize a higher price per acre.

The Norwegians, who numbered only 8,600 in Wisconsin in 1850, became the second largest foreign-born nationality by 1900. We know of the Norwegian immigrants of 1830–60 that they usually came from a farming background and sought a place on the land here. They were likely to be poorer, but more likely to be literate, than Germans or Cornish. They were probably more clannish and parochial than either. Enthusiastic religious controversialists, the Norwegians brought this enthusiasm to a high point in the New World. The state church in Norway was controlled by the aristocracy—the urban, officeholding class looked upon as aliens by the rural population. There was a continuing struggle between the official church and an evangelical movement within the Lutheran faith that was largely lay in inspiration. Religion looms large in Norwegian emigration literature.

Nevertheless, the impetus for Norwegian emigration was mostly economic. Norway shared in the astonishing European population explosion that began sometime in the eighteenth century. The country's population of 883,440 in 1801 was almost tripled by 1905, despite the emigration of more than 500,000 during the period. By 1845, the population was close to double that of 1801, over 80 percent rural, and dependent upon an almost inflexible 4 percent of the land surface which was arable, much of that in meadow. We usually think of the Norwegians as primarily a fishing and seagoing people who developed considerable industry. Yet in 1865 only 5 percent of the people engaged in fishing and 10 percent in trade and transportation. Mining and manufacturing had not yet developed on any considerable scale. The pressure upon the available land was tremendous. Of the 1,328,471 people in 1845, only 77,780 were independent landholders, while the remainder of the great rural population was an ever-growing body of cotters, tenants, farm laborers, and servants almost in the position of serfs. Norway had never had a feudal system, but it had an aristocracy and a rampant class consciousness.

The Norwegians were very responsive to American letters and to books about America. The pied piper of their immigration to America was Cleng Peerson, who spied out the land for the first Norwegian colonists of the sloop *Restoration* in 1825. He subsequently penetrated to Illinois, which became the target of the Norwegians. Ole Rynning, who settled in Illinois, was another. Norwegians congregated in the Rock River valley and spread northward into Wisconsin. Until the 1860s, when they began to favor Minnesota, Wisconsin was the center of their settlement in America. Seventy percent of the Norwegians in the United States in 1850 lived in Wisconsin, and they continued to come.

The Norwegians were attracted to Wisconsin for much the same reasons as the Germans. It seemed more like their homeland, from descriptions, than rival lands in Illinois, Missouri, and Texas. They were parochial, and tended to settle in colonies representing their own districts and dialects in Norway, spreading up the Rock River and then across westward from Stoughton and Madison. The Norwegian consul-general from

New York toured the West in 1847 and reported his observations of his countrymen settled there, describing each Norwegian settlement in Wisconsin in relation to the districts from which the inhabitants came: "Koshkonong Prairie stretches northwest from Lake Koshkonong to about eight or ten miles from Madison. This settlement is the largest in Wisconsin, and numbers about four or five hundred families from Telemarken, Voss, and Numedal. It consists mostly of prairie with a little timber. Only a few of the Norwegians live on the prairies, which are mostly inhabited by Irish and Americans."

The Norwegians did not come from a tradition of progressive agriculture, but were raisers of small grains and potatoes. Having worked holdings of marginal lands at home, they were accustomed to heavy labor with meagre return, and took what land was left, including rough hills and even swamps, to turn into productive farms.

To their Yankee neighbors, Norwegians were at first among the least acceptable of the European immigrants. One of the best-known expressions of this was the comment of Marshall Strong in an argument about Negro suffrage in the territorial council. Blacks were more civilized and adaptable to American institutions, he declared. "He had seen Norwegians living without what other people would have considered the most absolute necessaries of life, burrowed so to say in holes in the ground, in huts dug in the banks of the earth." Strong's prejudices aside, the Norwegian immigrants' struggles with their new environment were at an elemental level.

Ole Rolvaag, author of *Giants in the Earth,* had a theory that one's personality was so bound up with his native language that the adjustment to a new one was a traumatic experience. Norwegian women, abetting their imported clergy, did their best to keep their children within the Norwegian community they had created in the New World. Rolvaag's story, with the figure of Beret, the wife and mother, is a powerful evocation of the sense of alienation which the European immigrant lived with in America. It was particularly difficult for the women, who often learned no English. They had a feeling of being between two worlds, one to which they could not return and another into which they lost their children without being able to follow.

Part of the sense of leaving the Old World forever grew from the rigors of a sail voyage in steerage. There are countless tales of this, all hard to grasp in our time when hazards have so changed. On the vessel which brought Thorstein Veblen's father to America, every child died. Another narrative tells of an American ship sailing out of Hamburg in 1867 with 544 German immigrants aboard. Delayed by headwinds, the ship went south to cross and had her passengers aboard for seventy days. Of the 544 souls, 105 died on the voyage and 3 in port. The grim statistics tell us little of the imprint such an experience had on those who survived.

Marcus Lee Hansen reminds us that contemporary European observers often described their emigrants as belonging to the "anxious classes," which does not suggest a bold or revolutionary temper. "The bulk of them merely hoped to preserve what they had—not alone of property, but a status in society which was uncertain at home." They did not come to change American society, but came with the belief that our system of government would facilitate the acquisition of property and protect them in its enjoyment.

Settlers meant improved lands, roads, schools, a growing economy, and taxpayers. Nativism was never more than a minor political faith in Wisconsin, even in the early 1850s when there was a Know Nothing presidential candidate. Wisconsin became the first state to establish an office for the purpose of encouraging foreign immigration. In 1852 this official was located in New York City to work with the agents of steamship and railroad companies.

Smaller nationality groups are represented in Wisconsin's rich ethnic mix, each with its own history and consciousness of its cultural heritage. The Swiss and Dutch, for instance, were represented in the 1850 census, but numbered only 1,244 and 1,157 respectively. Because of their tendency to clan together, these smaller groups set the tone for their communities and are significant factors in local elections. Wisconsin politicians still are close students of ethnic preferences and prejudices.

How did this mixed population of domestic and foreign immigrants assimilate on the Wisconsin frontier? Not easily and not quickly, to be sure. Marshall Strong's comment on the Norwegians is indicative. Many Yankees referred to them as "Scandihoovian Indians" and used similar terms of derision for the Irish and Germans. The Norwegians had the virtue, from their Yankee neighbors' viewpoint, of isolating themselves, but the Germans and Irish seemed always to be underfoot, the German asserting his cultural superiority and the Irishman exhibiting a precocious political skill.

The Irishman accepted the Yankee's world and studied its levers of political power. The German considered the Yankee a pious fraud who professed a horror of gambling but was a confirmed speculator, a public teetotaler who probably nipped at a bottle in private, and a Philistine with pretensions to a culture that had no Goethe or Schiller. The Norwegian nursed his pride in silence.

All learned the American art of compromise. Immigrant Catholic priests organized temperance societies among their congregations, and

Norwegian pastors rebuked their flocks for holding Sunday picnics. American nativists learned that intolerance of the foreign-born was politically hazardous, and all parties proposed a generous franchise while discovering the virtues of the balanced ticket. The standard to which the European immigrant in this new Eden trimmed was that of the dominant Yankee.

Selected Bibliography

Bayley, Calvin. "Western Trip." *Wisconsin Magazine of History* 37:237–39 (Summer 1954). Excesses of speculation in Milwaukee.

Billington, Ray Allen. *The Protestant Crusade, 1800–1860: A Study of the Origins of American Nativism.* Chicago: Quadrangle Paperbacks, 1964. Saving the West from the pope.

Blegen, Theodore C., ed. *Land of Their Choice: the Immigrants Write Home.* St. Paul, 1955. American letters.

———. *Norwegian Migration to America, 1825–1860.* The standard on early Norwegian migration.

"The Cities of Wisconsin." *The Wisconsin Blue Book,* 1958, pp. 149–63. Madison, 1958. Short sketches with some material on early settlement.

Cochran, Thomas C. *The Pabst Brewing Company: The History of an American Business.* New York, 1948. Philip Best's 1847 letter to his in-laws.

Curti, Merle. *The Making of an American Community: A Case Study of Democracy in a Frontier County.* Stanford, 1959. A path-breaking study.

Curtis, John T. *The Vegetation of Wisconsin.* Madison, 1959. A reconstruction of the pioneer vegetation.

Detzler, Jack, ed. " 'I Live Here Happily': A German Immigrant in Territorial Wisconsin." *Wisconsin Magazine of History* 50:254–59 (Spring 1957).

Foreman, Grant. "Settlement of English Potters in Wisconsin." *Wisconsin Magazine of History* 21:375–96 (June 1938). A colonization scheme.

Fuller, Margaret. "The Promise of Milwaukee." In Walter Havighurst, ed., *The Land of the Long Horizons,* pp. 286–89. New York, 1960. View from the Waterside, 1843.

Gregory, John. *Industrial Resources of Wisconsin.* Madison, 1855. A strange jumble of a book, but interesting.

Hansen, Marcus L. *The Atlantic Migration, 1607–1860.* Cambridge, Mass., 1940. Concerned with European backgrounds.

Haygood, William C., ed. "Featherstonhaugh in Tychoberah." *Wisconsin Magazine of History* 45:172–85 (Spring 1962). English geologist's view of Madison and the lead region in 1837.

———. " 'God Raised Us up Good Friends': English Immigrants in Wisconsin." *Wisconsin Magazine of History* 47:224–37 (Spring 1964). Letters from two London house painters who settled at Fond du Lac in 1849.

Lucas, Henry S., ed. "Reminiscences of Arend Jan Brusse on Early Dutch Settlement in Milwaukee." *Wisconsin Magazine of History* 30:85–90 (Sept. 1946). Came in 1846, didn't like Yankees.

MacDonald, Sister M. Justille. *History of the Irish in Wisconsin in the Nineteenth Century*. Washington, 1954. Irish were second only to the Germans in pre-Civil War immigration.

Muir, John. *The Story of My Boyhood and Youth*. Madison, 1965. Pioneer Scottish immigrant of 1849 to Portage.

Quaife, Milo M., ed. *The Movement for Statehood, 1845–1846*. Constitutional Series, vol. 1. Madison, 1918. Marshall Strong's remarks on the relative merits of Norwegians and free Negroes on page 95.

Sanding, Ruth Gladys. "The Norwegian Element in the Early History of Wisconsin." Master's thesis, University of Wisconsin, 1936. Useful supplement to Blegen.

Schafer, Joseph P., trans. and ed. "Christian Traugott Ficker's Advice to Emigrants." *Wisconsin Magazine of History* 25:217–36, 331–55, 456–75 (Dec. 1941, Mar. 1942, June 1942). Most popular of the early German guides.

———. *Four Wisconsin Counties: Prairie and Forest*. Wisconsin Domesday Book, vol. 2, Madison, 1927. On the southeastern Lakeshore counties and their settlement.

———. *The Winnebago-Horicon Basin: A Type Study in Western History*. Wisconsin Domesday Book, vol. 4, Madison, 1937. Made use of original land and census records.

———. *Wisconsin Domesday Book, Town Studies*. Vol. 1, Madison, 1924. Turned out to be the only volume; twenty-four representative townships.

Still, Bayrd, ed. "Milwaukee in 1836 and 1849: A Contemporary Description." *Wisconsin Magazine of History* 53:294–97 (Summer 1970). From speculation to growth.

Trovatten, Ole Knudsen. "The Trials of an Immigrant: The Journal of Ole K. Trovatten." Trans. and ed. Clarence A. Clausen. *Norwegian-American Studies and Records* 19:142–59. Northfield, Minn., 1955. A voyage from Norway to Milwaukee in 1842.

Walker, Mack. *Germany and the Emigration, 1815–1885*. Cambridge, Mass., 1964. The German background.

Wittke, Carl. *The Irish in America*. Baton Rouge, La., 1956. A general history, but with frequent reference to Wisconsin.

PIONEER LIFE

12

Diversities of location, topography, resources, and opportunity within reach of the general economy of the country provided Wisconsin with a great variety of pioneer experiences. While the urban pioneer of 1850 could settle in Milwaukee, a bustling city of 20,000 inhabitants offering the amenities available in older American cities, German immigrants a few miles away were grubbing stumps and living on the edge of subsistence. At a greater distance from Lake Michigan, pioneering could include neighboring Indians of an uncertain temper and a real sense of isolation.

For the agricultural settler, all locations were not equal. Joseph Schafer, in his studies of land ownership and settlement patterns, found the Yankee settlers in possession of most of the desirable land southwest of Milwaukee, stretching behind the towns of Racine and Southport. Here was the open prairie which was easily broken to crops, interspersed with hardwood groves for fuel, fencing, and lumber. Not only was it most readily put to crops, but it was also close to the Lake and the urban centers growing there. This was the land taken by the Milwaukee Union, an association of settlers to hold their squatter claims in the absence of an applicable preemption law. Not all of these squatters were farmers, however, nor were they on the land. Choice claims were rapidly "settled" by Yankee speculators attracted to the Milwaukee townsite and other

Lake ports. Americans assumed that a preemption claim was the inalienable right of every citizen—a speculative windfall for the frontier town dweller. It was a lure which brought many nonagricultural settlers to the towns and pineries of Wisconsin.

Many German immigrants went north of Milwaukee into the heavy hardwood forests of Ozaukee and Washington counties, not because they preferred the timbered land, but because the Yankees had taken up the more desirable land and held it for prices running from $5 to $10 an acre. The heavily forested land could still be had for the government price of $1.25 an acre and yet was within reach of Milwaukee and Lake Michigan. Like the Yankees, the Germans intended to be commercial farmers, but they were not as sanguine about the development of public improvements that would put them in communication with their markets from the interior. The Yankee pressed inland with confidence, breaking more land to the plow than he could efficiently farm. Such prairie farming cost more for fencing, firewood, lumber, work animals, and equipment.

The German farmer, in contrast, laboriously cleared his forested acres, lived modestly in his log house, and invested his money first in an ample barn in the Pennsylvania Dutch manner. Contemporary observers often commented that the German took better care of his livestock than the Yankee, who let them run loose and provided them with little winter shelter. As roads penetrated inland, the Germans followed, clearing the remaining forest land. Watertown, for instance, on the first important plank road, had a large German population at the time Carl Schurz moved there in 1855. The pattern of settlement was not unvarying, of course, as the Germans took advantage of the fact that the Yankees and Irish more readily sold out for a profit and moved on to new ventures.

As a Norwegian immigrant song goes:

> We had come from a national quarry
>   Of land claims we didn't know beans.
> So the Yankee would settle the prairie
>   While we clung to the woods and the streams.

A Norwegian government official was apologetic about the condition of his countrymen as he found them on the Wisconsin frontier in the 1840s. He wrote of their "native and habitual squalor" which their American neighbors disdained. They lived "in genuine chalet manner" resembling life in the temporary shelters in the upland pastures of their homeland.

The Norwegians were not the only pioneers who lived in one room log huts on the Wisconsin frontier. A majority of the settlers had to build their own shelters. Hardwood lumber, planked by hand or by waterpower, was relatively expensive, hard to work with, and heavy. Pine lumber was available along Lake Michigan fairly early, as Chicago and Milwaukee demand created a market, but the expense of more adequate housing and the temporary nature of improvements on a squatter's claim, before purchase was assured, put many settlers in a log house in their early years.

Much, of course, depended upon the kind of housing to which people had been accustomed and what prospects would allow. The mountain peasants of Norway had to be educated to the advantages of better housing than they had known. The American, ordinarily on better land, usually thought of a frame house, or even one of brick or stone, as soon as materials were available. The level of expectation, based upon the familiar, was sometimes amusing. William Paddock, a young Vermonter living near Taycheeda in 1848, complained to his relatives back home that "there is not stone enough on a whole farm to stone a well" and allowed that "if I ever get money enough I think I shall come back to Vermont and buy me a farm." Reality triumphed, and he stayed in Wisconsin.

An often-repeated story, in accounts of immigrant travel to America, is that of the family that bought passage through to its destination only to find slender remaining resources drained by extra demands which could not be refused. A Dutchman who was part of the large immigration of 1854 recounted several such occasions. A typical one occurred in Boston when the family claimed their tickets through to Milwaukee. "They weighed our baggage, and we were assessed $18 more than we had expected, which so depleted our purse that we felt downhearted. I cannot decide whether we were cheated; a few said we were not, but others insisted we had been swindled."

Immigration to the United States was a large if very disorganized business activity, and this Dutch traveler described the callous rapacity of people engaged in transporting and housing immigrants along the regular routes taken. Having paid the puzzling extra tolls assessed along the way, he reached Buffalo. "We still had to travel nearly a thousand miles, and I did not have enough money left to pay for a single night's lodging for my family." He had a windfall when the other passengers were so seasick on Lake Erie he was able to buy, for small change, enough food to see them through to Milwaukee. "What would become of us in this land of strangers?"

Pioneers were like soldiers. They enjoyed telling the recruits how rough things were before the latter arrived. Nonetheless, one gets a fair appreciation of the quality of pioneer life from such accounts. Elisha Keyes recalled the arrival of his family, in 1837, at the claim his father had taken as the first settler at what became Lake Mills. It took two days from Milwaukee by ox team after their journey from Vermont. The claim, on a waterpower, was over three miles from the nearest neighbor and fifteen from Watertown, then only a single log house and the beginnings of a sawmill. "After crossing the river we struck across the opening, with no road, not even an Indian trail, seeing no human being, nor even a shanty, until after dark, when we struck the present site of Lake Mills, where, near the lake, we found a floorless shanty shingled with a hay stack. In this we made ourselves as comfortable as we could." His father built a log house before the winter. The house and most of its furniture were of the crudest manufacture. As Keyes wrote, it took some spirit of adventure to embrace opportunity in "this splendid country. . . . They did not at first realize the hardships they would be obliged to undergo, the privations they would have to endure, and the many discouragements that were sure to meet them in every step of their progress. If they had, I believe many of them would have remained at home."

Settlement followed across southern Wisconsin along the routes pioneered by teams hauling lead to the Lake Michigan ports, then north into Columbia, Marquette, and adjacent counties in central Wisconsin, and next along the Mississippi north of Prairie du Chien. Twenty years after the Keyes family reached Lake Mills, the family of Warren W. Cooke, who has left us a similar memoir of a pioneering boyhood, arrived by wagon from Indiana to settle in a coulee in Buffalo County. They arrived in June, raised a large tent, and lived in it for three months while building a double log cabin. "The making of these cabins—their different parts, the doors, windows, the rough slabs of green oak timber used in the making of shingles for roofing, the chinking of space between the logs, the blue clay mud taken from the creek bed for plastering all cracks between logs—all stand out 'on memory's walls' today . . . you must bear in mind that the cheapest of everything that could possibly be put up with was necessary, for we had not the means to do better at that time."

Not everyone, of course, pioneered on a shoestring. This was especially true of professional and business people who came to the growing towns. It is apparent that the family of Dr. James Albert Jackson was comfortably provided for in Staffordshire, where his step-father was a physician. In 1852, they were so captivated by a pamphlet about Madison sent by a distant relative "that we soon afterward 'pulled up stakes,' and forty of us came to Madison in 1853–54." They came by steamer— not in steerage—to Philadelphia, and from there by train, stopping every night in hotels, to Milton, the end of the line out of Milwaukee. Life in pioneer Madison, Dr. Jackson recalled, "was free and easy, and people lived without a care. Prices were low and taxes nominal, board averaged

$2.00 a week, and livery keep for one's horse and buggy $1.50. Money was not plentiful, but we did pretty well with what we had. . . . We had foolishly brought with us hardware and other supplies for fitting up our household, which was a useless expenditure of time and money, for we found that we could buy here everything that we needed even then."

Life may have been free, easy, and without a care for people of his circumstance living in a growing town, but what Dr. Jackson did not notice was that wages averaged about $1.00 a day for laborers in town and 75¢ for farm work. Cash was scarce and there was a good deal of barter and paying in kind. We know that many agricultural settlers within a few miles of Madison remembered the early years as anything but free and easy. Still, not everyone who turned to farming came without resources to weather the lean early years. George Dow, a Scotsman who immigrated to New York City in 1830, was interested in a townsite near Madison, now Rockdale, and around 1838 sent his young brother-in-law to investigate. The scout, in the late evening light, stumbled around among the stakes of the prospective town on the deserted site. Dow instead bought a claim on Lake Ripley, near present Cambridge, and sent out a man with practical farm experience, which he did not have, to create a farm and build a house for Dow's growing family. The family arrived in May 1842 with Mrs. Dow, a city girl raised in Glasgow and a resident of New York City until this bucolic venture, sitting on the rear of the wagon with her baby, prepared to flee for their lives should the "terrible beasts," as she described the plodding oxen, turn upon them. Fortunately James Stark, the hired man who carved the farm from the wilderness, stayed with the family for the balance of his life.

Mr. Stark's letters to Dow give a picture of pioneering for the relatively affluent somewhat at variance with Dr. Jackson's. It is largely a reflection of the difference between 1841, when Stark arrived, and 1853, when Jackson's family found everything they needed at hand. Stark's letters are full of lists of common articles which Dow was to forward or bring with him. Stark used hired labor to build the house. It was evidently an ambitious structure, even though made of logs, for he spoke of buying flooring, which must have been sawn. But he could not find bricks for the chimney and disapproved of the common practice of running stovepipe directly through upper floors and the roof, as the neighbors did. Many of the things that Mr. Stark ordered from Dow in New York proved to be available in Whitewater, but the frontier prices affronted him. Shopping facilities were limited. Madison he described as a collection of eighteen log houses and not much as a market. Dr. Jackson found it, twelve years later, a town of probably 3,000. A good comment on urban real estate is included in Stark's advice to Dow: "You had better before you leave N. York if you possibly can turn your Harlam lots into cash, and turn your whole attention to your Farm." So much for the relative value of lots in Harlem and the future Lake Ripley Golf Course.

What was it like for most pioneers in their first cabin? The Edwin Bottomley family spent the winter of 1842–43 in a shanty made of the outer slabs of logs trimmed at the mill. They were in relatively settled surroundings in western Racine County, where mill lumber, bricks, and other materials were readily available. Bottomley had a two story brick house built the next year, but life in the slab shanty tried their resolve:

> . . . winter as sett in sooner than usuall and the ground is now covered with snow and the Frost is very keen and would be called very cold weather with you [his parents in England] our house is not one of the Best for keeping the snow out and frost for we get snown on in bed which [when it] is heavy weather and when we get up in a morning we have to pull our shoes off the floor by main force for they freez to the floor very soon with having nails in them. . . .

Such inadequate quarters often had to do double duty, for new pioneers were constantly arriving to stop with relatives or friends. Those who lived along the traveled routes learned to sell this hospitality, or hardened their hearts. Everyone complained of the cost of travel and especially of food and shelter. One pioneer mother of 1843 whose family came overland from Detroit by wagon, eighteen days on the road in November with four sick children, recalled stopping overnight with a family, and her tears when the woman of the house gave her children warm biscuit. "It was the first morsel, except one, that they had received without money, in five weeks." She next found herself and family left with her brother while her husband made his location and put up a cabin. He returned to find "there we were in a pile, three of us in one bed, and nine of us in a little shanty 12 × 14 feet in size." Two of her four children died of smallpox. The remainder of the family spent a cold and hungry winter. It was not only the immigrants who remembered the long trip and early years with something akin to wonder that they had survived.

Many of the settlers found it difficult to furnish bread for their families during the time before they had land cleared and crops to harvest. Elisha Keyes recalled prayerful meetings when they considered butchering their oxen and were at a loss to find credit. "I have seen my father with his head bowed low upon his hands, in deep thought . . . and when my mother attempted to rouse him by the inquiry, 'Joseph, what is the matter?' he would lift his head and say, 'Olive, I know not where we are to get provisions to live upon much longer.' " The fears and the windfalls were shared with the neighbors. One such windfall for the Keyes family was the appearance of suckers in their small stream in early spring. It became a popular joke, among those who had weathered the starving times together, "that they did not make an attempt for months to change their shirts, the fish bones sticking through and preventing such an operation."

Silas Seymour, another Yankee, spent a winter living alone in his crude cabin on his claim near Reedsburg, eating "Irish Bannocks" of his own manufacture. These were short cakes minus the shortening. "I have not been able to get any meat of any kind yet . . . I see some lonesome times," he wrote to his sister. Silas was from western New York; therefore his loneliness was self-imposed. Earlier in the year he had visited former neighbors from New York who had moved to Madison and found so many of his own kind that "it seemed as though we were in York State again—so many of us together that had recently come from there." Silas received a duty letter from the daughter of the house. "I am now seated with my pen in hand to fulfill my engagement made nearly 3 months since to you." While she addressed Silas as "Respected Friend," her message was direct. "I think it a pity for young men like you and him [another New York bachelor] to live alone where there is so many young ladies that would esteem it a privilege to be your company if only you would let them know you wanted them." The letter is a curious mixture of Victorian convention and Yankee directness. Silas ungallantly returned to Covington, New York, for a cook to improve upon his "Irish Bannocks."

Even those pioneers who came under relatively comfortable circumstances sometimes knew periods of short rations. The recollection of food or the want of it is a common feature in pioneer reminiscences. One of those more comfortable pioneers, Amherst Kellogg, emigrated as a boy with his family from Canaan, Connecticut, in 1836. They were a large family with uncles who had gone ahead to investigate, place land claims, and settle before the others came on, and Amherst's father was able to set up in business immediately as a contractor in Milwaukee. Amherst remembered that they lived pretty well on arrival, but recalled that "the winter of 1837–38 was a very hard one for Wisconsin; for most of the people, potatoes and salt were the only diet, and for many it was hard to get even these." He was particularly struck by the expedient of one of his uncles, who served raw turnips in the evening, with a case knife, in lieu of the customary New England apple.

It might be assumed that pioneering meant learning to live off of the country, but Elisha Keyes remembered that "the early settlers were not good huntsmen, nor expert fishermen. They had to learn these high arts by practice. . . . It was a long time before any white man proved himself smart enough to shoot a deer. . . . There were deer in great abundance, prairie chickens, partridges, ducks and geese." The Norwegian consul observed that "wild game is found almost everywhere in Wisconsin. . . . As yet the Norwegian settlers pay little attention to hunting, because they have no time; but they have learned here what they hardly understood at home, to make use of wild game." An Englishman from the industrial midlands, James Jackson, was drawn to hunting immediately, even though he was a townsman in America as in England. Game, in pioneer accounts, was often something received from Indian neighbors who liked bread in exchange.

If the pioneer diet seems sometimes meagre and often wanting in variety, the answer is that it certainly was. Both Yankees and Europeans made the trip to the frontier on a diet of salt pork, dried peas, flour, and meal. These, and potatoes, turnips, and other root crops, were usually all that their established neighbors had to sell or lend them during the lean season while they were getting started. The American pioneer kept hogs and cattle but did not expect a cow to produce into the winter. In winter he missed the foods that gave his diet variety, especially apples and other fruits that took years to establish in a new country.

Pioneering added to the already considerable health hazards of the time. The practice of medicine and the regulations for public health were at a low level in the half century before the Civil War. Medical practice was in a state of near anarchy in which anyone could practice who felt a call. No form of charlatanry seemed too blatant. The broader movement of people scattered epidemic diseases readily, and the growing cities had few methods of defense. Rural America was a healthier environment in these years. Pioneering also added the hazards of inadequate housing and diet, the problems of adapting to a new climate and environment, sanitary facilities that were rudimentary or less, and men working with stock and with awkward, often unfamiliar tools.

Illness and death were constant companions on the journey to the frontier. These hazards were by no means confined to the European immigrants, who faced a long sea voyage. Before the completion in 1853 of a railroad link of sorts as far as Chicago, the trip from New England to Wisconsin commonly required about a month, and it took its toll, particularly of children and older people. Many accounts of such trips mention sickness along the way and rumors of smallpox, typhoid, and cholera. Cholera, the most frightening of epidemic diseases because of the swiftness of its onset, the agony of its sufferers, and the high mortality rate, was no stranger on the Wisconsin frontier. General Scott's troops brought it from Detroit to Chicago during the Black Hawk War, and it occasionally reached epidemic proportions in the Upper Midwest. The cities were struck the hardest. Milwaukee was visited by particularly severe outbreaks in 1849 and 1850. The Milwaukee *Sentinel,* in 1849, reported 209 cases with 105 deaths. The season of 1850 was more severe, with over 300 deaths recorded. The Chicago and Milwaukee papers tried to minimize the severity of local epidemics, while giving full publicity to the misfortunes of the rival city.

The authorities often blamed the immigrants for bringing the cholera, but it was nearly nationwide in epidemic years. Most of these epidemic diseases were associated with unsanitary conditions, and the growing cities offered a fertile field. The central district of Milwaukee developed a rudimentary sewerage system after 1845, but the residential districts were without even this service. Most homes had privies, and water came from private wells. The *Sentinel* was agitating for a unified sewerage system, based upon brick and pottery construction, in 1858, when the facilities which existed were shallow wooden pipes maintained by the street commissioners of the individual wards. It was 1869 before such a unified system was begun, under a board of public works, in the city of 70,000 people.

Hogs ran loose in Milwaukee's residential districts until the time of the Civil War. Efforts to control this nuisance were resisted by people who argued that the hogs were efficient street cleaners and a cheap source of meat for the city's poor. Opponents argued that the animals sometimes grew mean, were a hazard to children, and that no one ever owned a dead hog.

Medical opinion held that most diseases resulted from natural environmental and climatic conditions. For some years the Army Medical Corps gathered detailed weather information and descriptions of the topography, water, soil, timber, minerals, and air circulation around military posts, with the idea that some truths about disease control would emerge. Translated into common terms for the settler, this meant that some locations were more hazardous than others, although there was much leeway for conflicting opinions. Much depended upon the ability of the settler to become acclimatized to his new surroundings. If the newcomer managed to raise a few boils and experienced some diarrhea, these were looked upon as favorable signs of his adjustment.

Malaria was endemic throughout much of the Upper Midwest, including Wisconsin. The fevers accompanying bouts of the disease were so common as to account for the expression, "He ain't sick, he's only got the ague." Wisconsin was considered somewhat less subject to fevers than areas further south with longer summer seasons, but the settlers certainly had their share. Malaria offered great variety in its symptoms but was often very regular in its characteristic chills and fevers, which people learned to bear stoically and joke about. Sickness was a normal part of the turn of the seasons. Many pioneer letters contain detailed descriptions of the illnesses of family and neighbors. Death was a familiar visitor.

Pioneer life was difficult for women and children. Women in rural homes were fortunate to have in attendance a midwife with any knowledge of her calling. Children were raised, not reared, weaned by the almanac, and put on a diet of salt pork and cornbread at an early age. Life insurance companies had little interest in children: a pioneer Milwaukee company set its age limit at fourteen. Women were conceded the right to fits, vapors, or spells, but were expected to carry on.

The state of the medical fraternity was as low as the knowledge of matters of public health and personal hygiene would imply. The profession enjoyed no particular respect nor advantages of income. One Wisconsin practitioner reported his cash earnings for one year as $68. A young German doctor with a superior medical education for the time set up practice in Madison in 1855 and soon had a clientele. He was distressed, however, by the state of his profession:

> Of one thing though I must complain & justly; that is: of the lack of courtesy and attention among members of the Profession. I know as yet only one Physician here (except by sight) who was courteous enough to call on me. The cause of this rude treatment in the profession lies in the mixed character of its members and the comparatively low estimate in which society holds them; which gives equal standing to the quack & the charlatan, to the Homeopathist & Hydropathist with the scientific & phylosophic physician. The population here consisting largely of Yankees who are acceptable to all *isms* accounts for this fact, deplorable as it is.

It was a day of heroic remedies. Bleeding and calomel were standards, like "bake in a well greased pan." It was not always easy to bleed a patient who had a faint pulse and could not raise his head from the pillow, but doctors were resolute. The patient had to be pretty low before the doctor was called, even at 50¢ or $1.00 a call. Home remedies were readily traded and tried, and their efficacy was judged by the taste. Measles, for instance, called for "nanny tea" made with sheep dung. An account of the treatment, described by Dr. H. B. Willard of Jefferson County, of a case of typhoid fever in a boy of three, tells why the homeopath's patients at least had an opportunity to die of the disease while the patients of traditional physicians died of the cure:

> Willard made his diagnosis December 1, 1850, and prescribed calomel,

rhei (rhubarb extract), and soda every three hours, until a "brisk operation was produced," then camphor, ipecac, opium and soda. On December 4, the patient's head "appeared much affected, would roll it on
pillow and screem. Kept his hands on it." Willard blistered the nape of
his neck, applied mustard cataplasms upon the ankles, and prescribed
balsam, camphor, and turpentine internally. On the 5th he administered more calomel, blistered the right side of the child's abdomen, and
prescribed more balsam and turpentine. Two days later he prescribed
castile soap and rhei every three hours and turpentine and balsam between. He kept up approximately this same treatment until December
10, then "Blistered behind each ear. Mustard poultices to the ankles."
He continued the balsam and turpentine, and on December 12 administered ten grains of calomel. A few days later he gave the boy an enema.
Despite the heroic treatment the child recovered and by mid December,
Willard released him.

Loneliness was the most common pioneer complaint, and even the
Yankee from New England or western New York on occasion felt himself cut off from family, friends, and familiar surroundings. This feeling
was more acute among the European immigrants, who despite their tendency to flock together in communities representing their own district
and dialect, were in a stranger world than the Yankee. Obviously, for
most of them, the feeling that they had exchanged the dear and familiar
for a life of hardship was transitory. These were the people who wrote
the "American letters" which brought a continuing flood of their countrymen to share the hardships and opportunities.

Wisconsin pioneers belonged to a religious generation for whom the
church or meeting was first among the institutions fostering a sense of
community in new surroundings. Silas Seymour caught this spirit perfectly
in a letter written to the folks at home in Covington, New York:

> As for the *Society* in Baraboo—there is *none* yet. When I left there was
> not a house between my place and Reedsburg (a distance of 4½ miles).
> East and North there were folks one mile off. They have Christian
> meetings at Reedsburg one in two weeks; Methodist meetings in Butter-
> field's Settlement (5 miles off) once in four weeks. No school in the
> town (18 miles long and 9 wide) but there will be soon—several—as
> the inhabitants (except a few Irish) are "York State folks" and they
> won't live long without schools and meetings.

Wisconsin was an important mission field, particularly for the New
England churches. It was settled during a period of enthusiastic revival-
ism when young men at Yale, Amherst, Dartmouth, Williams, and And-
over felt a call to carry the gospel to new fields. The Methodist Church,
which was particularly successful on the frontier because of its use of a

lay clergy and a more comfortable theology, was a formidable antagonist for the American Home Missionary Society, organized jointly by the Congregational and New School Presbyterians in New England to save the West from error and worldliness. "The East must mold the new West, or the West will soon mold the East" was their theme. The Society supported, in part or in full, ministers who would accept a call to this mission field, and many of the men subsidized became memorable pioneers of their churches in Wisconsin.

These subsidized missionaries found what they were looking for: a worldly, secular, backslid, selfish, and materialistic society badly in need of reformation. Typical was a report from Racine, certainly a Yankee stronghold in 1844. The minister had spent his Sabbath morning counting the teams going by, presumably not to church, listening to a sportsman's gun, the village grist mill running, hogs being butchered within range of his meeting, and a tavern nearby, owned by a rival preacher of the Christian Church, that operated even while the owner was off spreading the Word. People simply broke away from old social restraints, it was claimed, and they had to be reached before they took Christian civilization down with them.

These enthusiastic endorsements of the drawing power of Mammon in the West must be taken with a grain of salt. A man who has traveled a thousand miles to fight Sin should not be disappointed by his antagonist nor should he disappoint his sponsors. But any reading in pioneer letters soon gives the impression that the average Yankee brought his religion with him and was ready to be churched. One also gathers that many husbands commonly allowed their wives to carry the burden of the vocal requirements of religion. Men shrank from the public spectacle of confessing a conversion experience, which often was expected. They were nonetheless regular in their support of and attendance at church.

Preaching, like medicine, offered an outlet for those with professional ambitions, and in some churches, notably the Methodist and Baptist, required a minimum of preparation. Silas Seymour, who felt such a call, asked advice of his uncle in Aztalan. "There is now a surplus of teachers and preachers in Wisconsin," the uncle replied," and many that are preparing. I heard a gentleman say he thought we should have to organize a missionary society and send some of them away. My judgment is, there is a lack now of these that are well qualified."

The school was the second institution that helped to draw a pioneer society together, often appearing almost simultaneously with the church. Jorgenson, in his history of early public education in Wisconsin, observes that "the early school legislation is evidence of a strong sentiment in favor of free schools in Wisconsin, but it is not in the laws that their origins are to be found. The most striking fact about early education in Wisconsin is that the movement for free schools was essentially a local one. Tax-supported schools were not created by territorial legislation; it would be much nearer the truth to say that they developed in spite of such legislation." Among the Yankee settlers, schools were commonly supported by informal cooperation before a district was organized. Organization often grew out of a desire to build a schoolhouse, although this was frequently accomplished without formal taxation.

The church and school were equally central to the German and Norwegian ideas of community. Both institutions, however, were the center of forces tending to oppose the processes of assimilation and to serve the separateness of the immigrant group. The Catholic Church, containing both the Irish and a large body of the German immigrants, had the more difficult task of serving both its national constituencies—which would grow in variety—and its traditional parochial school program.

It is not easy to characterize the emerging pioneer society. While Warren Cooke was enjoying the wilderness of western Wisconsin in which his family had settled in 1856, still twenty-five miles from their market and five from the nearest grocery in 1860, Milwaukee was a city of over 45,000, and the interior towns of Watertown and Madison had between 5,000 and 7,000. In 1847, Milwaukee merchants agreed to close their stores at 8:00 P.M., about two hours earlier than had been the custom in the busy season. The editor of the *Sentinel* saw, as a result of this, the need for organizing a Young Men's Association to assure the proper use of the new leisure. Leisure was no problem for other pioneers.

Watertown was a fair example of the small city which is still so characteristic of Wisconsin. Germans were in the majority, but the town had a fair share of the Yankee element and the Irish. It maintained both an Irish and a German Catholic Church, each with its own parochial school system. Two German Lutheran congregations maintained separate school systems also. In addition to these churches there were Methodist Episcopal, Congregational, Episcopal, and Calvinist Methodist churches for the Yankees, and German Methodist Episcopal, Moravian, German Baptist, German Adventist, Evangelical Reform, and German Protestant churches for the Germans.

Lodges and other organized societies in pioneer Watertown were also split along national and religious lines. The Odd Fellows organized in 1848 as a single group, but by 1854, "after national dissensions caused a rupture," the Germans organized their own chapter. The Irish Catholics organized St. Bernard's Temperance and Benevolent Society in March 1867. The German Catholics, in July, answered with St. Henry's Benevolent Society, which incidentally put the Germans on record as favoring temperance.

Watertown, like Wisconsin pioneer society in general, was an aggregation of separate but not equal social groups. The Yankees occupied seats of economic and political power, even in a community with an immigrant majority. Yankees controlled the mill sites until after the Civil War and were the entrepreneurs who built a farm machinery plant, woolen mill, wagon factory, and large cooperage works. A leading political and business figure of the town was Irish-born Patrick Rogan, who had come to Canada as a boy and lived for twelve years in northwestern New York before coming to Watertown. The names in the roster of local elected officials make it plain why Carl Schurz was influential in the state, as a candidate of the developing German political bloc, but had modest political strength in his home town. Until about 1860 the Germans controlled few local offices. Watertown, from the early fifties, was as heavily German as Milwaukee, but the Germans were similarly divided by religious and geographical differences brought from the homeland.

There were many centrifugal forces in pioneer Wisconsin working to keep it a fragmented society. Strong national groupings, languages, religions, mutual prejudices, American nativism, the temperance crusade, disagreements over the franchise, economic and social discrimination—all of these, and other influences, were divisive. They were to present a real test of Wisconsin's political and social institutions and American instincts toward accommodation.

Selected Bibliography

Ackerkneckt, Erwin, H. *Malaria in the Upper Mississippi Valley, 1760–1900*. Baltimore, 1945. One of the endemic diseases there.

Blied, Benjamin J. *Three Archbishops of Milwaukee: Michael Heiss (1818–1890), Frederick Katzer (1844–1903), Sebastian Messmer (1847–1930)*. Reprints of articles from *Salesianum*.

Burmester, Ruth Seymour, ed. "Silas Seymour Letters." *Wisconsin Magazine of History* 32:88–99, 328–38, 456–71 (Dec. 1948, March 1949, June 1949). A New York bachelor in the wilds of Wisconsin.

Cooke, Warren W. "A Frontiersman in Northwestern Wisconsin." *Wisconsin Magazine of History* 23:281–303 (March 1940). A pioneer boyhood.

Cross, Whitney R. *The Burned-Over District: The Social and Intellectual of Enthusiastic Religion in Western New York, 1800–1850*. Ithaca, N.Y., 1950. For an understanding of Wisconsin's native Americans.

Davenport, Garin and Katye Lou, eds. "Practicing Medicine in Madison,

1855–57: Alexander Schue's Letters to Robert Peter." *Wisconsin Magazine of History,* 26:79–91 (Sept. 1942). He found a lack of professionalism in pioneer medicine.

Gjerset, Knut, trans. "An Account of the Norwegian Settlers in North America." From a report by Consul General Adam Lovenskjold. *Wisconsin Magazine of History* 8:77–88 (Sept. 1924). About Norwegians settled around Lake Koshkonong.

Hansen, Marcus Lee. *The Immigrant in American History.* ed. Arthur M. Schlesinger. Cambridge, Mass., 1940. Essays on the immigrant.

Harris, Walter. *The Story of Medicine in Wisconsin.* El Paso, Texas, 1958. Not worth taking from the shelf.

Harstad, Peter T. "Disease and Sickness on the Wisconsin Frontier: Malaria, 1820–1850." *Wisconsin Magazine of History* 43:83–96 (Winter 1959–60).

———. "Smallpox and Other Diseases." *Wisconsin Magazine of History* 43:253–63 (Spring 1960).

———. "Cholera." *Wisconsin Magazine of History* 43:203–20 (Spring 1960). From his Ph.D. dissertation, "Health in the Upper Mississippi Valley, 1820–1961," University of Wisconsin, 1963.

Jackson, Alice F. and Bettina, eds. "Autobiography of James Albert Jackson, Sr., M.D." *Wisconsin Magazine of History* 28:20–36, 197–209, 325–50 (Sept. 1944, Dec. 1944, March 1945). The English family that came to Madison in 1853.

Johnson, Peter Leo. *Crosier on the Frontier: A Life of John Martin Henni.* Madison, 1959. First bishop of Milwaukee, 1843.

———. *Stuffed Saddlebags: The Life of Martin Kundig, Priest.* Milwaukee, 1942. Missionary companion of Bishop Henni.

Jorgenson, Lloyd P. *The Founding of Public Education in Wisconsin.* Madison, 1956. Pioneers and the school.

Kellogg, Amherst W. "Recollections of Life in Early Wisconsin." *Wisconsin Magazine of History* 7:473–98 (June 1924). Pioneering in the city.

Kennedy, Charles J. "The Congregationalists and the Presbyterians on the Wisconsin Frontier." Ph.D. dissertation, University of Wisconsin, 1940. The American Home Missionary Society subsidized ministers on the frontier.

Keyes, Elisha W. "Early Days in Jefferson County." *SHSW Collections,* vol. 11, pp. 416–36. Madison, 1888. The family that settled Lake Mills.

Kleppner, Paul. *The Cross of Culture.* New York, 1970. Ethnic and religious differences and politics.

Krueger, Lillian. "Motherhood on the Wisconsin Frontier." *Wisconsin Magazine of History* 29:157–83, 333–46 (Dec. 1945, March 1946). It was a man's world.

Leonard, Richard D. "Presbyterian and Congregational Missionaries in Early Wisconsin." *Wisconsin Magazine of History* 24:263–82 (March 1941). Westerners wouldn't stay put to be churched.

Lucas, Henry S., ed. "The Journey of an Immigrant Family from the

Netherlands to Milwaukee in 1854." *Wisconsin Magazine of History* 29: 201–23. Victimizing the immigrant.

Mathews, Edward. "An Abolitionist in Territorial Wisconsin: The Journal of Reverend Edward Mathews." *Wisconsin Magazine of History* 52:3–18, 117–31, 248–62, 330–43 (Autumn 1968, Winter 1968–69, Spring 1969, Summer 1969). A stern foe of sin.

Nelson, E. Clifford, and Eugene L. Fevold. *The Lutheran Church Among the Norwegian Americans.* 2 vols. Minneapolis, 1960. Sources are thin before 1860.

Paddock, William. "William Paddock Letters—1848." *Wisconsin Magazine of History* 33:87–91 (Sept. 1949). The Vermont boy who wanted rocks on his farm.

Pickard, M. E., and R. Carlyle Buley. *The Midwest Pioneer: His Ills, Cures, and Doctors.* Crawfordsville, Ind., 1945. Dedicated to "The Pioneer Doctor who boldly faced the wilderness; and to the Pioneer who Bravely Faced the Doctor."

Quaife, Milo M., ed. *An English Settler in Pioneer Wisconsin: The Letters of Edwin Bottomley, 1842–1850. SHSW Collections,* vol. 25. Madison, 1918. Escape from England's satanic mills.

Shepperson, Wilbur, ed. " 'The Natives are Grasping': A Welshman's Letter from Wisconsin." *Wisconsin Magazine of History* 43:129–32 (Winter 1959–60). Welsh tenant farmers found success in America.

Townsend, Georgia Dow, ed. "Letters of James Stark, 1841–1842: Friend and 'Most ob. Servant.' " *Wisconsin Magazine of History* 33:197–215 (Dec. 1949). Pioneering by proxie.

THE
PIONEER ECONOMY:
OPPORTUNITIES

13

Optimism was the key to the Yankee approach to the Wisconsin frontier. The journey there and the hard early years may, on occasion, have introduced a note of caution into their letters home, but the constant theme was of the possibilities for a "hardy, enterprising, self-denying, economical and industrious people," to use Silas Seymour's phrase. The European immigrant was often more somber in his appraisal. Edwin Bottomley, writing from his frontier farm to his former workmates in an English textile mill, put his expectations as hopes:

> Dear Freinds and fellow workmen you may wish to know how I like this cuntry for myself I like [it] very well and the more I Persever I shall like [it] Better you must be aware that a new Settler in this cuntry as to strugle with Difficulties but hopes of future reward (*which can not be realized in a cuntry wher Labour the sorce of all Real wealth is troden under foot By Monopoly Taxation and Oppression*) gives him strength to Persever I do not expect to realize a great fortune here But I do hope to place myself in circumstances on Day or another so that I can see my children smileing around me in contentment and be able to assist theire parents in theire Declining years and sooth the pillow of afliction. . . .

The note of opportunity assured was normally the possession of the dominant Yankee group, although it was communicable to the others. As for

179

really optimistic ardor, this belonged to the frankly speculative Yankee who had access to capital or credit.

The wish was often father to the thought. There were, indeed, water-powers and timber in abundance to be exploited, if not the assured fortunes anticipated by the most sanguine. Even lots in the Milwaukee townsite—as close to a sure thing as one can perceive in retrospect—had their bad times, and many opportunities proved less substantial. A glance at an early gazetteer will show that the townsite promotions far outran the realistic opportunities. This exuberance of expectation was expressed in many directions. James Doty and others supported comprehensive canal schemes based upon very dubious assumptions about terrain and stream flow. It was a common article of faith that Wisconsin harbored copper mines, "probably the richest in the world, and apparently inexhaustible," with iron ore equally abundant and easily worked. These expressions of faith in the extent of prime soils and the presence of mineral riches within easy reach have been associated with almost every American frontier. Wisconsin even had an oil boom in 1865–66. Sparta, a town of 1300 in 1866, supported a dozen companies allegedly engaged in petroleum exploration.

The combination of seemingly limitless opportunity, a chronic shortage of cash and credit, the high cost of labor and materials, and an abundance of resources awaiting development influenced the Yankee pioneer to applaud any economic activity that converted abundant resources into capital. Rather than a laissez-faire view of the role of government, the Yankee accepted the idea that any contribution that government could make to the release of economic energies was a good policy. The most obvious contribution was the conversion of public lands, which government owned in abundance, into capital for public works. The various land grants for canals and railroads in Wisconsin, eventually more than one-tenth of the state's total land area, were welcomed. Such direct subsidies for extensive public improvements were a common demand of the West.

The same prodigal disregard for future deployment of resources characterized the popular attitude toward poaching timber from public lands or claiming waterpower sites as agricultural preemption claims. The timber poacher sold the product or converted it into buildings and fences. If the squatter on a waterpower site did as Elisha Keyes' father did and converted it into a mill to serve his neighbors, there were few to begrudge him his claim. An immigrant from an economy of scarcity had a problem of adjustment. An English homesteader at Mazomanie marveled at his own prodigality. Logging on government land for timber for his house, he wrote: "The oaks I have cut down for the purpose would bring

£700 in England at 2/6 [2 shillings 6 pence] per cubic foot, for I cut a tree 40 or 50 feet long and just take the butt length off, and leave the rest for the prairie fires."

The problems of building an economy in an environment of abundant natural resources and scarce resources of capital and labor had some positive social implications. The Yankee pioneer, whose nativist tendencies were particularly heightened at this very time by the flood of European immigrants in his midst, found himself welcoming the immigrant for the muscle and gold he brought to the common task of subduing nature and building a community. The neighbor down the road might be a foreigner and a Papist, but he needed a road, could be taxed for a schoolhouse, and would support a subsidy for a canal or a railroad. All in all, he made a better neighbor than an absentee speculator.

The great cash crop of this frontier was wheat, which meant that farmers on the prairie lands and oak openings of Racine and Kenosha counties, and the Rock River Valley in the interior, were caught up in commercial agriculture from the first. The man trying to put 160 acres under the plow, with clearing and fencing to do, turned naturally to grain which was so well suited to an extensive, relatively careless style of farming. Wheat stored well and commanded a cash price at the Lake ports. For a few years in the 1860s, before grain culture swept westward, Wisconsin was the leading wheat-producing state.

The great disadvantages to this frontier wheat-farming were in the harvesting and getting the grain to market. Wheat ripens all at once, and the farmer has only a matter of days to get it cut and gathered before it begins to shatter. The grain farmers of biblical times would have recognized many of the tools and techniques of the wheat farmers of the Wisconsin frontier. Wheat was cut with a scythe, gathered, bound by hand, and stored in the shock to be threshed, cleaned, and hauled later. With labor short, the farmer often found himself with acres of wheat scattering on the ground, while the tools at hand limited him to cutting two or three acres a day. Other hands were needed to gather and shock it. Wheat culture provided work for new arrivals but not an abundance of cash to pay them.

The combination of its strategic location and the commitment of its pioneer agriculture to wheat put Wisconsin into the developing farm-machinery industry. Early inventors naturally addressed the troublesome problems of cutting, gathering, threshing, and cleaning the grain. On his farm near Janesville in 1844, George Esterly was tinkering with what may have been the first successful American harvesting machine. Jerome I. Case had established the J. I. Case Company at Racine in 1847 to produce his improved threshing machines. Esterly went on to perfect other machines and was manufacturing binders and mowers at his plant in Whitewater before the Civil War. After years spent in tinkering, a Wisconsin man perfected the standard twine binder.

The experimental temper of the times is suggested by a letter of John Greening's in 1847 to relatives in England, from his newly established home near Mazomanie. His observations concerned the unfamiliar in flora and fauna as well as his Yankee neighbors' curious habits. "Wheat is trod out upon the ground with oxen, except in some cases where they get a travelling machine, it is about as long as our English wagon, and the wheels that bear the machine along, work it. It is drawn by 4 or 6 oxen. They put on the front part of the machine about half a wagon load of sheaves and one man feeds it, while another takes the reins and drives around the fields." Here was custom threshing available on a remote frontier, as an alternative to the biblical ox treading the grain. Frontiers demand technical boldness and have traditionally been receptive to new technologies.

Given the economics of pioneer transportation, it is surprising that wheat culture advanced so rapidly into interior Wisconsin. In 1850, Rock County had more cultivated acres than Racine and Kenosha counties combined; most were devoted to wheat, despite the sixty- to one-hundred-mile haul to Lake Michigan. The farmers' eagerness for improved transportation is made manifest by considering his hauling problems. Assume a Rock County farmer with a crop of 500 bushels of wheat from 25 acres yielding 20 bushels an acre. These are close to average figures for the time, on new wheat land. Acreage was increased steadily, but yields declined as farmers cropped the same land. Assume a haul of sixty miles to Racine. Twenty-five bushels of wheat weigh 1,500 pounds, a heavy load for a team on roads which were only traces in many areas. But assume travel conditions allowed him to make twenty to twenty-five miles a day. The round trip required five to six days under these conditions. Twenty such trips would be needed to market his grain crop. The price of grain at the port towns ranged from a low of 44¢ to a high of 90¢ a bushel during the forties. Assume a 60¢ price, and the farmer's return would be $15 a load, or $300, less seed, for his main cash crop of the season.

Freighting grain was too expensive to be considered. Over fair roads, freighting cost about 15¢ a ton-mile, or $8.75 for our hypothetical farmer and his 25-bushel load for which he got a return of $15.00. Interior farmers were faced with the dismal fact that wheat, worth 87¢ in Buffalo in 1845, brought 62¢ in Milwaukee and only 35¢ delivered to the storekeeper in Lake Mills, fifty miles away. Yet the *Prairie Farmer,* in 1850, lauded "King Wheat . . . it pays debts, buys groceries, clothing, lands, and answers more emphatically the purposes of trade than any other crop." It is little wonder that pioneer Wisconsin was concerned first and foremost with problems of transportation.

This modest return on the principal cash crop turns us naturally to a second problem of the squatter farmer: how to pay for his acreage, machines, and other necessities that could not be acquired in barter or produced by his own labor. In a cash-short economy, the farmer doubly resented the money that went into unproductive land speculation. Absentee speculators hemmed him in with idle land and dumped precious cash into the till at the land offices. After the 1837 panic, many who could command cash saw the folly of speculation in wild lands and the wisdom of more secure investment in mortgages on the more strategically located productive lands of squatter farmers. The squatters responded with political action aimed at limiting the return on mortgages to 12 percent, and a determined push, in 1848–51, to limit the amount of land that could be held in one ownership. Neither of these campaigns was peculiar to Wisconsin. The second, which failed narrowly, originated in New York with George Henry Evans and Horace Greeley. The legal interest rate proved unenforceable in the face of the desperate need of squatters for funds to cover their land purchases when the land came on the market. The usual device was for the creditor to take a deed to half of the squatter's claim as security and then, through transfer charges, get a rate ranging from 50 percent to 100 percent on the use of the money in the face of rising land values. Lands that brought $1.25 into the federal treasury cost the owner from $2.50 to $3.50 after the cost of a loan was added.

Joseph Schafer points to "the treadmill routine of life" on a farm in the period "when practically all farm work was hard work, when cultivating was with the hoe, mowing with the scythe, reaping with the sickle or the cradle, binding and husking with the fingers, pitching with the two-tined fork. No relief could the harassed farmer find from the compulsory program of toiling 'the live-long day' in order to eke out a livelihood for the family." The opportunity to pull up stakes and make a new farm further west, or to try the western mines, was a form of relief.

Clearly, wheat farming was not profitable unless the farmer could reach his market economically. Plank roads were a brief enthusiasm, incorporated as private ventures authorized to collect tolls. What was required was the mobilization of community resources or the organization of capital beyond the capabilities of individuals.

Although Wisconsin provided for general laws of incorporation in the 1848 constitution, special charters were not ruled out, and they outnumbered incorporations by general statute almost eight to one before 1872, when this dual system was abandoned. From 1836 to 1848, the territorial legislature granted seventy-three corporate charters, of which forty were directly related to transportation improvement. Seventeen of these, all passed in 1848, were for plank roads. The others were for bridges, canals, railroads, and so forth. Charters for banks, insurance companies, and mining companies made up those not related to public improvements. Businessmen in other fields, whose enterprises would have benefited from the flexibility and advantages of limited liability for attracting capital, did not commonly adopt the corporate form. It took some time for men to recognize its use to a business not identified with a public purpose.

Banking, which one would assume to be necessary to meet the trade, exchange, and capital needs of a growing economy, excited a hostility at odds with the general pioneer cordiality toward local business enterprise. In common with many other western states and territories, Wisconsin's experience with her few territorial banks was unfortunate, and left a legacy of ill will which hampered effective political action as well as economic development. Territorial Wisconsin was Jacksonian Democratic in temper. Wisconsin citizens emerged from the chilling experience of the 1837 panic, and their own banking experiments, as monetary conservatives. They were adamantly opposed to chartering banks of issue, but troubled by the obvious necessity for the services which banks alone seemed equipped to supply. This confusion of purpose and policy grew out of the brief careers of two territorial banks.

The Bank of Wisconsin, chartered in 1835 at Green Bay, was a legacy from Michigan Territory. Wisconsin Territory chartered seven others, but all proved abortive, except for the Bank of Mineral Point and the Bank of Dubuque. The last need not concern us. Briefly, the provisions of the charters were that specie (hard coin) only could be accepted in payment for stock in the venture. When 10 percent of the stock had been subscribed, the bank could issue bank notes in the ratio of $3 for each $1 of paid-up stock and then lend the notes at an interest of no more than 7 percent. The theory was that the bank notes would increase the local money supply, by circulating at par, on the assurance that the bank had specie in its possession to redeem bank notes at their face value in coin.

The theory proved wrong in several respects. The first was the assumption that the stockholders could raise and would deposit coin in the amounts required. Another was the belief that banks could be regulated by charter alone, with no provision for audits or reports. Lacking these now elementary restraints, the incorporators played fast and loose with matters of capitalization, note issue, and general policy. Whatever the theory of the legislature, the prospective stockholders looked upon their bank charter as an opportunity to multiply their capital at a ratio of three to one and then to borrow it, on favorable terms, to finance their own land speculations. They gave little thought to banking as a business based upon services in commercial transactions or to short-term credits based upon deposits rather than upon capitalization and note issue.

The banks at Green Bay and Mineral Point engaged in what was known as wildcat banking. Both issued banknotes in considerable quantities, resulting in heavy losses which combined were close to $100,000. James Doty was involved in both. As one of the incorporators of the Bank of Wisconsin in Green Bay, Doty subscribed to a majority of the stock in the Mineral Point Bank when the promoters had the usual trouble selling stock on the charter terms. In lieu of specie, Doty gave a certificate of deposit against the Green Bay bank. The record of transactions from this point is not clear. Doty was such an effective lightning rod in territorial politics that investigation followed investigation on the part of the legislature and the attorney general. Nothing emerged but confusion. Doty evidently retreated from the Mineral Point venture. It was stripped by its cashier, who used the banknotes to buy lead for the Helena shot tower, which he controlled briefly.

In 1839 the legislature authorized the attorney general to commence suit against the Bank of Wisconsin in Green Bay for violation of its charter and apparent insolvency. The records and assets were seized. The required specie turned out to be a keg in the vault containing $86.20 in coin, a sufficient reason for suspending the redemption of the bank's notes for the past year. Paper assets included a draft on the Mineral Point for $61,507 and a personal note against James Doty in the amount of $17,987.32. Liabilities were approximately $100,000, estimated to be about half covered by debts owed the bank. The Mineral Point Bank left $34,137 of worthless notes in circulation, after redeeming $101,863 for amounts ranging from 10¢ to 50¢ on the dollar.

These examples demonstrate the desperation of the community for a medium of exchange. Notes of both banks were being used in transactions long after the banks had given up all pretense of redeeming them for specie as required by law. For example, a purser on a river packet operating on the upper Mississippi has left the following account: "At Dunleith, before starting on the up-river trip, we were handed by the secretary of the company, a *Thompson's Bank Note Detector,* and with it a list of the bills that we might accept in payment for freight or passage. We were also given a list of those we might not accept at all; and still another list upon which we might speculate, at values running from twenty-five to seventy-five percent of their face denominations." Not only did the purser have to keep track of current discount rates but he also had to consult his *Dectector* for counterfeits. Gresham's law was in full effect, and no one proffered coin for a debt or purchase. Every sale or day's pay could be a speculation, and the recipient often was not in a position to refuse or even to discount a dubious banknote. Western banknotes were commonly discounted about 12 percent in the East as a matter of principle.

There was, in Wisconsin, one conspicuous exception to this dismal banking picture, the Wisconsin Marine and Fire Insurance Company. A shrewd Scotsman, George Smith, came to Chicago in 1834 at the age of twenty-six, and by the time of the panic in 1837, had turned his small capital into an impressive fortune in strategically located land at Chicago, Milwaukee, Manitowoc, Sheboygan, and other points, as well as contracts for sales made. Possibly sensing the end of the boom, with its accompanying opportunities as well as hazards for his own numerous purchase contracts, Smith returned to Scotland to recruit capital from his neighbors for joint stock ventures to take advantage of his knowledge of midwestern real estate. He also proposed to enter into the banking business as a natural complement to dealing in real estate. Scotland was a pioneer in free commercial credit banking, a fact which was already transforming it into an urban, industrial country and sending its young men abroad looking for a better than 6 percent return.

Illinois, Wisconsin, and Michigan were fast becoming banking deserts, as the banks, incorporated before the panic, failed, and hostility toward banking mounted. People naturally associated banking with the irresponsible issuance of banknotes, and despite the demands of the rapidly growing economy of the 1840s for adequate banking and credit facilities, the voters of Wisconsin made chartered banks illegal. George Smith knew his way around this dilemma. He organized both his Chicago and Milwaukee banks as insurance companies, chartered by the legislatures, with the power "to receive money on deposit and lend it," as well as the usual powers of an insurance company.

Smith subscribed almost all of the stock in the Wisconsin Marine and Fire Insurance Company himself. There was never any doubt of his control or his purpose. He began at once to issue certificates of deposit, which functioned in the community as money, although his charter specifically forbade exercising banking privileges. The certificates were popularly known as "George Smith's money," and Smith, with the backing of the business community, successfully held off all political and legal efforts to close down the operation. The great secret of his success, aside from his single-minded business acumen, was that he was always prepared to redeem the certificates in gold, and this was not always easy. As Smith's notes spread abroad, with the confidence which they inspired, they were a threat to currencies issued by banks in neighboring states. Other bankers responded by gathering large amounts of Smith's deposit certificates and presenting them all at one time for payment (a regular feature of banking in the period). Smith met all such raids successfully.

When banking was again made legal in Wisconsin in 1853, 8 banks were started, circulating notes worth $300,000. This was less than $1 per capita, and by 1859, with 108 banks chartered, only about $9 per capita in state banknotes were in circulation. It becomes plain why the gold that the immigrants, especially the Germans, brought with them is so often mentioned in pioneer accounts. There was a variety of other coin, some Spanish from the lower Mississippi, as well as familiar eastern banknotes attracted to Wisconsin by speculation, high interest rates, and the generous discounts they could command when converted to western banknotes. But George Smith's money was the local standard.

The trouble with all money on the Wisconsin frontier at this time was that it found its way out of the local economy too rapidly. Jackson's specie circular of 1836 required hard money at the land offices, and only a portion of this remained in the area to meet federal commitments. Much of the cash that came in was seeking speculative opportunities and was immediately tied up in land in this manner. Then, too, the pioneer economy continually ran a deficit, buying goods and services outside. Buffalo provided much of Wisconsin's shipping, and it is estimated that Milwaukee, in the period 1835–41, imported goods valued at about $6,000,000, but exported only $500,000 worth. Even as late as 1849, this imbalance was an estimated $2,000,000 to $4,000,000 annually, and the imports had to be paid for with coin or convertible currencies. Milwaukee's was a deficit economy which had to generate more exports from its hinterland. This, of course, required adequate transportation inland and the facilities to handle the wheat crop and lumber. There was also the matter of financing farmers engaged in commercial agriculture and the loggers and mill men in the growing lumber industry. In all of these endeavors, George Smith's deposit certificates and management played a crucial role.

Not the least of George Smith's services was to bring in a young Scotsman named Alexander Mitchell to manage the Wisconsin Marine and Fire Insurance Company. By the 1870s Mitchell would be the acknowledged railroad king of the upper Mississippi Valley. But his more immediate service, in the years before the Civil War, was to finance, through the credit facilities of the bank which he bought from Smith in 1854, a variety of businesses in the community, especially those associated with the movement of wheat through the port. Another Milwaukee entrepreneur, Daniel Newhall, starting with a $300 credit, built a fortune as a wheat broker, owning extensive warehouses and a fleet of twenty vessels on the Lakes. Wisconsin had poor wheat crops in the late forties, as well as transportation problems, but by 1855 Milwaukee had exports valued at $12,500,000 and by 1860 almost that much in grain exports alone.

The urban frontier, of course, was an important part of the pioneer Wisconsin economy, a fact easy to overlook. A generous gazetteer estimate of urban populations in 1857 found 160,000 people living in eighteen towns and cities of 3,000 or more. Milwaukee had established clear hegemony as the metropolitan center, with over 45,000 in 1860 and no close rivals. Her rivalry was with Chicago. Among the other Wisconsin ports, Racine was the largest in 1860 with 7,800, Sheboygan had 4,250, and Kenosha 4,000.

Many of Wisconsin's smaller cities of 1860 are her small cities of today. Watertown, at 5,300, was a rival of Janesville (7,700), Madison (6,650), Oshkosh (6,100), and Fond du Lac (5,450). Portage (2,900) represented the northern interior, La Crosse (3,900) was the principal town on the Wisconsin side of the Mississippi, and Eau Claire (1,400) was just starting a rapid growth.

It would be difficult to assess all of the reasons for Milwaukee's emergence as the metropolitan center on the Wisconsin lakeshore. Location certainly had much to do with it. It was one of the few shelters, on a sometimes stormy shore, between the Door Peninsula and Chicago. It was far enough from Chicago to be a potential rival. It was one of the first prospective shoreline urban centers, along with Green Bay, able to offer clear land titles. Green Bay lost out in the rivalry, because the weight of population was settling farther south and the Fox-Wisconsin route never competed seriously with the pioneer railroads.

Among its more immediate rivals, Milwaukee was one of the first to build piers into the lake (in 1843) to facilitate the transfer of goods and passengers, which had had to be lightered ashore. She also developed her waterpower as an adjunct to the proposed Milwaukee–Rock River canal which was never completed, and by 1848 there were twenty-five manufactories using the power. This industrial activity was backed by growing facilities for handling the wheat harvest. Milwaukee was also the main point at which immigrant traffic and imports were disembarked, and a glance at similar rivalries, such as that on Puget Sound, where potential sites with a variety of advantages existed, will illustrate that the harbor which develops a higher volume of import traffic will win in the race for metropolitan hegemony. It becomes the wholesale, financial, legal, and service center, and this is what Milwaukee became, despite the fact that Racine sometimes surpassed her in the export of wheat in the 1840s. One can point to such factors as George Smith's banking business, or superior promotion, or early improvements such as Milwaukee's waterpower, or pioneer plank roads and railroads; but the battle was really won by the people who were attracted to Milwaukee to start a great variety of enterprises and small businesses.

The most pressing problem for Wisconsin's economy in this period was that of internal transportation. The urban center which succeeded ahead of its rivals here would be the link between a growing commercial agriculture and the developing American national economy. Milwaukee set the pace.

Selected Bibliography

Andersen, Theodore A. *A Century of Banking in Wisconsin*. Madison, 1954. Covers early banking well.

Croft, Josie Greening, contributor. "A Mazomanie Pioneer of 1847." *Wisconsin Magazine of History* 26:208–18 (Dec. 1942). Farming methods, credit, and the prodigal frontier.

Ebling, Walter H. "A Century of Agriculture in Wisconsin." *The Wisconsin Blue Book*, 1940, pp. 185–96. Madison, 1940. A good sketch of the pioneer period.

Feigenbaum, Harold. "The Pioneer Lawyer in Wisconsin." Ph.D. dissertation, University of Wisconsin, 1969. A description of the legal profession in the territorial period.

Gates, Paul W. *The Farmer's Age: Agriculture, 1815–1860*. New York: Harper Torchbooks, 1960. Hazards of pioneer wheat farming.

Hammond Bray. *Banks and Politics in America from the Revolution to the Civil War*. Princeton, 1957. The sectional struggle and the role of the banks.

Houkom, John A., ed. "Pioneer Kjaerkebon Writes from Coon Prairie." *Wisconsin Magazine of History* 27:439–45 (June 1944). Letter of 1856, mostly on prices and wages.

Schafer, Joseph. *A History of Agriculture in Wisconsin*. Wisconsin Domesday Book, vol. 1. Madison, 1922. Most of it is on pioneer farming.

Smith, Alice E. "Banking without Banks: George Smith and the Wisconsin Marine and Fire Insurance Company." *Wisconsin Magazine of History* 48:268–81 (Summer 1965). The only redeemable currency in the territory.

———. *George Smith's Money: A Scottish Investor in America*. Madison, 1966. The only safe "non-bank" in the territory.

———. *Millstone and Saw: The Origins of Neenah-Menasha*. Madison, 1966. Model study of a waterpower site.

Van Wagenen, Jared, Jr. *The Golden Age of Homespun*. New York, 1953. In case you want to tan a hide or card some wool.

Walsh, Margaret. *The Manufacturing Frontier: Pioneer Industry in Antebellum Wisconsin, 1830–1860*. Madison, 1972. Access to capital was the vital key.

THE
PIONEER ECONOMY:
TRANSPORTATION

14

Just as the present-day traveler sometimes finds the trip from airport to office or home more time-consuming than crossing half the continent by plane, the pioneer traveler found that he could approach Wisconsin on the east or west at speeds of ten to twenty miles an hour, but both speed and comfort were left at the water's edge. Indeed, such was the technological and entrepreneurial advancement of the American river steamboat that a popular recreation for ante bellum genteel southern families, to escape the heat and fevers of summer, was a trip to the Falls of St. Anthony on the upper Mississippi. While the southerner, surrounded with luxury, was making this seasonal pilgrimage, travel from the river's edge was a grim contest with a primitive system of roads, until the railroad reached Prairie du Chien in 1857. Then, released from dependence on animal muscle to get its products to waterside, the commerce of Wisconsin took on a new dimension.

The growth of the pioneer economy was of course directly concerned with the development of a transportation network. The internal river systems, which had proved adequate for the movement of products of the fur trade, could not serve the new economy effectively. The great problem was how to get things from the developing hinterlands to the ports on Lake Michigan and the Mississippi. The difficulties were in part technological, but even more, financial. It was a serious question whether the pioneer society could command the necessary collective resources to overcome its isolation, or could attract outside capital to the task on anything but the most ruinous terms. The most attractive outside aid was direct federal involvement, or subsidies which were sought with no doctrinaire embarrassment. If there was any objection to federal aid it was the oblique one that land grants inconvenienced the squatter by holding blocks of land off the market. Better than roads or canals, railroads were the more expensive, but the pioneers never doubted that they should have them, although the social cost of the railroads came high at this stage.

Wisconsin commerce was well served on the Great Lakes and the Mississippi in the pre-Civil War years. The cost of vessels was not prohibitive, and the shipowner did not have to worry about maintaining his right of way, which was in fact subsidized by the federal government. Congress abandoned early the doctrine that the Constitution was "a saltwater document" and undertook channel markings and improvement of harbors of refuge on the Great Lakes. Nor did the operator of a vessel ordinarily maintain terminals for his operations. If a lakeshore settlement was ambitious to become a port, it provided facilities for docking, cargo handling, and storage as an incentive for vessels to call. The unrivaled cheapness of water traffic insured the use of the convenient highway provided by the Great Lakes for bulky goods, and for some years it had little competition either for goods or passengers. It was 1855 before Milwaukee had a rail connection paralleling the Lakes. Lake commerce also had the advantage of subsidized connections to draw traffic to the Lakes. The most conspicuous examples of this were the Erie Canal, the Welland Canal, the canal and railroad systems of Ohio, Indiana, Michigan, and Illinois undertaken in the 1830s, and the canal at the Sault which opened Lake Superior in 1855.

Profits were high for vessel owners on the upper Lakes with the opening of the Erie Canal in 1825. The canal drew a flood of Yankees to settle the shores of Ohio, Indiana, and southern Michigan, and brought the desirable far shores of Lake Michigan into view. It was not unusual for a boat to pay for itself in a single season, and the optimism that resulted is reflected in a certain exuberance in ship design. The first propeller vessel, the *Vandalia,* was launched on Lake Ontario at Oswego in 1841, and a ship built at Cleveland in 1844, the *Empire,* was advertised as the largest steam vessel of its time, at 254 feet in length. Its builders boasted that it would have been longer if they could have found a straight place in the Cuyahoga River to launch it. Ship design on the Lakes tended to follow salt-water models. There was even more technical virtuosity displayed on the great American inland rivers at this time.

Sail dominated traffic on the Lakes until the 1880s, in spite of advances in steam vessels. By that time the technology of handling the common bulk cargoes of the Lakes, ores, coal, wheat, and limestone, began to eliminate sailing vessels, because their rigging was not suited to the new shore facilities. Characteristically, the sailing ships on the Lakes hit a peak of grandeur in design, size, and luxury after the sail had become economically obsolete. The *David Dow,* a five-masted vessel built for the bulk trade, was proudly launched at Toledo in 1881, but like others of its kind was eventually dismasted and pushed about as a barge. In like manner, the plush liners later built for the passenger trade were driven out of business by the competition of the railroads, and many rotted for years at the docks because they could not be converted to other uses.

The economics of the Lakes commerce were such that as early as 1837, in the months following the panic, a loose organization of carriers grew up to divide the remaining business and retire some vessels from use. This loose organization did not survive long, and Lakes carriage was normally competitive until the late nineteenth century. The great proprietary lines such as the Steel Trust fleet, Cleveland Cliffs, and Canada Steamship emerged in the present century. In 1838, there were 11 small steamers on the upper Lakes and one company running steamers in the immigrant trade. By 1845 there were three companies making scheduled runs out of Buffalo, with daily sailings. There were, by that year, 60 steamers and 320 sail on the upper Lakes, but the traffic was heavily one way in both passengers and cargo. It was in 1845 that young Isaac Stephenson arrived in Milwaukee and recalled that "the tide of immigration had set in. On some days during this period I saw as many as seven or eight hundred people land at Milwaukee on steamers from Buffalo, packing their belongings with them; and I have seen them by the hundreds in vacant lots bargaining for cattle and wagons."

James Stark, who came in May 1841, wrote to George Dow, his employer, that it cost him $10 on the lone steamer line then in operation, to come from Buffalo to Milwaukee. He thought this pretty steep: "Of course they have their own price." He could have come on a sailing vessel for about half as much, but did not want to spare the time. He left Buffalo on the 14th and arrived in Milwaukee on the 19th, while the journey under sail generally took three to four weeks. The steamers were not much safer than sail; usually heavily loaded and grossly underpowered, they added the hazards of fires and explosions. The steamer *Erie* blew up in 1841 with the loss of 170 lives. (The hull was raised later to recover the gold the immigrant passengers were carrying.) In 1847, the *Phoenix* burned off Sheboygan, taking some 200 lives, mostly Dutch immigrants. Any pioneer account of travel on the Lakes takes note of such disasters. The score for 1852 was six paddle steamers, seven propellers, and thirty-five sailing vessels lost.

The Upper Lakes fleet was still largely sail on the eve of the Civil War. In 1858 it was counted as 1,200 sailing vessels and 242 steam. The Wards, Samuel and Eber, illustrate the relative ease with which the fleet was expanded. Samuel Ward was a Vermonter who began in the carrying trade on the Erie Canal and soon turned to operating on the Lakes, building his own vessels. He moved to the St. Clair flats of Michigan, near timber, and continued to build schooners, although he later became the "steamboat king" on the Lakes of the 1840s. His nephew, Eber, took over and by 1854 had a fleet of fourteen steamers, six sail, and numerous tugs. The Ward vessels, later known as the Goodrich Line, were earning $240,000 net by 1851, and this was before the grain trade became big on the Lakes. Eber Ward's earnings in shipping enabled him to engage in opening up Lake Superior mining and took him into railroads and the iron and steel business. A generation later the steel companies were the nucleus of the United States Steel combine.

Thus Lakes carriage attracted capital, but also generated considerable in the hands of enterprising men like the Wards. At the same time, the range of the Lakes trade was expanded by the extension of public works. The Welland Canal around Niagara Falls was enlarged, by 1848, opening a channel eight feet in depth from the Atlantic into the Upper Lakes. The enlargement of the Erie Canal in the 1850s added to its usefulness, while the canal at Sault St. Marie in 1855 opened Lake Superior. All of this system of carriage was available to pioneer Wisconsin at the cost of developing facilities for the transfer of goods at the water's edge. The problem was to get products to the lakeshore and develop an export trade to offset the heavy imports of food, clothing, machinery, building materials, furniture, and so forth required by a building frontier.

Like the Great Lakes, the upper Mississippi on Wisconsin's western border had a well-developed commerce, capable of considerable expansion and financed from outside. The steamboat had replaced the keelboat on the river quite early, to meet the needs of the army posts at Prairie du Chien and Fort Snelling. Already in 1828, steamboat arrivals at Galena outnumbered keelboats by two to one, with 75 of the former. There were 30 steamboats calling regularly at Galena by 1837, and the business continued to grow as the lead trade reached its peak in 1847. As the lead trade declined, a new source of traffic on the upper Mississippi appeared in the stream of immigrants heading across the river into Iowa and upriver to Minnesota. Iowa grew from 43,000 to 675,000 between 1840 and 1860 and Minnesota from 6,000 to 172,000 in the decade after 1850.

Many of these people travelled part of the distance on the river and settled within hauling distance of a river landing. Wisconsin's population,
100,000 larger than Iowa's in 1860, was mostly tributary to the shore of
Lake Michigan, but the counties along the Mississippi enjoyed impressive growth in the period.

The next event in shaping the upper Mississippi traffic was the construction of railroads from Chicago and Milwaukee to the river. The railroad from Chicago reached Galena in 1856, and the Milwaukee and
Mississippi entered Prairie du Chien the next year. Oddly, the railroads
increased traffic on the river rather than inhibiting it, because the panic
of 1857 caught them before they could undertake the expensive and difficult task of bridging the great river. Until 1865, there were no bridges
across the Mississippi between Rock Island and St. Paul. Railroads termi-
nating at East Dubuque, Prairie du Chien, and La Crosse were halted on
the east bank until after the Civil War. The result was an increase of
traffic on the river, which served as a north and south feeder for the railroads, gathering wheat from Iowa and Minnesota. But by 1887, there
were fifteen railroad bridges across the upper Mississippi, which meant
that the railroads were performing their own feeder operations and the
river traffic was in precipitous decline. At this point, when the postwar
river steamer had reached a peak of size, specialization, and general impressiveness, it was clearly doomed.

While a part of the lead trade had found its way to Lake Michigan by
way of the seasonal wagon trains to Milwaukee, and by the Illinois and
Michigan Canal to Chicago after 1848, the bulk of it went downriver to
St. Louis and New Orleans before 1856, when the railroads reached the
lead region. The upper Mississippi had its limitations as an avenue of
commerce; it was generally closed by low water at the Rock Island rapids for at least three months, and sometimes for much of the year. In
addition, St. Louis and New Orleans neglected their port facilities. While
riverboat rates remained competitive with the routes through the Great
Lakes, insurance rates were significantly higher on the river, handling
and financing were more haphazard, and the route was long and slow.
The lead trade figured prominently in the arithmetic of the railroad pro-
jectors, but wheat provided the overwhelming bulk of their traffic by the
time they were built to the river. Wheat from the upper Mississippi never
flowed in quantity to New Orleans as it did on the Ohio. Handling facilities for grain downriver were inferior, and it was held that the heat and
humidity encountered had a deteriorating effect on grains and flour. By
1840 the grain trade from Ohio, Indiana, and Illinois was turning north
along the canals and railroads to the Lake ports, well before the upper
Mississippi country was producing much wheat. The population of

southwest Wisconsin, which was culturally and economically tied to the South, had been joined to the Lake Michigan ports economically well before the Civil War closed the lower Mississippi.

Technologically, the development of the riverboat was probably more interesting than the evolution of vessels on the Great Lakes. Starting in 1813 with a version of Fulton's *Clermont,* the western riverboat evolved into a long, narrow, shallow-draft, highpowered, nervous, and dangerous instrument of fast, luxurious travel. Immensely profitable and short lived, it evolved rapidly. Riverboats were built in unusually remote areas, wherever timber was available. George Dow's brother-in-law wrote from near Cambridge, Wisconsin in January 1842 that "they Built a Steam Boat on the Rock River last winter and sent it down to St. Louis in the Spring but the thing has never Returned." The average life of a Mississippi steamer was from three to five years, and it was not unusual for the boilers and machinery to see service in three or four boats before ending up ashore or unrecoverable. The machinery was developed by empirical engineers, mostly around Pittsburgh, and was simple, with wide tolerances, and operating on pressures up to 125 pounds. Boilers breathed visibly as they worked. Explosions, like navigational hazards, were common.

A man could be in the steamboat business on the river for as little as $2,000. Boats were smaller in the early years, usually in single ownership, and ran anywhere that there was business. They nosed up many a small stream, whistling the cattle from the water ahead, sometimes getting stranded in unlikely country until the next high water came to their rescue.

As the river business evolved, boats became larger, more luxurious, and more expensive. Because of the profits, they were a favored investment, often owned by a condominium. The inevitable tendency toward consolidation and monopoly gave rise to packet lines maintaining published schedules, with daily runs. The rivalries between river towns resulted in subsidies to start such lines and in fierce rate wars. The situation was generally quite fluid in the pre-Civil War years when packet lines came and went and boats changed hands rapidly. It is difficult to find figures on the number of boats operating on the upper Mississippi at any given time. Boats were readily moved many miles to a new base, often on a lease arrangement, or they might operate on subsidiary streams, such as the Minnesota River, until low water drove them back onto the Mississippi. Another source of confusion was the common practice of taking a boat into a yard, cutting her in half, and adding twenty feet or so to keep abreast of the trend toward larger vessels. These boats ordinarily reappeared under a new name. One authority gives the number of boats on the upper river in 1857 as 99, most of them owned or leased by the Minnesota Packet Company, which the Davidson Brothers of La Crosse took over in 1861. The railroads controlled many boats and lines in the postbellum years.

What has survived of this colorful era on the river, aside from the traditions, are the towns that were important ports in their days. Their demise has been slower than that of the boats on which their brief prosperity was built. The *Grey Eagle,* built in the 1850s in Cincinnati for Captain Daniel Harris of the Galena Packet Line, was 250 feet long, 673 tons burden, and could make eighteen miles an hour upstream. But sternwheelers, while more efficient than the sidewheelers, were less maneuverable, and the pride of the Galena Packet Line met her fate against the abutments of the hated Rock Island railroad bridge.

The name Galena Packet Line reminds us of Galena's dominance on the river. The visitor to Galena today may attribute its faded evidences of wealth and importance to the lead trade, but it is as intimately associated with the steamboat era. Although not directly on the Mississippi, the town was a port on the Fever River, which enters the larger river a little below the town. It was the wholesaling, financial, and distribution center on the upper Mississippi until the railroad from Chicago developed Dunlieth (now East Dubuque) in 1857. Galena's position as the center for the lead area gave it the commercial and financial sinews to control much of the traffic on the river until Chicago's rail line displaced it. Dubuque, Prairie du Chien, MacGregor, and La Crosse all give similar evidences of metropolitan pretensions a century and more ago, based upon their relation to the steamboat traffic. When the railroad from Milwaukee ended at Prairie du Chien, MacGregor had a mile of warehouses and ferried millions of bushels of grain across the river from Iowa to the railhead. Hercule Dousman ended a long acquisitive career, started in the fur trade at Prairie du Chien, by enlarging his fortune with steamboat and railroad ventures. Dubuque, in 1854, handled a dozen steamer landings daily and was a wholesale and retail center for a large area. The town had gaslight, paved streets, and omnibuses to mark its early dignity. La Crosse had a similar history as the home of the Davidsons, who built a monopoly on the river above Galena.

The Mississippi never held the importance for Wisconsin agriculture that it held for neighboring Iowa and Minnesota. This was partly because the rivers that flow into the Mississippi from Wisconsin were not suitable for navigation. The largest of these, the Wisconsin, was shoaled and did not develop as a carrier except for logs and lumber rafts. The others had falls and stretches of swift water which limited their usefulness to the movement of logs and lumber. Mississippi shipping was more important for collecting wheat west of the river for shipment to Milwaukee and

Chicago than it was as a commercial outlet for Wisconsin farmers. It was important for Wisconsin wholesalers, manufacturers of farm machinery, and merchants in the years before the railroads spanned the great river and left the steamboats rotting at their docks.

The most widely used forms of transportation in pioneer Wisconsin, serving mail, freight, and passengers, traveled on the roads. Roads were built and maintained by a variety of methods, but very few, even on well-traveled routes, were adequate. Wisconsin achieved a comprehensive railroad system long before most roads were brought beyond a primitive condition. A description of intercity and local public roads in the 1850s fits the condition of most throughout the nineteenth century; it was the bicycle craze of the nineties and the following age of the automobile that helped to bring about the change. Direct state responsibility for roads did not come until 1911. Wisconsin entered the twentieth century with only 17 percent of her rural roads having as much as a gravel surface, and there were few all-weather roads, even between major centers.

With the maintenance of the roads left to local county and township officials, who were elected by and directed crews of local taxpayers working out their assessments, the condition of the highways offered more adventure than ease. Farmers were naturally interested in their many local routes to the trading centers and not eager to tax themselves or to work on the improvement of those roads used as highways. Under the best of circumstances, a pioneer highway was of limited use when freighting costs were from twelve to twenty cents a ton-mile and portions of the road were nearly impassable for much of the year. Hence the enthusiasm for canals, briefly for plank roads privately built, and finally for railroads.

It is apparent, from numerous accounts, that those forced to use the pioneer roads for any distance remembered the experience. Frederika Bremer, traveling on the stage between Milwaukee and Madison in 1849, wrote:

I was shaken, or rather hurled, unmercifully hither and thither upon the newborn roads of Wisconsin, which are no roads at all, but a succession of hills, holes, and water-pools, in which first one wheel sank and then the other, while the opposite one stood high up in the air. Sometimes the carriage came to a sudden stand-still, half overturned in a hole, and it was some time before it could be dragged out again, only to be thrown into the same position on the other side. To me that mode of traveling seemed really incredible, nor could I comprehend how, at that rate, we should ever get along at all. Sometimes we drove for a considerable distance in the water, so deep that I expected to see the whole equipage either swim or sink altogether. And when we reached dry land, it was only to take the most extraordinary leaps over stocks and stones. They comforted me by telling me that the diligence was not in the habit of being upset very often!

A young man coming out from Vermont to work on Milwaukee's pioneer railroad in March 1852 came to the end of the existing railroad lines at Chicago and took the stage from there:

We left there at 6 o'clock Wednesday evening & road all night & all day yesterday & arrived here last night at 7 o'clock distance 90 miles fare $5.00. It was a very hard ride as the Roads were rough & the weather pretty cold for Vermont even at this season. We tipped over once but came out safe—driver hurt a little bit—& we had reason to be thankful that we were not all hurt as there were seven of us inside a coach shut up tight & heavily loaded with baggage.

Like Miss Bremer, this traveler was describing conditions on a main road in a scheduled public conveyance.

An Englishman, traveling a lesser road, from Mazomanie to Mineral Point in 1847, was most interested in the amazing endurance of American horses but did not fail to notice the condition of the road:

But the jolting was terrific, sometimes a foot deep in fine sand, and then loose stones, as big as a bushel basket, then mud half way up to the axles, then logs of timber as any size you like. Still on we dashed at a furious rate, but the bridges, aye the bridges. They get two huge trees 50 to 60 feet long, and lay across from bank to bank of creeks or small rivers. Then lay small poles across, just to stop a horse's foot from going thro, and that's all. They are truly corduroy, and you may think yourself lucky not to get a dozen of them in a day's journey.

How did this system of roads come into being? Intercity travel was generally on roads which had originally been built by the federal government, or authorized by the territorial legislature and built by the township road districts. A road still partly identifiable as the Military Road was built by troops stationed at Forts Howard, Winnebago, and Crawford, linking Green Bay and Prairie du Chien. A federal road, surveyed and contracted with federal funds, linked Green Bay and Chicago. Another connected Milwaukee with East Dubuque by way of Madison. On some planned federal roads only the bridges were built, for lack of funds.

Impetus for the Military Road connecting the Wisconsin forts came from James Doty, aided by his patron Lewis Cass, the secretary of war in 1832. Doty and Lieutenant Alexander Center were named to make the survey. The two men laid out the Military Road in 1832 and the Green

Bay to Chicago federal road in 1835. The traveler on Highway 18 from Madison to Prairie du Chien covers the route, along the Military Ridge, which was built by troops from Fort Crawford under the command of Colonel Zachary Taylor. Taylor had no great faith in the permanence of the project; he expected the road to disappear through washing, and the bridges through unchecked prairie fires. He had two furrows plowed to mark out the thirty-foot roadway, had the brush cleared, and rough bridges built where necessary. The job was more complicated between Madison and Fond du Lac by way of Fort Winnebago, a route broken by marshes and forests. Trees were felled and the stumps hollowed to hold the rainwater which would aid in rotting them. While this process went on over the years, the road was liberally dotted with foot-high stumps in forested areas. On wet land the roadway was corduroyed with reasonably straight poles of a common size. There was much drowned land between Fort Winnebago and Fond du Lac where in the wet season the road tended to float away. On the prairies, after the road boundary furrows grew dim, travelers had the problem of lining up with the next bridge. The wheel tracks of previous travelers were not always a reliable guide, because those who knew the route wandered in search of smoother going. From Fond du Lac, the road traversed the escarpment on the east side of Lake Winnebago and then struck the difficult portion down the lower Fox River, where fifty-six bridges were built.

Building the Military Road was one of the pioneer duties which took soldiers away from the manual of arms, to the distress of the inspector general. Congress could not be interested in appropriation requests for the maintenance and improvement of the road, after granting $5,000 in 1838 and a final $2,000 in 1845. The road had cost, altogether, $12,000 for 234 miles, exclusive of the army labor: an average of $51 a mile. Fortunately, the existence of the road attracted settlers who helped to maintain it, and the road was well traveled. Travelers sometimes found themselves doing informal road work to make a stretch passable.

Territorial roads were authorized under a general 1839 law, although many were established by individual statute designating the routes and providing for commissioners to see to the survey and compliance by the various township road districts. Roughly 300 such roads were authorized and about 250 were built. Road districts could levy a tax of one half of one percent on real estate and two days of labor on farmers in the district. Labor could be offered in lieu of money for the tax, which meant that funds were usually short. Available money ordinarily was used for bridging, and it was common to ask a charter for a privately owned toll bridge or ferry. The standards for road work were not high, partly from a lack of practical knowledge and partly because the job of overseer was elective. The job was passed around, was not usually sought after, and the voters preferred an easy boss. When pioneers got together to discuss their need for better transportation facilities they ordinarily meant toll roads, canals, and railroads to connect beyond their road districts. Nonetheless, the public road system, such as it was, served scheduled mail and stage coaches, freighters, and other travelers.

Plank roads cost about $2,000 a mile, about one-tenth as much as a railroad. Portable steam sawmills were used to cut the lumber, and an astonishing amount of heavy oak planking was required for the single-lane roads. Even when the farmer-stockholders worked out assessments by grading and laying the planks, a large crew was needed to run the mill and hurry the work. The farmers along the Racine to Rochester plank road mortgaged their farms at 12 percent to raise a required $15,000, Racine raised $10,000 by a bond issue, and private citizens subscribed another $25,000 to build the twenty-five-mile road to Rochester.

The plank road era was a brief one. The cost was nominal compared to a railroad or canal, and anyone could use them with his own wagon and team, but the increase in speed and carrying capacity was limited. An 1853 gazetteer noted seven out of Milwaukee totaling about 200 miles; Racine had three plank roads. Many more were chartered than ever were built, but they doubtless retarded railroad building by competing for scarce capital. Except for a few like the Milwaukee to Watertown, plank roads were not a great success. The oak planks and sleepers rotted quickly on the often water-logged dirt grades. Mud and water splashed up between the planks, making the footing insecure for the animals. Farmers avoided them during dry weather and when the ground was frozen, which reduced the income necessary to pay off the debt and maintain the roadway.

A surprising anachronism of pioneer travel in Wisconsin was noticed by a Swedish author, Frederika Bremer, when her luggage was lost temporarily but recovered by telegraph. "It is remarkable that in all directions throughout this young country, along these rough roads, which are no roads at all, run these electric wires from tree to tree, from post to post, along the prairie-land, and bring towns and villages in communication." Samuel F. B. Morse had trouble exploiting his invention after a small federal subsidy, in 1844, had helped him to prove its practicality. Others took hold of the telegraph, and Morse licensed franchises freely. The use of the invention spread rapidly, because it was cheap to build. A single iron wire was strung along the road or across country. By 1849, when Miss Bremer made her trip through Wisconsin, Milwaukee was connected by telegraph with Chicago and the East. Local lines reached to Green Bay, Watertown, and Mineral Point.

The telegraph was a novelty that failed to pay in its early years. A pioneer Milwaukee operator wrote that Val Blatz, the brewer, was the principal user of the Watertown line in the 1850s. He had one customer there with whom orders were exchanged by "lightning." The main line to the East depended upon the Milwaukee newspapers, which accounted for almost half of the revenues in the early years. The Civil War finally proved the usefulness of the telegraph, and commission merchants learned to use it to keep in touch with distant markets. It seemed a miracle to have, instantly, intelligence that had formerly taken a week to come by the Lakes. But men soon adjust to miracles.

Wisconsin's canal era did not produce any significant transportation routes, but the projects undertaken had an important economic impact. The principal results were the development of a useful waterpower for pioneer Milwaukee, the strange anomoly of the federal government maintaining dams on the lower Fox for which private interests still own the power, and a marvelous complication of land titles in the areas covered by canal grants or flooded by their works. The stories are too long and complicated to be told in detail.

It was natural that Wisconsin pioneers, many of them from the region so profoundly affected by the successful Erie Canal, would scheme to reach the interior by canals. Wisconsin towns on Lake Michigan looked to the lead trade as a basis for their canal schemes. One pioneer historian made the delightful comment that "a catfish drawing three inches of water would have found it difficult to ascend in a dry time, some of the rivers which our territorial statesmen petitioned Congress to have improved at Uncle Sam's expense."

Green Bay expected to lead in any such promotion because of its command of the traditional Fox-Wisconsin waterway used in the fur trade. The route had been the subject of some private efforts even before 1836. Daniel Whitney, who built the Helena shot tower, and Morgan Martin were involved in various schemes to eliminate the portages along the route.

Despite Green Bay's early start, it was Byron Kilbourn at Milwaukee who got the first federal subsidy, a land grant made in 1838, for the Milwaukee–Rock River canal. The scheme was to connect the Milwaukee River with the Rock River and then to work cross-country (with some pretty dubious engineering) to the lead area. Support for the project was less than total, for the grant covered the settlements of preemptors, and rival canal schemes were upset. James Doty, who had supported the Fox-Wisconsin route, was now pressing for a comprehensive canal scheme from Lake Winnebago into the Rock River and then up the Catfish (now the Yahara) into Four Lakes and thence to the Wisconsin River by canal. He owned townsite promotions at Fond du Lac, Madison, and some intervening points on this fanciful route. He professed to find great philosophical hazards for a free people in federal grants of land to a private company such as Kilbourn's. The grant, maybe because of these reservations, went to the Territory of Wisconsin for administration. Doty became territorial governor in 1841 and successfully blocked Kilbourn's operations. The Milwaukee–Rock River canal ended as a diversionary dam at Milwaukee, which became the source of power for the city's pioneer flour-milling and wood-working industries.

The Fox-Wisconsin canal continued to attract support because it offered a strategic connection between the Great Lakes and the Mississippi River over a long-familiar route. There were always sympathetic ears in Congress among those who speculated in Wisconsin lands or supported internal improvements. Morgan Martin finally won a federal land grant for the project, which was nearly rejected during Wisconsin's constitutional debates. The canal disasters of neighboring states, in the 1830s, were a grim reminder. A constitutional provision forbidding the state to engage in works of internal improvements was modified to allow it to administer funds from federal grants for the purpose.

The State of Wisconsin was in the canal-building business until 1853, when the funds realized from the sale of the federal lands clearly could not sustain the work. A board of public works had directed the finances and contracts with fair efficiency and no scandal. They were simply out of money. Martin, the prime contractor, now persuaded the state to turn the project and the land grant over to private operators, with guarantees of performance for its completion. Martin and his associates went in search of capital with the land grant as bait. They found it in upstate New York with men who had made money in wild lands along the Erie Canal and in the promotion of a Sault St. Marie canal. Chief among them were Horatio Seymour, Erastus Corning, and Hiram Barney. Seymour and Corning were men of wide interests, known nationally in politics and business. The price of their cooperation was high. Martin recalled sadly that "the big imported fish swallowed the little natives."

The new Fox and Wisconsin Improvement Company devoted its greatest efforts to the successful enlargement of the land grant by Congress, with a tortured interpretation of the terms. Although the little steamer *Aquila* made its much heralded passage through the waterway on a trip from Pittsburgh to Green Bay in 1856, during a period of high water, the canal was never of much practical use. Locks carried vessels around the rapids in the lower Fox, but the Wisconsin River was stubbornly ungovernable with its shifting shoals, and the drowned upper Fox remained a wild rice pasture.

Despite the resources of its new sponsors, the Improvement Company was allowed to become insolvent, went into receivership, and was bid in by the New York group with just enough to satisfy claims against the state. The New Yorkers emerged with the land grant and the appurtenances of the canals and locks. Their next step was to persuade the federal government to take over the work in 1872. It was a time of renewed enthusiasm for waterways as a means to keep railroad rates honest, and Governor Fairchild and Congressman Philetus Sawyer successfully pressed the suggested solution. The federal government reluctantly agreed to buy the canal improvements, but refused to send good money after bad to buy the waterpower rights. As a result, the federal government maintained the dams on the lower Fox for which private interests held the power rights. The waterway was recently closed on its upper reaches, having proved its lack of utility over the years.

Wisconsin built no railroad until a modest ten miles of line were built in 1850 out of Milwaukee toward Waukesha. The first phase of pioneer railroad construction ended in 1857, the year of another business panic, when every railroad in the state defaulted on its bonds. A total of 688 miles of railroad had been built. Two railroads had reached the Mississippi, at Prairie du Chien and La Crosse. The period of consolidation which followed belongs to the next era in Wisconsin's railroad history.

Early railroads were thought of in terms of local transportation to reach a city's immediate hinterland or to connect ports to the interior. While there were 3,200 miles of railroad in the United States by 1847, the average line was only nineteen miles long, gauges were not standard, and equipment was not exchanged. It was 1852 before one could get to Chicago by rail, and that with much transferring between lines. A young man who came to Milwaukee in that year to work on the Milwaukee and Mississippi Railroad described his two-day trip from Cleveland to Chicago. He rode on four different railroads, with long stretches by stage in between. The Michigan Southern took four hours to traverse thirty miles over a line "laid with strap iron & in miserable order." A ninety-mile stage trip to Milwaukee completed his journey, four days out of Cleveland.

Asa Whitney, who was in Wisconsin in 1845 to propagandize for a

Pacific railroad, was a bit ahead of his time. Most people looked upon railroads only as local feeders which were expensive and monopolistic by nature. On the other hand, they could haul large loads, haul them faster, and the rate was on the order of one-fifth as much a ton-mile as the rate for freighting by wagon. Furthermore, they could run in winter.

A real limitation upon those backing railroads was the railroads' initial cost. Estimates are difficult to make, but it is likely that a working railroad in the 1850s cost on the order of $20,000 to $25,000 a mile. It is little wonder that plank roads, at $2,000 per mile, seemed more practical for the sparsely populated miles between the lead mines and Lake Michigan. The rapid growth of population in Wisconsin, from 31,000 in 1840 to 305,000 in 1850, worked a change. Still, the equation was far from easy.

With the example of other states before them, the citizens of the new State of Wisconsin rejected the use of state revenues or credit for internal improvements. While some European capital was finding its way back cautiously into American railroads after the debacles of 1837, its owners had been badly burned in western railroads and could find profitable and secure investments further east. Eastern investors had little interest in Wisconsin railroad ventures, either. There were no land grants to sweeten them until 1856. Wisconsin citizens, determined to have railroads, were about to commit themselves to financial improvisation that would lead to grief.

The experience was to be widely shared. Enthusiasm for railroad promotion led to chartering more than one hundred companies in Wisconsin in the decade of the fifties. It must be emphasized that railroads were promoted. They were not simple business propositions to be constructed and managed on business principles. The state constitution did not prohibit the participation of municipal corporations in railroad financing or granting subsidies, and a compliant legislature broadened this power. Citizens fulfilled their patriotic duty by voting generous bond issues by town, city, or county to subsidize local railroad promotions. Municipal bonds got a better price than the securities of an unbuilt railroad. The municipality, in turn, received railroad securities which it was generally believed could not fail to make money, retire the debt, and put the municipality on the map with an operating railroad. It was an exercise in self-levitation that seldom failed in its appeal. Milwaukee, locked in a struggle with Chicago as well as with its smaller neighbors, awoke to find, in 1857 when the bubble burst, that it had bonded itself for $1,614,000 for this purpose: about $40 for every man, woman, and child of its population. Assessed valuation of property in the city was only $6,000,000. The debt was a heavy borrowing on its future. The railroad had defaulted on its bonds by the time citizens were working out this sad arithmetic.

The Milwaukee and Mississippi Rail Road Company did build a railroad, but its demands were insatiable. The central figure in the promotion was Byron Kilbourn, one of the principals in the Milwaukee townsite speculation, and a promoter of the Milwaukee–Rock River Canal and its land grant. The company found a new source of capital in 1850 when a farmer from Milton suggested that farmers along the route of the railroad should mortgage their farms and take railroad stock in exchange. His argument was that the stock would shortly pay 10 percent dividends, which would cover the 8 percent interest on the mortgages, the railroad meanwhile advancing the value of their farms. By 1857 more than 6,000 Wisconsin farmers had acted upon this sage advice, in the interest of various real and imaginary railroads, to the tune of $5,000,000 in mortgages. The railroad promoters, always pressed for cash, sold the mortgages at large discounts in eastern money markets, and the farmers found themselves facing foreclosure notices from strangers, while all they had in hand were defaulted railroad securities or stock, and often no railroad.

Kilbourn's railroad was built at heavy social cost. Filled with enthusiasm, local citizens did a good deal of clearing and grading without any exchange of cash, but enthusiasm and barter would not procure rails and rolling stock or build bridges. Before the end of 1851, more than $550,000 had been spent on a line that reached only to Waukesha. An outside observer of this bootstrap railroad building, a very young Vermonter with some engineering experience, wrote home:

> Conkey says that when he came on here to lay track for them . . . he never saw so green a set, not an engineer that ever saw any track laid & all were in a fix. . . . They never had an engineer on here that had ever been on another railroad. It seems that the said Byron Kilbourn the former Presdt was a scoundrel (to speak it plainly as it is said to me) & sunk a good deal of money for the Company. He appointed himself Chief Engineer & made a miserable location from Milwaukee to Waukesha, very crooked & about four miles out of the way.

There were other deficiencies to provoke the young man's scorn. The survey beyond Milton bypassed Janesville and struck for Madison. The citizens of Janesville were certain that the road would pass through their town, as prescribed in the railroad's charter, but the promoters were equally adamant, because Janesville offered no subsidy or other aid. "They are awfully green here in Railroading and do not manage well for their own interest," reported the young critic. The survey of the line was repeatedly jogged "to hit some village or somebody's sawmill." The exigencies of promotion invariably prevailed over engineering considerations. Few of those concerned realized that railroads presented rather special management problems. Carelessness about means extended to other people's money.

Congressional hostility toward land grants for railroads was crumbling after the 1850 grant to the Illinois Central. Wisconsin got two grants in 1856 to encourage railroad construction to the north and northwest. This was where the remaining public land was. People had been hostile to grants in the south, where the desirable farm land and settlement were. Grants in unsettled areas were applauded.

The federal grants were made to the state for disposition. Naturally, there were a number of companies prepared to qualify for these grants, and a lively competition ensued. Bryon Kilbourn, who had been forced out of the management of the Milwaukee and Mississippi Rail Road Company, appeared as the principal promoter of the La Crosse and Milwaukee Railroad. There followed one of the ripest scandals in Wisconsin legislative history, as Kilbourn and his principal lieutenant, Moses Strong, distributed nearly $900,000 in railroad securities to win the so-called St. Croix grant. They bought fifty-nine assemblymen, thirteen senators, the governor for $50,000, and a supreme court judge for an equal amount. The governor, Coles Bashford, had the wit to cash in his $50,000 in railroad bonds for $15,000 in cash, and moved to Arizona after legislative questions made him uncomfortable. No one was punished for the unseemly affair, and Kilbourn, testifying before an investigating committee, expressed satisfaction with his own role. Wisconsin citizens would have considered the Milwaukee promoters remiss had they allowed a competing Chicago promotion to carry off the prize with competing bribes. As for Governor Bashford, Kilbourn had offered the $50,000 with no corrupt intent. The governor had suffered some disappointment "in the direction which . . . the grant had taken. . . . On his part I believe he accepted it [the bonds] for the reason that he thought the company could well afford to make such a donation without doing it any material damage while to him the sum was large enough to confer a real benefit."

Most of Wisconsin's pioneer ventures in transportation improvement had ended in disappointment or disaster—victims of misguided enthusiasm, unrecognized economic realities, ineptitude, mismanagement, and plain dishonesty. It was Wisconsin's good fortune that the growing strength of her economy made it possible for a Milwaukee banker, who discovered his talent for railroad finance and management, to build a railroad empire tributary to the state's metropolis.

Selected Bibliography

Bender, Vilas A. "Morgan Martin and the Improvement of the Fox River." Master's thesis, University of Wisconsin, 1951. Martin lacked the tools, engineering skill, and money.

Bernd, John M. "The La Crosse and Milwaukee Railroad Grant, 1856." *Wisconsin Magazine of History* 30:141–53 (Dec. 1946). Bribery and scandal.

Bremer, Fredericka. *The Homes of the New World: Impressions of America.* Trans. Mary Howitt. New York, 1853. The stagecoach ride.

Clark, James I. *Wisconsin Grows to Statehood: Immigration and Internal Improvements.* Madison, 1955. Roads, canals, and railroads.

Clark, John G. *The Grain Trade in the Old Northwest.* Urbana, 1966. From a prize-winning dissertation.

Cropley, Carrie. "When the Railroads Came to Kenosha." *Wisconsin Magazine of History* 33:188–96 (Dec. 1949). Not very informative.

Cuthbertson, George A. *Freshwater.* New York, 1931. An interesting book on the technology of Great Lakes ship building.

Duckett, Kenneth W. "Politics, Brown Bread, and Bologna." *Wisconsin Magazine of History* 36:178–81, 202, 215–17 (Spring 1953). More on the 1856 railroad land grant scandal.

Fargo, Robert. "Robert Fargo—An Autobiography." *Wisconsin Magazine of History* 10:189–205 (Dec. 1926). Fargo worked as an operator on a pioneer telegraph line.

Fishlow, Albert. *American Railroads and the Transformation of the Ante-Bellum Economy.* Cambridge, Mass., 1965. There is an argument about the impact of the railroad on the American economy.

Goodrich, Carter. *Government Promotion of American Canals and Railroads.* New York, 1960. For the bigger picture.

Hartsough, Mildred L. *From Canoe to Steel Barge on the Upper Mississippi.* Minneapolis, 1934. Best on Wisconsin use of the river.

Hunt, Robert S. *Law and Locomotives: The Impact of the Railroad on Wisconsin Law in the Nineteenth Century.* Madison, 1958. Covers the pioneer promotions.

Hunter, Louis C., with the assistance of Beatrice Jones Hunter. *Steamboats on the Western Rivers: An Economic and Technological History.* Cambridge, Mass., 1949. Scholarly, readable, and interesting.

Karn, Edward D. "Roadmaking in Wisconsin Territory." Master's thesis, University of Wisconsin, 1959. Useful for knowing who built the first roads and how.

Kuehnl, George J. *The Wisconsin Business Corporation.* Madison, 1959. Material on early plank roads and turnpikes.

McCluggage, Robert M. "The Fox-Wisconsin Waterway; 1836–1872: Land

Speculation and Regional Rivalries." Ph.D. dissertation, University of Wisconsin, 1954. The best of several unpublished studies.

McCorison, Marcus A. "Peter Hotaling Brings a Steamboat to Lake Winnebago." *Wisconsin Magazine of History* 40:117–20 (Winter 1956). A Buffalo man got carried away by Wisconsin advertising.

Pommer, Patricia Joy. "Plank Roads: A Chapter in the Early History of Wisconsin Transportation, 1846–1871." Master's thesis, University of Wisconsin, 1950. There is not much published material on the plank road era.

Rice, Herbert W. "Early Rivalry among Wisconsin Cities for Railroads." *Wisconsin Magazine of History* 35:1–15 (Autumn 1951). There were 124 railroads chartered in Wisconsin, 1836–1859.

Schafer, Joseph. *The Winnebago-Horicon Basin: A Type Study in Western History.* Wisconsin Domesday Book, vol. 4. Madison, 1937. Good material on the Fox-Wisconsin waterway scheme.

Shaw, Ronald E. *Erie Water West: A History of the Erie Canal, 1792–1854.* Lexington, Ky., 1966. The canal was a vital link for Wisconsin.

Taylor, George Rogers. *The Transportation Revolution, 1815–1860.* The Economic History of the United States, vol. 4. New York: Harper Torchbooks, 1968. Useful general work.

Titus, Walter A. "Early Navigation on the Fox and Wolf Rivers and Lake Winnebago." *Wisconsin Magazine of History* 25:16–30 (Sept. 1940). From birchbark to some pretty queer contraptions.

Usher, Ellis B. "The Telegraph in Wisconsin." *SHSW Proceedings,* 1913, pp. 91–109. Madison, 1914. Not much available on the subject.

STATEHOOD IN
AN UNSTABLE UNION
1846–1865

part five

Local history, with its magnifying lens, often finds order and unity beyond the bounds of plausibility. This is especially so when Americans deal with the origins of their political institutions or with their Civil War. Founding fathers and fallen heroes inspire piety.

It will be suggested here that Wisconsin's founding fathers of 1846 did not remotely resemble the men of Philadelphia in the summer of 1787. They lacked the philosophical range and were impatient. Many of them were strangers to their electorates, strangers to one another, and certainly strangers to their task. It may be said that the second and successful constitutional convention was a cut above the first, and this may be so, but it was the 1846 convention that defined the issues and debated the alternatives.

Among the saving graces of both conventions was the adoption of a generous franchise allowing European immigrants to vote—white, male, twenty-one and over—after one year's residence with declaration of intent to become a citizen. The importance of this provision was tested in the 1850s, a decade of intense nativism and political uncertainty. Wisconsin's large foreign-born minority, unwittingly instructed by condescending Yankees, learned the uses of bloc voting. The new Republican party emerged from this experience shorn, at least officially, of some of the Yankee enthusiasms which most excited the wrath of the large German and Irish blocs against the Free Soilers. The claim that the Republicans captured a large portion of the German vote in 1860, however, is a dubious proposition.

Wisconsin, on the eve of the Civil War, was a society still growing pell mell—a population of 305,000 in 1850 swelled to 776,000 in 1860— and profoundly divided. The Yankee attitude is illustrated in a Thanksgiving sermon delivered in Plymouth Church of Milwaukee in 1856:

> Our city is distinguished for the largeness of its foreign population, and if we can do them good, while we avail ourselves of their assistance, we ought to be thankful for their presence. It may be a great disadvantage to us, to have so many foreigners among us, or, to speak more precisely, *to be among* so many foreigners. If we look upon them only as constituting so much political stock to trade in, or as mere tools for any purpose; we shall suffer. If we conform our habits to theirs, visit their dance-house on the Sabbath, saturate ourselves with their lager beer, and place ourselves on the one hand under the shadow of their infidelity, or on the other under the control of the Romanish Church— with no effort either to improve them in whatever respect they are defective, or to derive from them the benefits of their associations in whatever respect they are good; we shall suffer. It is possible to enjoy all the advantages of their presence, and avoid the greater part of the evils.

The challenge of civil war, to which Wisconsin responded with great sacrifice of blood and treasure, failed to unite this divided society. The embarrassing draft riots in the German communities of Ozaukee and Washington counties were not necessarily aberrations from a broad consensus. The Milwaukee *Seebote* warned emigrants that they had better choose Russia or Turkey rather than the United States, "the country of the lords of New England, where Germans and Irish must be annihilated, to make room for the negro."

Our view of the period has generally been colored by the ultimate military success of the Northern cause and the sacrifices that success cost. The commonly expressed judgment that Wisconsin was ready for the impending conflict, mentally and emotionally if not militarily, seems highly debatable. It was a retrospective and strictly Yankee view of the affair.

STATEHOOD

15

Sir, the time was when constitution-making was a rare affair, and many men found themselves suddenly enlarged by having a hand in the matter. But those days are gone by. It has become a common affair now. There are so many of them, and all so similar that I have little expectation of seeing any considerable number of great men indebted for their greatness to their seat here. It will therefore be quite as well to turn our attention to the business of making a constitution for the people, instead of making one for ourselves.

These words are so apt, both as description and criticism of the 1846 Constitutional Convention of Wisconsin, that it is a shame they cannot be cited as disinterested wisdom. George B. Reed, the delegate who spoke them to his fellows, was protesting the doctrinaire antibanking provisions which the convention had approved. Reed was correct in the substance of his protest, even though, as the brother-in-law of Milwaukee banker Alexander Mitchell, the source of his concern is suspect. It would be difficult to claim more than Delegate Reed was prepared to concede for the assemblage of prospective founding fathers, gathered in the capitol at Madison in the fall of 1846.

Professor James Willard Hurst has pointed out that Americans of the 1840s were impatient of the time and effort taken for constitution making. It did not represent the challenge that it had to an earlier generation:

Politics in the grand sense had been the focus of our creative energy from 1765 to 1800, when first the impact of imperial policy and then the novelty of new governments forced us to attend to problems of the organization of power. With these matters apparently settled, and confronting the challenge of the continent, the nineteenth century was prepared to treat law more casually, as an instrument to be used whenever it looked as if it would be useful. This instrumentalist view tended to put aside consideration of the larger problems of the organization or limitation of power and to take for granted the law's framework-setting function to an extent that did not do justice to its actual importance.

There is little that is remarkable in Wisconsin's course toward statehood. For some years it was the province of politicians and newspaper editors to yearn for this change of status. Governor Doty, for one, had identified himself with statehood and the return of the "lost territory" granted by Congress to Illinois and Michigan. Fortunately for statehood, the ever-popular Governor Dodge also agitated the question and was as ready as Doty to submit it to popular vote. Both laid a good deal of stress on the terms of the Northwest Ordinance of 1787, and assumed that when the population of the territory reached 60,000, the people should have the option to vote for statehood.

On the recommendation or insistence of Doty and Dodge, Wisconsin after 1841 voted on the issue almost yearly. The usual result was a very light vote, indicating indifference, and running about two to one against statehood. Interest plainly turned the other way early in 1846, when the legislature enthusiastically endorsed Governor Dodge's recommendation for yet another popular referendum on the matter, and provided the machinery for calling a constitutional convention should the referendum be favorable. It was: in a special April election, 12,334 voted for statehood and only 2,487 against.

In the summer of 1846, the census for which the legislation had provided showed a territorial population of 155,277. Comparison with the 1840 federal census of 30,945 showed that the territory had entered a period of explosive growth. Just ten years before, in 1836, a territorial census found only some 11,000 whites in the same area. There were changes to remark in the distribution of the new population. The lead district now held only 17 percent rather than the 28 percent of 1836. Green Bay had increased very little, while the Lakefront counties of Milwaukee and Racine had grown from 2,893 to 38,908. Population in 1846 was still mostly south of a line following the Wisconsin and Fox rivers from Prairie du Chien to Green Bay. There was only scattered settlement, of about 5,000, north of this line and along the Mississippi above Prairie du Chien. If the population figures by counties convey any surprises, they are in the growth of the interior counties. Rock County, for instance, grew from 2,867 in 1842 to 12,405 in 1846. Jefferson County grew from 1,594 to 4,758 in the same interval. Clearly, there were many communities which had barely formed at the time of statehood, and this would affect the constitutional convention that followed.

The rapid increase of population was one reason for the shift in sentiment from indifference to eagerness for statehood. There was every reason to expect that the change of status would be acceptable to Congress as well. Florida and Texas were admitted in 1845, affecting the balance between the slave and free states upon which the Missouri Compromise rested. Wisconsin and Iowa were the logical candidates to restore the balance.

If other reasons were needed to vote for statehood, a joint select committee of the territorial legislature provided them in reporting that the future state of Wisconsin would come into a handsome legacy of public lands: 500,000 acres, under the 1841 Land Law, in addition to the traditional section 16 of every township for school purposes and nearly 50,000 acres for a university. As a state, Wisconsin would receive 5 percent of the net proceeds from the sale of all federal lands within her borders. It was estimated that the share for 1845 would have been about $22,500. This figure exceeded the allocations made by a niggardly Congress for territorial legislative expenses that year.

Statehood also implied more dignity than territorial status. With that dignity, of course, went the selection of state officers and the end to territorial dissatisfaction with executive and judicial appointments through presidential patronage. While President Polk had made a popular choice by returning Henry Dodge to the governorship, Dodge's predecessors, Doty and Tallmadge, had not had such broad approval. The appointments of judges and federal attorneys had been jealously watched and complained of by the territorial bar.

Beyond these considerations loomed the presidential election of 1848. Serious sectional strains were appearing in the Democratic party nationally, centering on President Polk's war policy, which seemed to favor the southern slave interests. His contrasting mildness on the Oregon question was taken by many as evidence that the president lacked enthusiasm for adding northern territory. This might have been expected to further split the Wisconsin Democrats between the Yankees of the Lake, as the lead miners called them, and the Dodge Democrats, with their southern orientation. But Polk was a strict constructionist and vetoed a rivers and harbors bill in 1846, which enraged Democrats of both sections of Wisconsin. Southern Democrats settled above the Rock Island rapids of the Mississippi soon became western Democrats, with more flexible views on the role of the federal government with respect to internal improvements.

The campaigns of 1840, 1844, and 1848, built upon the popular campaign tactics developed by the Jacksonians, created an uncommon excitement for presidential politics. It was surely as distressing to be left out of this as it was to be denied United States senators and a vote in the House by the limitations of territorial citizenship. Politics was one of the few sources of organized amusement for everyone and a deadly serious game for many. Newspapers were generally dependent upon political factionalism just to keep afloat. There were many more of them than today, and their hold upon life was uncertain; a look at the newspapers published in Milwaukee or Madison in the 1840s and 1850s will satisfy one of that. There was always a political campaign of some kind going on, even if only to get someone removed or appointed. Wisconsin, after statehood and until 1884, conformed to the general pattern and elected state officers in biennial elections held in the odd-numbered years. In this way the excitement of filling the state offices did not dilute that of the congressional and presidential campaigns in the even years. United States senators were elected by the state legislators in the intervals between general elections.

It would have been strange had Wisconsin's citizenry not responded to the call of statehood in 1846. The population was here, the interest in national politics was intense, and politicians nationally looked to Wisconsin to mend a temporary sectional imbalance. Then, too, it was a period frothing with reform that found expression in political pressure groups and third-party movements, as the Jacksonian Democrats split apart and the Whigs slowly sank from view. State politics, constitution-making, and participation in national campaigns gave infinitely more scope to these reform enthusiasms than did territorial politics.

Frederick Jackson Turner claimed that the new western states established a broader definition of democracy and more progressive values in their constitutions than their predecessors had. His critics replied that the new states simply copied what others were already doing, and the best ideas came often from the older states in the East. Turner's defenders answer that the selection and modification of these ideas expressed what was creative and progressive on the frontier. Wisconsin's lawgivers had every temptation before them. They thought they had a clear mandate from the electorate, and models were being drawn all around them. Iowa had constitutional conventions in 1844 and 1846, Louisiana and Texas in 1845, and New York, which was Wisconsin's primary model, in the summer of 1846, just before the first Wisconsin convention. There were twenty new state constitutions adopted between 1838 and 1859, aside from a good number, such as Missouri's of 1845, Iowa's of 1844, and Wisconsin's of 1846, that were not adopted. In most of them, Democratic majorities were solemnizing the Jacksonian revolution, they thought. Wisconsin was no exception.

The 1846 constitution, which emerged from a convention described by a conservative Democratic editor as having "convened in disorder and ill humor, sat in confusion, and adjourned in disgrace," was decisively rejected by the electorate. That same electorate had decisively commissioned it, a few months earlier, in something resembling the form that it took. Despite its rejection, historical interest continues to center on the first convention, and justifiably, since the 1848 constitution, the one adopted, followed the earlier one closely. The 1846 convention almost exhausted public interest in constitution writing, but it brought into focus the issues of the day.

The delegates to the 1846 convention were nominated by party caucuses and elected on a partisan ballot. Of the 124 delegates, 103 were elected as Democrats, 18 as Whigs, and only 3 as independents. The leaders of the Democratic majority proclaimed their intention to write a Democratic constitution and saw no reason to act otherwise. Most of the important issues were debated in the election of the delegates: the prohibition against banking; limitations on state debt, particularly for internal improvements; enfranchisement of aliens who had declared their intention to become citizens; the long ballot and plural executive; an elective judiciary; a homestead exemption; women's property rights; and Negro suffrage.

Except in a few places, being a Whig in Wisconsin was a lonely career, and Whigs who ran for delegate had a strong tendency to take on a Democratic coloration. They foreswore nativist tendencies in the face of large foreign minorities who were enfranchised in the election of delegates, proclaimed wildcat banks an invention of the Devil, plumped for the homestead exemption, were against state support of internal improvements, and even favored an elective judiciary. There seemed to be general agreement on the issues and on the readiness of the voters to accept what were described as stern solutions.

Superficially, it would appear that a detailed understanding of New York politics in the period, which were infinitely more luxuriant and subtle than anything Wisconsin had yet achieved, should be helpful in understanding the vagaries of the Wisconsin 1846 Convention. Discussion in the convention, press, private correspondence, and letters to the editor was full of the terminology of New York politics: *Locofocos, Regency, Hunkers, Barnburners, Anti-renters, Tadpoles, Progressives, Greeleyites,* and variations thereon. The difficulty was that in a Wisconsin context, the terms acquired an Alice in Wonderland quality and meant whatever the user intended them to mean.

The New York influence in the convention went well beyond the 46 members listed as native New Yorkers. Fully 72 of them had some New York association, including education, residence, or business experience there. Patrick Rogan and Edward G. Ryan, for instance, listed among the 7 Irish-born members, both spent some years of their early manhood in New York; Ryan had his legal training there. Wisconsin was a Yankee society. A simple count of 103,000 native Yankees in the 1850 population of 305,000 does not give their true weight, any more than the count of 46 New York natives in the 1846 convention measures the influence of New York.

For geographic reasons, the basis of representation was set at 1 delegate for each 1,300 people, resulting in an unwieldy convention of 124 members. Only 9 members of the previous legislature were elected to the 1846 convention, a very thin leavening of experience for a constitutional body expanded to three times the size of the legislature and five times the size of the lower house.

In many areas, the electorate was equally novice. Delegate slates were chosen by party caucus on a countywide basis. Rock County's population, for example, had increased more than fourfold in the four years from 1842 to 1846. It had one councilman and two representatives in the 1846 legislature, and now elected ten delegates to the constitutional convention. Only three of them appear to have had significant political experience.

The unwieldy size of the convention, the newness and rapid growth of the larger counties, and a lack of acquaintance between electors and elected all prejudiced the chances for intelligent action. Another factor, which may seem an advantage at first blush, was that 1846 came before the railroad-building era in Wisconsin and before the lumber industry was well established. The energy expended in other directions might better have been devoted to defining the legal perimeters within which the railroads, lumber industry, and corporate enterprise generally were to operate. Workable concession and compromise is likely to start with mundane and definable interests. Spokesmen for conflicting public and private interests would have discovered one another more readily than they did in a fog of rhetoric about the various reform enthusiams of the times.

The large Democratic majority was at least faithful to its New York counterpart, which was irretrievably split in 1846 between the Van Buren, or Barnburner, faction (which was to emerge as the nucleus of the

Free Soil party in 1848) and the conservative, or Hunker, faction. It is usual to divide the Wisconsin Democrats between the followers of Governor Dodge, generally called Hunkers, and the Yankees in the southeast, who were variously labeled to identify their supposed radicalism. As we shall see, this division was not always helpful or accurate. A greater source of trouble in labeling was that the three Democrats who had the greatest influence on the proceedings, Marshall M. Strong and Edward G. Ryan of Racine and Moses M. Strong of Mineral Point, were to be erratic guides to any useful scheme of labeling.

Moses M. Strong was a clever parliamentarian, quick and forceful in debate. Twice he had been president of the legislative council, and he intended to be elected president of the 1846 convention. But this none-too-trustworthy legislative leader of the Dodge or Hunker faction, vain, quick-tempered, and ambitious, was given to bluster and improvisation rather than careful planning. Swaggering in to claim his prize, he was more of a Jacksonian bullyboy than many of his southern neighbors of the lead region, where his fondness for liquor and reputation for quick anger were not unappreciated.

Marshall M. Strong was a sort of legislative Hamlet, often caught in inconsistent positions, and he ended his part in the convention by resigning with a vow to oppose its results. Edward G. Ryan was razor sharp, as vain as Moses Strong, and a compulsive talker. For a short time he had edited a paper in pioneer Chicago when journalism was truly personal. True to his character, he had set out one time, with suitable publicity, to horsewhip a rival editor. His opponent took Ryan's whip away and literally sat on him in the middle of Clark Street. It was Ryan's second such humiliation, and after suffering others, he moved on to Racine and the practice of law in 1842. Marshall Strong recruited him for the county's Democratic delegate slate on the basis of their acquaintance.

The split in the Democratic party was out in plain sight. There were Yankees of the Lake who accepted such labels as progressive, Young America, Locofoco, and Tadpole, but the real division was between Governor Dodge and his supporters, who held all of the offices, divided the patronage, and ran the party, and the less-conservative newcomers, who were eager to take over. Many Yankee Democrats were conservative in temper or sided with the Dodge faction by sharing in the patronage. Many of the alleged radicals were one-issue men, and divisions grew from a lack of recognized leadership among them.

The splits among the Democrats presented an opportunity to the minority Whigs, who found their leader in the person of the lone delegate from Winnebago County, James Doty. Doty's politics were flexible. He owed his earlier appointment as territorial governor in 1841 to a Whig administration, but came to the 1846 convention as an independent. He later won election to Congress in 1848 as a Democrat. Though neither Whigs nor Democrats claimed him, he always found a following in Wisconsin politics. He enjoyed the politics of intrigue, at which he was a master. Ryan, in his perceptive convention reports published by the Racine *Advocate,* marked Doty as "the silent partner in this game" of thwarting the Democratic majority.

Doty found the divisions in the Democratic majority ready-made. Having an overwhelming majority, the Democrats characteristically afforded themselves the luxury of internal squabbles. The Dodge or Hunker Democrats were fighting over patronage. Moses Strong was at odds with Josiah Noonan, the postmaster at Milwaukee, who was Governor Dodge's principal lieutenant among the mixed Irish, German, and Yankee constituency there. This internal struggle among the party professionals turned out to be expensive. The convention included a crowd of Democratic strangers, most of them from the burgeoning Lakeside counties, who arrived with an assortment of radical notions and little sense of loyalty to the party leadership. These radical notions revolved around Negro suffrage, women's rights, reform of debtor law, limitations upon land ownership, and the abolition of capital punishment.

Moses Strong came to Madison assuming that the Democratic majority would assert its mastery by electing him to the convention presidency. Governor Dodge, as usual, provided no effective leadership for his followers. The "radical" Democrats, abetted by the Whig minority, pressed for the election of permanent officials as the first order of business. Don A. J. Upham, a Milwaukee Democrat whose sentiments were uncertain, led on the first ballot and won on the fourth. Upham was too amiable a man for the job, and Ryan noted James Doty's satisfaction with this result.

It is easy to exaggerate the conflict and disagreement which gave drama to the convention. The loose coalition of outsiders who, under James Doty's persuasion, thwarted the Democratic regulars again by giving the convention printing to Beriah Brown's *Wisconsin Democrat* rather than to the regular party organ, the *Wisconsin Argus,* could not accept Doty as a leader and did not find an effective one among themselves. The Democrats made an unwieldy majority, without cohesive force except for the individual delegate's need to defend his party orthodoxy. This response was frequently called upon by the trio who assumed the Democratic leadership. There was much of conventional wisdom upon which everyone was pretty well agreed. The problem was to find an issue which would separate the dissidents from their Whig allies and unite the Democrats.

The convention organized in committees to carry on its work. Ryan, who had taken a prominent role in the unsuccessful effort to get a Democratic caucus on the first day, was appointed chairman of the committee on banks and banking. The day after the announcement of committee assignments, Ryan astonished the convention by presenting for action the report of his committee. It developed that he had written the document entirely by himself, without calling a meeting of his committee. He had solicited the concurrence of individual members, but had ignored the lone Whig member. Ryan thought he had defined the issue that would unite a clearcut Democratic majority.

The banking proposals were truly Draconian. The legislature was never to have the power to authorize or incorporate anything resembling a bank. Anyone issuing any evidence of indebtedness which might circulate, like the certificates of deposit of the Milwaukee Marine and Fire Insurance Company, would upon conviction receive a prison term of not less than five years and be fined not less than $10,000. Other provisions were equally severe, to stop any possible improvisation that might be used in place of a bank note. The convention was stunned by Ryan's design and by his temerity.

The banking issue was one which cut across geographic and factional lines within the Democratic majority and mobilized the Whigs in opposition. The Whigs were ready to rule out wildcat banking, but not banking root and branch. Most Democratic delegates, except for some from Milwaukee who recognized the advantages of Alex Mitchell's bank, had taken positions hostile to all banks and bank notes. It was difficult to defend a sensible position on the subject without being shouted down as a monopolist. The ridiculous result was to remove Ryan's punitive provisions as proper subjects for legislation, but to leave intact the provisions prohibiting the incorporation of "any bank or other institution having any banking power or privilege," excluding even branches of any bank of the United States, and prohibiting the circulation of any bank note of less than $20 denomination. The purpose of this last was to prevent outside banks or the federal government from circulating smaller notes in Wisconsin. This raised interesting possibilities, should the federal government issue paper money, as it began to do during the Civil War.

Most of the delegates were aware that they had taken an untenable position on the banking matter, and a great deal of time was wasted bringing it to the floor again. But the hard-line coalition held on the measure each time. Ryan delighted in expounding his partisan position and his distrust of future legislative judgment. He was a heavy cross for many less-aggressive delegates to bear. Moses and Marshall Strong upheld him stoutly. In the eighth week, after members had been home to test local sentiment and feel the pressure from banker Alexander Mitchell and his friends, a crucial vote was taken on a motion to reconsider the banking article. The motion lost in a tie vote. The article had been passed a month earlier by a vote of 79 to 23. The defectors were nearly all Lake-shore Democrats.

Ryan was no radical. He was merely representative of the varied opinions found among the Democratic delegates which make them so difficult to categorize. Ryan was a member of the original Locofoco convention in New York City in 1835 when reformers led a workingmen's revolt against the Tammany organization. The Tammanyites turned off the gas in the hall, but the reformers were prepared with the new sulphur matches, known as "locofocos"; hence the name. This reform branch within the New York Democracy had various origins, including the Workingmen's party of the early 1830s, English radicals of both working and middle class origins, and American reformers. Locofocoism has some significance for Wisconsin politics over the long term. It was Edward G. Ryan's belief that the corporation was strictly an instrument of monopoly chartered by the state. The role of the state, he believed, was properly one of prohibiting any form of advantage to organized capital rather than of chartering privilege. The language is familiar; Robert M. La Follette often cited his debt to the ideas of Judge Ryan as he had heard them expounded in the 1870s.

Ryan and the two Strongs dominated but could not control the convention. All three opposed Negro suffrage. Moses Strong, chairman of the committee on suffrage and the elective franchise, held the most generous views among the three on giving the franchise to aliens seeking citizenship. All three voted against article 14 on the property rights of married women and exemption of a minimum homestead from sale for debt. Ryan was the only member of the trio who spoke and voted for the abolition of capital punishment. They agreed in opposing an elective judiciary. These matters, plus a movement to limit the amount of land under a single ownership (which did not come to a full debate or vote), constituted the truly radical proposals seriously considered by the convention.

Moses Strong was the self-appointed watchdog of the convention's time, to the irritation of other delegates, who found him long-winded and much given to self-justifying speeches. Marshall Strong, by a similar appointment, was the conscience of the convention—self-righteous and inconsistent. Ryan also spoke frequently, and no one appeared to challenge successfully the trio's domination of the proceedings. One delegate expressed his sorrow, after a Ryan speech, that they had not adopted a suggested rule "that a man should not talk any longer than he had anything to say."

Negro suffrage was made a rider on the 1846 constitution, to be voted upon separately. It was defeated, to no one's surprise, having been offered to placate the unknown number of Yankees suspected of favoring it. The number of acknowledged abolitionists was small, but vocal, and had a following. There were very few Negro citizens available to exercise the right that would be granted.

The enfranchisement of the alien immigrants was a matter of wider concern. The Democratic legislature had adopted a generous franchise in the session which set up the vote on statehood and provided for the election of delegates. Only six-months residence and a declaration of intent to become a citizen had been required of aliens. Many Whigs and conservative Democrats would have preferred more stringent requirements, but this was a hazardous position to advertise with such a large foreign-born population. Moses Strong favored the broad franchise; the Germans and Irish flocked to the Democratic banner. Ryan, who like many of the Irish-born had established his citizenship before coming to Wisconsin, favored an oath of allegiance in addition to the declaration of intent. This was distasteful to the large German minority. A year's residence, registration of intent, and the oath of allegiance became the final version.

Two provisions which raised almost as much resistance as the banking article, in the struggle over ratification, were included in article 14. They dealt with the property rights of married women and the homestead provision.* Section 1 proposed that a married woman should be entitled to hold property without its being subject to disposition by her husband. This was in contradistinction to the prevalent theory that the husband was the superior partner and properly had full control over what was his, theirs, and hers. It was a man's world, and both Ryan and Marshall Strong were horrified by this threat to it.

Section 2 of the same article, the homestead provision, had no connection with the familiar federal land law of later date. It was a measure designed to insure that a debtor's family should be protected by reserving from attachment the family home and forty acres or two town lots, to the maximum value of $1,000. This was an extension of the already successful movement to do away with imprisonment for debt, as well as a recognition that American society was based upon economic risk-taking. Josiah Noonan, the conservative Democratic postmaster of Milwaukee, referred to "those Horace Greeley provisions of the constitution—the rights of married women and exemption." Marshall Strong left the con-

---

* These provisions were borrowed from the constitution of Texas, which as one opponent uncharitably put it, was "filled with the scapegraces of all nations."

vention, pledged to defeat the constitution for containing these monstrosities. Ryan and Moses Strong accepted the convention's work and its identification with the Democratic party.

With enemies like Marshall Strong, Noonan, who had lately been editor of the principal Democratic paper in Milwaukee, Rufus King, Whig editor of the Milwaukee *Sentinel,* the allies of the Milwaukee Marine and Fire Insurance Company, and many influential men with commercial interests, the constitution had too few friends. The rival Democratic newspapers in Madison both supported it. Ryan and Moses Strong took the campaign trail in its favor, as did their quondam opponent James Doty. Their support was well publicized by the opposition. There was scarcely a hamlet in the territory where the support of at least one of the three was not the kiss of death. Supporters insisted that all opposition was inspired by friends of the banks and of banking privileges, preferring to ignore opposition to other controversial provisions. The constitution was defeated by a vote of 20,333 to 14,119, carrying only seven counties out of twenty-eight. It lost most heavily in predominantly Yankee counties, particularly Racine and Rock. It had strong support in heavily German areas, carrying Washington County by 1,478 to 353. Milwaukee County, heavily Democratic but the home of the Mitchell bank and the principal commercial center, rejected it by a close 1,996 to 1,678.

Wisconsinites generally were disgusted with the results; they remained in favor of statehood and impatient of delay. Morgan Martin, their congressional delegate, had succeeded in getting an enabling act through Congress, after the favorable vote on statehood in the territory, so that door was invitingly ajar, but apathy reigned toward any proposal to pay for another constitutional convention. There was some suggestion that the legislature should cure the worst defects of the instrument and submit it again to a referendum, but this seemed a dubious course. It was generally agreed that the bank article had been the real nemesis of the constitution and the issue which demoralized the Democrats more than any other. The party's difficulties were confirmed when Moses Strong demanded and won its nomination for congressional delegate, then lost the election to Whig John H. Tweedy of Milwaukee, who did not campaign. This was a sobering event for the Democrats, many of whom wished Strong every discomfort short of defeat.

Interest in a new convention began to build during the Strong-Tweedy campaign in the summer of 1847, and Governor Dodge called a special session to set up the necessary machinery. Profiting from the mistakes of the first convention, the legislation provided for a membership of sixty-nine, a little over half that of the 1846 convention. Although as divided as before, the Democrats elected forty-six delegates, to twenty-three for the Whigs. Continuing Democratic dissension gave the Whigs, with their larger minority, more of a voice in the second convention. Candidates were questioned closely on the controversial articles adopted by the 1846 convention and only six members of that first convention returned as delegates to the second. Among the new faces were many men who had been residents of the territory a relatively short time. It cannot be argued that the members of the second convention were very different in respect to their familiarity with one another or their electorate, but they had the advantage of being fewer and the example of their predecessors to consult. Morgan Martin, who had been retired from Congress by the nomination of Moses Strong as the Democratic candidate for territorial delegate, was elected president of the new convention. "It was composed of a large majority of conservative men and my task was far from difficult," he recalled later.

The second convention, which met from December 15, 1847, to February 1, 1848, did not accept the suggestion of several members that they simply revise the controversial sections of the 1846 draft, but their work was primarily a reworking of it. One authority, while claiming that the second convention created a new draft "from preamble to signatures," noted that the skeleton of the rejected constitution was only slightly altered, "and even the disputed provisions were changed less than was to be expected."

The hotly debated banking article of the 1846 Constitutional Convention was compromised in a manner calculated to mollify both friends and foes of banking: the legislature was authorized to take a referendum on the question of banks or no banks. Should the response be affirmative, any general banking legislation proposed by the legislature had to be returned to the general electorate for approval by a second referendum. Within five years this had been done, as the growing commercial economy demanded the services of banks.

The elective judiciary was retained, along with other 1846 provisions relating to the courts. The language dealing with the property rights of married women was discreetly dropped, to be adopted soon by the legislature. A neutral evasion, recommending exemption of "a reasonable amount of property" to be recognized "by wholesome laws," replaced the homestead exemption. This was one of the twenty-two sections in the Bill of Rights. Similar provisions had found their way into the constitutions of the respectable states of Michigan and Connecticut since the 1846 convention had borrowed the idea from Texas. No reference was made to Negro suffrage in the 1848 constitution. The provisions for white manhood suffrage remained essentially the same, except that the requirement of the oath of allegiance for aliens was dropped.

The new constitution was accepted with a general feeling of relief and little organized opposition. Only 22,591 electors voted on ratification in March 1848, whereas 34,350 had voted a year earlier when the 1846 constitution was rejected. Three-fourths of the light vote favored ratification. The rest of the statehood process went smoothly, and Congress passed the official admission act on May 29, 1848.

The 1846 constitution had answered a number of purposes. It defined the essential framework of the 1848 constitution, which still serves the state of Wisconsin. It also aired most of the enthusiasms which animated particularly those of Yankee background in the "fermenting Forties."

The story of Wisconsin's founding fathers is one worth notice, if only to counteract our tendency to assume that "there were giants in those days." The mantle of statesmanship will not cover the confusion involved. The confusion was much a part of the times and the inchoate state of Wisconsin's rapidly growing pioneer society. It was also a reflection of the inadequacies of available political leadership. As in other times, there were not many giants at hand, but men of ordinary clay consulting serviceable precedents.

Selected Bibliography

Alexander, Edward P. "Wisconsin, New York's Daughter State," *Wisconsin Magazine of History* 30:11–30 (Sept. 1946). Influence of New York on the Wisconsin constitution.

Andersen, Theodore A. *A Century of Banking in Wisconsin*. Madison, 1954. The bank issue in the constitutional conventions and after.

Beitzinger, Alfons J. *Edward G. Ryan, Lion of the Law*. Madison, 1960. Participant and commentator on the 1846 Convention.

Brown, Chester C. "A Comparative Study of Constitutional Development in the Old Northwest, 1847–1875." Master's thesis, University of Wisconsin, 1937. A useful view of constitutional changes and conventions in neighboring states.

Brown, Ray A. "The Making of the Wisconsin Constitution." *Wisconsin Law Review* 1949:648–94 (July 1949). A summary of the 1846 Constitutional Convention.

Fishel, Leslie H., Jr. "Wisconsin and Negro Suffrage." *Wisconsin Magazine of History* 46:180–96 (Spring 1963). The argument in the constitutional conventions.

Hill, Perry C. "Rufus King and the Wisconsin Constitution." *Wisconsin Mag-*

azine of History 32:416–35 (June 1949). New York Whig who edited the Milwaukee *Daily Sentinel and Gazette;* opposed the 1846 Constitution.

Hurst, James Willard. *Law and the Conditions of Freedom in the Nineteenth-Century United States.* Madison: University of Wisconsin Paperbacks, 1964. "The Release of Energy," the first of three essays, is on constitution making.

Jorgenson, Lloyd P. *The Founding of Public Education in Wisconsin.* Madison, 1956. Free public education was not widespread in the 1840s.

London, Lena. "Homestead Exemption in the Wisconsin Constitution." *Wisconsin Magazine of History* 32:176–84 (Dec. 1948). A popular debtor-law reform from the Texas constitution.

Paxson, Frederic L. "A Constitution of Democracy—Wisconsin, 1847." *Mississippi Valley Historical Review* 2:3–24 (June 1915). Paxson was Frederick Jackson Turner's successor at Wisconsin.

Quaife, Milo M., ed. *SHSW Collections.* Constitutional Series. Vol. 1, *The Movement for Statehood, 1845–1846.* Madison, 1918. Vol. 2, *The Convention of 1846.* Madison, 1919. Vol. 3, *The Struggle over Ratification, 1846–1847.* Madison, 1920. Vol. 4, *The Attainment of Statehood.* Madison, 1928. Massive, poorly edited and indexed, but it's all there somewhere.

Smith, Alice E. *James Duane Doty, Frontier Promoter.* Madison, 1954. The gentleman from Winnebago.

Still, Bayrd. "State-Making in Wisconsin, 1846–48: An Illustration of the Statehood Process." *Wisconsin Magazine of History* 20:34–59 (Sept. 1936). Ray Brown, "The Making of the Wisconsin Constitution," is clearer.

The Wisconsin Blue Book. Any recent issue will have a copy of the Wisconsin constitution with amendments.

THE UNEASY YEARS, THE 1850s

16

Although badly split by the fight over the 1846 constitution, the Democratic party still mustered a comfortable majority in Wisconsin politics. The surprise victory of Whig John Tweedy over Moses Strong in the election for territorial delegate in 1847 reminded the Democrats that the purpose of major parties is to win elections and distribute the patronage. The defeat was sobering in view of the greater rewards promised by statehood. The party managers, realizing the hazards of divisive factionalism, decided upon the nomination, at the head of their ticket, of a man who would give the least offense. Nelson Dewey, a Connecticut Yankee from Grant County in the lead region, was the compromise candidate. He was not allied with the Dodge faction, although a resident among the southern Democrats, and his background was that of a Yankee lawyer. He had represented Grant County in the territorial legislature and had served as both speaker of the assembly and president of the council. Dewey did not disappoint the hopes of more ambitious politicians in the party. He had two unexceptional terms as governor during which he did nothing to advance his own career. Retiring quietly at the end of 1851, he was scarcely noticed and died in obscurity and poverty in 1889. Dewey is remembered today for the home he built near Cassville, now a state park.

Unlike the federal government inaugurated in 1789, the new state government of Wisconsin was not a sharp departure from its predecessor, in form. It followed easily in the path of the territorial organization and built upon the territorial laws, administrative forms, and judicial decisions. There were new tasks, however, which went beyond the powers which Congress had conferred upon the territorial government. One of the most important of these was the management of a huge and growing body of state lands. Wisconsin eventually got over 10,000,000 acres, or about 30 percent of her land area, in the form of grants for common schools and higher education, public improvement subsidies, and swamplands. This land was patented to the state, and most of it was disposed of over a long period of years.

In addition to the traditional section 16 in every township reserved for school purposes, the state received the benefits of an 1841 Whig measure granting 500,000 acres to each state for internal improvements. The opposition of both constitutional conventions toward involving the state in internal improvements determined them to dedicate this land, also, to school purposes, roughly a million and a half acres. Added to this, but earmarked for the university, was a grant of two townships—46,080 acres. In 1850, Congress made another princely grant of what were loosely defined as swamp and overflow lands. By 1875, Wisconsin had claimed over 3,000,000 acres under this grant. The grant for the Fox-Wisconsin Waterway, made in 1846, was supplemented by grants of 2,400,000 acres for railroad subsidies, which like the earlier canal grants were made to the state. Most of this land was conferred on private corporations to carry out the improvements. The Morrill Act of 1862 made a further grant of 30,000 acres for each member of Congress, to be used for an agricultural and mechanical college.

The immediate problem for the legislature was to carry out the mandate of the state constitution specifying that school and university lands should be administered by a commission made up of the secretary of state, the state treasurer, and the attorney-general. The legislature was to designate the terms of sale and the investment of the proceeds, which were to form a permanent fund from which only the income would be used. In common with most of the public-lands states, Wisconsin appears to have frittered away her patrimony by unwise laws and culpable administration. This has been the theme of those who found the proceeds of early sales not at all commensurate with the value of the lands involved. The constitution provided that "the commissioners shall have power to withhold from sale any portion of such lands when they shall deem it expedient," and critics have pointed out that this provision was used very little to protect the funds, the commissioners acting rather in "hot haste" to get the lands on the market.

It must be remembered, however, that the legislators and administrators were operating within the framework of contemporary attitudes and political opinion. The pioneers, probably correctly, assumed that posterity was going to have an easier time than they paying taxes for necessary services. Agricultural pioneers were hostile to the withdrawal of lands from the market, whether by speculators, by the granting of designated tracts as subsidies for canals or railroads, or withheld by the state for future revenue. They might favor the purposes of the various grants, but wanted to retain preemption privileges on them at the minimum federal price.

The handling of the lands and funds, therefore, was in accord with current opinion. The terms varied for the various lands, but in general, sales were by auction, with a minimum price set by a local board of appraisers. The minimums above $1.25 were justified by the costs of administration and a generous credit policy not available on federal lands. A preemption right was recognized for bona fide settlers, and credit terms required only 10 percent down, with ten years to pay, on a mortgage drawing only 7 percent. Credit was even more generous on the 500,000-acre grant—nothing down and thirty years to pay—with a larger preemption claim allowed. Except for the section 16 lands, the granted lands had to be located and claimed by the state from the public domain. This placed much of the state land in unsettled areas which had not been open to sale, where it was surrounded by federal public lands.

The hot haste to get the lands sold, and their location in unsettled areas, had the obvious effect on the market: many of the tracts remained unsold, after being offered at the statutory public auctions. Contemporary critics blamed high appraisal prices, while later critics said that local appraisal boards set them ridiculously low. As with the federal lands, after the state lands had been offered at public auction and gone unsold, the commission could entertain private purchase offers at the minimum appraised prices. A 160-acre limitation on individual purchasers, contained in the legislation, was ignored after the land was offered at auction, and at this point there was ample opportunity for land speculators. But the decision to locate, appraise, and put the lands up for sale as quickly as possible was a popular one not chargeable to speculators alone or to administrative ineptitude.

The belief that there should be limits on the purchase of public lands was widely held. It appeared in urban politics through the National Reform Association, which grew out of the workingmen's parties of the 1830s, a reflection of the conviction that cheap or free lands influenced wages favorably by offering an alternative to industrial labor. The attitude of pioneer farmers toward absentee speculators coincided with this agitation. The leadership was also involved in antislavery, temperance, and other reform causes. The prejudice against absentee speculators, most active in 1848–51, was such that the land limitation forces briefly got the support of Governor Dewey and many of the legislators. A bill to set a 320-acre limit upon landholding came very near passage, although it is a question how serious its support was among the legislators who voted for it. For many, it was an impractical enthusiasm which could not be implemented in the face of federal land policies and laws, but it was simply not politic to oppose the legislation. The threat of its passage, however, brought out a determined and successful opposition whose most effective weapon was ridicule. One mocking resolution, offered at a Milwaukee mass meeting, was "that all property in the United States, the State of Wisconsin, and the City of Milwaukee [the legislation included a two-lot limit on urban property] ought to be equally divided every Saturday night, and oftener if considered necessary."

The real struggle, as it turned out, was over the use of the permanent funds created by the sale of the state land. In a capital-starved economy, any measure that turned a plentiful resource like land or timber into scarce capital met with approval. Now the question was who should have the use of the capital which was to form the permanent school fund. Here again popular opinion was served. While there was agitation to lend the fund to the Milwaukee and Mississippi Railroad, a broader sentiment favored lending it on liberal terms to farmers. This last was acted upon with a law authorizing loans of $100 to $500 at 7 percent interest, a very favorable rate at the time, on first mortgages on real estate. The effect of the law and its administration was to collect very small down payments on land sales and then lend the modest capital accumulated to the buyers.

It was argued that the early sale of school lands and the generous loan policy served to attract settlers and speed the building of the country. But it had other effects. Early sale by public auction left large tracts open for later private sale to speculative buyers unembarrassed by the 160-acre restriction, while the 1857 panic imperiled much of the principal of the school funds. Fortunately, the state retained title to lands with unpaid balances.

The idea of free public education was fairly well established in the territorial period in Wisconsin, a sentiment somewhat in advance of the times, for free public schools were not at all common in the United States until after 1865. A generous attitude toward public education dominated both constitutional conventions. It was felt that the public schools would be the most effective single instrument for the assimilation of immigrant children as well as an attraction for their parents to settle. Controversy revolved around the creation and administration of the school funds. The Democratic majority assigned the public improvement fund from the federal land sales and the 500,000-acre grant, similarly earmarked, to the school fund. This disposition of state land grants became so well established that the 1856 legislature assigned 75 percent of the returns from the swamplands grant to the school funds, specifically to the normal schools.

The school system set up by the new state did not go much beyond the territorial system in existence, and the 1848 school statute was such a hodgepodge that the legislature, recognizing its deficiencies, selected a commission of three to codify and rationalize school law. Michael Frank of Racine was the leader of the revision commission, but he was unable to achieve the reforms he thought necessary. The independence of individual school districts and boards was a serious defect, fostering a spirit of localism and partisanship in school matters. The county superintendents with authority, which Frank wanted, were not authorized until 1861. The constitution created the elective office of state superintendent, with duties prescribed by the legislature, but its powers were not extensive. While the superintendent apportioned revenues from the state school funds, they were not large enough to enhance his powers, which remained largely hortatory. The independent districts went their own ways, and there were few people involved in school matters who could be considered professionals, even among teachers and administrators. The local school boards were often the province of Protestant clergymen, who effectively set aside the statutory provision that public education was to be nonsectarian. One state superintendent defended the proposition that "an illiterate teacher is best for a school of beginners." Teaching was regarded and paid accordingly.

Aside from the schools, the legislature was busy with the requirements of local government in a rapidly growing and expanding population. Administratively, this meant the creation of twenty-eight new counties in the decade from 1850 to 1860. Towns and villages were discovering new responsibilities, as well as organizing to serve established needs. Milwaukee grew from 20,000 to 45,000 in the interval, and had problems which, as a municipal corporation created by the state, it often took to the legislature. The legislative record is full of this detail.

The executive and the legislature were also involved in setting up the new state institutions. New York had furnished models for constitutional provisions, criminal code, and code of court procedures, and it now provided a model for the state prison. It was a time of interest in the possible reform function of prisons as opposed to simple punishment, and the prisons at Cherry Hill, near Philadelphia, and at Auburn, New York, were leaders in this movement. With the building of the Waupun prison, beginning in 1851, Wisconsin, too, became a leader in penal administration. Taken from the Auburn model, which was based upon a theory of useful labor, learning skills, and earning privileges in common workshops, Waupun became another national model in this field. The prison was built under the direction of a commission of three appointed members, but became such a political football that in 1853 the legislature provided for an elected warden. This system prevailed until 1873, when the office again was made appointive, and a State Board of Charities and Reform made policy. The elective warden tended to act quite independently, which is bad in terms of administrative theory. But it is interesting that during the first twenty-five years of statehood, Wisconsin was looked to as an example of progressive prison administration, a reputation she had lost by the 1880s. Colonel Hans Heg, who is memorialized with a statue on the capital grounds at Madison as a Civil War hero, was one of the elected wardens, the Republicans having provided a place on the state ballot for the Norwegians in this manner.

The abolition of capital punishment had been pressed by Warren Chase in the constitutional conventions, but without success. The legislature took this step, largely at the instance of Marvin A. Bovee, a member of the state senate and one of the many New Yorkers in early Wisconsin politics. He saw the passage of his measure in 1853, putting Wisconsin in the van in this respect. Bovee devoted much of his life to writing and speaking on the subject to a national audience.

The School for the Blind at Janesville was the first state institution for the handicapped, taken over in 1850 from local supporters. Other state institutions were developed, as it was recognized that county support and maintenance were inadequate. The state prison was a logical outgrowth of the counties' reluctance to hold prisoners on long sentences in county jails. Similarly, the first State Hospital for the Insane at Mendota was opened in 1860, and in the same year, the State Reform School for boys at Waukesha. The creation of these institutions was the expression of humanitarian and reform impulses that were shortly overshadowed by the slavery issue. The generation of the 1880s would return to them and rescue the indigent and mentally handicapped from county jails and poorhouses.

The perfectionist temper in secular affairs is illustrated by an experiment in communal living, the Fourierist Phalanx at Ceresco (Ripon), on the same model as the more famous Brook Farm. Ceresco was a brief success, and noteworthy in that its members made a small profit in its liquidation. Its founder, Warren Chase, sat as a member of both Wisconsin constitutional conventions, skillfully advocating such advanced reforms as the abolition of capital punishment and perfect equality regardless of race or sex. Following a common diversion of the time, Chase immersed himself in spiritualism, and in 1853 left Wisconsin for California. An antithesis to Chase's liberalism was the variant Mormon colony at Voree in Racine County, led by James Strang. The colony moved to Beaver Island, Michigan, in 1849. Its story involves polygamy, intrigue, and murder, while Ceresco's was simply one of communal living quietly abandoned.

The elective judiciary, while not a Wisconsin innovation, was sufficiently new to make it remarkable, although seventeen other states had adopted the system by 1860. An argument during the conventions had centered on the merits of a separate supreme court as opposed to one made up of the district or circuit judges sitting *en banc*. The latter was adopted, but the writers of the constitution happily allowed the legislature to define court jurisdictions and to decide on the question of a separate supreme court, which they did affirmatively in 1852.

There can be no doubt of the vigor of the pioneer state circuit and supreme courts. Most judges were elected on a partisan ballot. Several ran on independent tickets but were identified as independent Whigs or Democrats. The voters seemed to have a weakness for Whig judges, even in districts which were normally Democratic. Whigs were assumed to have the virtues of their Federalist forebears when clothed in judicial robes. Certainly they acted independently enough, despite the manner of their selection. In the famous Glover case, Sherman Booth, who had aroused the citizens of Racine and Milwaukee to release the escaped slave Joshua Glover from jail, was arrested by a U.S. marshal, under the federal Fugitive Slave Act, for impeding justice. A writ of habeus corpus brought Booth into the state court of Judge Abram Smith, who discharged him and declared the Fugitive Slave Act unconstitutional into the bargain. This decision was taken to the state supreme court, which upheld Judge Smith and affirmed the unconstitutionality of the federal law. It should be pointed out that these events took place between March and July of 1854. In January 1854, Stephen A. Douglas had introduced his Kansas-Nebraska Bill overthrowing the Compromise of 1850 and reviving a militant antislavery sentiment.

An act of greater courage on the part of the supreme court came the following year in the contested election between William A. Barstow and Coles Bashford for the governorship. Barstow was the Democratic incumbent, while Bashford represented the new Republican party in its first major test. The Democrats had carried the other state offices easily, but Barstow was a heavy liability. His administration had been marked by accusations of corruption, and he was at odds with the popular leaders within his own party. The returns were not clearcut and the contest was close. The state board of canvassers, controlled by the Democrats, waited until the day before the inauguration, then counted Barstow in by 157 votes. Barstow had all the aces showing: possession of the office, the certificate of election from the official canvassers, and a Democratic attorney-general.

The Republicans went to the state supreme court to contest the election. They hired Edward G. Ryan, who although a Democrat, disliked Barstow. Ryan was a fixture of many landmark judicial decisions of the period, and with his associates was able to persuade the court that it had to go behind the official returns of the board of canvassers. The court did so and declared Republican Bashford the duly elected governor. Barstow denounced the usurpation of power by the court, but made the strategic error of resigning when he might easily have stretched an appeal over his two-year term. The Democratic lieutenant-governor, Arthur MacArthur (grandfather of General Douglas MacArthur), had been installed as governor by the Democrats. He was seized with the momentary delusion that the office was his, but he prudently reconsidered and surrendered it to Governor Bashford. It is argued that the prestige of the court prevented a threatened resort to violence by Democratic hotheads.

The passionately argued bank issue had been put off, rather than settled, by the second constitutional convention. When put to the voters in 1851, it carried in favor of state banks by an overwhelming majority. The votes represented a surprising shift in popular sentiment, a recognition of the necessary role of banks in the economy, and a tribute to the management of the Wisconsin Marine and Fire Insurance Company, which had been filling that role in spite of determined political efforts to put it out of business.

The cumbersome constitutional machinery retarded banking legislation and reforms but nevertheless worked. The 1852 legislature elected free banking, rather than charter banking, in the belief that it was more democratic to allow any group with the necessary capital to organize a bank under a general statute. The question of note issue was recognized as most crucial, requiring close regulation. It was decided to control this by having an elected state official, the bank comptroller, issue bank notes based upon the deposit of certain securities—state and railroad bonds— with his office. Bank note circulation could not exceed the value of the securities deposited. The notes were identified with the bank of issue, which had to redeem them in specie upon demand.

The techniques, if not the worst vices, of wildcat banking were still practiced. C. C. Washburn started a bank at Mineral Point and bought into another in Hallowell, Maine. He circulated the Hallowell notes among the Maine lumbermen in the Wisconsin pineries and the Mineral Point notes wherever he could. The purpose was to keep notes from coming back to the bank of issue for redemption. Bank notes issued in the northern counties amounted to ten to twenty times the amounts per capita issued by banks in the populous counties. Banking, for many promoters, was still a game of circulating notes and making it difficult for the holders to redeem them.

The state bank comptroller had little regulatory machinery at his command, beyond the control of the initial note issue and semi-annual reports required by statute. It was easy to get into the banking business under the general statute, and by 1859 there were 108 state banks. It was a chancy way to create needed bank credit, but it encouraged the growth of industrial capacity. Wisconsin's banks survived the 1857 panic, but the crisis posed by the Civil War took several under.

There was a lingering Jacksonian distrust of the corporation as an instrument of private business, yet a growing recognition of its usefulness in organizing capital for economic development. The constitution was ambivalent on the matter, as were the early legislatures. The constitution provided that corporations other than banks "may be formed under general laws," but not by special acts except "where, in the judgment of the legislature, the objects of the corporation cannot be attained under general laws." This constitutional provision looked in both directions and did not bring into being a truly general law for corporations.

A general statute covering a particular type of corporation was the usual pattern. Although such statutes were not limited to public purpose corporations—roads, railroads, bridges, ferries, piers, telegraphs, and so forth—these were a large share of the business of the legislature. An 1849 statute covered incorporations in manufacturing, mining, lumbering, agriculture, mechanical, and chemical businesses. Businessmen were not averse to using the option of special charters for their corporations, but not usually for suspect reasons. "The reader must scan their standardized clauses with a very careful eye if he would find the small variations which may represent the hidden grab or privilege which legend associates with the special charter era," according to James Willard Hurst. There was generally more evidence of legislative mistrust than of special privilege or corruption.

Positive concern with private economic development went beyond cor-

poration law. A geological survey of the state was begun in 1853 with
the optimistic expectation that vast workable deposits of lead, copper,
iron, coal, and other mineral resources would be found. Another contribution to the needs of private enterprise, at least in part, was the establishment of an office of commissioner of immigration, which Wisconsin
pioneered in 1852. Official pamphlets were broadcast, and the governor's
annual report was commonly made in a form for this purpose, with ex-
tracts printed in several languages. The city of Milwaukee joined in these
efforts, to increase the local labor supply as well as the flow of immigration through the port.

Wisconsin came to statehood at a time when the traditional major parties were in transition, and one of them, the Whig party, would shortly
disappear, while the Democrats had entered a time of trial. Territorial
politics had been highly personal in the early years, but were becoming
more traditionally partisan as statehood approached. The dissolution of
the minority Whig party, the serious splits in the Democratic party, and
the metamorphosis of parts of both into the Republican party are commonly explained in terms of the slavery issue. It is probably fair to say
that slavery and temperance were the paramount issues in Wisconsin politics in the early years of statehood, but with some qualification.

The antislavery issue was not a simple, direct one. There were shades
of antislavery sentiment ranging from uncompromising abolitionism to
simple disapproval of slavery by old-line Whigs and Democrats who yet
accepted it as legal under the federal constitution. Events were to blur
the distinctions and bring many of these people together in the Free Soil,
and subsequently the Republican, party. Temperance sentiment was likewise divided, and ranged from those who wanted to legislate absolute
prohibition to those who opposed any political solution for what they
considered an individual moral problem.

Opposition to temperance was well defined. Political conservatives objected to legislation on the matter as an unconscionable interference with
individual rights. The Germans were militant on the subject and rejected
the meddlesome prejudices of their Yankee neighbors. This was a continuous source of hostility between these groups. No one defended slavery
except by indirection: a strictly southern problem having no place in
Wisconsin politics.

The annexation of Texas and the Mexican War made slavery a burning issue in Wisconsin's first election after statehood. There had been an
abolition party, the Liberty party, in existence since 1840, with a small
but firm following in southeast Wisconsin. Agitating for abolition and
Negro suffrage, however, was a far cry from this general opposition,

which objected to the spread of slavery into the territories in competition with free labor and the small farmer. Support of the Wilmot Proviso, which would exclude slavery from the territories annexed from Mexico, was their political test, and "free soil" their war cry. There was no accompanying call for freedom, equality, and suffrage for the Negro in this agitation. Many antislavery men were profoundly anti-Negro.

The southern Democrats, in 1848, were in firm control of the party, with an incumbent president, James Polk. They nominated the first of a line of doughface candidates—northern men who accepted the southern view that Congress could not legislate on the subject of slavery—in Lewis Cass of Michigan, who rejected the Wilmot Proviso. A branch of the Democratic party in New York, known popularly as the Barnburners, broke away to form a third party, the Free Soil party, with former president Martin Van Buren as candidate.

The Free Soil revolt posed a problem for militant abolitionists of the older Liberty party. Should they stay pure, or should they join the larger new movement, which was not abolitionist, and try to win more than self-congratulation for their virtue? Sherman Booth, the leading publicist of the Wisconsin Liberty party, was persuaded to join the Free Soilers and carried others with him. Van Buren got a very respectable 10,418 votes in Wisconsin, to 15,001 for Cass and 13,747 for the national winner, Zachary Taylor.

The vote for Cass indicated the hold that the traditional Democratic party had on Wisconsin politics. They controlled the state government and the congressional contingent. Taylor, who like Cass had a long association with territorial Wisconsin where he had soldiered, represented a hardy tradition in American politics. A military hero from the Mexican War and a southerner, he professed to know nothing about politics and refused to abide by any party platform. If the Whigs should choose to tender their nomination to him, he would accept, and it was given to him on that basis. A branch of Whiggery which leaned toward antislavery sentiment, known as the Conscience Whigs, found Taylor too much to swallow and joined the Free Soilers or stayed at home. In Wisconsin, Free Soiler Charles Durkee, a former Liberty party man, won the congressional seat in the Yankee southeast.

The Free Soil vote stunned the Wisconsin Democrats who were inclined toward the Free Soil issue but refused to bolt their party. Despite the Democratic dismay, it was the Free Soilers who faced problems of survival. They were largely a one-issue party, made up of an odd collection of deserters from the two major parties and the Liberty party members. The new party had a congressman and a press—C. C. Sholes had started a paper called the *Barnburner,* in addition to his *American Freeman,* and there was Sherman Booth's *Wisconsin Freeman*—but nothing in the way of patronage. The Democrats courted fusion with the new party, but it soon became apparent that what they offered was a return to the fold for the Free Soil men as individuals. The logical fusion for the Free Soilers was with the minority Whigs, inasmuch as the Free Soil members held the balance between Democrats and Whigs in the legislature. But many Whigs could not swallow free trade, nor could the ex-Democrats, who were a majority in the Free Soil ranks, accept Whig protectionism.

Near disaster came for the Free Soil party with the Compromise of 1850, which presumably took their central issue out of politics. Members drifted back to their old party allegiances until the Free Soil party bore very much the complexion of the old Liberty party, with its hard core of abolitionists. It was a popular saying that Free Soil had gone up like a rocket and come down like a stick. Meanwhile, by some arm's-length cooperation, the Whigs and Free Soilers had reelected Durkee to Congress, and taking advantage of Democratic dissension, put Leonard Farwell in the governorship. Farwell was an odd candidate who resisted nomination and election. Holding large interests in Madison, he had little time for his new office, which was run by his secretary, Harlow S. Orton, later a state supreme court judge.

In 1853 Governor Farwell ran away from another nomination with real determination. Charles Durkee had lost his congressional seat the year before to a Democrat. The coalition between the Whigs and the Free Soilers had broken down, and the Free Soilers were determined to displace the Whigs as the second party in the state. Prohibition was their big issue.

Liquor had been controlled by licensing laws inherited from Michigan Territory. There were occasional campaigns for stronger regulation, but the early temperance movement accepted abstinence as a personal obligation. Temperance societies were seasonal phenomena, flowering with a burst of religious enthusiasm, then fading rapidly. These organizations flourished among the Yankees from the "burned-over" districts of New York, for whom the societies filled a social need. The Washingtonians, a popular society of the early 1840s, featured lurid confessions by reformed drunkards. On occasion, a travelling performer on the Washingtonian temperance circuit would backslide spectacularly, bringing joy to the skeptics and civil libertarians. Temperance taverns were kept in some areas, but they found it difficult to compete with the genuine article.

Agitation for sumptuary legislation began to make headway as temperance became a better political issue than abolition. It was not an issue upon which the major parties were sharply divided, and its supporters seemed worth courting. As a result, the territorial legislature adopted a weak local option law in 1846. Its failure led to an 1848 law requiring a liquor dealer to post a bond of $1,000 and authorized suit by dependents of drunkards to whom a dealer knowingly sold liquor. Milwaukee got an early start in its career of ignoring legislation of this character, but it felt threatened. Milwaukee's Mayor Upham, in tune with his German constituency, came out against a stronger bonding and licensing law in 1850, which, however, passed. In 1851, Upham was nominated by the Democrats to run for governor against Farwell.

The temperance forces were as dissatisfied with the licensing and bonding law as were the Germans, civil libertarians, and brewing and distilling industry. The Maine Law, total prohibition, became their aim in 1853; the Free Soil party was to be their instrument. They ignored the Whig's hopeful renomination of Governor Farwell (he resolutely refused to run; Henry Baird of Green Bay claimed the nomination) and nominated their own candidate, E. D. Holton of Milwaukee, an avid abolitionist and prohibitionist, hoping to attract the German vote on the antislavery issue. Their leadership was too strongly tainted with temperance and abolition, however, and Holton was beaten by Democrat William Barstow 30,405 to 21,886, with the Whig, Baird, getting only 3,304 votes. Interestingly enough, a referendum calling for the enactment of the Maine Law carried by 3,000 votes: many Yankee Democrats would vote for the issue but not for a temperance candidate on another slate. Barstow recognized that the Germans were learning to vote as a bloc, and paid them off with two vetoes of prohibition measures that passed the legislature.

The antislavery issue, which had been languishing since the Compromise of 1850, came to life in January 1854 with the Kansas-Nebraska Act and the issue of popular sovereignty. In March, the runaway slave Joshua Glover was forcibly released by a Milwaukee mob from a federal marshal's custody, initiating the long-drawn-out case against Sherman Booth. These events should have served the cause of the Free Soil party, but the party proved to be the harbinger and not the instrument of the new politics.

New men saw the need for a party built on the antislavery issue but free of the other commitments and enthusiasms of the Free Soil party leadership: abolition, prohibition, Negro suffrage, women's rights, land limitation, and nativist leanings. The new men were mainly Whigs who saw their party sinking after the humiliating defeat of Winfield Scott in 1852—he carried only Vermont, Massachusetts, Kentucky, and Tennessee—and Baird's miserable showing in the gubernatorial race in 1853.

The most active of the new men was a relative newcomer to Wisconsin, Alvan Bovay, who had been associated with the National Reform Association in New York. He was ideologically close to the Locofoco

Democrat tradition, but like Horace Greeley, with whom he had close ties, he was an uneasy member of the Whig party. Bovay had been attracted to Wisconsin by the communitarian experiment at Ceresco, and so, by this chance, Ripon became the official home of the Republican party. Searching for a name with as fundamental an appeal as *Democrat,* Bovay advanced the name *Republican,* and it was adopted by similar third-party movements in Michigan, Illinois, and elsewhere. Bovay's meeting at Ripon was followed by a mass meeting at Madison in July 1854, at which the new party took shape. The central issue agreed upon was the barring of slavery from the territories. Whigs and Free Soilers formally disbanded their old parties and joined the new banner.

The Wisconsin Republican party met instant success, taking the governorship and one U. S. Senate seat from the Democrats in 1855 (having won a majority in the legislature), and delivering the state's electoral vote to Fremont in 1856. The Democrats tried to bait the triumphant Republicans in the legislature by introducing prohibition legislation. This ploy was meant to divert the many temperance sympathizers in the Republican ranks, but the new party's leadership had had enough of this distracting issue and refused to rise to it. The virulent nativist outburst of 1856, which delivered 22 percent of the national popular vote to Know Nothing presidential candidate Millard Fillmore, was held to one half of one percent in Wisconsin. Nativism was a perilous political commodity with such large foreign-born voting blocs and the adherence of many of them to the Catholic Church. Know Nothingism had its appeal, of course, and a new paper, the *Milwaukee American,* identified with the nativist party. The Know Nothings in Wisconsin operated within the established parties by endorsement and repudiation of candidates. Because of the foreign vote which both courted, the Democrats and Republicans tried to pin the Know Nothing label on one another, but the Republicans were left wearing the albatross when the *Milwaukee American* endorsed Coles Bashford, their successful candidate for governor in 1855, and claimed to have insured his narrow victory. Politicians were nervous about disavowing the Know Nothing vote too vehemently, since in the nativist tradition it was a semisecret organization, and no one knew how large the iceberg was.

The Republicans struggled manfully, with their nativist identification, to make inroads on Democratic control of the immigrant vote. In 1857 they dumped Coles Bashford, who had been caught in the unsavory La Crosse and Milwaukee Railroad land-grant scandal, and nominated Alexander Randall, an ex-Democrat and Free Soiler, for governor. The Democrats found it difficult to exploit Bashford's disgrace, however, for the wholesale bribery associated with the land grant had been conducted by Democrats Byron Kilbourn and Moses Strong. In the tradition of the practical businessman, the pair had been nonpartisan in their vote buying. The one holdout whom investigators could turn up was a Republican state senator forever after known as Honest Amasa Cobb.

The 1857 election brought another new face to Wisconsin politics. In an effort to woo the stubbornly Democratic German vote, the Republicans nominated, practically sight unseen, a recent convert to the party, Carl Schurz, for lieutenant-govern'r. Randall won and Schurz lost, which was a reflection of Republican rank-and-file sentiment toward the Germans and of German sentiment toward the Republicans. Schurz turned out to be a great find for the party nationally and fixed the myth that he, with modest help, delivered the midwestern German vote, and the election, to Lincoln in 1860. Joseph Schafer, from his grass roots studies of pioneer Wisconsin, destroyed this myth for scholars if not for the general public. Schurz, one of the best advertised of the Forty-eighters, marched to a different drum than the more numerous Catholic and Lutheran Germans, who looked upon the Forty-eighters as morally and politically dangerous. Schafer found no perceptible shift from the Democrats, through 1860, in town after town where the German vote was decisive—including Schurz's home town of Watertown. Maybe one-fourth of the German Protestants voted for Lincoln, but this was a small share of the German vote. As for the Democrats, they were heading for their trial by fire in the heat of the Civil War.

Selected Bibliography

Andersen, Arlow W. "Venturing into Politics." *Wisconsin Magazine of History* 32:58–79 (Sept. 1948). Norwegian press and politics of 1850s.

Berthrong, Donald J. "Social Legislation in Wisconsin, 1836–1900." Ph.D. dissertation, University of Wisconsin, 1951. Some interesting material on early institutions and civil rights.

Blue, Frederick J. "The Free Soil Party and the Election of 1848 in Wisconsin." Master's thesis, University of Wisconsin, 1962. Sorts out the fragmented parties of the 1850s.

Byrne, Frank L. "Maine Law Versus Lager Beer: A Dilemma of Wisconsin's Young Republican Party." *Wisconsin Magazine of History* 42:115–20 (Winter 1958–59). The prohibition issue in antebellum Wisconsin.

Christman, Henry. *Tin Horns and Calico.* New York, 1945. Something on Alvan Bovay and New York politics, which were reflected in Wisconsin in the 1850s.

Clark, James I. *Wisconsin Defies the Fugitive Slave Law: The Case of Sherman M. Booth.* Madison, 1955. Wisconsin's venture in nullification.

Cole, Albert, Jr. "The Barnburner Element in the Republican Party." Master's thesis, University of Wisconsin, 1951. Helps to sort out the Locofocos, Barnburners, and Free Soilers.

Curti, Merle. "Isaac P. Walker: Reformer in Mid-Century Politics." *Wisconsin Magazine of History* 34:3–6, 58–62 (Autumn 1950). Henry Dodge and Walker were Wisconsin's first U.S. senators.

Derleth, August W. *The Shadow in the Glass.* New York, 1963. Novelist's biography of Nelson Dewey, rather dull.

Gregory, John G. *The Land Limitation Movement: A Wisconsin Episode of 1848–1851.* Parkman Club Publications, no. 14. Milwaukee, 1897. Gregory was hostile to the reform.

Hanneman, Richard L. "The First Republican Campaign in Wisconsin, 1854." Master's thesis, University of Wisconsin, 1954. Why the Democrats lost to the three-months-old Republican party.

Jorgenson, Lloyd P. *The Founding of Public Education in Wisconsin.* Madison, 1965. Useful on the disposition of the school lands.

Kroncke, Robert N. "Race and Politics in Wisconsin, 1854–1865." Master's thesis, University of Wisconsin, 1968. Republicans moved from antislavery position to support of Negro suffrage and civil rights.

Kuehnl, George J. *The Wisconsin Business Corporation.* Madison, 1959. General corporation laws did not catch on in the 1850s.

Langsam, Miriam Z. "The Nineteenth-Century Wisconsin Criminal: Ideologies and Institutions." Ph.D. dissertation, University of Wisconsin, 1967. On Waupun as a leader in penology.

McIntyre, Elwood R. "A Farmer Halts the Hangman: The Story of Martin Bovee." *Wisconsin Magazine of History* 42:3–12 (Autumn 1958). The abolition of capital punishment.

Patterson, Thomas H. "The Disposal of Wisconsin's Common School Lands, 1849–1863." Master's thesis, University of Wisconsin, 1961. The public got what it wanted.

Pedrick, Samuel M. *The Life of Alvan E. Bovay, 1818–1903.* Ripon, 1955. Father of the Republican party.

Schafer, Joseph. "Know-Nothingism in Wisconsin." *Wisconsin Magazine of History* 8:4–21 (Sept. 1924). The only summary available.

———. "Who Elected Lincoln." *American Historical Review* 41:51–65 (Oct. 1941).

Schlicher, J. J. "Bernard Domschcke." *American Historical Review* 29:319–22, 435–56 (March and June 1946). Milwaukee editor of German-language papers.

Smith, Theodore Clark. "The Free Soil Party in Wisconsin." *SHSW Proceedings,* 1894, pp. 97–162. Madison, 1895. See Frederick Blue above. This is the only published account.

Thomson, Alexander M. *Political History of Wisconsin.* Milwaukee, 1900. A rare book in more ways than one, deserves reprinting.

"Wisconsin's Former Governors, 1848–1959." *The Wisconsin Blue Book,* 1960, pp. 69–206. Madison, 1960. Some forgettable names.

Wyllie, Irvin G. "Land and Learning." *Wisconsin Magazine of History* 30:154–73 (Dec. 1946). About the University's lobby.

CIVIL WAR

17

Wisconsin on the eve of the Civil War was not a confident, united, economically sound society. The realignments of the 1850s had soured politics and separated the dominant Yankee group even more from their European immigrant neighbors. The rapid population increase of 154 percent, from 305,000 in 1850 to 776,000 in 1860, multiplied the strains of ethnic and religious differences. Nor had business recovered from the effects of the panic of 1857 before the threat of civil war brought another sharp break in commodity prices and distressing dislocations to the fragile pioneer economy of the young state.

The Whig party had quietly died early in the 1850s, and the Free Soil party, which aspired to succeed it, had given place to the instantly successful Republican party. The latter absorbed the revived antislavery issue, rejected the divisive prohibition issue, and officially disclaimed nativism. The charge of nativism regularly leveled against the Republicans undoubtedly helped the Democrats to stay in contention in Wisconsin, despite the disastrous blows that the party experienced during the Civil War and after. The source of continuing Democratic strength was the heavy influx of immigrants which Wisconsin was receiving. The number of foreign-born rose from 106,000 in 1850 to 277,000 in 1860. The German-born proportion increased from 36 percent in 1850 to 45 percent in 1860. There were now 124,000 German-born, and first-generation children of immigrant German parents made up a considerable portion of the 499,000 native born. While the 50,000 Irish-born of 1860 made them a not insignificant second, the Yankees were more concerned about the large and growing German contingent.

Much of the nativist fear was a reaction of the American Protestants to the growth of the Catholic Church. Early German immigration was heavily Catholic, the local Roman hierarchy was German-speaking, and already by 1853, the Catholic Church claimed 100,000 communicants in Wisconsin, which made it by far the largest church. Many Germans were Lutherans, as were most of the 23,300 Scandinavians, but the Lutheran community was divided into separate synods, and as Protestants, they did not excite the suspicions that attached to the Catholics.

Like the Norwegians, the Germans tended to settle in ethnic islands and to preserve their language and culture. Unlike the Norwegians, they were an urban as well as a farming people. Milwaukee, a city of 45,000 in 1860, was 50 percent foreign-born, and 70 percent of those were German. Some of the larger towns to the north and west of Milwaukee, particularly Sheboygan, Manitowoc, and Watertown, were likewise German, as were many lesser villages. The Irish-born made up only 7 percent of Milwaukee's population, but the Irish had a talent for making their presence felt. They were also more mobile than the Germans and Norwegians, as the manuscript censuses show, the Irish appearing in many villages, particularly those along the lines of the railroads built in the 1850s, and then moving on by the time of the 1870 census.

The native Americans were equally mobile, filling in and advancing the Wisconsin frontier as it moved westward and northward above the Fox-Wisconsin waterway and along the Mississippi on the west. Remember that by 1860, Milwaukee was connected by rail to the eastern shore of the Mississippi at Prairie du Chien and La Crosse. Not much railroad would be added in the next decade, nor would the Mississippi be bridged in Wisconsin until 1874. The railroad and population maps of 1860 coincide quite closely, except for the early advances upon the pineries along the Chippewa, the Black, the upper Wisconsin, and along the Mississippi and St. Croix rivers. A comparison of the 1850 and 1860 federal censuses shows that twenty-eight new counties appeared in the interim, and many more new towns and villages. Such rapid growth and movement contributed, along with the ethnic, religious, and political divisions, to the instability of the society.

Economically, Wisconsin was built upon a narrow base. Milwaukee, although milling, brewing, wood-manufacturing, leather, and other industries were becoming important in the city's economy, was primarily a commercial center in 1860. The transformation into an important industrial city was some years away. In 1860 only 7.5 percent of her people were engaged in manufacturing, compared to 18.1 percent by 1880, when the population was two and a half times greater. The railroads depended upon agriculture for over three-fourths of their freight revenue. Nor was agriculture in a happy condition. Wheat was still king in 1860, and while the year had provided the greatest crop to date, the threatened loss of the southern market drove the price down from 94¢ in August to 65¢ in December. Farmers faced the debts incurred in opening new land, the expense of mechanization, which was making rapid strides in wheat culture, the troublesome mortgages which over 6,000 of them had given as subsidies for railroads both built and unbuilt, and a currency crisis which was coming to a head because most of Wisconsin's bank notes were based upon bonds issued by southern states. The lumber industry, still in its infancy in 1860 although second to agriculture already, also saw prices sag disastrously between October 1860 and the beginning of hostilities the following spring. The ability of the local economy to sustain the costs and displacements of a major contribution to the coming war effort was no matter for optimism.

The politicians who controlled Wisconsin's destinies in 1860 were less concerned with the state of the economy, however, than they would necessarily be today. Neither the state nor the federal government assumed much responsibility for action in a downturn of the business cycle. Misgivings about economic danger signals were brushed aside in appraising the threat of southern secession.

Governor Alexander Randall, an ardent abolitionist who had pressed Negro suffrage in the 1846 Constitutional Convention, had followed a common Yankee pattern. He had come to Waukesha in 1840 from upstate New York, with a legal education, and moved from the Democratic party into the Free Soil party in 1848. Randall's Republicanism was quite new when in 1857 the Republicans found it prudent to dump Coles Bashford in his favor.

Randall understood the largely Yankee constituency of the Republican party. His task was to drive them away from any lingering loyalty to the Democrats, and in this he was aided by the ineptitude of the Wisconsin Democrats and the unpopularity of the Buchanan Administration in Washington. Randall focused upon the moral issues of slavery in the South and alleged Democratic sins at home. The Democrats were vulnerable on the basis of their national opposition to homestead legislation, which Buchanan vetoed in June 1860, and their traditional opposition to federal support of internal improvements. Both of these were issues which in the West ran across party and ethnic lines.

Led by Governor Randall, Wisconsin Republicans were counted in the radical camp on the issues of slavery and favored punishing the South should it dare secession. With an effective majority in the state legislature and control of the congressional delegation, they moved with confidence as the presidential year approached. In keeping with their radical leaning, Wisconsin delegates to the 1860 Republican convention went to Chicago pledged to Senator William Seward of New York. Abraham Lincoln better fitted the requirements of the Republican kingmakers. Wisconsin salvaged what it could from his victory, when Carl Schurz seconded the motion to make Lincoln's nomination unanimous.

Wisconsin Republicans were well satisfied with their party's platform and reconciled themselves to Lincoln. The Democratic party, meanwhile, pursued its destiny by dividing three ways. The Northwest's candidate, Stephen A. Douglas, took the campaign trail, visiting Wisconsin with formal appearances in Milwaukee and Fond du Lac. In Kenosha, a stronghold of Yankeedom in that day, he was jostled and booed, a prophetic reaction, for Lincoln beat Douglas handily in Wisconsin by a majority of 21,000 out of 152,000 votes cast. The southern and border Democrats, Breckinridge and Bell, drew fewer than 1,000 votes away from Douglas. Republicans won all three congressional seats.

In the confused time between Lincoln's election and assumption of office, the Republican governors were in a position to set forth the party line, and Randall understood this, taking an uncompromising stand against secession. Only recently the test of Republican loyalty, in Alexander Randall's eyes, had been a readiness on the part of militia commanders to accept his orders in contravention of federal orders to enforce the Fugitive Slave Law, which Wisconsin's Supreme Court and Republican party had declared null and void in Wisconsin. This embarrassing venture into states' rights was set aside as the issues of the Civil War were developed.

A fire-eater, Governor Randall gave thought to the emergency ahead. Given the limited size of the federal army and the number of southerners in its officer corps, it was clear that any coercion of the South—and Randall was committed to armed intervention to prevent secession—would depend upon the militias and volunteer regiments of the loyal states. With this in mind, he asked for legislation authorizing the organization of the volunteer militia into regiments and obligating $100,000 for the purpose of bringing it to a state of readiness.

President Lincoln called for a levy of 75,000 volunteers for three months, of which Wisconsin's share was to be one regiment of ten companies. A company of infantry counted 78 men, plus officers. In the patriotic fervor which attended the early days following the Confederate attack on Fort Sumter, Randall could easily have raised many more than this number of troops, but Secretary of War Cameron declined to receive them. In light of the long war to come involving mass armies, Lincoln's call seems ludicrous, and Randall's insistence that more men be called for a longer term truly prescient. But Lincoln's limited call complied with federal law, and neither the War Department nor the states were ready to handle and equip a larger levy. Randall continued the state's recruiting, and was prominent among the governors asserting leadership in the early months of the war. None of the northern governors could match Lincoln politically as he skillfully assumed control of the war effort. Randall, Wisconsin's governor, was energetic, but given to bombast and the accumulation of political liabilities.

Governor Randall prudently decided against running for a third term in 1861. He had spent money freely to supply the Wisconsin volunteer regiments and had made some injudicious purchases. More to the point, it was felt by many that he had allowed the bankers to drive too hard a bargain with the state in solving the financial crisis of 1861. Randall wanted to be a general, but Lincoln had enough political generals and sent him as minister to the Papal States, from whence he shortly returned to serve as assistant postmaster general and later as postmaster general under Andrew Johnson. He did not return to Wisconsin.

Randall's successor, Louis P. Harvey, served less than three months before he was tragically drowned in the Tennessee River while visiting Wisconsin troops. He was succeeded by Lieutenant-Governor Edward Salomon, a German-born attorney from Milwaukee and the Republican party's concession to this largest foreign minority. In his term, from April 1862 through 1863, this young man in his early thirties inherited all the vexatious questions attending the draft calls that came during those depressing months for the Union, as well as the false, but nonetheless unnerving, emergencies which attended the Sioux War. Furthermore, he had to deal with the irascible secretary of war, Edwin M. Stanton, who administered the draft nationally and who, with Lincoln, was gathering new and impressive powers in Washington. Salomon was a man who recognized political stakes, which he obviously cared about, but he sometimes cared about logic more. On one occasion, lecturing the legislature about a proper militia and draft law, he commented that "exemptions should be made as in all civilized countries. . . ." The legislature, called into special session to deal with the draft, left Salomon without any such civilizing legislation, which might have placed it on record as implementing unpopular federal conscription. Governor Salomon, who with some justice thought he deserved a second term in his own right, was dropped by the Republicans in favor of another Yankee from New York, James T. Lewis.

The Wisconsin militia is of more than passing interest for a generation that has been called upon to examine critically the military obligations of its young men. The concept of militia service was an old one, going back into colonial and British experience, and was still a part of the American scene in 1860. Basic to the idea of the militia was the notion that American military power should be essentially defensive and local. The federal government was actively discouraged from maintaining a standing professional army any larger than that required to discharge the police powers of the constitution. In the event of war, the state militia—the householder, armed and organized locally—would furnish the first line of defense while a volunteer federal army was brought into being. All efforts to tie the militia effectively to the federal government or to the national military establishment were successfully resisted. The last meaningful federal legislation on the militia had been passed in 1792 and 1808 and provided that each state should have an adjutant general appointed by the governor. His responsibility was to enroll, staff, and train the militia and to maintain an inventory of the arms to be provided from federal arsenals. But the adjutant general was a state officer answerable to the governor. Providing federal arms did not bring federal control.

The militia had proved consistent in one thing: it seldom met an emergency. It demonstrated almost total incompetence in the War of 1812. Militia officers, appointed by the state governor, or at company grade elected by their men, were not inclined to accept orders from regular army officers. Citizens detested muster days when the enrolled militia, men between eighteen and forty-five years of age, were legally subject to company drill. Legislators, who controlled the terms of militia service, obligingly changed the definition of the militia to an enrollment (usually by town or village officials) of those eligible, and did away with the muster days.

When men spoke of the militia they generally meant the volunteer militia, made up of companies recruited primarily for social purposes. Milwaukee, by 1859, had a regiment of ten companies, among whom the mostly Yankee Milwaukee Light Guard were the elite. The Guard had elaborate uniforms provided by the members themselves, featuring bearskin shakoes, and in the mid-fifties their annual ball was the most glamorous event on the Milwaukee social calendar. The social aspects of the volunteer militia are self-evident. The officer rosters of many companies, containing the names of political figures of the day, attest to its political role.

Of the ten Milwaukee companies, only three were made up of the Yankee element, and the other seven were German or Irish. The Germans had had only a company or two in the forties; the arrival of the Forty-eighters renewed interest and rivalries. The Irish, who were ahead

of the Germans in their political integration, recognized the political implications of the militia. It was one of their units, the Union Guard, that
was disbanded by Governor Randall in the summer of 1860 when he
suspected their officers of a higher loyalty to the United States than to
Commander in Chief Randall. This did not endear him to the Irish and
Germans, but they voted Democratic anyway.

The adjutants general, while making occasional efforts to revive the
enrolled militia, found themselves primarily involved with the volunteer
militia companies. The expense in money and time of belonging to a
well-turned-out, well-drilled outfit were such that many more companies
were born than survived their first year. The adjutant general was eter-
nally making out new commissions, revoking old ones, recovering the
federal arms and other equipment to be reissued, and trying, often without success, to get the reports dear to the military heart from the dilatory
militiamen. He reported 1,992 rank and file in the Wisconsin volunteer militia, organized into fifty-two companies, on the eve of war in
1861.

It was the volunteer militia that carried the burden of the belligerent
Governor Randall's hopes. Of the fifty-two volunteer companies, twenty-
six eventually volunteered for service and were accepted. While they volunteered as units, all of them lost men and had to recruit to fill the ranks,
and in the end they supplied only 40 percent of the first levy of troops
called for by Lincoln. Only seven of the twenty-nine brigadier generals in
the Wisconsin volunteer militia of 1860 saw service in the Civil War, and
only eighteen of fifty-two colonels, five of thirty-four lieutenant-colonels,
and five of thirty-three majors. Twelve Wisconsin men were to win generals' stars in the federal volunteer service. Only three of these were in
any way connected with the pre-war volunteer militia.

Wisconsin, of course, carried her full share of the burden in the Civil
War. The state of the records makes accurate statistics impossible, but
probably 82,000 Wisconsin men were in service—roughly one for every
nine citizens—and 12,216 died, over two-thirds of these from disease.
The loss ratio was about one in seven of those involved. Compare this
with the figure of 332,200 from Wisconsin in the armed forces in World
War II—about one for every ten citizens—with 8,149 deaths from all
causes, a loss ratio of one in forty-five. The two wars were of about equal
duration.

Governor Randall built the First Wisconsin Regiment around five of
the Milwaukee volunteer companies, ordering the others to report to
Camp Scott in that city. The camp was worse than primitive. Facilities
were so poor that the Milwaukee soldiers commuted daily from home,
and the others were housed in hotels and boarding houses. The state's

stands of arms were so scarce, heterogeneous, and in poor repair that they were not issued. The First Wisconsin shipped out for Washington, D.C., after a month, still without arms. By June they were in the field near Harpers Ferry, with arms from Washington, and the regiment had its first skirmish and battle casualties on July second.

Camp Randall, now a part of the university campus, became the principal training camp for the Wisconsin regiments; some 70,000 trained there. Training maintained the timeless elements of military routine: hurry up and wait, baseless rumor, bad food, petty tyranny, a general feeling of uselessness combined with an eagerness for change that promised no improvement, and the accumulation of intense dislikes for officers, the system, and the cause of the inconvenience—the enemy—in about that order.

If there is an element of difference that a World War II soldier might see between himself and the Billy Yank of 1861–65, it is that the latter was a real Jacksonian. One reads with surprise of the incidents of individual and mass insubordination that enlivened the training periods of many of the Wisconsin volunteer regiments. The rank and file assumed the right to elect their company officers, and since, unfortunately, most such officers knew no more of the military than the men in the ranks, the men found nothing unusual in pausing to debate an order. They did not accept military discipline as ordained from on high.

Discipline in the ranks was not the only problem. The Sixth Wisconsin, made up largely of German and Irish companies, expressed their displeasure with the food one day by breaking up the mess hall. The officers quelled the riot by sending to town for rations and stood treat from their own purses for twenty kegs of beer. The Eighth later repeated this exercise, burning down the cook shack. The men were issued rations to prepare for themselves. When they received orders to ship out, 200 members of the Eighth joyously charged the fence and made for town a mile away. Word reached the sheriff in time for him to close the saloons, and guard details rounded up most of the soldiers, except for a determined group found next morning serenading a house of ill repute.

The state was without funds on occasion, operating on devalued currency and dilatory federal aid. When Governor Harvey had to plead with the Seventeenth Wisconsin to ship out without a promised payday, the regiment rioted in his presence. Their officers were unable to handle the situation, requiring a regiment brought from Chicago to bring the men under control. There was much hard talk, a fire in the camp, and the Seventeenth departed late as well as short-handed. Madison endured the military much as it has its student population over the years. Girls and chickens strayed from their yards at their own peril.

For men who went almost directly to the field of battle, the training received at Camp Randall left much to be desired. The regular army was maintained as a separate organization, which meant that its officers were not available for training or staffing the volunteer forces. The volunteers afforded a real opportunity for a man like Ulysses Grant, but there were all too few such men with West Point training available. Very few states instituted separate training for volunteer officers. Wisconsin was not among them. It was strictly on-the-job training for everyone involved, and much depended upon the colonel of each new regiment. He was almost solely responsible for its organization, discipline, and training. The usual pattern was for officers to get together for skull sessions and bone up on the popular manuals of infantry tactics. Perfection in drill had a real purpose. The deployment of large bodies of infantry in the field was an intricate business.

Given the lack of organization, the volunteer militia companies were fortunate if they had had any training by files, platoons, and company. The Lemonweir Minute Men, not untypically, did not even know how to form up in ranks when they alighted from the train in Madison. Mostly raftsmen from the pineries, they made a colorful mob in their red raftsmen's shirts, or long johns, the company uniform, as they hiked in an unmilitary gaggle to Camp Randall. Those companies that took pride in their drill had not had an opportunity to exercise as regiments or brigades, and precious few officers had even seen these larger formations. Amasa Cobb, who gave up the speakership of the state assembly for a colonelcy, was embarrassed on one occasion when his horse shied, causing his notes for the day's drill to take to the wind. Colonel Cobb had to dismiss the regiment on the spot.

Colonels who knew too much could also be a problem. Colonel Joseph Vandor, of the Wisconsin Seventh, was a Hungarian with a military background. He was masterful in drill, a good disciplinarian, and his men swore by him. The Seventh was the first regiment to have rifles issued for training. Vandor even instituted bayonet drill, an unheard of refinement. His trouble was that he found many of his officers deficient in military science and discipline and said so. Colonel Vandor may have understood these things, but his officers understood American politics. They shortly had him removed. It is little wonder that being a private in the U.S. Volunteers in the Civil War proved to be an occupation of uncommon hazard.

As the war became less of a novelty, as wars do, the supply of volunteers began to dry up. We have noticed Governor Randall's initiative in accepting volunteers beyond the first federal levy. As he had foreseen, more calls were necessary, and Wisconsin was training its fifteenth and sixteenth regiments at Camp Randall by December 1861. The federal government assumed responsibility for the camp and training in January 1862, but the states were left with the responsibility for raising the quotas of troops assigned them by Secretary of War Stanton.

A number of factors made recruiting increasingly difficult. The war was not going well for the North, for one thing. The almost unbroken series of defeats and military standoffs that characterized the first two years were disheartening, and in these circumstances the vocal antiwar faction of the Democratic party found its voice. Edward G. Ryan provided the keynote in what became known as the Ryan Address, an arraignment of the Lincoln administration as "a conspiracy to subvert the government and set up a military despotism," and Wisconsin had an active contingent of Copperheads. While Lincoln received much criticism then and later for a disregard of civil liberties, an examination of Brick Pomeroy's *La Crosse Democrat* is evidence that the president stopped short of tyranny. Pomeroy variously characterized Lincoln as "a flat-boat tyrant" and "hell's vice-agent on earth." Pomeroy was widely quoted, and continued to publish.

The secretary of war unaccountably cut off recruiting in April 1862. Shortly, Lincoln had to issue two calls for volunteers, the first in July 1862, for 300,000 men for three-year enlistments, and the second in August, for 300,000 men for nine months. This second call was partly directed at the many who were reluctant to enlist for the longer term. As a case in point, the First Wisconsin, which originally enlisted for three months, was asked to accept a three-year term on being sworn into the federal service. Over a third of the men refused, including an entire company of Beloit College students who had planned to get a taste of the war during summer vacation. The solemn induction ceremony performed at the end of each regiment's training period involved the reading of the Articles of War, with its awesome list of infractions calling for the death penalty, and several of the freer spirits could be counted upon to drop out of ranks at this point.

Congress, doubting the ability of the states to raise these new quotas under a system of voluntary enlistments, provided the country's first draft law and thus gave new ammunition to the dissident Democrats. The wily Congress put the onus of implementing the draft squarely upon the governors of the states. Governor Salomon, confronted with a quota of 42,557 men for the two 1862 levies, wrestled with the problem of devising an equitable draft system based upon nonexistent militia rolls and only the sketchiest notion of where the previous volunteers had come from. A system of local bounties had come into use to fill the ranks of the volunteer militia companies. The larger cities were able to pay larger bounties, usually raised by subscription, with the result that boys from the rural counties volunteered for companies raised at places like Madison. This meant that their home counties were not credited with their enlistments when the puzzle of allocating the draft calls by counties had to be solved.

The governor realized that the application of the draft was a political hot potato. He tried to hand it to the legislature, which quickly tossed it back, at which point he did the next best thing and dragooned a prominent war Democrat, Levi B. Vilas of Madison, into administering the draft. Vilas worked through a draft commissioner and surgeon appointed for each county, but Governor Salomon could not escape the task of making up the county quotas.

All men between eighteen and forty-five were to be enrolled by the county sheriffs and draft commissioners. The first enrollment turned up 127,894 eligible males, of whom 28,012 had obvious physical disabilities. Again the system of bounties came into play as the counties were encouraged to fill their quotas with volunteers. The result was that rural counties lost more men to the populous centers.

Even people who gave wholehearted support to the war effort looked upon the draft as an unhealthy, alien importation, and upon those caught in its toils as vaguely disgraced. This attitude undoubtedly stimulated enlistments after July 1862. Those whose enthusiasm for the war was minimal, and there were many, held lightly the obligation to report when drafted. The many Democrats who looked upon the war as a piece of Republican folly instigated to free the slaves had their belief confirmed on September 23, 1862, when Lincoln issued the Emancipation Proclamation. Their sentiments were reinforced by the inequitable application of the draft, which recognized only occupational deferments. The draft law also included the grossly unfair deferment based upon furnishing a substitute, or payment of a commutation fee of $300.

A popular term of the time was the word *skedaddled,* to describe the many men who fled to Canada or found reasons to go west where the draft was not applied. Malingering, or simply dropping from view, were common expedients. The draft struck hardest in the heavily immigrant areas which had produced the fewest volunteers. (Washington County, just north of Milwaukee and heavily German, therefore had a high quota.) These were people less ready to adopt the expedient of going west or to Canada. They found the vaunted freedom, which they had been promised in official literature from Wisconsin's commissioner of immigration, a mockery. For many, this was simply another despicable Yankee trick to take their men, who were stubbornly clearing the heavy hardwoods, and throw them into distant battles to free the Negro from slavery. Most of them were profoundly unsympathetic to this objective. Indeed, some of the Lutherans, in synodical meetings, had squared contemporary slavery with the Old Testament and pronounced the "peculiar institution" a blessing. Much of the German-language press reflected these views, along with the most vigorous condemnation of Lincoln and the Republicans.

The results were predictable. There was a threat of overt action in West Bend, where a mob formed and some rocks were thrown, but the real outburst came in neighboring Ozaukee County at Port Washington. A group of rioters roughed up the draft commissioner, burned draft records, and invaded the houses of the commissioner and seven prominent Republicans, wrecking the interiors and burning the furniture. Governor Salomon acted decisively, ordering troops from Milwaukee, who arrested 130 of the rioters and marched them through the streets of Milwaukee, where trouble also threatened. Ozaukee County was put under martial law while the draft proceeded. The prisoners were tried by a provost marshal's court, an action resulting in one of the habeas corpus cases of the war. The case was won by Democrat Edward G. Ryan before the Wisconsin court. Lincoln prudently ignored the decision.

The federal government finally took over the administration of the draft in 1863, and some of the worst inequities were rectified. There were near riots, and two enrolling officers in Dodge County were shot, but not fatally. The assailant in one case posted bail and was escorted home to the music of a "Dutch" band. Except as a spur to enlistment, the draft was no great success. One student who did the arithmetic based upon various reports found that in the drafts levied through July 1864 there were 38,495 men called. Of these, 11,742 failed to report and were not apprehended, 5,097 paid the $300 commutation, 1,621 found substitutes, and 13,223 were discharged as unfit or for other causes. Of the 38,495 called, the draft produced only 6,812 soldiers.

General John Pope, who bore the blame for the Union defeat at Second Bull Run, served out much of the war in command of the U.S. Army Department of the Northwest, with headquarters in Milwaukee. Pope resisted calls from Wisconsin governors and local officials for assistance with mobs and threats against draft officers. He once characterized the local politicians who served as draft officers as "rash, imprudent men, whose zeal outruns discretion. . . . Who rather desire to stir up a fight . . . to rid themselves of offensive opponents." There was doubtless a large element of truth in this. The zeal of Republicans often accommodated the view that their Democratic opponents were overt traitors. Supporting this judgment was the fact that the Germans and Irish, who formed the unruly mobs resisting the draft, voted the Democratic ticket.

Because of varied terms of enlistment, ranging from three months to three years, Wisconsin furnished 91,379 men during the course of the war, but some served more than one hitch—hence the estimate of 82,000 altogether. If the larger figure is considered and the draft produced only 6,812, then nearly 85,000 enlistments were voluntary. Again, given the negative attitude of so many toward the draft and the war as a just cause, why did such a large number volunteer? Bell Irvin Wiley, in his *The Common Soldier in the Civil War,* tries to answer this question. One of his important sources was the collection of soldiers' letters and diaries in the Wisconsin State Historical Society. Wiley doubts that one soldier in ten had any real interest in emancipation of the slaves, although the New Englanders and upper midwesterners were more apt to be imbued with this spirit. Democrats who supported the war invoked the Union as the main object of their concern. "While the men in blue were not so irreverent toward high-sounding appeals . . . as were their khaki-clad descendants in World War II, yet American soldiers of the 1860s appear to have been about as little concerned with ideological issues as were those of the 1940s," Wiley concludes.

Certainly, social pressure and a reluctance to be drafted induced many to volunteer. One should not discount the excitement of young men who were eager to see action. An indication of this spirit was the odd reaction of the recruits at Camp Randall when they were given the news of the Union rout at the first battle of Bull Run July 21, 1861. After some confusion a ragged cheer went up. They were going to get to "see the elephant." The South was not crushed at the first meeting, as many had expected.

Going to war was for many a welcome relief from endless farm chores, or an exhilarating release from school or dull toil. The volunteer army, also, was intensely local. Communities resisted having their volunteers used as replacements and expected that they would be formed into company units. Many states made no effort to keep older units up to strength because of this sentiment. As a consequence, most men did their entire service surrounded by faces from home.

More curious, many volunteers enlisted for economic reasons. A majority of Wisconsin's soldiers were boys of the average age of nineteen or twenty. It was a measure of contemporary farm life that many of them expressed themselves as well satisfied with the rude accommodations and food supplied by the military. The standard seven hours of drill a day during training were no more monotonous than much farm work, while camp life offered endless diversions for boys accustomed to isolation. The $13 a month pay of the private was more money than many of them had ever seen, and added to the free board and room, was as high as and more certain than the wages of many day laborers. Bonuses that were commonly paid by both the federal government and local communities could amount to as much as $600 or more for volunteers by 1863.

The parochial character of the basic company unit made the volunteer army a poor agency for assimilating the immigrant. Many Wisconsin companies and even whole regiments were made up almost entirely of a single ethnic group; the War Department had ruled that only the officers of such units need understand English. There are more stories indicating ethnic exclusiveness and rivalry than the opposite. When Colonel Hans Heg's Fifteenth Wisconsin Regiment, made up of Norwegians, was at Camp Randall, there was a threatened move by some unruly Scandinavians to release some of their buddies from the guardhouse. An officer of the all-Irish Seventeenth, which was sharing the camp, called for a couple of platoons to mount extra guard. The entire regiment fell in for this welcome duty.

Service in the field, and the fact that many regiments had companies of different ethnic backgrounds, overcame some of this spirit. Common battle experience and the high rate of attrition contributed to a feeling of camaraderie. Wisconsin's famous Iron Brigade, for instance, was down to less than half of its normal complement of 4,000 men by October 1862, after taking part in several actions, including Antietam. After Gettysburg, less than a year later, it was down to 600 men, despite the addition of a new regiment after Antietam.

There is not space to follow the course of Wisconsin troops in the field. They served in almost every theater of the war, some with real distinction. Frank L. Klement, in *Wisconsin in The Civil War,* describes the Iron Brigade, made up of the Second, Sixth, and Seventh Wisconsin, the Nineteenth Indiana, and later, the Twenty-fourth Michigan, as "the most famous brigade in the entire Union Army." This is apparently not hyperbole. It was a war of crashing encounters, largely an infantryman's fight, with long charges across open ground in the face of light artillery, rifle, and musketry fire.

Looking back at the Civil War, one is struck by the pervasiveness of politics in the volunteer army from top to bottom and the attitude of business as usual on the part of the civilian economy. The pattern of local and state politics in the volunteer army was to be expected. The militia had always maintained a swollen officer corps, up to the brigade level, even when there were no troops and no real enrolled militia. Officer appointments were in the hands of the governor and were used more for political than for any military purpose. This attitude underwent no

great change with the war, especially as there were so few men with genuine military experience available to the volunteers. A field command
was a temptation for any politician worth his salt; the war was the training ground of many men who rose to the rank of colonel and general.

Wisconsin had its political generals, but the winnowing process brought
many officers to their proper level or sent them home. A major general in
the militia raised a volunteer company in his home town and remained
its captain throughout the war. Governors used appointments to satisfy
party leaders and ethnic voting groups and to woo Democrats. Governor
Randall appointed S. Park Coon, a former Democratic attorney general,
as colonel of the Second Wisconsin. This is often given as an earnest of
Randall's nonpartisan conduct, but should not be taken too seriously.
Many Democrats supported the war "for the preservation of the Union"
and found their way into the Republican party where the dispensation of
the loaves and fishes now resided. Coon, incidentally, turned out to be a
military embarrassment, and so was no great credit to Randall's nonpartisan acumen.

It must be remembered that much of the Civil War was fought almost
within earshot of Washington, D.C., as well as in the Ohio and Mississippi valleys. Politicians were in close touch with officers in the field,
many of whom operated in both roles. The close link between politics
and the military was reinforced by this continuous proximity.

One would expect that the agonizing death struggle being fought by
mass armies over the very fields, in the suburbs, and along the roads,
rivers, and railway lines of the country would have been reflected in a
stern mobilization of the civilian population and its economy. But it was,
in the popular expression, "a rich man's war and a poor man's fight."
John D. Rockefeller, Pierpont Morgan, Philip Armour, Grover Cleveland, James J. Hill, Jay Cooke, and Jay Gould were all men in their middle twenties or early thirties in 1861 who avoided serving in the army.
Their varied circumstances at the time are evidence that family, money,
or enterprise could insure against serving. Many families in humble circumstances lost the breadwinner, or the labor of their sons.

We can notice some interesting evidence that the influence of the war
and the military was less pervasive than one might expect. The British
novelist Anthony Trollope made an American tour in the summer of
1861. He visited Camp Scott in Milwaukee and recorded these melancholy observations:

> Wisconsin with its three quarters of a million of people is as large as
> England. Every acre of it may be made productive, but as yet it is not

half cleared. Of such a country its young men are its heart's blood. Ten thousand men fit to bear arms carried away from such a land to the horrors of civil war is a sight as full of sadness as any on which the eye can rest.

He observed that in the American army, "the men generally were taken from a higher level in the community than that which fills our own ranks" in England. Trollope was delayed between La Crosse and St. Paul by a regiment of Minnesota troops being brought down on the boat. He expressed surprise that "all means of public conveyance were not put absolutely out of gear" by the requirements of the army, but in La Crosse, as elsewhere, the agents of steamboat and railway companies made it amply clear to him that civilian passengers stood first in their regard. Troops were often moved in cattle cars, and army supplies were regularly disregarded in favor of commercial freight. General Pope once rebuked a zealous lieutenant for commandeering cars at Dunleith (East Dubuque) to move a badly needed supply of army oats which the local railroad agent persistently shunted aside in favor of civilian business.

As in the South, where the most unreconstructible rebels were apt to be women, some Wisconsin women were conspicuous for their patriotic zeal on public occasions. Recruiting of volunteers was brought to a high art and was one in which women could play an important role. Other opportunities for them to contribute were more private, or less certain in their organization and in the recognition of their usefulness by a male-dominated society.

The private contribution was that of thousands of wives and mothers who remained behind, many of them dependent upon the unkept promises of the community and the state legislature to sustain their families during the absence of the breadwinner. In a largely agricultural society, the enthusiasm for soldiering that seized upon the men left many farm families with a labor force made up entirely of women, children, and older men. Mrs. Mary E. Livermore of Chicago, a moving force in the organization of the United States Sanitary Commission, toured Wisconsin and Iowa in the summer of 1863. A lady of energy but conventional opinions, she observed women everywhere working in the fields and "at first it displeased me, and I turned away in aversion." Having overcome this first reaction, she walked into a field where six women and two men were harvesting. A woman of forty-five or fifty years who was driving the reaper said that she and her daughters were in the field because "my man can't hire help at any price."

"You are not German? You are surely one of my own countrywomen—

American?" Mrs. Livermore inquired. Assured that this was so, she recorded that her "eyes were unsealed."

Women stepped into other lines of work. Many entered traditional employment as teachers, domestics, seamstresses, and so forth, but the number of women employed in industrial and commercial pursuits also increased from 773 in the 1860 census to 3,967 in 1870. Three hundred sixty-two of these worked in sawmills, and many in the men's clothing industry, allied needles trades, and light manufacturing.

Women were better known for their volunteer work in the Sanitary Commission and in the organized aid societies engaged in making lint bandages and packing boxes for individual soldiers with hand-made articles, preserved foods, clothing, and sewing kits. Mrs. Cordelia A. P. Harvey, widow of Wisconsin's second wartime governor, is doubtless the best known of Wisconsin women engaged in war work. Women were slow to be accepted as nurses in army hospitals. Mrs. Harvey was one of a few Wisconsin women who worked in military hospitals as sanitary agents distributing supplies. Her great contribution was to prevail upon President Lincoln and Secretary Stanton to establish convalescent hospitals in Wisconsin to get wounded and ill men out of the fever-ridden military hospitals of the South. Other Wisconsin women made important contributions to the success and financing of the Sanitary Commission and to the founding of institutions for the care of disabled veterans and war orphans.

An interesting sidelight on the Northwest Sanitary Fair held in Chicago in 1863 was the incorporation of a German department. The ladies organizing the fair, for money-raising purposes, had Mrs. Governor Salomon take charge of soliciting and displaying handcrafts from "the German ladies of the Northwest." One was a needlework portrait of Mozart purchased for $150 by the Chicago Philharmonic Society. In all, the German department raised $6,000—$3,799 of it from Wisconsin contributions—and it was observed, somewhat patronizingly, that "the patriotism of the German women during our great struggle was manifested on this occasion." Mrs. Livermore, who expected to find only German women working in the fields, was a prime mover in the fair.

The Sioux War was another embarrassment for Governor Salomon. The war was real enough, but it was confined to the area west of the Mississippi. The Sioux, numbering over 10,000 in Minnesota and the Dakotas, had legitimate grievances and considerably more spirit than Wisconsin's Indians. They were not entirely dependent but were able to supply their needs from the buffalo herds ranging in the upper Missouri. A drunken argument at Acton, Minnesota, about fifty miles west of Fort Snelling, resulted in the massacre of some settlers, and making a virtue of their acts, the braves involved persuaded Chief Little Crow to turn the incident into a declaration of war. This was in August 1862. The raiding fever swept westward and into Iowa, with 737 whites murdered within seven days. The outbreak occupied the Minnesota volunteer militia, in training, and other troops as well. It coincided with the replacement of General John Pope as commander of the Army of the Potomac and the return of General George B. McClellan. Pope, posted to Milwaukee to chastise the Sioux, was, whatever his other limitations, calm, decisive, and a firm believer in the supremacy of civilian control, even when he had to force a sense of responsibility on the civilian authorities.

The Sioux outbreak resulted in an unreasoning panic that swept as far eastward as Indiana. Citizens in northwestern Wisconsin fled their homes, and there were even alarms just north of Milwaukee. Governor Salomon joined the panic briefly, demanding aid from Washington which he did not receive. He shared with others the belief that the Chippewa living in northern Wisconsin and the Winnebago who were scattered through central Wisconsin had been tampered with by Confederate agents and were in league with the Sioux. Neither suspicion turned out to be true. The Indians, justifiably, were more frightened than the whites by the threats of violence. The panic abated as swiftly as it had spread. Thirty-nine of the offending Sioux were ultimately hanged, and the remnants of the Winnebago were once more rounded up and sent west. It did not make a proud record, but attention was shortly diverted to the draft riots and incidents in Wisconsin. Pope forced the reluctant civilian authorities to handle most of the emergencies.

On the civilian front, political differences were exacerbated by the issues of the Civil War. Many Democrats were dismayed by the growing intransigence of what was loosely termed the Copperhead element, as represented by the extravagance of the Ryan Address and the shrill invective of Brick Pomeroy in the *La Crosse Democrat*. Conservative Democrats tried to maintain a responsible opposition based upon the states' rights doctrine, Republican corruption, and ineptitude in the conduct of the war—of which there was a surfeit—and economic grievances growing out of tariff concessions to eastern manufacturers, the tax burden placed on distilled spirits (the traditional use of much western grain), and the unconscionable rise of railroad freight rates on western products. As Alexander Thomson, an active Republican, commented, "these loyal Democrats paid their taxes, fought in the Union cause, sent their sons to fight, and did everything but vote Republican. For this last error they were never forgiven."

The Republicans made attractive terms for Yankee Democrats to make the transition to the new party. In the 1861 state elections, the Republicans adopted the Union party label and nominated a Democrat for lieutenant-governor. The Union convention was so devoid of Democratic support that this nomination was dropped in a regular Republican convention. The Union party label was revived when the War Democrats in 1862 held a convention separate from the regular party convention. This Republican policy paid off with many Democratic desertions to the Union party. It also brought dismay to many Republicans when the converts made off with assorted plums of office. Another expedient that paid rich dividends was the authorization of soldiers in the field to vote by special ballot. The ballots were collected by special commissioners, called "political commissars" by the Democrats. The soldier vote was consistently about 90 percent Republican and turned the balance in some crucial contests. Many doubted that the troops in the field voted quite that heavily Republican.

The Civil War was not instrumental in binding together Wisconsin's divided society; it brought burdens which were distributed with gross inequity. The Yankee elite maintained its position on the top rung of the ladder, while managing affairs with self-assured ineptitude. Wisconsin's contribution to the war was an important one. Fully one in ten of its population saw service in the armed forces. It is a melancholy source of pride that one in every seven of these died in that service.

Selected Bibliography

Abernethy, Byron R., ed. *Private Elisha Stockwell, Jr., Sees the Civil War.* Norman, Okla., 1958. Joined the 14th Wisconsin Volunteers at age fifteen.

Ambrose, Stephen E., ed. *A Wisconsin Boy in Dixie: The Selected Letters of James K. Newton.* Madison, 1961. Another member of the 14th Wisconsin Volunteers.

Andersen, Arlow W. "Lincoln and the Union: A Study of the Editorials of *Emigranten* and *Faedrelandet.*" *Norwegian American Studies and Records* 15:85–121 (1949). *Emigranten* was the only secular Norwegian paper of the time, both were Republican.

Balasubramanian, D. "Wisconsin's Foreign Trade in the Civil War Era." *Wisconsin Magazine of History* 46:257–62 (Summer 1963). The wheat trade with Canada was cut off by the growing hostility toward Britain.

Brobst, John F. *Well Mary: Civil War Letters of a Wisconsin Volunteer.* Madison, 1960. "Seeing the elephant."

Clark, James I. *The Civil War of Private Cooke: A Wisconsin Boy in the Union Army.* Madison, 1955. More about Wisconsin during the war than the title implies.

Cooper, Jerry M. "The Wisconsin Militia, 1832–1900." Master's thesis, University of Wisconsin, 1968. The ready defense that was never ready. An excellent thesis.

Dawes, Rufus R. *Service with the Sixth Wisconsin.* Edited, with an introduction, by Alan T. Nolan. Madison, 1962. Originally published in 1890, this is a prized account by the captain of the Lemonweir Minute Men.

Ernst, Dorothy J. "Wheat Speculation in the Civil War Era: Daniel Wells and the Grain Trade." *Wisconsin Magazine of History* 47:125–35 (Winter 1963–64). Took advantage of Milwaukee's new railroad connections to make a fortune in Iowa and Minnesota wheat.

Glazer, Walter S. "Wisconsin Goes to War: April, 1961." *Wisconsin Magazine of History* 50:147–64 (Winter 1967). Doesn't find the commonly accepted enthusiasm for the war in the opening weeks.

Hardgrove, J. G. "General Edward S. Bragg's Reminiscences." *Wisconsin Magazine of History* 33:281–309 (March 1950). Union Democrat who made the grade.

Hesseltine, William B. "Lincoln's Problems in Wisconsin." *Wisconsin Magazine of History* 48:187–95 (Spring 1965). Dealing with Republican governors.

———. *Lincoln and the War Governors.* New York, 1948. A compromise candidate and a minority president who showed the Republican governors how to play the political game.

———. "The Pryor-Potter Duel." *Wisconsin Magazine of History* 27:400–409 (June 1944). In calmer times it would have been called an undignified wrangle.

Horton, Jackson R. "The Demobilization of Wisconsin Troops after the Civil War." Master's thesis, University of Wisconsin, 1952. Wars and armies don't change much.

Hurn, Ethel A. *Wisconsin Women in the War Between the States.* Wisconsin History Commission Original Papers, no. 6. Madison, 1911. Mrs. Harvey and the Sanitary Fairs.

Jones, Robert H. *The Civil War in the Northwest.* Norman, Okla., 1960. General John Pope had to clean up after the Sioux War of 1862.

Kaiser, Leo M., ed. "Civil War Letters of Charles W. Carr of the 21st Wisconsin." *Wisconsin Magazine of History* 43:264–72 (Summer 1960). In case we forget what Sherman said about war.

Klement, Frank. "Brick Pomeroy: Copperhead and Curmudgeon." *Wisconsin Magazine of History* 35:106–13, 156–57 (Winter 1951).

———. "Copperheads and Copperheadism in Wisconsin: Democratic Opposition to the Lincoln Administration." *Wisconsin Magazine of History* 42:182–88 (Spring 1959).

———. *The Copperheads of the Middle West.* Chicago, 1960.

———. "The Soldier Vote in Wisconsin During the Civil War." *Wisconsin Magazine of History* 28:37–47 (Sept. 1944).

———. *Wisconsin and the Civil War.* Madison, 1963.

———. "Wisconsin and the Civil War." *The Wisconsin Blue Book,* 1962. Madison, 1962. The expert on Wisconsin in the Civil War.

Mattern, Carolyn Jane. 'Soldiers When They Go: The Story of Camp Randall 1861–65." Master's thesis, University of Wisconsin, 1968. Excellent, and heavily leaned upon here.

Merk, Frederick. *Economic History of Wisconsin During the Civil War Decade.* Madison, 1916. A Wisconsin history classic, reprinted by the State Historical Society of Wisconsin.

Miller, Willard F. "A History of Eau Claire County During the Civil War." Master's thesis, University of Wisconsin, 1954. A nice job about the home front in a frontier community.

Nolan, Alan T. *The Iron Brigade: A Military History.* New York, 1961. Wisconsin's most famous fighting unit.

Overy, David H. *Wisconsin Carpetbaggers in Dixie.,* Madison, 1961.

———. "The Wisconsin Carpetbagger: A Group Portrait." *Wisconsin Magazine of History* 44:15–49 (Autumn 1960). A variety of Wisconsin men went south to serve, or be served.

Porter, Daniel R. "The Colonel and the Private Go to War." *Wisconsin Magazine of History* 42:124–27 (Winter, 1958–59). Training the 16th Wisconsin at Randall.

Roddis, Louis H. *The Indian Wars of Minnesota.* Cedar Rapids, 1956. The bulk of it is about the Sioux War of 1862.

Schoonover, Lynn I. "A History of the Civil War Draft in Wisconsin." Master's thesis, University of Wisconsin, 1915. There were 38,495 names drawn, 11,742 didn't show up.

Schurz, Carl. *The Autobiography of Carl Schurz.* Edited by Wayne Andrews. Abridged ed. in one volume. New York, 1961. Schurz was an egotist, but he had an interesting career. An awkward figure in the Gilded Age.

Scott, Spencer C. "The Financial Effects of the Civil War on the State of Wisconsin." Master's thesis, University of Wisconsin, 1939. State and local financing of bonuses, bounties, relief, and raising armies.

Trollope, Anthony. *North America.* New York, 1951. Visit to Wisconsin in 1861.

Voegeli, V. Jacque. *Free But Not Equal: The Midwest and the Negro During the Civil War.* Chicago, 1967. The Midwest accepted emancipation but not equality or economic competition.

Wiley, Bell Irvin. *The Common Soldier in the Civil War.* New York, 1951. Why men fought.

Williams, T. Harry. "Badger Colonels and the Civil War Officer." *Wisconsin Magazine of History* 47:35–46 (Autumn 1963). The North had only 440 West Pointers in 1861.

Wittke, Carl. *The German Language Press in America.* Lexington, Ky., 1957. Wisconsin had a large share of them.

———. *Refugees of Revolution: The German Forty-Eighter in America.* Philadelphia, 1952. They had a lot of *amour propre* to appease.

A NEW
ECONOMY EMERGES
1860–1900

part six

The fur-trading and lead-mining frontiers of Wisconsin were harbingers of the economic development brought by American settlement. They were commercial and industrial frontiers dependent upon distant markets and sources of supply. They exhibited few characteristics of subsistence agricultural frontiers, but rather were based upon the exploitation of a limited resource which was exchanged for money.

The exploitative phase is a familiar one in the history of our trans-Mississippi frontiers. One thinks of the various mining frontiers following 1849, the slaughter of the great buffalo herds, the open-range cattle industry, bonanza grain farms on railroad grant lands in the Dakotas and California, and the lumber frontier on Puget Sound in the Pacific Northwest. Western industrial growth was often held in this initial phase, with ownership and control exercised by outside capital.

A significant difference can be discerned between the development of

Wisconsin's economy in the second half of the nineteenth century and
that of most other western frontiers, however. It represents, in many
ways, a transitional model somewhere between the more mature economies of the New England, Middle Atlantic, and older Lakes states and
the colonial economies of the trans-Mississippi West. This transitional
character owes much to geography and the historical moment, and something to individual enterprise.

Fronting on the two westernmost of the Great Lakes, Wisconsin was
the beneficiary of the rough economic democracy of the age of sail. The
hinterlands of her port cities started at their back doors. The first major
barrier was the Mississippi River, which served as a gatherer of commerce for the pioneer railroads until they managed to bridge it. Compare
Milwaukee's situation with that of Seattle, also a port city but with the
Cascade Mountains blocking her back door. Seattle saw the commercial
agriculture that she hoped to tap served by a water level route reaching
tidewater at Portland, her principal rival, and major national markets
were 2,500 miles away by land, thousands by sea. Milwaukee could realistically think of local railroad promotions to reach her hinterlands. The
Great Lakes and the Mississippi River were public highways to market
for wheat and lumber. The movement westward of grain farming and
lumbering gave the city advantages of location. The technological
changes in those industries favored the adaptability of Milwaukee's pioneer machinery manufacturers. The result was the accumulation of investment capital at home in lumbering, wheat processing and forwarding,
and manufacturing.

Wisconsin's industrial frontier preceded the consolidation of many industries, hence the importance of timing in comparison with other frontiers. A pioneer iron industry was developed with limited resources of
ore and hardwood charcoal at hand. Her growing metal-working and
machinery industries, served by lake carriage, were assured an economical supply of iron and steel after the pattern of this basic industry
changed. Being new and adaptable, these metal-working and machinery
industries shared in and fostered the various technological revolutions
which were a part of the dynamic growth of the extractive industries:
lumbering, milling, mining, and plains agriculture. As these industries
moved westward, Wisconsin-made machinery followed. Again a comparison with the Pacific Northwest is instructive. The difference was not all a
matter of geography. The timing of these two comparable frontiers was a
significant factor in defining the roles played by outside capital and the
ability of established firms, with national markets, to compete with or to
discourage nonextractive local manufacturing. Just as Wisconsin lumber-

men moved readily to the Pacific Northwest, Milwaukee-built machinery went into the mills there.

The influence of individuals is an imponderable. Would Wisconsin's industrial history have been so different without Alexander Mitchell, Edward P. Allis, Jerome I. Case, and others? One suspects that opportunity does not necessarily call forth the individual who can do the most with it. These men made a difference.

THE CIVIL WAR AND
THE ECONOMY

18

The Civil War interrupted the growth of Wisconsin's economy. Railroad mileage increased only nominally from 1857 to 1870. Immigration fell off markedly during the war. There were 356 corporations chartered in the flush years of 1853–1857, only 164 during the war years 1861–1865 —half of these in 1865 alone—and then in 1866–1870, a dramatic rise to 515. The last period saw a boom in mining ventures, and oddly, petroleum, clearly speculative in character.

The war came hard upon the heels of the 1857 panic and placed new strains upon the pioneer economy of Wisconsin. Recovery was rapid in the industrial states of the East, but prospects brightened more slowly in the West. Pioneer ventures depend upon a spirit of speculative buoyancy which takes some time to rebuild after a panic. Capital is easily frightened.

Wisconsin's lumber business, small as yet compared with the expanded industry that would come after the war, ranked second after flour milling among the state's industries, but was hard hit by the panic and got little encouragement until 1860. And Wisconsin's banks were mostly of the wildcat variety. While they rode through the panic with much difficulty, measures were not taken to cure their worst faults before the next emergency presented by the war.

Wisconsin law specified that state bonds acceptable as security for bank notes must pay at least 6 percent interest on their face value. The bonds of certain southern states were the most popular for this purpose; they paid the highest interest and usually sold at a discount, an evidence of how the general money market viewed them. In 1860, bonds of the state of Missouri with a face value of $31,250 could be bought for $25,000. Paying 6 percent on the face value, they returned $1,875 annual interest to the banker. The banker deposited them with the state comptroller and received in return $25,000 in bank notes properly countersigned. He could lend these at an interest rate of 10 percent and thus realize a profit of 17.5 percent on his invested capital.

Wisconsin ignored New York State's experience with the free banking system and the abuses to which it was prone. In particular, the Wisconsin law placed few barriers in the way of a determined wildcat operator. It was possible to have a broker buy the necessary bonds for a small down payment. One could start a bank with an actual minimum of $1,250 in cash. The law did not specify the location of the bank nor did it require that the bank make arrangements to redeem its notes through correspondent banks. It was to the advantage of the banker, interested only in the circulation of his own bank notes, to establish his bank where redemption would be inconvenient for the noteholder. One banker did this by naming his bank the Bank of Green Bay and printing the name on the bank notes, although the bank was actually in La Crosse. Obscure villages blossomed with banks of issue.

We may wonder how such money found acceptance anywhere. The answer seemed to be that any currency was better than none, and all of the 108 state banks existing in 1859 created only about $9 per capita of bank notes in circulation. This was little enough with which to conduct business, for we must remember that there was no national currency at this time, gold coin was hoarded or used to pay obligations for which local bank notes were either unacceptable or discounted too heavily, and checks were not in common use. Eastern bank notes and coin went East to pay for manufactured goods, or else into the mattress as the only constants in a wavering economy.

The assurances of the Wisconsin banking law were acceptable, except when tested by emergencies. People were accustomed to the inconveniences of discounts against their currency or playing host to an occasional worthless bank note. As an illustration of this complacency, the banks of Eau Claire had $536,764 of bank notes in circulation in 1860, compared with only $86,521 from all of the Milwaukee banks where genuine commercial banking prevailed. The population of the entire county of Eau Claire was just over 3,000, but it had floated about one-eighth of all the bank notes in Wisconsin.

The legislature tinkered a bit with Wisconsin's banking laws in 1858, but did not effect much change. The bank comptroller had no real powers to remedy the situation, and banks that had no offices or regular hours continued to circulate bank notes, many of them beyond the limits of their paid-up capital. One new element in the situation was a Bankers' Association, led by Alexander Mitchell of the Wisconsin Marine and Fire Insurance Company Bank. Supported by the more conservative bankers, who were actually engaged in commercial banking, the association endeavored to tighten regulation and require all banks to arrange for an agent (presumably one of the "responsible" banks) in Milwaukee or Madison to redeem their bank notes upon demand. Mitchell's group was not effective in getting any meaningful changes in legislation, but they represented a power that would be heard from in the future.

Wisconsin's economy was just making a recovery in the summer of 1860, when the new crisis posed by the coming election and the threatened secession of the southern states interrupted the growth in confidence and put the unstable banking system to a new test. As the threat of secession developed into an assured fact after Lincoln's election, the bonds of the southern and border states, which backed three-fourths of the Wisconsin bank notes, dropped steadily in price on the New York money market, where their legal collateral values were set. Missouri and Tennessee bonds, which had sold for 80 and 86 respectively in January 1860, fell to 67 and 75 a year later and to 37 and 27 by June 1861, after hostilities had begun. The comptroller called upon the affected banks to cover this erosion by retiring bank notes or adding collateral, but the situation was soon out of hand.

The trouble with heroic measures at this point, based upon the application of the strict letter of the law, was that they would sweep many of the conservatively run banks out of business along with the wildcatters. Into this situation stepped Alexander Mitchell and the Bankers' Association. In a couple of meetings held in April 1861, the Milwaukee bankers and forty-five allied country bankers discredited the bank notes of thirty-seven banks by giving notice that they would refuse to accept them at any discount. They listed the notes of the remaining seventy as sound and acceptable, although only about 8 percent of them were fully secured by satisfactory collateral as the law required.

The measures taken by the Bankers' Association were certainly extralegal, but Mitchell is generally credited with saving an essential part of the banking system. The association called upon the state bank comptroller to sell the collateral of the proscribed banks and retire their remaining banknotes. This operation siphoned what hard coin and good paper the offending banks had into the vaults of the association banks and eliminated the most questionable bank notes from circulation at a very considerable discount to those unlucky enough to hold them.

The man in the street was naturally apprehensive about the proposed actions of the Bankers' Association. Not knowing exactly which banks were going to pass through the fire successfully, citizens took inventory of the bank notes they had on hand and hastened to spend those that might be suspect. The haste to spend questionable bank notes was met by an equal reluctance on the part of creditors and merchants to receive them, with an accompanying disruption of normal business.

The Draconian measures of the Bankers' Association, however, did not restore stability. The state comptroller continued to levy upon the affected banks as southern bonds dropped further in value. Eighteen of the seventy approved banks were among the fifty-eight that failed to respond to his call for more collateral. The Milwaukee banks, having a relatively small amount in bank notes circulating in their own names, but being the mainstay of the Bankers' Association pledge to honor the notes of the seventy favored banks, were hard pressed. Members from outside of the metropolitan district loaded their questionable bank notes onto the Milwaukee banks for redemption. What worked once could work again and more effectively within the confines of the Milwaukee banking fraternity. They got together and determined to refuse the notes of an additional ten banks within the association.

The problem of privileged information has always been a thorny one for the insiders of the financial community, but one which they normally manage to resolve in their own interests. This occasion was no exception. The Milwaukee bankers cleaned out their tills of the newly defaulted bank notes and sent them floating out into the community with their blessings. Local businessmen and factory owners evidently had a fair idea of what was coming, for when the notice of the repudiation was published by the bankers at the close of business on Saturday, June 22, an unusual number of the discredited notes had found their way into the pay envelopes of Milwaukee's workingmen. The German community, with a high proportion of the workingmen and Jacksonian hard-money Democrats, had their Sunday leisure to consider this new evidence of Yankee perfidy. Monday morning found them out in force to vent their displeasure. They headed for Mitchell's bank, properly identifying that Scotsman as the most culpable Yankee. Mitchell, who had examined his own conduct and found it blameless, was at the bank with the mayor in tow, prepared to explain the facts of commercial life to the crowd, which through the filter of pioneer accounts written by complacent Yankees was henceforth to be known as a "lawless, largely German mob."

Mitchell and the mayor found it advisable to quit the scene hastily, as the crowd was in no mood for sweet reasonableness. The canny Scot had given enough thought to the persuasiveness of his case to order all valuables into the locked vault. The mob had to be content with some breakage and a bonfire of the furniture from a neighboring bank. Since it was June 1861, the state already had volunteer troops in training. Four companies were quickly gathered to deal with the situation. The Milwaukee bankers were probably justified in their original decision to discredit the bank notes in question, but not in the manner in which they chose to do it.

The pressure upon the state banking system was not relieved, even though the legislature came to its relief with what amounted to an unconstitutional suspension of the requirement of specie payment. The southern state bonds that stood behind most of the currency were sinking from the view of the New York market. Wisconsin bank notes were heavily discounted outside of the state's borders. Meanwhile the state, to meet the emergency expenses involved in raising and equipping the volunteer militia, attempted to float an unusual state bond issue of $1,000,000. The national money market had its problems without absorbing this bond issue, which seemed of dubious constitutionality. Added to the legal question were the determined efforts of the Grand State League to repudiate the infamous farm railroad mortgages. Wisconsin's credit was not good, and officials could not place the bond issue.

Again Alexander Mitchell came to the rescue. He perceived a way to combine the embarrassments of the state and the state's bankers in a mutually advantageous arrangement. An agreement was worked out whereby the state banks would replace the devalued southern bonds with the new Wisconsin bonds as collateral for their note issues. Mitchell had not remained solvent over the years by being all heart. Only 60 percent of the banks' payment for the new bonds was to be in coin and New York bank notes, 10 percent in their own bank notes, and the remaining 30 percent from the coupons on the Wisconsin bonds. The terms were certainly generous for the bankers, but the state was in no position to drive a better bargain.

These various measures worked a wondrous attrition on the amount of currency in circulation. The $6,800,000 in bank notes abroad in October 1860 had shrunk to $1,600,000 by July 1862. This added to the business crisis brought on by the displacements caused by the war. The shortage of currency made it difficult, even for business houses with the best credit ratings, to obtain operating funds. The artificial tightening of credit compounded the already acute situation and delayed recovery. After 1863, the national greenbacks, issued by the federal treasury as a method of deficit financing, eased tight credit and brought a steady inflation in prices.

The state's management of its financial emergencies was not any better than the general level of its military preparations. Governor Randall, whatever his virtues as an energetic and highly vocal war hawk, was careless about financial details. The agreement with the bankers had reduced the return on four-fifths of the special $1,000,000 state bond issue to an immediate 70 cents on the dollar. Before this deal was made, Randall's procurement officers had negotiated contracts for supplies to be paid for half in cash and half in the bonds. Contractors had generously applied a 40 percent advance in their prices to compensate for the questionable value of the bonds. Having accepted the prices, the state then paid most of the contracts off in cash and currency, fearing that the contractors would dump the bonds and depress their market further. The accounts which Governor Randall and his agents kept of these transactions were often less than sketchy. A hostile senate committee estimated that it cost Wisconsin nearly $100,000 to outfit 1,000 men, while neighboring states accomplished this for outlays ranging from $21,000 to $42,000.

Tax rates did advance during the war, but war financing was a matter of improvisation at both the national and state levels. In theory, the federal government reimbursed the states for the cost of equipping troops and for other expenses, but this was a slow process. Expenses borne by the state were of an unusual order. When the Union army was routed at First Bull Run, the state had to assume the expense of replacing lost weapons and other equipment for its troops. These costs were later assumed by the federal government, but many others for men in the field remained with the states—much of the care for the sick and wounded, for example. Governor Randall determined that it made sense to attach a civilian agent to each regiment to see to such details. The phrase *political boondoggle* was not in common use, but its equivalent was applied by Randall's opponents.

The largest and most constant expense was a $5-a-month subsistence allowance voted to soldiers' dependents, and the private soldier's pay of $13 a month, plus bounty money and the allowance, evidently tempted many patriots. The legislature was more ready to vote the allowance than the funds to pay it. Governors Harvey and Salomon were frequently forced to beg the legislature to meet this commitment. The state finally met much of the extraordinary expense by replacing some $3,000,000 of the state's permanent funds with new issues of state bonds. When Wisconsin eventually collected about $4,000,000 from the federal government, the money was placed in the general fund rather than being used to retire the bonds. Another way to lighten the load was to permit local taxing districts to adopt levies for the purpose of paying bounties to soldiers; the state was not directly involved in the bounty business. Politicians of a century ago lacked the services of academic economists to advise on the care and feeding of public debt. They may have understood less about the possible consequences, but they met their responsibilities in a manner familiar to their heirs.

In the 1860s, agriculture was the dominant interest of Wisconsin, and wheat overshadowed all other crops. Wheat culture had marched steadily westward. By 1860, Illinois and Wisconsin were numbers one and two, respectively, among all the states in its production. They were also the principal exporters, for the older wheat-growing states consumed most of their own production.

Southern Wisconsin, by 1860, was what one could term a mature wheat-producing area. It had railroad links reaching from Lake Michigan to the Mississippi, with well-developed grain-forwarding facilities at Milwaukee, Racine, and Chicago. Export flour mills were important industries at Milwaukee and on the waterpowers of the lower Fox. Mechanization of wheat farming proceeded at a rapid pace. The Wisconsin State Agricultural Society estimated that 3,000 reapers of various kinds were sold in the state in 1860 alone. Jerome I. Case was marketing 1,500 of his large ten-horse threshers annually, manufactured at his Racine plant. And 1860 was the year of Wisconsin's banner wheat crop, estimated at 29,000,000 bushels, probably on the order of one-sixth of the U.S. total.

But farmers were not happy in their apparent prosperity. While not much of Wisconsin's grain had found its way to markets in the South, particularly after the railroads intercepted the upper Mississippi in 1857, the price was affected by the threat to the large St. Louis grain market posed by secession. The Wisconsin price, a satisfactory 94 cents in August, fell to 65 cents by December 1860 and did not recover until the summer of 1862. By the summer of 1864, it had reached an astronomical $2.64 at Milwaukee in depreciated greenbacks, but the crop was exceedingly poor. Wheat was an increasingly unsatisfactory crop for Wisconsin farmers for a number of reasons: depleted soils, pests, a climate too harsh for the favored varieties of winter wheat, and the dubious blessings brought by the railroads.

The railroads put the Wisconsin wheat farmer in communication with a larger market and introduced new and capricious factors. Not only did the farmers find a mystery in the grain prices of the Liverpool market, but closer to home, he found his new partner in this wider venture, the railroad, given to greed. Where the railroads were without competition in the hinterland they charged what the traffic would bear. Throughout the 1860s, agricultural produce, principally wheat, furnished fully three-fourths of the freight traffic for Wisconsin's railroads. It did not take the railroads long to arrive at a community of interest at points where they were in competition, particularly after their consolidation got underway in the early sixties. As for the competition of the Mississippi, that was partly closed off by the war and by the railroads taking control of the packet lines. Railroad freight on a bushel of wheat from La Crosse or Prairie du Chien to the Lake was 10 cents a bushel in 1860. By 1865 it had doubled to 20 cents. The farmers would make trouble for the railroads as wheat prices fell.

The transition from a dependence on wheat was to be long and painful, but meanwhile some venturesome farmers tried crops that promised to satisfy war-induced demands. Great enthusiasm was generated for the growing of African sorghum and Chinese imphee, for processing as a sugar substitute. Madison became the center of this industry and for the machinery to extract the syrup. The state and county fairs of the period devoted considerably more space to sorghum and sorghum machinery than to dairying. Wool-raising was an answer to a wartime demand and the need to vary the use of land depleted by successive wheat crops. As wool prices soared, there were great hopes for sheep-raising. But with the end of the war, just as flocks were reaching the desired size, the return of southern cotton drove the price of wool down from a high of $1.05 a pound to 29 cents.

Wisconsin's first cheese factory was built in 1864, but the pioneers of dairying were less concerned with filling wartime scarcities than with finding a practical alternative to wheat on land which, owing to the railroads and growing urban markets, was climbing in value even as repeated grain crops sapped its fertility. Tobacco culture, oddly, did not increase significantly during the war, although the plant flourished in many places where it was grown for home use. Hop growing enjoyed a brief and profitable hour through a combination of distress in older hop-raising areas and the wartime growth of the brewing industry. The hop louse, which had put the New York hop yards out of business, soon made its way to Wisconsin, and the "hop craze" passed. Flax growing went the same route as wool raising, with the return of cotton as the basic textile. All in all, the war neither set Wisconsin agriculture in new directions nor left a golden glow of prosperous years.

Wheat milling was the leading industry in Wisconsin and remained so until the eighties, when lumbering and lumber milling finally took first place, but it made less growth during the war years than any major industry. Exports from Wisconsin increased only from 550,000 barrels in 1860 to 625,000 in 1865. The railroads had already worked a certain degree of consolidation of milling at Milwaukee and around Neenah-Menasha, but it remained largely a dispersed industry with a local character. The big advances in the technology of flour manufacture came after the Civil War, turning Minnesota and the Dakotas into prime wheat areas when machinery was developed that would make a more satisfactory product from the hard spring wheat. The failure of milling to make larger gains during the war probably had something to do with the structure of freight rates on the Lakes, which favored shipping wheat in the berry rather than as flour. The Buffalo milling interests had a hand in this, for Buffalo largely financed the forwarding of grain and flour from the west through agents who gave advances to millers, commission merchants, and even growers. Also, flour ground by the traditional method, with millstones, did not ship well for long distances; the germ of the wheat was crushed with the starch, which promoted souring. Finally, the various crises of Wisconsin's currency and credit structure inhibited the capital investment needed by the export-milling industry for expansion. The opportunity was clearly there, for Milwaukee's and Neenah's milling industry underwent considerable expansion and modernization immediately after the war.

The combination of expanded cultivation, the absence of some 80,000 men in the army, improved wheat prices after July 1862, and the continuing revolution in the technology of grain raising helped to expand the agricultural machinery industry in this period. Investment and capacity could not keep up with demand. Wisconsin manufacturers found themselves in a good position to control the machinery market growing across the Mississippi in Iowa and Minnesota. It must be remembered that the farm machines of the day involved more work in wood than in metal, and Wisconsin's southern counties furnished an abundance of good hardwoods. Aside from the well-publicized J. I. Case works at Racine, which became a major American farm machinery manufacturer during the sixties mainly because of its improved thresher, there were other important innovators and manufacturers developing in the state. George Esterly, at Whitewater, became an important inventor-industrialist manufacturing seeders, mowers, self-raking headers, and other machines of his own design. Less well known, Van Brunt and Company, in the village of Horicon, produced 60 seeders in 1861 and reached an annual production of 1,300 by 1866. Rowell and Company at Beaver Dam was almost as large in the same line. The farm wagon industry was widespread, and specialty manufacturers were to be found in many hamlets, turning out local versions of various agricultural machines.

Wisconsin's growing lumber industry went through more poor than good years during the Civil War, although the years beginning in 1863 were a time of rapid expansion and technological innovation in the sawmills. The cut for the winter of 1860–61, lower than in 1856–57, was estimated at 375,000,000 board feet, compared with 800,000,000 by 1866–67 and 1,200,000,000 in 1868–69. Much of the expansion came in the pine-rich river valleys of northwestern Wisconsin: the valleys of the Black, the Chippewa, and the St. Croix. The exploitation of these three river valleys was just beginning on a large scale in the 1860s.

A combination of troubles plagued the lumber business. The pineries tributary to Lake Michigan were dependent upon the Chicago market, which was easily glutted, drawing as it did upon Michigan and Wisconsin lumber. Prices there rose as high as $30 a thousand in the boom years before the 1857 Panic. They skidded disastrously and in 1858 fell as low as $4 or $5. There were many bankruptcies in these years. Prices began a tentative firming in 1860, but fell again with Lincoln's election and did not revive until 1862, when bonanza years began a period of rapid expansion.

The lumbermen in the pineries tributary to Lake Winnebago and Green Bay were then in clover. The Chicago market absorbed all they could send, at prices which held around $20, until 1865, when a brief depression interrupted this happy state of affairs. Unusually low water conditions in 1863 and 1864 kept the timber tributary to the Mississippi from sharing much of the prosperity. In the 1860s, these mills in Wisconsin depended upon the rivers for their logs and for carrying the rafts of cut lumber to market. Prosperity came for them in the years immediately after the war, when railroads expanded into the prairie wheat lands across the Mississippi, ending dependence upon the St. Louis market and finally upon rafting the cut lumber.

There were some industries that definitely benefited from the war and established their importance in the economy in this period. The firms of Plankinton and Armour, Layton and Company, and Van Kirk, Mc-Geach and Company made Milwaukee an important national center in pork packing. The meat was salted in brine and shipped in barrels, even the hams. The Union Army was fed largely on salt pork and beef, and Milwaukee packers shipped their products to eastern cities and as far as England. They processed 60,130 hogs in 1860, 133,370 in 1866, and 313,120 by 1871.

The tanning industry was another that expanded and centralized considerably in the sixties. The Civil War armies moved on shoe leather and by harness. The increased mechanization of farming was based upon horse-power, and horses required more elaborate harnessing than oxen. And the mechanization of shoemaking was given impetus by the demands of the war and by the invention, in 1862, of McKay's pegging machine for attaching the uppers to the sole of the shoe, creating centralized markets for shoe leathers tanned to a common standard.

The western tanning industry traditionally had been a village industry processing local hides on a custom basis. A number of factors made Milwaukee and other Lakeshore towns centers of a tanning industry on a larger scale, however. Most important of these, probably, was the presence of the chemical agents used in tanning, oak bark and hemlock bark; recent innovations had made hemlock bark as acceptable as oak. It required about a ton of the ground bark to tan 200 pounds of hide—about four or five average cowhides—and Milwaukee had ample quantities of both oak and hemlock tributary to her growing tanneries. The city also had its large German colony, among whom were skilled tanners plowing their earnings back into their businesses. Milwaukee had nine tanneries in 1860, only two of them substantial operations, and fifteen by the close of the war.

Although tanning underwent important changes of scale at this time, the basic chemistry of the process remained traditional until about the turn of the century. With the completion of rail links, the hides came to where the bark supplies were to be found. The Milwaukee packers were not an important source of hides, for they packed mostly hogs, and the tanneries worked principally with beef and calf hides. Nevertheless, leather production remained an important growth industry, among the first five in value of product in the state, until after 1920. The industry was dominated by men of German background well into the twentieth century, with Pfister and Vogel among the best known. The Wisconsin Leather Company, however, a rival in size, was built on plants at Two Rivers and Milwaukee by the Allen family from Cazenovia, New York.

Those acquainted with the history of American labor will recall that the Knights of St. Crispin was a pioneer national union organized among the shoemakers in Milwaukee in 1867. Shoes were still largely custom made, but the factory system was growing. The adaptation of the sewing machine to shoemaking in the 1850s, and McKay's machine in 1862, left only part of the process in the hands of skilled labor. Until the end of the 1860s, Bradley and Metcalf, an early boot and shoe manufacturing firm in Milwaukee, operated a loft building in which they rented space to craftsmen to do the necessary hand labor, with their own tools, on unfinished shoes. It is difficult to establish a ranking for the state's boot and shoe industry in the 1860s. The industry centered in New England, where about 90 percent of Milwaukee's shoe leather products found their market in the 1870s.

One industry which in particular was to be intimately identified with Milwaukee grew rapidly during the war and beyond. Brewing and malting were pioneer industries in Milwaukee and elsewhere in Wisconsin, because of the high quality of the state's barleys, the water supply, the abundant natural ice, and the large German population. The Civil War helped to convert the Yankees and other ethnic groups to beer drinking, as distilled liquor was forced to bear a war tax which rose to $2 a gallon. Milwaukee brewers doubled their output during the war, but they were a long way from solving the technological and marketing problems of reaching a national or even a regional market. The growing Chicago market absorbed some of the increase, but most of it was manfully consumed at home by a growing circle of lager beer lovers.

The foundry, metal-working, and machinery industries had established beginnings in Milwaukee and other Wisconsin cities before 1860. These generally small shops were able to grow as suppliers to other industries and because of the protection which distance and freight charges gave them, the availability of pig iron, blacksmith iron, and charcoal, and a population which brought the needed skills, particularly immigrants from Germany and Britain.

It would be impossible to trace the effects of the Civil War on the 3,064 factories listed in the 1860 federal census for the state. Milwaukee already had 22 percent of the state's industrial labor force, but this was only 7.5 percent of the city's population. One can still be surprised by the wide distribution of various industries and their persistence. For instance, a Beloit foundry went into the manufacture of paper-making machinery in 1855 because the owner's brother, a paper maker, had such difficulty getting parts for his machinery. This became the Beloit Machine Works, now manufacturing a large share of the nation's paper-making machinery. It was much more common, however, for small industrial enterprises to fail in a business slump.

The Civil War did not industrialize Wisconsin. A few favored industries were stimulated by the war, but others were retarded by the disruption of trade patterns and even more by the financial stringencies and crises resulting from Wisconsin's precarious banking and currency structure. Probably more decisive—and this has been noted by a number of students of the period—is that the attention of those who controlled sources of credit and capital in the port cities, primarily Milwaukee, had their eyes fixed on the flow of commerce and particularly the grain trade. This was natural, in view of the great growth of the trade and the emphasis upon railroad building. The lumber industry had not yet grown to the point where, as Robert Fries noted, "their problem was one of investment rather than acquisition of new capital." Several of Milwaukee's pioneer industrialists complained about the financial community's indifference to their credit needs. The war decade was over before Milwaukee's commercial bias recognized any new challenge from manufacturing. The emphasis upon extractive and processing industries continued.

Selected Bibliography

Andersen, Theodore A. *A Century of Banking in Wisconsin.* Madison, 1954. Rise of the national banks.

Ernst, Dorothy J. "Wheat Speculation in the Civil War Era: Daniel Wells and the Grain Trade." *Wisconsin Magazine of History* 47:125–35 (Winter 1963–64). Took advantage of Milwaukee Railroad connections to make a fortune in Iowa and Minnesota wheat.

Fish, Carl Russell. "Phases of Economic History of Wisconsin, 1860–1870." *SHSW Proceedings,* 1908, pp. 204–16. Interesting in view of later controversy over the economic impact of the war.

Gilchrist, David T., and W. David Lewis, eds. *Economic Change in the Civil War Era.* Proceedings of a conference on American economic institutional change, 1850–1873, and the impact of the Civil War, held March 12–14, 1964, at Eleutherian Mills–Hagley Foundation. Greenville, Del., 1965. Representative of a considerable literature on the subject.

Horton, Jackson Roger. "The Demobilization of Wisconsin Troops after the Civil War." Master's thesis, University of Wisconsin, 1952. It was difficult for many to find a niche in the civilian economy.

Merk, Frederick. *Economic History of Wisconsin During the Civil War Decade.* Madison, 1916. A Wisconsin history classic, reprinted by the State Historical Society of Wisconsin.

Schafer, Joseph. *A History of Agriculture in Wisconsin.* Madison, 1922. War shortages brought experimentation.

Sharkey, Robert P. *Money, Class, and Party: An Economic Study of Civil War and Reconstruction.* Baltimore, 1959. Also available in Johns Hopkins Press Paperback, 1967. Wisconsin's experience fits into this study of war finance and the changes it wrought.

KING WHEAT
DETHRONED

19

Wheat was the primary crop of Wisconsin agriculture in the pioneer period and continued its dominance well beyond the point when it ceased to pay its way satisfactorily. In the pungent phrase of William Dempster Hoard, one of the early prophets of the painful shift to dairying, "One reason why there is so much truth in the oft-reiterated remark,—'Farming don't pay'—is that there is not another business on the face of the earth that, in proportion to the numbers engaged in it, supports so many incompetents." Hoard happened to be arguing the merits of the silo, which was slow to find acceptance, but the comment could apply with equal force to the Wisconsin farmer's stubborn devotion to his first important cash crop.

The reasons for this long-term attachment to wheat are not difficult to discern. It was a relatively valuable product that stored well. Corn, which proved adaptable to the southern counties, could not compete with wheat in paying its transportation costs. Furthermore, wheat was better adapted to the needs of a pioneer farmer who had generally taken more land than he could handle and wanted much of his time for clearing, breaking, and fencing. Wheat could be sowed with a minimum of soil preparation; then it could be ignored until harvest time. After harvesting, it could be stored in the stack, to be threshed and cleaned later. Harvesting was the crucial operation, as the grain began to shatter when ripe.

The early development of grain-cutting machinery—the McCormick Company was producing reapers at its Chicago plant by 1848—solved the farmer's most pressing problem. He was no longer limited by the two and a half to three acres that a single worker could scythe by hand in a day, during the critical ten to twenty days that the grain and the weather might allow for the harvest. The revolution in grain-planting, reaping, and threshing machinery that followed rapidly, plus the development of transportation, shipping, milling, and financing facilities for the wheat trade, completed the work. Wheat, hopefully, was what paid for the mortgage and its high interest rates, put groceries in the pantry, and bought lumber for improvements. Wheat in the popular phrase, was King.

Improved wheat prices in the mid-fifties, largely a reflection of European conditions, coincided with the expansion of the pioneer railroad network. Only about 8 percent of Wisconsin's land was in farms by 1850, and less than half of that in cultivation. By 1860, the land in farms had increased to around 20 percent, and about 1,215,000 acres were in wheat, as compared to only 325,000 acres a decade earlier. It has been mentioned before that 1860 was a banner wheat year, with a crop of some 29,000,000 bushels, the largest ever raised in Wisconsin. In a sense, wheat farming in Wisconsin was in decline after 1860, although wheat acreage continued to increase. It reached about 1,875,000 acres in 1876, 50 percent more than in 1860, but the yield never again matched that of 1860.

Price fluctuations were less disturbing to the Wisconsin wheat farmer than the growing proof that the cereal was an unsatisfactory crop. Prices for wheat firmed in 1862, then reached unprecedented levels under the impetus of growing domestic and export demand and the inflationary pressure of the unsecured federal greenbacks. Prices reached a peak of $2.96 in May 1867 and seldom dropped below $1.00 a bushel until the end of the seventies. With this encouragement, Wisconsin farmers throughout the sixties maintained the state in second place among the wheat-producing states.

Dissatisfaction stemmed from declining yields on a thin soil which could not sustain successive years of cereal cropping. Other difficulties that went beyond soil depletion crowded in. Soft winter wheat was preferred by millers because it gave a higher yield of premium flour; therefore, most Wisconsin farmers raised winter wheat, with the frequent chance of winter kill in the severe climate. More serious was the appearance of pests, such as the chinch bug, and plant diseases, smut and rust, in the older wheat-growing areas.

As dependable yields disappeared and averages fell below 15 or 16

bushels to the acre, wheat farmers in older areas faced still another unpleasant reality. No matter what their farms might be capitalized at, land
adjacent to growing cities and towns, or served by the new railroads, was
too valuable for such unsatisfactory cropping. Valuations for tax purposes reflected the facts, along with rising tax rates. The dedicated wheat
farmer faced a choice. He could sell his appreciated acres and move his
wheat-growing equipment northwestward to cheap government land to
begin anew, or he could mortgage his new valuation and put the money
into stock, buildings, and different equipment for a more intensive type
of agriculture. The former was possibly the easier course, while the latter
raised the question of just what was available as a proven alternative to
wheat.

The federal census reports are not well adapted to following the migrations of individual farmers, but there is a recognized trend of wheat
culture and of farmers westward and northward. Rock County, for instance, in south-central Wisconsin, ranked first among the wheat counties
in 1849, fifth in 1859, and thirty-first in 1869. Green Lake County, well
to the north in the settled area of Wisconsin, ranked first in 1869. St.
Croix, Buffalo, and Trempealeau counties, bordering on the Mississippi
River in the northwest, ranked first in successive census years from 1879
to 1899.

This northwesterly shift in wheat farming showed the pattern of new
settlement. Wisconsin's population in 1850 was fairly well confined south
of the traditional Fox -Wisconsin water route from Green Bay to Prairie
du Chien. By 1860, it conformed roughly to a dipping line running from
Green Bay to the upper end of Lake Pepin, with a salient running north
along the western border—the Mississippi and St. Croix rivers. This new
area, designated by Joseph Schafer as the Old North, was primarily agricultural. The dip in the line excluded the sandy soils of the central counties: Portage, Wood, and Jackson. Lumbering was the dominant interest
in the northern half of the state, lying above the Old North, until about
the turn of the century.

Schafer, who published his history of Wisconsin farming in 1922, was
more sanguine about the agricultural possibilities of the New North than
it was possible for later students to be. He did note that the center of
wheat culture moved steadily westward, beyond Wisconsin into Minnesota, Iowa, and the Dakotas. The census of 1890 found 250,000 natives
of Wisconsin west of the Mississippi, 59,000 of them in Minnesota and
42,000 in Iowa. Probably 100,000 or more Wisconsin wheat farmers
took part in this exodus. Hamlin Garland, in *A Son of the Middle Bor-*

der, put into literary form the heartaches endured by his family in their several moves, from La Crosse County into Iowa and finally into South Dakota, chasing rising land values in new wheat land.

The great expansion of the lumber business after the Civil War had a tremendous impact upon the adjacent agricultural settlements. It provided a growing market for feed crops for the oxen and horses, as well as for diversified food crops and grain for the army of woodsmen and sawmill workers. It also gave winter work to the farmer and his team, drew railroads into the area, and opened new land. But, as Schafer observed, prairie farming was all the rage in these years, and most farm settlers left the work of clearing pine stumps from the Wisconsin cutover for a later generation.

It was recognized early that some form of animal husbandry was the most likely alternative to the widespread dependence upon wheat. When artificial fertilizers were lacking, the natural replenishment for the thin soils subjected to continual cropping of wheat would come from cover crops and feeding. Sheep raising was a favorite expedient, because these animals required little attention or outlay for shelter. They provided a regular revenue from their wool and could be eaten or sold as mutton. The large contingent of Yankee farmers, particularly those from Vermont, were disposed toward sheep raising, and the high prices for coarse wool in the war years encouraged it. In the southeastern quarter of the state, where Yankees were most solidly entrenched, sheep raising and the alternation of cover crops with cereals became popular. Even the collapse of high wool prices after the war did not sweep this form of husbandry aside, for at the time there were few alternatives. Sheep production, like wheat, tended to shift westward to cheaper land, and lingered on the hill farms in Wisconsin.

Corn, hay, oats, and other feed grains showed a steady rise as wheat acreage declined. In the twenty transitional years between 1869 and 1889, wheat acreage fell from 1,940,130 to 744,080, while corn acreage rose from 462,115 to 1,120,340; tame-hay acreage rose from 1,000,000 to 2,250,000, and oat from 600,000 to 900,000. Hog raising had an irregular expansion, showing the relative ease with which a farmer could move in and out of this activity, while the number of milk cows showed a slow but steady rise from 308,375 to 792,620. Raising beef cattle was more specialized, requiring a considerable outlay of capital and beyond the means of most farmers. There were stockmen who were breeders, but most were cattle fatteners who bought young stock for feeding. Successful stockmen were as close to an agricultural elite as the countryside afforded at the time.

Geographical expansion accounted for most of the growth in Wisconsin's agriculture between 1860 and 1890. There was an advance into the Old North, and the area in farms increased an average of about 3,500,000 acres each decade from 1860 to 1880, then slowed to less than half this rate in 1880–90. There were 7,893,587 acres being farmed in 1860 and 16,787,988 by 1890. The number of farms grew from 69,270 to 146,409 during the thirty years. The top agricultural counties remained much the same for the southern end of the state, which was settled first and had most of the best land.

All that has gone before raises the question of how long it took for Wisconsin's hard-pressed farmers to find salvation—stability and regular profits—with the dairy cow. The answer is that it took a long time, and the acceptance of a discipline that placed many demands upon the prejudices as well as the work habits of our pioneer agriculturalists.

The dairy cow accompanied the pioneer settler as a decidedly poor relation, walking at the rear of the wagon when she was fortunate enough to escape service under the yoke as a substitute ox. Her first function was to provide the oxen, and if a cow proved to be a good milker—one which provided a surplus beyond the needs of her calf—this was looked upon as a happy chance rather than a design of her breeding. The slow, clumsy, but steady ox was the mainstay of the pioneer farmer. Wisconsin oxen outnumbered horses and mules by a ratio of three to two in 1850. They were especially prized for the heavy task of breaking prairie sod, a task which might require six or eight oxen. Though slow, they were powerful and phlegmatic, and could subsist on much coarser feed than horses. But the machinery revolution, which did so much to fix wheat culture in the early years, was based upon the faster gait of horses and mules to turn the working parts of reapers and mowers at satisfactory speeds. By 1870, horses and mules outnumbered oxen by a ratio of five to one.

The ancestry of Wisconsin's pioneer cattle, a category that made few real distinctions among work animals, beef animals, and milk cows, was various. French cattle appeared at Detroit as early as 1707 and were widely dispersed among the French outposts. Later additions were brought in from the Ohio country by the British and American fur trade, by the Galena district lead miners, and by the U.S. Army for the posts at Forts Howard, Winnebago, Crawford, and Snelling. The emphasis in these acquisitions was upon beef animals; fluid milk and butter were not amenities ordinarily available at a fur-trading post or army fort. The first mention of milking stock is of the introduction by Morgan Martin of a Durham shorthorn bull, in 1838, whose progeny were looked upon as superior milkers.

The production of butter was strictly a kitchen function. Any pioneer housewife could produce something recognized as butter by the uncritical if the family was fortunate enough to have a cow that would surrender a little milk for the household. As a second-class citizen in the barnyard, the cow's rations and quarters were secondary to those provided for the working animals. She hustled for herself most of the year, and often was expected to make it through the Wisconsin winter on a bait of wheat straw behind the shelter provided by the stack and a rail fence. Dairying became the primary agricultural pursuit in Wisconsin before the end of the century. The changes involved were monumental. First, farmers had to be convinced that dairying was a real alternative to other forms of land use and would be more profitable over the long run. Dairying represented a long-term commitment not as easily adopted as alternate crops or livestock raised for wool or meat. Markets had to be developed, along with methods of reaching them, with a product of recognized dependability. Specialized skills had to be multiplied and standards of performance of unprecedented rigor imposed upon all producers. Beyond this, a milk surplus was a seasonal product. This had to be considerably modified in order to justify dairying as a primary activity for the farmer.

Just as the former Vermont hill farmers brought a predisposition for sheep raising as an alternative to the waning wheat harvest, many of the settlers from western New York had seen a transformation in agriculture there based upon dairying and market crops, with access to urban markets by way of the Erie Canal. Although it has often been assumed that the Swiss, German, Scandinavian, and other farmers of foreign extraction, more than the native Americans, were the dependable troops of the dairying revolution, it was the Yankee farmers who gave dairy pioneering its leadership. Local leadership and example were more important than national background in the development of dairy farming. Wisconsin by the 1850s had growing urban markets at hand, land of diminishing fertility yet increasing dollar value, and former York Staters who had seen the center of grain culture move westward. Many were ready to try other expedients than chasing after cheap wheat lands again. Chester Hazen, Willian Dempster Hoard, W. C. White, and many other New Yorkers showed the way.

Wisconsin's dairy pioneers concentrated on the production of butter. This was natural, since the adjacent towns and cities provided a clientele of middle- and upper-income people who would willingly pay a premium for a reliable product. Butter kept moderately well if carefully made and packed, particularly if a springhouse was available for cooling. It was the most practical way to market milk, given the difficulties of handling fluid milk and the much more complicated processes of cheese making. The trouble was that everyone who had a surplus of milk in season turned to butter making, and it was usually an indifferent product. Storekeepers commonly accepted butter for credit against customers' accounts. They treated it as a necessary accommodation, and few expected to turn a profit. The storekeeper was happy if a buyer from the city gave him his costs for the lot accumulated over the season. Usually he had paid a flat rate, regardless of quality, and wanted the buyer to take it on the same basis. The buyer sorted out the more saleable portions. The rest might end up as lubricant for wagons. Western grease, as pioneer butter was widely known, commanded little loyalty.

Cheese making was a better alternative for a variety of reasons. It used the whole milk, which was an advantage, because gravity separation of cream failed to remove a substantial portion of the butterfat. Cheese, if made with reasonable care and skill, kept better than butter and could be shipped farther. On the other hand, cheese making was beyond the skill of most householders; therefore the local price reflected the shipping costs from New York or Ohio, where dairying was further advanced. Cheese making as a full time commercial venture for the dairy farmer was limited by the skill required, the investment in equipment and storage space, and a sufficient supply of milk to operate economically.

The solutions to these problems came from New York farmers, who had faced the economics of agricultural survival a generation earlier than their former neighbors now in Wisconsin. Herkimer County had developed as a cheese center shortly after the Erie Canal brought the New York City market within practical range. Other New York farmers followed the lead, as wheat yields dwindled below an average fifteen bushels to the acre, and the flood of grain from the cheap lands of Illinois and southern Wisconsin put them out of competition. With more farmers turning to dairying as a likely alternative, they began to study the problems of penetrating the large British market, where cheese was acceptable as a substitute for meat. By 1850, New York produced over a quarter of the nation's butter and almost half of its cheese.

It was the industrialization of cheese making that converted a haphazard kitchen handicraft into a major agricultural undertaking. The factory system of cheese production was pioneered near Rome, New York, by a man named Jesse Williams, beginning in 1851. Williams was a skilled cheese maker whose product was eagerly sought by dealers for its uniformly high quality. What Williams did was to multiply his particular talent, by arranging to have neighboring dairymen deliver their milk to him while he devoted all of his energies to the manufacturing process and to developing the equipment needed to mass produce cheese. It sounds ridiculously simple until one considers all of the obstacles that stood in

the way of multiplying what was a relatively rare skill—dealing empiri-
cally with a complicated chemical process that was poorly understood
and that yet allowed only a modest leeway for error. An unnerving number of major or minor disasters could overtake a batch of cheese from
the point at which the cow ingested her feed—some plants affect the flavor of the milk—to the finished, properly aged cheese ready for sale. It
may seem less than disastrous until one considers that the factory system
came to involve the product of several hundred cows and the work of a
good many farm families. An occasional shipment of unpalatable cheese
could threaten ruin for a community.

An authority on Wisconsin dairying, Professor Lampard, insists per-
suasively that the acceptance of the factory system in cheese making represented the imposition of industrial discipline upon a class of the American population not heretofore noted for its ready compliance with exter-
nally applied rules and strictures. Americans have long assumed that the
most intractably Jacksonian among their nineteenth-century forebears
were those who sought independence on the land, particularly in the
Midwest, where agricultural diversity seemed practical. Why did they accept the yoke of servitude represented by a pleasant landscape dotted
with Holstein cows?

The answer lies partially in the inexorable facts of economic competition and the limitations imposed by climate, soils, and available markets.
Wisconsin farmers were committed from the start to commercial agriculture and had to solve the dilemma when wheat failed them. Many avenues were explored, and while dairying was not the exclusive solution,
90.5 percent of Wisconsin farms reported dairy cattle in 1899. Although
only 17.4 percent were primarily dairy farms, Wisconsin relatively was a
specialized dairy state. In playful language, Lampard summarized the elements of the transformation:

> With fervor born of religiosity and language lifted bodily from Old
> Testament prophecy and popular Darwinism, the Wisconsin leaders de-
> nounced the errors of wheat growing and proclaimed the glad tidings of
> redemption through dairying. They announced the certitude of survival
> in obedience to the "inevitable natural and progressive laws of . . .
> science," urged frugality in every phase of farm management, taught
> the saving virtues of precision and piety at each stage of manufacture.
> They revealed the working of a cosmic principle of "Qualitative Selec-
> tion," and preached an austere discipline of technical and intellectual
> fitness for a competitive universe in which the only sure token of grace
> was "extra" prices.

The story thus told may be a bit too short. What Wisconsin's dairy
pioneers did was to prove the practical nature of dairying as one of the
better options open to their neighbors, by making dairying pay, and pay

more consistently than other alternatives. The demonstration was accompanied by a great deal of proselytizing, showing that the Yankee enthusiasm for moral uplift did not disappear after 1865. Along the way, they made the agricultural college of the university into a significant national center of the dairy sciences, helping to solve marketing, processing, breeding, feeding, and other technical problems.

Dairying is a year-round, seven-days-a-week occupation regulated by the needs of the cows. The transition from the seasonal requirements of grain raising was not an easy one to make. Nor was the change in emphasis from an extensive, relatively careless form of cultivation, based upon cheap land usually rising in value, to a high-cost, intensive operation a simple shift for the farmer. A herd of a dozen mixed-breed cows could be had for $300 in the 1870s, when many were making the conversion, but it took probably $2,000 to $3,000 for a barn and other equipment to house the cattle, store feed, and handle the milk. Cheese production figures for 1877–78 indicate an average make of 323 pounds of cheese valued at $35 a cow. This provided little enough income to apply to capital outlay, labor, and feed. It does not, of course, take into account the use of whey for hog raising, or the natural increase of the herd, but it does explain why cheese factories commonly developed as independent enterprises, usually without any investment from the farmers who delivered the milk.

The increase of dairying appears as a steady upward curve, but the path to dairy prosperity was not smooth. Diversified farming seemed to be a safer hedge than a full conversion to dairy farming. There was much debate, into the 1890s, about the comparative virtues of the "dual purpose" cow and strictly dairy breeds. The idea, of course, was that both beef and milk could be produced from the same animal, a heresy that *Hoard's Dairyman* fought with support from most of the founding fathers of Wisconsin dairying. A Wisconsin atlas published in 1878 remarked that most cows with any pretensions to breeding lived in town and served a single family. Grade cattle, rather than purebreds, were the standard for many years. Much ink was spilled in farm papers arguing the virtues of the various breeds. By the early eighties, opinion began to favor Hoard's dairy breeds. By the nineties, the Holstein-Friesian and Jersey were clearly the most popular breeds.

The disciplinary demands of dairying extended beyond the farm, with its milking and feeding schedules. Cheese making also demanded a schedule. Given the execrable condition of both main and local roads in Wisconsin through most of the nineteenth century, it was often difficult to meet the factoryman's deadlines. The question of whether to add a late delivery to the day's make of cheese or to accept milk that might be turning—not unusual, with poor cooling and a long, slow, bouncing trip to the factory—led to many disputes between the cheese maker and his milk suppliers. The cooperative factory, in which the farmer had some interest as an owner, was not common before 1900, and it was difficult to maintain an identity of interest between the factory owner and the farmers. In this period the Grange, with its interests in cooperative ventures, had little impact upon dairymen. The factoryman was cast more and more in the role of a middleman who sought his financing from wholesalers and necessarily had his attention upon markets. To the farmers he appeared as an exhorter, calling for standards of performance from them that seemed unnecessarily strict. Indeed, the men who led in the founding of the Wisconsin Dairymen's Association in 1872 were the pioneer factorymen of the era. Their transition from dairying to the necessary emphasis upon manufacturing developed a growing antagonism between them and the farmers to whom they were giving leadership.

Dairying was gaining only tentative acceptance in the 1870s, as prices fluctuated, and an occasional good year for wheat was a siren call to the farmer. Prices and dependable markets aside, dairying was badly in need of some practical inventions or innovations that could measure standards of performance and extend the dairying season. The new school of agriculture of the University of Wisconsin, created with funds from the 1862 Morrill Act, seemed a most unlikely agency to produce them. In 1866, the school was advertising, without much success, for a professor of agriculture and for students. Farmers saw little use for "book farmers," and the university conceived of its mission as the training of "scientific farmers" with a firm grounding in trigonometry, physiology, astronomy, political economy, logic, aesthetics, and conic sections. The notion that mental discipline and theoretical knowledge constituted genuine education was not easily displaced. The school finally got a professor, in 1868, and a farm of 200 acres that now forms the western end of the Madison campus. Students were harder to come by. The first graduate of the agricultural course completed the course in 1878. He had a single prospective successor in 1881. The farm provided firewood for the university and a picnic ground for students and townspeople.

It was the dairy pioneers who rescued the university's program from a hostile legislature. They recognized the useful role that a more practical agricultural college could play, both in problem-solving research and in the propagation of dairying skills. The Wisconsin State Agricultural Society, founded in 1851, had proved to be too general in its interests; it often wandered into debate on Granger enthusiasms such as the currency issue which were of little moment to many dairymen. The Wisconsin

Dairymen's Association, on the other hand, was looked upon by many farmers as a special-interest group representing the cheese factory owners and largest dairymen. The College of Agriculture was to develop into a more neutral source of dairying leadership. This was accomplished through the appointment in 1878 of the pioneer dairyman Hiram Smith, of Sheboygan, to the university's board of regents. He promoted the appointment of William A. Henry, in 1880, to a new professorship strictly in agriculture, and Henry was connected with the program until his retirement in 1907. He served in various capacities, finally as dean of the College of Agriculture created in 1891.

Henry was a man of great energy, a keen judge of the talents of his staff, and a formidable lobbyist who made shrewd use of his own rural background in dealing with rural legislators and farm groups. He built the College of Agriculture into a position of national leadership in dairy science and allied fields. It was a staff member, Stephen M. Babcock, who gave the world the answer to one of the dairymen's most vexing questions.

The problem was to give an accurate measure of the butterfat content of milk by means of a quick and easy test, and Babcock's test became a world standard after its announcement in 1890. It involved chemical separation and centrifuging of a small sample in a graduated bottle, required only a simple apparatus and a few minutes, and could be done by almost anyone. Other tests of less reliability, requiring more time, equipment, and elaborate procedures, were quickly displaced. The problem solved was a better method of payment for milk based upon its quality rather than simply upon weight. Payment by weight invited fraud with a dipper of water, and angered those who sought quality in the operations. Babcock's test was said to have done more for the honesty of dairymen than the Bible. The test was extended to check individual cows and eliminate "boarders" who fell below a standard of quality.

Another contribution of the revitalized university program was in scientific work on feeds and feeding on the experimental farm. Dairying, a highly capitalized form of agriculture, was seriously limited in Wisconsin by the shortness of the season. Some cheese factories and creameries operated only four or five months of the year and few beyond six months. Farmers who kept their herds productive for longer terms had to improvise their own manufacturing processes on the farm. Making a virtue of necessity, they developed the notion, which was incorrect, that the longer a cow was dry, the more milk she would produce after freshening in the spring. Along with this bit of folklore went the practice of getting the cow through the winter on a minimum of rough fodder.

The preparation of silage worked a revolution in winter feeding and made possible a much longer milking season. The technique was not new, but became generally available only after 1877, when a French experimenter, August Goffart, published the results of twenty-five years of experimentation with the process. Dr. H. S. Weeks of Oconomowoc experimented successfully with it as early as 1880, using Goffart's book as his guide. Inspired by Dr. Weeks' success, other farmers built silos of their own design and tried the innovation. The majority of farmers preferred to consult their prejudices, formulated to deal with this new challenge to custom, and opined that the green fodder would spoil, eat away the cattle's stomachs, and cause them to lose their teeth. Dean Henry promoted a special appropriation of $4,000 from the legislature to build a silo on the university farm in 1881. The success of the first batch was not unequivocal, as one-fourth of the school's herd steadfastly refused to touch the stuff, but in subsequent experiments improvements in technique overcame the difficulties. The staff was soon advancing the case of the silo at farmers' institutes. William Dempster Hoard, in *Hoard's Dairyman* and frequent lectures, was also spreading the word, in his usual terms of exasperation. He was still at it in 1915. Hiram Smith kept careful accounts which showed that he could winter three cows for seven months on the silage made from green corn from one acre of land, while it took two acres of hay for one cow. Silage and corn permitted many farmers to double the number of cows in their herds and keep them in milk for a much longer term. Despite this manifest proof, it was many years before the silo became a really ubiquitous feature of the Wisconsin landscape. The University Experiment Station, as late as 1904, listed only 716 silos in a statewide census.

The development of the mechanical cream separator was another technological advance of great importance, particularly in the manufacture of butter. The invention was of European origin. Dr. Carl De Laval perfected his model in Sweden, and by 1885 the De Laval Company had introduced two models, suitable for farm use, which swept the market in the United States. Before this invention, creameries were severely limited by the space required for the shallow vessels used in gravity separation. Even after the introduction of mechanical separation, creameries opposed transferring this operation to the farm. Farmers accumulated their cream for occasional delivery, and it tended to a mixture of fresh and overripe that adversely affected the quality of the butter. The economy for the farmer in delivering cream, rather than delivering whole milk and hauling the skim back to the farm for feed, was so obvious that home separation was bound to become the norm. Creameries grew more numerous in the 1880s, and before 1900, home separating made possible large "centralizers" that received their cream by railway from many remote areas. Run on a more economical scale, the centralizers were competition for local cheese factories and creameries, but they encouraged the spread of dairying. Devoted to quantity rather than quality, they faded from the Wisconsin scene as the Wisconsin Buttermakers' Association, organized in 1902, fought oleo and indifferent butter to give the Wisconsin product a universal image of dependable high quality.

The vicissitudes of the dairy industry were many in its efforts to establish and hold markets. Because of its location and relatively smaller urban population, Wisconsin had to depend heavily upon exports both abroad and to the American city markets. So successful had they been that in 1881, the United States exported 148,000,000 pounds of cheese; cheese marketing was well in advance of the marketing of butter and other products, because of technologies and a pioneering emphasis upon cheese. By 1880, Wisconsin was fourth in the nation in cheese production, behind only New York, Iowa, and Illinois, all of which had much more agricultural land. Wisconsin was competitive because of a spread of quality standards, special rates, and handling negotiated with the railroads, and the development of boards of trade such as the famous one at Plymouth, Wisconsin, to create a reliable market for seller and buyer.

Most of the profitable British market, built laboriously over the years, was lost by 1890. Faced with the temptation of a market that readily took all they could produce, Wisconsin cheese makers had begun filling their cheddars with skim milk and lard, to expand supply. The result was the loss of the market to the enterprising Canadians. There was a period when Wisconsin's pride was falsely labeled "Canadian Cheese" in order to sell it. Before the damage was repaired, the slump in cheese prices had driven many dairymen into butter production, or selling to the newer condenseries. Similar experiences with sharp practice and slack standards plagued the newer butter and fluid milk industries, and helped turn Wisconsin dairymen to the state as an agency to set and enforce standards. William Dempster Hoard was elected governor in 1888, and the legislature responded to his recommendations by creating the office of dairy and food commissioner to enforce food, drink, and drug laws. Dairymen fitted easily into the progressive mold as a result of this, for regulation and the application of standards through the agency of the state held no terrors for them. The federal law of 1902 placing a tax on oleomargarine was viewed in Wisconsin as a progressive triumph.

An important element in Wisconsin progressivism was a readiness to make use of the academic expert. Wisconsin's dairy pioneers led in the successful transformation of the university's College of Agriculture into an agency devoted to practical research and instruction. Beyond the benefits to the industry from the research efforts of the faculty—Babcock's butterfat test; Henry's important work *Feeds and Feeding,* which was issued in its twenty-first edition in 1948, just fifty years after the original; the experimentation with and promotion of the use of silage; discoveries in the chemistry of cheese making which produced the cold-curing process and many other practical applications—the college also pioneered effective educational techniques for reaching an audience of farmers. Wisconsin farmers retained a healthy skepticism toward academic agriculturists, even in the face of Dean Henry's homespun approach. Oddly, it was not Henry nor his colleagues who originated what was to become the much-publicized prototype of the agricultural short course. It was two members of the university's board of regents, William F. Vilas, a Madison attorney, and H. D. Hitt, a farmer, who forced its introduction despite opposition from Henry and his associates.

The short course, instituted in 1886 after a shaky start with a faculty uncertain of the methods to use and still opposed in principal to the innovation, became a highly successful device for teaching scientific agriculture. Opened to boys with a common school education, the short course consisted of two twelve-week terms held during the winter season. In 1890, the same year the Babcock butterfat test was published, a short course strictly in dairying was inaugurated, drawing students from the regular short course, as well as mature men engaged in cheese making and creamery operations. Its graduates were in great demand. The regular short course began drawing about as well by 1894.

Even more successful, from the first, were the farmers' institutes, inaugurated by the legislature with a $5,000 appropriation in the same year as the short course, 1886. This was not a new concept as were the short courses, nor did it originate with the agricultural faculty, although they administered it. The institutes were placed with the university regents largely out of deference to Hiram Smith of the board of regents, in recognition of the role he and other pioneers of the Dairymen's Association had played in holding what they termed "experience meetings" to provoke discussion and interest in dairying. The *Wisconsin Blue Book* for 1891 lists locations and dates of fifty-eight institutes held in the previous year, indicating the extent of the audience reached.

There were other farm groups and associations. The Wisconsin State Horticultural Society, like the Dairymen's Association, served a special group which found the State Agricultural Society too generalized, too taken up with politics in the Granger period, and too involved with the management of the state fair. Horticulturists tended to be narrow in their interests, but they were more receptive to scientific discussions than most farm groups. They were working on the special problems presented by the Wisconsin winter, which was too harsh for most fruit trees brought from New England and New York. With the dairymen, they represented an interest group dedicated to solving production and marketing problems, rather than protesting the emergence of the new economic order that was pushing the farmer aside.

Lampard summarized the agricultural revolution that transformed Wisconsin after King Wheat had failed his subjects:

> Before the close of the nineteenth century, dairying had become the most viable "type-of-farming" in Wisconsin. The difficult period of experiment and adjustment now lay behind and after 1897, the industry went on to enjoy almost three decades of prosperity and expansion. Not before the second quarter of the present century did the dairy farmer find himself engulfed by the deepening economic crisis of American agriculture. Though other systems of farming might flourish here and there in the state, corn-hog, grain-cattle, truck-farming or specialty crops, the dairy and its related livestock activities were henceforth the chief concern of a majority of cultivators. Their task was to produce the raw material for a highly specialized branch of manufactures. Dairying, in short, had become Wisconsin's specialty.

Selected Bibliography

Be Beau, Wilfrid L. "A German Immigrant Farmer Pioneers in Northern Wisconsin." *Wisconsin Magazine of History* 38:239–44 (Summer 1955). 1883–1903 in the Chippewa Valley.

Cerny, George. "Cooperation in the Midwest in the Granger Era, 1869–1875." *Agricultural History* 37:187–205 (Oct. 1963). Based largely on The Wisconsin Grange.

Clark, James I. *Wisconsin Agriculture: The Rise of the Dairy Cow.* Madison, 1956. A summary in twenty pages.

Elston, Charles B. "A History of County Fairs in 19th Century Wisconsin." Master's thesis, University of Wisconsin, 1966. Yankees and immigrants shared a tradition.

Glover, Wilbur H. "The Agricultural College Crisis of 1885." *Wisconsin Magazine of History* 32:17–25 (Sept. 1948). Start of the famous "short course."

———. *Farm and College: The College of Agriculture of the University of Wisconsin, A History.* Madison, 1952. Trials of selling "book farming."

Hammer, Einar O. "One Hundred Years of Wisconsin State Fairs." *Wisconsin Magazine of History* 34:10–16 (Autumn 1950). A brief summary.

Hill, Charles B. "The First Combine." *Wisconsin Magazine of History* 35:263–66 (Summer 1952). Story of Hiram Moore, Green Lake inventor.

———. "John V. Robbins, Pioneer Agriculturalist." *Wisconsin Magazine of History* 34:230–32 (Summer 1951). A Cincinnati shoe manufacturer who pioneered dairying near Madison on a large model farm.

Lampard, Eric E. *The Rise of the Dairy Industry in Wisconsin*. Madison, 1962. Now the standard work on Wisconsin agriculture.

Luther, E. L. "Farmers' Institutes in Wisconsin, 1885–1933." *Wisconsin Magazine of History* 30:59–68 (Sept. 1946). Mostly in terms of personalities.

McCluggage, Robert. "Joseph Osborn, Grange Leader." *Wisconsin Magazine of History* 30:178–84 (Spring 1952). Pioneer of cooperative buying.

McIntyre, Calvin M. "William D. Hoard as an Agricultural Educator." Master's thesis, University of Wisconsin, 1966. Colorful, effective dairy leader.

Rankin, Stephen W. "Hiram Smith: Wisconsin Pioneer Dairyman." Master's thesis, University of Wisconsin, 1962. A neglected dairy leader.

Schafer, Joseph. *A History of Agriculture in Wisconsin*. Madison, 1922. First in his Wisconsin Domesday Book series. There is much about agriculture in the others.

Wisconsin Crop and Livestock Reporting Service. *A Century of Wisconsin Agriculture*, 1848–1948. Bulletin 290. Madison, 1951. A summary.

EMPIRE IN PINE

20

The true forest area of Wisconsin lay in roughly the northern three-fifths of the state. There were dense growths of hardwoods along the Lake immediately north of Milwaukee, but these were treated as an impediment to agricultural settlement. North of a rough line drawn southwest from Manitowoc to Portage and thence on a northwesterly course to the fall line of the St. Croix River lay a tremendous virgin forest inviting exploitation. Because its most valuable stands commercially were white and Norway pine, this forest was commonly called the pinery, although there were large tracts of mixed conifers and hardwoods which were not dominated by the pines. Any tract with an average of one or two large pines an acre was designated as pine land. As this would suggest, the lumber industry concentrated its attentions upon the pine, with little regard for the other timber until the end of pine was in sight. This end did not seem possible to most people until after the Civil War, when Wisconsin's pine-lumbering began to take a truly staggering toll of the standing timber.

The pine forests of Wisconsin were a part of a great forest belt stretching from New England through the Great Lakes, with Lake Erie marking its southernmost fringe. In the United States, this forest dominated the Michigan peninsulas and the northern three fifths of Wisconsin, then

Empire in Pine is the title of the standard history of the Wisconsin lumber industry from 1830 to 1900, written by Robert F. Fries (Madison, 1951).

swept northward through eastern and northern Minnesota into Canada. Wisconsin's pine was larger and thicker than that in Minnesota. Where soil and climate were favorable, pine grew to yields of 40,000 board feet an acre, or sixteen to twenty mature trees. In other areas, still designated as pine lands, the yield might be as low as 1,000 to 3,000 board feet. The Chippewa River, with an unrivaled pine forest in its watershed, was estimated to have tributary to it one-sixth of the pine west of the Adirondacks.

Pine, because of its desirable characteristics, could be brought a considerable distance and still compete successfully with more easily available hardwoods. Pine is a softwood, straight-grained, light but strong for its weight, easily worked with a handsaw or edged tool, maintains its dimensions when properly seasoned, and being resinous, resists rot. So advantageously was much of this premium timber placed in relation to water transportation that it supplied lumber to the Ohio Valley and areas east of Pittsburgh for many years before West Virginia's nearby forests were exploited.

Markets and technology developed together in the exploitation of Wisconsin's pineries. If Michigan pine found a ready market in the upper Ohio valley where hardwoods were abundant, it can be readily understood why Wisconsin pine lumber met an insatiable demand on the prairies of Illinois and westward. The effect of improved technology is illustrated by the movement in price from more than $60 per 1,000 board feet paid for cut lumber in Madison in 1836, to an average ranging from $15 to $20 at Chicago and sale points along the Mississippi for Wisconsin pine throughout the second half of the century. The average is only an educated guess, because lumbering was notoriously a boom-or-bust activity, despite a prevailing demand. The total cut was easily expanded, in the face of favorable prices, with predictable results—glutted markets and ruinously low prices.

Wisconsin's waiting pine forests seemed ideally placed for their developing markets. Tributary to Green Bay were the Menominee valley, the Peshtigo and Oconto rivers, and the lower Fox, which drained Lake Winnebago with its tributary rivers, particularly the Wolf. The rivers and streams carried the logs to the mills, powered the saws, and brought the lumber to Lake Michigan for delivery to the rapidly growing cities. The upper reaches of the Wisconsin River stretched into the pine lands, and the river's current delivered the lumber to St. Louis or intervening markets. Similarly the Black, the Chippewa, and the St. Croix tapped rich areas of pine and emptied into the Mississippi, which bordered the expanding prairie agriculture to the west with its great appetite for lumber.

The opportunities afforded by the standing timber, the rivers, and the growing markets were not long in finding exploiters. Daniel Whitney, who started a wide range of ventures from Green Bay, built a sawmill on the Wisconsin River in 1831. Earlier than this, both Colonel John Shaw and James Lockwood, of Prairie du Chien, had attempted lumber production on the Black and Chippewa rivers. From the time that the Indians ceded much of the pineries in 1836 and 1837, the mills multiplied thick and fast. By 1847, there were twenty-four on the upper Wisconsin alone, producing nearly 20,000,000 board feet of lumber, and the Green Bay district soon outstripped the mills on the Wisconsin. Chicago and other Lake Michigan markets encouraged competition with the lumber from the Lower Peninsula of Michigan. Oshkosh had established itself as the milling center for logs from the Wolf River by 1852, the year that La Crosse, located strategically at the mouth of the Black and La Crosse rivers, opened its first mill. The rich harvest of the Chippewa Valley timber was being tapped at the same time.

Until the 1850s, most of Wisconsin's mills were simple. Whereas the pioneer waterpowered mill of the 1840s afforded a good deal of leisure for the operators while a board was being produced, the 1860 mill called for an orderly processing of the cut lumber through trimmers, edgers, and related equipment. Steam power was available through belts from overhead shafts, the entire process was mechanized, and logs were disassembled in a production line. The sawdust and scrap were conveyed to the boilers, while other waste was manufactured into laths.

A mill with a capacity of 200,000 board feet a day chewed up a phenomenal number of logs in a year. It is difficult to deal in averages, for logs came in all sizes. Take, for instance, timber that ran 20,000 board feet an acre—an excellent yield—and it required ten acres of timber a day, or 400 good-sized logs. The spectacular pictures of log jams that were said to stretch for miles on the rivers begin to make sense. The annual cut in Wisconsin in 1853 was estimated at 200,000,000 board feet, and at 1,250,000,000 in 1873. A jam on the Chippewa River in 1869 contained 150,000,000 board feet of timber and choked the river for a distance of fifteen miles with logs that in places piled thirty feet high.

Those handling timber in the woods did not have the advanced technology of the sawmill. Tools were improved, along with certain techniques, but it was still human muscle that felled the trees, trimmed the trunk, and bucked it into logs, usually of twelve to sixteen feet in length. It was animal power that snaked the logs to the loader and then hauled the load to the riverbank or railroad. Steam was tried, but it was never adapted successfully, to felling, bucking, or the haul from the woods. In Wisconsin logging stories there is little mention of steam donkeys, spar trees, or highlining logs from the woods, a technique familiar in the Pacific Northwest. Steam was used for loaders, but steam tractors were not practical for many applications.

The railroad would work a real revolution in the later decades of the nineteenth century, but the use of specialized logging railroad equipment was not very common before 1890. Back in the sixties and seventies, when sawmill capacities were making great strides, the principal changes in the woods, to meet the new demands, were replacement of oxen with heavy draft horses, and hiring more and more hands to man the axes and saws.

In good times, the shortage of experienced labor kept wages in the woods relatively high. A. G. Ellis, the pioneer publicist of the industry on the upper Wisconsin River, estimated that already in 1857, 2,500 men were employed there, getting out about one-fourth of the 475,000,000 board feet of timber cut in all of Wisconsin in that year. The total cut had increased by three times that figure in 1873, when Knapp and Stout, who operated Wisconsin's largest mill at Menominee on a tributary of the Chippewa, had 1,200 men on the company payroll. The woods crews claimed the largest contingent of this army.

The lumber business was well along toward consolidation and integration by 1873, although there was always a place for the small operator, particularly in boom times. Before this it was common for the mill to contract the logging and driving, whether the timber was taken from company land or from private stumpage. More imaginative loggers contracted to supply logs which they found for themselves and without the formality of purchase, often on federal or state lands or the lands of absentee owners.

The logistics of logging, in the dead of winter far from supply points reached by dubious roads often closed by snowdrifts, were a challenge to the managerial abilities of the contractor. Those who were successful, whether owners of the logging outfit or hired "woods bosses," were men of varied talents. They had to be prepared to face down a mutiny, placate a cook, set a broken limb, or whip a bully, as well as make important managerial decisions and deal with the vagaries of a rugged climate. One of the best descriptions of these specifications put to practical use is contained in the autobiographical *Life of a Lumberman* by John Nelligan, a six-foot-two Irishman from New Brunswick who joyously recalled every fight he had had since his boyhood.

The tools and techniques of winter logging and the spring drive of the logs down the river to the mills had originated in the older lumber regions of the Northeast, mainly New Brunswick and Maine. Skilled woodsmen and rivermen were actively recruited there, although many were naturally attracted to the new pine frontiers in Michigan and Wisconsin. Isaac Stephenson, Philetus Sawyer, and Daniel Shaw were among the prominent Wisconsin lumbermen from New England states. Lumbering here was largely a Yankee trade.

In addition to the experienced hands who followed the timber westward on the Lakes, there was a steady flow of green hands from the farm. The wages, the lure of a rough communal life that promised a welcome change from the drudgery of farm life, and the fact that logging was a winter activity when farm work was minimal, brought many rural youths to the pineries. The mills and woods crew also created markets for farmers who moved into adjacent open lands. The off-season on the farm found them hauling supplies into the woods, hiring out with their teams, or cutting and hauling timber on their own. A season in the woods, and particularly the adventure of the spring drive, gave the returned farm youth something to talk about. Even more venturesome was a trip to St. Louis on a lumber raft. Apparently many of them discovered no particular talent for the work, which was rugged, risky, and offered even fewer comforts than the farm. One season in the woods or on the river usually sufficed.

There are many colorful accounts of the activities of the timber camp and particularly of the spring log drive, an organizational nightmare. All through the winter the various camps cut and hauled logs and stacked them along the available streams. Even at high water in the spring, many of the streams did not furnish enough water to float the logs to the main river. The technique was to build dams to create reservoirs in the upper watersheds. By a coordinated outflow from the reservoirs, a controlled high-water stage might be maintained in the main river for two or three weeks, time to get the logs to the mills. Wisconsin law was more than generous with respect to the riparian rights involved in dam building, both for power and log driving, for the works often involved flooding adjacent land and affected navigation rights on many streams.

A proper control of stream levels was further complicated by the fact that there might be several logging camps each on a tributary of a logging river. If everyone breached his reservoirs and tumbled his logs into the stream at will, the result might be a spectacular log jam and too much or too little water in the main river. The usual solution, as log drives mounted in size, was to form a company to build, maintain, and control the various dams, coordinate the drive, and operate the booms where the logs were sorted according to brands placed on them before they were put in the river. An example of such an enterprise was the Menominee River and Boom Company, superintended by Isaac Stephenson. Organized in 1867, the company controlled forty dams on the river and its tributaries, delivering 675,000,000 board feet of timber to the mills on the lower river in that year. Wisconsin lumbermen were highly skilled in the construction of timber-holding dams, power dams, rolling dams, and wing dams. Their skill once saved a Union fleet caught by low water on the Red River, deep in Confederate territory.

Another spectacular practice, introduced to Wisconsin river lumbering from New England and Canada, was the rafting of cut lumber to market. The early mills cut only rough lumber, the standard being boards of a generous one or two inches in thickness and twelve or sixteen feet in length. These were built into cribs twelve to twenty boards deep, depending on the depth and hazards of the river to be navigated. The cribs were bound together by heavier stringers secured by tough roots pulled through two-inch holes. Up to 7 cribs in lines made up what was called a "rapids piece," and these in turn were bound together by various means into larger rafts, as the more difficult navigational hazards were left behind. At the Mississippi, the smaller rafts were tied into giant rafts containing as many as 120 cribs, or about 600,000 board feet of lumber, covering over two-thirds of an acre. This was a typical Wisconsin River raft fleet. The Black, Chippewa, and St. Croix rivers were more easily navigated below the mills, hence the rafts were larger.

The sight of a fleet of rafts negotiating the white water on the upper Wisconsin or shooting the slot in one of the larger dams was a show not to be missed. Most of the rapids and falls of that day now lie under the slack water behind power dams. The rafts were guided by large oars at bow and stern. Pilots and skilled steersmen were always in short supply. At some rapids, resident pilots with their own crews took rafts through for a fee. A famous pilot at Little Bull Falls, at Mosinee, took rapids pieces through a quarter-mile stretch of water for $1 each, averaging thirty trips a day in season.

Added to the natural hazards of falls, rapids, and the Dells were the dams in the river. The law required that dams have a sixty-foot-wide chute, with a slide of heavy timbers, down which the rafts skidded to the river level below. Aside from the thrills which these natural and man-made barriers to navigation provided for spectators and crew, they were expensive in men and money. Forty lives were claimed by Wisconsin River lumber rafting in the 1872 season alone. No one seems to have kept count of those lost in the numerous log drives. The skill required meant high wages for raft pilots, who got $5 and more a day for a trip that took about three weeks to St. Louis, if all went well. In a season of good water, a pilot could make five trips and clear $1,000. A fleet of rafts making up a big Mississippi raft carried about eight hands, who made $1 to $2 a day in the 1850s, according to their skills. The river furnished the only motive power until towing became common on the

Mississippi in the seventies. Lumber rafting involved a great deal of walking, or "gigging back" as it was called, to bring the fleet through rough passages by pieces. The hazards, frequent duckings, and the discomfort associated with raft life usually convinced the green hands that one look at St. Louis was enough.

Lumber from the rafts was sold at various yards in the towns along the Iowa and Illinois shores, with St. Louis as the last prospect. Rafting was not a cheap means of reaching the market, but cost about $5 a thousand, added to an average value of $12 a thousand at the mill, this at a time when the cost of stumpage was a nominal $1 a thousand. Aside from wages, there were tolls for improvements in navigation, towage, and losses. Wisconsin lumber arrived at its destination in a sorry state. The roughly cut planks were water soaked and mud stained. Many of the rafts never reached their destination, having broken apart in the rapids or in shooting a dam. Sometimes a pilot error led a Mississippi raft into a blind channel in low water, where it was not worth the effort to retrieve it.

The wholesale and retail yards along the Mississippi ran their own sawmills to prepare the rough Wisconsin lumber for market. The Wisconsin sawmill operator often found himself in debt to the downriver wholesaler and retailer who, carrying less of the cost between forest and mill, put his quicker profits into assuring his supply at a favorable price. The earliest steps toward a vertical integration of operations on the part of the Wisconsin lumberman were the establishment of his own wholesale and retail outlets on the Mississippi, or in Chicago, or partnerships there. Some found it more profitable to float logs to mills along the Mississippi, where they could be worked into finished dimension lumber of a higher value than the water-soaked planks of the lumber rafts.

Lumber rafting lasted into the early eighties; the final raft on the Wisconsin was dispatched in 1883. Before rafting ended, there were improvements in the river to facilitate it, and Mississippi rafts grew in size. They were towed by steamboats rather than floated to market—one behind to push and a smaller one in front to steer. Some of these rafts were three or four acres in area; one from Chippewa Falls in 1870 was said to contain 2,500,000 board feet of lumber. Railroads reached many mills in northern Wisconsin by the seventies and made it possible for them to market directly to retail yards. Lumber rafting was not a feature of the business on the shorter rivers that fed into Lake Michigan. The Lake was too rough to permit it, so lumber was shipped by vessel or barge.

The penetration of the railroads into the pineries brought a technological transformation comparable to that in the mills when heavy steam engines and band saws replaced the speedy but wasteful circular saws. Wisconsin railroad building had lagged for a dozen years after the 1857 panic. Seven hundred miles of railroad had been built by 1857, but only an average of 45 miles a year were added until 1871. In the next dozen years after that, an average of 200 miles a year were added. Wisconsin's principal railroad, in the years immediately after the Civil War, was pressing construction beyond Wisconsin's boundaries, following wheat culture westward. The Chicago & Northwestern, Wisconsin Central, and what became the Omaha were opening the pineries. It was 1874 before a railroad bridge spanned the Mississippi in Wisconsin at Prairie du Chien. Once the leap was made, the days of the river gathering the grain for the railheads on the Wisconsin side were numbered. Rafting Wisconsin lumber was likewise becoming an anomaly.

A community of interest between the railroads and the lumber industry was inevitable, but the latter was oriented toward the convenient waterways. Apparently when lumbermen first considered the uses of the railroad, they thought of getting logs to the mill. By the seventies, most of the timber convenient to a stream had been cut. Suitable railroad spurs offered a means of getting to the remainder, supplemented by narrowgage lines and equipment. The railroad could also extend the logging season beyond the winter months, and had the advantage of being able to carry hardwood logs, which a river could not, at a time when the white pine in merchantable sizes was disappearing from many areas. It will be recalled that federal land subsidies for railroads, made in 1856 and 1864, were directed at subsidizing north and south lines with termini on Lake Superior. The purpose was to open lands in northern Wisconsin. Not only did this suit the needs of lumbermen for a much cheaper way of supplying the armies of men and animals working in the pineries and of opening new tracts of timber remote from log-driving streams, but the railroad land subsidies were mostly timber lands. Lumbermen, therefore, had ample incentive to take an interest in railroad building. This they did by investing in railroads, by selling them ties, bridge timbers, and lumber, by being generous with rights of way and other privileges, and by voting subsidies from the towns and northern counties which were often in the lumbermen's political control. When the Grangers were voting the regulation of railroad rates with the Potter Law of 1874, the northern counties, busy courting new railroad construction, were adamant in their opposition to regulation.

As Wisconsin's railroad network tied into the extended lines reaching westward, her lumbermen continued to send roughcut lumber down the rivers by raft for several years. This was not for want of capital, as Robert Fries makes clear. Lumbering was an extremely high-risk undertaking, but the rewards were equally high for those who were successful. The most successful lumbermen accumulated enough capital to make their problem one of finding investment outlets, but many lumbermen had invested in wholesale and retail yards at Mississippi River marketing centers. Others had built or invested in mills downriver and were sending logs down the Mississippi. It took time to establish new trade patterns, and railroad rate structures favored Chicago lumber wholesalers.

By about 1880, the old pattern was broken. A combination of western railroads, known as the Wisconsin Lumber Lines, granted favorable rates on lumber to Omaha, Kansas City, and intervening points. This meant that the mills added new machinery to finish, shape, and dry lumber for delivery direct to retail markets by rail. This brought another era of change in technology, scale, and complexity to the mills. It coincided with significant changes in the E. P. Allis Company of Milwaukee, one of the principal suppliers of machinery to the sawmills. Allis had divided his company into three primary divisions: flour mill machinery, sawmill machinery, and steam engines. The sawmill machinery division installed the first bandsaw in a Wisconsin mill in 1885. Mill capacities took a great qualitative as well as quantitative leap in the decade, reaching their peak about 1890, when the census takers found 1,033 sawmills in the state. Many of them were impressive ventures in scale and complexity. The annual cut reached over four billion board feet in 1892, three times that of twenty years earlier.

The risks in lumbering were imposed as actively by nature as by the business cycle, and they centered on the mill and timber owner. The sawmill that had not risen phoenixlike from its own ashes was a rarity. Because of the high incidence of mill fires, insurance was difficult to procure, even at prohibitive rates. One is impressed when reading contemporary histories of lumbering with the frequency of the loss of a mill by fire and the almost ritualistic phrase, "it was soon replaced by a new, larger, and in every respect more modern mill." Building mills was an active trade. As an instance, the newest steam mill built on the Menominee River in 1863 was totally destroyed by fire two years later. Its replacement—larger and more modern—was ready for business fifty-four days later. This element of risk doubtless accounts in part for the rapid adoption of new technology by the mills. Their profits made it possible to afford continual replacement and renewal.

The sawmill owner ordinarily accepted the losses associated with the delivery of lumber by rafting down the river. As timber became a more critical item, it was customary for the mill owners to extend their control backward to the stands of timber. With this ownership, they accepted a new list of impressive risks. By the time mill men began owning large tracts of timber, the loss from timber thieving was a decreasing hazard on privately owned lands, but still a hazard. Fire was the great peril in the forest, as it was in the mill. It was 1895 before the legislature attempted to create a system of fire wardens to prevent and fight forest fires. Fires burned unchecked throughout the nineteenth century; probably more prime timber was consumed by fires between 1850 and 1900 than ever found its way to the mills. The Peshtigo Fire of October 1871, which burned over much of a half dozen counties in northeastern Wisconsin and cost over one thousand lives, is the best known. Hundreds of lesser fires went unnoticed. Once the timber had escaped disease, infestation, or fire and was laid beside the log-driving stream for transportation to the mill, the hazards were not at an end. Too violent a spring runoff meant sawlogs irretrievably lost in the bogs, bracken, pastures and flooded areas generally. Excessively low water in the spring might leave them alongside the stream to await better conditions. Two summers in the stack gave the beetles and other pests an opportunity to render the logs totally useless. All in all, lumbering seemed a business balanced always on the edge of disaster.

That the lumber business was profitable is attested by the impressive fortunes, including that of Frederick Weyerhauser, that were made in Wisconsin timber. It was not a difficult business to get into, although staying might be a problem for some. John H. Knapp of Knapp, Stout and Company, Wisconsin's largest lumber firm by the seventies, started in 1846 with $1,000 inherited from his father. Some of his early borrowing stretched his credit, but he was well on his way to fortune, after weathering the 1857 Panic. Philetus Sawyer learned lumbering in New York and left there with $2,200. After a brief interval of farming, he went to work in the woods, worked in, rented, and finally in 1853 bought a small mill in Algoma, part of present Oshkosh. Within four years, Sawyer built the most imposing home in Oshkosh and was the wealthiest citizen from that time. Isaac Stephenson grew up in the lumber business in New Brunswick and Maine. He managed timber interests for others, in Michigan and Wisconsin, before going into business for himself as one-fourth owner of the N. Ludington Company in 1858. Stephenson was, by the 1870s, one of the wealthiest lumbermen in the Great Lakes area. Sawyer's biographer estimated Stephenson's personal fortune, in 1890, at twenty-five to thirty millions, Sawyer's as a more modest four or five million.

The Beef Slough Manufacturing, Booming, Log Driving and Transportation Company was a company on the Chippewa River, organized by large timber owners in the Chippewa valley and mill owners on the Mississippi for the purpose of shipping logs down the river to supply the Mississippi mills. After a long fight with the mill owners on the Chippewa, which featured court battles, legislative skirmishes, and threatened physical violence between rival crews on the river, the Mississippi mill men won out, under the able leadership of Frederick Weyerhauser, who operated a mill at Rock Island. Weyerhauser wisely consolidated his victory by buying into the larger Chippewa Falls and Eau Claire mills.

The Beef Slough War, as it came to be called, brought home to Weyerhauser and many others that they should concentrate belatedly upon the control of the remaining timber to insure their future operations. Weyerhauser bought tracts from speculators who had accumulated holdings through federal sales and particularly through use of Morrill Act scrip, much of which had sold for less than 55 cents an acre. Timber land bought with scrip in 1866–69 was being taken by Weyerhauser for $10 an acre in 1875, and as much as $44 an acre in 1880–82. These speculators did offer the advantage for Weyerhauser of large consolidated tracts. One owner with whom he dealt, Francis Palms of Detroit, owned 112,000 acres of Wisconsin timber. Paul Gates, in his research, made a list of sixteen such owners who each held from 10,000 to 118,000 acres. There were many lumbermen in the timber market before Weyerhauser, of course. Sawyer started buying timber on the Wolf River in the mid-fifties, a first tract of 25,000 acres he considered the basis of his fortune. It was good timber, well located. He acquired 11,500 in federal sales from 1865 to 1888, compared to 120,000 bought by Knapp and Stout from the same source in those years.

Along with the integration of the lumber business, forward and backward from the mill, went a drive toward consolidation. This first gave rise to efforts to control the disastrous drop in lumber prices, following the financial panic of 1873, by joining in an association to limit production. The lumber business was too widespread geographically and contained too many individual units to expect success in such an endeavor. Smaller regional associations, based upon price agreements rather than production quotas, proved a little more effective, but their real usefulness was in developing standards and grading practices. A more effective instrument toward consolidation or the centralizing of control could have come straight out of studies of J. P. Morgan and the interlocking directorates whereby the investment banker asserted a pervasive control over an industry. One of Lincoln Steffens' muckraking interviews was with a little-known titan of finance and industry, Frederick Weyerhauser. By the 1890s, Weyerhauser had a hand in the direction of eighteen lumber-manufacturing concerns. His direction was enforced by his commanding voice in the Mississippi River Logging Company and allied concerns that had achieved control over much of the remaining timber in Wisconsin.

Robert Fries notes that pioneer Wisconsin lumbermen engaged in such disparate activities as the fur trade, operating grist mills, steamboat lines, telegraph lines, farms, and electrical generation plants, manufacturing woolen cloth, barrels, boxes, and paper, conducting licensing businesses for patents, maintaining retail establishments with the broadest lines of goods, and dealing in real estate. Knapp, Stout and Company was:

> by the seventies . . . a huge and complex organization having virtually complete control of the Menomonie (Red Cedar) River valley. Its power and flooding dams occupied nearly every available site on the main river and its tributaries. Knapp, Stout and Company logging camps were scattered throughout the north woods. On the routes from the mill to the camps the company operated farms or large gardens to provide food for its workers. At important points down the Mississippi as far as St. Louis it had sales yards and finishing mills. A company steamer returned the rafting crews to their base. In 1870 the regular daily output of its main mill at Menomonie was three hundred thousand board feet of lumber, and a second mill turned out quantities of shingles and laths. The concern operated also a boarding-house that served two barrels of pork every day, a gristmill and grain warehouse, a general store that did an annual business of three-quarters of a million dollars, a foundry, a machine shop, a wagon and cooperage shop, and a pork-packing establishment. In 1877 its payroll listed fifteen hundred men. It also maintained stores, farms, mills, and warehouses at other places. During the depression following the panic of 1873 this huge and diverse enterprise was able to make a profit when other firms were facing bankruptcy.

The firm continued to expand, investing heavily in timber lands and acquiring smaller lumbering firms with land holdings. It promoted towns; Rice Lake in Barron County was the principal one. It moved into southern pine lands in Missouri, Arkansas, and Mississippi in the 1890s, as the end of Wisconsin pine came in view.

Isaac Stephenson's career exemplifies the same readiness to put his money and talents to any opportunity or need that promised profit, or sometimes, apparently, just the satisfaction of managing something well. He managed the Menominee River and Boom Company, building forty dams on it "without the advice of engineers and the advantage of modern mechanical contrivances," as he put it. He performed a similar service on the Peshtigo River, and took over the active management of the Peshtigo Company which carried on a large lumber operation and the manufacture of woodenware. Stephenson claimed to have originated the use of barges for delivering lumber to their Chicago yards when ordinary vessel carriage was too expensive. The Peshtigo Company, under his direction, promoted and carried out the construction of the Sturgeon Bay Canal, which made barging lumber shorter and safer. With all of this, Stephenson managed the N. Ludington Company and began his own lumber company at Escanaba, Michigan. He was a banker, one of the organizers of the Marinette and Menominee Paper Company, bought out the Peshtigo Company with Milwaukee partners, bought and managed timberlands in Louisiana as well as in Michigan and Wisconsin, aggregating 390,000 acres, operated a 900-acre farm near Kenosha, and had an interest in one of the large creameries nearby. Stephenson was active in politics, serving in the Wisconsin Legislature and as congressman and U.S. senator. Contracting an alliance with Robert M. La Follette, Stephenson financed a Milwaukee newspaper, the *Free Press*. It obviously rankled him that it failed to show profits as did his other enterprises, but he recognized its usefulness.

Stephenson offers an apt description of himself and many other men who built fortunes in lumbering. "These were days of large industrial enterprise and men of great capacity and breadth of view were required to encompass and make the most of the opportunities that began to appear upon the brightening horizon." Lumbering probably demanded talents beyond those of railroad building in a pioneer economy. The managerial abilities required were probably more varied, the logistics as difficult, and technological advances in lumbering more rapid. The lumberman was more accustomed to turning available resources into capital. Having achieved an impressive cash flow, he was quick to seize any new opportunity, or to turn a recognized need, such as for a grist mill, a boarding-house, a town, or a general store, into a profitable enterprise. The lumber barons were wasteful and piratical, but certainly contributed to the creation of a growing economy.

Lumber and timber products topped all other manufactured products in Wisconsin from 1890 through 1910, although the cut was on the decrease after 1890. While exceeded in value, into the 1880s, by the products of the grain-milling industry, lumbering involved the largest manufacturing investment and payroll after 1860. At its peak, from 1888 to 1893, it accounted for nearly one-fourth of all wages in Wisconsin, and in value of product represented more than grain milling, malting and brewing, leather, and foundry and machine shops combined.

As employers, lumbermen grew accustomed to a high turnover of labor, both in the woods and in the sawmills. The industry accepted this situation and did not seek to improve upon it. Where it had offered relatively attractive pay in the early years, it came to depend upon an abundant supply of transient and immigrant labor after the Civil War. In its peak years in the 1890s, lumbering ranked forty-sixth among Wisconsin industries in per capita wage. It was no longer a strictly seasonal industry geared to winter snows and the spring runoff. The average per capita annual wage in the lumber industry in 1897 was $386.09. It was the worst offender for payment in truck—scrip, or due bills, accepted at the company store. Knapp, Stout and Company, in the eighties, was still paying its employees only at the end of the season, enforcing use of the company store, and discounting a man's wages 20 percent if he quit before the season was completed. While mechanics lien laws protected the employee after 1860 by making it relatively simple to attach logs or lumber upon which he had worked, the employer's power to define the labor contract was practically unlimited.

Reading the autobiographies of Isaac Stephenson, or John Nelligan, or Richard Current's biography of Philetus Sawyer, one gets the impression of self-made men with a strong sense of responsibility and a paternalistic regard for their employees. But this regard was strongly tempered by prevailing attitudes about the prerogatives of the employer, the demand for unquestioning deference, and the arrogance of competence dealing with lesser clay. They respected and paid well the few highly skilled workers—sawyers, millwrights, pilots—and repaid dogged loyalty in the others when they knew about it. They considered themselves approachable and congratulated themselves on dealing with their men as individuals. It is questionable how successful they were in this.

The sawmill workers had a brief success with union organization and strikes in the 1880s, but the lumber industry was difficult to organize. It was scattered, there was always a high turnover of itinerant labor, not many jobs were highly skilled, and the owners could usually count upon the loyalty of county sheriffs and municipal officials. There was seldom any hesitance on the part of employers to use all of the traditional nineteenth-century weapons: the lockout, the blacklist, strikebreakers, and political pressure to call out the militia.

Wisconsin's pine forests were a one-time resource. There is every evidence that the lumberman, the citizen, and the legislator of 1880 were well aware of this fact. There was a ready recognition that the rate of the annual cut would soon end the virgin stands. In the rich timber of the Chippewa Valley, one can trace the loggers' progress. The Daniel Shaw Lumber Company contracted only for white pine in the 1860s, a minimum of eighteen inches in diameter at the small end of the log. By the 1870s, this had shrunk to twelve inches, by the eighties there could be no more than five logs to furnish 1,000 board feet, by the nineties eight logs, and only a small proportion were white pine.

James Willard Hurst has put this reckless destruction of a priceless resource in perspective. "What stands out as the dominant tone and character of the record," he comments, "is that on the whole contemporary community values supported, acquiesced in, or were indifferent or unseeing toward most of what private interest sought and obtained from law concerning exploitation of the Wisconsin forest." It was not necessary, then, for the lumbermen to outrage or subvert community standards to carry out their wholesale destruction of the forest.

Nineteenth-century American values applauded the conversion of the forest into capital for the creation of jobs, private fortunes, towns, bustling factories, and houses, barns, and fences on the prairies to the west. The prevailing view was that the natural use of land was for farms, and the troublesome forests had to be cleared to make way for this purpose. The preemption and homestead laws were unquestioningly applied to the pine lands. Railroad grants carried the express provision that the lands should be sold to small holders, for agricultural purposes, and not held off the market for an increase in the value of the timber. The record of this attitude is detailed and overwhelming. Conservationists of the time were generally concerned with the climatic implications of deforestation, or the flood control functions of the natural growth. Policy makers were impatient of any advice that was contrary to prevailing views, and they were not exposed to much of it. So far as the state legislature was concerned, the federal government effectively set land policies. It was the wholesaler and retailer of millions of acres. There existed no scientific standards to which to repair, no trained bureaucracy to enforce them had they existed to be translated into law, and no discernible public support for serious limitations upon prevailing practices, until the 1890s, when the question was already largely academic for Wisconsin. The federal government had disposed of all but 600,000 acres in Wisconsin by 1892, without considering any serious alternatives. Sixty years later, not over one-sixteenth of the former pine forest land in northern Wisconsin was in farms, but the state of Wisconsin, which fell heir to nearly 30 percent of the land, had exhibited no greater foresightedness.

The Wisconsin Cutover is a singularly unprepossessing monument to nineteenth century enterprise and an unsatisfactory substitute for the original forest, but we do its creators an injustice to charge them with simple, unbridled greed. The sad part is the realization that it was not at all the joyful adventure of the Paul Bunyan legends or jolly lumberjack stories. Like so much pioneering, it was accomplished at great social cost.

Selected Bibliography

Clark, James I. *The Wisconsin Pineries: Logging in the Chippewa.* Madison, 1956. A short summary, a few good pictures.

Current, Richard N. *Pine Logs and Politics: A Life of Philetus Sawyer.* Madison, 1950. As the title implies, there was a connection.

Everest, D. C. "A Reappraisal of the Lumber Barons." *Wisconsin Magazine of History* 36:17–22 (Autumn 1952). By a paper baron.

Fries, Robert F. *Empire in Pine: The Story of Lumbering in Wisconsin, 1830–1900.* Madison, 1951. The standard work.

Gates, Paul W. "Weyerhauser and the Chippewa Logging Industry." In Fritiof O. Anders, ed., *The John H. Hanberg Historical Essays.* Rock Island, Ill., 1954. Weyerhauser was late in his decision to control timber sources.

———. *The Wisconsin Pine Lands of Cornell University.* Ithaca, N.Y., 1943. Reprinted by the State Historical Society of Wisconsin. Madison, 1965. The hazards of holding timber were fearsome.

Hidy, Ralph, Frank E. Hill, and Allan Nevins. *Timber and Men: The Weyerhauser Story.* New York, 1963. A too-sympathetic approach.

Holbrook, Stewart H. *Burning an Empire.* New York, 1943. Has three chapters on Wisconsin timber fires.

———. *The American Lumberjack.* New York, 1962. A Collier Paperback reissue of his *Holy Old Mackinaw: A Natural History of the American Lumberjack,* New York, 1945.

Hurst, James Willard. *Law and Economic Growth: The Legal History of the Lumber Industry in Wisconsin, 1836–1915.* Cambridge, Mass., 1964. An important, large book, not for the faint of heart.

Kanneberg, Adolf. "Log Driving and the Rafting of Lumber in Wisconsin. Statutory Provisions and the Common Law of Wisconsin Pertaining to the Use of Navigable Water for Log Driving and the Rafting of Lumber." Mimeographed. Madison: The Public Service Commission of Wisconsin, 1944.

Lapham, Increase A., J. G. Knapp, and H. Crocker. *Report on the Disastrous Effects of the Destruction of Forest Trees Now Going on so Rapidly in the State of Wisconsin.* Madison, 1867. As reprinted for the State Historical Society of Wisconsin. Menasha, 1967. Not all of the reasons were right, but the effects were.

Larson, Agnes M. *History of the White Pine Industry in Minnesota.* Minneapolis, 1949. Supplements Fries and is more readable.

Nelligan, John Emmett, as told to Charles M. Sheridan. *The Life of a Lumberman.* Madison, 1929. What it was like.

Rector, William G. "Working with Lumber Industry Records." *Wisconsin Magazine of History* 33:472–78 (June 1950). Story of the Forest Products History Foundation.

———. "The Birth of the St. Croix Octopus." *Wisconsin Magazine of History* 40:171–77 (Spring 1957). No one else could use the river.

Reynolds, A. R. *The Daniel Shaw Lumber Company: A Case Study of the Wisconsin Lumbering Frontier.* New York, 1957. A good study of a me. dium-sized company in the Chippewa valley.

Stephenson, Isaac. *Recollections of a Long Life: 1829–1915.* Chicago, 1915. He made a huge fortune in lumbering.

Twining, Charles Edwin. "Orrin Ingram: Wisconsin Lumberman." Ph.D. dissertation, University of Wisconsin, 1969. A fascinating study of the marketing aspects.

———. "Plunder and Progress: The Lumbering Industry in Perspective." *Wisconsin Magazine of History* 47:116–24 (Winter 1963–64). It was a wasteful process, and the lumbermen knew it.

RAILS, COMMERCE,
AND INDUSTRY

21

Milwaukee owes much to the consolidation of her bankrupt, unfinished, pioneer railroad lines into a powerful railroad empire, with its managerial control firmly fixed in Milwaukee. Fortunate, too, that the railroad attracted the financial resources to follow the growth of economic opportunity westward and northward. The railroad empire was what we know today as the Milwaukee Road, or more properly, the Chicago, Milwaukee, and St. Paul Railroad. The guiding hand behind the creation of the empire was Alexander Mitchell's.

Mitchell was more than a passive witness of the promotional efforts which by 1858 brought into being railroad links with two Mississippi River towns, Prairie du Chien and La Crosse. He served as a director on both roads, providing valuable financial advice and contacts. A prudent investor, Mitchell did not take a large personal share in the feverish financing that characterized these pioneer railroads. But his bank was an important source of funds for others who pledged the security of their own property in exchange for cash to put into the railroads. Mitchell also advised the city on the various bond issues voted as subsidies.

Milwaukee liked to recall that she had " 'forged with her own hands and by her own unaided efforts, the Iron Chain that linked the shores of the Lake with the banks of the Mississippi.' " There was a bit of hyperbole in this. Probably not much over one-fourth of the cost of the Milwaukee and Mississippi Railroad was raised locally. This would include approximately 6 percent paid in cash by subscribers to the railroad's stock, $900,000 in the troublesome farm mortgages, and about $500,000 from bonds issued by the city as a subsidy in exchange for railroad stock. But at $25,000 a mile, the railroad, which built 203 miles of track to reach Prairie du Chien, cost at least $5,000,000. The costs of promotional management, and unsecured borrowing at ruinous interest rates running as high as 2.5 percent a month to keep the whole afloat, ran this figure higher.

Following the classic pattern of western railroad building, the local promoters provided—through subscriptions, subsidies, terminal and right-of-way grants, clearing and grading work exchanged for stock, and other aids—the basis for mortgage indebtedness with which to buy railroad iron, rolling stock, and heavy construction work such as bridging. This money was sought in New York and other money markets through bankers and brokers who specialized in placing such securities. They usually expected to get the securities, first-mortgage bonds ordinarily, at a generous discount, with some capital or preferred stock thrown in as a sweetener. This, with the higher rate of interest on bonds commonly paid by western roads, was supposed to make the bait attractive enough to capture the dollars of investors running a speculative fever. It did that, but it made western railroading financially hazardous.

The upshot of this type of financing and management was a spectacular debt with carrying charges to match, which even a potentially profitable railroad could not sustain in its early years. When the Milwaukee and Mississippi Railroad reached financial exhaustion and the Mississippi River simultaneously in 1857, it had a mortgage indebtedness of $6,000,000 in bonds and $3,500,000 in capital stock. Earnings were not within hailing distance of the carrying charges. It did not take the financial panic of 1857 to sink the frail craft. It went under along with all of the other Wisconsin railroads.

A bankrupt railroad was as much of an embarrassment to its bondholders as it was to its promoters. It was no simple task to foreclose the mortgage and take over the operation of the road. The Milwaukee and Mississippi Railroad, for instance, built the line from Milwaukee to Madison and then in 1853 absorbed the Madison and Prairie du Chien Railroad, a subsidiary company. Later consolidations took over spurs and feeder lines promoted separately. This proliferation of companies, and their reappearance under altered names after bankruptcy, reorganization, and consolidation, accounts for the jungle of names involved in any account of Wisconsin's railroad history. There were thirty-three new railroad companies chartered in Wisconsin between 1861 and 1867, yet only 130 new miles of track were built. This does not count numerous others that were projected but failed to get official charters.

The bondholders ordinarily looked to the brokers and bankers, from whom they had originally bought, to gather a phalanx of lawyers and care for their interests. This involved getting a committee representing a majority of the bondholders to request the appropriate court to order sale or reorganization of the property. The procedure normally required a liquidation of much of the capitalization represented by the common stock of the railroad, as well as a reduction of the bonded indebtedness, through the exchange of new securities for the old, to a capital base which the railroad could hope to carry. Bankruptcy made the common stock, representing management control, a highly speculative equity which depended upon the establishment of earning power to service the senior securities.

There were a number of factors which made the management of these reorganized Wisconsin railroads unattractive ventures. They had very little history upon which to base meaningful estimates of prospective revenues. They depended heavily upon the revenue from grain hauling, and the wheat crops in southern Wisconsin were increasingly unreliable, after the bumper crop of 1860. Northern Wisconsin was not yet an exciting prospect. The growing lumber industry depended upon the rivers to carry its logs and lumber rafts. Indeed, it seemed that it required large federal land subsidies to attract railroad building in that direction after 1866. But most of all, southern Wisconsin, where the bankrupt lines ran, was an exceedingly hostile environment in which to operate a railroad. The 6,000 farmers who had given mortgages to get the railroads built organized a Grand State League and various lesser leagues to thwart the mortgage holders or force the railroads to pay them off. Between 1858 and 1863, there were fourteen measures passed in the legislature attempting to repudiate these mortgages. Most of them were struck down by the courts, despite the efforts of the league to elect compliant judges. An 1863 statute attempted to assess the former La Crosse and Milwaukee 12 percent of its gross earnings for the purpose of paying off the farm mortgages pledged for its construction. Eventually a disputed land grant was used for this purpose.

The farmers were not hostile simply because of mortgages. The period of reorganization of the bankrupt railroads led inevitably to consolidations. The Chicago and Northwestern, which was to be one of the two giants dominating Wisconsin railroads, was organized in 1859. The Milwaukee and St. Paul was organized in 1863. This latter occasioned great excitement. There was angry talk of monopoly, with mass meetings to protest. The excitement went beyond debate, for there were a number of incidents of track and bridges destroyed, fires set, and obstructions placed on the rails, and at one time the Milwaukee and St. Paul found it necessary to abandon running trains at night.

It was in this unfriendly atmosphere that Alexander Mitchell began to build his railroad empire. It is a moot question whether Mitchell's interest stemmed from a desire to have Milwaukee as the center of a railroad network which he envisioned, whether he was protecting the investments his bank had in Milwaukee real estate and commerce, whether the railroads simply appealed to him as an investment that was badly out of favor and therefore undervalued by the market, or whether he saw speculative profits. Whatever his motives, Mitchell's primary interest became management and control of a successful railroad rather than speculation. He and his able general manager, Sherburn S. Merrill, consolidated existing lines, built many miles of new railroad, and took pride in the equipment, management, and operation of their lines. For a brief time, in 1869–70, Alexander Mitchell was the president of both the Milwaukee and St. Paul and the Chicago and Northwestern roads, aggregating more mileage than any rivals.

Mitchell had more working in his favor than simply the low estate to which Wisconsin railroads had fallen. He was backed by great wealth, and had a record of prudent financial management which permitted him to move with confidence, even in the money marts of Wall Street. His early mentor, George Smith, had $20,000,000 in the CM&StP at the time of his death in 1899. Mitchell had his confidence. The ever-present threat of political action against his railroad lines was not calculated to frighten Mitchell. He had protected his banking interests from political assault during years when his operations were loudly proclaimed to be illegal and unconstitutional. A pragmatist in politics, he usually belonged to the Democratic party, which had a habit of winning in Milwaukee. His purse was a handy instrument of political control. He could always put his money on a Republican like Matt Carpenter or Harrison Ludington when the Democrats affronted him. And finally, he was a calculating optimist. He believed that he could mold Wisconsin's ailing railroads into a functioning system that would return a dependable profit.

The future CM&StP, beginning in 1863, soon absorbed some smaller Wisconsin lines, and the La Crosse and Milwaukee, into a rail system which within a few years reached westward into Minnesota and developed feeder lines probing the southern edges of the pineries. Mitchell next engineered the absorption of the Milwaukee and Prairie du Chien, in 1866. Three years later, with money raised on a trip to his native Scottish heath, he purchased a controlling interest in the Racine and Mississippi, which had reached the River at Savanna, Illinois, in 1862. Mitchell's combination now held all of the lines running in an east-west direction to the Mississippi from Lake ports in Wisconsin.

Consolidation of the Mitchell interests in the 1860s, as noted, inspired occasional outbursts of antimonopoly sentiment. Mitchell and his supporters were able to blunt this sentiment by pointing to the competitive threat of Chicago-based railroads, particularly the Chicago and Northwestern, and the dangers of outside financial control and management. One of Mitchell's allies in financing the consolidations was Russell Sage, who had a financial interest in the former La Crosse and Milwaukee. Sage bore an unsavory reputation as a financial manipulator, which he later enhanced as an ally of Jay Gould and Jim Fiske. In 1875, Mitchell took Sage's measure in a head-on-confrontation, accusing him of being interested only in manipulating the railroad's stock. He enlisted a majority of the stockholders and threw Sage and his supporters off the board of directors, no mean feat for the Milwaukee capitalist.

Mitchell saw the agricultural frontier receding northwestward and proposed to follow it in order to gather Milwaukee's share of the grain harvest. Like the pioneer farmer who wanted to own only his own land and that adjoining it, a proper railroad tycoon expected to control only his "rightful territory." This was sometimes difficult of definition. Mitchell saw the Milwaukee Road reach Omaha, Kansas City, and points in the Dakotas; the ill-advised extension to Puget Sound came early in the twentieth century, long after his death.

The Mississippi River was a barrier but also a collector of traffic. The "Milwaukee" concentrated its building activity and acquisitions in Iowa and Minnesota during the ten years following 1863, in order to gather the grain harvest at MacGregor, Iowa, and La Crescent, Minnesota, opposite the company's railheads at Prairie du Chien and La Crosse. The interests of the Davidsons of La Crosse, who built a monopoly of the packet lines on the Mississippi in 1866, were not always synonymous with the railroad's interests, although they were allied. Milwaukee grain men were alarmed, in the late sixties, by the amount of grain being diverted down the river to St. Louis and New Orleans. But by 1872 fully 83 percent of the grain from Minnesota and Iowa was going by way of Milwaukee and Chicago again. In 1874 the Mississippi was bridged by the Milwaukee Railroad at Prairie du Chien and in 1876 at La Crosse. Milwaukee competed successfully with Chicago for a share of the grain trade. The Twin Cities and Duluth, by the early seventies, were diverting a large amount of the spring wheat from the northern plains.

A simple picture of the consolidation phase of Wisconsin's railroad history, beginning after the panic of 1857, can be gained if one thinks of the Milwaukee-based consolidation, which was to become the Chicago, Milwaukee, and St. Paul Railroad (CM&StP), as primarily stretching in a westerly direction, following the receding wheat frontiers. In contrast, the Chicago-based consolidation, the Chicago and Northwestern Railroad, drove primarily in a northerly direction in Wisconsin. The C&NW took over a line projected from Fond du Lac to Janesville. This cut across the lines out of Milwaukee and Racine to the Mississippi and also tapped the lumber mills tributary to Lake Winnebago. The Chicago-based road maintained its interest in a northern extension, building to Green Bay and beyond into the Upper Peninsula to the lumber mills and iron mines. Chicago was the largest lumber market in the country at the time. The distinction between the directional emphases of the rival systems is largely lost if one looks at a twentieth-century map of midwestern railroads, but it was self-evident in the 1870s. The two railroads soon recognized a community of interest, a fact emphasized by Mitchell's brief tenure as president over both simultaneously, and their exchange of board members.

Unmindful of the reaction of farmers and other shippers, Alexander Mitchell in 1870 controlled, through the two great consolidated systems of which he was president, all but 86 miles of the 2,300 miles of railroad in use in Wisconsin. Hostile public opinion made it advisable to abandon the public community of interest of the CM&StP and the C&NW, represented by Mitchell's dual presidencies, but their rivalry was benign. It was more profitable to exploit shippers in areas where they were not in competition and divide the traffic and revenues where they were.

Other railroads in Wisconsin were built in subsequent years, but most of them were absorbed by or operated in comity with the two larger systems. The West Wisconsin Railroad began its existence with a federal land grant in the pinery. Naturally enough, this attracted the interest of lumbermen, who developed it into a line that served the pineries, delivered its products as far west as Omaha, and reached Chicago over the lines of the C&NW. It was known popularly as the Omaha or the Wisconsin Lumber Line, and all in all received federal grants of 1,288,000 acres, much of it in timberlands. The C&NW bought a majority of its stock in 1882, but continued its separate existence. It was through this connection that Senators Sawyer and Spooner acquired an identification with the C&NW.

The Wisconsin Central line was built by Boston capital in the seventies, to earn federal grants in the pineries and create a link with the Northern Pacific and Lake Superior. It was largely the creation of the Colby family of Boston. Charles Colby moved to Milwaukee and was identified with the city and enterprises along the railroad during the years

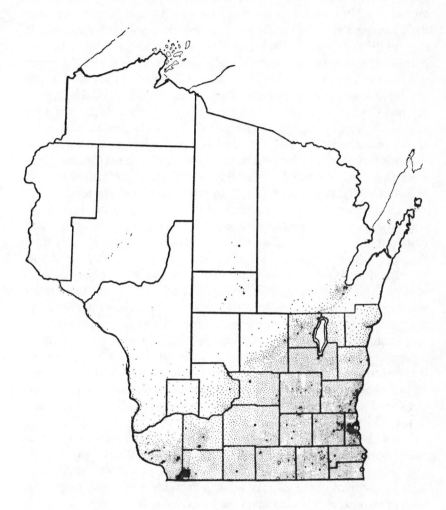

Map 10.   Population of Wisconsin, 1850. Each dot on the map represents 25 rural people localized by civil townships. In the 1850 census the population of the state was given as 305,391, only 9.4 percent of it urban (in population centers of 2,500 or more). This non-Indian population was confined to the south and concentrated in the Milwaukee-Lake area and the lead region of the southwest. Map by Guy-Harold Smith. Reprinted from *The Geographical Review,* vol. 18, 1928

of his active business career. The Minneapolis, St. Paul, and Sault St. Marie, popularly known as the Soo Line, was built in conjunction with the Canadian Pacific in the eighties, to carry the northern grain trade. It absorbed the Wisconsin Central in 1909. It became primarily a lumber, pulpwood, and mineral line serving northern Wisconsin and the paper mills on the lower Fox River. The Northern Pacific and the Great Northern, great trunk routes from the Twin Cities to the Pacific Northwest, reached Chicago over the Burlington and Northern, a Burlington Line subsidiary, which built a line in the middle eighties up the Wisconsin side of the Mississippi. The NP, GN, and Burlington formed a combination that was forced to dissolve by Theodore Roosevelt in the Northern Securities Case, since reversed. Green Bay achieved an independent connection to the Mississippi in 1873 with the Green Bay and Western.

As it did everywhere, the building of the railroad network in Wisconsin had a great effect upon the economies of the farm areas, towns, and cities it touched. The state had a commercial agriculture practically from the start. Farmers began raising wheat even where distance from export points and inadequate means of transportation made it a highly dubious venture. This headlong push of commercial agriculture into the interior was accompanied by an enthusiastic promotion of urban centers to serve the growing farm population, or with larger ambitions to develop into manufacturing centers. Some that were favorably located, particularly on a dependable waterpower of some size, made that transition. Others were destined to remain villages with a modest trading area. The early census reports show that even the villages of two or three hundred inhabitants developed some manufacturing beyond the ubiquitous flour and grist mill or saw mill.

The Lake ports had advantages of location for differentiated manufacturing not shared by interior points or those on the Mississippi. Milwaukee asserted her supremacy in this early. Already in 1860, the city produced one-fourth of the value of all manufactures in the state, despite the heavy emphasis in this total upon the broadly dispersed flour-milling and lumber industries. By 1880, Milwaukee produced fully one-third of the value of all manufactures. Flour and grist mill products for the state now equalled the value of manufactured products for 1860, and lumbering about two-thirds as much. All manufacturing for the state totalled $128,255,480, with Milwaukee accounting for $43,473,000.

It would be difficult to find an American frontier that did not exult in its limitless resources and opportunities while decrying the importation of manufactured articles creating an unfavorable outflow of funds. Milwaukee was no exception, lamenting in 1842 that large amounts of lumber

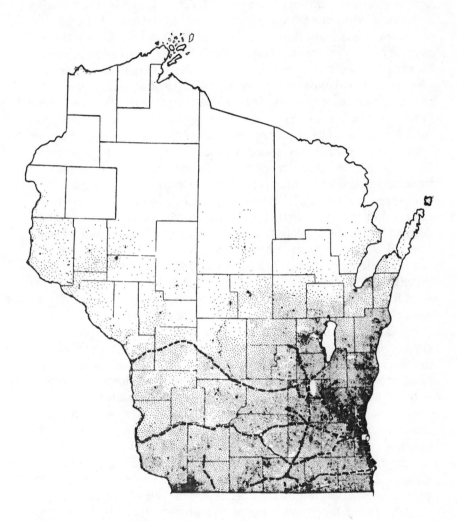

Map 11. Population and Railroad Development, 1860. Each dot on the map represents 25 rural people localized by civil townships. The location of approximately 7,000 Indians of northern Wisconsin is not shown. In the 1860 census the total population of the state was given as 775,881, of which 14.4 percent was urban (in population centers of 2,500 or more). The dashed line drawn represents railroads built before 1860. Population map by Guy-Harold Smith. Reprinted from *The Geographical Review*, vol. 18, 1928. Railroad statistics incorporated in the *Wisconsin Regional Plan Report*, 1934

were being imported, and in 1849 that exports of $2,000,000 in value did not yet counterbalance imports of $4,000,000. Along with the "viewing with alarm" went much "pointing with pride" to resources, both real and imaginary, which must draw the capitalist inevitably to develop the opportunity: ". . . we are sending our hard lumber east to get it back as furniture and agricultural implements, we ship our lead to St. Louis and New York, to pay the cost of bringing it back as shot, type, pipe. . . . we ship away our wool crop and import cloth, carpets, blankets, and other fabric; we give rags for papers, and hides for boots and harness, and iron ore for stoves—and our consumers all the while are paying the double costs of this unnecessary transportation," complained the Milwaukee Chamber of Commerce *Report* for 1871. The dirge could be duplicated from many sources over the next twenty-five years.

Despite the rhetoric of industrial opportunity, Milwaukee citizens concentrated their energies and capital upon the city's commercial possibilities. Alexander Mitchell lent money to men like Daniel Wells, Daniel Newhall, Alanson Sweet, and Angus Smith, who built warehouses, vessels, and elevators to handle commerce. Much of the animus against Mitchell's bank displayed in the 1846 Constitutional Convention came from Racine and other rival ports, in recognition of the role the "illegal" bank played in Milwaukee's growing commercial supremacy.

Milwaukee was the largest milling center and grain export point in the country in the 1860s. Her loss of primacy went largely unnoticed, as the flood of western wheat grew even while Milwaukee's share diminished. It was little wonder that the nabobs of the community, represented in the Milwaukee Board of Trade, were men with their attentions riveted upon commercial rivalries with Chicago and lesser competitors, railroad construction and consolidation, and facilities for shipping grain on the Lakes.

The growth of the city's industry caught the financial elite almost by surprise. There was doubtless an element of pique over this lack of foresightedness, that drove Edward P. Allis into the role of a political maverick when he ran for governor on the Greenback ticket in 1877. He came very near to losing his industrial enterprise, when he was forced through bankruptcy in 1876 as a result of the financial stringency of the time and his sound but ill-timed expansive policies. Allis, with other manufacturers who found themselves sitting below the salt in Milwaukee's business hierarchy, forced an investigation which showed that the railroads and other commercial ventures were loading an inequitable tax burden upon the city's growing manufacturing interests.

With a larger market area opening to her, more of her handicraft and artisan industries were susceptible to entry by the factory system. As an

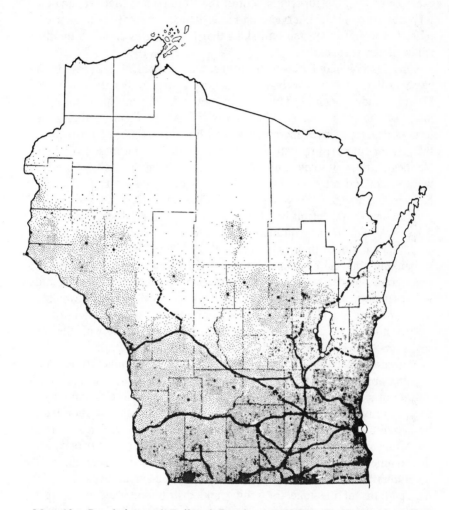

Map 12. Population and Railroad Development, 1870. Each dot on the map represents 25 rural people localized by civil townships. The location of approximately 6,000 Indians in northern Wisconsin is not shown. In the 1870 census the total population of the state was given as 1,054,670, of which 19.6 percent was urban (in centers of 2,500 or more). The three largest cities were Milwaukee (71,440) Fond du Lac (12,764), and Oshkosh (12,663). The solid line drawn represents railroads built before 1860, the dashed lines railroads built between 1860 and 1870. Population map by Guy-Harold Smith, reprinted from *The Geographical Review,* vol. 18, 1928. Railroad statistics incorporated in the *Wisconsin Regional Plan Report,* 1934

example of this, the superintendent of the Bradley and Metcalf shoe factory observed, in an interview in 1869, that of the 450 men then employed, not more than ten had skills that had been essential to the firm ten or fifteen years earlier.

Some lessons may be taken from this. One is that the craftsman in the city was likely to be absorbed by a factory system rather than to follow his trade independently. This was true even before machines mastered many of the processes. Another lesson is that the factory process was usually developed by a merchant with a line of credit back East, rather than by an enterprising craftsman who expanded his business from humble beginnings. Bradley and his partner, William Metcalf, started as wholesalers and retailers of factory-made shoes from the East. The pair had clerked together for Spofford and Tileston, a New York City shoe wholesaling firm. Metcalf had the foresight to marry Tileston's daughter. Tileston provided the youthful partners with a letter of credit for ten times the amount of their pooled capital. Bradley's family was well-to-do in banking and real estate in Haverhill, Massachusetts. A third lesson is that factory-made, standard goods drove the artisan out of his trade wherever they could reach his market economically. As Milwaukee's trade area expanded, the village shoemaker became a repairman or a retailer, although he probably continued to record his trade with the census-taker—unless he graduated to "merchant."

Milwaukee was not the only location for such manufacturing, but it had the obvious advantages of a growing urban market, a steady immigration of skilled and unskilled labor both native and foreign, and better access to raw materials and markets on the growing transportation facilities. Men coming with capital or access to it, and an eye for a business opportunity, usually saw Milwaukee first. As the railroad network grew, the commercial travellers representing Milwaukee wholesalers and manufacturers became a familiar sight in villages and small towns. The normal patterns of the time for selling and distribution were not long in coming to a frontier devoted to commercial grain-raising and extractive industries seeking cash markets to meet payrolls. The interval between pioneering on a partially self-sufficient frontier and the arrival of an advertisement for "The Spring and Summer Fashions" or "The Improved Little Giant Corn and Cob Mill" was a brief one.

One would not expect Wisconsin, lacking coal and cheap sources of ore, to develop heavy industry dependent upon these resources. But the business pages of the *Milwaukee Journal* often remind us that Wisconsin firms have long had an identification with the production of large machines and foundry castings of an impressive character. This identifi-

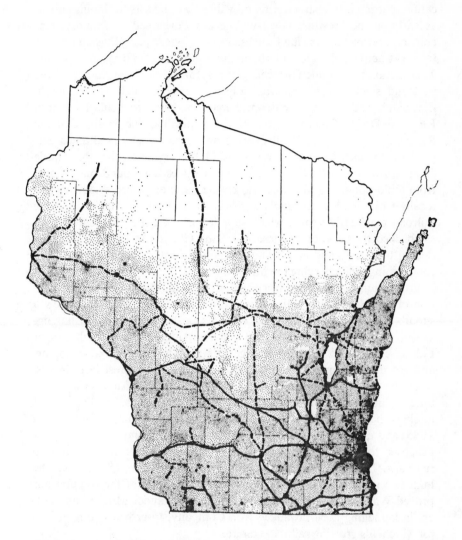

Map 13.   Population and Railroad Development, 1880. Each dot on the map represents 25 rural people localized by civil townships. The location of approximately 5,000 Indians in northern Wisconsin is not shown. In the 1880 census the total population of the state was given as 1,315,497, of which 24.1 percent was urban (in centers of 2,500 or more). Milwaukee was now a city of 115,587. The solid line drawn represents railroads built before 1870, the dashed line railroads built between 1870 and 1880. Population map by Guy-Harold Smith, reprinted from *The Geographical Review,* vol. 18, 1928. Railroad statistics incorporated in the *Wisconsin Regional Plan Report,* 1934

cation, particularly characteristic of Milwaukee, had its beginnings about as early as the brewing industry. The city developed its foundry, machinery, and metal-working business in the pioneer period, as an adjunct to its extractive industries: lumbering, wheat raising, milling, and mining. This fortunate conjunction took place before the concentration of the iron and steel industry in areas adjacent to coal, such as Pittsburgh, Cleveland, and Chicago. Wisconsin had iron ores, particularly at Iron Ridge in Dodge County, in the Upper Peninsula, and in the Gogebic Range, developed in the 1880s. The Iron Ridge ore was used much earlier than the eighties. The many lake vessels carrying on the wheat trade from Milwaukee looked for westbound cargoes and found one in coal from Ohio ports. Pig iron was also carried, and enough ore was smelted locally with charcoal to supply a growing foundry business. In 1855 the railroad reached Mayville, which supplied iron from a charcoal furnace established there. Another furnace in Sauk County, at Ironton, was producing that early and employing as many as 150 men in making charcoal, mining, and charging the furnace.

Production of iron on a large scale began, in 1870, with the completion of the plant of the Milwaukee Iron Company at Bay View, now a suburb of Milwaukee. This plant owed its existence to an interesting figure in the pioneer history of the iron and steel industry on the upper Lakes, Eber Brock Ward. Ward got his start in Great Lakes shipping, and got into iron making near Detroit through his interest in railroads, which he saw displacing shipping. He was a prophet of industrialization for the Midwest, and with a fortune of $3,000,000 made in shipping and mining—he was involved in the Sault Ste. Marie Canal, completed in 1855, and exploitation of the Upper Peninsula iron and copper mines— proposed to stake his fortune on the production of iron for the growing railroads. He expanded his operations to Chicago, in 1857, where he built two mills. The Civil War and the tariff policies of the Republicans proved Ward a prophet. In 1866 he joined Alexander Mitchell and others in launching the Milwaukee Iron Company, to provide railroad iron for Mitchell's growing railroad empire.

At his Detroit and Chicago plants, Ward was pioneering the introduction of the Bessemer process for making steel, but the Milwaukee plant was primarily an iron producer. The iron-rail market seemed inexhaustible, given the expansion of the railroads westward and the fact that iron rails wore out rapidly. This enlarged iron industry, called into being by the needs of the railroads, provided a base for the rapid expansion of the foundry and machinery industries in Milwaukee. They had started in 1840, when the infant town had an iron foundry. When John Gregory published his *Industrial Resources of Wisconsin* in 1855, he named six

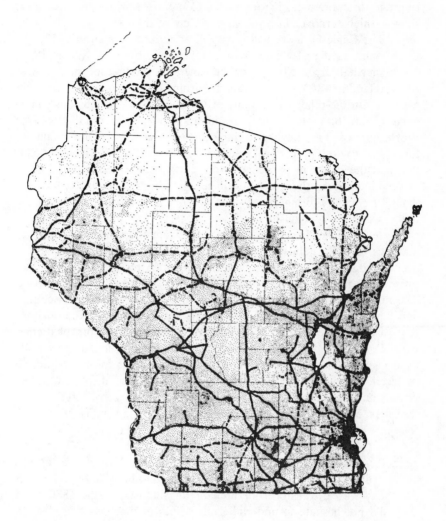

Map 14.   Population and Railroad Development, 1900. Each dot on the map represents 25 rural people localized by civil townships. In the 1900 census the total population of the state was given as 2,069,042, of which 38.2 percent was urban (in centers of 2,500 or more). Milwaukee was a city of 284,315. Ten years later it would have 373,857 people, far outdistancing the next largest cities, Superior (40,384), Racine (38,002), Oshkosh (33,062), and La Crosse (30,417). The solid line on the map represents railroads built before 1880, the dashed line those built between 1880 and 1900. Population map by Guy-Harold Smith, reprinted from *The Geographical Review*, vol. 18, 1928. Railroad statistics incorporated in *Wisconsin Regional Plan Report*, 1934

iron and three brass-casting foundries. Comparison with later directories shows a high turnover in ownership. A few of the foundries were fairly large. The Eagle Foundry had a payroll of about fifty men in 1853, and Decker and Seville's Reliance Works, taken over by E. P. Allis in 1860, was somewhat larger. Milwaukee industry built the first locomotive west of Cleveland in 1853 and was already turning out steam engines and mill castings. On the other hand, many of the businesses were obviously marginal; the attrition rate was high. As James Seville, partner in the Reliance Works expressed it, "anyone having sufficient 'nerve' to go into manufacturing had to do it on his own resources or 'bust.' " Local sources of capital, and the banks in particular, were chiefly concerned with the commercial interests of the city. Milwaukee's growing stake in heavy industry would frequently bring home the fact of the cyclical nature of the foundry and machine business.

These industries benefited, to a degree, from their unstable character and lack of well-established markets. They were able to move rapidly to accommodate themselves to new technologies. After the Civil War their prospective markets for machinery expanded with the railroad network. The railroad was a consumer of iron and machinery, as were agriculture and flour and lumber milling. It was very much the age of the tinkerer, the backyard inventor, the innovative mechanic, and the practical engineer. It was also an age concerned with the production of power, its transmission, and its application. Power increased as the metal turbine replaced the wooden waterwheel, the steam engine displaced waterpower, and twelve horse sweeps were developed to drive large custom threshers. Metal replaced hardwood wheels, gears, and shafts. Machinery tolerances were reduced, and metals had to meet higher standards.

E. P. Allis bought Seville and Decker's Reliance Works at a sheriff's sale in 1860, after the 1857 panic brought them to bankruptcy. The Allis Company was to transform the flour-milling industry in the 1880s, and Allis did not hesitate to undertake other lines of machinery production as opportunity beckoned. A capsule history of his firm illustrates the story of the growth of the foundry and machinery industry in Wisconsin during the last third of the nineteenth century—a story of opportunities seized.

Edward P. Allis was one of the many graduates of Union College, in Schenectady, New York, who cast their lots with pioneer Wisconsin. Visiting the West after graduation, the twenty-two year old Allis abandoned plans for a legal career, and instead went into the leather business in Milwaukee with a friend from home. Ten years later, in 1856, he sold out his interest, which by then included a share in a large tannery at Two

Rivers, as well as the wholesale and retail business in Milwaukee. Being of an entrepreneurial temper, Allis readily pushed his credit to the limit in order to seize an opportunity. It is interesting that he left the leather business, which was surely profitable. The Allens, his partners, built it into what was claimed, by the seventies, to be the largest tannery in the world. But there were elements in the business which doubtless robbed it of charm for Allis. There were three Allens, father and sons, in partnership with him, besides which the tannery business of the period was not innovative.

The availability of the Reliance Works in 1860 gave Allis the opportunity he was seeking. He had not been idle, but had improved his fortunes in the grain brokerage business. He borrowed to buy the Reliance Works and the Bay State Iron Manufacturing Company, moved the machinery to an acreage on Milwaukee's south side, and expanded his production into steam engines and other mill equipment. His move coincided with the conversion of many sawmills and flour mills to the more dependable steam power which could better meet the increasing power needs of larger mills and the speed requirements of circular saws. In 1873, Allis installed a new mill for the production of iron pipe, and filled large orders for the water systems of Milwaukee and Chicago. The company also supplied steam-pumping engines for Milwaukee's water system capable of supplying twenty million gallons daily.

Allis's risk-taking built his business to major proportions, with an average payroll of 400 men, but hazards went with the growth. As the depression of the seventies deepened, he found it increasingly difficult to meet obligations. In 1876, the reorganization of the Milwaukee Iron Company, to which he owed a large sum, forced Allis into bankruptcy. He emerged with the control of his company intact, but unhappy with Milwaukee's financial community for its infatuation with the wheat trade, and with the Republican party for its deflationary policies. This led him into his venture as Greenback party candidate for governor in 1877.

The 1876 experience with bankruptcy had little effect upon Allis's buoyant business temperament. That same year, he hired a Scots-Canadian millwright, William D. Gray, to take over the flour-milling machinery operations of his company. Gray was one of a number of American millwrights interested in the European roller mill process, which was particularly well adapted to milling the high protein, hard spring wheat of the northern plains. It was difficult to set the cumbersome buhrstones of the traditional mills so that they would crack rather than crush the berry of the wheat. C. C. Washburn, whose mills at Minneapolis were to form the base of present General Mills, lost one of his mills in an explosion in 1878. Washburn, a plunger, determined to rebuild the mill with the latest European technology. He sent his agent, William de la Barre, to study the process developed by Hungarian millers in particular. It is often represented as a great secret, but there were at least three millwrights in Wisconsin working on the roller process at the time: de la Barre, Gray, and John Stevens of Neenah. Whatever the mystery, the Edward P. Allis Company built the machinery for the new Washburn mill, a landmark in American flour milling which made the old-fashioned buhrstone mill a bucolic survival.

The year 1876 was celebrated with a great Centennial Exposition in Philadelphia. One of its outstanding attractions was the giant Corliss steam engine which drove the machines on exhibit in Machinery Hall. It was one of the marvels of that mechanical age, representing the highest state of the art. The next year Edwin Reynolds, an engineer who had helped to perfect the Corliss engine, came to the Allis Company, attracted by the offer of a free hand in the engine division. Reynolds gave Milwaukee and the Allis Company a world reputation as the center for the production of the heaviest class of low-speed engines used in mines, power plants, and public utilities.

For the sawmill division, Allis hired a Milwaukee millwright, named George Hinckley, who had developed several devices for the improvement of sawmill machinery. As sawmills increased in size, with more power available, the circular saw became a serious limitation upon increased efficiency, cutting a kerf at least $\frac{5}{16}$ of an inch wide, and even wider at high speeds. With increased speeds, as much as one-third of a log ended up as sawdust. There was great need for a more efficient high-speed saw.

French metallurgy was a world leader at the time, and it was there that a practical bandsaw for large work was developed. The new saw required a continuous band of steel, forty or fifty feet in circumference, that could operate at high speeds in much the same manner as a pulley. An American millwright, Jacob Hoffman of Fort Wayne, Indiana, developed the first practical bandsaw in this country in 1868. Allis saw the possibilities of the device and set Hinkley to solving some of the remaining technical problems. By the mid-eighties, the bandsaw was the standard in the larger mills.

The Edward P. Allis Company was Milwaukee's largest industry by the late eighties, with an average payroll of 1500 men. Allis was neither an engineer nor a mechanic. His genius lay in sensing the market for a new technological advance and hiring engineer-managers of outstanding ability, then giving them a wide latitude of decision in their divisions. The company's growth was based upon the technological changes that transformed Wisconsin's extractive industries.

As the Allis Company developed its capabilities in heavy machinery and power generation, new markets appeared. The iron and copper mines of the Gogebic and Upper Peninsula were among the deepest and wettest in operation. Allis engines and pumps raised the water and ventilated them. The same technology served to provide the draft for Bessemer converters and blast furnaces in Pittsburgh and Birmingham. Edward Allis died in 1889, just when the electric street railway was proving practical. Allis-built engines powered the generators of the dawning electrical age. The company had a national and international market even before 1901, when it was merged with heavy machinery concerns in Chicago and Scranton to become the Allis-Chalmers Company.

The story of Milwaukee's industrial growth was not, of course, the whole story of industrial growth in Wisconsin. But if one excludes the lumber industry, which was a widely dispersed industry converting a resource near its sites, Milwaukee's industries contributed nearly half of the value of manufactures in the period from 1870 to 1900. They represented the greatest variety, ranging from heavy machinery to paper toys, as well as the greatest collection of skills. This, of course, is to be expected, as Milwaukee by 1850 was developing into the only metropolitan city in Wisconsin. The lesser cities generally acquired an identification with one or two industries. In some cases this identification did not come until after 1900. The industrial histories of the smaller cities make interesting reading and matter for speculation. We might wonder why Manitowoc is identified with the aluminum products industry, for instance, or why Beloit is the largest producer of paper-making machines in the world, or how Sheboygan became identified with plumbing fixtures, chairs, and bratwurst, but we have not the space to pursue such inquiries.

The agricultural machinery industry was widely dispersed by the 1870s. Its technology was ingenious but simple, and the essential parts were often fabricated from hardwood. As the technology advanced, the industry became an important customer of the growing foundry and machine industries. Farm machines grew more sophisticated, with complicated metal parts, and a much larger capital outlay was required to produce the machines in quantity for a growing market at a price that the farmer could pay. The result was concentration in larger plants, particularly for implements used in grain growing. Many small firms survived by serving a localized market or by making simpler, low-cost machines, such as seeders or fanning mills, that could not pay for a long haul to market.

J. I. Case of Racine was one of Wisconsin's most conspicuous successes in the field of the higher-cost machinery. His threshers became the standard of the industry and found a national market, as did his portable steam engines for powering them. The larger plants that came to dominate the agricultural machinery industry were in the lake port cities of Milwaukee and Racine.

The Rock River valley had many waterpowers, a relatively concentrated agricultural population, and plentiful supplies of hardwoods, which invited participation in the manufacture of agricultural machinery. The area was among the early interior points served by competing railroads, thus making the transition to foundry and machine work easier, for pig iron from Milwaukee or Chicago could be brought in. The development of a variety of industries, particularly machine tools, dependent upon a highly skilled labor force, is as characteristic of the Rock River cities as it is of Milwaukee.

The principal exception to this distribution of agricultural machinery manufacturing was La Crosse, the point from which the Chicago, Milwaukee, and St. Paul Railroad advanced into Minnesota and northern Iowa. A lumbering and riverboat-building center, La Crosse attracted an enterprising population of Yankees, Germans, and Norwegians who developed various industries. La Crosse was Wisconsin's second city in 1890.

The tanning industry, like flour and grist milling, was a village craft persisting locally but also a significant industry concentrating in a few centers. Throughout the period 1865–1900, the leather industry was among the first five in the state. Wisconsin tanneries concentrated upon the staples of the trade—shoe leather and harness leather. The firms in Milwaukee were the most important, but Racine became an important tanning center because of its location between Chicago's packing plants and the barklands north of Milwaukee, furnishing tanbark.

The pioneer meat-packing industry was largely identified with Milwaukee also; the corn-hog economy was suited to southern Wisconsin agriculture. By 1861, there were six fair-sized packing plants in Milwaukee. It was one of those industries stimulated by the Civil War. The trend, as elsewhere, was to concentrate in larger firms. In 1890, there were only two Milwaukee firms, Cudahy and Layton, although meat packing was sixth in size for the state in value of product.* One recognizes the names of Philip Armour, who left Plankinton and Armour in the eighties to go to Chicago, and the Cudahys, who took over the Plankinton Company in 1888.

Beer, because of the dollars spent in advertising, has long been identified with Milwaukee and the German image of the city. The brewing in-

---

* "Value added" is probably a better measure of industrial activity, but it isn't as available as "value of product." Census figures are justly suspect but probably are better than those supplied by local booster literature.

dustry was established early there as in other German communities (unfortunately for the advertising, Milwaukee's first brewery, in 1840, was started by a Welshman making ale) and found a wider consuming public during the Civil War. In an excellent history of the Pabst Brewing Company, Thomas C. Cochran puzzled over the question of why Milwaukee became the site of a number of national breweries. It was not, he decided, simply because of the location, the water, Wisconsin's excellent barley, or the enthusiasm of Milwaukee's beer consumers. It was, rather, because Milwaukee was a relatively modest sized city within close range of much larger markets, particularly Chicago's. Nineteenth-century beer was temperamental, and many problems had to be solved before it could be supplied as a uniform product to points distant from the breweries. The large breweries in Chicago, New York, Cleveland, and Cincinnati had great urban markets at hand, and so did not worry about solving those problems. Milwaukee brewers did.

The great expansion of the export breweries took place in the seventies and eighties. In the census of 1890, malting and brewing ranked third in the state, after lumber and flour milling. It ranked first among Milwaukee's industries in that census only. The industry carried a heavy capitalization, most of it generated internally, with a relatively modest labor force. It created a market for a number of subsidiary industries, not all of them carried on within the brewery: cooperage, ice harvesting, refrigeration, malting, brewery equipment, saloon furnishings, and distinctive cartage equipment. Milwaukee's breweries were shipping one hundred carloads daily in 1891. It was claimed that they gave employment to about 46,000 people in that year, counting Spaniards cutting corks in Spain, but only 2,700 working directly in the city's breweries. The figure must have counted barkeeps, cooks fixing free lunches all over America, and a few really devoted customers.

Papermaking as a pioneer industry followed newspapers, appearing first in Wisconsin on the Milwaukee waterpower in 1848. Large amounts of clear water are required for manufacturing paper, and power on a much larger scale than most industries demand. Large-scale papermaking logically took root on the waterpowers of the lower Fox River, fed by the dependable reservoir of Lake Winnebago; the Fox falls 170 feet from the lake to Green Bay. Lumber and flour milling developed at the principal falls. Neenah and Menasha had thirteen flour mills by 1870 and were heavily dependent on that industry, but the migration of wheat raising westward put the mills at a disadvantage in relation to those built at Minneapolis. Milwaukee's superior rail connections kept her mills busy longer than those on the Fox. At Neenah-Menasha, the successor to flour milling was paper, the first mill installed in 1865. This was before the introduction of wood pulp; the mill used 1,000 tons of rags annually, gathered mostly in Milwaukee and Chicago. The first wood pulp mill in the area began operations in 1871 at Appleton. By 1890, wood pulp was coming into general use. Despite enormous expansion, the market for cheap paper was insatiable. Most of the paper mills on the Fox developed out of converted flour mills or from waterpowers formerly used for flour milling, whereas on the upper Wisconsin it was lumber money that was more commonly associated with papermaking. Paper and pulp had risen to eighth place among Wisconsin's industries by 1900, having increased in value of product almost ten times since 1880.

New Englanders naturally associated waterpowers with textiles. Particularly in the Rock River valley, woolen and cotton textiles were common local industries. Some important inventions in textile manufacturing came from Rockford, Illinois, the largest industrial city on the Rock and one often used as the model of industrial development in the valley. Appleton developed a woolen mill, which found its market in the specialized felts used in paper making.

Clothing manufacturing had a surprisingly large part in Milwaukee industry, even in 1850. By the 1890 census it employed the largest labor force in the city, counting those who worked at home or in tailor shops, making finished clothing from knit goods and woolens cut by the manufacturer. The city claimed the largest straw hat factory in the West and a wide market for hats and caps. Growth in the clothing industry was slow after the nineties.

Lumbering and flour milling were the dominant industries of the period 1865–1900, but both were in relative decline before its end. Manufacturing associated with the growing dairy industry was in fourth place by 1900. It was, of course, widely dispersed. The basic iron and steel industry was also in decline, as concentration of the industry favored sites closer to coking coal sources. Operations at the iron furnaces of Bay View persisted until 1930, when Wisconsin went out of iron and steel production. Industries using iron and steel flourished; their raw material came by water and rail at the lowest rates.

Weighing the relative importance of location, a skilled labor force, entrepreneurial enterprise, and availability of capital can lead to endless speculation. The enterprise of men like Edward P. Allis or J. I. Case was obviously crucial, but other favorable factors had to be present. The skilled labor force available in Milwaukee and the Rock River valley had much to do with the persistence of foundry, machinery, and heavy metal industries after Wisconsin's anemic iron industry succumbed. The accidental location of many Wisconsin industries in the nineteenth century seems to establish the competitive abilities of a variety of locations. A Beloit minister invented a superior windmill and began its manufacture there in 1867. Fairbanks, Morse and Company of Chicago, a sales agency for the Fairbanks scales made in Vermont, bought the Eclipse Wind Engine Company of Beloit, launching Fairbanks, Morse as a great manufacturing firm. A student at a Janesville business college worked his way by selling fountain pens, a relatively new item on the market. He decided that he could make a better product. The Parker Pen Company was the result. An itinerant peddler of German-made aluminum combs was given the use of shop space by a generous owner of a woodworking shop in Manitowoc in 1895. From this grew a complex of aluminum fabricating industries identified with Manitowoc and West Bend.

The years before 1900 were not only years of great industrial growth for Wisconsin but also years of experiment and adjustment. The problems of adjustment were most serious for those industries and cities that depended directly upon the rapidly disappearing forests or the westward-moving grain culture. The Lake port cities, which had concentrated on moving or processing the pioneer grain crop, adjusted easily because of their advantages of location. The lower Fox River cities retained their magnificent waterpowers after the flow of wheat to their mills was reduced to a trickle. Attracting capital was less of a problem than finding the right industry, which turned out to be papermaking. The Rock River cities were aided in their adjustment by the creation of a railroad network that put them in a competitive position. It was the lumber towns, now near a dwindling resource, that were to suffer serious adjustment pains. Some never made it; others experimented with feverish booster schemes with indifferent success.

Selected Bibliography

Alexander, J. H. H. "A Short Industrial History of Wisconsin." *Wisconsin Blue Book,* 1929, pp. 31–49. Summaries of census data.

Alexander, John W. *Geography of Manufacturing in the Rock River Valley.* Madison: University of Wisconsin School of Commerce, Bureau of Business Research and Service, 1949. Wisconsin's lesser manufacturing cities.

Association of American Railroads. *Wisconsin's Railroads: Their Part in the Development of the State, 1848–1948.* Washington, 1948. A pamphlet with useful information and a bibliography.

Atherton, Lewis E. *Main Street on the Middle Border.* Bloomington, Ind., 1954. No hicks without city slickers.

Branch, Maurice Lloyd. "The Paper Industry in the Lake States Region, 1834–1947." Ph.D. dissertation, University of Wisconsin, 1954. Centers on Wisconsin.

Bruce, William George. *Builders of Milwaukee*. Milwaukee, 1946. A mixture of biography and social, political, and economic history.

―――. "Old Milwaukee's Yankee Hill." *Wisconsin Magazine of History* 30:289–91 (March 1947). Defining the Yankee's place.

J. I. Case Company. *Serving Farmers Since 1842*. Racine, 1948. Better than most company histories.

Casey, Robert J. and Douglas. *Pioneer Railroad: The Story of the Chicago and Northwestern System*. New York, 1948. A literary flight, not very good.

Clark James I. *Edward P. Allis, Pioneer Industrialist*. Madison, 1958. The model entrepreneur.

―――. *Farm Machinery in Wisconsin*. Madison, 1956. Wisconsin was central for the industry, especially in grain.

Cochran, Thomas C. *The Pabst Brewing Company: The History of an American Business*. New York, 1948. Milwaukee brewers solved the problems of a national market.

Current, Richard N. "The Original Typewriter Enterprise, 1867–1873." *Wisconsin Magazine of History* 32:391–407 (June 1949).

―――. *The Typewriter and the Men Who Made It*. Urbana, Ill., 1954. A Milwaukee invention.

Derby, William Edward. "A History of the Port of Milwaukee, 1835–1910." Ph.D. dissertation, University of Wisconsin, 1963. Commercial Milwaukee did not welcome industrial Milwaukee.

Derleth, August. *The Milwaukee Railroad*. New York, 1948. Mitchell did not leave much for historians to work with—no problem for a novelist.

Eblen, Trudi J. "A History of the Kohler Company of Kohler, Wisconsin." Master's thesis, University of Wisconsin, 1965. Story of a family enterprise, lovingly told.

Elliot, Frank N. "The Causes and Growth of Railroad Regulation in Wisconsin, 1846–1876." Ph.D. dissertation, University of Wisconsin, 1956. Unorthodox financing and special tax breaks created a hostile public reaction.

Elliott, James L. *Red Stacks Over the Horizon: The Story of the Goodrich Steamboat Line*. Grand Rapids, Michigan, 1967. For buffs.

Glaab, Charles N., and Lawrence Larsen. "Neenah-Menasha in the 1870's: The Development of Flour Milling and Paper Making." *Wisconsin Magazine of History* 52:19–34 (Autumn 1968).

―――. *Factories in the Valley, Neenah-Menasha, 1870–1915*. Madison, 1969. From a Ford Foundation grant for urban studies.

Grist, Walter. *Allis Chalmers: A Brief History of 103 Years of Production*. New York, 1950. A company history.

Hilton, George W. *The Great Lakes Car Ferries*. Berkeley, 1962. Emphasis on the boats.

Hirshheimer, H. J. "La Crosse River History and the Davidsons." *Wisconsin Magazine of History* 28:263–76 (March 1945). Steamboat competition on the upper Mississippi.

Holbrook, Stewart H. *Machines of Plenty*. New York, 1955. Much of it is on J. I. Case.

Howard Publishing Company. *A History of the Wisconsin Paper Industry, 1848–1948.* Chicago, 1948. A centennial pamphlet.

Korn, Bernhard C. "Eber Brock Ward, Pathfinder of American Industry." Ph.D. dissertation, Marquette University, 1942. Ward built the Bay View Iron Works.

Kuehnl, George J. *The Wisconsin Business Corporation.* Madison, 1959. General incorporation became the pattern after 1871.

Lawrence, Lee E. "The Wisconsin Ice Trade." *Wisconsin Magazine of History* 48:257–67 (Summer 1965). A forgotten commercial enterprise.

Leonard, David. "A Biography of Alexander Mitchell, 1817–1887." Master's thesis, University of Wisconsin, 1951. Journalistic in style, but scholarly.

Marshall, Richard H. "Samuel Marshall, Pioneer Banker." *Wisconsin Magazine of History* 32:26–40 (Sept. 1948). Of the Marshall and Ilsley Bank.

Martin, Roy L. *History of the Wisconsin Central.* Boston, 1941. Not scholarly, but good research.

Miller, Willis H. "John Comstock, Pioneer Hudson Banker." *Wisconsin Magazine of History* 32:168–75 (Dec. 1948). Involved in local railroad promoting.

Schefft, Charles Ernest. "The Tanning Industry in Wisconsin: A History of Its Frontier Origins and Its Development." Master's thesis, University of Wisconsin, 1938. Interesting industry identified with Milwaukee.

Smith, James Bruce. "The Movement for Diversified Industry in Eau Claire, Wisconsin, 1879-1907." Master's thesis, University of Wisconsin, 1967. A study in boosterism.

Still, Bayrd. "The Development of Milwaukee in the Early Metropolitan Period." *Wisconsin Magazine of History* 25:297–307 (March 1942). Not beer, but a municipal conscience, made Milwaukee famous.

———. *Milwaukee, the History of a City.* Madison, 1948. A scholarly urban biography.

Taylor, Robert Hilton. "Men of Metal: A History of the Foundry Industry in Wisconsin." Master's thesis, University of Wisconsin, 1952. Useful on the early and middle years.

Wik, Reynold. "J. I. Case: Some Experiences of an Early Wisconsin Industrialist." *Wisconsin Magazine of History* 35:3–6, 64–67 (Autumn 1951).

———. *Steam Power on the American Farm.* Philadelphia, 1953. Case was a leader in the adoption of steam for farm machinery.

Williamson, Harold F., and Kenneth H. Myers II. *Designed for Digging: The First 75 Years of Bucyrus-Erie Company.* Evanston, Ill., 1955. Early lesson in attracting industry with a subsidy.

Williamson, Harold F., and Orange A. Smalley. *Northwestern Mutual Life: A Century of Trusteeship.* Northwestern University Studies in Business History, vol. 4. Evanston, 1957. Hard going.

Wisconsin Academy of Sciences, Arts, and Letters. *A Wisconsin Academy Profile in Wisconsin History.* Transactions 54, part a. Madison, 1965. Articles on business in the last half of the nineteenth century.

POLITICS AND THE MELTING POT
1865–1890

part seven

It is usual to discuss Wisconsin politics in the post-Civil War era in familiar terms: a comfortable, corrupt Republican majority occasionally jolted out of its complacency by a coalition of the disorganized but numerically dangerous Democrats and whatever elements of discontent were abroad. It was a period of exaggerated party loyalty for the very reason that the major parties were unsure of their differences in new areas of economic concern that called for political solutions. Ethnic sensibilities, religious tensions, urban-rural conflicts, and Yankee moral certainties introduced other wild cards into the political game. The picture of easy Republican dominance is partly a matter of convenience, fitting a complicated political story into a recognized mold, and partly the legacy of Robert M. La Follette, who found his villains in the party he meant to control.

Granger protest was a congenial topic for La Follette. He chose the railroads as the most malign political power in the state, and the short career of the 1874 Potter Law, a rate-regulation measure commonly referred to as the Granger Law, was a useful touchstone. La Follette, a keen student of Wisconsin politics, shunned appeals to ethnic and religious prejudices. He knew they ran deep and could be politically decisive when aroused. He was one of the unwilling victims of the Bennett Law controversy of 1890 and did not forget the lesson.

The lesson, of course, was that the native Americans—Yankees for short—continued to be the movers and shakers in state politics, but they could be moved and shaken by any significant shifts in the delicate balance between German Catholic Democrats and Lutheran Republicans. A too-confident assertion of Yankee social and cultural values as the necessary norms brought swift political retribution.

The Wisconsin melting pot worked imperfectly, and the working cannot be described with any precision. What we know is that there were no halcyon days. The pressure of immigration was continuous from both old and new streams of strangers. At the same time, Wisconsin's population was becoming more urban, rapid transformations in the economy were creating a self-conscious working class, old skills were displaced, new fortunes and unprecedented centers of economic power were being created, and everyone seemed to be on the move.

It all appears very contemporary, but without planners, pulse-takers, economic advisory councils, national union contracts, social insurance, or in-depth comment by familiar television personalities to tell the participants what it all meant. The wonder is that they made it to the turn of another century.

THE MELTING POT

22

Wisconsin in 1870 had a population of just over one million, 1,054,670. Only one in five lived in an urban place (over 2,500), altogether 207,099. Of that urban 207,099, one in three lived in Milwaukee (71,440). There were only eleven other cities of over 5,000 population. The two largest, Fond du Lac and Oshkosh, had 12,765 and 12,673 respectively.

Thirty years later, in 1900, the population had almost exactly doubled. But the rural population had gained only 51 percent, while the cities had increased by 281 percent. Two out of every five people now lived in town* or city, just about the national average. The national urban percentage in 1870 had been 25.6 compared to Wisconsin's 19.6—more than the difference between a fourth and a fifth. Wisconsin was hurrying to overtake the average. During the decade 1860 to 1870 two rural residents were added for every new one in an urban place. Between 1880 and 1890, these proportions were practically reversed.

---

* In Wisconsin, the term *town* legally designates an area, the township, usually six miles square, and it may be entirely rural. I have used the term in the popular sense, as an urban place which one thinks of as larger than a village but not as large as a city. The legal definitions present difficulties in ordinary language. For instance, in 1960, the City of Boscobel had a population of 2,608, the Town of Mount Pleasant (suburb of Racine) 12,358, and the Village of Menomonee Falls 18,276.

Milwaukee grew from 71,440 in 1870 to 285,315 in 1900, an increase of 400 percent. Smaller cities had also gained in spectacular fashion. La Crosse, Oshkosh, and Racine had populations just short of 30,000. Superior, which had not existed as a single city in 1880, had 31,091. Where there had been only a dozen cities of over 5,000 population in 1870, there were thirty-three by 1900. Seventeen were over 10,000, twelve of them over 15,000 and five over 20,000. The weight of urban population remained on the Lake Michigan shore and in the Fox and Rock River Valleys. Outside of these general boundaries only La Crosse and Eau Claire, across the state, had populations over 5,000 in 1870. By 1900 there were thirteen cities of over 5,000 scattered outside of the more populous areas: Antigo, Ashland, Chippewa Falls, Marinette, Marshfield, Menomonie, Merrill, Oconto, Stevens Point, Wausau, Superior, La Crosse, and Eau Claire.

Urbanization was a generalized phenomenon of the period. It is possible to list, although not to isolate, many of the factors accelerating the growth of Wisconsin's towns and cities. The growth of the major industrial and trade centers was largely a matter of their expanding marketing areas; they were serving a population that was growing geographically, in density, and in economic sophistication. The railroads were the principal agents of that expansion. Agriculture expanded with the railroads, as did the farmer's commitment to the market and mechanization. The number of farms in Wisconsin increased by almost 50 percent between 1870 and 1890. Resource-oriented industries grew similarly, geographically and in size and complexity.

The rapid growth of the cities, towns, and villages, the displacement of local crafts and manufactures by standard articles from city factories and wholesalers, and the growing commercialization of farming were all contributing new stresses and divisions to a society growing at a rapid rate. Much of the growth came from simply filling up the map. Some of the older, mainly agricultural counties in the south were stable or even lost population in this period. In others, the growth was primarily urban. These changes were not unique to Wisconsin, but the combination of an expanding frontier in agriculture and lumbering, rapid urban and industrial growth, and a continuous inflow of European immigration probably increased the internal stresses of society beyond those in more mature states or in states farther west, with simpler economies.

Even apparent stability proved illusory. A study of five villages in Grant County whose population showed almost no change in numbers between 1870 and 1900 revealed that 78 percent of the village families moved on between 1885 and 1895. Who were they and where did they go? Those questions remain unanswered, although the manuscript censuses indicate that they were mostly families whose heads were unskilled or semiskilled, had accumulated little property, and probably went to other villages or larger centers looking for work. They were evidently replaced by others moving off the land into the villages. A study of Trempealeau County found a similar high degree of mobility, running to 60 percent among farm operators in the decade 1860–70 and over 75 percent among business and professional men in the villages. Again, we do not know where they went. Probably some moved to larger population centers and others westward, or north to the pineries.

We can see a growing difference emerging, not just between city and farm but also between the village or small town and the farm and the city. The town dweller looked down the rails toward the city and identified his way of life with it. At the same time, he endorsed the rural view of the city as a menace to what he identified as American values. But this area of agreement did not imply a common bond between the farmer and the small town dweller, who usually came from the farm but felt he had transcended it. The farmer looked on the village inhabitant as a man who kept late hours and owed his living to the sharp practices he imposed upon his farm neighbors, nature's true producers. Laurence Larson, who made the transition from immigrant farm boy to university professor, tells us how the immigrant farmer viewed the townsman:

> At the county seat he saw men and women who lived in houses that looked palatial to his hungering soul. They wore what he regarded as fine clothes and there could be no doubt that they ate good food. They were believed to have an easy time; they held nearly all the public offices, from which they pocketed large salaries; at least, so the alien believed. They controlled the affairs of the county and the alien was sure that through this control they were able to lay exorbitant taxes on the poor farmers' land.
>
> The Yankees were "smart" and the immigrant had a lurking fear that he himself was not smart in the same way. Of course, he was handicapped all around; his ignorance of English put him at a disadvantage in all sorts of business transactions. It is therefore not strange that he came to believe that he was being exploited by the native businessmen, and often too the belief was well founded. Usury was a practice of which farmers complained most bitterly: in one case a helpless immigrant paid interest at the rate of fifty-five percent. In their resentment the farmers sought out the traders and businessmen who spoke their own idiom. They felt safer with them; at least they could make them understand what they thought of men whom they suspected of dishonest dealings.
>
> Lurid tales floated over the countryside detailing the alleged wickedness of the Yankee aristocrats in the little town. To the charges of idleness and dishonesty there was added that of coarse immorality, of which

the village doubtless had its share in the usual measure. Most of the immigrant farmers were desperately poor. They had many children and their daughters, in growing numbers, were finding work as domestic helpers in town. Some of them returned to their homes in shame. Incidents of this character were not allowed to be soon forgotten; every case added fresh fuel to the fires of bitter resentment that were burning in many homes where the alien tongue was spoken.

Hamlin Garland expressed a similar tension in his story "Under the Lion's Paw," and Wisconsin's Thorstein Veblen remarked that the "country town of the American farming region is the perfect flower of self-help and cupidity." Lewis Atherton in his *Main Street on the Middle Border* takes exception to Veblen's characterization, but Larson, Garland, and Veblen were authentic farm boys who went on to other careers.

Milwaukee's relations with the rest of the state reflected dislike and fear of the city's power and influence. Already by 1875, one in every ten Wisconsin citizens was a resident of Milwaukee County. The figure was one in eight by 1885. A decided urban tilt was well advanced in favor of the southeast corner of the state, with Milwaukee at its center. There was more involved than numbers. It had been the Milwaukee bankers, led by Alexander Mitchell, who had closed out forty-seven country banks in 1861 by refusing to honor their banknotes. It was Mitchell again who emerged in 1869 as head of both the Chicago and Northwestern and the Milwaukee Road, the two having swallowed all but a few miles of railroad mileage in the state. Milwaukee's population was nearly 50 percent foreign-born in 1870. The infamous Whiskey Ring of the Grant Administration was active there. Milwaukee's distillers and brewers could be counted upon to raise a slush fund to fight any liquor-control legislation, behind a phalanx of German and Irish voters. The county voted top-heavy Democratic majorities in every presidential election until 1880, while most of the state was stoutly Republican. A labor party emerged in Milwaukee politics as a repeated threat, with socialist leadership. Governor Jerry Rusk achieved tremendous popularity, in 1886, when he called out the militia to quell, with bloodshed, Milwaukee labor agitation for the eight-hour day. Milwaukee was different in a society that harbored many differences. The metropolis and its dominance were actively resented.

An element of difference between Milwaukee and rural or small town life of the period was the variety of living styles which the city offered. Among the refinements of the city were surfaced streets and public transportation, running water, sewers, street lights, gas for lighting, and after 1881, electricity. The presence of city shops and department stores, a broad representation of professional men, restaurants, theaters, and other cultural facilities made city living more attractive. Milwaukee supported a public high school after 1868, a normal school by the early seventies, and kindergartens after 1881. Teaching in the city was becoming professionalized by the seventies and increasing in specialization. It was 1907 before public technical and vocational education was available, a development in which Milwaukee pioneered, but there were evening schools and special schooling for deaf and blind children in the eighties. Not all children took advantage of the city's superior educational facilities. Fully one-third of Milwaukee's school-age youngsters were attending no school in 1868. There was no effective compulsory school law until the controversial Bennett Law of 1889.

Burr Jones, who grew up on a farm near Evansville in Rock County during the fifties and sixties, reminds us in his *Reminiscences* of the disparities in opportunity and experience between city and rural or small town life. Jones attended a seminary in Evansville run by the local Methodist church. He was urged to think about going on to college. "I listened to the suggestion more than willingly, but in those days I had never seen but two or three men who had gone through college, so far as I knew, and for a farm boy to make the attempt seemed a somewhat perilous adventure." Jones grew up in a homogeneous community with no families of foreign birth. He saw his first Irishman at age twelve, when the railroad was built through town. The simple rural background of Burr Jones's youth and the outlook which he recalled were not unusual. He was raised in one of the oldest settled sections of Wisconsin, within a few miles of Janesville, Madison, and Beloit. The relative isolation which his account reflects persisted in much of rural and small town Wisconsin.

The observation that ethnic and religious prejudices have persisted as powerful forces in American politics has now become a commonplace. This understanding has replaced the earlier assumption that ethnic bloc voting was a temporary aberration from responsible citizenship, encouraged by political bosses. Let proper assimilation take place and it would be eliminated, was the hopeful prediction of enthusiastic Americanizers of the 1920s.

Religion was considerably less of a uniting influence among the large German minority in Wisconsin than was their determination to retain their own cultural values and definition of what constituted the good life. But the Yankees unabashedly assumed that the constitutional prohibition that "no sectarian instruction shall be allowed" in the state's public schools had no reference to evangelical Christianity, so long as it was not too identifiably Congregational, Presbyterian, Methodist, or Baptist. The most vocal opponents of this assumption were the Catholics, although the German anticlerics and Lutherans shared in the opposition. German Catholics made up a good half of the 249,000 Catholic communicants in Wisconsin, according to the 1890 census. What might loosely be called the Yankee churches were credited with only 130,000. Their numbers and the anomalous position of the 170,000 communicants in the immigrant Protestant churches—161,000 of them adherents of the several synods of the Lutheran community—emboldened the Catholics. The German Lutherans were strong supporters of parochial schools, as were many of the Norwegians, but the Catholics bore the brunt of the attacks upon the sectarian school. They also bore the burden of counterattacks, arguing for tax sharing or tax relief and for support of Catholic eleemosynary institutions from general tax funds. They could count upon oblique support from the anticlerics for their position that readings and prayers from the King James Bible were improper and unconstitutional. Particularly in the 1870s, these issues were argued in the press and were used as political capital. The Catholic position on prayers and Bible readings in the public schools eventually prevailed in a landmark judicial decision by the state supreme court in the spring of 1890, known as the Edgerton Bible Case.

Local history tends to look at the more smiling aspects of American life. There is an implicit assumption that assimilation was going forward on an ascending curve. Interruptions were simple misunderstandings growing out of Yankee ineptitude, an excess of *amour-propre* on the part of immigrant groups, or an occasional embarrassing lapse of taste on the part of a bigoted minority of native Americans. The norm, undefined, was an amalgam of "Old Immigration" streams with the dominant Yankees and their cousins from the British Isles into a common culture which would draw upon the cuisine and best character traits of all concerned.

To give this positive approach to our earlier problems of integration its due, the subject has its ambiguities. One is reminded of the definitions of a pessimist and an optimist: the first seeing his glass as half-empty, while the other finds cheer in the thought that it is half-full. Let us examine the proposition from the viewpoint of the optimist.

The American-born Wisconsinite of the 1890s had a wider acquaintance with the foreign born than did his counterpart of the 1850s. He was most likely from rural and small-town New England or western New York, areas with a highly homogeneous population. The comments about foreign immigrant neighbors in Yankee letters written then give a clue to the attitudes that fed nativist sentiment. With one-third of the 1850 population foreign born, Know-Nothingism lacked viability as a political rallying cry, but it was surely less covert as a personal creed. The Yankee of 1890 had achieved a greater tolerance for his foreign neighbor through long acquaintance and it should not be overlooked that the principal nativist organization of the nineties, the American Protective Association, did not exclude the foreign born. Roman Catholicism was its bête noir, and the APA recruited very successfully among anticlerical Germans, Lutheran Germans, and Scandinavians.

Wisconsin was the goal of a steadily increasing immigrant stream, although the percentage of foreign born was dropping because of the growing base of native born, including the children of the foreign born. The foreign born still made up 30.7 percent of the state's population in 1890 and 27 percent in the state census of 1895. Germans and Scandinavians continued to dominate the immigrant stream. There were 268,469 German born in 1895, an increase of 8,650 over 1890, and 106,900 Scandinavians, an increase of 7,162. The other foreign born, totaling 148,508, had decreased 11,134 since 1890. Irish, British, and Canadians, in about equal proportions, made up 78,582 of the 148,508. The Poles, who were to be the third largest immigrant group within a decade, are not so easily counted, since Poland was divided among Germany, Russia, and Austria-Hungary. The 1895 state census counted 6,129 foreign born of Slavic ancestry. The federal census in 1900 counted 31,789, with 27,644 of them living in Milwaukee County and 2,750 in Portage County.

Another fact to remember when we speak of a spirit of toleration between the native born and the foreign born is the very real relationship between the two groups. We are no longer dealing with a majority of Yankees learning to put up with strangers. There were 1,686,880 Wisconsinites, according to the 1890 census. Of these, 519,200 were foreign born and another 726,835 the children of foreign-born parents. Only 434,650 had native-born parents. Fifty percent of the foreign born were Germans, and half of the native born were of foreign-born parentage. In 1850, one in eight residents of Wisconsin had been a German-born immigrant, which means that in 1890 a fair number of the 434,650 citizens of native-born parentage had German origins. This, rather than the impractical schemes of German intellectuals, was the reason for calling Wisconsin a German state. It was no such thing, for the Yankee stamp still was clear upon it. Even in Milwaukee, with its greater concentration of Germans than in the state as a whole, the German community as a cohesive and exclusive entity was fading by 1900. The city retained its foreign flavor but was unmistakably American.

Professor Bayrd Still remarked many evidences of the passing of the German community in Milwaukee as an ethnic island. The German-language press had nearly twice the circulation of the rival English-language dailies in 1884. By 1910, the proportions were more than reversed, with the German-language papers down to one to three in circulation. The social clubs, which had played such an important role in the German social, cultural, and political life, were losing their influence. Germans in the business community were identified in accordance with their economic or professional status rather than as Germans. The appeal of the Druids, Sons of Hermann, and other German lodges had waned, except for those who were late arrivals or who found their place only in the German community, a society of small shopkeepers and workingmen. There were fewer German musical, theatrical, and general cultural affairs every year. Things of a purely German identification were running low on new blood and meeting the active resistance of a generation of American born. The latter were critical of their fellows who were more fluent in German than in English and clung too firmly to things German.

Milwaukee isn't the best measure of acculturation and assimilation, for it is generally agreed that ethnic exclusiveness was more apt to persist in the enclaves of a large city, regularly receiving new recuits, or in a rural area settled by a closely knit group. Any Wisconsin resident today is probably aware of identifiable ethnic islands persisting in rural settings, small towns, and the city, to the delight of sociologists. But the tendency to modify or break them down was discernible even in the 1870s. Joseph Schafer, an indefatigable student of social change, worked from available land records and the manuscript censuses to reveal this process. For instance, the Germans moving into the Winnebago-Horicon Basin, displaced the more mobile Yankees, Irish, and British who preceded them. The town (township) of Burnett in Dodge County was almost solidly Yankee in 1850, 55 percent Yankee twenty years later, and nearly 75 percent of German birth or extraction by 1905. The number of farm families in the township had actually decreased from 168 in 1870 to 146 in 1905. Schafer concludes that "it is both interesting and significant to find a rural town with the social organization just described, which still thinks of itself as a Yankee community. This would be farcical were it not for its historical background. During many years, in the formative period, the Yankees were completely dominant, controlling the business of the town meetings, of the school districts, and maintaining the strongest, most popular churches. The Germans, who drifted in gradually, beginning in the middle 1840's, perforce learned English and their children, in many cases, as they emerged from the public schools or from the higher institutions of learning, were hardly to be distinguished from the children of Yankee settlers."

By contrast, other towns originally settled in large part by foreign born retained their German, Norwegian, or other ethnic identity over the years. Cities such as Fond du Lac, Oshkosh, and Beaver Dam present a fairly consistent picture. All three had large foreign-born populations as shown by the 1870 census, and these were often grouped by wards, although not usually as distinctly as in Milwaukee. The ethnic enclaves tended to lose their identity in the smaller cities by the end of the nineteenth century, although this generalization is subject to argument in specific cases. We simply do not know much about the mobility of individual families in these cities that seemed to be eminently stable in numbers of people. Fond du Lac, for instance, had 12,765 people in 1870 and 12,024 in 1890, but were they substantially the same people? We don't know.

As the Bennett Law controversy testifies, the dominant Yankee element placed great faith in the powers of Americanization of the Little Red Schoolhouse. This trust was not entirely misplaced. Atlhough Wisconsin has traditionally had a large parochial school enrollment, the *Wisconsin Blue Book* reports that only one-sixth of the children between seven and thirteen attending school in 1894 were enrolled in private or parochial schools as an alternative to public education. This indicates that many children from homes where a language other than English was regularly spoken were attending public school. Of course, public school did not always mean what it does today, for many schools in overwhelmingly German or Scandinavian districts were taught by, or overseen by, the pastor. In many Yankee communities, "public" schools were under the direction of local ministers and were equally sectarian in spirit.

Economic assimilation certainly preceded equality, in a social sense, for the immigrant. The Germans had the advantage of their large settlement in Milwaukee. Many German businessmen started modestly and grew with the city. As tradesmen and craftsmen, they benefited from a superior apprenticeship training in their homeland and a large market among their countrymen, who responded to ethnic advertising in the early years. Germans dominated several industries that grew rapidly: brewing, tanning, leatherworking, furniture manufacture, cigar making, and grocery wholesaling, to name a few. German medical and pharmaceutical education was highly regarded, as were German attainments in the arts.

While it is true that the recent immigrant was most likely to find his rung near the bottom of the economic ladder—including some immigrants with superior education in fields not in demand here—the established ethnic groups found the ladder scalable. A study of a number of villages of mixed ethnic character, in the period 1850–80, revealed that although native Americans were more likely to be the merchants, shop-keepers, and small manufacturers, foreign-born businessmen were far from a rarity. A perusal of the various gazetteers and business directories of the period will confirm this.

One can easily argue the divisive role that ethnic and religious differences have played in American politics, but the argument also works well in reverse. The balanced ticket was an early discovery of both major parties. The Republicans, laboring under the well-founded charge that they were heirs to the Whigs and nativists, were particularly apt students, as their state tickets will attest. It is interesting to see how nearly a representative body, such as the state assembly, mirrored the ethnic make up of the population. The Germans had only 4 members and the Irish 5 in the 1853 legislature. This reflects the frequent complaint that the Germans were slow to find the levers of American politics, while the Irish were particularly gifted. Twenty years later, the foreign born held 33 of the 100 seats—an accurate reflection of their numbers in the general population—with the Germans occupying 15 of those. The Irish born held only 6. The 6 Irishmen were all straight Democrats, while only 9 of the Germans clung to the traditional immigrant party. Of the remainder, only 1 had gone straight Republican, while the others were various brands of Greeleyites, Liberals, or Reformers. The point is that political parties adjusted to ethnic prejudices and diffused the largest bloc of immigrant votes, the Germans, well before social assimilation took place on a broad scale.

Just as the argument that political participation cut both ways—toward assimilation as well as ethnocentricity—one can argue that the immigrant press was an instrument of Americanization as well as ethnic separation. Students of the foreign language press observe that it was not, ordinarily, patterned on the press in the homeland, but was an amalgam of American press features and the familiar. It is easy to forget that a vital function of the immigrant press was to explain America, Americans, and American politics to citizens who could not read English. The perpetuation of a foreign language clientele and their immigrant culture may have been a vested interest of the paper, but it had to serve the other need to survive. Some editors readily accepted this responsibility, others were bent to it by necessity.

No one likes his world to be too complicated, and the Yankee was no exception. Well satisfied with himself, his unconcern with essential differences was a worthy match for the arrogance of the German intellectual who set the cultural tone of the German community in Milwaukee. It took the Yankees some time to draw the necessary distinctions between a Catholic from southern Germany, a Lutheran from the north, an anticlerical Forty-Eighter, and a socialist. While this was infuriating to the German-American, he liked even less being lumped with other foreigners. A typical comment was made by the anticleric Bernhard Domschke in response to the suggestion that the immigrant vote should combine in a third party to combat the Know-Nothings. It would destroy all German influence in politics by driving them "into a union with Irishmen, those American Croats," who were sunk in popery and barbarism, he wrote.

The lesson to be learned about the foreign born was that they presented considerable variety within each national group. The Germans, by far the largest group, were particularly fragmented. While they drew upon a common culture and literary language, they had little sense of unity until the era of Bismarck and the creation of a German state. Parochial in the extreme, German businessmen in Milwaukee were apt to know one another as "the Bavarian," "the Prussian," or "the Mecklenburger." They were further divided, and sharply so, into Catholics, Lutherans, lesser evangelical sects, and anticlerics. The last are generally identified with the Forty-Eighters, refugees from the unsuccessful revolution of 1848, although Milwaukee had a vigorous colony of freethinkers before these arrived. It was augmented again, after 1878, when Bismarck proscribed the Social Democrats, bringing socialists of various persuasions to the city. The anticlerics could claim a high proportion of the well educated who edited and wrote for the German-language press. Ambitious to take part in American politics after they gave up the notion of returning to a republican Germany, they kept one foot in the German community as intellectual arbiters, while many mastered English for the purpose of raising up the Yankees. The older, conservative, Democratic, Catholic and Lutheran Germans were called Grays, the anti-clerics Greens.

The Greens effected an alliance with the Republican Party in the middle 1850s. American nativists were pleased with the Greens for their vocal anti-Catholic stand, until it filtered through to them that these allies were denouncing all revealed religion. They were happier when they discovered that the Lutheran Church was evangelical in persuasion, and the Republicans began making inroads among the Lutheran Germans by the 1870s. Discovering shared prejudices must have been a powerful engine of acculturation. They held an abhorrence of Catholicism in common and could agree that the Irish were the worst of the lot.

The Irish were an important ethnic group in Wisconsin, not so much because of their numbers—they came early, but the Germans outnumbered them two and a half to one by 1860—but rather because of their influence in politics, the degree to which Irish nationalism became a part of the American heritage, and their identification with American Catholicism and its hierarchy. There were 50,000 in Wisconsin by 1860, but the percentage of Irish was declining. New Irish immigration fell off drastically, while German and Scandinavian continued at a high rate.

The Irish were, at least in most ways, a more homogeneous group than the Germans. They had more of a sense of nationality and were almost all Catholic, although Ireland exported a few radicals and anti-clerics. The early comers to Wisconsin were only a little more urban than the general population, even though many historians insist upon making a majority of them city dwellers. They did make up 14 percent of Milwaukee's population in 1850. By 1890, this was down to 1.7 percent— foreign-born Irish, that is—but they were still conspicuous as an ethnic group of political consequence.

Schafer found many Irish in Ozaukee and neighboring counties on the pioneer farms. About half of these early Irish had been in the States an average of seven years before coming to Wisconsin. In some ways, they fit the Yankee mold. They were highly mobile, took advantage of the public schools, and were prominent in politics and some of the professions.

When American nativism was at its height in the 1850s, the Germans and the Irish made common cause, but their reactions were different. Many Germans were confirmed in their separatism. The Irish, on the other hand, fought back belligerently and often effectively against being consigned to a second-class status in American society. Yankees identified Catholicism, which they considered a most pernicious foreign importation, with the Irish more than with the Germans, even though the Germans had a firm grip upon the Roman hierarchy in Wisconsin. But nationally it was leaders named Gibbon, Hughes, and Ireland who spoke for the Catholic Church in America.

Sharing a common religion with a part of the German community did not bring the Irish and the Germans together except in rivalry. They were estimated to be about equal in number as communicants in Wisconsin in the sixties, but the nineteenth-century archbishops of Milwaukee were Henni, Heiss, and Katzer. The running battle over appointments, down to the level of parish priests, was continuous. While Irish and German Catholics seldom strayed from the Democratic fold and could present a more or less united front to the Yankees, they had plenty of energy left over for each other. St. Patrick's Day and the German holidays in Milwaukee were often observed with fights that sometimes reached the proportions of riots. The Republicans were tempted to detach the alle-glance of one or the other group, making demagogic appeals to the Irish, particularly during the Fenian disturbances right after the Civil War. Chairman Edward Wall of the Democrats later bewailed his difficulties with both factions. The Irish demanded all of the patronage, in English, while the Germans sat back awaiting the opportunity to give him the knife for ignoring their claims.

The Norwegians, the third ethnic bloc of consequence, before the Poles began to muster large numbers in the nineties, outnumbered the Irish by the 1870s. As noted before, the Norwegians were happier arguing religion among themselves than discussing American politics. But they had a tradition of political freedom which was considerably more liberal than their theology, and they began to leave the immigrant's traditional allegiance to the Democratic Party in the latter 1850s, emerging as a block devoted to the Republican cause. A majority of them were farmers who shared in the agrarian discontent directed against the complacent Republicanism that characterized the years after 1865.

Wisconsin also became the home of immigrant Hollanders, Belgians, Danes, Swedes, Swiss, Austrians, Jews, and many others. The Yankees, who had their hands on the levers of power, took at their peril a simplistic view of these differences, as each group attained some measure of political sophistication. As close a student of politics as Robert La Follette made the error of trying to beat a Norwegian, James Davidson, with a Swede, Irving Lenroot, in his own primary. Ethnic politics generated a good deal of cynicism, but much mutual understanding as well.

Another instrument of acculturation was the common task for which the immigrant was invited to Wisconsin. It must be remembered that Wisconsin was the first state in the Old Northwest to establish an official agency to attract Europeans, beginning in 1852. The effort was abandoned for a few years, but taken up again in 1867 and continued beyond 1900. There was an appreciation that these people brought money, muscle, and skills which converted wild land to productive, tax-producing acres, and kept the labor market filled as industries expanded. Both Americans and Europeans came primarily for economic reasons, but the European soon learned that the Yankee liked to hear that they had come for religious freedom and political equality. The Yankees didn't realize how really chary they themselves were with these last two commodities.

Now we shall look at the pessimist's side of the process of Americanization. Remembering our comparison of the optimist's view with that of the pessimist, we will find that we sometimes are looking at the same influences, but in a different light.

The very fact that immigration continued in large numbers—the actual numbers of the foreign-born did not begin to decline until 1900—meant that there was a regular renewal of people who preferred the ethnic enclave, would never be comfortable in English, would give a new lease on life to the foreign-language press, and would abet the clergy and other conservative forces in resisting assimilation. That the older Scandinavian and German minorities continued to receive such a large share of the newcomers meant that these conservative influences were particularly strong with them.

Lutherans as well as Catholics have supported parochial school education for their children. The Catholics, wherever possible, ran a complete school program through the grades. In 1893, they claimed 279 schools throughout the state, with 44,669 pupils. The German Lutherans maintained a heavier commitment to parochial education than the Scandinavians. The Wisconsin Synod (German) maintained 149 schools with over 9,000 pupils in 1893, the Missouri Synod (German) 107 schools with 8,500 pupils and seven other synods, including the Scandinavians, another 63 schools with 2,464 pupils. The figures on the Lutheran schools are ambiguous because many of them were only weekend or summer schools. Maintenance of the parochial schools was a divisive issue within the Norwegian synods, with one faction supporting the public schools. The part-time church school was their answer, with an emphasis upon seminaries and institutions training teachers and ministers.

School laws in 1849 permitted instruction in foreign language, not through the influence of the foreign born, but probably because Yankee teachers were thinking in terms of the classical languages. Ethnic groups took advantage of this to offer instruction in their native languages in public schools where they were a majority. In 1852, however, a school law requiring instruction of traditional subjects in English was passed, and it was strengthened in 1867. The affected ethnic groups were able to force a change in 1869 which permitted instruction for one hour a day in a foreign language. All of this legislative maneuvering was accompanied by a certain acrimony which confirmed the discontent of the Protestant Germans and Scandinavians with the autocratic Yankees. The Catholics simply resorted to complete parochial instruction not subject to the law's regulation. Meanwhile, the best argument for instruction in English was, of course, the necessity of making one's way in an English-speaking society.

The greatest bar to integration of the new Americans was human nature and uninformed prejudice. This, of course, was a two-way street. Much has been written about German arrogance and resistance to Americanization, but it was largely a reaction to American nativism by those who identified themselves as Forty-Eighters. German-born intellectuals were contemptuous of Yankee attainments in literature, science, and the arts. Their view was spread through the German-language press. The achievement of German unity and Germany's emergence as a world power under Bismarck reinforced this pride. The Norwegians, on the other hand, suffered feelings of inferiority, coming from a backward agriculture and a low standard of living and seeing the Yankee as the replacement of the aristocratic and bureaucratic class that had been gladly left behind.

Nothing could match the superiority with which the native American viewed his foreign-born neighbors. This observation is reinforced again and again by statements of academic, religious, and secular leaders. A Wisconsin Baptist conclave in 1886 deplored that "thousands are here, without evangelical religion or even evangelical belief. They bring among us every form of error, and are industriously seeking the control of things, in this formative period of many of our communities. They furnish the soil for the growth of everything that is noxious. They introduce among us immense possibilities of peril. Statistics show that they supply a very large percent of the criminal and pauper classes. In our cities especially, the lowest and most vicious are found among the foreign born. . . . Here in Wisconsin, the Romish church is made strong and kept strong by immigration. Socialism receives all its power for its fiendish work from immigration."

Language and social customs were also great barriers to easy interchange. Yankee prejudice thrived on ignorance and ready generalizations: Germans turned the Sabbath into a beery holiday; Irishmen drank whiskey, had too many children, and owed loyalty only to the pope in Rome; Scandinavians worked their womenfolk in the fields like animals and lived rude lives. To know any of these beings as neighbors worthy of friendship was to know that they had risen above their inheritance, probably by fortunate contact with their betters.

The proposition that the Civil War eased ethnic frictions in Wisconsin has its limitations. At least seven of the state's regiments were based upon ethnic appeals to serve with men and under officers from one's own national group. Nor was the supposed comradeship of immigrants and native Americans "institutionalized in the Grand Army of the Republic." The GAR, started in Illinois and Wisconsin in 1866, was an organization of Yankee veterans which dwindled sadly after its organization. The passage of time and innumerable veterans' benefits and pensions by Congress expanded its constituency. Scandinavian veterans, in particular, enjoyed the benefits of their status, since they were identified with the Republican majority.

If the Yankee was learning to know his foreign-born neighbor better over the years, his enthusiasm for causes that required conformity to Yankee notions of morality did not abate. Temperance, which had been an embarrassment to the rising Republican party in the 1850s, revived with renewed force after the war. Supporters made no bones about who the enemy was. *The Christian Statesman* of Milwaukee regularly reported the skirmishes. The ladies of Ripon opened a campaign of prayers and singing in front of the saloons, while the crowd inside treated them to "sauerkraut" songs. If the birthplace of Republicanism could thus respond to the forces of righteousness how could they conquer Rome? The cities are the stronghold of the rum power, lamented *The Christian Statesman,* "so long as they hold in their hands the metropolis they occupy a vantage ground whence they pour floods of desolation upon every portion of the State." The temperance crusade was not all moral fervor but held strong overtones of nativism, of rural versus urban, of American Protestantism versus Catholicism.

The stronghold did not fall. But the passage of local option laws and local blue laws, directed against the German notion of Sunday as a day of relaxation with music, beer, games, and theater, could keep the smaller cities and villages sober and solemn. The argument that such measures infringed upon the personal freedom of others, advanced by the infuriated Germans and Irish, fell upon deaf ears. The most prominent of several temperance organizations that flourished particularly in the 1870s was the Good Templars. Like all of these organizations, it had a very unstable membership that varied during that decade from 8,000 to 20,000. It found its recruits in the smaller cities and villages. Natives of New York and New England were the bulk of its membership.

The Good Templars were not, as one would expect, primarily middle-aged women. There were usually more male than female members, and the young people between twenty and twenty-nine were the largest age group. The organization offered as much social appeal as moral uplift at a time when social occasions outside of one's church group were limited. It is interesting that in a day when the social club was such an important element in the lives of the German immigrants, the Yankees should find their social needs met in an organization devoted to substantially altering the immigrant's manner of living.

While deadly serious in intent, temperance agitation often seemed like simple meddlesomeness to those against whom it was directed. Members of the legislature could always be found who would introduce temperance legislation. One such bill, introduced in 1881 and known as the Anti-Treat Law, made it a misdemeanor subject to a $10 fine to stand anyone a treat in a bar or saloon. Members treated the bill as a joke but passed it, and it became law. The law was shortly repealed, but it stood as an example of the extent to which the Yankee would go to legislate the social behavior of other Americans. Yet assimilation went forward in a subtle way as the immigrants, in spite of cultural loyalties and angry rejection of Yankee impositions, tacitly accepted the values of American society. Immigrant Protestant churches gradually came to mirror the notions of Christian propriety held by the Yankees.

In the 1890 Assembly, when the Democrats unexpectedly overturned the normal Republican majority, there were 32 foreign-born members out of the membership of 100, very close to their proportion in the total population. Their biographies indicate that they were nearly interchangeable with their native-born colleagues. It is somewhat surprising that only one-fifth were Civil War veterans, although men from forty-five to fifty-five were the bulk of the veterans' age group. The proportion of veterans among the native- and foreign-born assemblymen was almost the same. Occupational groups also were nearly comparable: about 25 percent farmers in both groups, although Wisconsin's population was 65 percent rural. There were more lawyers in the native-born group, but more bankers in the foreign-born. Aside from the farmers, only 3 or 4 identifiable were men working with their hands, divided between the groups. Roughly twice as many, proportionately, of the native born listed education beyond common school. There may have been some problems of establishing equivalency here, although ten of the foreign born came to the United States before the age of ten and fully three-fourths of them before they were eighteen. The continental Europeans among them naturally came from countries with large identifiable ethnic groups. These groups tended to pick someone who had made it financially or professionally and who was in a transitional position between the two cultures. Fourteen of the foreign-born were from the British Isles or Canada, 10 were Germans, 6 Irish, 1 a Pole, and 1 a Dane.

In this discussion of native born and foreign born there has been no notice of the true natives. With few exceptions the Indians had, by choice, little part in the white society that surrounded them. On the reservation or off, they clung to what remained of their cultural values and style of life, seeking isolation from the meddlesome whites.

The Menominee Indians were probably the most fortunate. They had ceded all of their lands in Wisconsin preparatory to being moved westward, but were instead granted twelve townships within what had been their traditional range and which now comprise Menominee County. They were a more sedentary people than the Chippewa or Winnebago, depending on a combination of agriculture, hunting, and gathering nature's bounty, particularly the wild rice which is identified with their culture. The Stockbridge Indians, a New England tribe that came to Wisconsin in 1822, were given a reservation made up of two of the Menominee townships on the east. There were about 1,200 Menominee in 1885 and 300 Stockbridge. The Oneida, numbering about 1,500, occupied a reservation of 65,000 acres southwest of Green Bay. It was fair agricultural land, in the way of the acquisitive whites. Although they had adopted Christianity, the living style of the whites, and worked the land, they maintained a cultural and economic isolation.

After the Civil War, federal Indian policy was dictated largely by relations with the tribes farther west. The Dawes Severalty Act of 1887, which represented a rare agreement of sympathetic easterners and land-hungry westerners, was a culmination of this period of change in policy. Its inspiration was to break down tribal organization and force the Indians into white society, and it provided for breaking tribal lands into individual holdings. The result was that the Oneida and Stockbridge lost much of their land, after individual ownership became unrestricted. The Menominee, with a stronger tribal tradition, resisted the change and forced the government to fulfill many of its treaty obligations. Their relatively fortunate circumstances made them the model, in the 1950s, for yet another unhappy experiment in federal Indian policy.

There were some 1,200 Chippewa left in Wisconsin in 1885, most of them on four scattered small reservations across northern Wisconsin. Their isolation strengthened their attachment to traditional ways. A hunting and fishing people, they were able to move about quite freely. With the Winnebago, they were a familiar part of the pioneer setting on the upper Wisconsin, the upper Black, and west of there. They respected one another's ranges, but intermingled in some areas. Some Potawatomi and others were included in the democracy of free souls that had superseded tribal organization.

The Winnebago, authentic Wisconsin natives, suffered indignities that won them a chapter in Helen Hunt Jackson's *A Century of Dishonor,* published in 1881, a book that did much to focus popular attention on the plight of the nation's dwindling Indian population. Repeatedly removed to various reservations west of the Mississippi, the Winnebago persistently returned. They followed game and the berry harvests in the central sand counties and northward, occasionally working as farm harvest hands, but mostly just being themselves in a life style that affronted many whites, when they chanced to notice these carefree, itinerant neighbors. It was possible to generate a local Indian scare still in the seventies and eighties.

The Wisconsin legislature petitioned Congress to round up the Winnebago strays yet another time. This was done in 1873, using the military to collect them at points along the railroad and ship them to their reservation, which by this time was located in Nebraska. It did not take long for most to return to the accustomed haunts where they were free of the restrictions of reservation life and whites determined to improve their characters. It was a precarious existence, but the free choice among the unattractive alternatives left to them. Their persistence was rewarded with forty-acre homesteads, which most of them selected on poor land chosen with hunting and gathering in mind. They were less than indifferent farmers. The Winnebago seldom lacked a vocal minority of sympathetic champions among their white neighbors. One who knew them well commented that they were good company. And they were ahead of their time in their recognition of the recreational possibilities of Wisconsin's north country, to which they maintained an exemplary devotion.

Except for the Indians, it can be argued that the Wisconsin of 1850 was more homogeneous than that of 1890. There was a rough democracy in pioneer agriculture which was shared by a greater proportion of the population, both native and foreign born, in the fifties. There were certainly important gradations in terms of economic circumstance, access to credit, knowledge of opportunities, and political know-how, but the 1850s pioneers were working for themselves, sharing both hardships and a vision of the future. Industrial America had caught up with them before 1890. A self-conscious industrial proletariat seemed to be finding its identity. Native Americans equated this new phenomenon with the European immigrants. The old frictions over religious and cultural differences continued to exist, along with new fears of a growing class that seemed not to share the American vision of the future.

Selected Bibliography

Ander, Fritiof O., ed. *The Trek of the Immigrants: Essays Presented to Carl Wittke*. Rock Island, Ill., 1964. Some interesting ideas.

Babcock, Kendrick C. *The Scandinavian Element in the United States*. 1914. Reprint. New York, 1969. Still best on Norwegians in politics.

Barry, Colman J. *The Catholic Church and German Americans*. Catholic University of America Studies, vol. 40. Washington, 1953. Narrower than the title implies.

Blegen, Theodore C. *Norwegian Migration to America: The American Transition*. Northfield, Minn., 1940. On becoming Americans.

———. *Grass Roots History*. Minneapolis, 1947. History and literature from immigrant chests.

Blied, Benjamin J. *The Catholic Story of Wisconsin*. Milwaukee, 1948. "The roaming Yankees who speculated on every frontier were adamant Protestants."

Coleman, Peter J. "Restless Grant County: Americans On the Move." *Wisconsin Magazine of History* 46:16–20 (Autumn 1962). The population was stable only in numbers.

Cooper, Berenice. "Die Freien Gemeinden in Wisconsin." Wisconsin Academy of Sciences, Arts and Letters, *Transactions* 53:53–66 (1964). Mostly on the Sauk City congregation.

Erickson, Charlotte. *American Industry and the European Immigrant, 1860–1885.* Cambridge, Mass., 1957. Steamship companies, rather than industry, did most of the recruiting.

Gilsdorf, Gordon. *Wisconsin's Catholic Heritage.* Madison, 1948. A short, pious account, with some interesting statistics.

Haugen, Einar. "Norwegian Migration to America." *Norwegian-American Studies and Records* 18:1–23 (1954).

———. "Wisconsin Pioneers in Scandinavian Studies: Anderson and Olson, 1875–1931." *Wisconsin Magazine of History* 34:28–39 (Autumn 1950). Haugen succeeded them at the University of Wisconsin.

Hawgood, John A. *The Tragedy of German America.* New York, 1940. Study in cultural separatism.

Holmes, Fred L. *Old World Wisconsin: Around Europe in the Badger State.* Eau Claire, 1944. Ethnic jollification.

Holzman, Hanni M. "The German Forty-eighters and the Socialists in Milwaukee: A Social-Psychological Study of Assimilation." Master's thesis, University of Wisconsin, 1948. She conducted some interesting interviews.

Jarstad, Anton. "The Melting Pot in Northeastern Wisconsin." *Wisconsin Magazine of History* 26:426–32 (June 1943). A quick review of ethnic settlements.

Kaiser, Norman J. "A History of the German Theater of Milwaukee from 1850–1890." Master's thesis, University of Wisconsin, 1954. A persistent culture.

Kinzer, Donald. *An Episode in Anti-Catholicism: The American Protective Association.* Seattle, 1964. Wisconsin was supposed to have the largest APA membership.

Knaplund, Paul. "Rasmus B. Anderson, Pioneer and Crusader." *Norwegian-American Studies and Records* 18:23–43 (1954). Founder of Scandinavian studies at the university.

Korman, Gerd. *Industrialization, Immigrants and Americanizers: The View from Milwaukee, 1866–1921.* Madison, 1967. The immigrant "peck order."

Lang, Edward M., Jr. "The Common Man in Janesville, Wisconsin, 1870 to 1900." Master's thesis, University of Wisconsin, 1968. A study of status mobility.

Larson, Laurence M. *The Log Book of a Young Immigrant.* Northfield, Minn., 1939. Life in the immigrant Norwegian communities.

Laugesen, Peter N. "The Immigrants of Madison, Wisconsin, 1860–1890." Master's thesis, University of Wisconsin, 1966. Goodwill and animosity nicely juxtaposed.

Lucas, Henry S. *Netherlanders in America: Dutch Immigration to the United States and Canada, 1789–1950*. Ann Arbor, 1955. Has a chapter on Wisconsin.

McDonald, Sister M. J. *History of the Irish in Wisconsin*. Washington, D.C., 1954. Good on the Irish in politics.

———. "The Irish of the North Country." *Wisconsin Magazine of History* 40:126–32 (Winter 1956–57). Lumbermen and farmers.

Meloni, Alberto C. "Italy Invades the Bloody Third: The Early History of Milwaukee's Italians." The Milwaukee County Historical Society, *Historical Messenger* 25:34–45 (March 1969). Displacing the Irish.

Mulder, Arnold. *Americans from Holland*. Philadelphia, 1947. Chapters on Wisconsin.

Schereck, William J. *The Peoples of Wisconsin: Scripts of the Ethnic History Radio Series "Sounds of Heritage,"* Mimeographed. Madison, 1956. Who came where and why.

Stampen, Jacob Ola. "The Norwegian Element of Madison, Wisconsin, 1850–1900: A Study in Ethnic Assimilation." Master's thesis, University of Wisconsin, 1965. Used Norwegian newspapers.

Suelflow, Roy A. *Walking with Wise Men: A History of the South Wisconsin District of the Lutheran Church—Missouri Synod*. Milwaukee, 1967.

———. *A Plan for Survival*. New York, 1965. Includes the Scandinavian Lutherans and the Lutheran problems with English.

Swichkow, Louis J., and Lloyd P. Gartner. *A History of the Jews of Milwaukee*. Philadelphia, 1963. Candid, traditional in treatment.

Weisensel, Peter R. "The Wisconsin Temperance Crusade to 1919." Master's thesis, University of Wisconsin, 1965. More rural vs. urban than sectarian.

Wittke, Carl. *The German-Language Press in America*. Lexington, Ky., 1957. Wisconsin had seventy German-language papers current at one time.

———. *Refugees of Revolution: The German Forty-eighters in America*. Philadelphia, 1952. An important role in Milwaukee education and intellectual life.

———. *The Utopian Communist: Biography of Wilhelm Weitling, Nineteenth-Century Reformer*. Baton Rouge, 1950. Weitling settled in Milwaukee.

Zucker, A. E., ed. *The Forty-Eighters: Political Refugees of the German Revolution of 1848*. New York, 1950. Uneven collection of essays.

POLITICS
OF COMPLACENCY

23

Early in his struggles to take over control of the Republican party in Wisconsin, Robert M. La Follette developed, for a formal speech at the University of Chicago in 1897, an address called "The Menace of the Machine." It became a familiar refrain for the state's voters. La Follette was an accomplished orator who could command substantial fees on the Chautauqua circuit, even with his political speeches, and was indefatigable in seeking engagements, without fee, for appearances in Wisconsin. Reform was in the air. La Follette succeeded in identifying the popular mood with his political career.

A few years later, when La Follette had won the governorship but not yet the political war, he had the opportunity to filter "The Menace of the Machine" through probably the best known of the popular political muckraking journalists of the day, Lincoln Steffens. Steffens' description fixed upon Wisconsin politics, in the post-Civil War years, the image of a boss-ridden fief of the railroads and lumber barons. This it was, to a large degree, but simplification was the stock in trade of both La Follette and Steffens:

> During the two terms of District Attorney La Follette, important changes were occurring in the Wisconsin state system beyond his ken. Boss Keyes was deposed and Philetus Sawyer became the head of the state. This does not mean that Sawyer was elected Governor; we have

nothing to do with governors yet. Sawyer was a United States Senator. While Keyes was boss, the head of the state was in the post-office at Madison, and it represented, not the people, but the big business interests of the state, principally lumber and the railways, which worked well together and with Keyes. There were several scandals during this "good fellow's" long reign, but big business had no complaint to make against him. The big graft in the Northwestern state, however, was lumber, and the typical way of getting hold of it wholesale, was for the United States to make to the states grants which the state passed on to railway companies to help "develop the resources of the state." . . . This was business, and while it was necessary to "take care" of the legislature, the original source of business was the Congress, and that was the place for the head of the system. Keyes had wished to go to the Senate, but Sawyer thought he might as well go himself. . . .

It all looked very simple and straightforward. The Republicans dominated state politics, holding the governorship and usually a legislative majority in all but six years between 1855 and 1900, and therefore could dispose of things as they wished. The boss controlled the party machinery, with patronage, funds, and passes from the lumbermen and railroads, and therefore what they wished was how things were disposed. But it was never that simple. Although the machinery of party selection of candidates favored the political professionals, and it was an age when professionalism counted for more in politics than did issues, the basic problems of politics were pretty much the same as they are today: finding nominees who could attract the voters, and finding the money and talent to carry off a successful campaign.

Much has been made of the unwavering loyalty to party of the average voter in this period, but it was certainly the heyday of the third party, in Wisconsin as elsewhere in the Midwest. Between 1865 and 1890, a Republican gubernatorial candidate won more than 54 percent of the vote in only one election. The margin of Republican victory ran only from 50.2 percent to 53 percent in eight of the thirteen elections from 1865 to 1890, and in 1873 and 1890 the Republican vote fell to 45 percent. The statewide percentages give an impression of great stability, although close enough to keep any party boss up late on election night, but the county by county totals give an impression of greater swings. Populous Milwaukee County gave the Republican gubernatorial candidate 26 percent of its vote in 1867, 21 percent in 1873, 58 percent in 1879, 59 percent in 1886, and 43 percent in 1890. Dane County voted Republican in only eight of the thirteen state elections from 1865 to 1890, although the percentages represented modest swings.

Ethnic and religious divisions, reinforced by Civil War issues, may well have been the principal determinants of voting behavior from 1865 to 1896. The immigrant vote in Wisconsin was reasonably constant in these terms, but the large Protestant German vote, very generally distributed and difficult to pinpoint, swung invitingly loose at times.

Immigrant voting was decided partly by national party issues, but mostly by the issues formed immediately in Wisconsin where their American political experience began: liquor control legislation, Sunday blue laws, party recognition of their national group, or nativist slights against their religious or ethnic identification. As for the Yankee vote, it should be remembered that slogans involving the bloody shirt—"vote the way you shot"—were more exhortations than accurate descriptions of voting behavior.

It is true that Wisconsin politicians exhibited a certain cynicism about their calling. After the chastening loss the Republicans suffered at the hands of a Reform-Democratic ticket in 1873, Horace Rublee, cosily ensconced in Bern, Switzerland as American minister, wrote to Elisha Keyes, his successor as state Republican chairman, that he trusted Keyes now had the Republican troops so well drilled that none would be "more hard-fisted, horny-handed, and agricultural-looking than they [the Grangers] and that they will leave a trail of hay seed behind them wherever they go. . . . No lobby influences allowed about the legislature. Rigid economy in all directions in the Government. Corruption withered at its sources. The railroad barons shorn of their power. . . . Virtue everywhere triumphant or about to triumph! How do you, my unregenerate friend, find the world and existence therein in the presence of these great innovations?" Rublee, sometime editor of the *Wisconsin State Journal* and *Milwaukee Sentinel,* was mildly a reformer in politics, but was complacent about any shocks he sustained from a close acquaintance with the realities. His facetious statement reminds us of the political realities with which we live today.

Rublee's letter also reminds us that even Republican bosses in nineteenth-century Wisconsin were less than omnipotent. Elisha Keyes, long past the zenith of his power when La Follette invested him with fearsome political strength for dramatic effect, was something of a paper tiger at his best. As a perennial candidate for minor offices in Dane County, Keyes was a frequent loser. But politics fascinated him and he preferred it to plowing. He finally hit pay dirt by attaching himself to the fortunes of Governor Alex Randall, who became assistant postmaster general under Lincoln, and later President Andrew Johnson's postmaster general. Gaining appointment as postmaster of Madison, Keyes made himself useful to Randall and to Senators Timothy Howe and James R. Doolittle by organizing the post offices in the Second Congressional District, which he controlled as patronage chief, so that all postal employees paid off on call for political campaigns.

The other main source of money and favors used in campaigning came from the railroads. This was normal, since railroads represented the largest aggregations of capital in their day, and Congress and the state legislature controlled land subsidies, the acceptance of mileage against grants already made, the bridging of rivers, innumerable legislative necessities that arose, and protection against hostile legislation. Keyes, now known as part of the "Madison Regency," joined with Senator Howe's nephew in tending the flow of railroad passes and other considerations for the Chicago and Northwestern Railroad.

Keyes loved the intrigue of politics, and he could not wait to test his new-found power. He did so by attempting to "scoop"—scoop out of office—the secretary of state, Louis P. Harvey. Harvey replied by organizing the Union ticket in Wisconsin, which was to be the ticket Lincoln would run on in 1864. Harvey emerged as the successful nominee for governor on the combined Union and Republican tickets. Senator Howe endeavored to instruct Keyes. "Learn to guide and gratify public opinion," he wrote, "not oppose it." Keyes was not an apt pupil.

As the term Madison Regency or Ring implies, there were always other factions in the field contending for party control. Factions shifted from election to election, however, and the terms applied to them usually invested them with more constancy than was warranted. These often centered in Madison or Milwaukee. Federal and state patronage flowed from Madison, the capital, while Milwaukee was the main locus of economic power.

Alexander Mitchell, who financed and usually controlled the minority Democratic party from its center of voting power in Milwaukee, was quick to appreciate the political appeal of a new element in state politics, the veterans. Irritated by the advantages accruing to the Chicago and Northwestern by its ties with the Madison Regency, Mitchell supported General Lucius Fairchild for the Republican nomination to the governorship in 1865. Mitchell even deserted, publicly, his Democratic allegiance, ostensibly over Andrew Johnson's emerging reconstruction policies. But Fairchild was a timid politician and had pledged to the rival Regency and the congressional delegation that they would continue to control the state patronage. The popular general, with his empty sleeve conspicuously pinned across his breast, proved a satisfying vote getter. His alliances successfully stood off the challenge for the nomination from another general, C. C. Washburn, who was an avowed anti-Regency candidate.

Keyes, still in training as a power in the party, was meanwhile treading eggs. Johnson's reconstruction policies brought a split in the party at the national level, and the Republican Radicals rose to challenge the president. The split was particularly excruciating for Keyes; his principal patrons were Senator Doolittle and Postmaster General Randall, both of whom had returned to the Democratic fold and supported Johnson. But the main body of Wisconsin Republicans went with the Radicals, including another patron, Senator Howe. It has been suggested that Wisconsin Radicalism was strongly influenced by promises of support for the Fox-Wisconsin Waterway and other internal improvements from the pork barrel, but the litmus test of Radical Republican loyalty was applied rigorously. Keyes, in order to protect his postmastership, supported Doolittle, whom the legislature had commanded to resign for his apostasy. At the same time, Keyes levied tribute on his postal troops for the Radicals, trembling for his head all the while. He lasted the course, until 1868, when he broke into the clear again to support Grant. His greatest stroke was to get an early seat on the bandwagon of Matthew Carpenter, who won Doolittle's seat in the Senate in 1869.

Carpenter was a nonpareil who proved that any prospective boss had better be looking down the road for the man who is going to command his loyalty. As Carpenter's biographer described him, "he was not a veteran of either the antislavery crusade or the battlefield. He had no experience as a legislator, did not at first have the backing of a political machine, and had joined the victorious Republicans under circumstances suggestive of the opportunism of a camp follower. He owed his triumph over flagwaving heroes, original abolitionists, and veteran wheel horses of the Republican Party to 'his brilliant talents, his magnetic qualities as an orator, his reputation as a profound constitutional lawyer, and his earnest Radicalism.' "

Political legends have a way of growing. La Follette succeeded in inflating Elisha Keyes to awesome proportions. Witness the description, from the same biography, of Carpenter's portentous meeting with the great party boss. When Carpenter asserted his ambitions and prospects, "Keyes was perhaps the most astute political manager in Wisconsin's history. As chairman of the state central committee and head of the 'Madison Regency,' he generously distributed the federal patronage, made and unmade governors and senators, and controlled the party machinery with the iron hand of a 'Bismarck.' That a candidate [Carpenter] should have achieved such support without the aid of the organization dumbfounded him. 'Spontaneous uprising of the people, for the purpose of rebuking politicians,' Carpenter explained. 'If that is true,' Keyes replied, 'you can be elected.' " The response scarcely fits the descriptions as either astute or Bismarckian!

Succeeding Rublee as Republican State Chairman in 1869, Keyes added to his record for political omniscience by telling Governor Lucius Fairchild that David Atwood, publisher of the *Wisconsin State Journal,* was the Regency's candidate to succeed Fairchild, therefore Lucius should not give thought to an unprecedented third term. Fairchild, who had been devoutly hoping for a diplomatic appointment from President Grant or a chance at the senatorial seat now claimed by Carpenter, saw that a third term as governor was his only alternative to political oblivion. He recognized a new power on the horizon when he saw one and made an alliance with Congressman Philetus Sawyer of Oshkosh. Sawyer's stock in trade in his Fifth Congressional District was the Fox-Wisconsin Waterway. Fairchild made internal improvements his battle cry. With Sawyer's help, which was not inconsiderable, Fairchild defied Keyes and returned to the governor's chair for his third term.

If anyone was keeping score on the political successes enjoyed by Keyes, it should have been apparent that his average was pretty low. But he continued to wield power and tend to the distribution of the loaves and fishes under the protection of Senators Howe and Carpenter. Keyes was domineering, brusque in his manner, and assertive of his rights to command the patronage and favors which the party had to deliver. Politicians, more than most species, are respectful toward a man who announces that he has power. "Now if you don't like this letter shove it into the stove. I don't like you very well for reason that I conclude you reciprocate the sentiment," wrote Keyes to an associate. This could be unnerving to a fellow politician of a less assertive nature.

After his humiliation at the hands of Governor Fairchild, "Boss" Keyes moved on confidently to fresh disasters. C. C. Washburn, congressman from La Crosse, was an inveterate foe of the Madison Regency. A man of property, he is best known for his association with the milling interests at Minneapolis. Washburn was seized with political ambition whenever something more attractive than member of the House became available. He had contested the senatorial seat with Carpenter and made Senator Howe nervous. Howe, Carpenter, and Sawyer, the powers in the congressional delegation, passed the word down to Keyes and others in Madison that Washburn was to have the governorship in 1871. As a *quid pro quo,* Washburn promised never to contest the seats of Senators Howe and Carpenter. He sealed the promise in a letter to Jeremiah Rusk. Keyes was faced with the unpleasant task of marshalling the Republican armies to deliver on the promise. The "boss" had his orders and delivered.

The gubernatorial race two years later in 1873 was a debacle. Governor Washburn had recommended and signed a stringent liquor control bill, known as the Graham Law, which drove the Protestant Germans back into the Democratic fold, from which they had been straying to the Republicans. Mitchell had consolidated his railroad empire and now was making it pay off by charging what the traffic would bear. Farmers associated in the newly organized Patrons of Husbandry, popularly known as the Grange, were using the organization as a rallying point to oppose the railroads. A strange alliance of Grangers, Democrats, Liberal Republicans who had bolted from the party to support Horace Greeley against President Grant in 1872, Germans unhappy with the Graham Law, Alexander Mitchell, who was angry with Governor Washburn over a veto of a railroad bridge measure, and a new Reform party organized in Milwaukee, made up of disaffected from both major parties and financed generously by the brewers and liquor interests, all combined to sweep the surprised Republicans from the state house.

The next test of Keyes as boss would come when Senator Carpenter's term ran out in 1875. United States senators were elected by the state legislature, with each member of both houses having a vote. Senatorial politics, therefore, involved getting a party majority in the legislature. Senatorial candidates and their friends lobbied individual legislators or, more effectively, aided in the nomination and election of legislators pledged to the senatorial candidate.

The legislative nomination process was carried on at county conventions made up of delegates chosen in precinct and ward caucuses. The machinery of politics and nominations was usually in the hands of the party officeholders—those with a stake in the system. The interest of most of the local faithful was in the county courthouse. They normally were pleased and flattered to have politicians operating at the state or congressional level soliciting their support. The latter controlled more substantial patronage, railroad passes, hospitality at state conventions, and other attractions. Many deals were made involving support of a senatorial candidate in exchange for assistance in attaining a minor county office. The boss system reached down to the local level in a system of hierarchies. Nils Haugen tells how the leading political figure in his home town, River Falls, approached him one day in 1878 with the remark, "Haugen, we are going to nominate you for the assembly." It was plain that the decision had been made in an informal caucus of a few local politicians who could announce, in complete confidence of the outcome, that the county convention would ratify their decision. Haugen was nominated and elected, which started him on a political career.

Thus the senatorial incumbent, in control of much federal patronage and the prestige of his office, had a great advantage in the race. But Matt Carpenter had become a controversial figure. A man of great ability, he had established himself as a leader among the supporters of President Grant in the Senate at a time when the Senate was the dominant force in national politics. Matt enjoyed the good things of life with open gusto and defended the ripe scandals of the Senate and the Grant Administration with too much candor.

The Republicans returned a narrow legislative majority in the election of 1874,* but the brief voter flirtation with reform had upset many long-standing Republican arrangements. Republican legislators were nervous about embracing the cause of a man who had loudly defended the infamous Salary Grab and scoffed at the Credit Mobilier scandal. To his credit, Keyes went down with the ship—an act which was not instinctive with him. A resolute band of Republican legislators refused to caucus with the party regulars and held out against Matt's skilled blandishments and the peremptory demands of Keyes. The large Reform-Democratic minority finally joined the holdouts in a vote for a Republican long shot who was innocuous enough to be acceptable to the Democrats. This was how Angus Cameron, a railroad attorney from La Crosse, became a United States senator, to his considerable surprise. The important contest had been between Carpenter and C. C. Washburn, but the Democrats were not foolish enough to advance the fortunes of a Republican as prominent as Washburn.

Keyes's conspicuous record of failure, in everything except terrorizing the federal employees whose jobs hung by the thread of patronage, resulted in expressions of dissatisfaction. C. C. Washburn had no use for Keyes and the Madison cabal. He approached excongressman Philetus Sawyer with his complaints, for Sawyer was close to Senator Timothy Howe, a long-time patron of Keyes. The loss of the other senatorship to an outsider rankled Sawyer. He had favored Washburn. Despite the pleas of Howe—a political mariner who loved smooth water—to overlook Keyes's failures, Washburn and Sawyer demanded that Howe join them in dumping Keyes.

It was at this point that Boss Keyes showed this powerful coalition "where the bear sat in the buckwheat." In a hard convention fight, he

---

* State elections were held annually, in November, until 1884, when gubernatorial elections were changed from the odd years to the even. Before this, assemblymen were elected annually.

called in all of his political IOU's and won reelection as state chairman, in the face of Sawyer's challenge, by a vote of 172 to 40. It was this performance, probably, which won Keyes his inflated image of unchallengeable boss. It must be remembered that it was the political small-change of the party, those holding or aspiring to federal or state patronage, and bosses operating at the county and local level, who made up the membership of the convention. These men, understandably, looked upon Keyes as more immediately concerned with their destinies. Keyes evidently won some of them to his cause with the argument that he had often been rougher than his naturally kind heart willed because he had been forced to it by the tyranny of Senator Howe.

The Republicans backed a winner for governor in 1875. As so frequently happens, the Reform-Democratic coalition that had won in 1873 began to come apart, and Governor Taylor pleased few of them. The Republicans knew that a portion of the Protestant German vote was essential to Republican victory. They also recognized that the liquor control measure, the Graham Law, was the principal Republican error that had driven the Germans back into the arms of the Democratic party. The problem was to find a Republican who was untainted with nativism or temperance tendencies.

There was such a paragon ready at hand. Harrison Ludington, the Republican mayor of Milwaukee, had ingratiated himself with the German vote by refusing to enforce the Graham Law in the city. Ludington was a pioneer Milwaukee merchant who had made a fortune in the lumber business. His qualifications as a popular candidate were attested by the fact that he had won the office of mayor in heavily Democratic Milwaukee. Governor Taylor was having his political troubles, but not to a degree that could apparently beat him in 1875. The upshot of this was that there was no rush of candidates for the Republican nomination. Ludington was the enthusiastic selection of Sawyer and Senator Howe. Keyes had no candidate of his own and so accommodated himself to Ludington, who developed into a popular candidate. Ludington made no speeches, campaigning by visiting county fairs. The election was close, but he won by a few hundred votes. The Reform-Democratic coalition retained the other state offices.

Keyes went to the Republican national convention of 1876 pledged to the support of James G. Blaine, but Blaine failed to win the nomination and Rutherford B. Hayes became president. One of the new president's first official acts was an order forbidding federal office holders to take part in political management. Hayes was a civil service reformer and meant what he said. Keyes thought it prudent to offer his resignation as state chairman, for the Madison postmastership was his livelihood. His offer was accepted by the central committee with unbecoming alacrity. Horace Rublee returned to the post. But Keyes was not put out of the running by this action. He had a wide acquaintance and had been a source of favors, patronage, and railroad passes for a good many years.

Timothy Howe came up, in 1879, for his fourth term in the U.S. Senate. Howe was a colorless, indecisive man who thought himself a statesman and monetary expert. He was neither, but his eighteen years in office seemed sufficient to other ambitious men in the party. The hopeful candidates and their lobbies set up headquarters in the Park Hotel in Madison for what was to be a long siege. It required ninety ballots before a senator was elected. This process naturally took a great deal of legislative time, but many people professed to see this as an advantage; it kept the legislature out of other mischief.

C. C. Washburn, who was not a candidate, devoutly desired to scotch Keyes and the Madison Regency. He considered urging Sawyer to run, but rejected this course. Sawyer was barely literate and a figure of great fun to the opposition press. It was alleged that he signed his name P. Sawyer because he never mastered the spelling of Philetus. Sawyer was, nevertheless, in the field of four serious candidates. The others were Howe, the incumbent, Carpenter, who had lost out in 1875, and Keyes. Keyes showed his strength by leading in the early balloting, but after a long deadlock withdrew in favor of Carpenter, who won. He relied upon Carpenter to support him for Angus Cameron's Senate seat which would be up in 1881.

Sawyer acted like a man with no interest in returning to Washington after his unsuccessful try for the Senate in 1879. He had refused to run again for congressman in 1874, after ten years in the house, because his business demanded his attention. With characteristic candor he had written to Washburn, "I have kissed a-s enough for the privlage of doing peoples Chores and I have got *through*." Maybe it was the simple elegance of this statement that deterred Washburn from urging Sawyer to run for the Senate in 1879. Now, in 1881, with Cameron's seat up, Sawyer was resisting the blandishments of his political friends that he seek the senatorship. Certainly one persuasive argument, which must have helped to turn him about, was the knowledge that Keyes would probably be the strongest contender for the seat. Sawyer was not a vindictive man, but he was competitive and Keyes had beaten him within the party on a couple of occasions.

Sawyer had many of the attributes that Keyes found useful in political warfare: a bluff persuasiveness, a zest for the game, and a detailed knowledge of the levers of power at every level within the party. In addition, Sawyer possessed a kindlier nature than Keyes, which saved him from alienating men by bulldozing tactics. More to the point, Sawyer had a fortune of several million dollars, a son who was competent to look out for his lumber business, and a large interest in both a railroad and timber business which, in turn, had considerable stakes in politics at both the national and state levels. He did not hestitate to throw bread upon the waters. Steffens told of a possibly apocryphal conversation between Sawyer and Isaac Stephenson, a Marinette lumber millionaire who also had a congressional career: "Isaac," said Sawyer, "how much did you put in to get the legislature for Spooner that time?" "It cost me about twenty-two thousand, Philetus. How much did you put in?" "Why," said Sawyer, surprised, "it cost me thirty thousand. I thought it cost you thirty." "No, it cost me thirty to get it for you when you ran."

Added to his business successes, which enabled Sawyer to approach and persuade businessmen in a manner not open to Keyes, he had been ten years in Congress where he had learned all about patronage and political power. He had done favors, was a master logroller in getting federal appropriations for his district, and knew how to keep this memory green. Keyes and his supporters reacted instinctively to the new element that Sawyer was introducing among those with whom politics was a full-time profession or a profitable avocation. The word came from everywhere. "That old tub of guts Sawyer should know that money could not run the people of Wisconsin yet," wrote one. "The old man was 'buying up' all he could," reported another. Keyes got all manner of advice on catching Sawyer buying votes. It was said he would "have the office if it cost him $100,000." Apparently the unspoken rules of the game did not allow the distribution of one's own money.

Sawyer swept up the senatorial pot on the first informal caucus ballot. Keyes was relegated to the status of a local satrap. He continued to wield some power in Dane and adjacent counties in his usual peremptory manner, as experienced by the young Bob La Follette. Thirty years later, recalling his earlier struggles in something less than tranquility, La Follette simply invested Keyes with more actual power and malign influence than the Boss had ever wielded. After 1881, Keyes accepted his new role and approached Sawyer as a supplicant. He wanted the postmaster generalship in Garfield's cabinet, for Wisconsin is supposed to have played a crucial role in breaking the 1880 convention deadlock in favor of the dark horse from Ohio. But Sawyer had no reason to bestow any blessing upon Keyes. To compound the troubles of the deposed boss, Matt Carpenter died in January 1881, and Angus Cameron, who had just lost his senatorial seat to Sawyer, was selected to fill the unexpired term. Cameron had no reason, either, to be kindly disposed toward Keyes.

Sawyer's succession to power was a confirmation of the direction politics was taking in the period. Keyes represented the old style political figure who operated as a broker for those who wanted things done and would pay for the use of the machinery. Keyes was identified with the Chicago and Northwestern Railroad, but only as a political paymaster. Sawyer, on the other hand, had a large interest in the Chicago, St. Paul, Minneapolis and Omaha, known commonly as the Omaha, of which he was vice president. The C&NW and the Omaha were allied. As a director of Alexander Mitchell's bank, he was also on friendly terms with the management of the Milwaukee Road. Sawyer made more of his fortune from timber lands than from lumber operations, and his railroad connections were particularly valuable in this regard. Dumping Keyes to take over the direction of the Republican party in Wisconsin himself was in many ways simply good business. Sawyer was achieving a degree of integration in his operations by eliminating the political middleman.

Another rival force in politics with which Sawyer had to deal was the Grand Army of the Republic. The GAR had been an instrument to uphold the Radical Republican cause as well as the patronage interests of the Union veterans. With the election of Grant, the Radical cause required less strenuous support. Patronage and pension claims became the centers of attention.

Governor Fairchild was the most successful practitioner of veterans' politics on the Wisconsin political scene. Mustered out as a brigadier after losing an arm at Gettysburg, he parlayed this into a draft for the office of secretary of state in 1863 and governor in 1865 at the age of thirty-two. After three terms, Fairchild again had no place to go politically in Wisconsin. He gave Timothy Howe some nervous moments, but Howe's Senate seat was not up until 1873, and Fairchild was at liberty early in 1872. He yearned after the ease of a prestigious diplomatic appointment, while friends urged him to hold out for the cabinet and a possible chance at the presidency. Such is the heady wine of politics. Supporters talked to him about going to St. Petersburg as minister to Russia. Secretary of State Fish offered him the consulship at Liverpool. This wasn't St. Petersburg, but it was a lucrative post, for the consul collected various fees in a commercial port. He accepted it and was abroad in a variety of posts for ten years, until 1882, ending up in Madrid as minister.

Senator Sawyer, who had not been in military service, soon found the combination which assured him the sympathetic support of veterans and their organizations, without being a professional veteran himself. In the first place, the woods were full of ex-soldiers who were happy to settle for less spectacular political careers than Fairchild's and were happy to have Sawyer's support. The senator found a broader avenue to veterans' support through his official duties. Before long, his talents won for him a respected place in that exclusive club, the United States Senate. Unlettered and uncouth he may have been, but no one ever accused Philetus Sawyer of being unaware of whatever affected his vital interests, or of not keeping abreast of affairs. He found the Senate committee on pensions far behind on its work of processing the hundreds of private pension bills which Democratic President Cleveland was making a reputation by vetoing. Sawyer volunteered to act as a member of the committee. He moved the voluminous files into his home, where he set up his own private pension bureau. The fact that he had ingratiated himself with the new bride in the White House, Frances Folsom Cleveland, as her favorite senator, did not harm his efforts for those veterans and their dependents who were left out under general pension laws. Word of Sawyer's extra efforts on their behalf was soon widely known among the Boys in Blue.

Sawyer recognized the usefulness of the veteran's label. One of his first decisions, after knocking Keyes aside, was who should have the governorship in 1881. William E. Smith, an original partner in what is now the wholesale grocery firm known by the familiar brand name *Roundy's,* had just completed the traditional two terms. Sawyer and two associates settled upon Jeremiah Rusk, a tavern keeper and farmer from Viroqua who had risen to brevet brigadier general in the war. An unlettered man, Jerry Rusk was 250 pounds of geniality and sharp political judgment. Sawyer made the nomination privately, conveyed it to Rusk, and made it stick in the party convention that followed. Despite the circumstances of the nomination, Rusk was no puppet. He was a popular governor who exercised independent judgment and commanded the respect of the anti-Sawyer Republicans.

Sawyer's alliance with Angus Cameron was one of convenience. Cameron had the sense not to question the good fortune which had given him two unsolicited terms in the United States Senate. When his second term expired, he did not contest the issue. Sawyer had decided that he wanted the seat for his western Wisconsin ally and the attorney for his Omaha Line, John Spooner.

Fairchild, mistaking the enthusiastic welcome his Madison neighbors gave him on his return from ten years abroad for a second bolt of political lightning, decided to offer himself for the senatorship. Feverishly working the veterans' organization circuit, he was exhorted on every side that he was the one to deliver his beloved state from the baneful control of Philetus Sawyer. Sawyer reckoned with his own unpopularity and pulled the necessary strings from the background. Fairchild stood forth *sans* manager and *sans* organization, like a republican Roman defying the imperial decree. He was defeated in the first caucus vote by 54 to 25 and drank humiliation to the dregs.

John Spooner had been Governor Fairchild's fresh-faced personal secretary twenty years earlier. He was deferential to Sawyer, but more ally than subordinate. He carved out a distinguished national political career for himself, joining Nelson Aldrich, William B. Allison, and Orville Platt in "the Four" who ruled the United States Senate at the height of its power.

Sawyer was the leader of a triumvirate in Wisconsin Republican politics that ran things successfully, except for the minor and major mishaps that always lie in wait for seemingly impregnable despots in American politics. The reader is prepared for the successful challenge of Robert M. La Follette, but the triumvirate passed through a number of political fires before this occurred.

Joined with Sawyer and Spooner in the management of the party was Henry Clay Payne of Milwaukee. Understandably mistrustful of Elisha Keyes and his Madison allies, Sawyer based his control upon the party leaders in Milwaukee and upon the western allies of John Spooner, who lived in Hudson.

Payne, born in 1843, was the same age as Spooner. He had come to Milwaukee in 1863 from western Massachusetts to work in a dry goods firm. He made his way as a businessman, and found a career as a political manager useful to him. Raised as a Whig, young Payne watched with dismay as the Republicans lost the support of the non-Catholic Germans to Greeley in 1872, and to Farmer Taylor and the Reform-Democratic ticket in 1873. A natural organizer, Payne started a Young Men's Republican Club to energize the party faithful and win back the non-Catholic German vote. It was an uphill pull. The strength of the party was among the Yankees, and they could not resist flirting with nativism, temperance legislation, and Sunday blue laws. But Payne was persistent and methodical. He made voter registration, helping immigrants with the mysteries of citizenship, and politicking year around activities, all with a card-file record. Milwaukee County gave the Republican gubernatorial candidate 40 percent of the vote in 1871, 21 percent in 1873, but 58 percent in 1879, the rise due mostly to Payne's efforts. The Republican share of the vote in Milwaukee County remained above 50 percent until disaster struck again in 1890 with the wholesale alienation of the German vote.

Payne refused the offer of the Milwaukee postmastership from Senator Carpenter, who recognized his usefulness. He later accepted it from Senator Howe and formed his alliance with Howe and Sawyer, who were longtime political allies. Politics was good to Payne. He became a director of a Milwaukee bank, the Milwaukee Road, the Milwaukee Gas Light Company, and various land-development companies. He was one of the organizers of the pioneer telephone company in Milwaukee and subsequently its president. He became the local head of the street railway company. Henry Villard, in 1890, gathered the competing street car lines and pioneer electric power companies into the Milwaukee Electric Railway and Light Company, a monopoly utility over which Payne presided. Payne was anything but a popular figure in Milwaukee and Wisconsin generally in the 1890s. He acted like a true monopolist with political clout, which he was.

Payne traveled far in politics, too. He was the patronage chief of the local triumvirate for years. His talents as a political manager were recognized early beyond the borders of Wisconsin. He served as national committeeman from Wisconsin from 1880 until after the turn of the century. Importuned to accept the chairmanship of the party nationally in 1888, he refused, but was western manager for the McKinley campaign in 1896. A friend and supporter of Theodore Roosevelt, he held the traditional political manager's post in Roosevelt's cabinet of postmaster general. He was state chairman for four years from 1888, and continued as the real manager while other men acceptable to Sawyer, Payne, and Spooner held the title.

Managing the election of his protégé, John Spooner, to the United States Senate, Sawyer was confirmed in his public image as the genial despot whose rule was unchallenged. New York papers took notice of him as "a shrewd manager of caucuses and conventions" who recognized "the power of money and judicious use of it in politics" to attain his unquestioned position as "the Republican 'Boss' of his State." How well did the "shrewd manager" manage?

Nationally, the best a state boss could be expected to do was to be in the camp of the winning nominee of his party for president and then deliver the votes. Sawyer was a longtime personal friend of James G. Blaine, the successful nominee in 1884, but Grover Cleveland won the election, although Blaine carried Wisconsin. Wisconsin Republicans persisted in the notion that Jerry Rusk and Lucius Fairchild were presidential timber. Sawyer professed to be for Rusk, Blaine, and Walter Q. Gresham, in that order, in 1888. The triumvirate mounted a campaign for Rusk, whether for bargaining position or for the outside chance of being kingmakers would be hard to say. Spooner, the orator, nominated

Rusk, but after two ballots, most of the Wisconsin delegation went to Harrison early and held until he won. Rusk got a cabinet post.

Wisconsin Republicans were in confusion in 1892 after losing control of the statehouse and legislature in the disaster of 1890. Spooner had lost his Senate seat to Democrat William F. Vilas of Madison. Payne doubted that Harrison could succeed himself, which proved correct. Not only did Cleveland beat Harrison, but Wisconsin voted Democratic in a presidential race for the first time since 1852. Spooner, who had hoped for Republican victory and a chance at the aging Sawyer's seat—he was seventy-six in 1892—found himself involved in a misunderstanding over the matter, while the Democrats won and sent John L. Mitchell, Alexander's son, to the Senate. The year 1896 brought a return to Republican control in Wisconsin and nationally, but Spooner was warning Sawyer of what presaged: "The faction which now seeks to gain control of the state is made up of many tireless workers," and La Follette was commanding them.

The Republican disaster in the state in 1890 was not caused by the rise of Populism, which found only a slight foothold in Wisconsin, nor by a resurgence of a suddenly vital Democratic party. It developed, in large measure, from an obscure passage in a little-noticed piece of legislation and an unexpected gubernatorial candidate. William Dempster Hoard was not the choice of the ruling triumvirate. Spooner had given the nod to Horace Taylor, his neighbor from Hudson, but Hoard swept the convention after the popular Governor Rusk, completing seven years in office, announced that the convention should be an open one. Horace Rublee, editor of the *Milwaukee Sentinel,* was on the lookout for a candidate who would not be beholden to Payne and his friends. He found one in Hoard, who was well known around the state as publisher of *Hoard's Dairyman* and a popular platform performer at farmers' institutes. Far from being a choice even acceptable to Sawyer, Payne, and Spooner, Hoard was completely independent of them and once threatened to "message" the legislature about Payne's lobbying efforts in favor of oleomargarine for the Milwaukee meat-packers.

It was during Hoard's term that the much-discussed Bennett Law was passed. This was a new compulsory school law with the added feature that a school, in order to be legal within the terms prescribed, was required to give instruction in reading, writing, arithmetic, and American history *in the English language.* This feature, largely ignored at first, soon brought a storm of protest from both the Catholic and Lutheran Germans and the Lutheran Scandinavians, who combined in an unlikely alliance. The Republicans again, as in 1873 with the strong liquor control law, had alienated the German Protestants. Hoard accepted the challenge, to the despair of Payne and Spooner, and waged the 1890 campaign squarely upon the rightness of the Bennett Law and the sacred character of the "Little Red School." Combined with other campaign liabilities which the Democrats exploited, this swept the Republicans from office. They lost the governor's chair, the legislature, and all but one of the congressional districts. Certainly it was a lesson in the perils of being a party boss in a democracy.

The Democrats did not offer much of an alternative to Republican rule. The largest base of Democratic votes was in Milwaukee County among the Catholic Germans, Irish, and Poles. It was boss-ridden in the sense that the ethnic vote was more manageable in blocs, by local political managers, and the interests of the voter did not extend much beyond his neighborhood and ethnic group. At the state level, the party was a holding operation awaiting the election of a Cleveland and the accompanying federal patronage.

Challenging Milwaukee control of the party were Democratic figures such as William F. Vilas of Madison and Ellis B. Usher of La Crosse. Vilas, the most prominent, served as Cleveland's postmaster general and secretary of interior. Vilas, like Cleveland, was a thoroughgoing Bourbon. He had no sympathy with the reform or liberal elements of his party, although he was equally unsympathetic with the antilabor position of the Mitchell forces in Milwaukee. Usher held reform views in which he sometimes attempted to educate Vilas, but with indifferent success. Vilas, like Sawyer, saw no necessary conflict between business and politics. He got an appointment as Indian agent for a former employee of a lumber firm in which he himself had stock. While the firm was not directly benefited, the idea was to hurry Chippewa lumber to market.

Another leader in Democratic politics was Edward C. Wall of Milwaukee, who succeeded Usher as state chairman in 1890. More than anyone else, Wall was the architect of the stunning Democratic victory in 1890. Like Payne, he was a political technician who knew that political victories were not hammered together in October of an election year. More sensitive than Payne to conflicts of interest between his business and political connections, Wall had similar connections. He was manager of the Badger Electric Company in 1890 and had an office in the same building as Henry Clay Payne. The two were both business and social friends. Maybe symbolically, Villard's North American Company, which owned Payne's loyalty, absorbed Badger Electric in 1893. Wall was a competent political organizer, but his technique was based too much upon the divisiveness of ethnic and religious issues, which were decisive in 1890.

Economic and political issues of consequence were surely less important in the politics of the period 1865 to 1890 than they became in the La Follette period. Voters reacted more readily to appeals to party loyalty and to ethnic and religious prejudices. It is a simplification to say that the Republicans, in 1873, lost because they were insensitive to the issues posed by the arrogance of the railroads. Both Governors Fairchild and Washburn addressed themselves to the issue and called for some form of regulation or control. But it was characteristic that Fairchild viewed that issue as a threat to his voter appeal rather than an opportunity. The same approach was repeatedly evident in addressing what passed for burning national issues in the period: the money supply, the tariff, internal improvement subsidies, and civil service reform, to name a few. In the main, major party politics was a professional game which paid off for those economic interests that financed the use of the playing field. But it was never as simple as this sounds. The voters were not as easily managed as the political professionals supposed, and they could, if aroused, change the rules of the game.

Selected Bibliography

Berthrong, Donald J. "Andrew Jackson Turner, 'Work Horse' of the Republican Party." *Wisconsin Magazine of History* 38:77–86 (Winter 1954–55). An editor in politics.

Conlin, Joseph R. "The Politics of Reconstruction in Wisconsin, 1865–1866." Master's thesis, University of Wisconsin, 1962. Asserts that Reconstruction policy was more important than Wisconsin internal improvements.

Current, Richard N. *Pine Logs and Politics: A Life of Philetus Sawyer.* Madison, 1950. The man and the book are central to the politics of the era.

Dearing, Mary R. *Veterans in Politics: The Story of the G.A.R.* Baton Rouge, 1952. Dissertation done at Wisconsin with Wisconsin models.

Deutsch, Herman. "Carpenter and the Senatorial Elections of 1875 in Wisconsin." *Wisconsin Magazine of History* 16:26–46 (Sept. 1932).

———. "Disintegrating Forces in Wisconsin Politics of the Early Seventies: The Ground Swell of 1873." *Wisconsin Magazine of History* 15:282–96 (March 1932).

———. "Disintegrating Forces in Wisconsin Politics of the Early Seventies: Railroad Politics." *Wisconsin Magazine of History* 15:391–411 (June 1932).

———. "Yankee-Teuton Rivalry in Wisconsin of the Seventies." *Wisconsin Magazine of History* 14:262–82 (March 1931). Best on politics of the 1870s.

Fowler, Dorothy Canfield. *John Coit Spooner: Defender of Presidents.* New York, 1961. Spooner became a power in the Senate.

Hantke, Richard W. "Elisha W. Keyes, the Bismarck of Western Politics." *Wisconsin Magazine of History* 31:29–41 (Sept. 1947).

———. "Elisha W. Keyes and the Radical Republicans." *Wisconsin Magazine History* 35:203–8 (Spring 1952). The Keyes Papers are important for the period.

Haugen, Nils P. *Pioneer and Political Reminiscences,* edited by Joseph Schafer. Madison, n.d. A prominent Norwegian politician, later allied with La Follette.

Holzhueter, John O. "The Wisconsin Editors and Publishers Association, 1853–1877." Master's thesis, University of Wisconsin, 1966. They lived and breathed politics.

Merrill, Horace S. *The Bourbon Democracy of the Upper Middle West, 1865–1898.* 1953. Seattle: Americana paperbacks, 1967. Conservatives in charge.

———, *William Freeman Vilas: Doctrinaire Democrat.* Madison, 1954. Vilas was the principal Wisconsin Democrat of the Cleveland era.

Miller, Curtis W. "Rufus King and the Problems of His Era." Master's thesis, Marquette University, 1963. King edited the *Sentinel* for sixteen years.

Ross, Sam. *The Empty Sleeve: A Biography of Lucius Fairchild.* Madison, 1964. It is difficult to take Fairchild as seriously as his contemporaries did.

Russell, William H. "Timothy O. Howe, Stalwart Republican." *Wisconsin Magazine of History* 35:90–99 (Winter 1951). U.S. Senator from 1861 to 1879; his contemporaries mistook him for a statesman.

Thompson, E. Bruce. *Matthew Hale Carpenter: Webster of the West.* Madison, 1954. Matt was surely more interesting than this book.

Thomson, Alexander M. *A Political History of Wisconsin.* Milwaukee, 1900. Lively, informed, and a deft partisan.

Wight, William W. *Henry Clay Payne: A Life.* Milwaukee, 1907. Unfortunately all that is available.

Williams, Helen J. and Harry. "Wisconsin Republicans and Reconstruction." *Wisconsin Magazine of History* 23:17–39 (Sept. 1939). Conlin, above, is arguing with them.

Wood, George H. "A Diamond in the Rough—A Study of the Administration of Governor Jeremiah McLain Rusk, 1882–1889." Master's thesis, University of Wisconsin, 1970. A "ring" politician of some independence.

POLITICS
OF PROTEST

24

Complacency was the common hallmark of the men who controlled, within limits, the destinies of the two major parties in Wisconsin during the quarter-century following the Civil War. They were content with the machinery of American politics as they found it, and adapted it to their own uses. They had few forebodings about the growing political and economic power of the rising corporations, viewed the public domain as undeveloped opportunity for anyone who could seize it, and accepted a world shaped by the Yankee ethos—within the bounds of practical politics. Any challenge to their complacency was viewed as a threat rather than an opportunity. Yet they were supreme opportunists. "What do the people want on the financial question? More money?" inquired the beleaguered Matthew Carpenter of Elisha Keyes, as he felt his senatorial toga being tugged from his shoulders in 1874. He went on to woo the popular will with speeches castigating the "charnel-house of corporations," while his nervous political supporters argued, correctly, that the railroads should recognize that no man in the Senate was more zealous in their service.

Senator Timothy Howe was more representative of the breed than that joyous brigand, Carpenter. Remarking the contrast between his own character and Carpenter's, Howe wrote that "he always acts and never deliberates while I always deliberate and never act." The necessity for action made Howe nervous. He preferred quiet, and performing his office without offense to those who put up the money to keep him there.

Governor Lucius Fairchild shared Howe's political instincts. His biographer concluded that Fairchild viewed issues of popular discontent "only as 'dangers' rather than opportunities for political capital." He invariably refused a role of real leadership, but preferred to be "a man acceptable to all factions because he was the party's willing tool."

Elisha Keyes, who acted as the political agent for the Chicago and Northwestern Railroad in Madison, was not a man discontented with the political world as he found it. It is easy enough to find Republican rhetoric directed against the railroads in the messages of Governors Washburn and Fairchild, and even in speeches by Keyes. It is another thing to interpret them as serious threats to those interests. Nor could one look for anything other than opportunism, conservative in intent, from the leaders of the minority Democratic party, Alexander Mitchell and the Bourbon William F. Vilas.

Issues were like attractive candidates. They had to be trimmed to and exploited as political capital. There was always the risk that candidates and the electorate might take them seriously. The risk was minimized if the bosses could retain control of the machinery of party politics, keep the influential newspapers in line, and retain an iron grip on the patronage and sources of political funds. Philetus Sawyer did this more successfully than most because he, personally, had both political skill and the kind of economic power that spoke with most authority in Wisconsin politics—lumber and railroads. But a Wisconsin political boss was more analogous to a steersman on a lumber raft than to the pilot of a river steamboat. In fast water, the raft needed a lot of luck.

Just as we tend to overrate the powers of the bosses in the politics of the time, we often oversimplify the forces of political protest. The assumption is that the label "agrarian unrest" explains the luxuriant flowering of the third-party movements between 1872 and 1892 that have been gathered under the convenient titles Grangers, Greenbackers, and Populists. This overlooks much in Wisconsin politics. The temporary overthrow of Republican rule in 1873 is commonly attributed to a Granger revolt, although the general Granger contribution seems to have consisted in the disgruntled farmers staying home on election day rather than voting their traditional Republican ticket. While the term *Greenback* conjures up a picture of debt-ridden farmers demanding relief from a return to gold, the unlikely leader of the ticket at its high point was the Milwaukee industrialist Edward P. Allis. The Populist party in Wisconsin was largely the creation of a Milwaukee labor leader, Robert Schilling, and a significant share of its votes came from the larger cities.

By and large, Wisconsin farmers voted traditional party loyalties but were responsive to agrarian economic issues. Traditional party loyalties were more apt to be broken by appeals to, or assaults upon, ethnic or religious prejudices than by economic issues. Third parties were the province of reformers and disappointed office seekers who hoped to catch a tide of protest at flood. A minority of metropolitan workingmen were developing a consciousness of themselves as a class apart, with interests outside of the traditional American political parties. German socialists formed the nucleus of this proletarian protest, but native Americans and British immigrants contributed recruits. Political revolts against traditional Republican rule were usually combinations of these forces of protest, often illogical combinations. The role of the minority Democrats was to exploit this protest. The Democrats could offer a statewide political machine and an outside chance at national patronage. It was difficult for third-party politicians to resist this bait. If they took it, the Bourbon Democrats ran the risk of losing control of their own party.

In 1873, loyalty to the Republican cause had been loosened, particularly for the German Protestants and liberals, by the Liberal Republican bolt from President Grant in 1872. German-Americans had been affronted by the insults heaped upon Carl Schurz, a leader of the bolt who was a national leader with German background and education. The stringent liquor control measure, the Graham Law, passed with the endorsement of Republican Governor C. C. Washburn, was a direct assault upon German cultural values, originating in the ethnic and religious prejudices of the Yankees.

As to those who more readily recognized the political requirements of their economic interests, we may look beyond the brewers, distillers, and publicans who were willing to pay to have the Graham Law repealed. The arrogance of the railroads drew admonitory words even from Republican politicians. It was assumed that these were directed toward the recently organized Grange audience. But a growing number of merchants, shippers, and grain brokers were equally alarmed at the growing power of the railroads over elevator space and rates, as well as shipping costs. One of the most articulate spokesmen of this view in the legislature was Francis West, a Milwaukee grain broker. West lost his fight to get an elevator rate law and pronounced the supposedly tough Potter Law a fraud.

A powerful statement of prevailing sentiment was voiced by Edward G. Ryan. Ryan's June 1873 address to the university law school remains a vital document because one of his auditors was the young Robert M. La Follette, who later professed that the occasion was one of the turning points in his remarkable career. Ryan's predictions were in these words:

> There is looming up a new and dark power. I cannot dwell upon the signs and shocking omens of its advent. The accumulation of individual wealth seems to be greater than it ever has been since the downfall of the Roman Empire. And the enterprises of the country are aggregating vast corporate combinations of unexampled capital, boldly marching, not for economical conquests only, but for political power. . . . For the first time really in our politics, money is taking the field as an organized power. . . . The question will arise, and arise in your day, though perhaps not fully in mine, which shall rule—wealth or man; which shall lead—money or intellect; who shall fill public stations—educated and patriotic free men, or the feudal serfs of corporate capital.

Ryan's speech was printed in the *Milwaukee Daily Sentinel,* the leading Republican paper, indicating that the old Democratic partisan had struck a popular note. The election that fall bore this out. Milwaukee Democrats, sensing an opportunity, called a convention for a "Reform Party," not identified with the Democrats, only to find a similar call in the field from dissident Republicans. The two joined, financed by Milwaukee liquor interests and Alexander Mitchell, both of whom were unhappy with Governor Washburn. Washburn remarked in a letter to a business partner that "the combined powers of darkness, Whiskey, Beer, R. Roads & a sprinkling of Grangers, have been on my trail and are confident of my defeat." They achieved it.

Led by a Dane County farmer prominent in the Grange, William R. Taylor, the Reform-Democratic ticket that had been hastily put together swept the state offices and legislative elections in November 1873. Legislative elections were held annually then, electing all of the assembly and half of the senate. It was not exactly a Granger victory as generally represented, although a Grange leader was at the head of the ticket. The rural vote was down 41,000 from 1872—a presidential year—contrasted with only a 3,000 decrease in the urban vote. Even allowing for a population that was 80 percent rural, this was a significant disparity. The Republican vote for governor was down 12,000 from the 1871 winning vote of 78,301; the Reform-Democratic vote was up 12,500 from the 68,910 that Democrat James R. Doolittle received that year. Taylor's vote in Milwaukee County was nearly double that of Doolittle's two years before and made up 13 percent of Taylor's total. It was not a Granger vote.

The reformers recognized one element of their support by repealing the offensive liquor control law and replacing it with a less punitive measure. It was the problem of railroad regulation that stumped them. Farmer Taylor, as the governor was popularly known, was ambivalent on the subject. He was enough of a politician to recognize the hazards, and Alexander Mitchell had been among his supporters. Mitchell, who financed the Democratic party in Milwaukee when it served his purposes, whipped the Democratic members of the coalition into line with the argument that Milwaukee's interests, as the principal terminus of the Chicago, Milwaukee, and St. Paul Railroad, would be hurt by any antirailroad measure.

The legislature was soon awash with railroad bills upon which few could agree. The Republicans, who recognized that their negative record on railroad control had kept many of their rural voters at home, set about fishing in these roiled waters. A bill written by Republican Senator Robert Potter of Wautoma was substituted for the Reform-Democratic party bill. The Republican bill was a stronger one setting maximum rates, providing for a three-man railroad commission which could only reduce rates, and requiring comprehensive financial reports. Among other promises, the reform coalition had pledged an economical session of the legislature. The Republicans, with a majority of one in the senate and a degree of party discipline unavailable to the coalition, held the reform party's feet to the fire. The Republicans could not lose. If the bill passed, they could take credit for belling the cat. If the bill failed, the failure would be charged to the reformers who could not agree upon or pass their own measure.

The Reform-Democratic coalition accepted the lesser evil and passed the Potter Law. The two major railroads, on advice of eminent counsel, served notice on Governor Taylor that they would not abide by the law. Taylor was in an awkward position. Enforcement of the maximum allowable rates depended upon an individual shipper or passenger bringing suit against the agent who had overcharged him, not against the railroad. This was a most unsatisfactory state of affairs, which the administration retrieved rather well. The attorney general decided to seek an injunction compeling the railroads to abide by the law or forfeit their corporate charters. At this point, Chief Justice Luther S. Dixon of the state supreme court resigned, and the governor had the opportunity to appoint his successor. He appointed the irascible Edward G. Ryan, after ascertaining his position on the Potter Law. Ryan proved to be a brilliant appointment. He wrote a landmark opinion, upholding the right of the state to assert jurisdiction over the railroads, which a federal court also upheld. The railroads capitulated, but succeeded in having the law repealed with the return of the Republicans to power.

Reform continued to have voter appeal for a season, but it was a difficult enthusiasm to sustain. The liquor interests had no reason to continue their support and Mitchell had withdrawn his favor. Following Mitchell's lead, a majority of the Milwaukee members of the coalition opposed Taylor and the Potter Law as detrimental to the city's interests. The Republicans were out assiduously wooing the Grangers, who were mostly Yankee farmers with strong ties to the party, and the German Protestants whom they recognized as the swing vote they must have for success.

The Republican strategy paid off in the crucial 1874 legislative election on which Matt Carpenter's senatorial seat was riding. They took back twenty-three seats in the assembly and held their narrow majority in the senate. The Reform-Democratic coalition was not swamped, capturing three of the eight congressional seats. Reform was still running strongly. The Republicans had managed to share in it by taking up railroad regulation as their battle cry.

The coalition of reformers and Democrats was badly split by 1875 when the governorship and other state offices were up. Governor Taylor had lost the support of the Democratic leaders in Milwaukee who were sympathetic with the railroads. Inclined earlier to temporize with the railroads, Taylor got his back up in response to their intransigent refusal to accept the Potter Law. This ambivalence won him few supporters, and the railroads returned their financial support to the Republicans. As one Republican politician put it, "The railroads had found out to their sorrow that a dull-brained demagogue is a worse enemy than an intelligent enemy." Taylor was not a dull-brained demagogue but neither was he a success in leading the coalition of reformers and Democrats.

The conservative Bourbon Democrats out-state were unhappy with the coalition because of their fear that the reform element would take over control of the Democratic Party, and they made common cause with Alexander Mitchell and the Milwaukee Democrats in trying to dump Taylor. They were not successful in this. Taylor won renomination, but went on to lose a close race to Harrison Ludington. Governor Ludington presided over repeal of the Potter Law, and railroad passes for political service came back into style. A railroad official wrote to Elisha Keyes: "There was a time when the R.R. men were badly off-color in this state; but by fasting and prayer and by sacrifices they are now able to look the honest granger in the left eye and charge him 4¢ a mile. . . ."

The Bourbon Democrats firmly returned the party to its accustomed conservative course by excluding the reformers from any positions of power. They preferred party control to coalition victory. Many of the reformers were men who wore their party ties lightly, and they became slightly shopworn as they shifted their allegiances from one third-party to the next. A generous view of them would be that they were impatient of the professionalism of politics, the influence of wealth and economic power, and the careful avoidance of genuine issues in major party politics. A view commonly held by party regulars was that the reformers were simply politicians whose qualities did not warrant their sharing in the management of the major parties. This turned them for gratification of their ambitions to every third-party movement that came along. "The barnacles around every court house [and] ignorant itinerant ministers," Gabe Bouck, an abrasive Oshkosh Democrat of statewide prominence, called them. "An able, learned man but deficient in common sense," was a Republican editor's description of Dr. O. W. Wight, who styled himself the originator of the Reform Party in 1873. "He is a man with just enough of talent and culture to render his asininity conspicuous. It is a sight for the poulterer to see him clucking around the brood of Reform chickens under his wing," commented another Republican leader of Wight.

The dissolution of the Reform-Democratic coalition coincided with the rise of another third party that attracted the support of many reformers. The Greenback party, or Anti-Monopoly party as it was often officially known, grew out of the depression conditions following the panic of 1873. The argument over the part played by the money supply in the economy went back at least as far as the Jacksonian era, but was rekindled by the inflationary financing of the Civil War, the expansion of debt in agriculture and manufacturing that accompanied wartime demand and the expanding economy, the fall of many commodity prices after the war, and the depth and length of the depression of the seventies. The problem was aggravated by the victory of the hard money theorists in 1873 when the Resumption Act was passed, establishing a return to specie—a gold base—as desirable national policy. Favoring hard money was an old Jacksonian prejudice, but the discomforts of the depression created a generation that learned to sit for long hours listening to abstruse explanations of the money question.

The railroad issue had proved to be one upon which agrarians in Wisconsin could not agree. Farmers and townsmen served by railroads wanted regulation, while those not yet served opposed legislation that might slow investment in new railroad lines. Milwaukee businessmen accepted Mitchell's argument that regulation hurt their interests. The money question proved equally divisive. Many saw resumption of specie as a plot by eastern creditors to get back gold dollars for cheap greenbacks loaned to the debtor West. The farmer, who had borrowed heavily when wheat was $2.50 a bushel in 1865, needed little convincing while trying to pay off with 77-cent grain. Some were easily convinced that malign influences were tampering with the value of the dollar. The Midwest discovered Wall Street and the 1870s version of the "Eastern Establishment." At the same time, Jacksonian prejudices in favor of hard money, and unhappy recollections of experiences with paper money, caused others to resist the siren call.

As with other issues that caught the popular imagination, the politicians of the major parties were in a quandary. Both Republicans and Democrats played with the paper money heresy, the latter more readily in search of a new coalition with which to beat the Republicans. The conservatives in both parties were kept busy reading out the heretics. This made a third party alternative more certain. The press of the regular parties generally treated the Greenbackers as a joke, except for Edward P. Allis, George Esterly of Whitewater, a successful farm machinery manufacturer, G. M. Steele, president of Lawrence College, and other "respectable" men led astray by the new religion. For the rest, Greenbackism infected the "court hourse barnacles" and congenital third-party types.

Another group that succumbed to the virus were some of the prominent labor leaders of the day. Labor unions suffered massive losses in the depression. Where there had been thirty unions claiming national organization in 1873, only nine remained by 1877. Many union leaders were inclined to be doctrinaire and fond of theories about the common concerns of all producers against the moneyed classes. The bounds of legitimate union activity were narrow indeed by the precepts of prevailing legal theory and the conventional wisdom. This encouraged unionists to think in terms other than bread and butter union issues. A delightful story concerns Greenback candidate Allis, on his way to New York to address a bankers' convention, stopping in Cleveland to persuade union leader Robert Schilling to come to Wisconsin as a publicist and speaker for the cause. The bankers discovered in time that Allis was not simply a respectable Republican industrialist with some interesting views on finance, and headed him off. Schilling proved to be as he had been represented. He was to be intimately associated with labor organizations and third-party causes in Wisconsin for the next twenty years.

The Greenback campaign was a failure in Wisconsin. It represented one of those perennial efforts to unite the farmer and urban laborer in a common cause. The test was not a fair one, since the Democrats adopted a soft-money platform and many Republicans were paper-money men publicly. Allis got one-seventh of the vote in an election won by the Republicans. He fortunately returned to his entrepreneurial role. A sample of Allis's rhetoric illustrates the oratory that was lost to the state: "Our bounteous Creator has not ceased to smile upon us as of old. His glad sunshine and gushing rain-drops have bathed our land until it has laughed with rustling crops, and the farmers' garner is all too small to hold the golden fruit. . . . Our forests and prairies are crying aloud for the sturdy caress of the axe and plow, and our mountains are groaning as in labor, from their precious burden. . . ."

Greenbackism had broad appeal, but it was essentially a one-issue movement. Because the money question was one upon which every politician felt he had to stand somewhere, the Democrats were stampeded to a soft-money plank and nominated a prominent Greenbacker for governor in 1877. The Republicans took a similar stand in favor of paper money. Horace Rublee called a rump convention to rectify this error and help win back the German Protestant votes. The Germans were hard-money men, unfazed by American rhetoric on the subject of the money supply. The depression had begun to moderate and the issue receded until its return a generation later in the cry for free coinage of silver.

The Social Democrat party entered the lists in 1877, but was somewhat ahead of its time. It was associated in the popular mind with the German community in Milwaukee. If one looks at the "Summary of Gubernatorial Vote" in subsequent volumes of the *Wisconsin Blue Book,* he will find that respectable people politely averted their eyes from this immigrant gaucherie. No total appears for the Social Democrat gubernatorial candidate, although he drew more votes in Milwaukee County, where both were residents, than Greenbacker candidate Edward P. Allis. The Social Democrat candidate was not a "crout-eating Dutchman" but a respectable Scotsman named Colin Campbell, who refused to run if the German socialists tried to repudiate the women's suffrage plank in the platform. Milwaukee socialism was to go through several transformations before it emerged as a real power in Milwaukee and Wisconsin politics.

The rise of socialism in Milwaukee is correctly ascribed to the heavily German character of the city's work force, although the socialists did recruit numerous English-speaking workmen and intellectuals to the cause. The German Forty-eighters were considered liberal bourgeois by the socialists, who called them "swollen ones" (*Geschwollenen*). The socialists were recruited from the German skilled workers and owed inspiration to the teachings of Karl Marx, Ferdinand Lassalle, and the First International. These influences kept them split between political action, trade union organization, and various utopian schemes for the reorganization of society. The centennial year, 1876, inspired considerable socialist activity, as did the accompanying depression and the general labor unrest. This was the background of Socialist Colin Campbell's candidacy for governor.

Alarm over the spectre of socialism proved premature. Interest in the movement rapidly faded, to revive again in 1886 as an accompaniment to the eight-hour-day agitation. Until Victor Berger Americanized social-ism in Milwaukee after 1893 and made it synonymous with honest, hu-mane, municipal administration, socialism played the role of spoiler in trade union organization and independent political activity.

What the American majority, which was deeply hostile to socialism and militant labor, failed to see were the conditions that were creating a proletariat groping toward a recognition of itself. It has been the easy course to ascribe this to immigrant groups that rejected American values. The common answer was to call for exclusion by ethnic or class identifi-cation—usually synonymous—and an effort through school and sumptu-ary legislation to Americanize, or compel conformity, of those already here. Despite the fact that Wisconsin had the largest proportion of for-eign-born of any state east of the Mississippi River and continued both official and unofficial efforts to attract more to the business at hand, her citizens reacted in typical fashion to the question of exclusion. It is not difficult to find statements by German-born or other well-established mi-norities deploring the free immigration of eastern and southern Europe-ans into their midst.

If the German immigrants provided most of the socialist ideology, the conditions of industrial labor provided the discontent. The big Milwau-kee firms operated with a labor turnover which averaged as much as 350 percent annually in some years. Hundreds of men might be taken on who worked only a few hours, days, or weeks on a particular job. The rail-roads and the lumber industry were equally prodigal. These industries fostered abuses which were noteworthy even in a time when working conditions generally were scandalous. Both depended upon a continuous flow of recruits from among recent immigrants, farm boys, and some skilled labor from older regions. The railroads took no interest in the financial responsibility of their subcontractors. It was common for con-struction laborers to be stranded without their pay. The lumber industry frequently exploited its labor because of the isolation of its operations. Blacklisting, control of local officials, introduction of scabs, and use of the militia were common weapons against organized labor.

The lumber industry and railroad construction had to compete with the opportunities in frontier agriculture and the westering urge of foot-loose men. The same factors increased the difficulty of organizing the workers to confront the employers, except in the mills. The millowners were ready to use women and boys to operate the machines where labor was troublesome.

Milwaukee labor was of a different order. While much employment was highly seasonal and there was a great turnover of men in the shops, the pool of labor from which the industries drew was urban in character. Many of the men were skilled or semiskilled, and identified themselves with certain industries if not with individual shops. The pool of unskilled labor, which floated from one plant gate to another in good times as well as slack, was made up largely of immigrant newcomers, especially of Poles, who began arriving in numbers in the eighties and were the second largest foreign-born group by 1890. The older ethnic groups were well established by the eighties and were as conscious of their superior status as any Yankee. Germans, British, Irish, and Scandinavian foremen exercised their prejudices freely. There were many bosses. Foundries and machine shops commonly let work to their skilled hands by bid or piece, and these in turn hired their own crews from among the semiskilled and unskilled.

The aristocracy of labor in the shops drew its membership from native stock and the older immigrant groups. The few unions which were effective were found among the skilled, were craft oriented, and took no interest in common laborers or the newer foreigners. Union leaders, most of whom spoke English or German or both, considered the Poles, Hungarians, and Italians incapable of meaningful union membership. Other elements of the skilled, for example the shoemakers and the coopers, were being displaced by new machine processes and factory production methods which eliminated their skills. The times were out of joint for many needing only leadership to call the whole industrial system into question.

The appearance of a self-conscious proletariat owed as much to these conditions of employment as it did to a growing socialist movement. As individual industries grew to the point where they were employing men by the hundreds and then thousands, the balance swung more heavily in favor of the employer. At the same time, the older notions of state or guild intervention in behalf of the employee were being lost. The power of the state, through the courts and the intervention of the police power, with the use of troops, was becoming a commonplace in protecting the interests of the employer. Much of popular opinion reflected the conventional wisdom drawn from laissez-faire doctrine and social Darwinism. Unionism was thought pernicious enough, but socialist doctrine was completely outside the pale. If economic conditions decreed that men must work for ten to twelve hours a day for a wage of $1.00 to $1.50, it was not only futile but also evil to try to interfere with this natural working of the system. Those who tried were not adaptable to the American system and must be drawing their inspiration from abroad.

Unionism was a fragile growth in this environment. It flowered in good times when business would bargain, but was easily crushed when hard times made employers more militant. There was the beginning of such a flowering in 1878 as the long depression ameliorated. Several trade unions appeared and won demands. But the strike, even for skilled craftsmen, was a chancy instrument where a majority of the society actively distrusted labor organizations and responded affirmatively to the right of the strikebreaker to work. In July 1881 the sawmill workers in Eau Claire, some 1,000 strong, called a quick strike to demand a cut in the hours worked from twelve to ten a day, and protested the withholding of 20 percent of a man's wages until he had finished the season. The millowners were better organized and promptly imported strikebreakers, meanwhile deploring the fact that most of the strikers were single men "without property interests in Eau Claire, or permanent homes anywhere." It was not explained why this had not militated against them when they were hired. The men attempted to turn the strikebreakers out and halt the machinery. Governor Smith responded to a call for the militia from the millowners, who presumably owned permanent homes. The strike leaders were clapped in jail, guarded by the militia. Operations were resumed on the basis of the twelve-hour day.

In the face of such effective opposition, it is not strange that bread and butter unionism had a difficult time taking root, nor that socialism and other utopian panaceas, to be achieved by education and political action for the reformation of society, found an audience among workingmen. Union activity often foundered on an injudicious mixture of craft unionism, industrial unionism, and utopianism.

The Knights of Labor was such an organization. Based upon the principle of one big union for all producers, the K of L was opposed to the use of the traditional weapons of unionism. Society would be remade through education and the adoption of cooperation by all producers and consumers. The union won its following, however, by leading a successful strike in 1885 against the railroads controlled by Jay Gould. The national organization of the Knights, made up of a conglomeration of trade and industrial unions and local assemblies made up of workers, small shopkeepers, and anyone else interested, blossomed.

Robert Schilling, who had come to Wisconsin to campaign for the Greenback ticket in 1877, moved to Milwaukee in 1880. An organizer of considerable talent, Schilling was at heart an educator and propagandizer whose philosophy coincided with that of the Knights. A skilled bilingual debater, Schilling was facile, inconsistent, but effective. He had come up through the coopers union to positions in the national leadership of various unions and third parties in Cleveland, his former home. He could sound radical, though no radical. His forte was composing ringing statements of principle upon which a variety of factions could coalesce into minor parties of dubious political effectiveness.

Schilling became state organizer of the Knights, as the Greenback movement sank from sight. He took over a German-language labor paper, the *Volksblatt,* in addition to a Greenback sheet he was editing. The Knights grew rapidly in Wisconsin and tended toward militant trade unionism in the Milwaukee tradition. Schilling became militant by force of circumstance. The Knights organized the sawmill workers in many large mills. Schilling became a forceful figure in negotiation for the men who were striking for the ten-hour day. He won a little for them—a ten-hour day at ten hours' pay, but a minimum of $1.25 a day. The settlement also involved union recognition, which was a step forward.

As Schilling became more militant, the conservative, utopian national leadership of the Knights tried to control him, but he was succeeding. By early 1886 the Knights had 15,000 members in Wisconsin—one-third of them in Milwaukee—and were gaining momentum. Schilling found a new enthusiasm in the Eight-Hour League, which had a large following in Milwaukee. Assailed on the right by the national leadership of the Knights and Frank Flower, a conservative Knight who headed the new Wisconsin Bureau of Labor Statistics, Schilling found a serious challenge from the left in the reviving socialist movement headed by Paul Grottkau. Grottkau, a Prussian aristocrat of good education, was considered by many the peer of Carl Schurz as an orator in German. He had been associated with Johann Most, and in Chicago with August Spies and the anarchist movement, but had broken with them. Grottkau, who had been brought to Milwaukee by a socialist German businessman, contested with Schilling for the leadership of the Eight-hour League.

The league was a great success in the number of people it could turn out and the militance it inspired. Egged on by Grottkau and other radical leaders while Schilling counseled caution, the movement came to a head in the first days of May. It ended on May 5, 1886, when the Kosciusko Guard, called out by Governor Rusk, fired into a crowd, a large number of whom were Poles determined to call out the workers of the huge Bay View Iron Works. Five people were killed and four badly wounded. Governor Rusk became a national hero. It was the day after the more famous encounter in Haymarket Square, Chicago. Schilling blamed "old Know Nothing, Jerry Rusk," for the bloodshed in Milwaukee.

A large share of the eight-hour agitation was carried on by the Knights. About 14,000 workers were out from the large plants in the city on the day before the Bay View Massacre. In the aftermath, wholesale indictments were issued by a grand jury, against Schilling and Grottkau among others. Schilling's indictment was on the lesser charge of instigating a boycott of a cigar manufacturer who refused to deal with his union. His case resulted in a hung jury, but Grottkau and six others received jail sentences.

Schilling struck back by organizing a People's party on a platform of labor and middle-class reforms, with a full slate of candidates for state and local offices. To the consternation of the Republicans and Democrats, the People's party swept the Milwaukee County elections and sent a member of Congress. It was not strictly a labor party, for the appeal extended to former Greenbackers and those who saw the events of the previous May as evidence of the malign power of organized wealth. The victory was brief and of little consequence. The alarmed Republicans and Democrats combined in a Citizen's Ticket, in 1888, and narrowly defeated Schilling's party when the socialists withdrew their support from him. Horace Rublee, in moments of depression, had been predicting Schilling as mayor and Grottkau as chief of police.

The 1886 election, which exploited grievances fresh in many minds, was Schilling's high point. In 1891 he was the national secretary of the People's party, or Populist party as it is more familiarly known, but the Populists had little impact in Wisconsin. The party was largely Schilling's creature, with a largely urban constituency. It drew only one-fifteenth of the vote cast for governor in 1894, its peak year. The Knights of Labor was melting away behind him more rapidly than Schilling could recruit and organize new assemblies. Labor was to find its political outlet in a new socialist movement, built by Victor Berger, and in the support of Robert La Follette's progressive movement, which was to capture control of the Republican party.

The strings of ethnic and religious prejudices were regularly plucked by both of the major parties, gingerly as a rule, as any appeal to one group could bring a strong reaction from another. Political protests based upon these prejudices are generally summed up as the responses of immigrant groups. Nevertheless, the Prohibition party was doubtless based as much upon nativist prejudice, however blandly stated, as it was upon moral fervor and religious conviction. The Episcopal Bishop of Wisconsin attempted to bridge the chasm between Yankee bluenoses and the immigrants. The Germans, he wrote, should not expect to introduce their traditional sociable Sunday to America, where it "instantly passes into a license for immorality and vice. . . . they must be content to give up the custom, or be held responsible for the flood of evil to which it opens the gates." The assumption of the article was that the Yankee version of the Sabbath was one which all newcomers were bound to accept.

The drive for legalizing temperance, or prohibition, started with territorial politics. It was accurately identified, by both proponents and opponents, with the Republican party from the party's beginning, but Republican politicians recognized the German Protestants as their swing vote and managed, especially after 1873, to equivocate on the issue. Finally disillusioned with the GOP, a Prohibition party was organized and offered candidates in state elections from 1881 onward. The party drew only 8,000 to 17,000 votes. The Republicans whittled away at this number by introducing and passing occasional liquor control bills so that only hard-core prohibitionists voted their principles in the third party.

Closely allied with the temperance and prohibition agitation was the drive for women's suffrage. Much of the leadership was interchangeable; women's organizations and feminine fervor were welcomed in the war against liquor. In 1869, Elizabeth Cady Stanton and Susan B. Anthony stumped Wisconsin to arouse interest in women's suffrage, but Wisconsin was not conspicuous for its support of the issue, on the part either of its women or its male politicians. It is common to blame the prejudices of the German community for this. The top membership of the Wisconsin Women's Suffrage Association has been estimated at 500, achieved in 1893, and the organization's treasury was considered to be in prime condition if it contained $135. Some prominent nineteenth-century leaders who deserve mention were Mathilde Franziska Anneke, editor of *Frauenzeitung* and a prominent Milwaukee educator, Dr. Laura Ross Wolcott, a pioneer woman physician, and Olympia Brown, a Universalist minister in Racine. Woman's suffrage was dropped from the 1865 Negro-suffrage measure after being passed by the state senate. A limited women's suffrage, for school elections only, was passed in 1886. Wisconsin was the thirteenth state to adopt the measure. It was lost in the following year when Olympia Brown brought a suit to protest the refusal of her ballot in a municipal election. She argued that the mayor and city council appointed the school superintendent and passed the school budget. The supreme court decided that school elections were not well-enough defined and voided the voting law. Victory came only with passage of the nineteenth amendment to the federal constitution.

The Bennett Law and other political dissatisfactions toppled the Republicans from power in 1890, for only the second time since the Civil War. It was a clean sweep. Cleverly exploiting the religious and ethnic issues involved, Chairman Edward C. Wall combined the German Catholic and Lutheran vote to create a Democratic victory.

Wall's problem was that he kept returning to the same well. He failed to recognize a shift in voter motivation from the old ties of party loyalty, determined largely by ethnic and religious affiliations, to a growing interest in issues based upon economic questions, the special problems of urban areas, and the means of making the political machinery more effective. La Follette sensed this change and used it to take power within the traditional majority party. Victor Berger also recognized it and turned the Socialist party into an effective political party with a local base in Milwaukee. The Democrats absorbed the Populists in 1896, but turned the politics of protest into a single note played on a silver horn. The Bourbons retrieved the shell of the party and waited—and waited. La Follette took the center of the stage and could not be persuaded to relinquish it, finally, until his death in 1925. Much of Wisconsin's political story is his after 1896.

Selected Bibliography

Beitzinger, Alfons J. *Edward G. Ryan: Lion of the Law*. Madison, 1960. The judge who made the Potter Law stick.

Brownsword, Joanne J. "Good Templars in Wisconsin, 1854–1880." Master's thesis, University of Wisconsin, 1960. An important Yankee social institution.

Bureau of Labor and Industrial Statistics of Wisconsin. *Second Biennial Report, 1885–1886*. Madison, 1886. Covers the year of Bay View, calls for immigration restriction.

Burton, William L. "Wisconsin's First Railroad Commission: A Case Study in Apostasy." *Wisconsin Magazine of History* 45:190–98 (Spring 1962). Railroads convinced much of the public that they were being abused.

Clark, James I. *The Wisconsin Labor Story*. Madison, 1956. Useful summary.

Cosmas, Graham A. "The Democracy in Search of Issues: The Wisconsin Reform Party, 1873–1877." *Wisconsin Magazine of History* 46:93–108 (Winter 1962–63). Alliance of reform, the liquor interests, and German Protestant deserters from Republicanism with the Democrats.

Daland, Robert T. "Enactment of the Potter Law." *Wisconsin Magazine of History* 33:45–54 (Sept. 1949). The Republicans boxed in the reformers.

Engberg, George B. "Collective Bargaining in the Lumber Industry of the Upper Great Lakes States." *Agricultural History* 24:205–11 (Oct. 1950). Brief summary of the 1880s in Wisconsin.

Fredman, L. E. *The Australian Ballot: The Story of an American Reform*. East Lansing, Mich., 1968. Robert Schilling was a leader in this essential reform.

Gavett, Thomas W. *Development of the Labor Movement in Milwaukee*. Madison, 1965. The Knights and political action.

Graves, Lawrence L. "The Wisconsin Woman Suffrage Movement, 1846–

1920." Ph.D. dissertation, University of Wisconsin, 1953. Wisconsin was not a leader.

Hunt, Robert S. *Law and Locomotives* *The Impact of the Railroad on Wisconsin Law in the Nineteenth Century.* Madison, 1958. On the separation of management and ownership and the political problems of control.

Korman, Gerd. *Industrialization, Immigrants and Americanizers: The View from Milwaukee, 1866–1921.* Madison, 1967. Sources of labor and its relations with early industry.

Marsden, K. Gerald. "Patriotic Societies and American Labor: The American Protective Association in Wisconsin." *Wisconsin Magazine of History,* 41:287–94 (Summer 1958). Taken from the APA newspaper, the *Wisconsin Patriot.*

Neu, Charles E. "Olympia Brown and the Woman's Suffrage Movement." *Wisconsin Magazine of History* 43:277–87 (Summer 1960). Protested a limited, local suffrage.

Orsi, Richard J. "Humphrey Joseph Desmond: A Case Study in American Catholic Liberalism." Master's thesis, University of Wisconsin, 1965. Desmond was important in the Edgerton Bible case and the Bennett Law fight.

Small, Milton, "Biography of Robert Schilling." Master's thesis University of Wisconsin, 1953. Schilling was the central figure in labor politics of the eighties.

Treleven, Dale E. "Railroads, Elevators, and Grain Dealers: The Genesis of Anti-monopolism in Milwaukee." *Wisconsin Magazine of History* 52: 205–22 (Spring 1969). Grain dealers were squeezed by Mitchell, who controlled elevators, railroads, and credit.

Ulrich, Robert. "The Bennett Law of 1889: Education and Politics in Wisconsin." Ph.D. dissertation, University of Wisconsin, 1965. Mostly newspaper opinion, with little synthesis.

Unger, Irwin. *The Greenback Era: A Social and Political History of American Finance, 1865–1879.* Princeton, 1964. In case you want to unravel the "money question."

Wegner, Janet C. "The Bennett Law Controversy in Wisconsin, 1889–1891." Master's thesis, Brown University, 1966. On University Microfilms, SHSW. 1966. Competent history.

Wyman, Roger. "Wisconsin Ethnic Groups and the Election of 1890." *Wisconsin Magazine of History* 51:269–93 (Summer 1968). The Bennett Law election that scooped the Republicans.

THE LABORATORY
OF DEMOCRACY
1890-1919

part eight

Robert M. La Follette dominated thirty years of Wisconsin political history from the mid-nineties to his death in 1925. Although he remained essentially a regional figure, his impact upon political thought and action was national. He possessed a unique blend of moral fervor, political gifts of a high order, a receptivity to ideas, human warmth, and consistency of ideals and actions that set a high standard. He was also imperious, judgmental, and usually unwilling to concede any honesty of motive to political opponents. He was, in other words, a bundle of human inconsistencies, but this only adds to the interest that students find in a political career that had such a tremendous impact upon his state. La Follette's goal was the American presidency, but he enjoyed the fullest of political careers despite the failure of this ambition.

The best recent scholarship has been done on La Follette's early career. Until very recently, the voluminous La Follette Papers were available only through 1906. The family constituted itself as the keeper of the legend, making it difficult to present a fully rounded sketch. This, and the man's combination of political opportunism with a consistency of laudable purpose which he well served. But there is an urge, occasionally, to kick a prop from under the legend.

The following chapters deal mostly with politics, but a history of Wisconsin progressivism does suggest economic and social change. Two frequently used pictures of the La Follette career make the point. The first shows him haranguing a county fair crowd from a farm cart, around 1900. Except for the clothing, the scene might have been dated anytime between 1870 and the turn of the century. The second shows him in 1924, listening to the election returns by radio. One must keep in the back of his mind the times: Thomas Edison, Henry Ford, Hollywood, the interurban, even John L. Kraft teaching Americans to buy processed cheese in a package.

The twenty years preceding American entry into World War I were immensely productive in adjusting the relations of state government to the requirements of the economic and social order that had emerged in the last third of the nineteenth century. La Follette rightly keeps the center stage, although politics and administration provided a number of men and women of force and ideas.

As La Follette predicted, American involvement in the war diverted attention from the unfinished business of progressivism. In Wisconsin especially, it cut much deeper than that.

LA FOLLETTE

25

Dealing with the La Follette legend is a difficult exercise. Seldom has a major American political figure so successfully converted his campaign autobiography into the commonly accepted story of his political career. When progressivism waned as an active political force, men tended to remember themselves as early recruits in what was once an exciting cause, but was now a commonplace. La Follette was conceded his central role, and if many of his contemporaries found him abrasive, the years have helped to translate this into the image of Fighting Bob.

Recent scholarship on La Follette has centered upon his early career and his role as the molder of a progressive faction which took over control of the Republican party in Wisconsin after a ten-year struggle. Was he the independent fighter against bossism in his early years in politics that he remembered himself to be? Did progressivism in Wisconsin start with La Follette's determination to return his party to the service of the whole people? Did the Bob who accused Theodore Roosevelt of invariably settling for half a loaf of progressive reform himself settle for only a full loaf in his dealings with Wisconsin's legislature? Were his political enemies truly corrupt hirelings of corporate wealth—men more often malignant than simply misguided—and surely dishonest?

The questions suggest the legend and the difficulty of reaching a balanced account. La Follette's sincerity is self-evident. The problems involve checking on a highly selective memory and judging a superbly endowed political man who was gregarious and eager to please, but self-righteous and judgmental at the same time. A political weathervane in his early career, he remembered only that he had never compromised his political beliefs. A man with a great talent for friendship, he left a large number of disillusioned and embittered friends along his political trail. His very human failings found small place in the accounts of friends, family, and supporters who celebrated his very considerable accomplishments and shared his disappointed ambitions to reach higher office.

Albert O. Barton, Madison journalist who served as La Follette's secretary in Washington for a time, accurately summarized the mixed feelings of La Follette's contemporaries as well as the opinion of later scholars: "It has been a serious question with many people whether or not, at least in its first years, the La Follette reform movement was inspired by any other motive than the personal ambition of La Follette. But to whatever degree his personal ambitions were the inspiration of the uprising, it must be said he had a remarkable facility or fortune in making himself and his cause interchangeable in the public mind, making it possible for him to press his propaganda while his friends rather urged support of the man."

Robert M. La Follette was the first Wisconsin governor to be born in the state, coming of Scots-Irish and French Huguenot stock who had pioneered in Kentucky and Indiana before his father moved the family to Primrose township in southeastern Dane County in 1850. Robert was born in a log cabin there in 1855. His father died when the boy was eight months old; his mother was remarried six years later to a man many years her senior. Belle Case La Follette wrote that her husband never expressed his feelings to her about his mother's remarriage: "He had never known his father, but his devotion to his memory was almost morbid."

The family lived with hard times during the boy's youth. Robert became the main support of his mother and sister at an early age, an older brother and half-sister having married. He moved the family to Madison in 1873 when he was eighteen, determined to get a university education, which he did, while continuing as the family breadwinner. His evident ability and ambition were accompanied by a sociable nature and a talent for leadership. He accepted the values of his peers and teachers, that is, he was bent upon improving his prospects through the virtues accepted by middle-class Americans of the time.

Graduated in law, La Follette turned at once to a political career. His recollection was that "Boss" Keyes opposed him in his successful race for district attorney of Dane County in 1880. The contemporary record,

however, indicates that La Follette had the support of what he later identified as "the machine" and "the boss," although Keyes was being humili-
ated by Philetus Sawyer in his own race for the senatorship. The "boss"
surely had little time to spare for the minor local race in which La Follette
was engaged. Thoroughly defeated, Elisha Keyes lost not only the state
chairmanship of the Republican party but also the postmastership of
Madison. He was replaced in the latter job by George Bryant, a wealthy
farmer, politician, and war veteran of Madison who became La Follette's
patron and supporter.

The congressional race of 1884 was made to order for a youthful
comer. Keyes and the incumbent Republican split the party in the
election of 1882, giving the seat to Democrat Burr Jones for one term.
La Follette, with the active backing of George Bryant, who was allied
with the powers of the party, Senator Sawyer and Henry Payne, carried
the nomination and election. La Follette was indeed opposed by Elisha
Keyes on this occasion, but Keyes was no match for La Follette's new
party connections.

La Follette in Congress was no rebel. Aided in his career by the affable Senator Sawyer, he became the useful ally of the equally affable William McKinley and an ardent supporter of the tariff bill which bore Mc-
Kinley's name. He did conceive a dislike for the imperious Henry Payne,
who represented Philip Armour and other meat-packers engaged in promoting oleomargarine. Given the dairy constituency in La Follette's district, this distaste was not a political liability. He spoke in favor of a special tax on oleo in 1886, thus gaining credit with Wisconsin dairymen
and their political mentor William Dempster Hoard, in the years to
follow.

La Follette's congressional career was cut short in the election of
1890, which was a Republican disaster in Wisconsin as elsewhere in the
Midwest. The Bennett Law and the McKinley Tariff were more than the
party could bear. La Follette returned to his law practice in Madison and
to the study of the Republican party's future prospects.

The party bosses had more problems than time for reflection. Both
Senators Sawyer and Spooner were swept from office before the Democratic wave subsided. Worse, the Democrats proposed to collect from the
bondsmen for a series of Republican state treasurers who, by right of
immemorial custom, had been pocketing the interest on deposited state
funds. The money had been treated as a party slush fund, which was the
feature most offensive to the now triumphant Democrats. What made the
Democratic proposal interesting was that Sawyer was a bondsman for
amounts running into six figures.

Sawyer, worried by the prospective loss at the hands of those whom he
considered political brigands, called upon his former congressional col-

league for aid. La Follette may have had his doubts about the old man's interest in him as an attorney, but he met with Sawyer in a public parlor of the Plankinton House. La Follette came away convinced that the millionaire political boss had tried to pay him to see that his brother-in-law, Robert Siebecker, the judge in the case, came to the "right" decision.

The incident occurred in September 1891. Devout La Folletteites often date the beginning of the progressive movement from this meeting. Doubters question whether La Follette did not leap to a conclusion about Sawyer's intent as a first step in his campaign to displace the older man as effective head of the party. Sawyer had already lost his U.S. Senate seat to Democrat William F. Vilas, but remained the acknowledged leader of the Republican Party. La Follette's subsequent actions may have been foolhardy, bold, or simply his response to a moral imperative. He told Judge Siebecker of what he considered a bribe attempt. The judge disqualified himself in the case. Sawyer came forward with an "explanation" before the allegations were more than a rumor. La Follette responded with his dramatic version, and the die was cast. Sawyer's biographer returns a Scotch verdict of "not proven" but leans toward La Follette's version. Equally puzzled, Nils Haugen, a La Follette ally in Congress and later, expressed his reluctance to reach a decision in the matter to former House Speaker Thomas B. Reed. "You never can tell about these old commercial fellows," responded Reed.

The popular legend has it that from this point, La Follette began his long and determined campaign to wrest his party from the hands of the triumvirate of Sawyer, Spooner, and Payne, representing the power of personal and corporate wealth which had corrupted politics. La Follette's weapons were various. He was one of the most compelling orators in American politics of the time. He supplemented this talent with a tireless energy, great attention to detail, an astonishing memory for names and faces, a charismatic gift, and a highly developed political sense.

Whatever his personal assets for political leadership, La Follette was following a course which many of his friends thought would lead to political oblivion. This was a serious matter for a man of thirty-six who had just completed three terms in Congress, where he gained many firm party friends, including a future president, William McKinley. La Follette had clearly dedicated himself to a political career, and he meant to have it within his chosen party. He did not accept the ostracism to which Sawyer, Payne, and Spooner tried to consign him. An acknowledged attraction on the stump, he forced the leadership to a grudging use of his services. It was plain, however, that he was organizing for revolt.

La Follette in revolt was slow to discover reform, except in the narrow sense that he believed the old party leaders to be cynical and corrupt. He meant to replace them. The elections of 1894 promised a return of the Republicans to power. The Democrats had ridden the issues, represented by the Bennett Law and the tariff, to the end of the line and were hurt by the severe depression which began in 1893. La Follette, searching for allies within the Republican ranks, found a power base and reform.

Sawyer was seventy-seven in 1893. The other two members of the party triumvirate, Spooner and Payne, were only fifty, but in years of leadership the three had grown long in the tooth, careless, and arbitrary. La Follette, from a new generation, found a ready constituency among many of the younger men in the party. His associations with the university as an alumnus, and his strategic location as a Madison resident, reinforced his personal attractiveness for this element. Young attorneys, sharing his background, readily responded to his appeals. Like La Follette, they were young men on the make. Old Elisha Keyes observed that "Mr. La Follette successfully appealed to these young men on the ground of self-interest, all the while, of course, putting up a show of very great seriousness and solemnity. [He] pushed them for local offices wherever he could, and told them that if they would join his standard they would break up the old ring and have a chance at the political crib themselves."

Former Governor William D. Hoard was another recruit. Angered by the triumvirate's reluctant support of the Bennett Law in 1890, and venomous toward Henry Payne for lobbying in the interests of oleomargarine, Hoard, who had an enthusiastic following with the growing dairy industry, enlisted with La Follette.

A third element in La Follette's power base was the Norwegian vote, the second largest immigrant vote after the German. Unlike the Germans, the Norwegians were overwhelmingly Republican and therefore had not been courted as assiduously by the party managers as had the German Protestants. They were a self-conscious minority bloc and resented this neglect. They were also looking homeward to an intensely democratic Norway which was implementing a social service state. La Follette had the advantage of having been raised with Norwegian neighbors, and could speak some Norwegian. He was also a political friend of Nils Haugen, with whom he had served in Congress. Haugen was the sole Republican congressman to survive the Wisconsin election of 1890. Although no factionalist, Haugen felt he had been ill-used by Sawyer and Spooner in patronage matters and was ripe to have his distrust converted into action.

La Follette and his friends persuaded the reluctant Nils Haugen to run for governor. Haugen's reluctance was based upon his relatively secure seat in Congress, which he would have to relinquish to make the race for the nomination, but against La Follette's considerable powers of persuasion his protests became progressively weaker. With characteristic energy, La Follette converted the offices of La Follette, Harper, Roe, and Zimmerman into a campaign headquarters. Thousands of letters and circulars went out emphasizing the necessity for those interested in delivering the party from the iron rule of the "bosses" and their "corrupt machine control" to rally to Haugen.

It was customary for a number of regional candidates to enter the gubernatorial race in the Republican party. Many of these candidacies were simply strategic, to hold a block of convention votes for trading purposes. State convention delegates were chosen by county conventions, which in turn were influenced by congressional district conventions lumping together the counties within the district. The 1894 state convention had a field of eleven candidates, in which Haugen ran third, after William Upham and Edward Scofield, both wealthy lumbermen eminently satisfactory to the established party leaders. Haugen did not fade in the balloting but increased his vote each time, until Scofield withdrew on the sixth ballot in favor of Upham.

Haugen returned to his law practice and a later career as a progressive bureaucrat specializing in taxation and railroad legislation. It was a disappointing sequel, and he was one of many who drifted away from La Follette in later years. As a cautious politician, he had sought and received assurances of Sawyer's neutrality toward his candidacy. In his memoirs, he blamed La Follette for continuing a feud that Sawyer would gladly have dropped, thus insuring Haugen's defeat. The feud was La Follette's principal stock in trade at that point in his career, according to many who agreed with Haugen.

La Follette and his circle were the gainers from Haugen's sacrifice. They developed a style of campaigning relatively new to Wisconsin politics. At the core was their "literary bureau," an active group of ambitious supporters throughout the state, oriented to the issues of reform within their own party and kept energized by frequent communications and the growing reputation of La Follette as an implacable rebel within the ranks. They played traditional politics as well, securing control of the party in important Dane County. What they lacked in 1894 was a body of well-defined reforms of broad appeal. Antiboss, antiring, antimachine slogans were not enough.

Recent scholarship on the politics of progressivism disagrees somewhat about the sources of La Follette's familiar array of more specific reforms: the direct primary, anticorruption legislation, railroad regulation, and railroad tax reform. One contention is that many of these ideas were supplied by the men who helped mount the Haugen campaign in 1894. La Follette, who emerged from this band of equals as their political general, made the ideas his own. Another student argues that the reform impulse, and particularly the drive for the direct primary or significant changes in the caucus and convention system, came out of the growing problems of the cities. It was too easy for arrogant utility managers like Henry Payne to manage the political machinery in order to thwart efforts at control over franchises, taxes, and so forth. The ward caucus had become an instrument of corruption because it was too easy to pack such meetings. The Keogh Law of 1891 was the first of a series directed at reform of the nomination process in ward caucuses in Milwaukee.

La Follette in his autobiography said that he had never heard of the direct primary in 1896, when he turned his attention to the lessons of his defeat in the state convention that year. Haugen's biographer claims that Haugen had been talking about the need for an effective corrupt practices act and modifications of the caucus and convention system since 1892, when he concluded that a man of modest means could hardly afford a political race if he was not a machine candidate. Suggestions for the primary device were not lacking. California had experimented with such legislation since 1866. Books and articles had appeared on the subject in the late 1880s when the Australian ballot was widely adopted. La Follette and Sam Harper, his principal strategist, put together the basic primary plank of the coalition in the months after losing the gubernatorial nomination in the 1896 convention.

La Follette was generous in his credits to Albert R. Hall, whom Haugen credits as the true "father of the 'Progressive' movement in Wisconsin." Hall was a Civil War veteran who had been raised in Minnesota after a Vermont boyhood. A successful businessman, austere and purposeful, he came to the Wisconsin assembly in 1891 from Dunn County, where he had moved in 1880. He was no freshman legislator but a seventerm member of the Minnesota assembly, three terms as speaker.

Hall soon established a reputation as a single-minded crank. In season and out, he pressed for legislation to outlaw the distribution of free passes and free transportation by the railroads. Passes had become such a well-established political commodity that legislators, officials, governors, and judges looked upon them as part of the natural order of things. A clear distinction in the political peck order was recognized between those who were important enough to have their passes discreetly delivered to them and those who had to stand in line outside the railroad lobbyist's hotel room to receive their quotas from his secretary. All concerned were quick to express indignation at the suggestion that this largess could in any way affect their official actions.

While Hall pressed the free pass issue as the most blatant example of railroad influence, he made himself an expert on such matters as railroad taxation, rate structures, and pointed comparisons between the railroads' reports to stockholders and those to the state for taxation purposes. The railroads replied with a determined effort to retire him from the assembly. Hall was a friend and ally of Nils Haugen, who brought him and La Follette together. After Haugen's defeat in the state convention, the reform coalition turned to Hall's defense and gained a new appreciation of the issues which he was pressing. The railroads were to become a central La Follette issue.

The gubernatorial campaign of 1896 diverted La Follette from developing the reform issues clearly; the nomination was fought for on familiar ground. Governor Upham had approved a measure which forgave the former Republican state treasurers from the judgments against them, thus relieving their principal bondsmen, Philetus Sawyer and Charles F. Pfister. Upham was clearly marked for retirement by this act of generosity, but Edward Scofield was waiting in the wings to take up the burden for the regulars. La Follette, after some coyness, while his intimates concocted a complicated strategy based upon multiple candidacies and geographic divisions, jumped into the race with his usual energy and determination, causing them some embarrassment. The signals soon got straightened around, as La Follette asserted his primacy in the reform coalition. It was a near thing for the regulars. La Follette believed that he went into the convention a winner, then watched helplessly as the ring, backed by corporate wealth, bought up or foreclosed on his delegates. He claimed that Pfister came to him with the news that "we've got you skinned," and warned La Follette to behave, for which he would be rewarded.

The election of 1896 was a critical one in Wisconsin, as elsewhere in the Middle West. The Democratic triumphs of 1873 and 1890 proved to be temporary, whereas 1896 represented a shift to the Republicans that would endure until 1932. Voter behavior before 1896 had been determined largely by ethnic and religious affiliations and loyalties fixed by the Civil War. Catholics were practically by definition Democrats. This meant the Irish, the Catholic Germans (about half of all Germans), the Poles, and other smaller Catholic groups. The Democrats could also count a large minority of native Americans, including many of Yankee stock, who had weathered the Civil War without changing their traditional party allegiance. The Republicans counted a majority of the Yankees. They also won the loyalty of a large majority of the Scandinavians, the English, the anticlerical Germans, and many of the non-Lutheran Protestant Germans. The German Lutherans constituted a large share of the swing vote between the two parties.

Republican Edward Scofield won a massive 61 percent of the vote in 1896, and Democratic fortunes went into decline. The marked shift from politics dominated by the worn issues defined by the Civil War was accompanied by a relaxation of rigid party loyalty based upon ethnic and religious identification (although these remain powerful indicators), and by a rising interest in issue-oriented politics. La Follette was a considerable influence in this shift. The task of identifying his voter constituencies is not complete.

Convinced that he had been sold out in the 1896 convention, La Follette had the satisfaction of knowing that his drive for the nomination had given the party bosses a scare. Time was on his side. Much of the young blood in the party was identified with his cause. Sawyer was eighty years old and tired. Pfister, who aspired to the leadership, was inept. Spooner returned to the senate in 1897 to cultivate statesmanship, which he much preferred to state politics. Payne, the political operator, was highly unpopular for his utility connections in Milwaukee and found national politics more congenial and rewarding. He became Roosevelt's postmaster general in 1902.

Bob La Follette was not one to wait for time to hand him his prize. Having crystalized his thinking in the model direct-primary bill, he accepted an invitation to deliver a Washington's Birthday address at the University of Chicago in early 1897. His speech, titled "The Menace of the Machine," rang the changes on bossism, corporate influence and corruption, and the need to make political parties responsive to the electorate through the adoption of his direct primary bill. He developed the speech into a standard and worked the county fair circuit with it in the summer and fall. Crowds were fascinated by a political orator out of season, particularly one who roasted his own party so thoroughly, and La Follette was an orator of great power and conviction.

La Follette was essentially a single-issue man. He became a firm believer in concentrating his fire on one or two reforms until he carried the day. Hall's railroad pass issue and tax reform were not forgotten, but La Follette's enthusiasm was reserved for the direct primary.

Edward Scofield has suffered for standing between Robert La Follette and his ambition. No corruptionist, Governor Scofield accepted the political system as he found it, but he was affronted by the patchwork system of state accounting and handling expenditures. He introduced the first governor's budget in Wisconsin and established a central accounting system as far as he was able. A temporary tax commission to study tax reform was created in 1897, with his support, and a permanent one in 1899. But Edward Scofield is remembered for using a railroad pass to frank his household goods from his home in Oconto to Madison, including "one cow, crated." La Follette made that cow famous.

By all of the ordinary rules of politics, Scofield deserved a second term. He was less than zealous in his treatment of some railroad express-car tax legislation and a party pledge to redeem Albert Hall's cherished antipass campaign, but he could argue from substantial technicalities in both instances. La Follette made an early announcement of his intention to unseat Scofield, encouraged this time by a group of prominent Milwaukee reformers organized as the Republican Club of Milwaukee. The members objected especially to the close alliance between their own party leaders and Milwaukee's utility interests. Some members were in the Mugwump reform tradition, while others, like La Follette, were interested in political power as well as reform. Francis E. McGovern, a future rival for leadership of Wisconsin progressivism, was among the latter.

It was a vitriolic campaign, with Scofield as the principal target. The progressive forces were strong enough to write into the platform much of their program: tax equalization, antipass and antilobbying planks, and reform of party nomination procedures. Despite the acrimony between progressives and stalwarts, the progressives were given the treasurer and attorney general nominations. The second-term tradition was strong, and Scofield won by a fair margin. As in 1896, La Follette cried fraud but accepted the results. He did not take part in the campaign because of a characteristic illness which often overtook him after a particularly intense pursuit of his destiny.

The accommodating politician in La Follette overshadowed the stern moralist and reformer in 1900. He had besieged the Republican convention three times, counting 1894 when Nils Haugen was his surrogate, and returned empty-handed. In politics it does not pay to become a prominent but perennial loser. La Follette was understandably nervous. He always ran with great energy and did not lose gracefully. He cultivated patience, but he was not a patient man.

It was symbolic that Philetus Sawyer died in March of 1900. The old leadership was passing from power, and new men were coming to the fore among the stalwarts. Emanuel Philipp was one of them. They found a conciliatory La Follette, full of reasonableness, but backed by more potential convention strength than ever. In Philipp's words, "the white winged dove of peace had become the emblem of the Wisconsin republieans and she no longer lived in terror of being cooked or eaten raw by frenzied factionists." Deciding that they might well lose a fourth bloody battle and reap the consequences, the stalwarts elected surrender with conditions. They were met with friendly interest.

In his autobiography, La Follette recalled that he had been bemused by the importance Philipp and Congressman Joseph Babcock attached to an interview to which they conducted him with Marvin Hughitt, president of the Chicago and Northwestern Railroad. La Follette's recollection was that he dealt forthrightly with Hughitt's questions, recognizing that Babcock and Philipp were admitting surrender while hoping to salvage something from the wreckage. Philipp evidently felt that La Follette was more conciliatory than La Follette remembered, for after quizzing the candidate at length, he personally pledged $1,250 to La Follette's campaign and undertook to get contributions from the railroads, which were forthcoming after the Hughitt interview.

Close friends among La Follette's supporters were alarmed by the candidate's amiability with the enemy. This was as much in character as his vitriolic attacks from the stump. He admitted to a talent for "stirring up the animals" from the platform, but he was courteous and agreeable in personal relationships. His judgmental tendencies increased as his ambitions reached further and he met larger frustrations. In 1900, his readiness to use all means at hand to seize the prize for which he had fought so long certainly matched the eagerness of his opponents to avoid a fight without conceding everything.

La Follette's conciliatory stance in 1900 paid him more dividends than it did the stalwart leaders. He had the stronger hand showing, of course; the progressive swing within the party was a strong tide. La Follette successfully rode that tide and identified it as his own creation. There was much of egotism in this, but much smart politics as well.

Money had always been a problem for the progressives—even reform politics must supply patronage for the faithful as well as funds for publicity. La Follette had been undecided about running in 1900 because of financial difficulties. He was rescued by a genuine gold-plated angel, Isaac Stephenson, an immensely wealthy lumberman. Stephenson had served three terms in Congress and aspired to the U.S. Senate seat that fell vacant in early 1899. He felt that commitments had been made to him, but the stalwart leaders ignored his claim. Aggrieved over this snub, Ike became a progressive. The La Follette group amused him by the excess of circumspection with which they approached the money bag, but the visits were frequent. La Follette and his circle had bought a Dane County weekly in 1897 which they named *The State*. Stephenson, in 1901, gave the progressives a real boost when he bought the *Milwaukee*

Free Press, a daily, shortly after Pfister acquired the much larger *Milwaukee Sentinel* as the stalwart organ. Like Nils Haugen, Ike wrote his memoirs in later years after falling out with La Follette. He estimated that his training period with the latter had cost him $500,000, but he did not regret the education.

With the 1900 nomination clinched, La Follette conducted the campaign with little reference to state issues and reform. Even crusty Governor Scofield, who was visited by no forgiving spirit, could not provoke a fight. But what the campaign lacked in excitement La Follette tried to supply by making 208 speeches in sixty-one counties with ten to fifteen appearances each day. His standard speech was devoted only about one-tenth to state issues, mostly a discussion of his direct primary proposals, with any discussion of railroad taxation or regulation significantly missing. He could have been more leisurely. He won 62 percent of the vote.

The immediate problem, after feeding the office-hungry in the time-honored tradition, was to muster his troops and see what could be done toward realizing some of the reforms now identified with his advocacy. Albert O. Barton, friendly historian of La Follette's rise to power, characterized the Wisconsin governorship as "in the main a clerical position, by courtesy made ornamental." Barton's point was that this was not La Follette's view of the office. The new governor broke tradition by appearing in person to read his first message to the legislature. It was a document in his style, the longest message yet, uncompromising and demanding. La Follette demanded that the legislature pass his direct primary bill and Albert Hall's railroad taxation measures.

The stalwarts felt abused that the harmony promised by the campaign proved so short-lived. They fought a rearguard action in the assembly (which narrowly passed the direct primary bill), secure in the knowledge that they controlled the senate. La Follette's direct primary measure was lost there, but the stalwarts foolishly passed an unworkable substitute, rejecting all progressive amendments, which drew a stinging veto from the governor. La Follette's severest critic, Emanuel Philipp, conceded that the veto was justified but not the tone of the veto message. The governor, commented Philipp, was girding for a long period of intraparty warfare which he was prepared to wage, while the stalwarts were unprepared for such warfare. The railroad tax bills died in the senate without a vote, and met defeat on the floor in the assembly.

If nothing else had been accomplished by the session, La Follette had established his issues for 1902. He dramatized them by vetoing a dog-licensing bill with references to the legislature's lack of interest in true tax equalization between the farmer or homeowner and the railroads.

The veto message was a piece of calculated demagogy that infuriated some progressive legislators as well as the hapless stalwarts. But it was good politics.

The stalwarts were fumbling about looking for leadership. They were not as cohesive a group as the La Follette legend has made them, for many were men with moderate reform records. Their common denominator was a hearty dislike for the governor and his assumption that anyone who opposed him in things great or small did so from dishonest motives. They organized a Republican League of Wisconsin, promptly branded the Eleventh-Story League from the location of their headquarters in a Milwaukee office building. Unfortunately the league found its leader and principal financial angel in Charles Pfister, who fit the description of a ham-handed corruptionist well. Some league members writhed under charges that they were corporation hirelings organized by a ruthless machine to do the railroads' and others' bidding. In rebuttal, they pointed to the formidable machine that La Follette had built upon his Dane County base. There were elements of truth in both accusations, but one must concede a more disinterested character and purpose to the La Follette machine. It was his eternal righteousness that galled.

The campaign of 1902 found La Follette at his combative best. He had his issues in the unredeemed platform pledge of his party and he had a new stump technique. Long gone was the harmony of 1900 as he invaded assembly and senatorial districts of stalwart members to "read the roll call" on their voting records. It was divisive, but effective. However, again the stalwarts controlled the senate. Again La Follette pressed for his direct primary, ad valorem taxation of the railroads, and a strong railroad commission.

The railroads were reconciled to a change in their tax base, which had long been a license fee based on a percentage of gross earnings. A tax commission created during Scofield's administration pointed out that the railroads were undertaxed if the tax were computed on the basis of their real estate and personal property holdings. The railroads paid 58 percent of the state's tax revenues in fiscal 1902. They recognized the ease with which the license fee percentage could be raised by an unfriendly legislature. It had advanced from an initial 1 percent to 4 by 1900, and the tax commission suggested a new rate of 5.5 percent. An ad valorem tax, based upon general tax rates, might be preferable. The change was accepted with better grace than La Follette ever conceded.

There was no reconciliation on the part of the railroads to peaceful acceptance of a strong railroad commission. Their defense was to point to the dire effects of the Potter Law of 1874, which was alleged to have halted all railroad building for a term of years. The truth was that whatever dire effects the Potter Law had grew out of the intransigence of the railroads. An acquiescent Republican legislature had repealed the law within two years. Nonetheless, the legend was useful. The railroads marshalled lobbyists, politicians, and large shippers who enjoyed a favorable rate structure. La Follette lost on his commission bill, but the issue was useful to him in engineering a third term draft for 1904.

The direct primary bill was, of course, an assault upon the machinery of the party and its managers. Emanuel Philipp, who was to become the most skillful manager among the stalwarts, commented that this supposedly boss-ridden faction could not produce a competent boss in its hour of need. Stalwart strategy, he noted sourly, was concocted in Washington by Senators Spooner and Quarles, with Congressman Joseph Babcock as runner. Spooner's popularity with Wisconsin Republicans cut across factional lines, mostly because he was remote from party management in the state. He chose to fight the direct primary before the general electorate by attaching a referendum provision in the senate, where the stalwarts had a working majority. The progressives accepted the challenge. The stalwarts assumed that the direct primary was such a radical departure from the cautious experimentation with caucus reform of the past dozen years that they should have little trouble persuading the voters to reject it. Many moderate progressives agreed with this view. This was another stalwart error in judgment.

La Follette was not a politician who suffered from overconfidence at election time, and 1904 was a crucial year with his cherished primary bill on the ballot as a referendum measure. Since it was a presidential year, delegates to the national convention, as well as the state ticket nominations, were to be chosen at the state convention. This was the first time that both slates were to be handled by a single convention.

The 1904 state convention, in the old red brick armory adjacent to the Madison campus of the university, was to become famous. The party factions were contesting with ferocity county elections of delegates through the caucus-convention system. There were cries of foul, and rival slates claiming legitimacy. The progressives professed to smell an overt plot of the stalwarts to take over the management of the convention by force. The stalwarts, for their part, held a similar conviction. For years the state convention had been held in Milwaukee, but La Follette had succeeded in 1902 in moving it to his home ground. His organization took firm control, even using barricades and special guards. The stalwarts claimed that they were counted out of all of the contested delegates by the La Follette-controlled credentials committee.

The unhappy stalwarts withdrew and held a rival convention, which nominated a separate slate of delegates and candidates for state offices. They gained a small triumph when their delegates were seated at the national convention—Henry C. Payne was postmaster general—but even this victory was set aside by the state supreme court, after the event. There were no triumphs elsewhere for the stalwarts. La Follette won the governorship easily, with over 227,000 votes, while the stalwart candidate polled only 12,000. The direct primary referendum carried in a surprisingly light vote.

La Follette's big issue in 1904 was his railroad commission bill, upon which he rang the familiar changes, calling the roll on votes hostile to the measure in his numerous county fair appearances. Another of his devices was the recitation of intrastate rates on farm commodities, comparing them with more favorable rates in the neighboring states of Iowa and Minnesota. Emanuel Philipp issued a stalwart pamphlet in rebuttal, *The Truth About Wisconsin Freight Rates,* which never caught up with La Follette's dramatic generalizations. Philipp was right that freight rate-making was complicated, and built upon years of experience and response to many pressures; but Wisconsin was not pioneering a new field this time. Thirty states had railroad commissions already, and the railroad's arguments from the 1874 Potter Law were growing thin. La Follette finally had his working majority in the legislature and would have his law. Even the stalwarts and Democrats endorsed some form of regulation.

La Follette's leadership was less effective than the legend assumes. He was an orator rather than a debater, and his stump performances on the subject did not add up to a coherent bill or arguments for one; he did not do his homework. The result was that the progressives lacked forceful executive leadership and were often in disagreement among themselves. This gave the railroads and their friends their chance. The final measure carried a burden of compromises that should have tested the governor's resolve.

There were extenuating circumstances which inclined La Follette to accept the despised "half a loaf" in this instance. Senator Quarles's term was up in 1905, and La Follette was pledged to the support of his principal financial angel, Isaac Stephenson, for the seat. But there were other ambitious progressives ready to contest the issue, despite the knowledge of La Follette's pledge. Friends of the governor undertook the relatively easy task of persuading him that he would have to sacrifice, in the interest of party harmony, and accept the senatorship for himself. He agreed to do so on condition that he would remain in the governor's chair to see his program through. The railroad commission bill was the principal item.

With Theodore Roosevelt's Washington beckoning, it was an impatient La Follette who watched his legislative troops being mauled by the enemy. Nothing will turn a disciplined faction into a loose coalition so rapidly as success at the polls. The railroad commission bill that finally emerged for his signature was a weak one compared to the strong laws recently passed in other states. For obvious reasons, La Follette preferred to declare himself pleased with the results. The railroads were immensely relieved. The commission was not given rate-fixing power, but rather powers of investigation, review, and revision, and these were subject to stays and injunctions by the courts.

La Follette wanted to appoint Nils Haugen as the strong head of the new commission, but the state senate would not confirm him. The effective head of the three-man commission, although not its first chairman, was Balthazar Meyer, a professor of political economy at the university in Madison. who had done his graduate work there under Richard Ely. Meyer was essentially a mediator who set the commission in a narrow, unaggressive role. The progressives easily adopted the line that their railroad commission was so fair and scientifically informed that even the railroads were forced to pronounce it "a high-grade commission." This the railroad men did, but for quite different reasons. Meyer wrote articles for railroad journals and much mutual admiration was displayed.

Having set his railroad commission in motion, La Follette departed for Washington to take up his duties as a senator. He sized up his principal rival for leadership of Republican progressivism and found him wanting. "President Roosevelt," wrote La Follette, "acted upon the maxim that half a loaf is better than no bread." For himself, he declared, he was accustomed, in matters of legislation, to "the most thorough and complete mastery of the principles involved, in order to fix the limit beyond which not one hair's breadth can be yielded."

Selected Bibliography

Acrea, Kenneth. "The Wisconsin Reform Coalition, 1892 to 1900: La Follette's Rise to Power." *Wisconsin Magazine of History* 52:132–57 (Winter 1968–69). Emphasizes the roles of La Follette's peers in reform.

Barton, Albert O. *La Follette's Winning of Wisconsin.* Madison, 1922. The received version by La Follette's one-time secretary.

Brandes, Stuart Dean. "Nils F. Haugen and the Wisconsin Progressive Movement." Master's thesis, University of Wisconsin, 1965. Wants credit for Haugen and Albert Hall.

Caine, Stanley P. *The Myth of a Progressive Reform: Railroad Regulation in*

Wisconsin, 1903–1910. Madison, 1970. When La Follette accepted half a loaf.

Haugen, Nils P. *Pioneer and Political Reminiscences.* Edited by Joseph Schafer. Madison, n.d. Norwegian-born progressive who had his differences with La Follette.

Helgeson, Arlan. "The Wisconsin Treasury Cases." *Wisconsin Magazine of History* 35:129–36 (Winter 1951). Compounding Republican troubles in 1890.

Hicks, John D. "The Legacy of Populism in the Middle West." *Agricultural History* 23:225–36 (Oct. 1949). La Follette as a model of Populist ideology.

Kennedy, Padriac M. "Lenroot, La Follette, and the Campaign of 1906." *Wisconsin Magazine of History* 42:163–74 (Spring 1959). The attempt to dump Governor Davidson.

La Follette, Robert M. *La Follette's Autobiography: A Personal Narrative of Political Experience.* 1913. Reprint. Madison, University of Wisconsin Press, 1960. How La Follette made his version the standard.

La Follette, Belle Case and Fola. *Robert M. La Follette.* 2 vols. New York, 1953. The official biography.

Lahman, Carroll P. "Robert M. La Follette as Public Speaker and Political Leader, 1855–1905." Ph.D. dissertation, University of Wisconsin, 1939. Uncritical, but contains valuable interviews.

Lovejoy, Allen F. *La Follette and the Establishment of the Direct Primary in Wisconsin, 1890–1904.* New York, 1941. The history of agitation for the primary.

McDonald, Forrest. "Street Cars and Politics in Milwaukee, 1896–1901." *Wisconsin Magazine of History* 39:166–70, 206–12 (Spring 1956). On the innocence of the Milwaukee Electric Railway and Light Company.

Manning, Eugene A. "Old Bob La Follette: Champion of the People." Ph.D. dissertation, University of Wisconsin, 1965. La Follette as demagogue. Naive.

Margulies, Herbert F. *The Decline of the Progressive Movement in Wisconsin, 1890–1920.* Madison, 1968. Best published to date.

Maxwell, Robert S. *La Follette and the Rise of Progressivism in Wisconsin.* Madison, 1956. Goes only to 1912, misses much recent scholarship on La Follette's early career.

———. "La Follette and the Election of 1900: A Half-Century Reappraisal." *Wisconsin Magazine of History* 35:23–29, 68–71 (Autumn 1959). Surface stuff.

Philipp, Emanuel L. *The Truth About Wisconsin Freight Rates: Views of Shippers and the Press.* Milwaukee, 1904. Chasing La Follette with the Truth.

———. *Political Reform in Wisconsin: A Historical Review of the Subjects of Primary Election, Taxation and Railroad Regulation.* Milwaukee, 1910. The articulate stalwart.

Snow, Carlton James. "A Reformer and His Heritage." Master's thesis, University of Wisconsin, 1970. On Nils Haugen's Norwegian background.

Stephenson, Isaac. *Recollections of a Long Life, 1829–1915.* Chicago, 1915. Ike Stephenson put up the money for La Follette.

Thelen, David P. "The Boss and the Upstart: Keyes and La Follette." *Wisconsin Magazine of History* 47:103–15 (Winter 1963–64).

———. "Robert M. La Follette, Public Prosecutor." *Wisconsin Magazine of History* 47:214–23 (Spring 1964).

———. "La Follette and the Temperance Crusade." *Wisconsin Magazine of History* 47:291–300 (Summer 1964). Best on La Follette's early career.

———. *The New Citizenship: Origins of Progressivism in Wisconsin, 1885–1900.* Columbia, Missouri, 1971. Urban problems and the progressive impulse.

Twombly, Robert C. "The Reformer as Politician: Robert M. La Follette in the Election of 1900." Master's thesis, University of Wisconsin, 1964. First you have to win!

THE FRUITS
OF PROGRESSIVISM

26

The stalwarts regularly celebrated the political demise of Robert M. La Follette, only to have "Fighting Bob" cast off the winding sheets and ruin the wake. He seemed to thrive while teetering on the edge of political oblivion. Lesser politicians challenged him at their peril, but it was a peril regularly courted.

La Follette disappointed his principal financial supporter, Isaac Stephenson, by taking for himself the Senate seat for which he was pledged to support the older man. Stephenson was angry and unconvinced by La Follette's justification for the substitution, but remained in the La Follette camp for a time.

La Follette was shifting his career and his interest to Washington. Nevertheless, he expected to retain his position of leadership in state politics, but he discovered that that leadership, given the new political rules of his own imposition, was more difficult than in the days of Philetus Sawyer and Elisha Keyes. The problem, for a true-blue progressive, was how to manage without the appearance of management. La Follette never really solved it, nor did his heirs.

The progressive lieutenant-governor, who stepped into the governor's chair in January 1906 when La Follette finally resigned to take his seat in the Senate, had every reason to expect that he would have La Follette's support to succeed himself. His expectation was disappointed.

La Follette and his inner circle decided that Governor James Davidson, the first Norwegian to achieve the office, lacked the necessary qualifications to give executive leadership to the progessives. It was a gratuitous slap at the important Norwegian vote and at Governor Davidson. The stalwarts joyously took up Davidson's cause. They saw it as a providential opportunity to heal the party's wounds and end La Follette's disruptive influence.

Davidson won an easy victory, defeating La Follette's candidate, Irvine Lenroot, in the primary by 109,583 to 61,178 and going on to a solid victory in the general election. For once La Follette accepted the defeat with outward grace and supported Davidson in November, but damage had been done. La Follette demanded loyalty, but it sometimes appeared to be a one-way affair. Nor did La Follette have the satisfaction of being proven correct about Davidson. The governor surprised him by a vigorous exploitation of the popularity that La Follette's opposition had given him. He built up a political organization of his own, largely at the expense of the La Follette faction.

Governor Davidson worked successfully with the progressive-dominated legislature, which had further reforms to press. The regulatory functions of the railroad commission were extended to other public utilities: express and telegraph companies, street railways, telephone, electrical, and water companies. A beginning was made on state supervision of the issuance of stocks and bonds by utilities. An investigation of the practices of insurance companies had been instituted by Governor La Follette in 1905, growing out of sensational disclosures from a similar investigation in New York. Davidson withstood the considerable pressures brought to bear by the major insurance companies and signed legislation putting them under comprehensive regulation.

La Follette did not abandon his attempts to manage his following, but his control of internal party affairs did not improve greatly. The truth, of course, was that he was simply the leader of a loose coalition, not the commander of a disciplined army. It is probably unfair to blame him for what appeared to be a lack of control at crucial times.

Senator Spooner unexpectedly resigned in 1907, giving the progressives the chance to fill the other senate seat. La Follette quickly redeemed his earlier pledge to support Isaac Stephenson, but progressives Irvine Lenroot and William H. Hatton also entered the race. Stephenson, probably with some justice, felt that La Follette could have called off Lenroot and marshalled more support. He won, but he was convinced that La Follette had done less in his behalf than he had a right to expect. La Follette, on the other hand, thought he had an understanding that the elderly lumberman would be content with the honor and not contest the seat in the regular election the following year. He was wrong.

La Follette's ambitions for himself did not slumber. He came to the Senate with a reputation which allowed him to ignore the senatorial custom that junior members were seen but not heard for a decent interval. Congress was dealing with what became the Hepburn Act, an expansion of the Interstate Commerce Act regulating railroads, and La Follette jumped into the fray. As the presidential sweepstakes of 1908 loomed, he was able to see himself as the logical heir of Theodore Roosevelt. He announced his readiness to take up the burden.

Nils Haugen and Isaac Stephenson both recalled their amusement that La Follette and his circle could take these presidential ambitions seriously. Ike hedged his opinion by financing a modest headquarters at the convention for La Follette. He also complained that the officious aides would not allow him in to see his tenant. History confirmed that La Follette was not the heir apparent. Roosevelt easily passed the honor on to his chosen successor, William Howard Taft.

With the imprimatur of the popular Roosevelt upon the Taft candidacy in 1908, Stephenson and Davidson allied themselves with the Taft forces to sweep La Follette's troops out of still more party posts. "The La Follette crowd was cleaned out, horse, foot, and dragoon . . . and the platform just as the conservative wanted it," crowed unreconstructed old Elisha Keyes. Davidson went on to win a second term, while Ike Stephenson bought the first Wisconsin preferential senatorial primary in a sharp contest. The "Bobolettes," as the stalwarts derisively named the La Follette faithful, gained no glory in the contest. After Stephenson won, they mounted a legislative investigation of the victory. Stephenson admitted to spending $107,000 from his ample purse. However, the investigation seemed inspired as much by spite as by concern for political purity.

The next election year, 1910, was surely a crucial one for La Follette. His own senate seat was up, which was an advantage, giving him a more legitimate role to play than that of kingmaker or spoiler. He formed an alliance with Francis McGovern, a new progressive leader who had arisen in Milwaukee politics and was seeking the governorship, and the combination of La Follette and McGovern was too much for the alliance of moderate progressives and stalwarts opposing them for control of the party.

La Follette immediately turned to challenge Taft's leadership at the national level. Taft had rediscovered his own conservatism and an abiding dislike for La Follette. La Follette had his own troubles. No matter how hard he ran, Theodore Roosevelt was always there ahead of him, denying him a chance at the prize. It is a familiar story how Roosevelt returned to politics and swept up most of La Follette's national support in the ill-fated Bull Moose campaign of 1912. La Follette sulked in his tent. Less familiar is the story of the 1914 debacle which overtook progressivism in Wisconsin, with La Follette playing a now-recognized role.

La Follette's brand of politics helped lead some Wisconsin voters away from strict party identification and from ethnic-religious voting as a matter of faith. But issue-oriented voting became the province of a minority. While La Follette's support was amorphous, it was real enough. Born Republicans continued to vote the straight party ticket, which confirmed his determination to stay within his traditional party. The large Scandinavian vote, dependably Republican since the 1850s, was inclined toward progressivism by background and the recognition accorded it by the progressives. The huge German vote was much less identifiable, but Milwaukee wards made up of skilled workers voted for La Follette. He did, evidently, have support from what might be described as the working-class elite. Farmers in poorer rural counties, particularly in the northern and western parts of Wisconsin, tended to be stoutly antimachine and antirailroad. Much depended upon tenuous political alliances and ethnic, economic, geographic, and personal ties. The large Catholic vote continued to favor the Democrats. The urban middle class, more prosperous farm areas, and Yankee-dominated precincts and wards generally favored the stalwart Republicans.

It is difficult to recapture the kinetic style of La Follette campaigning. Early and late, Bob was out on the hustings firing up the hardshells, and convincing the "fair-minded Democrats" by denouncing the villains of his own party. He captured Democratic votes by this technique. They recognized that in most years the real contest was in the Republican party. William Jennings Bryan treated La Follette with considerable deference, endorsing him in preference to a conservative Democrat in 1902.

The keys to La Follette's success were his image as a fighter, a growing acceptance of his definition of politics, sympathy with the progressive temper, his readiness to lend his talents to advance the careers of young men in exchange for their loyalty, and tenuous alliances with politicians having some political following independent of him. Isaac Stephenson, James O. Davidson, and later, Irvine Lenroot and John Blaine, all developed such followings in La Follette's shadow. In particular, his relationship with Francis E. McGovern of Milwaukee, who won the governorship in 1910, falls into this class.

Progressivism developed within the Republican party in Milwaukee independently of the La Follette machine. Stalwart leadership there in the nineties was in the hands of Henry C. Payne, Charles Pfister, and

Emanuel Philipp. Payne and Pfister were involved in the ownership and management of utilities, while Philipp had close ties with the railroads and breweries. Payne was president of the Milwaukee Electric Railway and Light Company. Consolidation and the rapid growth of the city brought the company aggressively into politics, and Payne was expected to deliver. He was powerful, arrogant, and self-assured. Utilities, contractors bidding on streets and sewers, organized vice, and other interests were turning Milwaukee into a city with an unsavory reputation for corruption.

The severe depression that began in 1893 drew attention to the costs of rapid growth, the boom psychology of the eighties, and corruption. Concerned community leaders organized the Milwaukee Municipal League. The organization was typical of the time in that it concentrated its attentions upon economy, efficiency, control of franchises, clean politics, and a civil service law for the city. It was interesting in that it offered a forum for a broad cross-section of community leaders. Populist Robert Schilling, an active member, argued reform with banker John Johnston and *Sentinel* editor Horace Rublee. There was general agreement that municipal elections should be nonpartisan in character.

Enthusiasm for reform, based upon calls for honesty and efficiency in the mugwump tradition, was hard to sustain. It was even more difficult to get politicians to agree to abandon traditional party ties in favor of nonpartisan elections. The nonpartisan argument had grown partly out of the brief success of Robert Schillings' Union Labor party in 1886–87, following the eight-hour-day agitation and the Bay View Massacre: Democrats and Republicans offered a combined Citizens Ticket to head off this threat from militant labor. The growing strength of the Social Democrats—Victor Berger's socialists—was convincing the mugwump element anew that nonpartisan fusion of reformist Republicans and Democrats was necessary.

Two Milwaukee politicians who did not agree with the nonpartisan approach were Francis E. McGovern and Victor Berger. McGovern's brand of Republican progressivism was to go well beyond the La Follette program, especially in the areas of industrial and social welfare legislation. He owed much of his interest in this type of legislation to Victor Berger.

Berger Americanized Milwaukee Socialism and made it into a respectable alternative to the scandal-ridden Republicans and Democrats in municipal politics. His Social Democrat party, which fielded a full ticket for the first time in 1898, built from 5 percent of the Milwaukee County vote in that election to 33 percent in 1908. They were second in both 1906 and 1908 in three-way contests with the Republicans and

Democrats, and won the mayor's office in 1910 for one term. This record persuaded conservative Democrats and Republicans to return to coalition tactics in 1912 to defeat the "reds." McGovern scorned coalition and "nonpartisan" politics, preferring to offer progressive alternatives to socialism. He made his initial mark in politics as district attorney for Milwaukee County, a seat the Socialists came within an ace of winning away from him in 1906. McGovern saw the Socialists as a threat to his constituency.

Socialist strength was squarely based on the German working-class wards in Milwaukee. Victor Berger, who started his career in American politics as a single-taxer, provided the party with a wider base. He broke with the Marxian socialists and adopted a gradualist philosophy receptive to piecemeal reforms. Education of a majority to accept the inevitability of socialism by way of the ballot, rather than by revolution, was Berger's creed. He helped persuade Eugene Debs to assume the leadership of the party nationally. A native of Indiana, Debs was America's most popular radical leader. At the local level, Berger recruited a number of native Americans: Frederic Heath of impeccable Yankee ancestry; Winfield Gaylord, a Mississippian who had been a Methodist minister; Carl Thompson of Michigan and Gilbert H. Poor of Louisiana, both clergymen; Carl Sandburg, who would later win literary fame, and Daniel Hoan, who became Milwaukee's famous Socialist mayor for twenty-four years. Another source of strength was the close link between the Milwaukee Socialists and union labor, especially the Federated Trades Council and the Wisconsin Federation of Labor (AFL) leadership.

Milwaukee Socialism was important to socialism nationally, but our concern is with the part played in Milwaukee and Wisconsin politics. The party regularly ran candidates in state as well as national elections, but local politics offered the best chance to win elections, more exciting than educating voters for the distant socialist millennium.

The German intelligentsia and a working class schooled in bread-and-butter unionism was not a broad enough base for socialist victory. And then there was the Catholic clergy, most of whom rejected socialism vehemently and claimed many German and most of the Polish workingmen as parishioners. Berger, an Austrian Jew by birth, was an agnostic and enthusiastic controversialist who enjoyed tilting with the priests. The Socialists, to succeed locally, had to attract middle-class votes on the basis of arguments outside the normal socialist rhetoric. They found these issues in municipal corruption, waste, debt, home rule, and public ownership of the troublesome utilities.

The records of Republican politicians and Democratic mayor David Rose were eloquently in the Socialists' favor. The district attorney, Mc-

Govern, got grand jury indictments in 1904–5 against twenty-four persons involved in municipal corruption. The Socialists had appropriated the issue by pointing up the tainted character of recent administrations of both Republicans and Democrats. They held aloof from McGovern's indictments, charging that the real offenders, the bribe givers, escaped, while the minor officials who accepted the bribes suffered the full force of the law. Their newspapers and leaflets, given wide distribution by a corps of devoted Socialists, convinced a wider electorate that the Social Democrats had the answers. The party won nine aldermanic seats in 1904. Their discipline, honesty, and readiness to work for realistic solutions converted many non-socialists to the idea that the party could be trusted with local affairs within the practical limits imposed by the city charter. The lessons of growing socialist success worried McGovern and his friends.

La Follette had a minority representation among Milwaukee progressives; the majority accepted the local leadership represented by the ambitious McGovern. In 1910, as in earlier elections, the cooperation between the La Follette and McGovern forces was by a treaty arrangement between equals who needed each other. Milwaukee, with nearly one-sixth of the state's population, was the logical center for a serious rival to La Follette's power within the progressive movement, and aside from philosophical differences, McGovern was as ambitious as La Follette and able. "If the McGovern crowd try to make any trouble he would find that he isn't as big a man as he thinks when it gets down to a question between you and him," wrote Irvine Lenroot to La Follette in 1906. The comment defines the relationship of all three. La Follette preferred subalterns to allies.

That McGovern was not La Follette's man from the first is amply clear. One can therefore draw a distinction between the reforms instituted by La Follette as governor and the astonishing legislative record of 1911 under McGovern's leadership. Political reforms, so much at the heart of the La Follette program, were advanced under McGovern's leadership, but his interests went well beyond them to fundamental economic and industrial legislation. The 1911 legislature created the first workmen's compensation program and an industrial commission to administer it, factory safety legislation, and hours for working women and children. The first successful state income tax law was implemented; a highway commission was created to administer a highway construction program; a comprehensive waterpower conservation law was adopted, along with new forest reserve laws and a forest commission. A state life insurance fund was created which, still in existence, anticipated the "yardstick principle" of the New Deal's Tennessee Valley Authority. Special laws encouraging the formation of farm cooperatives, fostering loans for farm improvements, and extending agricultural education were spread on the books. A typical progressive innovation was the Board of Public Affairs, with a broad mandate to study all branches of state and local government and make recommendations which would lead to greater efficiency.

It is manifestly unfair to label the accomplishments under McGovern's leadership as simply the fruition of reforms advanced by La Follette. They went well beyond La Follette's basic concern with the machinery of democracy, the curbing of monopolies, equitable taxation, and regulation of irresponsible financial power. At the same time, however, La Follette's largely rural following provided votes and much of the legislative leadership that brought McGovern's program into being. McGovern was responding to urban pressures and threats of Socialist success, while the La Follette progressives reflected a general temper of the times congenial to reform, and a receptivity to the suggestions of informed experts. Wisconsin, and particularly the close link between Capitol and campus in Madison, figured in many magazine articles of the time. Typical was one titled "A University That Runs a State" that appeared in *World's Work* in April 1913.

The indefinable Wisconsin Idea, which came into currency during the progressive era, is probably better summarized by some of the popular cliché phrases of the time than by the hyperbole of "a university that runs a state." "The expert on tap, not on top," "the boundaries of the campus are the boundaries of the state," "the service university," "applying the scientific method to legislation," "the democratization of knowledge," all suggest a congenial interchange between campus and Capitol.

There are a number of strands to the story of the relationship of the University of Wisconsin with the progressives at the other end of State Street. The traditions of that link appear today in the products of the ever-expanding public relations that characterize the contemporary university, and in the rhetoric of administrators who commonly confuse these efforts with reality. John R. Commons, whose name should head any list of professional scholars who shaped legislation and its administration in the progressive era, commented that "the faculty of the University of Wisconsin has always been perhaps nine-tenths on the conservative or reactionary side." He might have added that at any given time, nine-tenths of the faculty occupied itself with other scholarly concerns and had no interest in the boundaries of the university, or its impact upon practical politics. He did add, "I was never called in except by Progressives, and only when they wanted me."

While the University of Wisconsin has a self-conscious tradition of service to the state and its people, this was no invention of the Wisconsin progressives. The service university was a natural outgrowth of the rise of state-supported universities in the last quarter of the nineteenth century. Wisconsin was one of the leaders in developing university extension, and later, beginning with La Follette, furnishing experts to help shape legislation and administrative machinery. It established a reputation as a model in this. But it would be erroneous to assume that progressives gave more enthusiastic financial support to the institution than did conservatives, although the latter may have displayed less enthusiasm for professional scholars as social engineers.

La Follette's link with the university was a natural one. He was the first graduate of the institution to achieve the governorship, and as a resident of Madison he had maintained close ties there. He managed the appointment in 1903 of his classmate, Charles R. Van Hise, to the presidency of the university. Van Hise was devoted to the expansion of the university and its functions as a service institution. He was ably abetted in this by two faculty members of national stature, economist Richard T. Ely and historian Frederick Jackson Turner. These two helped to attract other scholars who were to function at both ends of State Street. A list, compiled in 1911, showed forty-six professional people connected with the university who were serving the state government directly in some capacity. A trend began with La Follette, who instituted a Saturday Lunch Club to bring together progressive officials and legislators and members of the faculty.

La Follette had met John R. Commons in 1902, when as an expert on taxation for the National Civic Federation, Commons discussed with him the new system of ad valorem taxation of railroad property. Commons came to the University of Wisconsin in 1904, and La Follette turned to him to draft a comprehensive civil service law, which was passed in 1905. Commons, in his autobiography, tells of meeting Charles McCarthy, who created the first legislative reference library out of a modest job as a document cataloguer for the Wisconsin Free Library Commission. McCarthy, a dynamic Irishman who had taken a doctorate with Turner, became a key figure in the impressive legislative accomplishments of 1911. Immodestly, McCarthy set himself the task of building "one state in the country whose written law will be to some degree better than that of other states." Disclaiming any influence over the legislative process except as an expert providing form and terminology, he was accurately identified by indignant stalwarts as a primary source of advanced progressivism. When in 1946 his admiring biographer published a book entitled *McCarthy of Wisconsin,* there was no confusion about who was *the* McCarthy of Wisconsin.

Governor Francis McGovern was an even more congenial figure for the university sociologists and economists than was La Follette, who never entirely abandoned the notion, which appeared in his early speeches, that city tenements were the source of criminals and incendiaries, quite unlike the honest husbandmen with whom he identified himself. La Follette found McCarthy useful, but dealt with him through intermediaries, while McGovern's relationship with McCarthy was much closer. McCarthy, of course, had had several more years to ingratiate himself with the sources of power around the Capitol by 1910, and was ambitious to expand his influence.

McGovern took command with a sure hand. Although he talked of harvesting the seed already sown, he was paying his respects more to his own faction of progressivism than to La Follette's followers. Those followers had found recent years confusing, with La Follette gone to Washington. Davidson's popularity in the governorship was a powerful counterforce to La Follette's influence, as well. Moderate progressives aligned with the stalwarts, under the leadership of Davidson in 1908 and 1909, to take over both the organization of the party and the legislature. McGovern found the confusion useful for building his own following.

La Follette, searching for new issues, tried to make tariff revision a key one. He may have been somewhat out of touch. State political waters were further muddied by a drive for local option to control the sale of liquor. La Follette always refused to take a position on the issue, arguing that it could only divide and confuse those interested in true reforms. Temperance legislation was always attractive to his Scandinavian supporters, who voted for him anyway, but it was political death with the much larger German population. McGovern, whose main strength was in populous Milwaukee County with its German majority, had no difficulty identifying himself as an out-and-out wet. This won him votes, and financial support from the brewers.

More than any previous year, 1910 was a progressive year. Even the Wisconsin Republican stalwarts felt compelled to use the label and came out for workman's compensation and extended regulatory powers. As for the Democrats, their platform could have been written by La Follette himself that year. McGovern, urged on by his own inclinations, his supporters, fear of growing Socialist success among his constituency, and competition from both stalwarts and Democrats, staked out the most advanced position. La Follette endorsed him out of political necessity, to bolster his own position as much as from conviction. The advanced progressives in the 1909 legislature had set up committees to study workmen's compensation, implementation of income tax, banking legislation, a state highway program, conservation, and regulation of water power development. These were the seeds of the harvest to which McGovern referred in his first message as governor. He had a progressive majority in the legislature, plus thirteen Socialists of Berger's persuasion who were ready to cooperate in social welfare and industrial legislation.

The Democrats, squeezed between the Socialists and progressives, had a bad year in 1910 in Wisconsin, although they made significant gains as the agents of progressive reform in the Northeast, Ohio, and Indiana. They charged McGovern and Berger with vote trading. Socialists clearly voted for McGovern in a statewide contest, while they voted for their own candidates in Milwaukee city and county elections. The Socialists responded that the progressives, unlike the Democrats, treated their party as a legitimate competitor. It will be recalled that McGovern refused to join other Republicans and the Democrats in calling for nonpartisan municipal elections. This was Berger's position too. He correctly saw it as a maneuver permitting Republicans and Democrats to gang up on the Socialists under the guise of a nonpartisan ticket.

It has often been remarked that the progressives of whatever stripe generally sounded more radical than they really were because they accepted the basic tenets of capitalism. But their rhetoric was directed against capitalism's most successful practitioners: Rockefeller, Morgan, et al. However, all progressives, including the Milwaukee Socialists, were pursuing approximately the same constituency, which had a keen appreciation of the politics of the possible.

The passage of the workmen's compensation act in 1911 was a fair sample of pragmatic politics in action. The architect of the legislation was John R. Commons, professor of economics at the university. Commons believed in the free play of all the economic interests involved, both in the framing and administration of such legislation. His genius lay in finding incentives which would enlist the support of the major interests involved: organized labor, the large employers, and the public. To this end, he established an advisory board made up of enlightened employers, labor representatives, and public members. The areas of common agreement discovered made the legislation seem almost inevitable. Indeed, the need for such legislation had been agitated in Wisconsin, as elsewhere, for some years, and not by labor alone.

The key group, of course, was the employers. Some of the larger employers in manufacturing had responded before 1911 with various plans designed to mitigate the unsatisfactory adversary proceedings, provided by the common law, in industrial accident cases. They were not unmindful that a more uniform system would force less conscientious or marginal employers into more equal labor costs. Commons built other incentives into the legislation. Participation was made voluntary, but some protections for the employer under the common law were removed to encourage participation. Labor, in turn, gave up certain rights under common law in exchange for the employers' participation. Employers were given the option of insuring through a state-administered fund or by comparable coverage with an insurance carrier. (The latter provision gave rise to Employers Mutual of Wausau and other mutuals, because stock companies, failing to block passage of the law, raised rates.) Finally, employers were rated individually for premium purposes according to what their accident experience cost the fund under the state plan. This provision offered an incentive for accepting safety regulation and inspection, which led to the acceptance of an industrial commission to discharge this function.

The general public accepted workmen's compensation readily on the argument that industry should pay for its own dead and wounded. It was made more palatable to rural progressive legislators by excluding employers of fewer than four men, ruling out most farmers.

The Wisconsin Industrial Commission, also largely the creation of Professor Commons, was promoted in the same manner. The legislation accepted the notion of a commission with broad power and ample discretion. Safety codes covering each industry were devised by advisory committees representing employers, employees, outside experts, and the public. Commons and McCarthy came up with a new definition of the court-accepted language of what should constitute "reasonable conditions" for purposes of safety. "Reasonable" was defined as "the highest degree of safety, health and well-being of the employees that the nature of the industry or employment would reasonably permit." The object, of course, was to permit the raising of standards of safety with the state of the art.

The parting of the ways which always threatened between La Follette and McGovern came a long step closer in 1912. La Follette was deserted by a majority of the progressives nationally in favor of the belated candidacy of Theodore Roosevelt. The Roosevelt forces recruited McGovern as their candidate for temporary chairman of the Republican National Convention, hoping to unite the Roosevelt and La Follette supporters to stop the Taft men. La Follette was not amenable to the arrangement, refusing all deals with Roosevelt. "I have been suspicious of that bunch for a long time," he commented about McGovern and his Milwaukee contingent. The feeling was certainly mutual.

McGovern, more astute and ambitious that his predecessor, Davidson, had built a political machine that slighted progressives in the western part of the state where La Follette had strength. La Follette's men needed McGovern's political power in the Lakeshore counties more than ever in 1912, when the Democratic ticket was headed by the progressive Woodrow Wilson. Roosevelt's Progressive party did not field a state ticket in Wisconsin but there were some strange goings on. McGovern forthrightly endorsed Roosevelt, although himself on the regular Republican ticket with Taft. La Follette, more equivocal, was suspected of supporting Wilson. Necessity required that he support McGovern at the head of the state ticket. He did so with reluctance. The arm's-length alliance benefited La Follette. His faction was able to purge the progressive organization of McGovern men in many areas where they had established beachheads.

The division went beyond the party organization. McGovern's second administration, in sharp contrast with the first, was a total disaster, with the La Follette men in captious opposition to anything originating with McGovern or his supporters. Charles McCarthy even warned La Follette that his followers seemed prepared to defeat good progressive legislation simply to deny McGovern any credit for its passage. That, apparently, was the idea.

The progressive debacle of 1914 has been charged to the now unrelenting feud between La Follette and McGovern. Emanuel Philipp, the most persuasive politician among the stalwarts, had emerged as their principal spokesman and gubernatorial candidate. The faction-ridden progressives, recognizing that La Follette could not hope to knock heads in privacy and emerge with a single, balanced ticket, attempted a conference to agree upon candidates. The attempt proved fruitless. The La Follette group ran a true-blue "Bobolette," Andrew H. Dahl, against moderate progressive William Hatton, Philipp, and three minor candidates in the Republican gubernatorial primary. Dahl and Hatton split the progressive vote, giving the nomination to Philipp, who had the endorsement of a stalwart convention which he had called. La Follette's recently passed "Mary Ann" law, which was supposed to answer this problem by counting second-choice votes in a primary, proved a flop. Voters either ignored the option or gave the second choice to one of the minor candidates rather than to a serious contender. Hoping to salvage something from the wreckage, the La Follette progressives used another device provided by their election laws. John J. Blaine solicited enough signatures to get on the general election ballot as an independent candidate. It was a sacrifice play.

McGovern, who wanted to be senator more than governor, won his primary race for Stephenson's vacated Senate seat against a stalwart and a La Follette progressive. With the exception of Philipp, all of the statewide races were won by progressives who went on to win in the general election. All, that is, except McGovern. Philipp's Democratic opponent was a Bourbon of the deepest dye who could not attract progressive support, but McGovern was opposed by a Wilson Democrat of the progressive strain. The Democrat, Paul Husting, won a narrow victory over Mc-Govern.

McGovern's defeat, and the victory of stalwart Emanuel Philipp at the top of the state ticket, were not entirely chargeable to the feud between La Follette and McGovern. The truth was that enthusiastic progressivism had about run out its string. Just as everyone, including stalwarts, found it good politics to adopt a progressive stance in 1910, by 1914 a mild conservative tide was running. The regulatory state, which came to fruition particularly with the 1911 legislature, was proving expensive. The newly instituted income tax, which had shifted much of the expanded tax burden from agriculture to industry, had not appreciably reduced the property tax as promised. Industry, which had not made its case very clearly when the income tax law was passed, now found its voice and claimed the income tax put Wisconsin industry and business at a competitive disadvantage. There were ready listeners. It became the style to complain about extravagance, a complaint which *La Follette's Weekly* took up with the rest of the press McGovern and the university became primary targets. One of Philipp's promises was to obliterate "McCarthy's Bill Factory." "Do you want a democracy or a bureaucracy?" asked the Taxpayers' League. "Do we want a State University or a University State?" cried the state superintendent of schools.

The 1914 election brought another premature celebration of the demise of La Folletteism. La Follette progressives joined stalwarts in making McGovern the sacrificial goat for the alleged excesses of his brand of progressivism. Phillipp's victory was a qualified one, however, as the other state offices were won by progressives. They also held a majority of both houses in the legislature. But they had trimmed to issues which belonged to Phillipp. Also, a long list of ten progressive-sponsored constitutional amendments to the state constitution went down to defeat at the hands of the voters. It was an election that continues to invite post mortems. Clearly there was a deep vein of conservatism running through Wisconsin's progressive majority.

Selected Bibliography

Ameringer, Oscar. *If You Don't Weaken: The Autobiography of Oscar Ameringer*. New York, 1940. Socialist leader who came to Milwaukee in 1910.

Burkel, Nicholas Clare. "Henry Allen Cooper: A Political Profile." Master's thesis, University of Wisconsin, 1967. Congressional progressive, contemporary of La Follette.

Campbell, Ballard. "The Good Roads Movement in Wisconsin." *Wisconsin Magazine of History* 49:273–93 (Summer 1966). Summary and bibliography.

Carstensen, Vernon. "The Origin and Early Development of the Wisconsin Idea." *Wisconsin Magazine of History* 39:181–88 (Spring 1956). "Groping" becomes "sifting and winnowing."

Cavanaugh, Cyril C. "Francis E. McGovern and the 1911 Wisconsin Legislature." Master's thesis, University of Wisconsin, 1961. Narrowly conceived.

Cavanaugh, James A. "Dane and Milwaukee Counties and the Campaign of 1912." Master's thesis, University of Wisconsin, 1969. Dane was surprisingly conservative.

Clark, James I. *Robert M. La Follette and Wisconsin Progressivism.* Madison, 1956. Short sketch for school use.

Commons, John R. *Myself.* Madison: University of Wisconsin Press Paperbacks, 1964. A notable progressive career as legislative technician.

Ely, Richard T. *Ground Under Our Feet.* New York, 1938. A progressive influence on the University faculty.

Erlebacher, Albert. "Herman L. Ekern: The Quiet Progressive." Ph.D. dissertation, University of Wisconsin, 1965. One of the few La Follette subalterns who stayed the course.

Fitzpatrick, Edward A. *McCarthy of Wisconsin.* New York, 1944. Published when people knew it meant Charles McCarthy.

Foss, Robert H. "Theodore Kronshage, Jr." *Wisconsin Magazine of History* 26:414–25 (June 1943). Political ally of McGovern.

Keeran, Roger R. "Milwaukee Reformers in the Progressive Era: The City Club of Milwaukee, 1908–1922." Master's thesis, University of Wisconsin, 1969. Answer to socialism and civic corruption.

Korman, Gerd. "Political Loyalties, Immigrant Traditions, and Reform: The Wisconsin German-American Press and Progressivism, 1909–1912." *Wisconsin Magazine of History* 40:161–68 (Spring 1957). Most of the German-American press was conservative.

Kreuter, Kent and Gretchen. *An American Dissenter: The Life of Algie Martin Simons, 1870–1950.* Lexington, Ky., 1969. An important Milwaukee Socialist.

McNamara, Sallee. "The Record Re-examined: The Stalwarts, the Progressives: Education and Public Welfare in Wisconsin." Master's thesis, University of Wisconsin, 1965. The progressives were no more generous than the stalwarts in terms of appropriations.

Margulies, Herbert F. "The Background of the La Follette-McGovern Schism." *Wisconsin Magazine of History* 40:21–29 (Autumn 1956). No love lost.

———. "The Decline of Wisconsin Progressivism, 1911–1914." *Mid-America* 39:131–55 (July 1957).

———. "Political Weaknesses in Wisconsin Progressivism, 1905–1908." *Mid-America* 41:154–72 (July 1959). See his book noted above.

Muzik, Edward J. "Victor L. Berger: A Biography." Ph.D. dissertation,

Northwestern University, 1960. On University Microfilms, SHSW. Milwaukee's Socialist leader.

Olson, Frederick I. "The Milwaukee Socialists, 1879–1941." Ph.D. dissertation, Harvard University, 1952. On University Microfilms, SHSW.

——. "The Socialist Party and the Union in Milwaukee, 1900–1912." *Wisconsin Magazine of History* 44:110–16 (Winter 1960–61).

——. "Milwaukee's First Socialist Administration, 1910–1912." *Mid-America* 43:197–207 (July 1961). A limited mandate.

Ondercin, David G. "Governor Francis E. McGovern's Senatorial Ambitions." The Milwaukee County Historical Society, *Historical Messenger* 25:71–75 (March 1965). He didn't even want to be governor.

Quint, Howard H. *The Forging of American Socialism: Origins of the Modern Movement.* Columbia, S.C., 1953. Contains much on the national role of the Milwaukee Socialists.

Vance, Maurice M. *Charles Richard Van Hise, Scientist Progressive.* Madison, 1961. La Follette friend and university president.

Vecoli, Rudolph J. "Sterilization: A Progressive Measure." *Wisconsin Magazine of History* 35:190–202 (Spring 1960). Eugenics and progressivism.

Wachman, Marvin. *History of the Social-Democratic Party of Milwaukee, 1897–1910.* Illinois Studies in the Social Sciences, no. 1. Urbana, 1945 More complete studies are unpublished.

Weibull, Jorgen. "The Wisconsin Progressives, 1900–1914." *Mid-America* 47:191–221 (July 1965). Swedish professor interested in ethnic identifications.

Woerdehoff, Frank J. "Dr. Charles McCarthy: Planner of the Wisconsin System of Vocational and Adult Education." *Wisconsin Magazine of History* 41:270–74 (Summer 1958).

——. "Dr. Charles McCarthy's Role in Revitalizing the University Extension Program." *Wisconsin Magazine of History* 40:13–18 (Autumn 1956). Energetic? Yes. Modest? No.

Wyman, Roger E. "Voting Behavior in the Progressive Era: Wisconsin as a Test Case." Ph.D. dissertation, University of Wisconsin, 1970. An important study combining the computer and traditional historical tools.

PROGRESSIVISM
FALTERS

27

"The people are tired of this progressivism and will welcome any-thing that will bring about a change," declared Emanuel Philipp, an unabashed stalwart. Philipp's election to Wisconsin's governorship in 1914, which brought the portly conservative into his first race for elective office, appeared to confirm this campaign judgment. Although he won by a plurality, with only 43 percent of the vote in a five-man field, the prin-cipal competitor was Democrat John C. Karel, whose conservatism was even more frightening to progressives than that of the winner. Between them, Philipp and Karel, looked upon as arch-conservatives by progres-sives in both parties, gathered in 80 percent of the vote in the gubernato-rial contest.

The La Follette group had frittered away its party majority in a pri-mary free-for-all. John Blaine, a La Follette faithful, ran as an indepen-dent in the general election but got only 10 percent of the vote. The out-generaled Republican progressives rallied to Philipp in sufficient num-bers to insure his victory over Democrat Karel, ignoring La Follette's vigorous campaigning for Blaine. Philipp's triumph was doubly sweet for the discomfort which it visited upon La Follette. Many moderate pro-gressives embraced the cause of Emanuel Philipp with varying degrees of enthusiasm. One may conjecture that the spectre of a revitalized Demo-cratic party in Wisconsin held its terrors, even for progressives faced with a stalwart takeover in their own Republican party. The Republicans kept two-thirds of the seats in the state legislature, with progressives holding a majority of these. What progressives did not see was that their movement was becoming middle-aged in political terms. Ambitious young Republicans turned to Philipp's leadership just as they had to La Follette's earlier, because the ranks of the latter's faction were already filled with established officeholders and candidates.

Politicians have been known to trim their sails to the winds of change. "We should be looking after *our own* in the legislature," wrote La Follette to the faithful Herman Ekern. "What have we there that we can bank on? We should get a lineup in the Senate. We should have a candidate for Speaker. We must fight every minute to hold our own men and make an issue against the enemy." The enemy, of course, was stalwart Emanual Philipp. But the troops did not rally to La Follette's call to battle. Lawrence Whittet, a Philipp supporter who was the new governor's chief adviser and later his secretary, was elected speaker, with Philipp's assistance. A stalwart was elected president pro-tem of the senate as well. Many progressives were marching to a new drum and no longer heeded their longtime leader.

Emanuel Philipp was a bluff and honest man. He set about immediately to redeem the platform upon which he had campaigned. Progressivism, he declared, was extravagant and the cost too high for the services rendered. Boards and commissions had proliferated which usurped legislative and executive functions, while harassing citizens with unnecessary regulations and examinations. He was careful to exempt from this indictment the Railroad Commission and the Industrial Commission, which had large and vocal constituencies. He claimed to have discovered some fifty others that could profit from drastic pruning.

Economy had become the best currency of the hour. Philipp had great success with homely examples of a parade of civil servants visiting his model farm, where each carried out some meddlesome duty such as inspecting the milk cans or checking the scales. Farmers were impressed by a millionaire—Philipp readily confessed to this and campaigned in his Pierce-Arrow, a luxury automobile of the period—who had started as a Wisconsin farm boy. Built along generous lines, Philipp developed a style of campaigning that suited his solid figure: direct, conversational, devoid of theatrics, and highly effective.

He charged full tilt at some specific targets. The direct primary, he said, had departed too far from the traditional patterns of politics and resulted in a breakdown of party responsibility. Charles McCarthy's "bill factory" he would abolish out of hand. And the university, an overgrown institution filled with overweening professors functioning as "experts" for the progressives, when they should have been attending to instruction in their classrooms, had to be cut down to a reasonable size and budget (the university's appropriation had almost doubled in the three years from 1911 to 1914). Worse yet, some of the most prominent professors were sowing the seeds of socialism among Wisconsin's youth who were "leaving there with ideas that [were] un-American."

The university was not a helpless target for conservative wrath, nor was it entirely blameless. The institution had reached true university status in the nineties. Elements of the enlarged faculty responded enthusiastically to the yeasty combination of La Follette's crusade, President Van Hise's call to service in solving any and all problems of government, industry, and the individual citizen, and the aggressive promotion, by Charles McCarthy, of a revitalized university extension division and the competing vocational education system. Under this prodding, the extension division's budget rose from $20,000 in 1907 to $125,000 in 1912, plus another $60,000 in fees. The division had sixty-three branches around the state, including centers with permanent staffs at Milwaukee, La Crosse, and Oshkosh. Each of these cities was also the site of one of the state's normal schools, which introduced interesting possibilities for conflict between the two systems. The extension division also started a correspondence department, after surveying the market being served by private correspondence schools. Not resting content with this excursion into fields cultivated by free enterprise, the division in 1915 bought six huge tents, along with the other necessary appurtenances, and launched its own venture into summer Chautauqua. The university's Chautauqua was the standard blend of entertainment, uplift, and instruction that was staple in the Midwest towns and small cities of the period.

Irritating as this competition must have been in certain quarters, the main thrust of Governor Philipp's brief against the university was that it was becoming too omnipresent in the state's political life, that it had grown inordinately at the expense of other elements in the public educational system, and that it was the disseminator of unorthodox doctrines, particularly socialism. Philipp, who read widely and was himself an author, was certainly acquainted with two popular books, published in 1912, that were enthusiastic descriptions of Wisconsin progressivism offering a beacon to less-enlightened states: *Wisconsin, An Experiment in Democracy* by Frederic C. Howe, a nationally prominent figure in the progressive movement, and *The Wisconsin Idea* by Charles McCarthy. Both emphasized that the marriage of higher learning with service to the state was a German concept, and Wisconsin, said McCarthy, was essentially a German state. Germany, echoed Howe, identified science with politics more closely than any other nation, and Wisconsin had made this German idea her own. Nineteen-fourteen was not far away.

Howe followed another familiar line which was more to the point at issue. "The university," he wrote, "is largely responsible for the progressive legislation that has made Wisconsin so widely known as a pioneer." Many of the new breed of civil servants attracted to state service under Wisconsin's merit system "were trained in the university under the group of men in the economics and political science departments, which have always been a source of radical university opinion." He characterized the university as the fourth branch of government in Wisconsin and "the nerve centre of the commonwealth, impelling it to action in almost every field of activity." McCarthy, who saw himself as a force often impelling reluctant university administrators to action in his pet fields of activity, extension and vocational education, was somewhat less ecstatic about the university's role, but took essentially the same tack.

Governor Philipp had sworn to bring both the university and Mc-Carthy to heel. These objectives appeared in his first message to the legislature. Bills were introduced in both houses to place the legislative reference service in the state law library, abolish McCarthy's job, and thus close down his offending "bill factory." McCarthy, a strong personality, had both friends and enemies in the legislature. Philipp did not leave the examination of McCarthy up to the legislators, but joined in an unprecedented two-day grilling of the persuasive chief of the legislative reference library, held in the governor's office. McCarthy fenced successfully with Philipp over the issue of McCarthy's influence with legislators for whom his office drew up bills. He stoutly denied that he would or could "put any ideas in their heads."

The governor passed on from questions about McCarthy's influence to a concern with his political beliefs. After some preliminaries, he asked, "Are you a Socialist?" McCarthy responded that he believed in the Panama Canal. Evidently Philipp was enjoying the exchange, for McCarthy, by his own account, boldly followed with a reminder that Wisconsin's railroad commission had been characterized as socialistic at the time it had been created, and now the governor himself spoke of it with approval. Philipp, whose fortune was based on a refrigerator-car-leasing business regulated by the commission, relaxed and began to joke with the relieved McCarthy.

The pattern of the McCarthy interrogation revealed much about Emanuel Philipp's character. He could be persuaded that his initial assumptions were incorrect, or open to considerable revision. Charles McCarthy remained in his job, kept his reference service intact, and soon became a trusted adviser of the governor. President Van Hise, as spokesman for the university, was to have a similar experience. Philipp was set upon the creation of a central board to direct the affairs of the university, the normal schools, and the public schools. The central board plan, which had an attractive simplicity to it for the allocation of state support, was not new with Philipp, but he had expressed his determination to implement it and had broad support.

Van Hise was in a difficult position. Widely acknowledged as one of the nation's most competent university administrators of what had become, in a brief span of years, one of the top public universities in the country, Van Hise epitomized the widely admired Wisconsin Idea far beyond the borders of the state. Before becoming the president and reorganizer of the burgeoning university, Van Hise had brought it distinction as a geologist of international reputation with outstanding talents in research, generalization, and exposition. His entire career had been spent at Wisconsin, where he had started as an undergraduate. This was a part of his difficulty. He had been a classmate and continued a close friend of Robert M. La Follette, who had made plain his determination to see Van Hise elevated to the presidency. As governor, La Follette succeeded in this objective in 1903, after the resignation of President Charles Kendall Adams. Matching La Follette's determination, Van Hise was no reluctant candidate.

Having won the prize, Van Hise faced the active dislike of Governor Davidson for five full years, from 1906 through 1910. Davidson, whose alliance with the stalwarts was important to him after La Follette's efforts to defeat him in the 1906 primary, appointed a number of conservatives to the board of regents. The president's relations with some of these men were strained but correct, while with others he was able to attain a degree of cordiality and work with them effectively. Van Hise was a man of optimistic temper and active plans. He was a vigorous exponent who welcomed debate, often growing heated, but he was never a man to harbor a grudge and he credited his opponents with the same disinterestedness. Even from Davidson, Van Hise won respect and occasional support. The years from 1904 through 1912 saw the progressive temper on the ascendant nationally. With Wisconsin a "laboratory of democracy" and the university an energizing agency of progressive reform, Van Hise's role was important as an able spokesman and a formidable force in the eyes of conservatives.

Following Governor Davidson were the euphoric progressive years with Francis McGovern in the governorship, leading a sympathetic legislature. McGovern's feud with La Follette and the growing criticism of the costs of Wisconsin progressive reform were capitalized upon by Emanuel Philipp. The new governor came to the task of reshaping the university with much the same attitude as that with which he had approached Charles McCarthy and his "bill factory." But Van Hise was as worthy an antagonist as McCarthy. With their prerogatives threatened by Philipp's central educational board scheme, the regents, faculties, and friends of the university and the normal-school system thwarted the governor in his plans by winning support in the legislature and extinguishing, with well-directed blasts, a widely publicized report on the university by an "efficiency expert." Philipp got his central board, but in an emasculated form which survived only until 1923.

Governor Philipp, like Van Hise, bore no grudge for his defeat and grew to be a useful friend to the university. This was largely the story of Philipp's efforts to reverse the progressive revolution. Everywhere that he looked for evidences of radicalism or an officious bureaucracy discharging useless functions he seemed to discover well-qualified civil servants performing socially or economically useful services. If there had been a progressive revolution, it had certainly lacked much in the way of radical content. Socialist Victor Berger had been saying this all along, but neither conservatives nor progressives were listening to him.

Governor Philipp illustrates the familiar dilemma of the critic when he is placed in command. The ship of state inevitably looks quite different to the man on the bridge than it does to a man in a small boat dead ahead. Philipp reacted like any responsible commander. He became alert to repel boarders, and soon doubted the advisability of stopping the ship to catechize and reassign the crew. The promised dismantling of the progressive ark turned into a minor shifting of ballast, even before the problems of the European war inevitably began to swell the crew even more. Emanuel Philipp's light shines today in the progressive firmament as the Intelligent Stalwart who accepted Truth.

World War I was a traumatic experience for Wisconsin. The *Milwaukee Journal* has scarcely recovered to this day. In an official history of the newspaper, written by staff members and published in 1964, it is recalled that the newspaper won a Pulitzer Prize in 1919 for being "one of the first newspapers of the United States to recognize the absolutely uncivilized methods employed by the German government in conducting its war against civilization. . . . In its editorials, from the very beginning of the War, it had followed an absolutely and unswervingly American attitude. In a city where the German element had long prided itself in its preponderating influence, the *Journal* courageously attacked such members of that element as put Germany above America." German names and cultural values were sufficient proof of a disposition to disloyalty in the eyes of self-appointed patriots. As the *Milwaukee Journal* historians put it, "who knew what might have happened if the forces opposing the war effort had not been broken?"

Lacking a Pearl Harbor—the decisive blow which leaves no alternative save war—the United States drifted from its 1914 position of strict neutrality toward its eventual entry on April 6, 1917. The United States had grievances against both sides for violations of its rights as a neutral, but the culminating grievance was the announcement, in January 1917, of the resumption of unrestricted submarine warfare by the German government. Suffice to say that American opinion on participation was less than unanimous in 1917, and Wisconsin in particular was badly divided over the issue. While not an accurate reflection of the numerical division of Wisconsin opinion, nine of the state's eleven congressmen, plus Senator La Follette, voted against the declaration of war. The emotional pitch of the country made this a hazardous course in April 1917, and a source of deep distress to many Wisconsin citizens who embraced the patriot's role with a passion that denied absolutely any previous or present doubts about the wisdom of this course.

There were many threads in the antiwar sentiment in Wisconsin that ran through the neutral years to April 1917, and exacerbated this society of immigrants and their children during the nineteen months of American participation in the war and the difficult years that followed. One must say that there can be no criticism of Wisconsin's contribution to the conduct of the war. The state gave more than its share in men, money contributed to loan and philanthropic drives, increased food production, and the conversion of industry to war needs. The draft was carried out in exemplary fashion, without obstruction, and the 32nd Divison of the National Guard, made up of Wisconsin and Michigan men, established an enviable combat record in the American Expeditionary Force. Still, there were many who suffered from a sense of humiliation that Wisconsin was stigmatized in the rest of the nation as essentially pro-German in attitude. The humiliation was exaggerated by the emotional patriotism which served so many as a substitute for rational discussion of America's course.

Robert M. La Follette became the principal storm center, in national as well as Wisconsin politics, for his steadfast opposition to American participation in the war. Although not an obstructionist once the country was committed by the Congress, he refused to retreat from his position that American participation was a tragic mistake, and built his subsequent political career largely upon a justification of that position.

La Follette cannot be faulted on the consistency of his opposition to America's involvement. His record on the shifting issues from 1914 to 1917 followed a line of logic which makes his insurgent Republican cohorts look like shuttlecocks in a brisk crosswind. La Follette remained inflexible. He suffered a relatively brief but virulent martyrdom for his views. Later, he enjoyed the personal and political rewards of justification, exoneration, and a feast of personal apology from many who had been most bitterly against him.

The La Follette position was straightforward. He never strayed from President Wilson's position of August, 1914—strict neutrality. Nothing in the aims and arguments of the belligerents could possibly be of enough concern to the American people to justify their participation, he maintained. The true business of the United States should be the implementation of reform on the model suggested by La Follette's Wisconsin. He saw the war spirit as the certain nemesis of continuing public interest in progressive reform. In every public debate of issues leading to the final American commitment, he measured the proposals against this conception of the war.

La Follette opposed preparedness, an issue which captured the public imagination in 1915 and brought Woodrow Wilson to a reversal of his initial opposition. There was much of faddishness in preparedness. Sunday supplements and popular magazines blossomed with articles exhibiting our military and naval helplessness. The regular army in 1914 numbered only 93,000 officers and men; the navy was somewhere in third place internationally, behind Britain and Germany, roughly comparable to that of France. Suddenly everyone became an amateur strategist, citing expert testimony on how simple it would be for the Italians or Hungarians to land an invading force on our undefended shores. German and Japanese capabilities were of more serious concern.

An enlarged naval establishment appealed to a majority as the appropriate response, but progressives who were persuaded of this exhibited considerable ambivalence at the thought that the principal beneficiaries of the program would be the hated steel trust. La Follette made his position clear with a comment about "Morgan and his dollar-scarred heroes of the Navy League." Accepting the inevitability of enlarged naval appropriations, La Follette introduced a resolution calling for the nationalization of the armament industry to take the profits out of preparedness and war. This suggestion was not acted upon, of course, but the resourceful senator left his mark upon the 1916 Revenue Act. With the assistance of progressive Democrats, he managed to get the inclusion of a surtax on large incomes, a special tax on munitions, and a federal inheritance tax. La Follette continued to call for pay-as-you-go taxation during the course of the war, with emphasis on the device of an excess profits tax.

A continuing controversy before April 1917 concerned the advisability of demanding strict adherence to American neutral rights under the traditional doctrines of international law. Both sides in the struggle repeatedly violated these rights, but the German breaches were more frequent and grievous because of the nature of submarine warfare and the increasing amount of business the United States was doing with Britain and France. Many Americans were willing to forego certain rights of travel and trade, given the inclusive nature of modern warfare. President Wilson's response was his doctrine of strict accountability, to which La Follette answered with a proposal that the United States call a conference of neutral nations to consider general disarmament, banning the shipment of arms to belligerents, and means to bring economic pressure upon the warring powers to cease hostilities. This was in early 1915, and the senator's suggestions received a good deal of attention outside of Congress.

A year later, La Follette supported the Gore-McLemore Resolution to keep Americans from traveling on the vessels of belligerent nations. He maintained that the *Lusitania,* sunk in May 1915 with the loss of 124 American lives, had been carrying munitions, and cited this as reasonable grounds for restricting the citizen's right to travel in the war zone. La Follette had long since parted company with Wilson over the issue of loans to belligerents through American banks. Their most dramatic confrontation came in February 1917, when Wilson appealed for legislation to permit him to arm American merchant ships against submarine attack. With the connivance of Republican stalwarts, who wanted to force Wilson to call a special session, La Follette led the insurgents in a filibuster against the bill which succeeded in killing it for that session. Wilson angrily denounced the insurgents as a "little group of willful men, representing no opinion but their own." A few weeks later the president called for a declaration of war, and La Follette spoke and voted against it—one of only six in the Senate.

It was with this record of opposition to American participation in the war that La Follette won a new constituency in Wisconsin politics. While supporting legislation necessary to the conduct of the war, he opposed conscription for foreign service, continued to support a rather quixotic scheme for a national referendum on any declaration of war, and hammered away at those interests making a profit from the war. He assessed blame for the war more or less equally among the belligerents and condemned America's increasing support of the Entente as the reason for German intransigence over the observance of our neutral rights.

La Follette was not unaware of the fact that his stand was popular with many German-American voters back home, but it is certainly unfair to charge that he was making a grandstand play for their votes. He was just as aware that he was losing large numbers of long-time supporters, particularly after the die was cast in favor of American entry. He was wounded repeatedly as old friends turned their backs upon him, often with angry words. It must be remembered that he ran for reelection in the summer and fall of 1916 when his stand was still popular with most Wisconsin progressives. Germany had backed away from her policy of unrestricted submarine warfare after the sinking of the *Sussex,* killing Americans, in 1916, and did not resume the policy until early in 1917. Neutrality was a popular doctrine in Wisconsin in the fall of 1916. Old La Follette progressives responded readily to the familiar villains called up by the senator: Wall Street bankers arranging British loans, British imperialists intent upon using Uncle Sam as a cat's-paw, the steel trust and munitions makers generally, and the corrupt politicians doing the bidding of these malign interests. He easily won reelection with 60 percent of the total vote.

It is no exaggeration to say that a huge minority of Wisconsin citizens were of German background in 1914. They were the most widely dispersed ethnic group and the largest to be found in many towns and cities, as they were in metropolitan Milwaukee. While they were one of the least homogeneous groups in religion and politics, they preserved a cultural unity based upon a vigorous German-language press, pride in German contributions to literature, music, the arts, science, education, and government, a sense of German nationalism inspired by Germany's comparatively recent unification and rise as a world power, their influence in both public and parochial school systems in the state, and the persistent tension which continued between German and Yankee cultural values. This tension seemed to center on the liquor question because of a Yankee obsession with the issue, which carried with it overtones of nativism and religious intolerance. An unfortunate consequence of this was that German organizations devoted to propagandizing their cultural values and defending civil liberties were subsidized by the brewing and distilling interests. This link was not overlooked by those pressing the temperance cause, and it tended to vitiate German efforts to win a sympathetic hearing outside of their community.

Wisconsinites of German and Austrian background responded predictably to the issues raised by the European War. Some nationals, motivated by an initial patriotic fervor, returned to their homelands for military duty, accompanied by suitable fanfare. Drives were held to raise money for the German Red Cross and similar relief agencies. An effort was made to sell bonds of the German government, after the Wilson administration backed down on its initial decision that the sale of bonds of belligerent governments violated our neutrality. What they were asserting was that other Americans should adopt a neutral stance and display an equal deference toward the claims of either side in the war. There was a struggle to influence American public opinion, and the Germans steadily lost ground.

German-Americans were fairly well organized for the propaganda campaign waged in the United States, but their ineptitude was monumental. The National German-American Alliance, organized in 1901, claimed a national membership of 2,000,000. The largest chapter, 100,000, was in Pennsylvania. Wisconsin's chapter claimed 37,000. While the avowed purposes of the alliance were to promote German culture and language, it had evolved into the opposite number of the Anti-Saloon League and the Prohibition party, both militant organizations. The war simply gave the prohibitionists another handy club with which to beat the alliance, claiming that it was an alien organization subsidized by the German government to promote its ambitions for world domination. The alliance was no such thing. The German government had remained, for the most part, blissfully ignorant of the organization as well as its aims and purposes. The alliance would have resented any effort to control or influence it. It was, indeed, handsomely subsidized at the national and local levels, but by American brewers.

German-Americans were unskilled at influencing general American opinion. They were active enough, but never struck the happy medium between angry officiousness and irritating impracticality. A group of German-American businessmen bought the *Milwaukee Free Press,* which had been a progressive organ, to propagate their views to a general audience. They used it to warn against British perfidy and the Yellow Peril, and for self-congratulations on the low state of American military competence as evidenced by the unfortunate military expedition into Mexico in the summer of 1916. The coincidence that the Wisconsin National Guard had been called into service on the Mexican border made such comment even less advisable. If the alliance sought friends, it found them in the Ancient Order of Hibernians, which joyfully celebrated British military disasters. Alliance members even feted the enthusiastic prohibitionist William Jennings Bryan, after his resignation as Wilson's secretary of state over differences about American neutrality. They drank his health in grape juice, which must have given pause to the brewers paying their bills.

Another voice of antiwar sentiment, forthrightly expressed, was that of Milwaukee Socialism. American socialists, a decidedly mixed group running the gamut from hardline Marxists and militant Oklahoma tenant farmers to Victor Berger's gradualists, were affronted by the supine acquiescence displayed by European socialist parties, which had put national loyalties before socialism's international aspirations by supporting their respective governments. Meeting in St. Louis at the same time President Wilson was asking Congress for a declaration of war, American socialism declared its solidarity with internationalism, and adopted a militant antiwar position two days after the declaration had passed Congress. Berger, who had tried to moderate the antiwar plank, voted for it and defended it. He was a confirmed Francophobe, a position he had made abundantly clear, and had been an apologist for the Central Powers. After the United States entered the war, Berger repudiated support from pro-German elements, but not convincingly, in view of his earlier editorial stand. The Socialists benefited from the growing disenchantment of German-Americans with Woodrow Wilson and the Democrats. Socialist Daniel Hoan started his long tenure as Milwaukee's mayor in 1916. Wilson lost Wisconsin in the same year. Governor Philipp, who was firmly neutralist, stood off the challenge of the La Follette progressives in the primary and won a second term.

Popular sentiment swung swiftly behind the war after April 6, 1917. The experience of the town of Monroe in Green County is indicative. Testing La Follette's call for a referendum on the issue of war, the town took a vote, which came out 954 opposed to U.S. entry and 95 in favor. Three days later Congress declared war. Monroe held an official celebration of that event.

The phenomenon of almost hysterical conformity which seized the American people after the declaration of war in 1917 has often been remarked. It took a particularly virulent form in Wisconsin. As expressed by the head of one of several patriotic organizations that sprang up, the Wisconsin Defense League, "Wisconsin, and least of all Milwaukee, must not, and shall not, subscribe, or be accused of subscribing, to any doctrine that does not venerate the constitution, love the flag, and keep step to the music of the Union." There was acute sensitivity about charges that Wisconsin was less than totally loyal, because of the adverse publicity that attached to La Follette's continuing criticism of American policies leading to the declaration of war, war finance measures, profiteering, conscription, and the repression of dissent. La Follette was a favorite target for the growing ranks of superpatriots, but any individual with a German name, according to a widely publicized notice of the American Defense Society, "unless known by years of association to be absolutely loyal, should be treated as a potential spy." Socialists, of course, were simply identified as Germans whose disloyalty was a fact. Not everyone who supported the war effort wholeheartedly was guilty of this simplistic silliness, but a disheartening number of men who for one reason or another were in the public eye fell victim to it. Richard Lloyd Jones, editor of the *Wisconsin State Journal,* which had supported La Follette until 1917, raved, "The arch reactionaries in Wisconsin today are the supporters of Bob La Follette. They are the cowardly pussy-footers who by their cheap and underhanded methods of weakening our national defenses are helping autocracy and not democracy; they are playing the brewers and the Kaiser's disciples in America."

Americans of German ancestry reacted variously to the spirit of vigilantism that was directed against them. The easy course for many was to join in the hue and cry against everything German. This was not necessarily an insincere reaction, particularly for those who had established successful business and professional careers in the wider society around them. They had consciously rejected sentimental attachment to things German long since, and were impatient with their compatriots who rejected full assimilation, whatever the term implied. But most German-Americans found it difficult to deny a heritage of which they were proud. One did not have to be devoted to the aspirations of Kaiser Wilhelm II to find references to himself as "the Hun" and "a potential spy" somehow objectionable.

President Wilson, no civil libertarian despite his devotion to British political models, demanded of Congress specific acts outlawing disloyal conduct. Congress complied in legislation open to the broadest interpretations. Wisconsin, as one would expect, was the scene of a disproportionate number of prosecutions under these and state statutes. One student found that the largest number of indictments in Wisconsin, under federal loyalty laws, were prosecuted in the western judicial district of the state among a much smaller population than that of the eastern district. He concluded that the small town was the real center of reaction and superpatriotism, where war hysteria pitted neighbor against neighbor. Ninety-two indictments under the Espionage Act were returned in Wisconsin, including the following counts, some of them multiple: thirty-five for criticizing U.S. policy, thirty-six for praising Germany, thirty-two for saying that it was "a rich man's war and the poor man's fight," nineteen for criticizing coercion in the sale of war bonds, fifteen for statements critical of drives for war charities such as the Red Cross, nine for remarks about wheatless and meatless days, seventeen for comments derogating the Allies, and nine for insults to the flag. The context of many of these counts was a comment over a glass of beer or a remark dropped in a personal conversation. Surprised citizens found themselves subject to heavy fines, while others received sentences to the federal penitentiary at Leavenworth. As an example, a Madison druggist paid a $2,000 fine for an overheard remark that the Kaiser was a better friend to his people than was the U.S. Government to its people.

Such a record depended upon a zealous prosecutor and eager informants. The latter were organized in various patriotic organizations, some with the official blessing of the Department of Justice or the state. The Milwaukee chapter of the American Protective League, an outfit semiofficially attached to the Department of Justice, claimed that it investigated 10,000 enemy aliens and 2,400 reports of sedition. It seems dubious that the war effort was seriously impeded by an overheard scurrility on the president's ancestry, but it could get one a year in Leavenworth. The suspicion is not unfounded that one could as well read "union labor" or "socialist" for many of the zealously investigated "subversives" subjected to the scrutiny of self-appointed patriots.

Examples abound of vigilante action. A favorite device was for a committee of patriots, including the local banker to accept a note pledging the man's property, to visit a farmer and tell him what amount in war bonds he was to purchase with the enforced loan. A minor form of coercion was to post his land with signs reading, "The Occupant of these premises has refused to take his just share of Liberty Bonds. DO NOT REMOVE." More direct methods included yellow paint, night visits with a rope, or official-appearing notices to report to an organization office and explain anonymous charges of sedition or disloyalty.

La Follette was correct in his assumption that the war spirit would divert people from an interest in progressive reform. His efforts in 1916 to bring about the defeat of Governor Philipp as a threat to progressive legislation already on the books generated little interest. Philipp actually was not such a threat. He was caught up in the same issues as La Follette: neutrality and then loyalty. It was a rare progressive who disagreed with La Follette's views on the war but remained with him on domestic issues. Most of them joined wholeheartedly in an effort to drive him from public life.

La Follette became the victim of a misunderstanding which illustrated perfectly the hazards of responsible dissent. He was a speaker before a convention of the Nonpartisan League in St. Paul in September 1917. League officials, subject themselves to demoralizing harassment by patriots, asked him to speak extemporaneously and avoid the war as a topic. But Bob was primed on the subject and inevitably took it up in his usual lengthy presentation. He prefaced a point with the remark that he would not deny that "we had grievances against Germany." The Associated Press reported it as "we had *no* grievances against Germany" and the fat was in the fire. La Follette was burned in effigy on the campus of the university; the faculty, almost to a man, signed a round robin condemning him for bringing "aid and comfort to Germany." The Associated Press belatedly admitted its error, but not in time to calm the storm. Senator Frank Kellogg of Minnesota, where the offending remark had alledgedly been aired, led an effort to have La Follette expelled from the Senate. The petition remained in committee until the end of the war, which came within days of the 1918 elections. Both events were important. The Republicans found themselves in control of the Senate by one vote—La Follette's! The matter was dropped.

Victor Berger, who did not have La Follette's wide following, was treated to a worse martyrdom for his opposition to the war. The St. Louis platform of the Socialist party was repudiated by many prominent Socialists, particularly those who had helped give the party an American image. In Milwaukee these included Algie Simons and Winfield Gaylord. Simons became a publicist for the Wisconsin Defense League, insisting that the St. Louis platform was treasonous. He gladly joined in efforts to silence Berger.

Troubles for Berger began when Postmaster General Burleson cut off the *Milwaukee Leader's* second class mailing privileges by administrative order. He contemptuously ignored the German-language Socialist paper *Vorwaerts*. Berger failed to get his paper's mailing privileges restored, and Burleson even halted the delivery of mail to the *Leader* so that sympathizers would have difficulty subscribing. While many Socialists deserted for the cause of patriotism, new recruits rallied to the cause.

Berger would not be downed. Senator Paul Husting was killed in a hunting accident, and Governor Philipp's opponents forced a special election in the spring of 1918. All of the divisive factors in Wisconsin politics were present in the election. Irvine Lenroot, who started his political career as a La Follette progressive and favored lieutenant, had deserted to Roosevelt and then to the Republican regulars. He was one of the two Wisconsin congressmen who voted in favor of the declaration of war in April 1917, and he became the conservative Republican candidate. The La Follete progressives persuaded James Thompson, a popular Norwegian-American attorney from La Crosse, to oppose Lenroot in the primary. Joseph E. Davies of Milwaukee, who was serving on the Federal Trade Commission, was pressed by local Democrats and the Wilson Administration to preserve the seat for the Democrats. Charles McCarthy, for reasons known mainly to himself, declared himself a Democrat and filed against Davies. Victor Berger, who had run for Congress unsuccessfully and regularly since 1912, ran on the Socialist ticket.

The unfortunate Thompson, who had expected to run on the usual progressive economic issues, found himself, willy-nilly, running on La Follette's war record with the newly founded *Capital Times* of Madison as his principal newspaper support. The paper was organized by William T. Evjue, former business manager of the *Wisconsin State Journal,* which had defected from the progressive cause. Thompson ran Lenroot a surprisingly close race, 70,772 to Lenroot's 73,186. Davies got 57,282, while McCarthy was nowhere with 13,784. Berger polled a substantial 38,564 votes in his unopposed primary.

The Socialist candidate for the Senate in 1916 had received only 11,479 votes in the primary and 7 percent of the total vote in the general. Berger had a strong 15 percent. Hysterical patriots added Thompson's nearly 28 percent of the primary vote to Berger's 15 percent and had visions of the Socialist as a winner in a three-cornered contest with Lenroot and Davies. Frantic efforts were made to get Lenroot to withdraw in favor of Davies, but the attendant aspersions on Lenroot's loyalty only infuriated Governor Philipp and others. Lenroot was an easy winner in the final. Berger ran third, with 26 percent of the vote. The new politics of fear viewed Berger's percentage with dismay.

Berger, heartened by his vote in a statewide contest, ran again for congressman in Milwaukee's fifth district in the regular fall elections of 1918, for the fourth consecutive time, and won handsomely in a three-way contest. But between his election and the first meeting of the new Congress, he was brought to trial on charges of conspiracy, under the 1917 Espionage Act. The charges were based mainly upon editorials written by him, but finally boiled down to a charge that he had counseled evasion of the draft, the proof offered being small contributions of money he had made to an IWW defense fund and to the Young People's Socialist League, which did counsel draft evasion. Berger had little sympathy with either radical organization, but he had the misfortune to have his trial before federal judge Kenesaw Mountain Landis in Chicago. Landis had gained notoriety when he slapped a fine of $29,240,000 on the Standard Oil Company in 1907. Still an advocate of heroic measures, he sentenced Berger to twenty years and set bail, while out on appeal, at $25,000, with $100,000 in property as surety.

It was 1921 before the Supreme Court set the verdict aside on the grounds that Judge Landis had displayed his prejudice in a variety of indiscreet comments about the defendant. The government dropped the charges. But meanwhile, Berger left for Congress under sentence for having obstructed the war effort. America was in the grip of the Red Scare which followed the war and the Russian Revolution. The House refused to seat Berger. A new election was ordered, which he won. Again he was refused his seat. He was defeated in 1920 but returned in 1922 and was seated without incident as the only Socialist in Congress. There he was an ornament of sorts.

Emanuel Philipp maintained a relatively moderate attitude on the loyalty issue. He remained a neutralist into 1917, although pessimistic about the chances of avoiding war. When war came, Philipp's concern was that Wisconsin should acquit herself well. He was irritated by any inference that her citizens were less than devoted to victory, once the die had been cast. His calm assurance of this saved the state government from some asinine actions on occasion. The Democrats tried to take advantage of the governor's apparent imperturbability by seizing upon loyalty as the particular possession of their party and the Wilson administration. They enjoyed reminding the Republicans of their divisions. Vice President Thomas R. Marshall, speaking in Madison just after the special senatorial primary in March 1918, told Wisconsin Republicans, "if the vote at the primary is based upon the charges and counter-charges you have made against each other, you are about half for America, half for the Kaiser, and all against Wilson." Given the poor showing of the Wilson administration's candidate in the primary, he could easily afford this gambit.

Governor Philipp's obvious distaste for indiscriminate charges of disloyalty got him into trouble in the regular elections of 1918. Superpatriots turned the Republican gubernatorial primary into a flag-waving contest. Their leader was State Senator Roy P. Wilcox of Eau Claire, who took out after Philipp as pro-German. This assured that the governor would run on his record for a third term.

Philipp had joined the hue and cry against La Follette, who had never conceded him an honest motive. But as one La Follette supporter stated the case, he considered Wilcox "five times as vicious as Philipp from the standpoint of progressive Republicans." Wilcox, however, quickly attracted the support of many prominent progressives who had deserted La Follette over the loyalty issue. He adopted a position of economic liberalism, which few took seriously, but his main thrust was a fervent Americanism as defined by himself. "Your call puts loyalty to our country and her cause as the first requisite for public office and the supreme political issue of the day. . . . There must never be in this state in the future any indifference, lukewarm support, faltering or compromise."

The issue joined between Philipp and Wilcox left no apparent alternative for the La Follette forces. They went again to James Thompson, who had run a good race in the spring against Irvine Lenroot for the Senate, but Thompson had not enjoyed the experience and refused. Before they could find another candidate, they were surprised by the announcement of James N. Tittemore, president of the American Society of Equity and of the Wisconsin Farmers' Union, that he was a Republican candidate for governor. Equity had a varied career in Wisconsin. Established in 1903, it had, like other state chapters, drifted away from the parent body. Its principal interests in the state were in cooperative livestock, tobacco, and grain marketing. At its peak, in 1920, Equity claimed 40,000 members in Wisconsin. After disastrous ventures in politics and a rapid expansion of unsucessful cooperatives, its remnants were absorbed into the Farmers' Union.

Tittemore was the one who led Equity into politics seriously. He took advantage of the discontent of Wisconsin farmers, who found feed and other costs rising more rapidly than the prices received for meat animals and milk. Equity had always had an ideological bent, generally supporting progressives in politics. The membership was pushed further in the direction of radical farm politics by the presence in northern Wisconsin of the Nonpartisan League, which had won the governorship and the lower house in North Dakota in 1916. The league set itself an expansion program into neighboring states in 1917. In Wisconsin it was largely a part of the La Follette movement, although meetings were called in the name of Equity and the NPL. Tittemore was a spellbinder who yearned for political office and used Equity as his instrument. A convention made up of Equity, the NPL, and representatives of organized labor met in Madison in May 1918 and endorsed Tittemore's candidacy, but without designating the party.

Caught off guard by this move, the La Follette inner circle decided that the better part of a bad bargain was to support Tittemore. Their real purpose, which they admitted privately, was to draw votes away from Wilcox. They stumped for Tittemore, and he had the support of the *Capital Times,* whose publisher, like Tittemore, was an enthusiastic prohibitionist. Wilcox was a Catholic, opening another dark side of Wisconsin politics, the influence of which is difficult to evaluate.

The Republican primary fight, as expected, was between Philipp and Wilcox, who hated one another. The results were in doubt for some time, but Philipp barely managed to win by a vote of 71,614 to 71,164 for

Wilcox. Tittemore was well behind, with 45,357, but it was probably the La Follette group's strategy that tipped the balance. The unlikely alliance of Philipp and La Follette continued in the organization of the official party convention, which included the party nominees for the state offices and for the legislature. The progressives who had supported Tittemore held the balance between the Philipp and Wilcox supporters. They supported the governor's faction in organizing the convention and writing the platform. Wilcox, who was present as a holdover state senator, made a brutal speech against an endorsement of Governor Philipp's war record. Philipp easily won in November, although he narrowly lost his home county, Milwaukee, to Emil Seidel, the popular Socialist candidate.

Emanuel Philipp had begun his career as governor with the avowed purpose of rolling back progressivism. He had not succeeded in this purpose, partly because of his open-minded approach to the problems of government, and partly because the European war had gradually pushed other matters aside. The war forced the creation of an even larger bureaucracy and increased the tendency for people to look to administrative agencies to find solutions for problems.

But what of progressivism as a spur to political action? Could La Follette, who had lost much of his old constituency to the cries for loyalty, win them back? What would happen to his new German-American constituency, who had been generally cool toward Old Bob until he made his neutralist stand?

La Follette was not cheered by the prospect ahead as the war came to a close. "Democracy in America has been trampled underfoot, submerged, forgotten," he wrote his old friend Louis D. Brandeis. "Her enemies have multiplied their wealth and power appallingly. She has thousands of Morgans against her now. But she calls to us as never before. I fear it will be some time before an appeal to her can get much of a hearing."

Continuing his note of pessimism, La Follette remarked in a letter to his family that Brandeis had urged him to take up his leadership again. "There is nothing to lead. The forces of democracy which we have been organizing for twenty years have been scattered to the four winds by this mad stampede for democracy in Europe—led by the enemies of democracy in America. What have we left to fight with?"

The mood would change. The old fire horse would answer the bell again. He would experience an outpouring of affection and sweet vindication from Wisconsin voters that would spur him to new efforts. Yet he had posed the crucial question for the next decade. "What have we left to fight with?"

Selected Bibliography

Bedford, Henry F. "A Case Study in Hysteria: Victor L. Berger, 1917–1921." Master's thesis, University of Wisconsin, 1953. The Joe McCarthy era looking at World War I.

Cary, Lorin L. "Wisconsin Patriots Combat Disloyalty: The Wisconsin Loyalty Legion and Politics, 1917–18." Master's thesis, University of Wisconsin, 1965. Trouble for German Americans.

Child, Clifton James. *The German-American in Politics, 1914–1917.* Madison, 1939. The German-American Alliance and its mistakes.

Conrad, Will C., Kathleen Wilson, and Dale Wilson. *The Milwaukee Journal: The First Eighty Years.* Madison, 1964. Celebrates the 1919 Pulitzer Prize for thwarting "the Hun" in Milwaukee.

Curti, Merle, and Vernon Carstensen. *The University of Wisconsin: A History, 1848–1925.* 2 vols. Madison, 1949. A highly readable study of a great university.

Falk, Karen. "Public Opinion in Wisconsin During World War I." *Wisconsin Magazine of History* 25:389–407 (June 1942). Naive.

Finnegan, John P. "The Preparedness Movement in Wisconsin, 1914–1917." Master's thesis, University of Wisconsin, 1961. Was the voice Paul Revere's or that of the steel trust?

Gisselman, Dana Lee. "Anti-Radicalism in Wisconsin, 1917–1919." Master's thesis, University of Wisconsin, 1969. A lesson in uncritical loyalty.

Kennedy, Padraic C. "La Follette's Foreign Policy: From Imperialism to Anti-Imperialism." *Wisconsin Magazine of History* 46:287–93 (Summer 1963). A friend of McKinley, an enemy of Taft.

Margulies, Herbert F. "The La Follette-Philipp Alliance of 1918." *Wisconsin Magazine of History* 38:248–49 (Summer 1955). To beat Roy Wilcox.

———. "Anti-Catholicism in Wisconsin Politics, 1914–1920." *Mid-America* 44:51–56 (Jan. 1962). Political correspondence shows many covert references.

Martin, Lawrence J. "Opposition to Conscription in Wisconsin, 1917–18." Master's thesis, University of Wisconsin, 1952. La Follette had distinguished support in 1916.

Maxwell, Robert S. *Emanuel L. Philipp: Wisconsin Stalwart.* Madison, 1959. An admirable conservative and worthy political foe of La Follette.

Miller, Melvin H. "Chautauqua and the Wisconsin Idea." Wisconsin Academy of Sciences, Arts and Letters, *Transactions* 52:159–68 (1963). An expansive university.

Nelson, Charles A. "Progressivism and Loyalty in Wisconsin Politics, 1912–1918." Master's thesis, University of Wisconsin, 1961. Democrats claimed a corner on loyalty.

Reinders, Robert C. "Hoan and Milwaukee Socialism during World War I."

Wisconsin Magazine of History 36:48–55 (Autumn 1952). Mayor Dan Hoan walked a narrow line.

Saloutos, Theodore. "The Wisconsin Society of Equity." *Agricultural History* 14:78–95 (April 1940).

———. "The Decline of the Wisconsin Society of Equity." *Agricultural History* 15:137–50 (July 1940). James Tittemore's political vehicle.

Shannon, David A. "The World, the War, and Wisconsin: 1914–1918." Milwaukee County Historical Society, *Historical Messenger* 22:43–56 (March 1966). The American experience intensified.

Stevens, John D. "Suppression of Expression in Wisconsin during World War I." Ph.D. dissertation, University of Wisconsin, 1967. Wilson encouraged it.

Trattner, Walter I. "Julia Grace Wales and the Wisconsin Plan for Peace." *Wisconsin Magazine of History* 34:203–13 (Spring 1961). A plan for mediation that received broad support for a time.

BETWEEN THE WARS

part nine

The La Follettes continued to dominate politics in Wisconsin during the two decades between the World Wars. Old Bob won triumphant vindication in his Senate race in 1922, and went on to his last dramatic campaign in the 1924 presidential race. His sons took over after his death in 1925. Neither was endowed with the full balance of political gifts possessed by their father, but they were not simply lesser men exploiting the family name. Their enduring impact was less than the father's. Both were more deeply disappointed in their political careers.

The decade of the twenties was soured by the aftermath of the war. The emotional commitment engendered by American participation astonished the generation involved, but not before years of indulgence in action and reaction. Wisconsin's large German-American population bore the brunt of much opprobrium and distrust. Old political balances were upset. The sense of direction provided by progressivism was largely lost, although not for want of serious economic and social problems needing solutions.

The Great Depression of the 1930s provided, finally, a rediscovered sense of purpose. Philip F. La Follette, as leader of a new progressive coalition, wanted Wisconsin to give leadership in finding solutions for the economic crisis. He was not able to master a dependable political majority for the attempt before the New Deal centered both economic and social legislation in Washington, forcing the states to follow in the national wake. Phil La Follette's ambitions and frustrations carried him out of the mainstream to political oblivion.

THE 1920s

28

It is difficult to characterize the decade of the 1920s in Wisconsin politics. Wisconsin gave Warren G. Harding 71 percent of its vote in the opening year—an overwhelming majority not equalled before or since—and closed it with stalwart Republican Walter J. Kohler winning the governorship by a comfortable margin of 55 percent in 1928. Victor Berger died in August 1929 correctly predicting that his once vigorous Milwaukee socialist movement would not long survive him. La Follette had gone in midyear of 1925, leaving to his sons and other political heirs the increasingly difficult task of controlling the Wisconsin Republican party.

Wisconsin's farm population, an important element in the support of La Follette's political movement, fell in absolute numbers during the decade, declining from 35 to 30 percent of the population. Farm income in the state hit a peak of $549,000,000 in 1919, fell precipitously to $320,000,000 in 1921, and recovered slowly to a level of $439,000,000 in 1929, when a second collapse occurred. As elsewhere, the prosperity of the 1920s belonged largely to business and industry. Wisconsin farmers were dismayed by the trend of the postwar years. The federal government had intervened during the war to set livestock and milk prices. Farmers rightfully felt that they had been encouraged to increase production, and many had made commitments for land, machinery, and improvements in a spirit of optimism unjustified by events. They were faced with rising

459

prices for the things they bought, higher taxes imposed by the postwar inflation—the chairman of the state tax commission estimated in 1923 that a levy of $100,000,000 was required to buy the same services and supplies covered by $60,000,000 five years before—and sharply lower prices for farm products. Milk receipts in 1922 were only two-thirds of what they had been two years before, and hog prices were cut in half.

The federal census of 1920 marked almost an equilibrium between the urban and rural populations in the state. Twenty years before, the rural population had a comfortable margin of three to two. Between 1910 and 1920, it had increased only 4.4 percent, the urban had increased 23.9 percent. One in four Wisconsinites, by 1920, lived in the three heavily urbanized counties in the southeast corner—Milwaukee, Kenosha, and Racine. The proportion had been less than one in five in 1900. An impressive increase of population, at least in percentage terms, had taken place in the northern counties, where the lumber industry had lately completed its work by denuding the area of its merchantable pine timber. This marginal agricultural population had been attracted there by high-pressure salesmanship, in which state agencies played a prominent role.

Organized labor in the immediate postwar period appeared strong, radical, and militant to those not sympathetic to it. Significant gains had been made through federal legislation in 1916: the La Follette Seamen's Act, the Adamson Act for trainmen, and the provision of the Clayton Act supposedly exempting unions from antitrust law actions. Probably more significant was President Wilson's appointment of Samuel Gompers, longtime head of the American Federation of Labor, to the Council of National Defense. Wilson was simply assuring the cooperation of organized labor in the war effort, and accomplished it most effectively. The leadership of the AFL in Wisconsin was dominated by socialists who at first followed the Socialist party's resistance to the war. Public and membership pressures modified this stand after the United States entry into the war.

Milwaukee was the center of the Wisconsin labor movement and of the important metal-fabricating industries, but the two were not synonymous. The metal industries had successfully resisted unionism with a variety of weapons. The piecework system, employed in many shops, militated against successful unionism, as did the continual flow of immigrant labor into Milwaukee, the seasonal nature of the work, and the customary turnover that ran as high as 200–300 percent annually in some large shops. The employers pursued a consistent antiunion policy coordinated through a variety of organizations, beginning with the Milwaukee Foundrymen's Association organized in 1898. They regularly employed labor spies, strikebreakers, blacklists, and the courts as weapons.

By 1919, wartime industries that had dealt generously with the craft unions were undergoing conversion or phasing out—shipbuilding, for instance—and therefore were a poor base for militant unionism. Management, along with much of the public, cherished a view of the war industry worker as pampered, prodigal with his inflated pay, and enjoying a haven from military service. The view colored the public's perception of organized labor generally. Milwaukee industrialist Theodore Vilter commented on the new prosperity of labor in the wartime economy: "There is now turkey or duck on many tables where they have not been before and it is going to take great effort to reconcile them to their accustomed sausage and sauerkraut when the time comes and they must go back to it."

Organized labor was the power base of socialism in Milwaukee and an ally of progressivism. The favorable conditions of the wartime employment market toward the AFL had encouraged the Federated Trades Council of Milwaukee to an organizational drive. From a union membership of 20,000 at the war's beginning, the drive carried union membership in Milwaukee to 35,000 in 1920, then lost 40 percent in the years following. But the gain was mostly among the meat cutters, furriers, tannery workers, flat janitors, and workers in the service trades. The metal trades unions made little gain. Employers responded with welfare capitalism and an Americanization campaign that used the facilities of the public schools, university extension, the YMCA, and popular fears of radicalism and disloyalty. More helpful, if unwelcome, to the employers was a drop in industrial activity in the postwar years. Wisconsin industrial employment dropped a dizzying 28 percent between 1919 and 1921. It did not recover to the 1919 level until 1927. The consumer price index rose from 43.4 in 1915 to 76.4 in 1921.

Looking back, the immediate postwar years would seem to have been an ideal time for conservatives to proceed with the work of dismantling the machinery of the progressive state from which Governor Philipp had been diverted by the war. Organized labor was clearly on the defensive in the face of rising unemployment and a series of unsuccessful strikes both locally and nationally which reacted unfavorably upon public opinion. The Boston Police Strike, the Seattle General Strike, and strikes in the steel and soft coal industries, all in 1919, contributed to the so-called Red Scare, which briefly but virulently ran its course. The Socialist party split disastrously with the expulsion of the growing left wing, which was ideologically tied to the Bolsheviks and Spartacists. National membership fell from the 108,504 claimed in 1919 to near 26,000 in 1920. Victor Berger abandoned his long-established separatist policy and began looking for allies to join in a fusionist third-party movement.

Many long-time La Follette supporters had noisily deserted their leader over the issues raised by the late war. Irvine Lenroot was the most prominent of these and seemed to have established a solid political base independent of his former mentor. The rise of James Tittemore, the president of the Society of Equity, was looked upon as a threat to La Follette's remaining farm support. Hopeful Republican stalwarts saw yet another eclipse for La Follette.

But Wisconsin politics had simply entered a new era of confusion. Although he had lost supporters, La Follette had recruited a new following of German-Americans who applauded what others marked as willful intransigence when his country was at war. Events soon turned the tides of popular opinion to running full in Bob's favor. He had expressed serious doubts about the proposed peace terms for Germany in May 1918, and took an early position in opposition to the Versailles Peace Treaty, and particularly to the League of Nations, which Wilson was determinedly embedding in the treaty. La Follette's stand on these issues was in advance of majority opinion in Wisconsin, but it was an accurate reflection of where the let-down from Wilsonian rhetoric and the reassertion of a traditional anti-British sentiment would lead it. Governor Philipp and Senator Lenroot were, by the spring of 1919, weakly echoing La Follette. Further strengthening La Follette's hand was the decision in January 1919, by the U.S. Senate, to drop the expulsion resolution growing out of his St. Paul speech to the Nonpartisan League. Many progressives who had condemned La Follette in hot haste were moved to repent that judgment.

The rampant, uncritical patriotism of the war years had not run its course with the armistice and the rehabilitation of Old Bob, however. Just as the superpatriot of 1918 had found the enemy within the city gates, especially among his neighbors of German ancestry, his avid search for new dangers was rewarded with a melange of un-American hazards in the society around him. The prohibition amendment was adopted nationally in 1919. It was greeted in Wisconsin with something less than unanimous enthusiasm; brewing had been the fifth largest Wisconsin industry. Aside from the total collapse of this flourishing industry, so closely identified with the state's metropolis, and the virtual disappearance of malting barley as an important cash crop for Wisconsin agriculture, there were many who looked upon prohibition as a totally unwarranted invasion of private rights as well as a hypocritical reflection upon their style of life.

Part of the propaganda for the passage of prohibition took advantage of the wartime spirit by identifying liquor and the saloon with the Kaiser and the hated "Hun." There were, however, many cross-currents: the traditional Yankee churches versus the "immigrant" churches, and rural versus urban values. Some ethnic groups, notably the Norwegians, were identified as ardent dries. Because the issue cut across party, ethnic, and social lines so erratically, La Follette still refused to deal with it as a political issue, which it certainly was.

The Red Scare of 1919–20 also came to reflect upon the German-Americans. There was an exaggerated fear of domestic revolution, fed by the wave of strikes across the nation which accompanied the sharp rise in living costs and the totally unplanned conversion of industry from the high levels of wartime production. The Seattle General Strike, as a case in point, started with the shipyard workers. Hysterical press coverage convinced many Americans that the Bolshevik Revolution had found a foothold on Puget Sound where the IWW (Industrial Workers of the World) had been active in the lumber industry. Seattle, like Milwaukee, was the center of an active labor movement as well as a center of American socialism. Patriots were not inclined to draw distinctions between Victor Berger's brand of gradualist socialism and Marxism, although the American communists were expelled from the Socialist Party in 1919 and there was no love lost between the two. Both were associated in the popular mind with things German. Berger edited a German-language newspapers and was the dean of Milwaukee socialists. He had been indicted and convicted for supporting the IWW, among other things. The Germans of Milwaukee had elected him to Congress and then reelected him when he was refused his seat. What seemed clear to everyone who wanted such opinions confirmed was that the Germans had invented communism and had successfully introduced it into Russia, effectively removing her from the war, and were now succeeding in the same treachery within Wisconsin's very borders. Wisconsinites of German extraction deeply resented the simple-minded equating of things German with the presumed threat of radicalism, and of an antiprohibition stand with immorality and treason.

Notwithstanding Harding's lanaslide victory in Wisconsin in 1920, it was a progressive year in the state. Deserted by the German-American voters, the Democratic party was sinking toward its lowest point in state politics. The meaningful contests were in the Republican primaries. La Follette easily swept the presidential preferential primary. The Wisconsin delegation held firm for "Old Bob" through the last ballot and took no part in the break in the deadlock which carried the national convention for Harding.

The state primary in 1920 was an interesting contest. Many progressive voters who evidently had made their peace with La Follette's war record still reacted to Roy Wilcox's calls for a militant Americanism. At the same time, labor and farm groups were conferring on an advanced progressive program. The Nonpartisan League, which now claimed nearly 30,000 members, mostly among farmers in northern and southeastern Wisconsin, sought alliances with Milwaukee Socialists and organized labor. They supported the Railroad Brotherhoods in their drive for government ownership of the railroads, which had come under government operation during the war. They advocated public ownership of stockyards, terminals, elevators, packing plants, "and all other public utilities and all natural resources, the private ownership of which is made the basis of monopoly"—language similar to that of La Follette and his supporters. A loose coalition of labor organizations, socialists, progressives, and radical farm groups, known as the Farmer-Labor League, came into being. La Follette rejected an invitation to run for the presidency on their ticket, but he was interested.

The Nonpartisan League met in Madison in the summer of 1920 to endorse candidates for state offices. John Blaine won the league's support for the governorship with a rousing speech. "I believe in going the full length . . . because it is the best kind of Americanism we can preach. . . . Private monopolies must be abolished. The railroads, the forests, the ship yards, the mines, the water powers must be returned to the people. . . . Those who have not earned what they have, must lose it. Regulation is ineffectual. Nothing but ownership by the government will remedy these ills."

It does not take much familiarity with Wisconsin's subsequent legislative history to know that there was more bombast than substance in the rhetoric of three-term Governor John Blaine on this occasion. There is more than a suggestion in Blaine's career of the eye on the main chance. As a young attorney in Boscobel, he responded to La Follette's invitation for someone in Grant County to carry the progressive battle there. He had done yeoman service in the movement for nearly twenty years before moving into the sunlight of an independent political career that would disturb La Follette's sons and heirs.

There were many elements in Blaine's 1920 victory. Roy Wilcox was again in the race, and Emanuel Philipp was as determined as ever to thwart him, which he did by persuading a popular Milwaukee conservative who had seen service with the 32nd Division to run. Blaine, with La Follette's support, was an easy winner in a field complicated by other progressive candidates, the issue of prohibition enforcement, and the perennial religious issue, for Wilcox was a Catholic. Bigotry was to have its day in the twenties.

Blaine's victory as the spokesman for a militant farmer-labor coalition provokes some cynicism, since he was to run successfully again in 1922 as "the Economy Governor." There is a certain incongruity between his radical posture as the spokesman for government ownership of "railroads, the forests, the shipyards, the mines, the water powers" and his emergence two years later as the champion of economy in state government.

Blaine evidently had gauged his constituency correctly. The Nonpartisan League shortly faded from the scene as an aggressive political force as did the Society of Equity. Much of the militancy of the 1920 election was diffused by the normal obstacles to a coalition made up of organized farm groups and labor. Many of the leaders found a new outlet in the triumphant re-election campaign of La Follette in 1922, followed by his independent candidacy for the presidency in 1924, which carried Wisconsin.

Wisconsin progressivism, as reconstituted after the war, was not the vehicle it had been. A large contingent of German-Americans had moved in, attracted by La Follette's anti-Wilson stand and the civil libertarian views of the progressives. Blaine made political capital from this last issue. He was a stoutly outspoken foe of the Ku Klux Klan, which found fertile soil in Wisconsin society and was an uncertain political force here for three or four years. Blaine also supported organized labor in its efforts to prevent the use of the courts and the injunction by management in labor disputes. Pointing toward a contest with Irvine Lenroot for his U.S. Senate seat in 1926, Blaine took a stand as an uncompromising wet, while Lenroot was closely identified with prohibition enforcement. The longtime La Follette position of circumspect neutrality on this issue made Blaine's position all the more conspicuous.

If Blaine's political career in the 1920s appears opportunistic, it is a reflection of what much of Wisconsin's progressivism had become. It was a tired, middle-aged movement which supported in office a number of spent political volcanoes. The formerly vital links with the university were mostly broken or unused. Charles McCarthy, who as chief of the legislative reference service did much to forge these links, died in 1921. Van Hise had died in 1918, estranged from La Follette. He was followed in an interim presidency by Edward Birge, who was cautious, conservative, and dominated by a conservative board of regents mostly appointed by Emanuel Philipp. President Birge forbade the use of campus facilities for appearances by Oswald Garrison Villard, Lincoln Steffens, Scott Nearing, and Kate Richards O'Hare. The latter, the Socialist candidate for vice-president in 1920, was given space for her Madison appearance in the State Capitol Building with progressive legislators and state officers in attendance. They were clearly making a point to the university administration for its timidity.

The progressive legislature of 1923 accomplished the possible, despite rhetorical flourishes. Tax reform was the main issue, but there was no agreement and no legislation. Some minor labor legislation, including a limitation upon the use of injunctions and a definition of peaceful picketing, was passed. A summary in the *Wisconsin Blue Book* pointed to the better-advertised accomplishments. Military training at the university was made optional, and the budget of the national guard was slashed. The conservative board of regents of the university was enlarged, with the requirement that two representative farmers and two representative laborers be included. A prideful achievement was that no state funds should be used for the purchase of history or other textbooks "which falsified the facts regarding the war of independence, or war of 1812, or which defamed our nation's founders or misrepresented the ideals and causes for which they struggled and sacrificed or which contained propaganda favorable to any foreign country." The final determination was to be made by the state superintendent, after a hearing, which could be requested by five interested citizens. This squares curiously with the progressive solicitude for civil rights, but accords with the reassertion of the isolationist spirit fostered by La Follette.

The brief rise and decline of the Ku Klux Klan in Wisconsin between 1922 and 1927 tells us something about the society in which it flourished. Highly adaptable, the Klan of the twenties took advantage of whatever prejudices came its way. It identified itself with aggressive protestantism, was hostile to the Catholic Church, Negroes, Jews, and foreigners generally, upheld Americanism, which in the Midwest it equated with support of President Coolidge, and was a champion of prohibition and the general code of morality associated with that law.

The Klan in Wisconsin was not a rural phenomenon. The first provisional Klavern was organized in 1920 aboard the U.S. Coast Guard vessel *Hawk* in Milwaukee harbor, and the members held their first meetings as the Milwaukee Businessmen's Club. The Wisconsin Klan fortunately never developed strong leadership, and remained a relatively benign organization appealing to the prejudices and fraternal instincts of those who felt the need to associate themselves with nativist, Protestant values. Whenever the head office in Atlanta, which was devoted to the selling of Klavern charters, memberships, and sheets, sent a hard-shell southern evangelist to Wisconsin to release innocent girls from nunneries, put down the Negroes, and damn the Jews, the state membership would go into serious decline. Too many affable neighbors—and voters —were Catholic, Wisconsin had only 5,201 Negroes counted in the 1920 census, and one of the most popular statewide politicians was State Treasurer Solomon Levitan.

A student of the Klan's career in the Midwest estimates that Wisconsin never had more than 40,000 members at one time, but it attracted crowds of 15,000 to 20,000 to its special functions. Possibly as many as 75,000 belonged at some time. The areas of Klan strength are significant. Milwaukee, Kenosha, and Racine counties had the heaviest representation. These were also the areas which received most of the post-1900 immigration of Polish and Italian Catholics and Russian Jews. A consuming embarrassment for Socialists Victor Berger and Mayor Dan Hoan, was the tendency for German Socialists, whose most conspicuous opponents were the Catholic clergy, to join the Klan. It was at once an assertion of a hard-won nativism and an anticlerical pose.

The Klan also won active support in the Fox River valley, in Dane, Green, and Rock counties in south-central Wisconsin, and in Eau Claire and La Crosse counties. Rusk County in the Cutover, with a heavy population of Polish newcomers, was also Klan territory, with the Poles as targets, not members. Similarly, Dane County membership was aimed at the Italian population in Madison, originally attracted by the marble work on the State Capitol—some had become bootleggers to the community after prohibition. The Klan successfully appealed to Protestant German-Americans, who now identified with the dominant Protestant, Yankee culture.

Governor Blaine, the progressive Republican, was triumphantly re-lected in 1922 with over 76 percent of the vote. La Follette was also on the ballot, which accounted in large measure for the progressive sweep. But there were cross-currents which continue to puzzle students. One concludes that the prewar decline of progressivism was not simply "an interlude in an otherwise prolonged and uninterrupted progressive continuum extending from the 1890s into the 1920s and beyond. The war so jarred society in Wisconsin as to generate new issues, new alignments . . . a new mood of anger and bitterness. . . . With the termination of the war in Europe, the relative power of the various factions changed, but otherwise the war situation continued." Frank R. Kent of the conservative Democratic *Baltimore Sun,* wrote that La Follette "is the 'Old Guard' in Wisconsin. He is the boss out here, and his machine, when you scrape off the camouflage, is the old-style political machine, run in the old-style political way and for the old-style political purposes—namely, to keep him and his friends in power."

The stalwart faction of the Republican party in Wisconsin was a study in frustration. Governor Philipp's reelections in 1916 and 1918 had been personal victories. In 1920, the stalwarts tried to win control of the party on the issue of loyalty, but their leader, Roy Wilcox, was anathema to Philipp, who helped to defeat him in the primary. The Democrats who had moved over into the Republican party were presumably mostly conservative German-Americans who, although conservative, made the change because they preferred La Follette's definition of loyalty. That they made such a move is plain. The Democratic primary for governor drew 73,000 votes in 1914 and only 25,000 in 1920. There was a steady erosion in the years between. The party's fortunes continued at a low ebb until 1932.

The conservative Republicans, who were probably correct in their conviction that a majority of Republican voters were conservative at heart, simply had no weapons with which to combat the popularity of Old Bob. His record on the war and his isolationist views probably brought him more votes in 1922 and in 1924 than did his economic radicalism.

With La Follette's death in June 1925, it became increasingly difficult for the progressives to control the Republican party in Wisconsin through the device of the primary. Robert M. La Follette, Jr., was an easy victor in the special primary held in the following September to fill his father's seat. Blaine was successful in his race against the incumbent, Irvine Lenroot, for the other U.S. Senate seat. But the progressives lost their hold on the governorship in 1926.

Blaine, who had started his career as an early supporter of La Follette, had built his own following in the governorship and was an independent force in the progressive movement. The La Follette boys, Young Bob and Phil, treated him with respect but caution; their distrust of Blaine is apparent in Phil's memoirs. But they were agreed with Blaine upon the candidacy of Herman Ekern for the governorship in 1926. Ekern had all the right credentials and was a faithful La Follette follower through thick and thin, but he was no match for a glad-handing joiner who was to be the founder of a Wisconsin political dynasty in the office of secretary of state, Fred Zimmerman. The Republican stalwarts abandoned their own candidate to support Zimmerman, who billed himself as a progressive but was not conceded an honest title to the label by either Blaine or the La Follettes.

It is instructive that stalwart Republican political appeals and writings in the twenties are in many ways almost a carbon copy of the La Follette fulminations of the nineties. The La Follette machine was a juggernaut that crushed honest dissent, they claimed, and rolled up majorities with its host of political time-servers and dishonest appeals to voters' prejudices. The stalwarts further asserted that, because they were honest and unmanaged, they were steam-rollered by the disciplined ranks of the progressives, who accepted dictation from an inner circle composed of La Follettes, Blaine, Ekern, and one or two others.

Discipline of a sort was achieved by the stalwarts. They invented the voluntary committee, an unofficial party organization outside of the official party structure defined in La Follette's direct primary law. It didn't work too well in 1925 and 1926, but it delivered the governorship to stalwart Republican Walter J. Kohler in 1928. Zimmerman, who was neither fish nor fowl in the factional alignments but had been preferred to Ekern by the stalwarts in 1926, was unceremoniously dumped. La Follette progressivism was in political trouble again.

Labor made some minor legislative gains, assisted by the progressive rural legislators, who did not mind embarrassing Milwaukee manufacturers so long as the legislation did not apply to farm labor or cooperatives. Organized labor also began a systematic lobbying effort in Madison through the twenties. This brought some results in legislation designed to control the use of the injunction in labor disputes and requiring the registration of "detective agencies" engaged in union sabotage. But a perennial proposal, originating with John R. Commons and his students, for unemployment insurance on the model of the 1911 workmen's compensation act for industrial accidents, got nowhere until Phil La Follette won the governorship.

Aside from property tax relief, farm progressives had less to ask in the way of legislation. The longtime war against the railroads had been translated to the federal level. Farm progressives placed great faith in the cooperative movement in the twenties. Wisconsin was a leader in cooperative legislation. The Department of Markets was created in 1919, and its duties and powers expanded in subsequent legislation. It was given investigative powers over cooperatives and engaged directly in their organization and management, as well as providing marketing information and advice. Agriculture in Wisconsin was already heavily subsidized in 1920 and became more so.

Farmer groups were unhappy with the university's College of Agriculture for its lack of interest in marketing problems and continuing emphasis upon greater production in a period when overproduction seemed a clear danger to farm prices. Dean Harry Russell of the College of Agriculture was a favorite target. Russell, who worried about radicalism and the returning veteran, continued the efforts of his predecessor to persuade new farmers to take up farming in the Cutover of northern Wisconsin.

The problem of the cutover lands in northern Wisconsin was one for which legislation finally provided imaginative answers of a pioneering sort in the Wisconsin progressive tradition. The problem was an old one, essentially an argument over the use of the pinelands after the timber was gone. Private enterprise preferred agriculture, even though the evidence of the time showed that most of this land could not provide a living for a farm family. Public officials and most of the nonfarm population in the northern counties wanted desperately to believe in this solution. The legislature and state executive agencies managed to look in both directions. In 1895, the legislature provided funds for the widely circulated *Northern Wisconsin, a hand-book for the homeseeker,* prepared by Dean Henry of the College of Agriculture, and in 1897 set up a forestry commission to study the utilization of the land for reforestation.

Progressive philosophy tended toward an extensive reforestation program, but private promoters were rapidly enlarging the problem. One of the most imaginative, James L. "Stumpland" Gates, claimed to have sold 456,000 acres between 1898 and 1902, and he was only one of literally hundreds of companies and individuals dealing in lumber company lands and lands that had reverted for nonpayment of taxes. Many of the ethnic colonies still existing in the area are traceable to the activities of promoters, encouraged by state agencies and official policy. As late as 1923, the State Department of Agriculture's division of immigration boasted that it had "been in touch with 10,000 new settlers . . . during the past eight years. These industrious people are changing the northern wilderness of slashings to productive dairy farms with fine buildings and herds." The mute evidence of many more than 10,000 failures can be seen in Wisconsin's Appalachia.

Forestry as a solution had a slower start and more opposition. A forestry board was created, in 1905, which began with the management of 220,000 acres of state and federal land. This was augmented by annual grants to buy land to fill in blocks for proper management. The program was challenged as unconstitutional, and to the chagrin of conservationists, the challenge was upheld by the state supreme court in 1915.

It was 1924 before the conservationists were able to get a constitutional amendment removing the disability. By that time, there was wide disillusionment with the results of the years of enthusiastic and indiscriminate promotion of agricultural settlement. With the constitutional roadblock removed, a forest crop law was passed in 1927 encouraging the counties and private owners to put land into forest plantation, under a tax plan which recognized the long-term nature of this land use. The 1929 zoning law extending the concept of city zoning to the county was even more imaginative. Counties could zone lands as out of bounds for agricultural settlement. It was a final recognition that an unsuccessful farmer, settled on unsuitable land in an isolated place, was anything but a taxable asset to the county.

Wisconsin industry was particularly vulnerable to the economic collapse that followed the stock market crash in October 1929. This statement must be qualified by noting that dairy-related industries—butter, cheese, and condensed milk—had climbed from fourth place in 1900 to first place in 1920. Lumber and timber products had been first in 1900: $57,634,816 in value of products, as compared to $20,120,147 for dairy-related manufacturing. These proportions were more than reversed by 1925, when dairy-related industries turned out $209,260,354 in value of product. Lumber and timber products, with only $56,374,753, had fallen to eighth place in the state's industries. Dairy products were more depression-resistant than lumbering, and the industry was even more dispersed. But the implications for those areas that had been dependent upon lumbering and had a marginal agriculture were not good. The paper industry took up some of the slack there. It climbed from eighth place in 1900 to fourth in 1925, and the value of product had increased nine times, while the total value of product for all industries increased on the order of five times in the same period. The paper industry, like food products, was considerably more depression-proof than the more cyclical heavy-goods industries with which Milwaukee and the Rock River valley were identified.

As today, when one discusses Wisconsin industry in the 1920s he must look particularly at Milwaukee and the adjacent area. With 17.4 percent of the population in 1920, the city produced fully one-third of the industrial output of the state. The first five industries there were leather, meat packing, foundry and machine shops, engines, and boots and shoes. The first industry was less than twice the size of the fifth. Brewing, which had ranked well toward the top in 1910, had disappeared from the list after prohibition. Leather, still first in Milwaukee in 1920, was on its way downward. The motor vehicle industry, with Nash Motors at Milwaukee and Kenosha, various small independents, particularly in the truck field, and the General Motors plant at Janesville, emerged as Wisconsin's second industry in 1925. The heavy emphasis upon motor vehicles, foundry and machine shop products, and engines, particularly of the heavy type, made the industrial center of the state particularly vulnerable to any downturn in the national economy.

The heavy industries, especially, had followed the normal American pattern of growth and consolidation. The pioneer industrial giant in Milwaukee, the E. P. Allis Company, became part of an international combine, Allis-Chalmers, in 1901. Milwaukee Harvester became part of In-

ternational Harvester in 1904. The Milwaukee Iron Company at Bay
View went through a series of title changes as a subsidiary of a subsidiary of U.S. Steel. The Bucyrus Company was a combine put together by
the Morgan syndicate in 1911. The Milwaukee business, banking, and
industrial community was mature enough to maintain an important voice
in the affairs of these new combines, although ultimate control was in
New York or in other financial centers. There was a marked concentration of industry after the turn of the century.

Another industrial trend in the period was a broader dispersion of industry, although Milwaukee, the only major city, did not decline in importance. One indicator is the percentage of wage earners in manufacturing. Milwaukee had 32.6 percent of the state's total in 1909 and 35.8
percent in 1929. Part of this increase, however, came through annexation. The new pattern showed up in cities in the 10,000–25,000 class,
where the proportion of wage earners increased from 9.9 percent to 15.7
percent in the same period. Wausau, Beloit, Manitowoc, Janesville, Fond
du Lac, Eau Claire, Appleton, and Waukesha were among them. Industries related to motor vehicles had much to do with this change.

Of the 265,000 manufacturing wage earners in Wisconsin in 1929,
some 120,000 were in metal fabricating and related trades: foundries,
machine shops, motor vehicles, and electrical equipment. Forest products and wood-working accounted for another 50,000, and food industries for only 25,000.

The manufacturers had another bone to pick with the progressives
that went beyond rural cooperation with organized labor. Wisconsin's pioneer income tax law had been passed without much regard to the burden it would place upon industry. The original argument was that a
property tax took no cognizance of ability to pay and that the urban taxpayer could more easily conceal personal property assets—stocks, bonds,
savings accounts, other investments—than could a farmer whose personal property stood on display in home, barnyard, and field. This was
borne out by the initial results of the state income tax. Milwaukee
County citizens paid 42.5 percent of the first levy, and 315 taxpayers
paid 39 percent of the total. The whole emphasis of the income tax law
was upon the methods of locating and taxing rather than upon the distribution of the burden.

The inflation of the war years added to taxes generally. Predominantly
rural counties were the hardest hit. The obvious solutions, for them, were
some form of statewide equalization and a further shift of the cost of
government from real property to the income tax. One solution adopted
was to shift a greater levy on industry in a 1925 tax law which cancelled
the personal property tax write off against the income tax. This may

sound technical, but a growing concern of such agencies as the University's Bureau of Business and Economic Research to prove that Wisconsin's tax system worked no competitive hardship on industry indicates a sensitivity to the issue which any casual newspaper reader is aware of yet today.

The logical closing point for a survey of the twenties is October 1929. Just as the tensions of the First World War and the immediate postwar years profoundly influenced Wisconsin politics and society, the aftermath of the Great Crash of 1929 would set new cross-currents in motion.

Selected Bibliography

Barlow, Raleigh. "Forest Policy in Wisconsin." *Wisconsin Magazine of History* 26:261–79 (March 1943). Background of the 1927 Forest Crop Law.

Brownlee, W. Elliot, Jr. "Progressivism and Economic Growth: The Wisconsin Income Tax, 1911–1929." Ph.D. dissertation, University of Wisconsin, 1969. His contention, that industry had little voice in framing the income tax.

Brush, John Edwin. "The Trade Centers of Southwestern Wisconsin: An Analysis of Function and Location." Ph.D. dissertation, University of Wisconsin, 1952. A geographer's treatment of town, village, and hamlet.

Campbell, W. J. *History of the Republican Party in Wisconsin under the Convention Plan, 1924 to 1940*. Oshkosh, 1942. To thwart progressive domination.

Carstensen, Vernon. *Farms or Forests: Evolution of a State Land Policy for Northern Wisconsin, 1850–1932*. Madison, 1958. Problems of the Cutover.

Clark, James I. *Cutover Problems: Colonization, Depression, Reforestation*. Madison, 1956.

———. *Farming the Cutover: The Settlement of Northern Wisconsin*. Madison, 1956. Summaries for school use, good pictures.

Daffer, James H. "Progressive Profile: John James Blaine from 1873 to 1918." Master's thesis, University of Wisconsin, 1951. Blaine emerged as an independent force in the progressive politics of the 1920s.

Helgeson, Arlan C. *Farms in the Cutovers Agricultural Settlement in Northern Wisconsin*. Madison, 1962.

———. "Nineteenth-Century Land Colonization in Northern Wisconsin." *Wisconsin Magazine of History* 36:115–21 (Winter 1952–53). Fervent promotion created Wisconsin's Appalachia.

Hutchinson, Edward P. *Immigrants and Their Children, 1850–1950*. New York, 1956. Interesting on economic assimilation.

Kane, Lucile. "Settling the Wisconsin Cutovers." *Wisconsin Magazine of History* 40:91–98 (Winter 1956–57). Promoters and enthusiasts.

Karges, Steven B. "David Clark Everest and Marathon Paper Mills Company: A Study of a Wisconsin Entrepreneur, 1909–1931." Ph.D. dissertation, University of Wisconsin, 1968. Best on the paper business and the interesting Wausau Group.

Knaplund, Paul. *Moorings Old and New: Entries in an Immigrant's Log.* Madison, 1963. Came as a young man from Norway in 1906; became a distinguished historian at Wisconsin.

Kolehmainen, John I., and George W. Hill. *Haven in the Woods: The Story of the Finns in Wisconsin.* Madison, 1951. Most of them in the Cutover.

Korman, Gerd. *Industrialization, Immigrants and Americanizers: The View from Milwaukee, 1866–1921.* Madison, 1967. Assimilation under forced draft.

La Follette, Robert M., Jr. *Back to Boscobel: A Tribute.* Joint Resolution, Wisconsin Sessions Laws, 1935. Madison, 1935. Memorial on John J. Blaine.

Lucker, Jeffrey. "The Politics of Prohibition in Wisconsin, 1917–1933." Master's thesis, University of Wisconsin, 1968. Wisconsin underwent a change of heart after 1920.

MacKay, Kenneth Campbell. *The Progressive Movement of 1924.* 1947. Reprint. Columbia University Studies in History, Economics and Public Law, 527. New York, 1966. The last campaign.

Mallach, Stanley. "Red Kate O'Hare Comes to Madison: The Politics of Free Speech." *Wisconsin Magazine of History* 53:204–22 (Spring 1970). The progressives vs. a conservative university administration.

Margulies, Herbert F. "The Election of 1920 in Wisconsin: The Return to Normalcy Reappraised." *Wisconsin Magazine of History* 41:15–22 (Autumn 1951). Wilson simply did not represent "Reform" in Wisconsin.

Middleton, George. *These Things are Mine.* New York, 1947. Memoirs of La Follette's son-in-law, mostly about New York theater people.

Morlan, Robert L. *Political Prairie Fire: The Non-Partisan League, 1915–1922.* Minneapolis, 1955. The league was a minor factor in Wisconsin politics but claimed much.

Morris, William W. "An Early Forest Plantation in Wisconsin." *Wisconsin Magazine of History* 27:436–38 (June 1944). On Walter Ware, pioneer of reforestation.

Muzik, Edward J. "Victor L. Berger, Congress, and the Red Scare." *Wisconsin Magazine of History* 47:309–18 (Summer 1964). A tawdry chapter.

Platt, Chester C. *What La Follette's State is Doing: Some Battles Waged for More Freedom.* Batavia, N.Y., 1924. Wisconsin progressivism was running down, but he didn't know it.

Plumb, Ralph G. *Recollections of an Amateur Politician.* Manitowoc, 1959. Liked the pre-La Follette politics of his youth.

Schlabach, Theron F. *Edwin E. Witte: Cautious Reformer.* Madison, 1969. One of many Wisconsin technicians who went on to important federal service; an architect of social security.

Schumann, Alfred R. *No Peddlers Allowed.* Appleton, 1948. Biography of Sol Levitan, unlikely progressive.

Shideler, James H. "The LaFollette Progressive Party Campaign of 1924." *Wisconsin Magazine of History* 33:444–57 (June 1950). A wild card in a stacked deck.

Slatin, Alfred. "Wisconsin Progressivism in Transition: A Study of Progressive Concepts, 1918–1930." Master's thesis, University of Wisconsin, 1952. Progressives getting petulant.

Solberg, Erling D. *New Laws for New Forests: Wisconsin's Forest-Fire, Tax, Zoning, and County-Forest Laws in Operation.* Madison, 1961. Highly technical.

Titus, Walter A. "Two Decades of Wisconsin Forestry." *Wisconsin Magazine of History* 30:187–91 (Dec. 1946). Titus was in the 1927 legislature.

Voigt, W. R. "A Survey of Manufacturing in Wisconsin." Ph.D. dissertation, University of Wisconsin, 1938. Useful survey of census reports, 1900–1930. See also *Wisconsin Blue Book,* 1929, "A Short Industrial History of Wisconsin."

Weaver, Norman F. "The Knights of the Ku Klux Klan in Wisconsin, Indiana, Ohio, and Michigan." Ph.D. dissertation, University of Wisconsin, 1954. An excellent work.

Wilson, F. G. "Zoning for Forestry and Recreation: Wisconsin's Pioneer Role." *Wisconsin Magazine of History* 41:102–6 (Winter 1957–58).

———. "Forestry in Wisconsin." *Wisconsin Blue Book,* 1942, pp. 177–85. Author a forestry consultant in the program.

Wyllie, Irvin G. "Bryan, Birge, and the Wisconsin Evolution Controversy, 1921–1922." *Wisconsin Magazine of History* 35:294–301 (Summer 1952). An undignified exchange.

DEPRESSION DECADE

29

The central concern of the 1930s in Wisconsin, as elsewhere, was the Great American Depression. In severity and length, it was the most serious crisis the American economy had faced. There are many indices that illustrate the completeness of the collapse of economic activity. Value added by Wisconsin manufacturing dropped from approximately $960,000,000 in 1929 to $375,000,000 in 1933. The number of industrial jobs fell from 370,000 in 1929 to 232,000 in 1932, while wage payments fell nearly 60 percent. Manufacturing wage earners, only about 28 percent of those gainfully employed, took about 40 percent of the loss in wages and salaries experienced in the interval between the prosperity of 1929 and the nadir of the years 1932–33.

The plight of the factory worker gave no comfort to the man engaged in agriculture. The farmer was somewhat more secure about food and shelter for his family, but he saw a drastic decline in income and the value of his property. The cost of servicing his debts did not decline, property taxes rose, as local governments were forced to meet emergency relief costs, and the prices of commodities the farmer bought did not decline on the same scale as did farm commodity prices. As ever, industry was better able to maintain its prices and restrict production by reducing its labor force. Taking 1929 prices as the base, farm commodity prices

476

fell from 100 to a low of 43 in 1932. The same index for commodities the farmer bought fell only to 71 at their lowest point.

A recital of economic statistics fails to convey the sense of helplessness in the face of overwhelming catastrophe which gripped people. By 1933 the burden of relief in Milwaukee County had risen from less than 1,000 families in January 1930 to one in every five families, and the burden was entirely on the county. The city had its breadlines, soup kitchens, and homeless men, but distress cut deeply into the homes of skilled workers and the middle class. As if to complete the disaster, Wisconsin agriculture shared in the drought which settled in the Midwest in the early 1930s and in 1934 became the most severe on record in the state.

It is certainly a truism that the economic collapse of the 1930s, bringing such critical dislocations to a highly interdependent urban-industrial society and increasingly commercialized agriculture, turned attention as never before to the various levels of government for solutions. Proud of the leadership it provided to progressive reform at the state level since the opening of the century, Wisconsin brought something unique to its attack upon the problems of the depression. This fact may be conceded, in part, simply on the basis that most of the states foundered in the face of the enormity of the problems of welfare and relief. A modicum of aggressively purposeful activity was bound to attract notice. Interest in this resurgence of Wisconsin progressivism was heightened by the appearance of Philip F. La Follette, the younger son of Old Bob. Phil was to dominate Wisconsin politics throughout the thirties.

Old Bob's popularity, which in Wisconsin transcended his economic and political doctrines after 1919, served to pass his Senate seat on to his elder son, Robert, Jr. The family grip on the Republican primary was becoming tenuous, however, when the combination of the depression and Phil's energy and political acumen brought him to the governorship in 1931. Senator Bob and Governor Phil provided good copy for reporters. Following in what was now a family tradition, Senator La Follette was taking an independent line as a principal critic of President Hoover's policies. He was establishing a reputation as an expert in the fields of unemployment and federal finance and spending. Phil, who suffered an early attack of presidential fever, proposed to make Wisconsin a model for the nation in solving the problems posed by the depression. The Wisconsin Idea probably furnished more technicians than original ideas to the New Deal, however.

Phil La Follette, possessing more self-confidence than he was ever able to implement with effective political support, served six turbulent years as Wisconsin's governor. But he was imaginative and offered legislative programs in 1931 that appeared later in one guise or another as part of the New Deal. Franklin D. Roosevelt, a fellow governor with realizable ambitions in 1931, kept an eye on the La Follettes, to be sure. The Democratic party of Wisconsin in 1930 was conservative and vestigial, and Roosevelt knew what he was about in flattering the brothers who spoke for an identifiable liberal faction in Wisconsin politics. It is doubtful that he was dependent for ideas upon Wisconsin's governor, especially since most of them were in the public domain anyway. Aside from lessons in political obstructionism from Republican and Democratic conservatives, Phil La Follette learned that there was no Wisconsin solution to the problems of Allis-Chalmers, J. I. Case, Nash Motors, and other major state industries. The White House was the driver's seat, and like his father, he never came close. Another Roosevelt took it.

By 1930, Wisconsin had undergone appreciable changes since the turn of the century, many of them accelerated in the postwar years. A population which had been three-fifths rural in 1900 was now more than half urban. Wisconsin lagged just a little behind the national average in population growth and urbanization. As usual, Wisconsin tended to fall between the averages struck by the other Great Lakes states and those immediately to her west. The growth was uneven: the Milwaukee metropolitan area accounted for 60 percent, between 1920 and 1930, while there was an erosion of population in many of the northern counties as well as in others with a stable agriculture and no substantial urban centers. A line drawn from the approximate center of Grant County, in the southwest corner diagonally to Marinette County, on the Michigan border, falls entirely within counties with losses, some ranging as high as 14 percent. Another cluster of such counties fell in the northwest quarter of the state. The growth occurred in the industrial counties along the Lake, in the Fox valley, and in Dane and Rock counties with their major cities.

The stream of European immigration, which still in 1930 gave Wisconsin a higher than average number of foreign born, had been curtailed by the war and the immigration restriction laws which shortly followed. The percentage of foreign-born fell from 22 in 1910 to 13 in 1930. Nearly half of the population over sixty-five years of age were in this 13 percent. Possibly a more meaningful indication of ethnic composition and influence is given in the combined number of foreign born and those with one or both parents of foreign birth. This number, 1,477,367, was just slightly over half of the state's total 1930 population of 2,939,006. Those of German background were almost 43 percent of the 1,477,367, the Poles 9.4 percent, and Norwegians 9.2 percent.

Wisconsin retained many ethnic islands in 1930, although it is impossible to judge their degree of assimilation. The larger cities and rural areas were most likely to perpetuate these islands. Characteristically, the Poles, who were late-comers and therefore near the bottom of the economic ladder, continued the practice of bloc voting in specific ethnic terms. About half lived in Milwaukee County in readily identifiable neighborhoods. Older national groups were fading into the more generalized divisions of religion—Catholic versus Protestant—or socioeconomic class. Catholics made up about half of those professing church membership, which included roughly two-thirds of the population, and the various Lutheran synods claimed two-thirds of the Protestant half.

Acculturation or assimilation is difficult to define. Second and third generations from the older immigrant groups were rediscovering their ethnic heritage as something worth preserving, while newer groups were turned inward by a sense of barriers in the society around them. A useful distinction has been offered by the sociologist Milton Gordon between what he defines as cultural as opposed to structural assimilation. Structural assimilation occurs as members of an immigrant group cease to regard themselves as different in any significant way from the general society around them. This, of course, implies that the general society returns the compliment. Cultural assimilation, by this definition, has been achieved when an immigrant group uses English easily, identifies itself as American in political loyalty, and accepts a basic sense of American values of work, education, success, and so forth. It is not easy to determine when these changes have been accomplished, since they involve individual points of view and cannot be measured finally. Many people would make a continuing distinction based upon religion, while others would be indifferent to this, but hold firmly to some national stereotypes—Italian gangsters, credulous Poles, authoritarian Germans, stubborn Norwegians, alcoholic Irishmen, and so on. The processes of the melting pot are further complicated when we introduce differences based upon race and color.

The movies, too, were a powerful common cultural influence in the lives of most Americans by the 1920s. A newer influence was the radio. The 1930 census showed that 59 percent of Wisconsin urban families and 38 percent of rural families had radios.

Socioeconomic differences were more apparent within an urban environment. The assumption that some of these gaps were steadily being closed—between the working class and the expanding white collar class for instance—is certainly correct. If industry successfully thwarted unionization in the postwar years, it did so by being somewhat less cavalier, providing some health and other benefits, and recognizing the usefulness of more stability in its work force. This and a sharing of public utilities had raised working-class living standards relatively.

We tend to think more, of course, of the differences between urban and rural styles of life and the lure which the city represented. Much had changed by 1930. Wisconsin had only 4,120 miles of gravelled and 718 miles of concrete roads in 1920. By 1930, these totals had increased to 28,500 and 3,660 miles respectively, and 84 percent of farm families had an automobile, as compared with only 50 percent in 1920. However, by way of contrast, only 16 percent of the rural homes had water piped into the house, only 8 percent had bathrooms, and only 26 percent had electricity.

A large third of the state's school-age children were not enrolled in any school in 1880. By the turn of the century, compulsory attendance was generally enforced. Wisconsin's excellent vocational and continuing-education system for working teenagers was established by the 1911 legislature, public school bus laws were passed in 1917 and 1919, and the school year steadily lengthened to near the present standard in both city and rural schools. Free union high schools for rural children were provided by a 1921 law, although over half of rural school children were still enrolled in the state's 6,347 rural one-room schools in 1930. With an approximately equal distribution of children between urban and rural school systems, there were only 31,836 enrolled in the county high schools, compared with 77,779 in city high schools. In other words, a child's chances of going on to high school were nearly two and a half times better in the city than in a farm or village environment. The radio, the automobile with vastly improved roads, and the movies, available in small towns as well as cities, were bringing urban and rural standards together, but the distance remained more than geographical. Wisconsin's farms lost 40,000 in population during the decade, mostly young people, while Milwaukee's population rose 21 percent and the suburbs 78 percent.

One commodity available in every urban area, but to only one in six Wisconsin farm homes in 1930, was electric power served by a power line. Another 10 percent of the farm homes had costly generating engines with storage batteries. Electric power on the farm not only did some of the outdoor and household chores but it also made the difference between indoor and outdoor plumbing and lighting. It put the farm home in the market for appliances that were widening the gap between rural and urban living styles. This can be easily overlooked in comparing urban and rural life styles of forty years ago.

Appleton, Wisconsin, had a pioneer central generating plant, supplied by the Edison Company, which began operations in 1882, the same year as Edison's more famous New York City plant. The Appleton plant was the first to be run by hydro power. Other generating plants followed as this new technology found an eager market, conceived of almost entirely in terms of municipal lighting as a competitor to manufactured coal gas. Another technological advance, the trolley car, came in the late 1880s with the application of electric power to urban transportation. It rapidly replaced the horse car and the competing cable car for most applications.

The availability of electric power for urban transportation, elevators, and factory machines had a profound effect upon the American city. Suburban living became possible for all classes, the central city was taken over for business purposes, and powered machinery was released from its dependence upon water power or steam power with their complicated drive mechanisms.

In a history of Wisconsin's electric power industry, Forrest McDonald summarizes this pioneering period of the industry:

> The general trend in the organization of the business, evident by the mid-nineties, was toward incorporation. Furthermore, a clear pattern of corporate growth was followed with astounding regularity in the major cities of the state. In the early 1880's, one or more lighting companies were established. In the late 1880's, an electric-powered street car company was formed. In the early 1890's, the lighting and/or the street railway companies went into bankruptcy or receivership, after which the companies were reorganized and merged. The new light and traction company, usually had a new central station competitor before 1895. In 1896, the companies went bankrupt again and were reorganized, with the erstwhile competitor acquired and merged in the process. In 1900 or 1901 another receivership and reorganization took place, this time with the local gas company also being merged. By the end of the quarter-century, electric, gas, and street railway service were unified under one ownership, usually a single company. . . .

Simultaneously with the appearance of the automobile there developed an enthusiasm for connecting adjacent cities by means of interurban trolleys. Their promoters saw the auto as a rich man's toy, and a look at any intercity highway in 1910 must have been reassuring. John I. Beggs had started as manager of Milwaukee's street railways and by 1901 was Wisconsin's utility tycoon. He managed consolidated light, traction, and gas companies in Milwaukee, Racine, Kenosha, and the Fox valley for the North American Company, an eastern utility holding company, and a number of local companies owned by Beggs and fellow Milwaukee investors. A traction man, Beggs expected the expansion of the electric power business to be based upon the interurban, which was cheaper to construct and much more flexible than the competing railroads, and able to operate on trolley lines. His vision was of an interurban system running from Chicago to Green Bay, with branches to cities as distant as Madison, Janesville, and Beloit. Beggs had achieved a continuous link from

Kenosha to Sheboygan by 1909, branching off to towns about halfway to the interior cities. There the system ceased its growth, as Beggs lost control of the various enterprises and of the North American Company board. The new management was more interested in the potential of the urban market, which proved fortunate as the various interurban lines lost out to autos, trucks, buses, and improved highways. Wisconsin had 26,690 motor vehicles registered in 1912, 303,246 in 1920, and 800,000 in 1930. Interurban lines were becoming a curiosity.

The harnessing of Niagara Falls in 1896, for the production of hydroelectric power, was another technological breakthrough which resulted in a rush for the development of the many waterpowers in Wisconsin to exploit the "free coal." It turned out not to be free, and broke many an enthusiastic entrepreneur. The technology was primitive; cost figures for site, dam, equipment, and distribution system were totally unrealistic, while owners and the public entertained exaggerated notions of the value of an undeveloped power site. McDonald characterized a typical development, the Kilbourn Dam at Wisconsin Dells by Magnus Swenson of Madison, as a comedy of errors. Swenson paid $1,500,000 for the site, a cost which was twice that per kilowatt of fully developed power at Niagara Falls. Technical problems delayed construction and ran the costs of construction from the $1,500,000 estimate to $4,000,000, at which point, in 1909, the promoter discovered he did not have a customer closer than the Milwaukee market. Beggs took advantage of Swenson's distress to give him just enough return to keep the facility out of receivership. Similar stories, with variations, describe many of the pioneering hydro developments. Wisconsin had over 400 hydroelectric dams in operation by 1934, but two-thirds of the electric power was generated by steam. Water flow varies seasonally, while huge interest charges do not. Steam plants are better able to meet peak load requirements, and fuel costs are offset by the interest charges against hydroelectric plants during low-water seasons.

The inevitable happened. Like the railroads, the electric utilities found a rapidly growing market, but the capital requirements to serve it were enormous and the time between spending and earning was long. By 1930, some 90 percent of Wisconsin's electric power production was controlled by three giant holding companies: the North American Company based in New York, Standard Gas and Electric controlled by H. M. Byllesby of Minneapolis, and Middle West Utilities Company directed by Samuel Insull of Chicago. Insull, in particular, is associated with the art of pyramiding utility companies into complex structures of fantastic financial leverage. The leverage worked in reverse with equal efficiency, as the debacle of 1929 proved.

Aside from financial leverage, the holding companies, and particularly Insull's organization, developed efficiencies of scale and use of technical personnel that brought relatively economical electrical power to the urban consumer. The utilities learned to accept and appreciate the progressive style of regulation pioneered in Wisconsin under the Railroad Commission. The commission guaranteed the utilities "a reasonable return," protected them from competition, developed scientific measures of valuation and rate review with uniform accounting practices, and regulated security issues which assured a market for them. But the Railroad Commission could not order service. Urban areas were the major markets. Most rural areas were considered less than marginal markets, and so only one out of six Wisconsin farmers enjoyed electrical service. This was a serious differential between farm and city life in a time when the relative isolation of the farm was disappearing.

His relative economic disadvantage bothered the farmer more than the difference in living standards between city and farm. Despite the increasing commitment of both federal and state governments to the farmers' problems of production and marketing, the farmer was acutely aware that farm prices had not recovered during the 1920s from the sharp drop that came immediately after the war. He was assured on all sides that farming was now a business and not simply a way of life. The number of farms declined almost 6 percent from 1925 to 1930, the first decrease. The commitment to dairying had increased to 125,000 of the 181,767 farms. The average mortgage indebtedness increased. Milk prices began to decline in the fall of 1928, and by 1932 farm prices generally had fallen far more than the prices farmers paid for machinery, parts, and petroleum products.

Wisconsin farmers were accustomed to radical rhetoric and to organizations—mostly processing and marketing cooperatives—that combined self-help with moral earnestness and the threat of political action. The Nonpartisan League and Society of Equity had frightened conservatives in the immediate post-war years, but by the late twenties the NPL was gone and Equity was fading. The creation of the Farm Bureau locally was usually a joint effort of farmers, businessmen, through the chamber of commerce or a like organization, bankers, metropolitan business interests, national firms such as Sears and Roebuck and International Harvester, and the United States Department of Agriculture, through the county agent system, for which the department provided matching funds. The sponsorship of the Farm Bureau naturally made it highly suspect in the eyes of La Follette followers, as did its frank economic and political conservatism.

Aggressive and well-financed elsewhere, the Farm Bureau Federation made indifferent progress in Wisconsin. It was without the conspicuous cooperation from business and government that it enjoyed in other areas. The forces that normally supported it, in Iowa and Illinois, for instance, joined in Wisconsin to form the Wisconsin Council of Agriculture in 1928. The council was conservative in orientation and rejected the idea, which recurs so often in Wisconsin politics, that farm and labor organizations should make common cause. The farmer, said the council, "is a business man carrying large inventories. He must take chances on the markets that gyrate with the weather and world-wide conditions. As an individual, he is the world's greatest producer of new wealth, under the most speculative conditions and on the narrowest margins."

The prospects of a farmer-labor coalition were not bright as the 1930s opened, although unemployment was becoming a serious problem, and farm prices were deteriorating at a more rapid rate than general prices. Organized labor, subject to a dwindling membership throughout the 1920s, represented only 10 percent of Milwaukee's labor force in 1929. Milwaukee was its stronghold. Victor Berger died in 1929, leaving the *Milwaukee Leader* with a debt of $250,000 and losing $6,000 monthly. The leadership of the Wisconsin Federation of Labor and the related Federated Trades Council in Milwaukee was more concerned with problems of the battered unions than with Socialist political problems. The party and its newspapers passed into the hands of Mayor Daniel Hoan and his secretary, Thomas M. Duncan, who was also a state senator and leader of the five Socialist members of the legislature. This contingent had seen better days, but could claim two senators while the Democrats had none. Political control in Wisconsin was clearly between the stalwarts and progressives within the Republican party.

If the possibilities of a new coalition of farmer-labor organizations did not look particularly promising, there remained the La Follettes. Robert, Jr., won a stunning victory in his 1928 reelection to the United States Senate, but the stalwarts had organized the Republican Voluntary Committee in 1925 and in 1928 took command of the governorship with Walter J. Kohler of the Sheboygan plumbing fixture family. Kohler appeared to be assured of reelection in 1930. He had been an effective governor by the prevailing standards, was well regarded as an astute politician, had organized support and financial backing, and was a wealthy man. The fragmenting effect of the Wisconsin electoral system, a legacy from the elder La Follette, was well illustrated by Kohler's position. The other state offices—lieutenant-governor, secretary of state, treasurer, and attorney-general—were all occupied by La Follette progressives who had won by wide margins in primary and general elections. Apparently there was a reluctance on the part of these comfortable officeholders to challenge Kohler. At least there are few contradictions of Phil La Follette's version of the 1930 primary. He waited modestly in the wings, prepared to support any likely progressive who should step into the breach. No one else having ventured forth, Phil took up the burden with the consent of his brother and other progressive leaders. The general consensus was that Kohler was well entrenched, and Wisconsin would pass up the chance to have a La Follette for both senator and governor.

A tide was running and it favored Phil, however. The depression was almost a year old by the September primary, and Kohler had followed President Hoover's policy of minimizing its seriousness. Then the governor made the further mistake of being nettled by the brashness of young La Follette, who was just thirty-three but certainly no neophyte in politics. It was a common observation that Phil was the son who had inherited Old Bob's political sense, oratorical ability, and zest for the campaign trail. His picture had been on the cover of *Time* magazine in October 1928, and liberal pundits were fond of putting the rhetorical question "What will Phil do?"

What he did was to run away with the Republican gubernatorial nomination, beating Kohler by 128,000 votes. Phil had struck a rich political vein in Wisconsin's banking system. He had been making the rounds of business club luncheons in the towns and small cities, finding a favorable reception. Wisconsin had a loose banking law which went back to 1903. It was easy for a small town bank to get started, with the result that state banks multiplied rapidly and often unwisely; there were 243 by 1900 and 827 by 1921. As an extreme example the village of Rockland, population 120, had two state banks in 1920. The distress in agriculture, after 1920, took a heavy toll in bank failures well before 1929. After 1929 the attrition rate rose.

Branch banking was illegal, but the bankers discovered a new device, in effect a holding company, whereby they could set up a corporation centered in a metropolitan bank and then buy controlling interests in small country banks with the stock of the corporation. This was known as group or chain banking. While it had the effect of strengthening the banking system, the connotation of a "chain" controlled from Milwaukee or Madison convinced many businessmen and farmers that credit in their local banks was too dependent on the metropolitan bankers. The formation of these bank corporations reached a peak in 1929. While the bankers insisted that their combinations were simply a necessary response to the threats of Twin Cities and eastern orporations swallowing Wisconsin banks, the public was alarmed by the trend.

Phil rode the wave of popular apprehensions directed against group banking, the multiplication of chain stores in the retail field, and the rise of giant holding companies controlling the production and distribution of electric power. He proposed special taxes to equalize the competitive advantages of the chains, substantive changes in the utility laws, and revising the debt limits on municipal corporations to permit them to buy or build competing power facilities.

With his easy victory over Kohler, Phil La Follette was certain of winning in November. The progressives also won enough of the assembly seats to carry control, but the state senate remained narrowly in the hands of the conservatives. It has been argued that had this balance been in La Follette's favor Wisconsin might well have furnished the nation with a working model for many New Deal programs, but one based upon a more coherent economic and political philosophy.

Governor La Follette began with two basic assumptions: that the depression signaled a fundamental change in the American economy requiring a new role for government in correcting imbalances, and that the central role in implementing change belonged to the executive. He was in the La Follette tradition. He sounded more radical than he was, and had boundless confidence in his own judgment and his ability to persuade others. He frightened and enraged conservatives with both his ideas and his abilities.

Phil La Follette offered a more scholarly view of the ills of society than did his father. His favorite explanation was derived from the 1893 essay of Wisconsin's Frederick Jackson Turner, "The Significance of the Frontier in American History." That history, declared La Follette, had carried us beyond the influences and opportunities of an open frontier. The horizontal frontier of space was gone and new "perpendicular" frontiers of opportunity had to be opened by collective action. This, he said, had been the aim of the progressive movement from its inception. America had solved the technological problems of producing abundance but had failed to provide for an equitable distribution. Government—collective action—must be reorganized to give it the power to take positive action beyond the role of regulator and honest broker.

The La Follettes had a tradition of complete solemnity about their rhetoric. Phil was sketching in the grand manner, but was a bit hazy on how to implement "the neighborhood cooperation of the simpler days of the frontiers." He reopened the old progressive fight for the initiative—direct democracy—on the theory that the executive would have the advantage in carrying a controversial measure to the people. He wanted to reorganize state government in a manner which would give the governor direct responsibility for originating measures, with the advice of an executive council made up of citizens and legislators. La Follette found the legislative process excessively slow and uncertain and would have reversed the roles, giving the executive the power to make changes within a broad mandate and giving the legislature the power to veto after leisurely debate. He would be called a dictator and worse for his particular vision of the future.

As for legislation of more immediate economic consequence, La Follette leveled his guns at the electric power industry, which had provided some of the more spectacular examples of frenzied finance on the now discredited stock exchange. His basic argument was that in areas of natural monopoly, the right of reasonable regulation was an insufficient protection for the consumer. Wisconsin's Railroad Commission, which regulated utilities, furnished justification for this view. It had become conservative, had scarcely taken into account the economies of scale and technology achieved since 1907, and could not require service to marginal areas neglected by the power companies. Phil proposed that legislative and constitutional changes be made to permit both the state and municipal corporations to enter the field of power production and distribution in competition with private utilities, or to buy them out. He called for a new public service commission with greater authority over the ownership and management of utilities.

He asked also for greater control over banks and chain or group banking, but he recognized the political realities and did not press this. A surtax on chains (bank and store) was more popular. The responsibility of the state to share the burdens of relief with local government was recognized, hence the need for new revenue sources and relief for the property tax, which was increasingly difficult to collect.

The progressives rejected outright relief as inimical to a sense of self-respect. Governor La Follette asked for expanded public works, particularly highway building. His only success in this area was an accelerated program of railroad underpasses and overpasses which the railroads agreed to help finance. He suggested a program that would put unemployed young men in reforestation work in northern Wisconsin. This has been represented as a model for the Civilian Conservation Corps of the New Deal, but it was an idea in wide currency. Senate conservatives killed it.

Another parallel to the New Deal was the proposal that industry and business accept an employment stabilization act in exchange for the right to fix prices and divide markets through councils representing business and the public interest. The resemblance to the program of the National Recovery Act, implemented by the New Deal in 1933, is obvious. But this program too was shelved by the conservatives in the state senate.

Organized labor, despite its relative weakness throughout the nine-teen-twenties, had maintained an active lobby in Madison that worked with some success through Socialist and progressive Republican legisla-tors. An unemployment insurance bill had been pushed in successive ses-sions. Its time came in the special session of 1931–32. Its success, in a heavily rural state, owed much to the argument that industrial unemploy-ment should be a cost upon industry rather than upon the overburdened general taxpayer. Farm labor was effectively exempt. The further argu-ment that unemployment insurance would help to raise consumption, particularly of foodstuffs, was also used. Some key large employers were persuaded that the law would help to stabilize employment and give more efficient managements a competitive advantage. The insurance would be funded on the basis of experience rating for individual employ-ers. Wisconsin was the first state to pass unemployment insurance, but economic conditions delayed its operation until the federal program was passed in 1935.

Another Wisconsin first in the field of labor relations was the passage, in 1931, of a unified state labor code. It was primarily a codification of legislation already on the books, but went beyond this in such areas as restraints on the use of the injunction. The legislation made it clear that the state actively encouraged collective bargaining. Organized opposition to the passage of the act was curiously restrained. Within the year similar legislation, known as the Norris-La Guardia Act, was enacted at the fed-eral level. This was more influential in encouraging unionization than the state legislation, which it naturally overshadowed.

A summary of legislation proposed and passed in 1931–32 has about it the ring of liberal success, but La Follette had pinned his hopes upon his public-power program and his economic policies. Although the legis-lature gave him much of the public-power program, they would not ap-prove the provision for municipal competition with private utilities and the constitutional amendments necessary for state entry into the field. The private utilities were not seriously threatened by the program as it was enacted, nor was the other economic legislation passed regarding business stabilization. The governor, in short, had what he considered a grand design but was unable to implement it.

The year 1932 was not a good one for incumbents, and Phil La Fol-lette turned out to be no exception to the rule. The depression had deep-ened while he was trying to provide an activist contrast to the disheart-ened President Hoover. Two years is scarcely a breathing spell in poli-tics, but between 1930 and 1932 Wisconsin's gross farm income fell from $350,000,000 to $199,000,000, employment declined another 33 percent, there were 116 more bank failures, and 1,500 businesses closed. Franklin D. Roosevelt ran a cautious and sometimes contradictory campaign, but conveyed a promise of vigorous leadership to millions. His politics would test, and finally break, the peculiar pattern of Wisconsin politics that had been largely the creation of the La Follettes.

La Follette smelled defeat in 1932, and it came early. He lost the Republican primary to Kohler by a margin of nearly 100,000 votes. What was more ominous for the progressives was the growth of the Democratic vote in the primary. The disgruntled La Follettes supported Roosevelt in the general election and the Democratic state ticket, the latter with less enthusiasm. Although the Democratic party in Wisconsin was conservative and received little help from the popular Roosevelt, the combination of progressive support, worsened economic conditions, and Roosevelt's landslide victory found the dazed Democrats in command of the governorship, the assembly, five congressional seats, and a senatorship. Their candidate for governor in 1930 had won only 28 percent of the vote.

The Wisconsin Democrats did not thrive on their unexpected good fortune. Governor Albert Schmedeman was nearing seventy when elected and had grown up in a conservative party with a tradition of minority opposition. He watched Roosevelt courting the La Follettes, with their liberal following, and was otherwise made to feel uncomfortably like a stepchild. Then he inherited other troubles at home. Wisconsin dairymen were organized in rival groups which could not agree on tactics. The Wisconsin Milk Pool, a militant group centered in the Fox valley, called two milk strikes in February and May, 1933. The larger Farm Holiday Association and the Wisconsin Council of Agriculture refused to join the action. Both strikes were accompanied by violence. Two men were killed in the May strike, and Governor Schmedeman called out state troops. It was a situation in which no one could win.

The Democrats went on to other political misfortunes. Hungry for patronage, they attempted to set aside the sacrosanct civil service system, but without success, after a long fight. They defeated a progressive move to incorporate the initiative in the constitution and a measure to permit municipalities to compete with private utilities. Both had broad popular support. Schmedeman was accused of truckling to his party conservatives and to the utilities. Given relations with the national administration, the inexperience of the Wisconsin Democrats, and their conservative temper, the necessary state cooperation with the New Deal was less than exemplary.

The La Follettes maintained their organization and tested the political winds. Phil's defeat in the 1932 primary and the brothers' public support of Roosevelt meant that the family's traditional hold on the Republican party in Wisconsin was lost. It was problematic how many of their progressive voters had deserted to the New Deal. The thought of moving into the Democratic party was distasteful and equally problematic. Bob, whose Senate seat was up in 1934, likely could have won in the Democratic primary, but his vote-pulling power would have been lost to other progressive candidates. Roosevelt would have welcomed him into the Democratic party, but the president's enthusiasm for Phil, never warm, was rapidly cooled by Phil's refusal of several important federal posts and subsequent public criticisms of the New Deal. Phil was making no secret of his own ambitions, or of his assessment of Roosevelt as a fellow master politician who lacked Phil's deep understanding of economic issues—an assessment which Phil resolved in his own favor on the basis of dubious evidence.

The natural alternative to joining the Democrats was to form their own third party, a notion the La Follettes had frequently entertained but rejected because of the anemia such parties are prone to in national politics. Meetings were held and the possibilities canvassed. The La Follettes' hands were forced by a combination of progressive intellectuals, the Wisconsin Federation of Labor, and militant farm groups who after the milk strikes of 1933 found themselves in sympathy with labor union tactics. There was much talk at the time, not just in Wisconsin, of the impossibility of either the Democratic or Republican parties ever becoming an adequate vehicle for liberal or radical change.

The problem faced by the organizers of what became the Farmer Labor Progressive League was that the La Follettes commanded the loyalty of most progressives throughout the state, and the La Follettes could not and did not let the FLPL run away with the third-party movement. They had held mixed views on the subject, but these were resolved by this outside threat of a third party, which was probably encouraged by Phil.

The FLPL people were powerless to prevent the La Follettes, who had the political power, from taking over. As pragmatists they had reconciled themselves to this result, and hoped to push the La Follette progressives toward the left in exchange for their support. It was a pressure which Phil easily withstood. The result was not a unified party but a coalition; although Phil liked to think of himself as a grand strategist, he remained a political tactician. The La Follette progressives failed to build urban strength, and instead continued to operate on the basis of a personal following. A roster of this following was contained in "a little black book" supposedly started around 1912 by the elder La Follette when he feared that Frank McGovern was building a personal machine within the progressive movement at his expense. The La Follette machine usually sat unused, to be cranked up at election time with letters, calls, and personal appeals. It was an economical machine to operate, running largely on sentiment, references to "the Cause," and La Follette oratory. Anyone reading Phil's memoirs will be struck by the family's reverence for the latter.

The patchwork Progressive party found a ready-made electorate in Wisconsin, where voters distrusted both Democrats and regular Republicans. Again Phil was prevailed upon to lead the state ticket, but this time his brother Bob was on the ballot with him. Whatever misgivings Bob had about "too much La Follette" being served up to the voters were suppressed by the close relationship that the family maintained. Phil was as indispensable on the ticket as Bob. He furnished the fire and the grassroots politicking. Phil won a close race with Governor Schmedeman, while the regular Republicans trailed badly. Bob won more votes than the combined total of his Democratic and Republican opponents.

Again, as in 1931, Phil found himself confronted with a hostile state senate. He had returned to the promotion of public power, but could get nothing effective through. Another ambitious scheme involved mounting a strictly Wisconsin public works and relief program, which he intended as a model to contrast with Roosevelt's handling of these twin problems. The program had the pleasing prospect of $100,000,000 in federal funds which Wisconsin was to match and operate through a Wisconsin Finance Corporation, issuing script for public and private work. This, too, died a slow death in the hands of the conservatives.

Phil was bitter, but he had his issues. The FLPL was expanded to include the Socialist party, which was competing with Progressive candidates in crucial urban districts. The Socialists demanded a price which they never collected from Phil, although the FLPL adopted the socialist slogan "production for use." Phil's executive secretary, Tom Duncan, still in good standing with the Socialist party, undertook to confine the FLPL to the Lakeshore, while La Follette remained aloof. FLPL was a troika difficult to manage. The socialist third was split between a right wing managed by Dan Hoan and Tom Duncan and a growing communist left wing. The labor third got involved in the CIO schism from the main body of the AFL, and the Progressives varied from left-wingers to the members of the Wisconsin Council of Agriculture. Phil La Follette ran on nerve and confidence in his ability to bridge the gaps. When he looked at Franklin Roosevelt, he saw himself as the philosopher statesman who had a coherent plan to replace the chaos of Roosevelt's political expediency. When he looked to the left, he saw himself as the saviour of responsible capitalism.

The 1936 election brought the Progressives back in greater force and to their first control of both assembly and senate. But the initiative in the fields of relief, unemployment insurance, public works, social security, rural electrification, agricultural assistance, and labor emancipation had largely passed to the federal government. La Follette and his Progressives were reduced to the role of followers of Roosevelt's programs, carping at details. The central problem of the 1930s was the economic emergency, and the story in Wisconsin, as elsewhere, was the shifting strategies of the New Deal and its many alphabetical agencies.

A passive role as implementor of state legislation to conform to federal standards was not Phil La Follette's style. But he could not revive his plan for a strictly Wisconsin relief and public works program based upon a lump sum grant of federal funds, which Roosevelt had tentatively agreed to in 1935. The president was understandably suspicious of Phil's ambitions, and had worked out an arrangement with Madison banker Leo Crowley, who was first chairman of the Federal Deposit Insurance Corporation and later administrator of Lend-Lease, to channel New Deal patronage to the Progressives in Wisconsin. Phil turned again to his public-power program with a proposal for the Wisconsin Development Authority modeled on the Tennessee Valley Authority's charter. The WDA bill was enacted, but the courts prevented its intended use.

La Follette was determined to use his power while he had a legislative majority. The most effective lobby within the Progressive alliance remained the Wisconsin Federation of Labor and its Socialist allies. Phil, who was aware of his political weakness with urban labor, put his influence behind a new comprehensive labor bill known as the Wisconsin Labor Relations Act, similar to the National Labor Relations Act of 1935. A coalition of Democrats and Republicans fought the bill for being too favorable to unions, but La Follette rammed it through. A special session in the fall of 1937 enacted a package of La Follette bills in one of the most acrimonious legislative battles on record. The principal measure, in La Follette's eyes, was a government reorganization act reversing somewhat the roles of the executive and legislative branches in ordering administrative changes. Other enactments created a Wisconsin Agricultural Authority to operate in marketing, a Department of Commerce to promote industrial development, and some changes in tax law.

The cost of this belated Progressive legislative success was high. La Follette was widely berated as an aspiring tyrant. Even the longtime La Follette ally, William T. Evjue, publisher of the *Capital Times,* described the last days of the special session as "a week in which democratic processes were abandoned and executive dictatorship was in the saddle." Evjue was in the process of transferring his sometimes erratic allegiance to Roosevelt, as Phil became increasingly critical of the president. A more sympathetic Progressive who was in the legislature later commented that "Tom [Duncan] and Phil always kept them guessing. They were master manipulators; they ran the show. They were smart; they did not wear well but they were good."

If La Follette progressivism in the hands of the younger son, Philip, offered a reasonable alternative to the centralizing tendencies of the New Deal, it never had a true test. In the end it was an echo, and the Progressive party was not able to escape La Follette's limitations and subordination to his ambitions. Bad luck and faulty judgment played into the hands of Governor La Follette's opponents. The CIO moved into organizing the employees of farm cooperatives and soured the alliance between farm organizations and labor within the FLPL. Thomas Duncan, the governor's executive secretary, was involved in a personal tragedy which ended his usefulness. La Follette took the lead in the removal of the university's president, Glenn Frank, in a maneuver that was readily interpreted as political spite, whatever the merits of the removal. Finally, the governor, whose ambitions were transcending the boundaries of the state, in 1938 launched his untimely creation, the National Progressives of America.

Phil was clearly influenced by the success which Hitler's National Socialism had achieved in mobilizing public opinion and a spirit of unity, with elements of dramatic staging and a sense of national purpose. Given the subsequent history of Nazism, it is grossly unfair to associate La Follette with the malignancy which it represented. What Phil fervently believed was original thinking on his own part was usually highly derivative. He was not alone among self-confessed liberals who were looking for a formula for harnessing fascism's sense of purpose to democracy's seemingly faltering confidence in its destiny. Phil simply dismayed fellow progressives by mounting his own design, which contained enough elements of the ridiculous to embarrass his friends. The unlikely staging of the event was in the Stock Pavilion of the university in Madison. The center of attention, aside from the candidate for greatness, was a cross in a circle said to represent the power of the ballot, and the circle the power of unity and the multiplier of a people united. Bemused critics saw it as an attenuated swastika while others used a ruder term. National Progressivism was stillborn.

Wisconsin politicians have generally credited the Wisconsin voter with either more perversity or lack of judgment than he or she possesses. So sure were some of Phil La Follette's dedicated opponents that he was practically unbeatable for an unprecedented fourth term that they subscribed to a *Milwaukee Journal* scheme for a coalition of Republicans and Democrats against him. The Republicans, no strangers to quixotism in their mature deliberations, were so certain of defeat that there was little crowding at the primary starting gate. The honor of opposing La

Follette was easily conceded to a wealthy Milwaukee industrialist, Julius Heil.

The coalitionists' candidate withdrew in favor of Heil, who went on to an easy victory in November, La Follette, embittered and a tragic figure in light of his early promise and youthful success, divorced himself from Wisconsin politics and took up the cause of the isolationists of America First. Neither Phil nor Bob advanced much beyond the views of Old Bob on this subject. Julius Heil went on to dismantle the legacy of the Progressives. A gregarious, irrepressible bungler, he opened the way for one more Progressive victory which proved as abortive as the rest.

Selected Bibliography

Altmeyer, Arthur J. "The Wisconsin Idea and Social Security." *Wisconsin Magazine of History* 42:19–25 (August 1958). Traces it through Bascom, La Follette, Van Hise, Ely, and Commons.

Andersen, Theodore A. *A Century of Banking in Wisconsin.* Madison, 1954. He manages to cover the 1930s without mentioning Phil La Follette—it is doubtful that many bankers did.

Backstrom, Charles Herbert. "The Progressive Party of Wisconsin, 1934–1946." Ph.D. dissertation, University of Wisconsin, 1956. In a political science framework, useful.

Carley, L. David. "The Wisconsin Governor's Legislative Role: A Case Study of the Administrations of Philip Fox La Follette and Walter J. Kohler, Jr." Ph.D. dissertation, University of Wisconsin, 1959. He found Phil more interesting.

Carstensen, Peter. "The Progressives and the Declining Role of State Government in Wisconsin, 1930–1938." Senior honors thesis, University of Wisconsin, 1964. Phil's missed opportunities.

Clark, James I. *Wisconsin Meets the Great Depression.* Madison, 1956. He also leaves out Phil La Follette, except for brief mention.

Doan, Edward N. *The La Follettes and the Wisconsin Idea.* New York, 1947. Journalist supporter of Bob Jr., accurate but uncritical.

Garlock, Fred L. *Country Banking in Wisconsin During the Depression.* U.S. Department of Agriculture technical bulletin no. 777. Washington, D.C. 1941. Reasons for small bank failures.

Hanna, Frank A. *Wisconsin during the Depression: Industrial Trends and Tax Burdens.* University of Wisconsin Bureau of Business and Economic Research bulletin no. 5. Madison, 1936. Figures on the impact of the Depression.

Hicks, John D. *My Life with History: An Autobiography.* Lincoln, Nebr., 1968. He knew Glenn Frank before their careers at Wisconsin.

Jacobs, Herbert. "The Wisconsin Milk Strike." *Wisconsin Magazine of History* 35:30–35 (Autumn 1951). Walter Slinger and the Milk Pool.

Keeth, Kent H. "The Profile of a Progressive: The Political Career of Orland

S. Loomis." Master's thesis, University of Wisconsin, 1961. Public power expert.

La Follette, Philip F. *Adventures in Politics: The Memoirs of Philip La Follette.* Edited by Donald Young. New York, 1970.

Larsen, Lawrence H. *The President Wore Spats: A Biography of Glenn Frank.* Madison, 1965. Frank's firing was a cause celèbre.

Laufenberg, Wayne E. "The Schmedeman Administration in Wisconsin: A Study of Missed Opportunities." Master's thesis, University of Wisconsin, 1965. Not FDR's brand of Democrats

Lilienthal, David E. *The Journals of David E. Lilienthal.* Vol. 1, *The T.V.A. Years, 1939–1945.* New York, 1964. He started his public career with Phil La Follette.

Long, Robert E. "Wisconsin State Politics: 1932–1934, The Democratic Interlude." Master's thesis, University of Wisconsin, 1962. Unprepared for the unexpected victory.

McCoy, Donald R. "The National Progressives of America." *Mississippi Valley Historical Review* 44:75–93 (June 1957). Phil La Follette's abortive third party.

McDonald, Forrest. *Let There be Light: The Electric Utility Industry in Wisconsin, 1881–1955.* Madison, 1957. Sympathetic but informative.

Mermin, Samuel. *Jurisprudence and Statecraft: The Wisconsin Development Authority and Its Implications.* Madison, 1964. Phil's power authority ran aground.

Miller, John Edward. "The Elections of 1932 in Wisconsin." Master's thesis, University of Wisconsin, 1968. The Republican progressives bolted to FDR and the Democrats.

Moriarty, Francis J. "Philip F. La Follette: State and National Politics, 1937–1938." Master's thesis, University of Wisconsin, 1960. Phil's national ambitions were showing.

Nelson, Daniel. "The Origins of Unemployment Insurance in Wisconsin." *Wisconsin Magazine of History* 51:109–21 (Winter 1967–68). Or see chapter 6 of Nelson's *Unemployment Insurance: The American Experience.* Madison, 1969. Triumph for John R. Commons and his students.

Palmer, Edgar Z. *The Prewar Industrial Pattern of Wisconsin.* Wisconsin Commerce Studies. Madison, 1947. Mainly from 1940 census data, with comparisons.

Richardson, Lemont Kingsford. *Wisconsin R.E.A.: The Struggle to Extend Electricity to Rural Wisconsin.* Madison, 1961. Phil's grand schemes came down to standard REA.

Saloutos, Theodore, and John D. Hicks. *Twentieth-Century Populism: Agricultural Discontent in the Middle West, 1900–1939.* Lincoln, Nebraska: Bison Paperbacks, n.d. Light on Wisconsin in the 1930s.

Schmidt, Lester Frederick. "The Farmer-Labor Progressive Federation: The Study of a 'United Front' Movement among Wisconsin Liberals, 1934–1941." Ph.D. dissertation, University of Wisconsin, 1934. How do you get organized labor and farmers to pull in double harness? You can't for long.

ADJUSTMENTS TO MATURITY, 1940–1970

part ten

The national emergency of World War II exploited what Wisconsin had at hand: industrial capacity convertible to the production of machines and other staples of warfare, a highly trained and productive labor force, and an agriculture adjusted to the export of high-value meat and dairy products. What emerged from the war was a mature economy at new production and employment levels, but not a greatly altered one, except as it reflected the general rise in living standards and economic security. Wisconsin since the war has had small share in industries benefiting from federally financed scientific research or the vast sums spent for the sophisticated hardware of newer wars and alarms.

Wisconsin's population, too, has matured. There has been a steady out-migration to areas offering more economic opportunity. This flow has included many young people with better than average educations. The smaller counterflow into the state has included a higher proportion of disadvantaged. Wisconsin's areas of economic opportunity have narrowed to a few urban centers of continuing growth.

Wisconsin's agriculture has been shrinking in acreage, in number of farm families, and in number employed. Much of this attrition has taken marginal farms, of which the state has all too many, out of production. There remains a serious imbalance of population and economic opportunity between the populous southeastern quarter and much of the rest of the state.

Politically, the period since 1940 has seen the demise of the Progressive party and of Milwaukee Socialism. They have been displaced by a revitalized Democratic party that now challenges the Republicans on equal terms.

What one misses in the post-World War II years is a sense of Wisconsin's difference from midwestern and national norms. The spirit is still here, as one would expect with a comparatively stable population in possession of a heritage in many ways unique, but the substance dwindles.

PROBLEMS OF
A MATURE ECONOMY

30

As the historian approaches his own times his diffidence should increase. One thinks of Milo M. Quaife writing his *Wisconsin: Its History and Its People* during the Harding years. He congratulated his readers that pioneer railroad promoter Byron Kilbourn, with his moneybags, "was actuated by a standard of public morality which, happily, is unknown to Americans of the present generation" and "one studies history to little purpose who assumes that no progress has been made since . . . in the task of elevating society to a higher plane of conduct and living." The ripe scandals of the Harding Administration began to break while his manuscript was being set in type. There are hazards in basing judgments about the past upon satisfaction with the present.

We are, therefore, warned against too many certainties in dealing with the last three decades. We need only to remind ourselves that most Americans during the New Deal years accepted the idea that a plateau of population and economic growth had been reached. The World War II years were thought to be a temporary interruption to the problems of the depression decade: a sluggish economy and a stabilized population growing steadily older. The subsequent growth of the national product from just under one hundred billion dollars in 1940 to almost a trillion by 1970 was as unexpected as the dramatic rise in the national birth rate from 19.4 per thousand in 1940 to a rate of 25 in 1955. The problems of the years since 1940 have been quite different from what many experts anticipated. Much of what follows must be taken as tentative and impressionistic.

We are concerned with the impact of these years of change upon Wisconsin. Wisconsin is close to a national average in many ways—area, population, income—but at the beginning of the war it had a more mature economy than the areas that have attracted spectacular increases in population and economic activity since 1940. Wisconsin's manufacturing, with its emphasis upon metal founding and fabrication, machinery, tools, vehicles, and electrical components, naturally shared vigorously in the production of war goods. The war emphasized the growing mobility of the American population. Population shifts in Wisconsin accelerated, most noticeably from the countryside to the city, a trend that had almost reversed during the depression years of the 1930s before the war reestablished it. The urban percentages of population were 52.9 in 1930 and 65.9 in 1970.

A closer examination of the shifts of the 1940s shows that Wisconsin's cities were not the only attractions. The out-migration exceeded the in-migration by a sum sufficient to reduce the expected natural increase of population by one-sixth, 66,000, within the state. The state's rural farm population lost 235,000 in the decade, but rural nonfarm population increased 135,000 to partially offset this. It was primarily young people who were leaving the farm, while the villages and hamlets, making up the rural nonfarm population, were gaining. Some of these were satellite villages around the cities, and some outlying villages attracting retired farmers. One more figure is worth attention. Over 70 percent of the farm girls ten to fourteen years old in 1950 were gone by 1960. Gone to the city or town, not down the road to marry a young farmer. The trend has continued. Farm boys leave home at only half the rate that the girls do, but boys leave the village and small town more readily than the girls.

All of these shifts—out of the state, rural to urban, farm to village, northern Wisconsin to urban areas, and young people away from the countryside—raise worrisome questions. What is becoming of the family farm? Are the villages and small towns turning into old people's homes? Can the Wisconsin economy offer attractive opportunities to hold the educated young people who make up a large part of the steady out-migration? Is the population distribution seriously out of balance and threatening the quality of life in many areas?

World War II did not do as much to reshape Wisconsin's economy as it did that of some other regions of the country, notably in the West and Southeast. Wisconsin shared with the Great Lakes industrial complex a developed capacity and labor pool engaged in industries directly convertible to war production. The conversion was rapid and employment boomed. Shipbuilding, primarily small naval vessels, was the largest single war industry.

It was in a largely negative sense that federal policy during and after the war helped to determine the shape of Wisconsin's postwar industrial development. There was a deliberate effort to decentralize new plants built with federal funds. The coastal areas and regions with milder climates were favored. Nor was it predictable that the war production of the 1940s would be transformed into a "defense" industry that thirty years later would consume tax dollars nearly equal to the gross national product of 1940. Or that the hardware of defense would be in such exotic fields as rocketry, nuclear energy, electronics, space, and sophisticated instrumentation. One needs only a superficial knowledge of Wisconsin's industry to appreciate some representative figures: of 28,108 defense contract awards in 1963, Wisconsin received 219, California 5,836, Texas 1,203, and Washington State 1,042. Texas and Wisconsin were about equal in value of manufactures in 1940. Texas's was 56 percent greater by 1967. Wisconsin got 0.5 percent of 1964 arms expenditures compared to 20.4 percent for California and 6.1 percent for Texas.

What of the other industries that have enjoyed an above-average growth rate since World War II: petroleum and chemicals, office machinery, electronics, commercial and military aircraft, and a number of new industries with advanced technology and scientific research? While Wisconsin is represented in some of them and provides important components in what are called high-science industries, it has a greater share in the mature industries that are primarily users of technology rather than scientific innovators. The state's young people trained in scientific specialties usually look elsewhere for employment. And the Milwaukee financial community probably deserves a reputation for conservatism. It has not conspicuously encouraged entrepreneurial innovation, but has preferred established payrolls and attracting branch plants of national companies. These find Milwaukee's skilled labor force an asset, and they approve the local concern with stability.

Milwaukee's mix of manufacturing industries is good in that no single sector overshadows everything else. It is the nucleus of a large industrial center marked by great diversity, although the emphasis is upon durable goods. A large part of its production is in machines, tools, and components used by other industries rather than sold directly to consumers. It is a mark of its industrial variety that the city is best known for its production of beer, which is not its major industry.

There are useful comparisons to illustrate the growing diversity of

Wisconsin's industries. Electrical machinery tripled its employment, from 9,713 to 27,745, during the World War II decade. It continued to grow, employing 54,836 in 1967. Other machinery manufacturing had a much larger employment base, with 42,821 in 1940. This nearly doubled during the war decade, had a very modest growth during the 1950s, then spurted again from 82,120 to 113,625 between 1960 and 1967. Much of this growth came from the expansion of small-engine manufacturing and related equipment. Expansion of employment in other, longer-established industries has been relatively modest: food products, metal fabrication, paper, printing and publishing, furniture, and chemicals. Employment in other traditional industries declined: in leather, textiles, lumber and wood products, and primary metals. In the manufacture of transportation equipment it has been highly variable, reflecting the fortunes of the state's largest employer, American Motors Company.

Wisconsin ranks sixteenth in population, losing fifteenth place to Georgia in 1970, but retains eleventh place in the value of manufactures. The state's growth rate in population has been below the national average. It has held its position in manufacturing, which accounted for 43 percent of wages and salaries in Wisconsin in 1965 compared with a national average of 33 percent. While much of Wisconsin's manufacturing is in relatively slow growth industries and some that are obviously shrinking, there is continuous change in the relationship of industries. Wisconsin's diversified industrial economy, with its large stable elements —food processing, paper, printing, and publishing—and rapid growth sectors such as electrical machinery and equipment, does not suffer by comparison with other states. The state maintains its traditionally lower-than-average rate of unemployment. Technologically oriented, Wisconsin industry has taken advantage of trends in the national economy such as the great increase in spending for leisure-time activities. For example, it holds a dominant position in the production of outboard motors and small gasoline engines and in promoting their use.

Wisconsin industry does not lack agencies and organizations devoted to taking its pulse, worrying over its symptoms, discovering new hazards to its health, and prescribing for all of them. The first state to institute a successful income tax, Wisconsin maintains a higher level of state and local government service than the national average, with a slightly less than average per capita base of wealth and income. Wisconsin's income taxes make up a larger share of revenue, and sales tax a smaller share, than the average. In 1971, state and local taxes amounted to $145.48 per $1,000 of personal income, third highest in the nation, while the state ranked twenty-seventh in per capita income before taxes. This, of course, has meant higher cost to industry, but does not prove that it counters other favorable factors. Wisconsin was traditionally on a pay-as-you-go basis, with a consequently lower debt ratio than other states. It rates high in terms of highways, education, labor skills and training, recreation and conservation, and the assurance that the tax dollar is honestly spent.

Wisconsin is at the outer edge rather than the center of the industrial and financial complex that rims the southern shores of the Great Lakes. This position offers some advantages, but the largest markets lie eastward through Chicago, as do the necessary supplies of metals and fuels for resource-short Wisconsin. The struggle to maintain an equality of freight rates with Chicago has occupied Milwaukee businessmen over the years. The car ferries which carry trains to points in Michigan are part of this contest. The heavy expense of developing the Port of Milwaukee as a municipal undertaking, to make it a major factor in the disappointing St. Lawrence Seaway traffic, is another response to Chicago's easy dominance.

The St. Lawrence Seaway, fervently promoted in the Midwest for generations, became a reality in the 1950s after Canada threatened to undertake it alone. Great expectations were held for the opening of "America's fourth seacoast" by completion of the seaway in 1959. Milwaukee, which in 1920 was the first Great Lakes port in the United States to set up a public port authority, had high hopes. Marking the end of the seaway's tenth year of operation, *The Wall Street Journal* had a lead article: "St. Lawrence Seaway, Completing 10th Year, is Awash in Problems: Its Traffic is Off, Debt is Up And It is Getting Obsolete; Some Ships Curtail Runs."

The headline sums up the seaway's fortunes to 1973. You cannot run a fourth seacoast successfully that is open only eight months of the year. Shipping general cargo, which is where the profits are, requires a spread of special facilities and auxilliary services. Eight major ports on the Lakes simply cannot sustain these on the basis of a limited season, in competition with the all-weather services of New York and its connecting railroads. Although use of New York's port is costly and often inconvenient, ships find it less convenient to make the long voyage in to the Lakes, paying substantial tolls, to look for cargo among the many ports. As a consequence, the Port of Cleveland was estimated to handle only 3 percent of the goods manufactured in the area in 1969. Milwaukee's port, credited with 12 percent of its potential traffic, was doing a little better. It is difficult for the layman to make an accurate assessment of the relative success of the seaway. At least it can be said that the varied facilities and activities of the port pay their way, while the seaway, which was supposed to amortize its initial debt and be self-sustaining, had to be rescued after it proved unable to pay even its interest charges.

Shipping on the Lakes remains primarily a business of moving basic commodities. Coal imports are steadily declining, while petroleum and natural gas pipelines have cut into water shipments. The car ferries accounted for 25 percent of Milwaukee's traffic in 1967. Development of more seaway traffic is imperative, and much depends upon improvements in the seaway's capacity and techniques for lengthening the shipping season. There is nothing particularly unusual about other aspects of Wisconsin's participation in the changing patterns of American transportation.

Surveys of Wisconsin's industries frequently show that while the state has some individual companies that are considered major by contemporary standards, the average Wisconsin company is relatively smaller than the degree of industrialization of the state would lead one to expect. This is another way of saying that much Wisconsin industry is marginal in financial power and competitive advantage. A phenomenon of the 1960s that could be compared to the growth of trusts around 1900 was the rise of the conglomerates. These giant corporations expanded rapidly in diverse fields by taking advantage of the high multiples their shares enjoyed in the stock market. They bought control of laggard companies that were rich in asset value but had their stocks selling at low multiples. Another favorite target was the smaller company of promise that wanted strong financial backing for rapid expansion. A survey of Wisconsin companies at the peak of the conglomerate craze showed that in a twenty month period to August 1968 there were forty-eight state firms acquired by conglomerates or firms controlled outside the state. Prominent among the acquiring firms were Litton Industries, National Cash Register, Beatrice Foods, Sunstrand, W. R. Grace, Tenneco, and ITT. Among the prominent Wisconsin companies acquired were Louis Allis Company, Falk Corporation, Waukesha Motors, George J. Meyer Company, Hamilton Manufacturing, Miller Brewing, and Nekoosa-Edwards, the smallest representing assets of $30,000,000 and the largest $50,000,000. Earlier transfers included such well-known firms as Fairbanks-Morse, Walker Manufacturing, FWD, Marathon Corporation, Line Material Industries, Speed Queen, and Ray-O-Vac. Wisconsin-based firms have not been conspicuous in this style of growth.

Wisconsin's industries have been concerned with their resource base for a long time. For many of them it has been inadequate within the state. An iron industry based upon charcoal smelting provided iron for the pioneer industries. The more ambitious iron works at Bayview operated in one form or another until the 1920s. The state had a speculative boom in the iron deposits of the Gogebic Range that flourished briefly in the mid-eighties. There was a real basis for the boom in particularly rich ores suitable for the Bessemer process and commanding a premium. The developed mines in the vicinity of Hurley supplied a lion's share of the ore for the reduction furnaces accessible to the Lakes, but the ore bodies all slanted steeply and were expensive to work. The easily worked and more extensive Mesabi ores began taking over the market in the 1890s, but the value of the Gogebic ores kept them in operation for years with the expansion of the steel industry.

Wisconsin's iron mines were known for their extreme depth and the awesome quantities of water that had to be pumped from them continuously. The last active mine in the Hurley iron district closed down at the end of the 1960s. Still, the ore continues to be of interest to the major mining and steel companies. They have much of it under long-term leases, but have developed other sources in Quebec and Newfoundland reached by the St. Lawrence Seaway.

The disappearance of an in-state iron industry has been no great inconvenience to Wisconsin's iron- and steel-using factories, for the Great Lakes insure favorable freight rates for supplies, as does the customary railroad rate structure. The shift by the vital metal-using industries to out-of-state sources of supply, however, is a reminder that Wisconsin is short of a number of basic resources. Her industries have had to learn to accommodate to this. Technology moved beyond the wood-burning locomotive and charcoal iron, and incidentally removed the sources of cordwood as well, leaving the state largely dependent upon fossil fuels. These are simply not present, at least not in commercial quantities, in Wisconsin. Imported coal, petroleum products, and natural gas have made up the deficiency.

There was a time when water power was thought to be the answer to increasing energy demands. Hydroelectric power provided approximately 50 percent of Wisconsin's electricity by 1928. In 1968, only about 9 percent of Wisconsin's power came from this source. For the remainder, the state now depends mostly upon coal-fired steam plants. Wisconsin in 1973 had three nuclear power plants in operation or building. A recent rise in public concern over pollution hazards puts the rapid expansion of this method of power production in question. Given the increasing awareness of environmental deterioration, there is an advantage for Wisconsin in having coal mined in neighboring states. Its neighbors must deal with both the environmental problems and a drop in tax revenues as coal, oil, and gas supplies are depleted. The eventual shortage will be a generalized problem not peculiar to Wisconsin.

The lumbering and metal-mining industries have long since adjusted to the depletion of their basic resources by simply going out of business. Wisconsin's paper industry, on the contrary, has adjusted successfully. Despite the fact that the industry must now import wood and pulp from as far as Montana, it has maintained its dominant position nationally. This success is owed to imaginative technology, adapting to specialty products of high value, heavy advertising, the fact that paper mills are heavily capitalized, and that it is not unusual for a paper machine to remain in practically continuous operation for a half-century or more. The real hazard seems to be that as the paper industry follows the general trend toward giantism, the older, less-competitive mills get closed out on the basis of decisions made in distant boardrooms. Another hazard to the paper industry is the heightened interest in environmental pollution. A paper mill is particularly vulnerable because its pollution sources are multiple. Vast quantities of water are required which are subject to chemical, thermal, and pulp contamination that are tremendously expensive to correct.

Environmental deterioration is also threatened by the growth of population, personal income, and leisure. Rural towns and counties have been poorly prepared to protect themselves, and the state has been slow to move with authority into matters of traditionally local concern. Local autonomy has been jealously guarded, especially where local tax revenue is involved.

The retreat of population from wide areas in northern, central, and southwestern Wisconsin and the lack of economic opportunity there have created problems. Rural Wisconsin, particularly the large northern region commonly known as the Cutover, has been intensively studied. The university was an early leader in developing the fields of agricultural economics and rural sociology. Study led to a variety of suggested solutions, some of them discussed above. Development of land not suitable for agriculture for recreational use has long been a popular solution.

A moderate summer climate, with lakes, streams, and renewing forests led northern Wisconsin's economic development toward an emphasis upon serving tourists and vacationists. Increasing affluence and leisure time, more automobiles, and better highways placed the area within the range of a constantly growing clientele. Economists calculated that over 56,000,000 vacation-recreation visits (use for one day or part of a day) were made to Wisconsin by non-residents in 1960 and 144,000,000 by resident tourists. The rate of recreational use has greatly increased with the improvements in the interstate highway network and wider ownership of camping trailers, boats, and other recreational equipment. The growing popularity of skiing and, more recently, snowmobiles has added a new dimension.

Tourism and the tourists' dollars have seemed a fortunate harvest for otherwise poor areas, but no economically viable alternatives have been offered to support a population already there. Good! Let them learn to operate ski lifts, rent boats, stake out compliant deer, and change the sheets in sylvan motels. Occasionally some senior citizen has been heard to grumble that the Dells of the Wisconsin once were pleasant, rustic, and subject to less relentless huckstering, but such is the price of progress.

Governor Gaylord Nelson established a national reputation as a leader in preserving the environment with his advocacy of Wisconsin's pioneering Outdoor Recreation Act in 1961. The act pledged $50,000,000 over the next decade toward environmental planning, land acquisition, and an interesting program of easements to insure continuing scenic values along state highways. One object of ORAP, as it is popularly known, is "to observe and record the many values in the Wisconsin landscape that make it an outstanding recreation state."

Attracting tourists and vacationers from neighboring states generates problems as well as profits and tax revenues. An overwhelming majority of these visitors are city dwellers. Wisconsin has a great concentration of its urban population in the southeast corner of the state where its recreational needs are in direct competition with those of Chicago and neighboring cities. Crowded highways, parks, lakes, and resorts are the result. A large part of the cost of providing facilities for these multitudes naturally falls upon the state or local divisions of government. As a private enterprise, seeking tourists and vacationers has its drawbacks. The business is seasonal, usually requires a large outlay of capital for success, and has a large number of business failures.

Another source of pressure upon available recreation land and the environment is increasing private development. One answer to crowding for the reasonably affluent is to buy a piece of vacation property. A 1965 study made an estimate of 92,000 vacation homes in the state compared to 55,000 in 1959 and a probable 120,000 in 1970. The number of available sites that could be purchased from private parties was obviously limited. An increasingly popular alternative is to buy a lot in a development. These tract developments range from modest subdivisions by farmers to operations involving thousands of lots, the creation of artificial lakes, and expensive advertising campaigns. Wisconsin citizens hold to the notion that this conspicuous tampering with the environment, subdividing, and ownership of desirable waterfrontage, is largely the work of Chicagoans. It is not. A 1970 survey indicated that only about 15 percent of sales of vacation lots were to people living outside of Wisconsin.

Whatever the apprehensions about new patterns of ownership, the hazards to the environment are real enough. A legacy of the progressive tradition in Wisconsin is the belief that a highly professional bureaucracy, backed by enlightened legislation adequate for the task, will save us from either rapacity or folly. This depends upon the presumption that there exists close liaison between the state's experts and those making decisions at the local level. The presumption overlooks the temptations offered to a poor county by a large real estate development to raise the tax base substantially. The usual result is an eagerness to embrace temptation and a display of generous tolerance toward the developer's shortcomings.

What are the shortcomings? For one thing, neither developers nor their prospective customers are eager to pay the added $1,000 or so per lot required for a central sewerage system. The results of several hundred individual disposal systems clustered around a shallow, artificial lake take some years to become evident. Soil scientists estimate that about 60 percent of the state is not suitable for septic tanks because of soil conditions or the high ground-water table. Local officials are reluctant to enforce standards that would embarrass the developers.

Other problems came to the fore in the areas of the heaviest concentration of population. Milwaukee, with other major American cities, witnessed the flight of its middle class population to the suburbs and an influx of the new urban poor, overwhelmingly black, filling in behind them. Much retail trade and light industry followed, or led, the rush to the suburbs. The result was uncontrolled urban sprawl, as farmlands were platted to residential and business properties, ahead of adequate traffic arterials, other essential services, or the sketchiest planning. The city was unable to follow these fleeing taxpayers by the traditional method of annexation. The surrounding towns had to agree to annexation and they were not eager to share the city's growing financial burdens or to give up certain tax benefits of remaining separate.

The need for cooperative planning was apparent as the population in the Milwaukee, Racine, Kenosha metropolitan area swelled by 35 percent in the thirteen years following 1950. A regional planning commission for the seven counties in the southeast corner of the state was created in 1960, by executive order, meaning that its powers were limited to persuasion and example. The proliferation of federal aid programs offering funds for use in solving urban problems gave the commission more authority; it was the logical planning instrument. In 1967, the legislature created a department of local affairs and development to give technical aid and to act as an intermediary for local or regional planning bodies and state and federal agencies.

Paradoxical as it may sound, among the major industries built upon the natural and human resources gathered here, agriculture has probably been the most successful in adjusting to its resource base in Wisconsin. It is paradoxical because few industries seemed so beset with chronic problems which defy solution: overcapitalization, overproduction, uncontrolled prices, an over-age work force that does not attract youthful replacements, a ridiculously low average return on capital invested and labor input, and an unusually high rate of business closures. Yet farming, because each operator was forced to adapt to the resources available within his property lines, made its painful adjustment early, cooperatively, and with massive aid levied upon the general taxpayer. One may argue that much of that aid was based upon the premise that it was necessary to save the American family farm. That institution remains, despite frequent alarms to the contrary, the standard farm operation in Wisconsin.

Devotion to dairying and livestock contributes to the continuing health of the family farm in Wisconsin. Technological and scientific advances have contributed less to economies of scale and to reducing labor requirements in dairying than in most other farming. Wisconsin therefore has a larger proportion of its work force on the land: 12.3 percent, compared to 8.7 percent for the United States generally. The average size of Wisconsin farms also reflects this. In 1969 the national average was 390 acres, for Illinois 242 acres, for Iowa 239 acres, for Wisconsin 183 acres. A much larger proportion of Wisconsin farms falls within the 50- to 500-acre range, with few very large or very small farms. The percentage of owner-operators is high, of tenant operators low, compared to national averages or the averages of neighboring states.

Milk production accounted for 55 percent of Wisconsin's gross farm income in 1970. About 90 percent of crop acreage goes into livestock feeding. Although the state ranks first in the nation in production of vegetables for processing, this involves a relatively minor part of farmed land. The state is properly advertised as the top dairy producer. In a day when fresh milk can be marketed hundreds of miles from its source, Wisconsin is the supplier that makes up milkshed shortages in urban areas as far away as Texas.

Dairy farming is a highly capitalized operation. Milk cows and the buildings and necessary equipment for their care are expensive. Because of the nature of the commodity, the dairy farmer is subject to rigid requirements and continuous inspection. The returns do not often match the capital outlay or the effort. In 1966 it was calculated that the average Class A dairy farmer (authorized to market fluid milk) earned a return of only $1.08 an hour for his labor. There were 132,500 dairy herds in the state in 1951. This number had fallen to 65,400 by 1969, but milk production was twice what it had been thirty years earlier. Production figures indicate a dramatic rise in individual production as a result of breeding and feeding practices. At a peak in numbers in 1956 there were 2,600,000 cows in Wisconsin. This number fell to 1,900,000 in 1968, but 6 percent more milk was produced.

Rising production did not save farming from serious problems. It is hazardous to compare one year with another in agriculture because of the many uncontrolled variables, but the following example represents a trend which figures for the intervening years confirm. Between 1950 and 1964, the production costs for Wisconsin farmers rose 41 percent, gross farm income rose 25 percent, but net income was 2 percent less than in 1950.

Wisconsin farmers have faced the problems presented by these figures in a variety of ways. The most obvious way is by getting out of farming. As one would expect, the attrition has been heaviest among marginal operators. There were in 1969 57,896 full-time farmers with gross sales below $10,000 annually; 25,734 of these fell below $5,000. Within a sixteen-month period, just following the compilation of these figures, 7,200 operators quit dairying. A survey of their reasons was revealing. Twenty percent quit because of inadequate income, another 20 percent because feed or labor was priced too high, 8 percent because of general dissatisfaction, and another 7 percent because sons were not interested in staying on the farm or had been drafted and alternate labor was hard to find and harder to pay.

The ideal of the family farm obscured some awkward statistics. Of the 57,896 farms that in 1964 grossed from $2,500 to $10,000, very close to half of the families were judged to be living below the poverty level. These farms experienced the greatest attrition in numbers during the years of the study, 1959 to 1964, but the 5,868 full-time farmers whose sales fell below $2,500, of whom fully two-thirds lived below the poverty level, lost only 167 members in the five-year period. The part-time farmers and those partly retired, who contribute very little to the agricultural economy, were also very persistent, numbering about 23,000 or one-fifth of all farmers in the state. Full-time farmers living below poverty levels accounted for another one-fourth. While as one would expect, the poverty-level farms were most prevalent in the northern counties, a rich agricultural county such as Dane had one-fifth of its farm families in this category. Price County, in the north, had 38 percent of its farmers below the poverty level.

Federal farm programs were not of much help to the marginal operator. Their emphasis was upon limiting productions or taking production out of normal channels. One might assume from this that the marginal farmers would fill the ranks of the more militant farm organizers, but such evidently has not been the case. The best known, the National Farmers Organization, had its start in Iowa in 1955, organizing to withhold from market a significant amount of farm production to force processors to contract at prices guaranteeing a fair return. A 1965 study indicated that NFO members were recruited largely from commercial farmers in southern Wisconsin who were operating larger-than-average farms and marketing more than the average of milk and livestock. They had larger gross incomes than the average in either the conservative Farm Bureau or the liberal Farmers Union. The NFO was also estimated to have passed the Farmers Union in membership and was briefly a close rival of the Farm Bureau. As part of its strategy, the NFO kept its membership secret, but sampling gave a fair estimate. It was clearly past its peak well before 1970. Farm organizations tend to have fluctuating memberships, but claimed a little over a third of all Wisconsin farmers in 1965. The profiles indicate that the most successful farmers belonged to the top three organizations.

The NFO faced the same problems as its predecessors in promoting successful holding actions. Farmers did not agree on tactics and many were either apathetic or actively hostile to NFO methods. More important, it was easier for processors to curtail operations or to find alternative supplies than it was for farmers to dump their milk, hold animals ready for market, or find alternate markets. More farmers apparently felt that development of the cooperative movement, particularly in marketing, offered more hope for improvement. Over 80 percent of Wisconsin farmers in 1965 bought supplies, equipment, or services through cooperatives. Half of the dairymen and one-third of the livestock men marketed through cooperatives that were joining into increasingly larger units for bargaining power. Nonetheless, a report on the state's farm economy for 1970 noted that farmers were still losing the race. Farm prices were up only 3.5 percent for the year, while prices farmers paid were up 4 percent. A spectacular surge in farm prices occurred in 1972–73, but predictions from that at the time were hazardous.

A couple of less-immediate threats have troubled Wisconsin agriculture. The growth of corporation farming has resulted in legislative debates as well as disagreement between federal and state agencies over the statistics and their implications. Corporate farms are particularly significant in vegetable production for canning and freezing. They are less important in livestock feeding and dairying. A good many farms of the latter sort have been large family operations incorporated for a variety of reasons. Apologists point out that corporate farms controlled less than 3 percent of Wisconsin's crop land in 1968 and were not a great threat to the family farm, which remained more adaptable to changing demands.

The other less-immediate danger to Wisconsin agriculture comes from pressure for other uses for farm land. The pressure comes as an advantage for many marginal farms. It provides a market for land that has sustained poverty level living conditions for farm families over the years, by converting it to recreational uses for urban dwellers. The new uses are many: bucolic settings and tax write-offs for affluent city families, vacation-home developments, resorts, golf courses, and even hunting preserves with conditioned game birds guaranteed to fly within easy range. Less comforting in its long-range implications is the growing demand for land by the heavy concentration of population in the southeast quarter of the state where the best farmlands are located. Somehow one regrets that a traffic interchange with a service station and hamburger franchise represents a higher use of Wisconsin's limited class A land.

Manufacturing and agribusiness—a term invented by someone whose ideal evidently was not the family farm—do not, of course, tell the full story of Wisconsin's economy, although they do tell more of what is characteristic than do facts about other sectors of the economy. Wisconsin has the usual quota of Sears stores, supermarkets, shopping centers, gas stations, medical clinics, schools, and interstate highways. Some employment statistics tell us much about the changes that have taken place since 1940 in the general economy.

The growth of manufacturing employment in Wisconsin has lagged a little behind the average for the United States in the period since 1950,

EMPLOYMENT IN WISCONSIN

Occupations	1940	1950	1960	1970
Nonfarm	786,400*	1,021,000	1,191,900	1,677,000
Manufacturing	270,000*	427,700	460,400	512,605
Wholesale & retail	137,150	214,400	243,900	331,000
Government	—	119,200	163,200	265,000
Service & miscellaneous	—	97,600	144,300	231,000
Transportation & utilities	60,600*	77,500	74,500	81,000
Contract Construction	39,870*	49,100	56,000	62,000
Finance, Insurance, real estate	24,770*	32,100	45,700	61,000
Farm	274,000*	251,900*	212,500	165,000

Sources: *The Wisconsin Blue Book*, 1940, 1950, 1960; *Wisconsin Statistical Abstract*, 1972.
  * Total number employed. Others are annual averages.

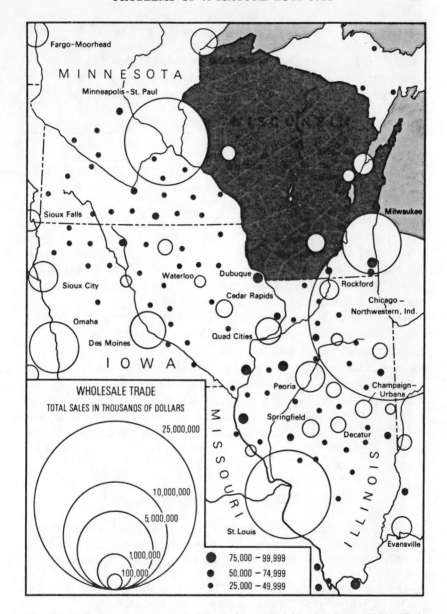

Map 15.   The Wholesale Trade in Wisconsin and Neighboring States, 1970. Wholesalers in Milwaukee and other Wisconsin cities have been severely limited by the more favorable circumstances of wholesalers in Chicago as well as by the development of wholesale centers to the immediate west, particularly at Minneapolis-St. Paul. Wisconsin cities have logically concentrated on manufacturing, for which they are well located. Map adapted from the 1970 *National Atlas of the United States,* based upon 1963 census data   *UWCL*

but remains above that average in the percentage of personal income derived from this source and in the percentage of labor force involved
(Wisconsin 27.3 percent, U.S. 25.1 percent, in 1970). Other sectors of
the economy are generally healthy, as evidenced by the growth of per
capita personal income. Wisconsin has maintained a position just below

AVERAGE PER CAPITA INCOME

	1929	1940	1950	1955	1960	1965	1969
Wisconsin	$684	$552	$1477	$1816	$2176	$2729	$3632
United States	705	592	1496	1876	2215	2765	3687

the national average, which considering that employment in the troubled
agricultural sector has stayed above the average (Wisconsin 9 percent,
U.S. average 5.9 percent in 1970), and that much of its manufacturing is
cyclical, shows a basic resilience. The construction industry, a bellwether
because it reflects industrial, business, private housing, and governmental
expansion, has been very active in postwar Wisconsin.

With Chicago on one side and the Twin Cities on the other, Wisconsin's wholesalers have stiff competition in a compressed trade area. One
is not surprised by the dominance of Chicago, but Minnesota wholesale
business consistently ran nearly 50 percent higher than that of Wisconsin
throughout the 1960s, while Minnesota's retail trade on the average was
only 90 percent of Wisconsin's, a reflection of the greater reach of the
Twin Cities wholesalers to the west and into northwestern Wisconsin.
The state of Wisconsin remains strong as a producer in a national economy in which distribution and services take an increasing slice from the
consumers' dollars.

Selected Bibliography

Anderson, Raymond L. "Problems of Private Land Use for Recreation in
    Wisconsin." Ph.D. dissertation, University of Wisconsin, 1959. Why ecolo-
    gists despair—he was disturbed that there was so much lakefront left un-
    developed in 1959.
Becker, Folke. "Trees for Tomorrow." *Wisconsin Magazine of History* 36:
    43–47 (Autumn 1952). Private enterprise and reforestation.
Berquist, Gordon F., Jr., ed. *The Wisconsin Academy Looks at Urbanism.*
    Special monograph from papers given at the ninety-third annual meeting
    of the Wisconsin Academy of Sciences, Arts and Letters, Milwaukee, May
    1963.
Brandsberg, George. *The Two Sides in the NFO's Battle.* Ames, Iowa, 1964.
    Background of the Farmers Militant.

Curran, Donald J. "The Financial Evolution of the Milwaukee Metropolitan Area." Ph.D. dissertation, University of Wisconsin, 1963. Tax problems of the metropolis.

Davis, Richard S. "Milwaukee: Old Lady Thrift." In Robert S. Allen, ed., *Our Fair City*, pp. 189–210. New York, 1947. Lighthearted.

Dorner, Peter. *Farming Changes in Wisconsin, 1940–1960*. University of Wisconsin College of Agriculture Experiment Station, bulletin no. 561. January, 1963. An example of many studies available.

Fuchs, Zahava, and Douglas C. Marshall. *The Socioeconomic Composition of Wisconsin's Population, 1900–1960*. University of Wisconsin College of Agriculture and Life Sciences, Department of Rural Sociology, Population Series. Wisconsin's Population, no. 12. Madison, May 1968. Largely shifts in types of employment.

Giese, Kenyon E. "An Analysis of the Sauk County National Farmers Organization." Master's thesis, University of Wisconsin, 1965. They were the more prosperous farmers.

Kerstein, Edward S. *Milwaukee's All-American Mayor: Portrait of Daniel Webster Hoan*. Englewood Cliffs, N.J., 1966. Shallow stuff.

Krueger, Anne O. *The Impact of the St. Lawrence Seaway on the Upper Midwest*. Upper Midwest Economic Study, study paper no. 8. Minneapolis, 1963. Points out the limitations.

Leopold, Aldo. *A Sand County Almanac and Sketches Here and There*. New York, 1949. Available in Oxford Paperback, 1968. Wisconsin's famous environmentalist.

Marshall, Douglas C. *The Story of Kenosha County, Wisconsin: Population Change in an Urbanized Area*. University of Wisconsin Agricultural Experiment Station, research bulletin no. 241. Madison, 1964. Farmers move out and younger urban types move in.

The Milwaukee Journal Company. *Wisconsin's Balance Sheet*. Milwaukee, 1953. Prospects for the economy.

Munch, Peter A. "Segregation and Assimilation of Norwegian Settlements in Wisconsin." *Norwegian-American Studies and Records* 18:102–40 (1954). Ethnic loyalties and identifications are persistent.

Murphy, Earl F. *Water Purity: A Study in Legal Control of Natural Resources*. Madison, 1961. A bit dated already.

"The Natural Resources of Wisconsin." *Wisconsin Blue Book*, 1964.

Nesbit, Robert C., comp. *Wisconsin since 1940: A Selection of Sources*. Madison, 1966. Supplement to Raney's 1940 text.

Saupe, William. *Poverty-Level Farming is Wisconsin*. University of Wisconsin College of Agriculture and Life Sciences Research Division, special bulletin 11. Madison, May–June 1968. It is not confined to the cutover.

Schenker, Eric. *The Port of Milwaukee: An Economic Review*. Madison, 1967. Background of the seaway.

Schmandt, Henry J., with William H. Standing. *The Milwaukee Metropolitan Study Commission*. Bloomington, Ind., 1965. Trying to deal with urban problems.

Schmid, A. Allan. "Water and the Law in Wisconsin." *Wisconsin Magazine of History* 45:203–15 (Spring 1962). On the 1840 Milldam Act and consequences.

University of Wisconsin College of Agriculture and Life Sciences, Department of Rural Sociology Population Series. Madison, 1961–. We keep taking the pulse.

Willoughby, William R. *The St. Lawrence Seaway: A Study in Politics and Diplomacy*. Madison, 1961. Best on origins of the seaway.

Wisconsin Academy of Sciences, Arts and Letters. "The Natural Resources of Northern Wisconsin, a Wisconsin Academy Profile." *Transactions* 53, part a, 1964.

Wisconsin Crop-Reporting Service. *Wisconsin Dairying in Mid-Century*. Bulletin 331. Madison, 1955. Beginning of the trend toward consolidation.

Wittke, Carl. "American-Germans in Two World Wars." *Wisconsin Magazine of History* 27:6–16 (Sept. 1943). Reflects concern with American Nazism.

Note on the bibliographies for chapters 30 and 31. Much of the material for these near contemporary chapters came from newspapers and other ephemera, state and university publications of an interim nature addressed to a variety of problems, and information from the *Wisconsin Blue Book* series. Some samples of the references are offered above.

REALIGNMENTS, SOCIAL AND POLITICAL

31

The Second World War ended a long period of chronic unemployment and underemployment which had reached disastrous proportions in the Great Depression of the 1930s. Almost 14 percent of Wisconsin's labor force was unemployed in 1940, much lower than a few years before, but still one in seven. This figure dropped sharply immediately after 1940 and stood at just under 3 percent for Wisconsin in 1950, slightly below the national average, a position the state has rather consistently maintained into the 1970s. The change has had profound psychological as well as economic effects. Income levels for wage earners have greatly altered living standards and expectations. Over two-thirds of Wisconsin's labor force earned less than $1,000 annually in 1940. By 1950, 36 percent earned more than $3,000, and by 1960 62 percent. The consumer price index doubled during the twenty-year period, but average per capita income was four times as great. Wisconsin's is now a consumer-oriented society with a high proportion of participants, both as employees and as customers.

Another less-obvious change has been the blurring of the traditional distinctions between the old established ethnic groups in Wisconsin society. This is a difficult generalization to prove, for there is much self-conscious preservation of immigrant heritages from a variety of motives: commercial exploitation, community identification, an interest in folk art, the urge to preserve an identification with a cultural heritage, and an appreciation of the historical value of artifacts and memorabilia. This is not to' deny the persistence of ethnic awareness in a great variety of forms, but the melting pot is working. Community celebrations with an ethnic identification have become primarily civic promotions. The problem frequently is to keep folk art and social organizations alive rather than ethnically exclusive.

Ethnic distinctions are related to religious differences, and Wisconsin society has become more secularized. An indication of a more secular attitude toward a public question was the pronounced lack of organized resistance in 1967 to carrying parochial school children on public school buses. A similar provision had been defeated by a five to four margin in a 1946 constitutional referendum. Backed strongly by the Catholics, who claimed 35 percent of Wisconsin's population, the amendment was fiercely opposed by an organization of Protestant sects. The *Wisconsin State Journal* called the campaign on the measure "one of the most bitter in the state's history."

The issue was on the ballot again in April 1967. An analysis of the vote indicates that there was a greater interest in it than in companion amendments on the ballot, but the voters confounded most observers by approving the measure 494,236 to 377,107. The debate on the amendment was subdued, and featured defections by Lutheran clergymen from the hard line of 1946.

A considerable change in the level of education of Wisconsin citizens doubtless contributed to the secular trend. Wisconsin had nearly 6,000 one-room country schools in 1940. Only one-third of farm boys and girls of sixteen and seventeen were enrolled in schools in 1940. This had risen to 88 percent by 1960, and the number of one-room schools by 1965 had been reduced to 35. College education also had a dramatic rise. Less than 8 percent of young people in the age group 20–24 were enrolled in school in 1930. This figure rose to 31.8 percent in 1960, almost twice the average for the United States. The percentage of urban youth enrolled rose from 9.5 to 40.1, and that of farm youth rose two and a half times, to 8.5 percent.

The tremendous growth of public higher education in the 1960s has placed serious burdens upon the taxpayer and the schools. Enrollment in the state university system grew from 14,338 in 1959–60 to 61,890 in 1969–70; on the University of Wisconsin campuses from 27,005 to 65,257. The two systems were merged under a 1971 statute.

Not only has there been a secularizing influence in higher education, and even on church school campuses, but parochial school education at the elementary and high school level, too, has been in serious crisis. The

Archdiocese of Milwaukee closed eight grade schools in the city in 1970. Parochial school enrollment below the college level fell almost 20,000 between 1968–69 and 1969–70, while public school enrollment rose by 30,000. About 18 percent of those enrolled through the high school grades were in parochial schools, compared with 24 percent in 1965. Apparently parental attitudes have changed more rapidly than building mortgages have been amortized. A growing sentiment for some form of tax support for parochial schools may be as much a response to the financial implications for the public schools as it is a sign of growing tolerance. Young people are largely unconcerned with religious distinctions and with ethnic differences. They have an awareness of their own ethnic origins as a mildly interesting event in their families' past.

One phenomenon of post–World War II that qualifies generalizations about a loss of active ethnic consciousness has been the rise of militance among racial minority groups, particularly Milwaukee's growing black community, but among Chicanos and American Indians as well. Opposition to black aspirations centers in Milwaukee's Polish community, which feels most directly threatened economically and socially. This opposition doubtless gives a heightened sense of ethnic identification to those in the blue-collar neighborhoods where the more recent immigrant groups are the conspicuous elements, but race prejudice is endemic in American society and not their particular possession. Their response is both racist and socioeconomic in origin.

The history of blacks in Wisconsin before World War I is that of a small but highly visible minority carrying the heavy burden of discrimination that obtained everywhere in American society. We read of the unusual individuals who rose above the barriers surrounding them to achieve success, or vignettes of those who demanded their legal and human rights from the startled community.

There were only 996 blacks in Milwaukee County in 1910, roughly one-third of all those in the state. They were almost all in the cities, strictly ghettoized, with very limited employment opportunity. Most large industrial plants were still segregated at the beginning of World War II. The public image of the black in industry was of imported gang labor used for strike breaking or for heavy, dirty jobs.

World War I brought a modest influx of blacks, but nothing like the numbers attracted to other major Great Lakes cities. By 1930 there were 7,500 in Milwaukee, two-thirds of the total in the state, crammed into a part of the present core area west of the Milwaukee River in a segregated community. They were not so numerous that the surrounding society felt threatened, but it did not let down the barriers. Milwaukee was looked upon as a relatively tolerant community with an officialdom that was, at best, not actively hostile toward black citizens. But despite the temporary opening of employment opportunities in many formerly segregated plants during World War II, it was still "last hired, first fired." A 1952 survey of 4,786 black jobholders in the metropolis found only 10 in the professions, 47 in clerical jobs, 345 in skilled labor positions, and 1 salesgirl in a major, downtown store. The black unemployment rate in 1960 was 11.4 percent compared to 3.9 percent for whites.

Progress in job opportunities and housing was much slower than the continued in-migration. It says something about the relative attraction of Milwaukee that blacks continued coming, although at a slower rate than in the 1950s. In 1950 Beloit had the highest proportion of blacks in the state, with 4.7 percent. By 1970 Milwaukee's population was 14.7 percent black. As these figures indicate, they are overwhelmingly an urban population—about 98 percent—and Milwaukee's 105,000 was 82 percent of the state's total.

A disadvantaged minority mostly from southern rural backgrounds, Milwaukee's newer black citizens lacked education, job skills, or acceptance by the white community as they expanded the city's traditional black community. Welfare is not strictly a black problem, but the necessity for welfare touches a much larger proportion of black families. Wisconsin's welfare expenses, as elsewhere, mounted rapidly. They were at a level of $60,000,000 in 1959 and increased to $239,400,000 in 1969. Comparable expenditures in Milwaukee County were $14,460,000 and $88,665,000. The rise of black militancy in Wisconsin was greeted, as elsewhere, with a mixture of concern, consternation, and indignation. Migrant farm labor, principally Chicano, met a similar response to its more orderly protest. Most Wisconsin citizens have little familiarity with racial minorities. Typically, the state showed sympathetic concern with the creation, by executive order, of a human rights commission in 1945. Finally funded by the legislature in 1949, the commission functioned as an instrument of persuasion and public education, but now has a panoply of open housing, fair employment, and public accommodation laws to enforce.

Any general description of Wisconsin's economy, the socioeconomic status of the population, the blurring of ethnic and religious lines, and the influence of education, requires qualification. It is plain that there are essential differences between living in Milwaukee, where the county contains one-quarter of the population of the state, 1,054,063, in Oshkosh with 53,221, and in Boscobel with 2,520, all defined as urban. Another qualification is the influence of geography. Maps based upon county dif-

ferences in average income, farm value, education level, value of manufactures, employment rates, and numerous other indicators show a consistent pattern. Draw a line from Green Bay to Madison, then south to
Janesville-Beloit, and the eighteen counties east of the line contain
2,940,280, or 67 percent, of the state's 1970 population of 4,366,766.
With the exception of the isolated centers of La Crosse, Eau Claire, Superior, and the scattered paper industry, one has also delineated most of
the important manufacturing in the state. In a ranking of all counties by
socioeconomic status (education, labor-force status, occupation, and income) of their citizens, only five of the southeastern eighteen counties
rank outside of the first eighteen. These five are primarily agricultural
counties, with only 10.4 percent of the population of the eighteen-county
area. The lowest quartile of counties in the statewide ranking includes
nine counties in the Cutover, four in the driftless area in the southwest,
and Adams, Washburn, and Marquette counties in the center.

The map confirms that over two-thirds of the state's population and
economic activity is confined to a small quarter of its area. Much of the
remaining area may be characterized as a sea of underprivilege, underemployment, and inferior soil, broken by conspicuous islands of prosperous farmland and economically active urban centers. State averages do
not convey any sense of this contrast. Waukesha and Burnett counties
are at opposite ends of the socioeconomic rankings as they are geographically. The average income per household in Burnett County in 1968 was
$5,818; in Waukesha County it was $13,635. Of the Burnett County
households, 36.5 percent had incomes below $3,000, certainly poverty
level in 1968. Only 7.3 percent of Waukesha's families fell below $3,000
income; 54.7 percent earned over $10,000.

This inequality of income and the concentration of higher income levels in the urbanized counties reminds us that great expanses of Wisconsin
are at a disadvantage, where wealth depends primarily upon the resources of the soil. Dairying offers the best use for much of the agricultural land, but successful dairying depends more and more upon a heavy
application of capital, technology, and management skills. In the northern counties, where much marginal agriculture remains, half of the farm
people left the land between 1940 and 1960. The economy of the area
has not generated alternate employment for them.

Wisconsin's Indian population of nearly 19,000 in 1970 was a newly
conspicuous group of the rural poor, although their greatest concentration is the 3,700 living in Milwaukee. Conspicuous is the proper word,
for Wisconsin Indians have caught the militance of other racial minori-

ties. But they are scattered across northern Wisconsin in a variety of
small reservations, while some, like the Winnebago, have no traditional
landholdings. There are six small Chippewa reservations, small remnants
of Oneida and Stockbridge-Munsee moved here in the 1820s, a few
Potawatomi, and the largest tribe, still in their ancestral home, the
Menominee.

The Menominee have had the most attention in recent years. Congress
and the Eisenhower administration seized upon the outworn notion that
the Indian would benefit from an end to his dependence, and the Menominee were made a test case. Their former reservation became Wisconsin's seventy-second county, and the land was turned over to a corporation, Menominee Enterprises, with the tribal members as stockholders
in a complicated trust arrangement. The company has been unable to
provide the necessary tax base for the county. Its principal resource is
timber, a business with a limited future on a sustained basis. The managers of the trust and Menominee Enterprises turned to a developer to convert part of the land, lying on a string of lakes, into vacation-home sites.
While the land involved is only a small fraction of the former reservation, it is a choice portion, and there is much dissension over the decision. There is a proposal in Congress to restore the Menominee lands to
reservation status.*

Milwaukee has a long-standing reputation as a strong union town,
probably the most completely unionized major city in the United States.
There are a variety of reasons for this: the European tradition of organization, particularly among the skilled German and British workmen; the
close link between the unions and the Milwaukee Socialists dating from
the mid-nineties; an exceptionally high rate of industrial employment
(41 percent) for the work force; an interesting mixture of intransigence
and enlightened benevolence among the city's large employers, both attitudes contributing to labor's solidarity; and the nature of much of the
industrial employment during the formative years of the unions—seasonal, frequently capricious, yet dependent upon skilled workmen most
able to enforce demands.

The local success of Victor Berger's Socialist party, in a symbiotic relationship with organized labor, created a tradition of strong labor influence in local affairs which moved beyond Milwaukee to adjacent industrial cities. Some observers are of the opinion that this political muscle
extends beyond what labor leaders can realistically deliver, but labor endorsement and support are considered valuable political assets.

Labor influence has not been confined to the industrial cities. Both
formal and informal alliances with the progressives over the years, plus

---

* Note to the Second Printing: The Menominee lands were returned to reservation status by Congress in 1975.

continuity and skill in lobbying in Madison, have resulted in a body of
Wisconsin labor legislation that set precedents for other states and the
nation: recognition of the rights of collective bargaining, workmen's
compensation, unemployment insurance, safety and health, and practices
in arbitration, among others. Two elements outside of the labor movement contributed to these gains: the university and its traditions, and the
support of rural legislators.

The university's contribution to Wisconsin and American labor theory, legislation, and the administration of programs can be summed up in
the names of a distinguished list of scholars, in particular Richard Ely,
John R. Commons, Charles R. McCarthy, Edwin E. Witte, Selig Perl-
man, Arthur J. Altmeyer, Paul Raushenbush, and Elizabeth Brandeis
Raushenbush. Ely and Commons established a school of labor economics whose traditions have permeated the university. Charles McCarthy
was the father of the nation's first comprehensive continuation school
system in Wisconsin, more commonly known as the vocational and technical schools, started in 1911. The state now has thirty-five full-time
campuses, and the Milwaukee Area Technical College is the largest of its
kind in the country. The program has had much to do with the attraction
which Wisconsin labor holds for industry. The School for Workers, a
university program attached to the Extension Division, is a continuing
recognition of the service university's obligation to meet the special needs
of labor as well as of agriculture and industry.

Wisconsin labor made spectacular gains in membership, legal status,
and bargaining power during the New Deal years. Phil La Follette's Progressives in 1937 passed the Wisconsin Labor Relations Act, popularly
known as the Little Wagner Act. The law, with a comprehensive list of
unfair practices of employers but not of unions, was bitterly contested by
employers' organizations, but their influence was at a temporary nadir. A
board, very similar in powers to the National Labor Relations Board,
administered the act.

After this victory of very considerable dimensions, things began to go
sour for labor. The New Deal was a deathblow for the Socialist party. It
is ironic that the economic conditions which should have favored socialism turned voters to the new liberalism represented by the New Deal.
Disgruntled with La Follette's Progressives and the Farmer-Labor Progressive Federation, the Socialists withdrew and found not opportunity
but political oblivion.

The split between the American Federation of Labor and John L.
Lewis's Congress of Industrial Organizations came in 1937. The Wisconsin Federation of Labor had always been sympathetic to industrial
unionists and it made serious efforts to heal the opening breach between

the national organizations. In the end, national policy prevailed, and the two began a bitter competition. Lewis readily welcomed Communists as organizers of the CIO. They were tough and dedicated. As a result, Communist leadership came to dominate a number of unions, with their most important base in the United Auto Workers (UAW). The huge local at the Allis-Chalmers plant, with about 7,000 members, left the AFL for the CIO under such leadership. The CIO took over hitherto un- organized shops at Bucyrus Erie, Harnischfeger, Heil, Harley-Davidson, Briggs and Stratton, and A. O. Smith. The AFL did not shrink from the fight and also grew in membership, despite substantial losses to the CIO.

Joined in battle with powerful antiunion employers and with each other, under the favorable aegis of the New Deal and La Follette Pro- gressives, the AFL and CIO sometimes forgot the realities of Wisconsin politics. The fragile alliance with the farm vote, through the rapidly fail- ing Farmer-Labor Progressive Federation, was broken by union efforts to organize the employees of some farm co-ops. The response came from the Wisconsin Council of Agriculture, representing cooperatives and the conservative Farm Bureau, which set out to counter labor. The result, although there were many other factors involved, was the defeat of Phil La Follette in 1938 and the election of a conservative governor and legis- lature dedicated to reversing some of labor's legislative gains.

The Wisconsin Labor Peace Act of 1939 derived from the same phi- losophy as the later national Taft-Hartley Act of 1947. The act hedged some of the protections given in 1937 to unions and emphasized a list of unfair union practices, in contrast to the former act's concentration on unfair employer practices. The bias of the 1939 law was that drives for unionization and other demands were usually inspired by outside orga- nizers. The intent of the law was to insulate the workers from this influ- ence and to give the employer more room for maneuver in countering. The arithmetic of such contests does not bear out the inspiration of the law, for the unions won about 85 percent of them. The act has been modified substantially in recognition of this, and both unions and em- ployers have accommodated to the realities of union power in our more affluent economy.

As one would expect in a highly industrialized state with a tradition of vigorous unionism and conservative, independent employers, whom some observers have considered more parochial in their attitudes than is common among the managers of national industrial concerns, Wisconsin has had its share of spectacular labor disputes. The long struggle from 1941 to 1946 to rid the Allis-Chalmers affiliate of its Communist leader- ship was one such. This struggle was complicated by a long history of company intransigence, then cooperation with that leadership. This was possible because of a natural limitation upon Communist leadership imposed by the rank and file, whose interest in ideology was generally less than minimal. The company found the leadership comfortable, and took up arms only when the red issue served the purpose of thwarting union gains. Walter Reuther finally established the authority of the UAW over the local in 1946 and purged the Communists. The Kohler strike of the 1950s represented another failure of the employer to recognize the permanence of New Deal labor legislation, and the end of benevolent paternalism as a working relationship.

The AFL and CIO finally abandoned their rivalry, at least formally, in Wisconsin as well as nationally. The combined membership added up to about 262,000 in 1958 when the merger took place. The AFL made up about two-thirds of the total and tended to dominate the new organization, but the spirit of industrial unionism was always strong in Milwaukee. The liberal element within organized labor is generally identified with the industrial unions.

Labor seems always to be at some sort of crossroads. Although fat and powerful compared to the leaner times not far behind, organized labor has its problems. As industry expands, blue collar jobs do not expand in proportion. The most dynamic areas of union expansion are among white collar workers in industry, services, and government, especially the latter, and Wisconsin has given leadership in this field. The American Federation of State, County, and Municipal Employees, fastest growing of this new style of union, was founded in Madison in the 1930s. But for the traditional unions, the white collar unions present difficulties because their motivation and outlook are so different. Another concern is that the powerful, unaffiliated Teamsters Union has moved in on the new white collar union field. Oddly, this concern with the different aims and attitudes of white collar or professional workers comes at a time when the blue collar worker is escaping to the suburbs with his new affluence, away from the union hall and the neighborhood where socialism was once a live issue.

Wisconsin, in 1970, elected its third Democratic governor since 1958, a state of affairs which continues to astonish older Democrats as well as Republicans. The Republicans maintained control of the state senate and most courthouses, but the two United States senators have been Democrats since 1962, and the congressmen are split in favor of the Democrats five to four. Observers of the Wisconsin political scene concede that the state now has two parties, on the national model, which contest rather evenly. This was a long time in coming. One might make a good case for setting 1855 as the last date when this condition prevailed.

The Progressive party of the 1930s was a La Follette creation, although it attracted support from elements who were less than enthusiastic about Phil La Follette. The problem was that they had no alternative political home. The conservatives had firm control of both major parties. The old stalwart faction held uncontested sway over the Republican party after the progressive element followed Bob and Phil into the Progressive party in 1934. The Democratic party in Wisconsin was of the Bourbon model—a German-Irish-Polish marching society, with a Catholic base—led by conservatives awaiting the patronage that a Democratic president would dispense. They got it with Frankin D. Roosevelt, plus an astonishing sweep of state offices in the Roosevelt landslide of 1932. Wisconsin's Democrats did not take advantage of their brief hour, and Roosevelt recognized that the voters who were temperamentally his followers were in the Progressive ranks. He therefore wooed the La Follette brothers assiduously, but to no avail, while the Wisconsin Democratic leadership maintained its conservatism.

It was a variety of circumstances that turned the Democratic party of Wisconsin toward the New Deal–Fair Deal pattern. Phil La Follette, misreading the political signs, attempted to launch his Progressive party on a regional or national basis in 1938. As he expressed it himself, he took a chance on becoming a national political leader or the William Jennings Bryan of Dane County. No one ever accused him of being either. The National Progressives of America was launched but sank at dockside. Phil was following the isolationist course set by his father, which continued to have an appeal in the Midwest, and he was convinced that Roosevelt was abandoning domestic liberalism for foreign adventure. He was hoping to build a third-party alliance of economic liberals and isolationists from the ranks of the two major parties. His brother, the senator, was reluctantly dragged along behind the younger brother's ambitious obsession in a brief blaze of publicity which he found unpleasant. Phil's move caught many progressives by surprise. They were affronted by the Nuremberg trappings in which he indulged, and learned little from his rhetoric: ". . . break the chains which bind us . . . go forward together to provide work, security, and comfort for all our people and preserve democracy in our nation." How? "Make no mistake, this is NOT a *third* party. As certain as the sun rises, we are launching THE party of our time." The sun rose, but the miracle of Ripon was not repeated.

Phil was defeated in his bid for reelection in 1938 by Julius Heil, a Milwaukee industrialist who was not one of the Republican inner circle. The ease with which Phil went down was a shock to Republican regulars, who had not seriously contested Heil in the primaries. The Democrats, reflecting the conservative temper of the party, agreed to a coalition against La Follette. The principal Democratic candidate withdrew after the primary in favor of Heil.

The Progressive party in Wisconsin did not die with Phil's defeat and withdrawal from an active political role. Julius Heil was a controversial governor, therefore the Progressive nomination in 1940 was briskly contested and drew more votes than the Democratic primary. The Progressive candidate, Orland Loomis, ran a close second to Heil and more than doubled the vote of the Democratic contender, a ghost from the past, Francis McGovern. Loomis won in 1942 but died before taking office. His lieutenant-governor, Walter Goodland, an independent Republican in the old progressive tradition, assumed the office. Loomis's abortive victory was the end of the line for the Progressive party.

Daniel Hoan, as observed earlier, had become disillusioned with his Socialist support before his defeat in 1940, after twenty-six years as Milwaukee's Socialist mayor. He turned temporarily to the Progressives, then led what became a general exodus. Hoan ran for governor as a Democrat in 1944—not yet a nomination to be prized, judging from the primary vote. But Hoan, a dynamic political personality, turned the contest with the popular Governor Goodland into a real race. Although Walter Goodland in November 1944 was approaching his eighty-second birthday, his age was not the liability one would expect. It simply enhanced his natural attitude of crusty independence which accorded well with the unusual circumstances of his original elevation to the governorship. Wisconsin politicians cultivate an attitude of independence with respect to the regular party organization—a legacy of La Follette's 1906 primary law. The same spirit allowed voters to accept the longtime Socialist, Dan Hoan, as a bona fide New Deal Democrat at the top of the ticket.

Hoan's role was that of Pied Piper for the Democrats among former Socialists and Progressives seeking a new political allegiance. He proposed to revamp the Democratic party in Wisconsin into the liberal party. His contribution was his hold upon the labor vote on the Lakeshore and his willingness to campaign for the liberal farm vote. This he sought in the northwestern part of the state among the Scandinavian farmers who had been mainstays of the La Follettes. He did not reap the harvest but he prepared the ground.

The election of 1946 is looked upon as the crucial one in post-World War II Wisconsin politics. Robert M. La Follette, Jr., who had squeezed out a victory in 1940 as a Progressive, had arrived at a political crossroads. Could he do anything with the moribund Progressive party, or was it the political graveyard it appeared to be? Should he accept the blandishments of Dan Hoan and stand as a Democrat? Or did his instincts rightly tell him to return to his father's Republican allegiance and wrest the party from the firm grasp of its stalwart heirs? He chose the latter course.

The gamble and the magic of the La Follette name almost paid off, but Bob was not the politician his father was, nor did he have the energy of his younger brother. He disliked campaigning and regularly took refuge in his work in the Senate, where he was an important member. Comic relief was provided by the Republican stalwarts, under the leadership of state chairman Thomas Coleman, a Madison banker. They rammed through a law to prevent La Follette from changing his political allegiance on a moment's notice, but Governor Goodland vetoed it. The governor was solemnly informed that he was tampering with his own political future. Although not given to hilarity, the governor did see some humor in this threat to a man of eighty-four. He went on to win a third term and, having shown them, died the following March.

Bob La Follette compounded his own difficulties. He endorsed Ralph Immel—who fit the La Follette pattern as a loyal subordinate—in the primary race against Goodland for the governorship. It was a gratuitous slap at Goodland, for many La Follette supporters had an attachment to "Old Woof Woof," as Goodland was affectionately known. Then La Follette, pleading urgent Senate business, ignored the canvass. The stalwarts were desperate to defeat La Follette's invasion of their preserve, but dubious about their self-anointed candidate, Joseph R. McCarthy. McCarthy's career has been generously covered as a result of his subsequent notoriety, but suffice it to say that he was an unknown quantity in Wisconsin politics.

The Democrats, displaying a political slyness that did them little credit in the light of subsequent events, decided that McCarthy would be much preferable to La Follette as an opponent in the November election. Having no very serious contests at the top of their ticket, an undetermined number took advantage of Wisconsin's primary law to vote in the Republican primary for McCarthy. This election has been analyzed ad nauseam, even weighing the Communist vote, but the upshot was that La Follette was retired from the Senate seat held by the family since 1905. In the end, the election of Joseph R. McCarthy as Republican senator from the State of Wisconsin was a boon to the struggling Democratic Party.

The Democrats received an infusion of progressive blood after the official demise of the Progressive party in 1946. But there was an element of uncertainty in the departures after the funeral. It depended upon where home was. A Progessive in Dane County knew where to go—to Democratic headquarters. In a majority of Wisconsin counties, however, it was not so simple. Party headquarters, in any meaningful sense, meant the Republican party, which had been Old Bob's political home.

The Democrats began a slow reconstruction from bases in the urban-industrial counties on the Lake and the second most populous county, Dane, with its growing city of Madison containing the Capitol and university. Dan Hoan helped to bring the mass labor votes of the Roosevelt New Deal into the party. Madison provided much of the leadership in terms of both liberal ideology and political technology. The university was of only secondary significance in this. Professors tend to be long on political conscience but shun canvassing a block. Their wives are better at this.

The Wisconsin Democratic party shows its disparate origins. The labor vote of Milwaukee is a dependable source of support for Democratic incumbents, while Madison Democrats bleed visibly for lost causes: Adlai Stevenson, the Hubert Humphrey of 1960, Eugene McCarthy in 1968, and George McGovern in 1972.

Many men and women took part in the building of the new Democratic coalition. Due credit can be given to only a few. First should come Senator Joseph R. McCarthy, Republican, who discovered the menace of domestic Communism in 1950 and embarked upon a course of political disruption which ended with his official censure by his senatorial colleagues in 1954, after which he lost the limelight and died before facing a campaign for reelection in 1958. Joe McCarthy's career rightly belongs to the national politics of the era, except insofar as he provided a rallying cry for Wisconsin's Democrats. Wisconsin's Republican leadership would not repudiate McCarthy. The Democrats found him an issue upon which they could agree, helping to submerge their own substantial differences.

William Proxmire, a carpetbagger in the eyes of many of his fellow politicians, moved to Wisconsin from neighboring Illinois in 1949 with a view to building a political career. He built it upon the party foundations established by others who had seized control from the Bourbons and, through the Democratic Organizing Committee, had begun to give the party a broad, liberal base. Proxmire's contribution was to extend the geographic boundaries of the party, which was only sketchily represented in most counties outside of southeast Wisconsin. A tireless campaigner, he ran unsuccessfully for governor three times, and built from a discouraging 37 percent against Republican Walter J. Kohler in 1952, to 49 percent against the same opponent in 1954, and 48 percent against Vernon Thomson in 1956. Proxmire's zeal carried him into courthouse squares where a Democratic gubernatorial candidate had not been seen within the memory of most voters. Young attorneys, raised in the La Follette progressive persuasion, were emboldened by this example to contest offices in local elections and give Democrats a base where Republicans had formerly run uncontested. Democrats held only 75 of the 542 courthouse elective posts in 1954 and contested none, or only 1, in 23 counties. In 1954, they held office in only 17. By 1958 they were contesting most courthouse and legislative seats, and won courthouse offices in 38 counties. There were many sacrificial goats, but sometimes surprising victories.

Proxmire, much like La Follette a half-century earlier, was in danger of becoming a perennial also-ran whom voters would cease to take seriously. He saved the situation by a gratifying six-to-four win over Walter J. Kohler for the United States Senate seat vacated in 1957 by the death of Joseph R. McCarthy. The question, which has since been answered affirmatively, was whether the Democrats had succeeded in building a state-wide base for the party. Gaylord Nelson won the governorship in 1958 and stepped from there to the United States Senate in 1962. Another Democrat with a progressive family background, John Reynolds, succeeded him in the governorship. The Republicans returned to control with Governor Warren Knowles (1965–71), but the Democrats held a majority in the assembly in 1965 for only the second time since the 1930s. This is an indication of the persistence of Republican dominance in rural and small-town Wisconsin. Statewide races are more evenly contested, with much depending upon national trends and political personalities with statewide recognition.

The postwar Democratic party is clearly an amalgam of the Progressive party of 1934–46 and the New Deal Democrats. It continues the progressive tradition of open primaries in which candidates and factions frequently exhaust their purses and tempers before the general election contests with the Republicans. The Republicans, by contrast, continue a policy of endorsement through the voluntary party organization, which in both parties is more important than the official party organization defined in La Follette's primary law. Elections and candidacies are clearly more issue-oriented than formerly, although religious affiliation, which has largely subsumed ethnic differences in American politics, plays a prominent role on occasion. That the postwar Democratic party is a new coalition is illustrated by the fact that of fifteen top Democratic counties, only four had been Democratic strongholds before 1946. Four of the leading Republican counties had been Democratic before.

The Democrats depended heavily upon organized labor for financing, volunteer workers, and the mechanics of campaigning in the early years of the party's metamorphosis. The advent of television and other factors escalated the costs of campaigning an estimated four times between 1950 and 1964. The Republicans can count upon a larger share of their budget from large donors, although the Democrats can expect their share to rise with continuing success at the polls. Political campaign contributions, especially large ones, are not always ideologically motivated. Through various organizational devices, both parties have achieved a support base that includes a larger number of small individual contributions than is usual in state politics. The result has been to minimize labor's role in Democratic politics more effectively than could Republican efforts, such as the 1955 Catlin Act, to control labor organization contributions.

The Wisconsin voter is a composite of independence, indifference, ignorance, and sophistication. Voters readily cross party lines to enjoy themselves in the primary, a habit which offers some strange statistics for national pundits. The presidential primary of 1964 was an example of this, when George C. Wallace, the southern segregationist, drew nearly 34 percent of the Democratic vote. Dire conclusions were drawn. Those who knew Wisconsin politics saw this in another light. Wallace's opponent was the incumbent governor, John Reynolds, standing in for the incumbent president, Lyndon B. Johnson. There was no contest in the Republican primary. Voters took the occasion to express an opinion about John Reynolds, who had built a political career upon opposition to the sales tax and then, responsibly to be sure, signed a bill increasing the tax. Wallace drew only a token vote in 1968.

Indifference is endemic with the American voter. After many pages extolling the political awareness of the Wisconsin voter under the tutelage of La Follette and Victor Berger, it is embarrassing to discover that the neighboring states of Illinois, Minnesota, and Iowa, on the average, turn out a higher percentage of voters. Milwaukee ranked a low twenty-sixth among thirty-nine major cities in this regard in 1962, and about 10 percent below the state average. It is reflex Democrats who stay at home. As for ignorance, with campaign costs rising spectacularly, it was natural that party officials should spend some of the money to find out what they were buying. It came as a shock to find that the successful Republican candidate, Warren Knowles, was recognized by name by only 44 percent of the voters in 1964. A prominent state senator since 1941 and three times lieutenant-governor, it was not because he hid his light under a bushel basket.

It may be agreed that Wisconsin voters have used the primary to assert a sturdy independence. They do not appreciate seeming to be managed. The Republicans are now in the process of questioning the wisdom of preprimary endorsement, which has occasionally backfired. Joseph McCarthy exploited this with a mixture of defiance and parochialism— "It's good to be back in the United States again," meaning away from the East Coast. It was about as close as he came to La Follette's style and constituency. He was one of many who cultivated the image of the beleaguered candidate rejected by the party organization, a rewarding stance in many cases, especially in a state which offers so little in the way of patronage and regimented organization men.

Wisconsin state government today is the inheritor of a proud tradition. Whether it is described vaguely as the Wisconsin Idea or as the legacy of the elder La Follette, it defines a level of expectation in terms of honesty, competence, humane motivation, and service that is a cut or two above the average among the states. Wisconsin citizens and civil servants are aware of this tradition and the position of leadership which the state has come to think its due in terms of innovative legislation and efficient, but not officious, administration. It sometimes falls short of these expectations, but the belief has had its value for a society which tends to conservatism and a provincial outlook.

One might argue that a number of factors contribute to a spirit of accommodation among competing interests, a concern for the environment, and a readiness to accept the aims of the "service state." Some argue that Catholic theology—and Wisconsin is one of the most Catholic of states —is more tolerant of human error and more readily accepts a broad social service role for the state. Another suggestion is that the Norwegians in particular, and the Germans, were conditioned to the social service state, either directly or by a lively interest in the reforms undertaken in their homelands after they left. It has been noted that Wisconsin has more people involved in agriculture than the average, with the consequence that urban-rural conflicts are more subject to accommodation. Despite the weight of Milwaukee's population, it is not as massive compared with the state's total population as are neighboring Chicago, Minneapolis-St. Paul, and Detroit. Many urban Wisconsinites live in medium-sized cities of under 50,000 where citizens still pay some deference to the dairy cow. Finally, to see Illinois is to appreciate that Wisconsin has unique environmental values worth preserving.

There is not space for an extensive review of Wisconsin's state government. Anyone interested may profit by spending some time with a recent issue of the *Wisconsin Blue Book*. The legislature has lately been tampering so industriously with the organizational structure of the executive and administrative machinery of the state, as well as with local government, that any specific description will soon be outdated. This is a measure of recent growth in budgets, personnel, and responsibilities. Two areas of responsibility, which absorb a huge share of state and local budgets, are education and social welfare. Both have recently been reorganized. Evidence for this concern with the definition of programs and their administration may be readily grasped by comparing figures. The state spent, from all funds, a total of $301,252,320.70 in fiscal 1949–50, $575,346,256.47 in fiscal 1958–59, and $1,882,473,889.00 in 1968–69. The multiples have been escalating.

Wisconsin government may be unique in some other respects. It continues to operate under a constitution written in 1847, the oldest among the states. While considerably amended, this has been done with moderation. Compared to most state constitutions it is brief and general in tone, and the legislature has considerable power. Like the state, county governments have a weak executive structure in theory, except for Milwaukee and Dane counties, which have elected county executives but retain boards of supervisors. Cities have generally followed the weak executive precedent. There has been continuous pressure for home rule for both counties and cities, and it has been achieved to a large degree in practice if not in name. There is wide latitude for local discretion, with the state bureaucracy depending upon persuasion, expert service, and a definition of standards to accomplish state policies. Wisconsin is unusual with respect to the number of governmental tasks carried out at the local level.

Wisconsin derived a tradition from its role as an innovator among the states, a jealous regard for doing things the Wisconsin way which has resulted in conflict with the federal government over methods and standards. But this spirit of independence was paid for as federal aid proliferated and Wisconsin was slow to seek its share. The advantage was all with the federal government, and Wisconsin is settling into a pattern of conformity in order to share in the benefits. More and more, Wisconsin has come to reflect national norms while insisting upon a uniqueness which like our ethnic differences becomes a less active part of our daily lives.

Selected Bibliography

Adamany, David. "The 1960 Election in Wisconsin." Master's thesis, University of Wisconsin, 1963. Extension of Epstein's *Politics in Wisconsin.*
———. *Financing Politics: Recent Wisconsin Elections.* Madison, 1969. Informed account by a participant.

Blachman, William L., "The Kohler Strike: A Case Study in Collective Bargaining." Ph.D. dissertation, University of Wisconsin, 1963. More like non-bargaining.

Campbell, W. J. *History of the Republican Party in Wisconsin.* Oshkosh, 1942. Formation of the voluntary party organization.

Coady, Sharon. "The Wisconsin Press and Joseph McCarthy: A Case Study." Master's thesis, University of Wisconsin, 1965. McCarthy used the press.

Donoghue, James R. "The Local Government System of Wisconsin." *Wisconsin Blue Book,* 1968.

Epstein, Leon. *Politics in Wisconsin.* Madison, 1958. Good background and analysis.

Gavett, Thomas W. *Development of the Labor Movement in Milwaukee.* Madison, 1965. Brings it up to 1959.

Gore, Leroy. *Joe Must Go.* New York, 1954. Leader of a recall movement against McCarthy.

Governor's Commission on Human Rights. *Handbook on Wisconsin Indians.* Compiled by Joyce M. Erdman. Madison, 1966.

———. *The Migrant Labor Problem in Wisconsin.* Madison, 1962. The other minorities.

Griffith, Robert W., Jr. *The Politics of Fear: Joseph R. McCarthy and the Senate.* Lexington, Ky., 1971. Good coverage on the early McCarthy and his role in Wisconsin politics.

———. "The General and the Senator: Republican Politics and the 1952 Campaign in Wisconsin." *Wisconsin Magazine of History* 54:23–29 (Autumn 1970). Eisenhower and McCarthy: The insult to General Marshall.

Haferbecker, Gordon M. *Wisconsin Labor Laws.* Madison, 1958. The Wisconsin Employment Peace Act of 1939 and its administration.

Haney, Richard Carlton. "A History of the Democratic Party of Wisconsin since World War II." Ph.D. dissertation, University of Wisconsin, 1969. Democratic activist writes of his party.

Hendra, Jane Catherine. "The 1960 Democratic Campaign in Wisconsin." Master's thesis, University of Wisconsin, 1961. The view from state headquarters.

Herberg, Will. *Protestant, Catholic, Jew.* New York: Anchor Paperbacks, 1960. Ethnicity in politics is now expressed largely by religious affiliation.

Johnson, Roger T. *Robert M. La Follette, Jr., and the Decline of the Progressive Party in Wisconsin.* Madison, 1964. Not the politician his father was.

Marshall, Douglas G. "Nationality in the Rural Midwest." In Arnold M. Rose, ed., *Race Prejudice and Discrimination: Readings in Intergroup Relations in the United States.* New York, 1951. Wild Rose, Waushara County.

Milwaukee Journal. Series on recreational land use. April 12, 19, 26, May 3, 10, 1970. Hazards of "improvement" of land use.

O'Brien, Michael James. "Senator Joseph McCarthy and Wisconsin, 1946–1957." Ph.D. dissertation, University of Wisconsin, 1970. McCarthy's impact on state politics.

Otto, Luther B. "Catholic and Lutheran Political Cultures in Medium-Sized

Wisconsin Cities." Master's thesis, University of Wisconsin, 1963. A lot of theory and some interesting questionnaires.

Ozanne, Robert W. "The Effects of Communist Leadership on American Trade Unions." Ph.D. dissertation, University of Wisconsin, 1954. Ideology is hard to sell to American labor.

Scoble, Harry M., and Leon D. Epstein. "Religion and Wisconsin Voting in 1960." In Lawrence H. Fuchs, ed., *American Ethnic Politics.* New York, 1968. The nature of religion-based voting.

Scovronick, Nathan B. "The Wisconsin School Bus Campaign of 1946." Master's thesis, University of Wisconsin, 1947. The referendum and the press.

Shannon, David A. "Was McCarthy a Political Heir of LaFollette?" *Wisconsin Magazine of History* 45:3–9 (Autumn 1961). No.!

Shannon, William V. *The American Irish.* 2d ed., rev. New York, 1966. Has sketch of Joe McCarthy.

Slocum, Walter Lucius. "Ethnic Stocks as Cultural Types in Rural Wisconsin." Ph.D. dissertation, University of Wisconsin, 1940. The distinctions hold, he says.

Steinke, John. "The Rise of McCarthyism." Master's thesis, University of Wisconsin, 1960. On the 1946 primary.

Uphoff, W. H. *Kohler on Strike: Thirty Years of Conflict.* Boston, 1966. A study in paternalism and its failure.

Valentine, John. "A Study in Institutional Americanization: The Assimilative History of the Italian-American Community of Madison, Wisconsin." Master's thesis, University of Wisconsin, 1967. Outsiders have no conception of the distinctions made within an ethnic group.

Vinyard, Clarence Dale. "Pre-primary Endorsement in Wisconsin." Master's thesis, University of Wisconsin, 1958. Adjustment to the La Follette primary.

White, Theodore. *The Marking of the President, 1960.* New York, 1961. Interesting chapters on the Wisconsin primary.

Witte, Edwin E. "Labor in Wisconsin." *Wisconsin Magazine of History* 35: 83–86, 137–42 (Winter 1951). Useful review.

REFERENCE
MATTER

APPENDIX 1
Governors and Elections

Governors and Major Opponents	General Election	Term
Territorial		
Henry Dodge, *Dem.*	Appointed	July 1836–Oct. 1841
James D. Doty, *Whig*	"	Oct. 1841–Sept. 1844
Nathaniel P. Tallmadge, *Dem.*	"	Sept. 1844–May 1845
Henry Dodge, *Dem.*	"	May 1845–June 1848
State		
Nelson Dewey, *Dem.*	19,538	June 1848–Jan. 1850
John H. Tweedy, *Whig*	14,449	
Nelson Dewey, *Dem.*	16,649	Jan. 1850–Jan. 1852
Alexander L. Collins, *Whig*	11,317	
Leonard J. Farwell, *Whig*	22,319	Jan. 1852–Jan. 1854
Don A. J. Upham, *Dem.*	21,812	
William A. Barstow, *Dem.*	30,405	Jan. 1854–Mar. 1856
Edward D. Holton, *Free Soil*	21,886	
Arthur MacArthur, *Dem.*	Lt. Gov.	Mar. 1856–Mar. 1856*
Coles Bashford, *Rep.*	36,198	Mar. 1856–Jan. 1858*
William A. Barstow, *Dem.*	36,355	
Alexander W. Randall, *Rep.*	44,693	Jan. 1858–Jan. 1860
James B. Cross, *Dem.*	44,239	
Alexander W. Randall, *Rep.*	59,999	Jan. 1860–Jan. 1862
Harrison C. Hobart, *Dem.*	52,539	

* The Supreme Court set aside Barstow's certificate of election and awarded the 1855 election to Bashford. MacArthur, the lieutenant governor, served for four days.

Governors and Major Opponents	General Election	Term
Louis P. Harvey, *Rep.*	53,777	Jan. 1862–Died Apr. 1862
Benjamin Ferguson, *Dem.*	45,456	
Edward P. Salomon, *Rep.*	Lt. Gov.	Apr. 1862–Jan. 1864
James T. Lewis, *Rep.*	72,717	Jan. 1864–Jan. 1866
Henry L. Palmer, *Dem.*	49,053	
Lucius Fairchild, *Rep.*	58,332	Jan. 1866–Jan. 1868
Harrison C. Hobard, *Dem.*	48,330	
Lucius Fairchild, *Rep.*	73,637	Jan. 1868–Jan. 1870
J. J. Tallmadge, *Dem.*	68,873	
Lucius Fairchild, *Rep.*	69,502	Jan. 1870–Jan. 1872
C. D. Robinson, *Dem.*	61,239	
C. C. Washburn, *Rep.*	78,301	Jan. 1872–Jan. 1874
James R. Doolittle, *Dem.*	68,910	
William R. Taylor, *Dem.*	81,599	Jan. 1874–Jan. 1876
C. C. Washburn, *Rep.*	66,224	
Harrison Ludington, *Rep.*	85,155	Jan. 1876–Jan. 1878
William R. Taylor, *Dem.*	84,314	
William E. Smith, *Rep.*	78,759	Jan. 1878–Jan. 1880
James A. Mallory, *Dem.*	70,486	
Edward P. Allis, *Greenback*	26,216	
William E. Smith, *Rep.*	100,535	Jan. 1880–Jan. 1882
James G. Jenkins, *Dem.*	75,030	
Reuben May, *Greenback*	12,996	
Jeremiah M. Rusk, *Rep.*	81,754	Jan. 1882–Jan. 1885*
Nicholas D. Fratt, *Dem.*	69,797	
T. D. Kanouse, *Prohibition*	13,225	
Edward P. Allis, *Greenback*	7,002	
Jeremiah M. Rusk, *Rep.*	163,214	Jan. 1885–Jan. 1887
Nicholas D. Fratt, *Dem.*	143,945	
Samuel D. Hastings, *Prohibition*	8,545	
Jeremiah M. Rusk, *Rep.*	133,247	Jan. 1887–Jan. 1889
Gilbert M. Woodward, *Dem.*	114,529	
John Cochrane, *Peoples*	21,467	
John M. Olin, *Prohibition*	17,089	
William D. Hoard, *Rep.*	175,696	Jan. 1889–Jan. 1891

* The constitution was amended in 1881 to change the election of state officers and the legislature to the even years, and regular sessions were changed from annual to biennial.

Governors and Major Opponents	General Election	Term
James Morgan, *Dem.*	155,423	
E. Y. Durant, *Prohibition*	14,373	
David F. Powell, *Labor*	9,196	
George W. Peck, *Dem.*	160,388	Jan. 1891–Jan. 1893
William D. Hoard, *Rep.*	132,068	
George W. Peck, *Dem.*	178,095	Jan. 1893–Jan. 1895
John C. Spooner, *Rep.*	170,497	
William H. Upham, *Rep.*	196,150	Jan. 1895–Jan. 1897
George W. Peck, *Dem.*	142,250	
David F. Powell, *Peoples*	25,604	
Edward Scofield, *Rep.*	264,981	Jan. 1897–Jan. 1899
Willis C. Silverthorn, *Dem.*	169,257	
Edward Scofield, *Rep.*	173,137	Jan. 1899–Jan. 1901
Hiram W. Sawyer, *Dem.*	135,353	
Robert M. La Follette, *Rep.*	264,419	Jan. 1901–Jan. 1903
Louis G. Bomrich, *Dem.*	160,674	
Robert M. La Follette, *Rep.*	193,417	Jan. 1903–Jan. 1905
Davis S. Rose, *Dem.*	145,818	
Emil Seidel, *Soc. Dem.*	15,970	
Robert M. La Follette, *Rep.*	227,253	Jan. 1905–Jan. 1906
George W. Peck, *Dem.*	173,301	
William A. Arnold, *Soc. Dem.*	24,857	
James O. Davidson, *Rep.*	183,558	Jan. 1906–Jan. 1909*
John A. Aylward, *Dem.*	103,311	
Winfield R. Gaylord, *Soc. Dem.*	24,437	
James O. Davidson, *Rep.*	242,935	Jan. 1909–Jan. 1911
John A. Aylward, *Dem.*	165,977	
Harvey D. Brown, *Soc. Dem.*	28,583	
Francis E. McGovern, *Rep.*	161,619	Jan. 1911–Jan. 1913
Adolph J. Schmitz, *Dem.*	110,442	
William A. Jacobs, *Soc. Dem.*	39,539	
Francis E. McGovern, *Rep.*	179,360	Jan. 1913–Jan. 1915
John C. Karel, *Dem.*	167,316	
Emanuel L. Philipp, *Rep.*	140,787	Jan. 1915–Jan. 1917
John C. Karel, *Dem.*	119,509	
John J. Blaine, *Ind.*	32,560	

* Robert M. La Follette resigned in Jan. 1906 to go to the Senate. Lieutenant Governor James O. Davidson completed the term.

Governors and Major Opponents	General Election	Term
Oscar Ameringer, *Soc. Dem.*	25,917	
Emanuel L. Philipp, *Rep.*	229,889	Jan. 1917–Jan. 1919
Burt Williams, *Dem.*	164,555	
Rae Weaver, *Soc.*	30,649	
Emanuel L. Philipp, *Rep.*	155,799	Jan. 1919–Jan. 1921
Henry A. Moehlenpah, *Dem.*	112,576	
Emil Seidel, *Soc.*	57,523	
John J. Blaine, *Rep.*	366,247	Jan. 1921–Jan. 1923
Robert McCoy, *Dem*	247,746	
William Coleman, *Soc*	71,126	
John J. Blaine, *Rep.*	367,929	Jan. 1923–Jan. 1925
Arthur A. Bentley, *Dem.*	51,061	
Louis A. Arnold, *Soc.*	39,570	
John J. Blaine, *Rep.*	412,255	Jan. 1925–Jan. 1927
Martin L. Lueck, *Dem.*	317,550	
William F. Quick, *Soc.*	45,268	
Fred R. Zimmerman, *Rep.*	350,927	Jan. 1927–Jan. 1929
Charles B. Perry, *Ind.*	76,507	
Virgil H. Cady, *Dem.*	72,627	
Herman O. Kent, *Soc.*	40,293	
Walter J. Kohler, *Rep.*	547,738	Jan. 1929–Jan. 1931
Albert G. Schmedeman, *Dem.*	394,368	
Otto R. Hauser, *Soc.*	36,924	
Philip F. La Follette, *Rep.*	392,958	Jan. 1931–Jan. 1933
Charles E. Hammersley, *Dem.*	170,020	
Frank B. Metcalfe, *Soc.*	25,607	
Albert G. Schmedeman, *Dem.*	590,114	Jan. 1933–Jan. 1935
Walter J. Kohler, *Rep.*	470,805	
Frank B. Metcalfe, *Soc.*	56,965	
Philip F. La Follette, *Prog.*	373,093	Jan. 1935–Jan. 1937
Albert G. Schmedeman, *Dem.*	359,467	
Howard T. Greene, *Rep.*	172,980	
Philip F. La Follette, *Prog.*	573,724	Jan. 1937–Jan. 1939
Alexander Wiley, *Rep.*	363,973	
Martin L. Lueck, *Dem.*	268,530	
Julius P Heil, *Rep.*	543,675	Jan. 1939–Jan. 1941
Philip F. La Follette, *Prog.*	353,381	
Henry Bolens, *Dem.*	78,446	
Julius P. Heil, *Rep.*	558,678	Jan. 1941–Jan. 1943
Orland S. Loomis, *Prog.*	546,436	
Francis E. McGovern, *Dem.*	264,985	

Governors and Major Opponents	General Election	Term
Orland S. Loomis, *Prog.*	397,664	Died before taking office
Julius P. Heil, *Rep.*	291,945	
William C. Sullivan, *Dem.*	98,153	
Walter S. Goodland, *Rep.*	Lt. Gov.	Jan. 1943–Jan. 1945. Served Loomis' term
Walter S. Goodland, *Rep.*	697,740	Jan. 1945–Jan. 1947
Daniel W. Hoan, *Dem.*	536,357	
Alex O. Benz, *Prog.*	76,028	
Walter S. Goodland, *Rep.*	621,970	Jan. 1947–Died Mar. 1947
Daniel W. Hoan, *Dem.*	406,499	
Oscar Rennebohm, *Rep.*	Lt. Gov.	Mar. 1947–Jan. 1949 Completed Goodland's term
Oscar Rennebohm, *Rep.*	684,839	Jan. 1949–Jan. 1951
Carl Thompson, *Dem.*	558,497	
Walter J. Kohler, Jr., *Rep.*	605,649	Jan. 1951–Jan. 1953
Carl Thompson, *Dem.*	525,319	
Walter J. Kohler, Jr., *Rep.*	1,009,171	Jan. 1953–Jan. 1955
William Proxmire, *Dem.*	601,844	
Walter J. Kohler, Jr., *Rep.*	596,158	Jan. 1955–Jan. 1957
William Proxmire, *Dem.*	560,747	
Vernon W. Thomson, *Rep.*	808,273	Jan. 1957–Jan. 1959
William Proxmire, *Dem.*	749,421	
Gaylord A. Nelson, *Dem.*	644,296	Jan. 1959–Jan. 1961
Vernon W. Thomson, *Rep.*	556,391	
Gaylord A. Nelson, *Dem.*	890,868	Jan. 1961–Jan. 1963
Philip G. Kuehn, *Rep.*	837,123	
John W. Reynolds, *Dem.*	637,491	Jan. 1963–Jan. 1965
Philip G. Kuehn, *Rep.*	625,536	
Warren P. Knowles, *Rep.*	856,779	Jan. 1965–Jan. 1967
John W. Reynolds, *Dem.*	837,901	
Warren P. Knowles, *Rep.*	626,041	Jan. 1967–Jan. 1969
Patrick J. Lucey, *Dem.*	539,258	
Warren P. Knowles, *Rep.*	893,463	Jan. 1969–Jan. 1971
Bronson C. La Follette *Dem.*	791,100	
Patrick J. Lucey, *Dem.*	728,403	Jan. 1971—
Jack B. Olson, *Rep.*	602,617	

Source: *Wisconsin Blue Book*, 1970, pp. 682–83; 1971, p. 308. The returns from 1848 through 1960 were corrected against the canvass reports and differ in some places from returns published in Blue Books before 1962.

APPENDIX 2
Wisconsin Votes in
Presidential Elections

Year	Candidates	Popular Vote	Percent	Electoral Vote
1848	Lewis Cass, *Dem.*	15,001	38.3	4
	Zachary Taylor,* *Whig*	13,747	35.1	
	Martin Van Buren, *Free Soil*	10,418	26.6	
1852	Franklin Pierce,* *Dem.*	33,658	52.0	5
	Winfield Scott, *Whig*	22,210	34.4	
	John P. Hale, *Free Dem.*	8,814	13.6	
1856	John C. Fremont, *Rep.*	66,090	55.3	5
	James Buchanan,* *Dem.*	52,843	44.2	
	Millard Fillmore, *American*	579	.5	
1860	Abraham Lincoln,* *Rep.*	86,113	56.6	5
	Stephen A. Douglas, *Dem.*	65,021	42.7	
	Other	1,049	.7	
1864	Abraham Lincoln, *Rep.**	83,458	55.9	8
	George B. McClellan, *Dem.*	65,884	44.1	
1868	Ulysses S. Grant, *Rep.**	108,857	56.2	8
	Horatio Seymour, *Dem.*	84,707	43.3	
1872	Ulysses S. Grant, *Rep.**	104,994	54.6	10
	Horace Greeley, *Dem. & Lib.*	86,477	45.0	
	Other	834	.4	
1876	Rutherford B. Hayes, *Rep.**	130,668	51.0	10
	Samuel J. Tilden, *Dem.*	123,927	48.4	
	Other	1,536	.6	

* Candidates marked with asterisk were winners in the national election.

Year	Candidates	Popular Vote	Percent	Electoral Vote
1880	James A. Garfield, *Rep.**	144,398	54.1	10
	Winfield S. Hancock, *Dem.*	114,644	42.9	
	James B. Weaver, *Greenback*	7,986	3.0	
1884	James G. Blaine, *Rep.*	161,157	50.4	11
	Grover Cleveland, *Dem.**	146,477	45.8	
	Other	12,254	3.8	
1888	Benjamin Harrison, *Rep.**	176,553	49.7	11
	Grover Cleveland, *Dem.*	155,232	43.7	
	Other	22,829	6.6	
1892	Grover Cleveland, *Dem.**	177,325	47.7	12
	Benjamin Harrison, *Rep.*	171,101	46.0	
	Other	23,155	6.3	
1896	William McKinley, *Rep.**	268,135	59.93	12
	William J. Bryan, *Dem.*	165,523	36.99	
	Other	13,751	3.08	
1900	William McKinley, *Rep.**	265,760	60.06	12
	William J. Bryan, *Dem.*	159,163	35.97	
	Other	17,678	3.96	
1904	Theodore Roosevelt, *Rep.**	280,164	63.23	13
	Alton B. Parker, *Dem.*	124,107	28.01	
	Eugene V. Debs, *Soc. Dem.*	28,220	6.37	
	Other	10,523	2.37	
1908	William H. Taft, *Rep.**	247,747	54.51	13
	William J. Bryan, *Dem.*	166,632	36.67	
	Eugene V. Debs, *Soc. Dem.*	28,164	6.11	
	Other	11,878	2.61	
1912	Woodrow Wilson, *Dem.**	164,230	41.07	13
	William H. Taft, *Rep.*	130,596	32.65	
	Theodore Roosevelt, *Prog.*	62,448	15.61	
	Eugene V. Debs, *Soc. Dem.*	33,476	8.37	
	Other	9,216	2.26	
1916	Charles E. Hughes, *Rep.*	220,822	49.38	13
	Woodrow Wilson, *Dem.**	191,363	42.79	
	Allan Benson, *Soc.*	27,631	6.11	
	J. Frank Hanly, *Prohibition*	7,318	1.63	
1920	Warren G. Harding, *Rep.**	498,576	71.09	13
	James M. Cox, *Dem.*	113,422	16.18	
	Eugene V. Debs, *Soc.*	80,635	11.5	
	Aaron S. Watkins, *Prohibition*	8,647	1.23	
1924	Robert M. La Follette, *Prog.*	453,678	54.44	13

Year	Candidates	Popular Vote	Percent	Electoral Vote
	Calvin Coolidge, *Rep.**	311,614	37.39	
	John W. Davis, *Dem.*	68,096	8.17	
1928	Herbert Hoover, *Rep.**	544,205	53.1	13
	Alfred E. Smith, *Dem.*	450,259	44.23	
	Norman Thomas, *Soc.*	18,213	1.79	
	Other	4,154	.41	
1932	Franklin D. Roosevelt, *Dem.**	707,410	63.5	12
	Herbert Hoover, *Rep.*	347,741	31.1	
	Norman Thomas, *Soc.*	53,379	4.8	
	Other	6,278	.58	
1936	Franklin D. Roosevelt, *Dem.**	802,984	63.8	12
	Alfred M. Landon, *Rep.*	380,828	30.3	
	William Lemke, *Union*	60,297	4.77	
	Norman Thomas, *Soc.*	10,626	.84	
	Other	3,825	.29	
1940	Franklin D. Roosevelt, *Dem.**	704,821	50.14	12
	Wendell Willkie, *Rep.*	679,206	48.32	
	Norman Thomas, *Soc.*	15,071	1.07	
	Other	6,424	.45	
1944	Thomas E. Dewey, *Rep.*	674,532	50.37	12
	Franklin D. Roosevelt, *Dem.**	650,413	48.56	
	Other	14,207	1.05	
1948	Harry S. Truman, *Dem.**	647,310	50.69	12
	Thomas E. Dewey, *Rep.*	590,959	46.28	
	Henry Wallace, *People's Prog.*	25,282	1.98	
	Other	13,249	1.03	
1952	Dwight D. Eisenhower, *Rep.**	979,744	60.95	12
	Adlai E. Stevenson, *Dem.*	622,175	38.71	
	Other	5,451	.34	
1956	Dwight D. Eisenhower, *Rep.**	954,854	61.58	12
	Adlai E. Stevenson, *Dem.*	586,768	37.84	
	Other	8,936	.59	
1960	Richard M. Nixon, *Rep.*	895,175	51.77	12
	John F. Kennedy, *Dem.**	830,805	48.05	
	Other	3,102	.18	
1964	Lyndon B. Johnson, *Dem.**	1,050,424	62.09	12
	Barry M. Goldwater, *Rep.*	638,495	37.74	
	Other	2,896	.17	
1968	Richard M. Nixon, *Rep.**	809,997	47.95	12
	Hubert H. Humphrey, *Dem.*	748,804	44.33	

Year	Candidates	Popular Vote	Percent	Electoral Vote
	George C. Wallace, *Ind.*	127,835	7.57	
	Other	2,560	.15	
1972	Richard M. Nixon, *Rep.**	989,430	53.42	11
	George S. McGovern, *Dem.*	810,174	43.74	
	John Schmitz, *American*	47,525	2.57	
	Other	4,868	.27	

Sources: *Wisconsin Blue Book*, 1954, pp. 535–37; 1970, p. 681; 1972 election figures courtesy of Legislative Reference Bureau Information Library.

APPENDIX 3
Population of Wisconsin

Year	Population	Increase	% Increase	Urban	Rural	% Urban
1830	3,245	—	—	—	—	—
1836	11,683	8,438	247.7	—	—	—
1840	30,945	19,262	164.0	—	—	—
1850	305,391	274,446	886.9	28,623	276,768	9.4
1860	775,881	470,490	154.1	111,874	664,007	14.4
1870	1,054,670	278,789	35.9	207,099	847,571	19.6
1880	1,315,497	260,827	24.7	317,204	998,293	24.1
1890	1,693,330	377,833	28.7	562,286	1,131,044	33.2
1900	2,069,042	375,712	22.2	790,213	1,278,829	38.2
1910	2,333,860	264,818	12.8	1,004,320	1,329,540	43.0
1920	2,632,067	298,207	12.8	1,244,858	1,387,209	47.3
1930	2,939,006	306,939	11.7	1,553,843	1,385,163	52.9
1940	3,137,587	198,581	6.7	1,679,144	1,458,443	53.5
1950	3,434,575	296,988	9.5	1,987,888	1,466,687	57.9
1960	3,952,765	517,202	15.1	2,522,179	1,429,598	63.8
1970	4,418,083	465,318	11.8	2,910,418	1,507,313	65.9

Sources: *Wisconsin Blue Book*, 1970, p. 716; 1971, p. 204, for 1970 figures. The federal census has not been consistent in its definition of urban population. In general it has been defined as population centers of 2,500 and over.

APPENDIX 4
One Hundred Years of Wisconsin Cities

(In order of population in 1910)

CITY	1870	1890	1910	1930	1950	1970
Milwaukee	71,440	204,469	373,857	578,249	637,392	717,372
Superior	1,122	11,983	40,384	36,113	35,325	32,237
Racine	9,880	21,014	38,002	67,542	71,193	95,162
Oshkosh	12,663	22,836	33,062	40,108	41,084	53,104
La Crosse	7,785	25,090	30,417	39,614	47,535	51,153
Sheboygan	5,310	16,359	26,398	39,251	42,365	48,484
Madison	9,176	13,426	25,531	57,899	96,056	171,769
Green Bay	4,666	9,069	25,236	37,415	52,735	87,809
Kenosha	4,309	6,532	21,371	50,262	54,368	78,805
Fond du Lac	12,764	12,024	18,797	26,449	29,936	35,515
Eau Claire	2,293	17,415	18,310	26,287	36,058	44,619
Appleton	4,580	11,869	16,773	25,267	34,010	56,377
Wausau	1,349	9,253	16,560	23,758	30,414	32,806
Beloit	4,396	6,315	15,125	23,611	29,590	35,729
Marinette (Incorp. 1887)	—	11,523	14,610	13,734	14,178	12,696
Janesville	8,789	10,836	13,894	21,628	24,899	46,424
Manitowoc	5,168	7,710	13,027	22,963	27,598	33,430
Ashland (Incorp. 1887)	—	9,956	11,594	10,622	10,640	9,615
Chippewa Falls	2,507	8,670	8,893	9,539	11,088	12,351
Watertown	7,550	8,755	8,829	10,613	12,417	15,683

City	1870	1890	1910	1930	1950	1970
Waukesha	2,633	6,321	8,740	17,176	21,233	40,274
Stevens Point	1,810	7,896	8,692	13,623	16,564	23,479
Merrill						
(Incorp. 1883)	—	6,809	8,689	8,458	8,951	9,502
Antigo						
(Incorp. 1885)	—	4,423	7,196	8,610	9,902	9,005
Beaver Dam	3,265	4,222	6,758	9,867	11,867	14,265
West Allis						
(Incorp. 1906)	—	—	6,645	34,671	42,959	71,649
Grand Rapids						
(Wisconsin Rapids)	1,115	1,702	6,521	8,726	13,496	18,587
Baraboo	1,528	4,605	6,324	5,545	7,264	7,931
South Milwaukee						
(Incorp. 1897)	—		6,092	10,706	12,855	23,297
Menasha	2,484	4,581	6,081	9,062	12,385	14,879
Marshfield						
(Incorp. 1883)	—	3,450	5,783	8,778	12,394	15,619
Neenah	2,655	5,083	5,734	9,151	12,437	22,902
Rhinelander						
(Incorp. 1894)	—	2,658	5,637	8,019	8,774	8,218
Oconto	2,655	5,219	5,629	5,030	5,055	4,667
Menominee						
(Incorp. 1882)	—	5,491	5,036	5,595	8,245	11,275

Sources: U.S. Census, 1870, 1880; *Wisconsin Blue Book*. The list is limited to cities of 5,000 population and over in 1910 simply to make a manageable list of some interest, and because the 1910 census was the last that did not have numerous metropolitan suburbs listed as separate urban centers of over 5,000.

GENERAL
BIBLIOGRAPHY

Some useful titles not in the chapter bibliographies

Austin, H. Russell. *The Milwaukee Story: The Making of an American City.* Milwaukee, 1946.

―――. *The Wisconsin Story, The Building of a Vanguard State.* Milwaukee, 1964.

Barton, John Rector. *Rural Artists in Wisconsin.* Madison, 1948.

Bowman, Francis F. *Why Wisconsin.* Madison, 1948.

Clark, James I. *Chronicles of Wisconsin,* Madison, 1955–56.

―――. *Education in Wisconsin.* Madison, 1958.

Davis, M. G., comp. and ed. *A History of Wisconsin Highway Development, 1835–1945.* Madison, 1947.

Donoghue, James. *How Wisconsin Voted, 1848–1960.* Madison, 1962.

Doudna, E. G., *The Making of Our Wisconsin Schools, 1848–1948.* Madison, 1948.

Evjue, William T. "Wisconsin: A State That Glories in Its Past." In Robert S. Allen, ed., *Our Sovereign State.* New York, 1949.

Gara, Larry. *A Short History of Wisconsin.* Madison, 1962.

Gray, James. *Pine, Stream and Prairie: Wisconsin and Minnesota in Profile.* New York, 1945.

Hesseltine, William B. *Pioneer's Mission: The Story of Lyman Copeland Draper,* Madison, 1954.

Hutton, Graham. *Midwest at Noon.* Chicago, 1946.

Lord, Clifford L., and Carl Ubbelohde. *Clio's Servant: The State Historical Society of Wisconsin, 1846–1954.* Madison, 1967.

McAvoy, Thomas T., ed. *The Midwest: Myth or Reality?* South Bend, Ind., 1961.

Marshall, Douglas G. *Wisconsin's Population: Changes and Prospects 1900–1963*. Madison, 1967.

Maxwell, Robert S. *La Follette*. Great Lives Observed Series. Edited by Gerald E. Stearn. Englewood Cliffs, N.J., 1969.

Murray, John J., ed. *The Heritage of the Middle West*. Norman, Okla., 1958.

Nute, Grace Lee. *Lake Superior*. American Lakes Series. Edited by Milo M. Quaife. Indianapolis, 1944.

Nye, Russel B. *Midwestern Progressive Politics: A Historical Study of Its Origins and Development, 1870–1958*. Rev. ed. East Lansing, 1959.

Perrin, Richard W. E. *The Architecture of Wisconsin*. Madison, 1967.

Quaife, Milo M. *Lake Michigan*. American Lakes Series. Edited by Milo M. Quaife. Indianapolis, 1944.

Smith, Alice E. *The History of Wisconsin*, Vol. I: *From Exploration to Statehood*. Madison, 1973. The first of a six-volume series.

Wells, Robert W. *This Is Milwaukee*. New York, 1970.

Wisconsin Academy of Sciences, Arts and Letters. "Wisconsin's Contribution to Humanitarianism and the Good Life." *Transactions* 54, part a, 1965.

WPA Writers' Program. *Wisconsin: A Guide to the Badger State*. American Guide Series. New York, 1941.

INDEX

Photographs are from the Iconographic Collections of the State Historical Society of Wisconsin unless otherwise indicated. A list of negative reference numbers follows.

1. View of the Mississippi River from the Iowa side near Prairie du Chien, 1836. Fort Crawford is on the low ground beyond the islands.

WISCONSIN: A PICTORIAL HISTORY

PRAIRIE DU CHIEN and Fort Crawford were on the military frontier after the War of 1812. It was at Prairie du Chien, the second oldest permanent settlement in Wisconsin, that traders from Montreal, New Orleans, and St. Louis rendezvoused with the Sioux of the Missouri country in the eighteenth century. Having failed to win this strategic point in the war, the Americans won *de facto* jurisdiction at the peace table and built Fort Crawford there.

2. Fort Crawford as it appeared after the rebuilding of 1830; from a painting by Mrs. O. G. Briggs, wife of an officer at the fort.

Pattashgas of the Wisconsin.

EUROPEANS and Americans had a consuming curiosity about the American wilderness, and descriptions of it by artists and literary travelers were popular. At the time that these sketches were made, steamboats called regularly at Galena, Prairie du Chien, and Fort Snelling. The Fox-Wisconsin route was a favorite tour for travelers prepared to rough it.

LA BAYE, Fort Edward Augustus, and Fort Howard sum up the history of Wisconsin's oldest city. Charles de Langlade, of French and Ottawa parentage, led western Indian forces for the French against the British and for the British against the Americans. Pierre Grignon, Sr., principal trader (bourgeois) at Green Bay, married de Langlade's daughter.

In 1829 Caleb Atwood met Peter Rindisbacher, a young Swiss artist, at Prairie du Chien, and obtained these drawings: the son of a Winnebago chief (3, *above, left*), a wading bird, the Pattashagas (4, *above, right*), and a prairie wolf (5, *below*).

Prairie Wolf.

6 (*above*). Fox River settlements, from the window of Fort Howard; from an 1818 map.

7 (*right*). Green Bay and settlements, from the same map.

8 (*above*). Augustin Grignon, who went from fur trading to land holding.

9 (*below*). Rachel Grignon, wife of Augustin Grignon's nephew. Daughter of John Lawe and a Chippewa mother, she often wore Indian dress.

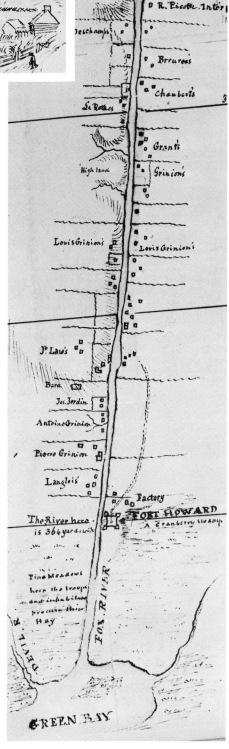

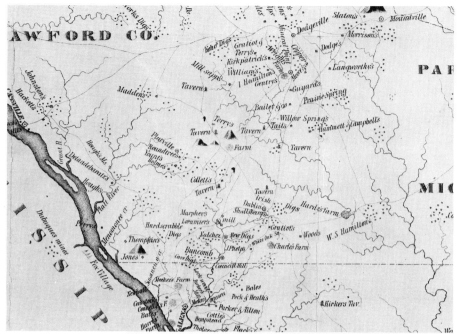

10. The lead country, from a map published by R. W. Chandler of Galena in 1829. Part of the legend reads, "Springs of purest water are found in abundance. The interior is healthy, no local causes for fever exist except near the Mississippi."

THE GALENA lead district was the scene of a true mining rush, unique because the federal government managed it and collected royalties. American settlement in Wisconsin began here at the time when Milwaukee was a minor trading post run by Solomon Juneau.

11. A view of the lead region; from *Harper's Magazine*, 1851.

12, 13. Steel engravings of miners at work.

LAND WARRANTS
For 40 Acres,
Also For
160 Acres,
FOR SALE,
At greatly reduced Prices, for CASH, by

WASHBURNE & WOODMAN.

Mineral Point, May 8.

14. In 1844 Cyrus Woodman teamed up with Cadwallader C. Washburn at Mineral Point to deal in lands and timber.

15. The land to be cried at public auction by President Van Buren's proclamation included Fond du Lac and acreage to the south of there.

BY THE PRESIDENT OF THE UNITED STATES.

In pursuance of law, I, **MARTIN VAN BUREN,** President of the United States of America, do hereby declare and make known, that a public sale will be held at Green Bay, in the Territory of Wisconsin, on Monday, the fourth day of June next, for the disposal of the public lands within the limits of the undermentioned townships and fractional townships, to wit:

North of the base line, and east of the meridian.

Townships fifteen and sixteen, of range thirteen.
Township thirteen, of range fifteen.
Townships twelve, fourteen, and sixteen, and fractional township eighteen, of range sixteen.
Township thirteen, and fractional townships sixteen and seventeen, of range seventeen.
Fractional township twenty-seven, of range twenty-six.

Lands appropriated by law for the use of schools, military, or other purposes, will be excluded from sale.
The sale will be kept open for two weeks, (unless the lands are sooner disposed of,) and no longer; and no private entries of land in the townships so offered will be admitted until after the expiration of the two weeks.

Given under my hand, at the City of Washington, this fifth day of January, Anno Domini 1838.

M. VAN BUREN.

By the President:
JAMES WHITCOMB,
Commissioner of the General Land Office.

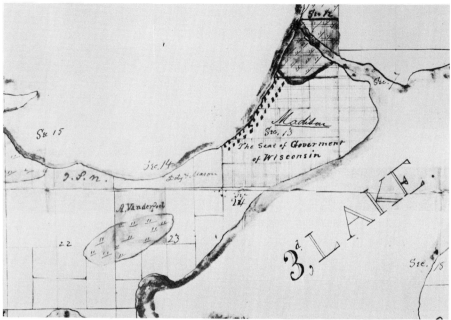

16. A manuscript map from the papers of Aaron Vanderpoel, a partner in James Doty's Madison land speculation.

BECAUSE the pressure for federal land sales began in the lead region, the surveys began there and worked eastward. James Duane Doty found the peninsula through the Four Lakes ignored by speculators, who were crowding the banks of the Rock and Wisconsin rivers with townsites. Imagination, a shoestring of credit, and legislative log rolling of a high order, and the result—Madison.

17. James Doty, territorial governor and later the governor of Utah.

18. Stevens T. Mason, a partner in the Madison land speculation and later the first governor of the state of Michigan.

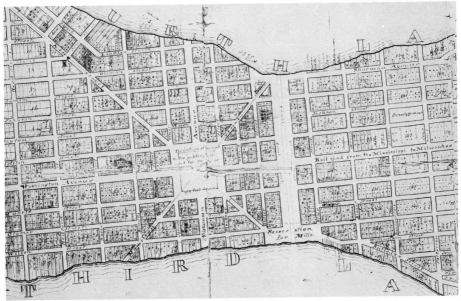

19. Doty's plat (1836) of Madison, indicating the lots that went to legislators.

20. The first house in Madison, 1837; copy of a painting done from memory in 1869.

21. A view of Madison in 1851 by Johann B. Wengler, a traveling artist, showing the capitol, center.

22. Kenosha about 1844, when it was still called Southport.

WISCONSIN was an urban frontier, based on commerce, a pioneer commercial agriculture, extractive industries, and desperate financing. The idea of a wildcat bank was to put the bank where the banknote holder could not conveniently get to it. Alexander Mitchell's bank was always solvent. He led the forces of righteousness in closing out the wildcatters—after floating their banknotes into the workmen's pay envelopes. Righteousness paid.

23. A bank note of the Batavian Bank of La Crosse.

24. Oshkosh about 1855, from an early daguerreotype.

25. A sketch of the bank riot of 1861, drawn in 1897 by Frederic Heath (see Figure 74).

26. Alexander Mitchell's first bank (1831); Mitchell (27, *right*); his Milwaukee residence (28, *below*).

Picture made by John Gaddis Company E, 12th

29. "The Twelfth Wisconsin Volunteer Infantry on their march from Quincy to Hannibal, June 13, 1862."

SERVICE in the Civil War started as an adventure for many young men. Their greatest enemies turned out to be inept leadership, boredom, disease, death, and the Rebels, in about that order.

30. "The Alarm at Humbolt, Tennessee, July 28, 1862."

31. "Skirmish . . . near La Marr, Mississippi, November 12, 1862. Sixteen rebels killed, 125 taken prisoner, 2 Union troops wounded."

32. "A rich rebel planter's house near Natchez. . . . The corporal is reading a newspaper from the north . . . the rest are making arrangements for their noon lunch. Sketched on the spot by John Gaddis, October 1863." Gaddis, a member of Company E, 12th Regiment, Wisconsin Volunteer Infantry, did many such sketches, which he distributed to friends and comrades after the war. The originals of illustrations 29, 30, and 31, with others, are in the GAR Memorial Hall, the Wisconsin State Capitol.

33. Lucius Fairchild as a young man.

34. Fairchild shortly after he returned from the gold fields.

CALIFORNIA was the adventure of the 1850s, the Civil War of the 60s. Then what did a maimed hero do? Politics, in the GOP and the GAR, led to the governorship and even presidential ambitions. One settled for what was available—a minor diplomatic career and a comfortable existence surrounded by Gilded Age amenities. He had walked with kings.

35. Fairchild (seated second from left) and other officers and their wives at the Iron Brigade's Virginia camp.

36. General Grant and his wife (third and fifth from left) and Fairchild and his wife (eighth and ninth from left), with the Big Gun at Newcastle-on-Tyne, England, 1877.

37. General Bryant, commander in chief of the Grand Army of the Republic (left), and Fairchild (center) in the Fairchild dining room, 1890.

38. Mrs. Fairchild (seated) in a Worth of Paris gown, with her daughter Caryl.

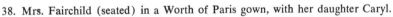

Railroad Mass Meeting
Hammond.

Come, Farmers and Business Men who do business at Hammond Station, and express yourselves on the Railroad Question, at the Town Hall, over McGovern & Deneen's store, Thursday, July 2, 1874, at 5 o'clock P. M.

"The generation between 1865 and 1895 was already mortgaged to the railways, and no one knew it better than the generation itself." HENRY ADAMS

39. A poster from the year the Potter Act passed.

40. A railroad trestle (from a stereopticon view).

41. A Norwegian family using a reaper.

42. A farmstead.

ANDREW DAHL, a photographer with a gallery in Deforest, worked in south central Wisconsin from 1873 to 1879. Many of his customers were Norwegian. He sold them stereopticon views (25 cents each) of their farms, churches, pastors, and associations, and took portraits for their family albums as well.

43. Norwegian pastor and his family at tea, Wiota.

44. The main street of Black River Falls, from Van Schaick's studio.

45. A circus performer.

CHARLES VAN SCHAICK was a local photographer (and town character) in Black River Falls in the late nineteenth and early twentieth century. He took formal portraits like the one on the left; and he also took snapshots and presented a lively scene of local life.

46. A Grand Army of the Republic parade.

47. A rural family.

THE ROMANCE of logging provided millions for a select few, and for others ill-paid, seasonal, difficult, and dangerous work in raw surroundings.

48. Lumbermen with their ox team. The men stood still; the oxen didn't.

CORPUS
CHRISTI
═══ DAY ═══

AT RESERVE, WIS.

Thursday, June 3

9 a.m. Religious Services And Procession

"Sermon: "Catholic Suggestions for Permanent Peace."

By Rev. P. J. O'Mahoney
─── OF SPOONER, WISCONSIN ───

2 p. m. Addresses:

Hon. Roy P. Wilcox
State Senator on "Current Topics."

DR. CARLOS MONTEZUMA
Full-blood Apache Indian of the University of Illinois
"The Plight of the Indian."

4 p. m. Indian Program
AND COUNCIL
Congressman A. P. Nelson has been invited

49. Carlos Montezuma was a leader of the Indian movement of the early 1900s.

50. The wigwam endured both as shelter and as a tourist attraction.

SOME INDIANS farmed the new scientific way and got involved in politics and progress; others became ornaments for the village fair.

51. An Indian street show in Black River Falls.

52. A Winnebago family in their best, photographed by Van Schaick at the turn of the century.

53. Clearing the land for farming near Valley Junction.

54. Dr. Christian Bohmer's sons with their brother-in-law (third from left) in late 1850s.

THE URBAN German was here in numbers enough to make his own world —a comfortable one with reasonable opportunities and a restrained *gemütlichkeit* that would not affront Yankee sensibilities. For other immigrant groups who came later, life was often a struggle, and they did not forget that many of those who were making it difficult bore German names.

55. The Sauk City Humanist Ladies Aid. A part of the German community.

56. Robert Homberger and A. E. Marquart in the Farmer and Citizen's Bank, Sauk City, 1914.

57. A New Year's greeting card.

58. Goldie Meyerson (Golda Meir) plays the part of Liberty in a pageant of a labor-oriented Zionist group in 1919.

59. Robert M. La Follette about 1880, when he was elected district attorney of Dane County.

60. Campaigning at Cumberland, Wisconsin, in 1897.

"Tyranny and oppression are just as possible under democratic forms as under any other. We are slow to realize that democracy is a life and involves continual struggle." ROBERT M. LA FOLLETTE

61. In his special campaign train in 1900, a year of Republican harmony.

62. Belle Case La Follette with her sons Robert, Jr., and Philip, about 1905.

63. Belle Case La Follette in Blue Mounds addressing farmers (about 1916). She also traveled the Chautauqua circuits speaking on woman suffrage in these years.

64. Robert, Jr., Mrs. La Follette, and Philip at the Senator's funeral in 1925.

65. Philip La Follette as governor of Wisconsin in 1935, with some of the Progressive Old Guard.

66. Women take the place of men at Nash Motors during World War I.

"Wealth has never yet sacrificed itself on the altar of patriotism in any war. On the contrary, it has ever shown itself eager to take advantage of the misfortunes which war always brings to the masses of people." ROBERT M. LA FOLLETTE

67. In Baraboo, anti-German sentiment led to book-burning, demonstrations, posters, and flag waving.

68. Defense Food Board Women's Committee sells parched corn at the Madison public market in 1918—3,000 pounds were sold!

THE GREAT WAR brought Liberty Bonds, war gardens, and patriotic zeal— *"to conduct an educational campaign in Milwaukee in behalf of Americanism and in opposition to revolutionary radicalism,"* as the American Constitutional League of Wisconsin put it.

69. A parade in Menominee, Wisconsin, celebrating the signing of the Armistice, November 11, 1918.

70, 71. Street scenes in Milwaukee, taken by J. R. Taylor, an early newspaper photographer, about 1910.

72. Berger's 1918 campaign poster defaced with anti-Socialist, anti-German sentiments.

73. Workmen board a streetcar at Chainbelt. Photograph by J. R. Taylor.

SOCIALISM was abetted unwittingly by industrial leadership that was heedless, arbitrary, self-assured, and complacent about political mismanagement—so long as it was in the hands of the right people. Victor Berger built Milwaukee Socialism—cynics called it Sewer Socialism—on this base, offering honesty and social conscience as an alternative. His gradualist views did not allay the fears of those who chose suspicion of their neighbors as a creed.

74. Victor Berger and Frederic Heath in Berger's room, 1897.

75. "Old Slovenly's Den"; from the *Wisconsin Farmer* of 1858.

"The Babcock test can beat the Bible in making a man honest."

No SINGLE innovation had greater significance for factory or farm than the butterfat test introduced by Stephen Moulton Babcock at the University of Wisconsin in the spring of 1890. The University had begun with the notion that a scientific farmer should have a firm grounding in aesthetics and conic sections, but was brought around to a more practical view that established its favor with Wisconsin farmers.

76. Doctor Babcock and an electric centrifugal butterfat tester, 1926.

77. A foot-powered milking machine.

78. Dean William Henry sponsored an expedition in 1896 to northern Wisconsin to demonstrate the fertility of the cutover.

79. A professor of agriculture lectures to a group of boys. Short courses spread to everyone and everywhere.

80. Milwaukee workers about 1910.

JUST OVER the edge from progressivism was the militance of unheeded labor and the farmer caught in the squeeze between costs and what the market offered. But they have never learned to trot in double harness.

81. The milk strike: farmers dumping milk cans, January 10, 1934.

82. Workers mill in the streets at J. I. Case, March 15, 1934.

83. A Farmer-Labor headquarters, January 23, 1936.

84. Milwaukee office of the State Employment Service, before World War I.

85. Cutler-Hammer workers receive an E for Effort during World War II.

86. The Case strike of 1960.

87. Opening a fund-raising campaign in Milwaukee, April 1, 1971.

WISCONSIN's cities and family farms are intact but threatened—the flight to the suburbs and the demand for land in the heavily populated southeast have endangered the tax base of the cities and resulted in urban sprawl over much of the state's best farmland. Yet it is in the state's tradition to believe that concerned citizens, backed by a skilled bureaucracy and enlightened legislation, can prevent man's rapacity or folly from destroying the world in which he lives.

88. Farmstead near Gilmanton, May 12, 1963.